AUTHENTIC WITNESSES

PUBLICATIONS IN MEDIEVAL STUDIES

Edited by

JOHN VAN ENGEN

Former editors: Philip S. Moore, C.S.C., Joseph N. Garvin, C.S.C., Astrik L. Gabriel, and Ralph McInerny

THE MEDIEVAL INSTITUTE

The University of Notre Dame

Volume XVII

Authentic Witnesses:

Approaches to Medieval Texts and Manuscripts

MARY A. ROUSE AND RICHARD H. ROUSE

University of Notre Dame Press
Notre Dame, Indiana

© 1991 by
University of Notre Dame Press
Notre Dame, Indiana 46556
All Rights Reserved

Manufactured in the United States of America

Library of Congress Cataloging-in-Publication Data

Authentic witnesses: approaches to medieval texts and
manuscripts / [edited by] Mary A. Rouse and Richard
H. Rouse.
   p. cm. — (Publications in medieval studies; v. 17)
   ISBN 0-268-00622-9
   1. Books—History—400-1400. 2. Books—History—
1400-1600. 3. Manuscripts, Medieval—History.
4. Literature, Medieval—Criticism, Textual. 5. Learning and scholarship—History—Medieval, 500-1500. 6.
Transmission of texts. 7. Scriptoria—History.   I. Rouse,
Mary A.   II. Rouse, Richard H.   III. Series. IV. Series:
Publications in medieval studies; 17.
Z6.A96 1990
091—dc20   89-40389

To the memory of

RICHARD WILLIAM HUNT
Teacher and Friend

Contents

Introduction   1

FORM AND FUNCTION

1. Roll and Codex: The Transmission of the Works
   of Reinmar von Zweter   13

ANCIENT AUTHORS AND MEDIEVAL READERS

2. *Potens in opere et sermone:* Philip, Bishop of
   Bayeaux, and His Books   33
3. The Medieval Circulation of Cicero's "Posterior
   Academics" and the *De finibus bonorum et malorum*   61

FLORILEGIA: CONTENT AND STRUCTURE

4. The *Florilegium Angelicum:* Its Origin,
   Content, and Influence   101
5. *Florilegia* and the Latin Classical Authors
   in Twelfth- and Thirteenth-Century Orléans   153
6. *Statim invenire:* Schools, Preachers, and
   New Attitudes to the Page   191
7. The Development of Research Tools
   in the Thirteenth Century   221

BOOK PRODUCTION: STATIONERS AND *PECIAE*

8. The Book Trade at the University
   of Paris, ca. 1250–ca. 1350   259

MEDIEVAL LIBRARIES

9. The Early Library of the Sorbonne   341
10. The Franciscans and Books: Lollard
    Accusations and the Franciscan Response   409

BACKGROUNDS TO PRINT

11. Correction and Emendation of Texts in the
    Fifteenth Century and the Autograph of the
    Opus Pacis by "Oswaldus Anglicus"   427

12. Backgrounds to Print: Aspects of the
    Manuscript Book in Northern Europe
    of the Fifteenth Century   449

EPILOGUE

13. Bibliography before Print: The Medieval
    De viris illustribus   469

Subject Index   495

Manuscript Index   511

Introduction

*The books of the Middle Ages are the most endur-
ing visible legacy of its flowering. Despite the losses
caused by revolutions and wars and periodic
neglect, they have survived in their thousands,
authentic witnesses. . . .*
— Richard W. Hunt*

History, in contrast with prehistory, is the written record of man-
kind. The medieval portion of this written record, in any of its several
manifestations, is our field of inquiry. Our question of the written record,
however, is not primarily "what?" (what does the text say, what does it
mean?). Our questions are "why?" and "how?" Why was it written—
from what source? and for what purpose? How was it written (the
mechanics, both material and intellectual)? Why at this time? Why by
this (or these) person(s)? Why in this specific form? How and why does
it differ from its analogues—in an earlier time, a later time, a different
place? How and why has it been preserved and disseminated?

For historians to question the why and how of the essential basis of
history itself is a salutary exercise that needs redoing from time to time,
lest we gradually lose touch with historical reality.

The following studies, while varied in topic and ranging widely in
time and place, are unified by the questions they pose and by the meth-
odology they use to arrive at an answer. They share common assumptions regarding the genre to which they belong, the genre of literary history or, more specifically, the history of texts. A constant element in this
genre is the desire to sort out the life of a text, from the evidence of its
surviving manuscripts and the traces they have left. In this kind of history, texts replace human beings as the protagonists. Like people, texts
can be examined individually, for themselves as texts, or in groups as a
genre. Like human beings, they have family trees; they are conceived and
born at a time and place; they grow, perhaps changing form radically in

---

*In *The Flowering of the Middle Ages*, ed. J. Evans (London 1966) 166.

the process; and eventually die and are preserved for future readers in libraries—and, to stretch the simile, they may ultimately be consumed by and reborn in new texts of a different era: ashes to ashes, dust to dust, texts to texts. The manuscript is the evidence through which the investigation is carried out; it is both a means of investigation and an object of investigation itself. It is a link, not just intellectual but physical, tangible, visible, between moments in time.

A manuscript is a unit, within which the written text and its physical surroundings interact. The physical support (quires made up of bifolia of given dimensions and given material), the marks that are applied to the physical material (whether letters or images, written, painted, or drawn, by reed, brush, or quill), and the significance of these marks in the minds of author, painter, reader (the text conveyed by the script, the message and symbolism transmitted by an image) mutually affect one another and merge to comprise one specific manuscript; in this sense, every manuscript is a *unicum*. To study any one element in isolation—the ruling, or the layout, or the form of the letters and the script, or the words of the text itself—without the others is to cut apart what was both conceived and perceived as a unit. Each of the three, the material base, the script or image, and the text, is a changing or evolving thing, a product of a compromise between traditional norms and the contemporary needs of the audience which it was to serve.

We have consistently attempted, in our studies, to set the manuscript or manuscripts with which we are dealing into the proper historical context—to discern what the framework is, and to see just how and why the manuscript fits into this frame. It is a natural result of our historical training to want to see an entity as it was perceived by its creators and users, and to place physical object, script form, image, and text into the appropriate historical setting. A manuscript is a product of a given historical environment and must be understood in its own terms. One cannot, for example, date small twelfth-century schoolbooks on the basis of criteria established from the study of large monastic books; the two come from different environments, the one experimental and the other conservative, with different needs, the one placing a high priority on portability and compactness, the other valuing authority, continuity, monumentality. Placing in context, however, is not a simple process of matching the right manuscript with the right setting by fitting Tab A into Slot B, so to speak; but rather it is the task of identifying, excavating, and often reconstructing the setting as it appears to have been from the evidence of the manuscripts themselves, studied in conjunction with the politics, theology, liturgy, art, and literature of the period.

The goal, from first to last, is a clearer understanding of the human beings behind the page, the individual people and the societies that produced and used these manuscripts. Every manuscript that survives was created not casually but deliberately, as a result of someone's decision that it should exist, as a result (in some cases) of someone else's request of the maker that it be made, as a result of common or group decision that it should be made in this fashion and not another. Subsequently, virtually everyone who owned it, everyone who read it seriously, every copyist who made a copy from it, each of them left marks, made notes, entered corrections, added an index, composed a continuation — in short, left revealing personal and cultural fingerprints. The fingerprints do not necessarily tell us the names of the makers or users of the manuscript, but invariably, and directly, tell us a great deal about them. A manuscript can be regarded as an archeological find — on a level with potsherd, midden heap, post hole — and, like all such, can be examined for every drop of information it will yield, pertinent to the society to which it belonged. The vast advantage of a manuscript, over the other items mentioned, is the fact that it is articulate. Like a potsherd, a manuscript has meaningful and measurable physical properties; unlike the potsherd, a manuscript also has a voice.

The articles gathered here range in subject from the transmission of ancient authors and the invention of the subject index, to late medieval spirituality and the invention of printing. Their content spans the period between the Gregorian reform of the eleventh century and the Protestant reformation of the early sixteenth century. They have been selected to represent the various themes of medieval literary history that have occupied our attention. An obvious thread running through them is a simple desire to know how things worked: how the great concordance to the Bible was compiled, how the production of books in pecia at the medieval university was organized, how a vernacular poet carried his songs. But the central theme in any history of texts and books must be that of change and renewal: Parchment that is written on, in one set of circumstances in late antiquity, may in the sixth century be scraped clean and written on again, leaving poignant evidence of a civilization in which blank parchment is more valuable than ancient literature. A literary genre (for example, the one traced below in the EPILOGUE) may continue to attract writers, from one century and country to another and another and yet another: perceptibly the same genre, but perennially renewed and re-formed, in content, in structure, in purpose, to suit the needs and practices of different cultures. The lectern-size Bible written in a monastic scriptorium at the end of the eleventh century may in the course of the twelfth have the space in its margins and between its lines filled with the new biblical gloss that is emerging in the cathedral schools, and will, by the middle of the thirteenth century, be marked from beginning to end with the standardized chapter-divisions adopted at the University of Paris. The studies collected here evince an abiding concern with change, as manifested in text and book: recognizing that change occurred, examining as precisely as possible the nature of the change, trying to understand why this change was made at this time by these people.

*   *   *

In surveying these interests, we begin at the beginning with FORM AND FUNCTION: There is a relationship between the physical form of an artifact and the function that it is meant to serve; therefore, the physical form of a manuscript is evidence of the purpose for which the manuscript was made. This fact, simple and direct, is the inevitable starting point for any study of the manuscript as an object. At the most basic level is size: a book's physical dimensions reflect the image its maker had of the book he was making, the use it was to serve, and how it was to be read, whether as a lectern book or a portable pocket book (to take the extremes). The physical size of the surviving manuscripts involved helps to delineate the circulation of any medieval text; for, while the number of manuscripts tells one about the extent of circulation, it is the physical element—the size, the quality of the parchment, the elaborateness (or the lack) of decoration—which tells one about the social *locus* of circulation, whether among impoverished students, or comfortable burghers, or wealthy prelates. One need only reflect whether all manuscripts of the Canterbury Tales share the size and beauty of the Ellesmere Chaucer, to make the point.

On a more complex level, the change from papyrus roll to parchment codex in late antiquity was an effort to adapt the form of the book to the needs of an authoritative faith, with its exegesis based on internal comparisons. In like manner, the continued survival and use of the roll (now made of parchment) for certain specific purposes reflects the compatibility of that format with the tasks in question. Thus the roll was used—probably never ceased to be used—both for certain administrative records and for literary texts, because of the roll's portability and legibility for the clerks and poet/singers who, each for their own purposes, needed to glance over large portions of a text at a time, and needed to carry their written matter with them as they traveled.

*   *   *

It is sometimes forgotten that medieval people lived in and were surrounded by the physical remains of antiquity, Roman roads, buildings, coins, gemstones, and the products of the late Roman book trade. As the location of a Roman road not infrequently determined the loca-

tion of a medieval abbey which survived long after the road had disappeared, so also the shape and form of Roman manuscripts determined
the physical appearance of their medieval copies. These products of the
late Roman book trade survived deep into the Middle Ages, at times to
the fifteenth century; where they were, the circumstances of their movement and rediscovery, is a study in how one culture perceived another
and adapted what survived to its own needs.

It is within this context that we consider the relationships between
ANCIENT AUTHORS AND MEDIEVAL READERS. The study of the
transmission of ancient Latin texts rests on two foundations: (i) the filiation of the surviving manuscripts, based on collation of the text, and
(ii) a knowledge of the circumstances of the production and use of the
surviving manuscripts (when, where, by whom). Until recent years, the
emphasis was almost entirely upon establishing filiation, which is necessary to reconstruction of the text, rather than upon dating and localizing
the surviving witnesses to the text, which is not. In fact, until recently it
was normal practice for editors simply to repeat the descriptions and the
dating of the manuscript witnesses from the previous edition, without a
fresh look. At times even the identifying press marks were obscured
beneath appellations such as *vetus parisiensis*. The manuscript was considered just the necessary vehicle which carried a text through an unfortunate time of barbarism in which such texts deteriorated. It is too much
to expect classicists of earlier days to have been particularly sympathetic
to the Middle Ages. This prejudice has fortunately been eliminated by
those who have demonstrated the value to editing of reexploring carefully the manuscript witnesses to any given text.

Books tell us how the past survived, how later generations selected
what was of use to them, rearranged it to suit their needs, and discarded
what was not of interest. For medievalists, the soundly constructed
stemma codicum of virtually any text is a valuable witness to contacts
between times and places, with a peculiar kind of precision and validity
afforded by no other source. The philologists' skeleton, when clothed
with historical flesh, will point to the ninth-century abbeys, the new
houses of the twelfth century, papal Avignon, and the reform councils,
as the crossroads where North and South and old and new met.

*   *   *

FLORILEGIA are crossroads in a different sense: Our studies of
various *florilegia* have been inextricably involved with many of the other
aspects of our work that are represented in this volume, in particular the
production of alphabetized reference tools, the transmission of classical
literature, and the history of medieval libraries. Collections of extracts

have for the most part been ignored by scholars because they do not contain original thought. A formal *florilegium*, however, is not an idiosyncratic notebook of random jottings, but a consciously created selection of excerpts, made for a purpose, and often surviving in more than one copy to confirm the fact that—however much it may fall short of one's preconceived standards—this is a piece of literature. As yet, we do not even know what medieval *florilegia* exist today, as real works in multiple copies. Consider, for example, that the twelfth-century *Florilegium Angelicum* was used by a major twelfth-century author, Gerald of Wales, and survives today in over twenty manuscripts that range in date from the twelfth to the fifteenth century and include what is probably the dedication copy; yet the existence of this work was unknown, until a study (published in 1973) excavated it. How many other *florilegia* exist today as actual works in multiple copies, whether *florilegia* of ancient and patristic authors, or canon and civil lawyers, or ancient and medieval physicians, at present we simply do not know.

Florilegia by definition are not original in their content. This in itself is not an unmixed curse: It has always been recognized by the textual scholar that the extracts in a *florilegium* testify to the existence of their source, even though the extracts are usually not much help in reconstructing the source-text itself. But while *florilegia* lack originality in content, their structure and organization are often ingeniously original. In structure and organization, collections of extracts reflect the ingenuity of writers in marshalling the written authority of the past and making it accessible—and relevant—to their present. The transition from random to rational and, finally, to alphabetical order reflects the institutionalization of scholarship, for better or worse. The sophisticated apparatus of some *florilegia* make them almost as easy to consult as a well-indexed product of the printing press.

Certain authors, among them Ennodius, enjoyed a larger medieval circulation in *florilegia* than they did in whole manuscripts. The well-read Gerald of Wales quotes Ennodius, but Gerald's whole acquaintance with this author comes from the *Florilegium Angelicum*. *Florilegia* were a conscious, recognized genre in the Middle Ages. For centuries the authorities were read largely in the form of extracts rather than as *originalia* or whole works. The *florilegium*, containing all that was most essential of the Fathers or the Ancients, formed the extent of a writer's vision of the literature of the past. It is, hence, an important part of literary criticism to know what intermediate sources an author may have used in writing his work. No study of a medieval text, from the viewpoint either of its composition or of its circulation, can be complete without an examination of the pertinent *florilegia*. Any study of the *mentalité* of an age will benefit from seeing concrete examples, in the contemporary *florilegia*, of just what that age judged to represent adequately the essence of its written heritage. In their own way, *florilegia* are as revealing of their society and their age as are the contents of successive editions of the *Encyclopedia Britannica*.

* * *

Two things, the adoption of ALPHABETICAL ORDER for the arrangement of concepts and the invention of techniques of reference required by the SUBJECT INDEX, taken together constitute a major change in medieval society's perception of its relationship to the written heritage. To arrange the words of Holy Scripture or the basic tenets of theology in the nonrational order of the alphabet required a substantial wrench in attitude to inherited authority, on the part of a society that firmly believed in a rationally ordered universe.

The appearance of the concordance and the subject index has traditionally been attributed to the invention of printing. It was proposed that, because print rendered uniform the amount of text upon each page throughout all copies of a given edition of a work, only at this point could one refer to a given portion of the text. This argument overlooked the fact that texts have other elements suitable for reference, book and chapter units or similar subdivisions that do not vary by copy. In actuality, it was a change in need rather than a change in technology that was responsible for the creation and adoption of the alphabetical concordance and subject index. The demands placed upon texts by the emergence and growth in the thirteenth century of literate professions such as parish priests, lawyers (canon and civil), professional civil servants, physicians, and estate managers, to all of whom the written word was a basic tool: These go much farther to explaining the revolution represented by the appearance of alphabetical tools.

* * *

Sensible interpretation of manuscript evidence by art and literary historians must be grounded on a clear understanding of how the manuscripts were produced. BOOK PRODUCTION is seldom investigated as a subject in its own right. Rather, it is treated as a route to information about the production of one specific book, or it is a by-product of discoveries made in the process of investigating the history of a given text. While the study of book production must be solidly grounded in the examination of individual books, it can best advance if it addresses the question directly and as a whole.

It is evident that book production was organized in various and quite different ways, dependent upon time and place: the commercial production of the late Roman city, production in the monastic scriptorium of the High Middle Ages, school production involving the emergence of the great glossed page and university production via exemplar peciae, urban commercial production of the late thirteenth and later centuries, production in the country noble household or court, production in the scriptoria of the renewed religious orders on the eve of print, and, at virtually all times and places, personal production by individuals of books for their own use. The organization of each of these types of production is quite different from the others because of the varying social context, audience, and market. We have said before that in order to render manuscripts useful as historical evidence one must try to ascertain the individual manuscript's date and place of origin as well as the circumstances of its production and use. The history of manuscript production and of the manuscript book trade is an integral part of this endeavor.

*   *   *

Concern with manuscript production is one end of a chain; interest in MEDIEVAL LIBRARIES is the other. The great majority of medieval manuscripts that survive today belonged at one time to some medieval library, even though only a small percentage bear an *ex libris* note. For example, although perhaps as many as 100,000 manuscripts that were once in medieval English libraries today reside, uprooted, on the shelves of English and Continental institutional libraries, the medieval home of only 6,000 or so is known. Surviving medieval library catalogs, ranging from large institutional inventories to wills of individual book owners, contribute to reconstructing what was once in medieval Europe's libraries. They are an aid to ascertaining the provenance or *Bibliotheksheimat* of surviving manuscripts, in those cases where a telling correspondence between the inventory description and the manuscript permits identification. Some day, one can hope, the medieval catalogs will all be edited; at present, we still have far to go.

This is the traditional use made of medieval book inventories: they are tools to establish availability and provenance. We are struck by the fact, however, that catalogs and inventories contribute additional and often unanticipated evidence for both intellectual and social history. These book lists are also reference tools and, often, administrative documents, and they merit study as such. Naturally, they offer a wealth of evidence for the history of medieval archive and library organization; perhaps unexpectedly, they also reveal the schemes of classifying knowledge that were accepted in a given intellectual context. Initially simple inventories of property, no different from the prior's list of the candles on the altars, institutional library catalogs served as mere lists of objects that could be checked off at the annual audit. The books themselves were stored in great chests or armaria, when they were not in the hands of individual members of the community; the collection of books, in its entirety, comprised "the library." Only with the maturing of collegial units at the universities and the development of the houses of the mendicant orders does the word "library" begin to refer to a room, a specific place where books were kept and read, with books (often bearing shelfmarks or benchmarks) arranged in fixed order on pulpits or benches, and requiring catalogs that were guides to their physical location. Looked at in this fashion, medieval libraries and their catalogs are, like *florilegia*, of interest for their organization, their ingenuity, as well as for the more obvious reason, their content.

* * *

The printing press with movable type, child of that technological focus said to epitomize the European West, is traditionally described as an invention that altered the course of European history. And so it did. Yet a focus primarily on the changes in society wrought by the press tends to obscure the features of continuity between manuscript book and printed book and, more important, to divert attention from the historical BACKGROUND TO THE INVENTION OF PRINTING. The press was more than an isolated piece of hardware; it was a cultural artifact, typical or even emblematic of its time and place. The printing press—like the parchment codex, the alphabetical index, or the adoption of paper—came about in response to a need; in this instance, the response was closely tied to the needs of those fifteenth-century religious communities for whom the written word played a central role in their religious experience and their way of life: Carthusians, Brethren of the Common Life, Windesheim Congregation, Crosiers, many others. Their care and concern for the dissemination of religious texts in manuscript, and their insistence on accuracy in these handwritten texts, foreshadow the age of the printed book and, ultimately, help to create the conditions for the birth and successful growth of the press.

* * *

While the studies collected here are unified both by their focus on the history of medieval texts and manuscripts and by the questions they ask of these materials, we would not for a moment deny the fact that they vary in topic and range in time and place. One of the perpetual delights, as well as one of the continual hazards, of following wherever the books lead, is the fact that we are forever being dropped without warning into new topics where we are total innocents, and we must attempt to become Instant Experts (on the German Minnesänger of the thirteenth century, on the twelfth-century Anglo-Norman episcopate, on Lollard readers in fourteenth-century Oxford libraries, and so on). The repeated scramble to master a historical framework new to us is at the same time exhilarating and terrifying. Obviously, we have not always succeeded as well as we wished; and we could not even have come close, without a lot of help form generous friends, lavish of their time and their expertise. Their names turn up in notes to all the articles, and we thank them once again.

Despite the liberal help of colleagues, we can be sure that errors remain, particularly errors of judgment. In reviewing these articles for publication, we find, for example, that some of the things which we once knew for certain are now open to question. If we were writing these again, especially the early ones, they would be different pieces. That is only natural. Yet we decided, upon reflection, that we would *not* write them again, which would only falsify the record. As is frequently the case with collected articles, there are inevitable overlaps and repetitions from one to another of the articles in this volume, since each was originally written to stand on its own. We have corrected typographical errors and errors in fact; but in the main we are content to let the articles stand as originally published.[1]

---

[1] Articles 2, 3, 4, 6–8, 10, 11, and 13 in this volume are of joint authorship; nos. 1, 5, 9, and 12 were written by Richard. This explains why some articles speak in the first person singular, and others in the plural.

Form and Function

chen sin. dar blinder rehte gelovbe in. swer werliche war rehter
smæher. da sich der gæhe tor in un vgæhe. des winscher alle vn
dannoch eines. daz wis got beidiv welle geben. vogr vn ewar
ren disiv leben. daz symon niht habe mit in gemeine.

Der Babest der hat richiv chint. die nimmer er swa si gesezzen
in den landen sint. mir in so reizt er sinen segen. si walent mit
un silber vn golt. div richen chint sint in so trut. daz er mir
flegen chome vngerne vf ir deheines hort. daz wolde got
war er den habelosen chinden halp so holt. e daz daz arme sin
halp zehtte beherte. so ist der riche vf siner widerverte. der pan
ist ime gar abe entrennet. sin war in vnschuldich sagt. swaz
ab ime der arme chlagt. so muz er doch den himel haben vberret

Swer penner vn pannen sol. der sol hoeten daz sin   (nie
pan. ihr si vleischliches zorns zorns vol. swa zorn in panne stechet
der pan ist niht reht gotes pan. swe panner ingot vn mit got. der
panner als ein reht gesegent gotes bot. swe ovch den pan niht
forhtet. der diincher niht gar ein wiser man. swer vndstal
schirnt. vlucher. panner. vn vinde helsnen rovber vn brenner
der wil nur boden swerten strizen mach daz geschehen ingotes
namen. so sol sich sant peter schamen. daz er des nie gepflach

Reht vn vnreht habent gestriten.   (bi sine zuin.
si habent lant vn levt vil vngeliche enzwei gestriten. vnrehe
hat mere gesindes. so hat daz arme reht die minneren schar
vnreht hat hohe dienstman. ez vn der babest lachent erwein
ein ander an. da bi ster reht vil æbriich. do von wirt romisch
lop zuhtlich geswer sint arme ez si daz reht ist doch vil kriege. e
daz er sinnv midiv bein gebiege. ez machet e vil offenbare daz
vnreht ber gewinnet hat. vnreht intrihter livte war. daz cheint
fet. wan fur einen trygenæte.

Wes siumest dvdich antichrist. daz dv miht chvmst fir ellv wilde

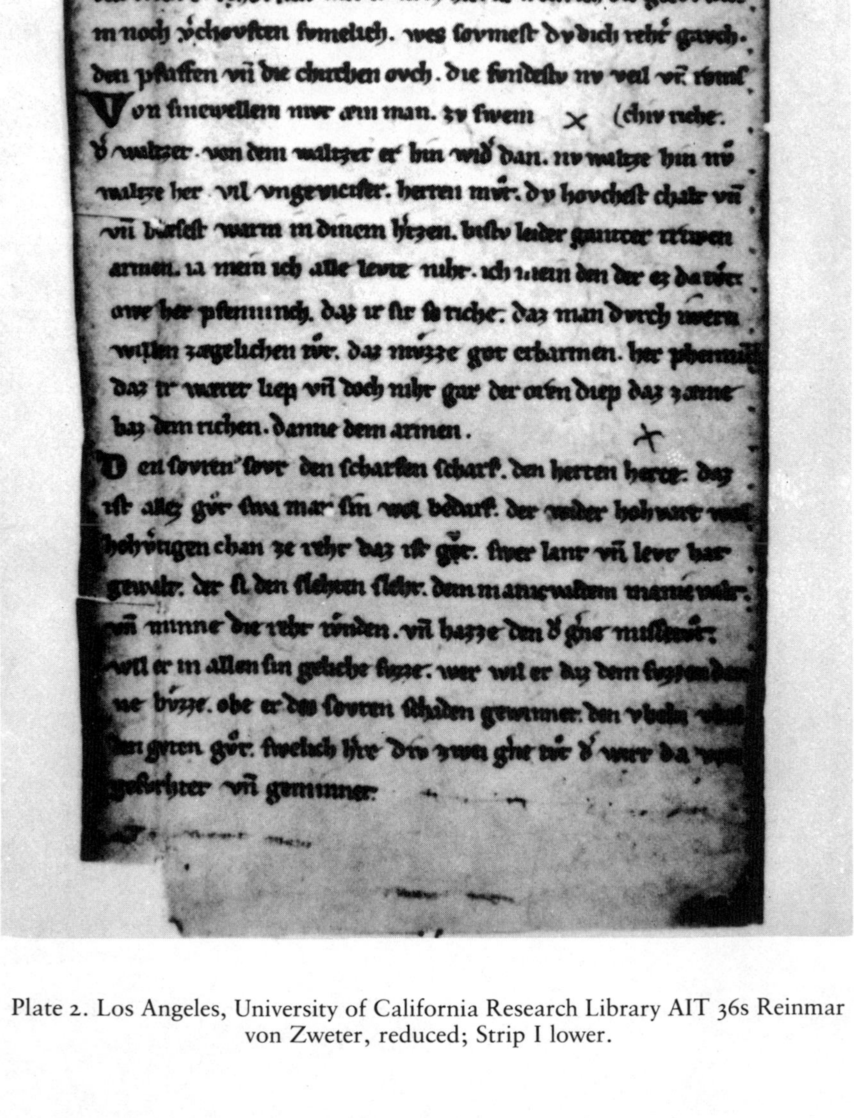

Plate 2. Los Angeles, University of California Research Library AIT 36s Reinmar von Zweter, reduced; Strip I lower.

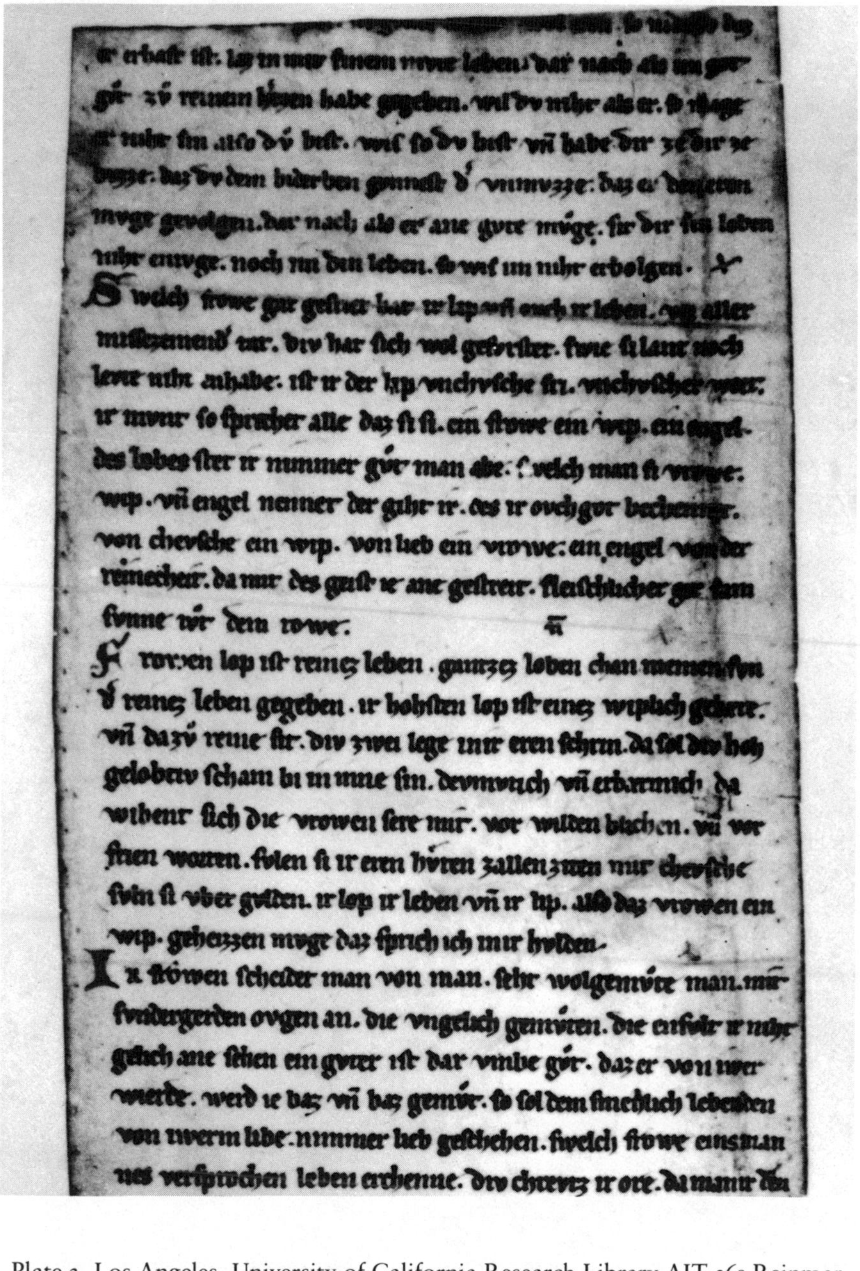

Plate 3. Los Angeles, University of California Research Library AIT 36s Reinmar von Zweter, reduced; Strip II upper.

Plate 4. Los Angeles, University of California Research Library AIT 36s Reinmar
von Zweter, reduced; Strip II lower.

1. Roll and Codex: The Transmission of the Works of Reinmar von Zweter*

In the process of searching the fifteenth-century printed books in the University Library for fragments of medieval manuscripts, I found two fragments (Plates 1–4) of a mid-thirteenth-century roll containing the songs or *Sprüche* of the Minnesinger Reinmar von Zweter.[1] Born around 1200, place of origin unknown, he tells us only, "Von Rîne sô bin ich geborn, in Ôsterrîche erwahsen, Bêheim hân ich mir erkorn . . ." Reinmar is thought to have grown up in the school of Walther Von der Vogelweide and lived in Austria at the court of Leopold VI and Friedrich II, or in the service of Friedrich's son Henry. From 1236 to 1240 or so he was at the Bohemian court of Wenzel I. From there began a period of wandering, through Meissen and Mainz and elsewhere. His last datable *Spruch* is from 1248, and he is thought to have died around 1260.[2] Reinmar's *Sprüche* were gathered a generation or so after his death, with the songs of his fellow Minnesänger, into those famous collections of court poetry now in Heidelberg, Liederhandschrift D and the famous

*Originally published in *Münchener Beiträge zur Mediävistik und Renaissance-Forschung* 32 (1982) 107–123.

This paper is given in homage to Professor Bernhard Bischoff.

I should like to thank Mrs. Mary Rouse, Mr. Terry Nixon, Mr. Brooke Whiting, Dr. Nigel Palmer, Professor Franz Bäuml, Professor Helmut Gneuss, and Professor Peter Ganz for their considerate help with various portions of this article. For a full study, and a transcription, of the text of the fragments, see F. Bäuml and R. Rouse, "Roll and Codex: A New Manuscript Fragment of Reinmar von Zweter," in *Beiträge zur Geschichte der deutschen Sprache und Literatur* 105 (1983) 192–231, 317–330.

[1] The text of the fragments was kindly identified by Professor Burghart Wachinger.

[2] Regarding Reinmar see E. Gierach in *Verfasserlexikon* 3 (1943) 1068–1071, and Roethe (n. 8 below) 1–92.

illustrated Manesse codex (Lhs. C). It is the purpose of this article to describe the new fragments, to place them in the transmission as it is known today, and to offer some comments on the place of the roll in the transmission of the *Sprüche*.

The two fragments were used as flyleaves in a copy of St. Thomas *Summae theologiae secundae partis pars secunda*, printed in Strasbourg ca. 1470 by the printer of Henricus Ariminensis (Hain 1455), which is now in the Research Library of the University of California, Los Angeles (AıT 36s).[3] The volume bears the *ex libris*, "Monasterii Emmerami Ratisbonae" written vertically between the columns of the table of contents on f.ii. It came to the abbey soon after it was printed, probably under Abbot John Tegernpeck II (1471–93), who purchased a large number of printed books for St. Emmeram.[4] The title and the press mark are written on the front pastedown by Laurentius Aicher, librarian of St. Emmeram in the 1480s. The volume is probably identifiable with no. B. 14 in the great catalog of his successor, Dionysius Menger, prepared in 1500–1501.[5] Holes in the rear cover of the book indicate that it was chained. The volume was bound soon after its arrival at the abbey. It is a typical St. Emmeram binding of the late fifteenth century, being whittawed deerskin over oak boards, ruled and decorated with large and small rosette stamps.[6]

The two fragments of Reinmar's poetry became part of this volume when it was bound by the abbey, being added as flyleaves to this, fortunately for us, rather large book, seven stanzas at the front and seven

---

[3] The book was part of the library formed by the English scholar, G. K. Ogden (1889–1957), which was acquired by the University of California in 1958. Ogden apparently acquired the volume, along with other incunabula now also at UCLA, from the library of Eduardo J. Bullrich, whose bookplate appears on the middle of the front pastedown, and whose library was sold by his brother-in-law D. L. Alvear at Sotheby's on 17–19 March, 1952, lot 375. See A. Hobson, "Notes on Sales," *The Book Collector* 1 (1952) 116–117, referred to me by Dr. Ch. de Hamel.

[4] Concerning St. Emmeram, see Bernhard Bischoff, "Literarisches und künstlerisches Leben in St. Emmeram (Regensburg) während des frühen und hohen Mittelalters" and "Studien zur Geschichte des Klosters St. Emmeram im Spätmittelalter (1324–1525)," in his *Mittelalterliche Studien* 2 (Stuttgart 1967) 77–155.

[5] Regarding the library see, besides the works in the previous note, the introduction to the library catalogs by Christine E. Ineichen-Eder, *Mittelalterliche Bibliothekskataloge Deutschlands und der Schweiz* 4.1: *Bistümer Passau und Regensburg* (Munich 1977) 99–142 and, for the volume in question, 339 lines 6083–6086.

[6] I am grateful to Dr. Christine Eder, who examined the volume on the occasion of the 1980 meeting of the Medieval Academy of America at the University of California, Los Angeles; she confirmed that we were dealing with a St. Emmeram binder, and identified the hands of the abbey librarians. For similar bindings see E. Kyriss, *Verzierte gotische*

stanzas at the rear. The two strips are written by the same hand, are almost identical in dimensions and preparation, and were once in all probability part of the same longer strip. They are about five inches in width and fourteen inches in height. Each strip has been pricked down both sides, indicating that we have the original width of the pieces of parchment in both cases. We are not, in other words, dealing with a two-column page cut in half. Neither parchment has been ruled, the column being narrow enough that the writer was able to maintain an even line on the basis of the pricks alone. On both strips, the text is written on one side, the hair side, of the parchment only.

The two strips can be described as follows: I (front flyleaf) 389 × 119 mm., 59 long lines. Seven stanzas. Incomplete at the beginning (opens with the last seven lines of the eight- or nine-line stanza) and at the end (closes with the ninth line of the seventh stanza, only the upper half of which is visible). II (back flyleaf) 391 × 120 mm., 55 long lines. Seven stanzas. Incomplete at the beginning (opens with the last four lines of an eight- or nine-leaf stanza). Apparently the end of the text, to judge from the space left after the last line.

The two texts, though in verse, are written in long lines. The verses, hence, are not hung on the left margin. The stanzas, however, are set off from one another, each beginning at the left margin with a small knobby or swollen two-line initial. The text in both strips has been carefully corrected by the writer.

The fragments are in good physical condition and reveal something about when and where they are written and what in specific they are. They are written in a well-formed, upright vernacular book hand with few abbreviations. The hand is conservative and shows no discernible school or chancery influences. The date of Reinmar's activity, the 1240s, provides a *terminus post quem*. The occasional appearance of the digraph *æ*, and the absence of the functionless decorative hairlines that appear in later German book hands, suggest a date in the middle of the thirteenth century. Other features of the script that might be noted are these: there are frequent letter unions, single *i* is ticked frequently, the small two-line initials are knobby and swollen; both the teardrop *a* and the double-looped form of *a* are employed, as well as the two forms of *r*, the straight and round (Arabic-2) form. The only punctuation mark used is the *punctus*. The diphthong and umlaut are in the form of a small *o* or *e* above the vowel.

Einbände im alten deutschen Sprachgebiet (Stuttgart 1951) 29–30, and plates (Stuttgart 1953), p. 29 and pls. 65.8, 66.

The hand resembles that of Petzet, Glauning plate XXI C (MS Germ. 94, Life of St. Ulrich),[7] first quarter of the thirteenth century, and plate XXVI A (Munich Germ. 91, Benedictine Rule), of the mid-thirteenth. It is a larger and more formal script than that in XXXI B (MS Germ. 191, Hartmann von Aue, *Iwein*), also of the mid-thirteenth century, and earlier than either XXXV (MS Germ. 18, Wolfram von Eschenbach, *Parzival*), s. xiii, or XXXVI (MS Germ. 44, Ulrich von Lichtenstein, *Frauendienst*), s. xiii ex., both of which show the numerous decorative flourishes that are lacking in the Reinmar fragments. In fact, the latter are closer in character to XVI B (MS lat. 19411, *Du bist min, ich bin din*), of the end of the twelfth century. On paleographic grounds, then, the two pieces can date from as early as the external and linguistic evidence will allow, namely, the mid-thirteenth century. Their place of origin remains uncertain. Both the language of the texts and the final home of the fragments suggest that they originated in Bavaria.

It is interesting to conjecture what these two strips of parchment may have been. They are not parts of a book, i.e., leaves cut up for scrap by a binder. The pricks down both sides of the two pieces show clearly that they were strips of parchment rolled up, like genealogical histories of the kings, when not being read. Their strip or roll form and the fact that they are written on one side of the parchment only, as well as their plain, unembellished appearance, would argue for the suggestion that the two strips are the remains of an object frequently depicted in the great illustrated court collections of Middle High German lyrics, such as the Manesse codex, but not hitherto properly explained, namely, a poet's (or singer's) roll. Their discovery is intriguing, because Middle High German vernacular lyric is reconstructed primarily from later copybooks or court collections. The actual rolls on which the poet or singer may have kept his songs, being ordinary, unbindable, and generally ephemeral, had no reason for being preserved and were discarded when they were worn out or otherwise superseded.

It appears, then, that we have two pieces from a mid-thirteenth century poet's or singer's roll, which was used at the end of the fifteenth century by a binder at St. Emmeram to form flyleaves of an early printed book.

II

The two parchment strips contain fourteen of Reinmar's songs or *Sprüche*, including one that was hitherto unknown. For that reason, and

---

[7] E. Petzet and O. Glauning, *Deutsche Schrifttafeln des 9. bis 16. Jahrhunderts* vols. 2–3 (Munich 1911–1912).

since the strips are almost certainly older than any other surviving manuscripts of Reinmar's works, one of course would like to know where the
texts of these strips fit, in the presently established transmission of
Reinmar's poetry. Do they figure among the ancestors of the known
codices, or are they merely derivative manuscripts? Or, as I shall suggest, are they neither?

In all, some *239 Sprüche* attributed to Reinmar are known, as well
as a number of doubtful attribution that travel with them. The standard
edition is that of Gustav Roethe, published in 1887.[8] Roethe's edition is
an effort to reconstruct the "original" text, following the rules established by nineteenth-century classical philologists; the method is not well
suited to the task at hand, because it creates an ideal text that never
existed in reality.

Although this edition is nearly 100 years old, no new manuscripts
of Reinmar's works have come to light since that time (until now), and
Roethe's reconstruction of the transmission remains generally accepted:
The earliest and largest surviving collections are Heidelberg Universitätsbibliothek MS. Germ. 350, called D (s. xiii ex.),[9] which contains 193
Sprüche; and the near-contemporary Heidelberg MS. Germ. 848 (the
Manesse codex), called C (s. xiv in.), which contains 219 *Sprüche*.[10]
Lying behind these and the later surviving manuscripts (which contain
only bits and pieces), Roethe postulates a collection X of 159 *Sprüche*
compiled, with Reinmar's assistance, in 1240/41 and arranged in careful
topical order; and he postulates a second collection Y, which incorporated X wholesale and added some 33 or 34 of Reinmar's later *Sprüche*
not arranged in any discernible order, compiled after X and before D
and C. D reproduces Y entire, according to Roethe. C draws, probably
via an intermediate excerpt or abridgement, from Y and X, and on other
unnamed sources (Roethe treats the *Sprüche* in C as 21 separate parts,
each with its own history); but the sequence of the *Sprüche* in C differs
almost entirely from that in D.[11]

In addition to C and D, there are fragments from two or three
other manuscripts of the early fourteenth century that probably contained, in the same sequence, the corpus of 193 poems in D.[12] The first
of these (T) possibly from Kloster Schönrain survives in fragments at
three libraries: (a) Ysenburgisches Archiv auf Schloss Büdingen (Fürstlich

---

[8] G. Roethe, ed., *Die Gedichte Reinmars von Zweter* (Leipzig 1887).

[9] B. Wachinger, "Heidelberger Liederhandschrift cpg 350," *Verfasserlexikon* 3 (Berlin
1981) 597–606.

[10] G. Kornrumpf, "Heidelberger Liederhandschrift cpg 848," ibid., 584–597.

[11] Roethe 93–141.

[12] Ibid., 141–147.

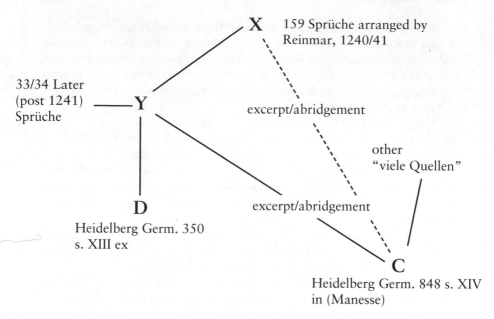

X 159 Sprüche arranged by Reinmar, 1240/41

33/34 Later (post 1241) Sprüche — **Y**

excerpt/abridgement

other "viele Quellen"

D

Heidelberg Germ. 350 s. XIII ex

excerpt/abridgement

C

Heidelberg Germ. 848 s. XIV in (Manesse)

Transmission of the *Sprüche* of Reinmar von Zweter as described by Gustav Roethe

Ysenburg-Büdingensches Archiv 54), 8 leaves, *Sprüche* 10–17, 55–58, 61–67, 74–77; (b) Basel Universitätsbibliothek NI₃, n. 145, 2 leaves, *Sprüche* 88–91, 117–121 (beginning); and (c) Marburg Staatsarchiv, 2 leaves, *Sprüche* 111–114, 121 (end)–124. The two other bifolia, U and V, survived respectively in Berlin Staatsbibliothek Germ. 923 (*Sprüche* 21–29, 79–87) and in Halle Leopoldinisch-Carolinische Akademie der Naturforscher (*Sprüche* 110, 116, 112–115). U and V may represent two other collections, or, despite anomalies in decoration, they may be two fragments of a single manuscript. In sum, only four or five large compilations of Reinmar's *Sprüche* are known to have existed. Otherwise, the manuscript witnesses consist of bits and pieces, mixed with the works of other poets or added to flyleaves and margins, with the *Spruch* as the unit; these are the analogues of Roethe's 21 separate sources of C. This fact has been obscured by the understandable focus of editors on the two famous compilations, C and D. The earliest of these, Heidelberg Universitätsbibliothek Germ. 357 ff. 19v–20, s.xiii² (A), contains *Sprüche* 19, 162, 211, under the name of Truchsess of St. Gall.[13] Surprisingly, Roethe

[13] G. Kornrumpf, "Heidelberger Liederhandschrift A," *Verfasserlexikon* 3 (1981) 577–584.

found A's text of these three random and misattributed *Sprüche* superior
to those of C and D, and used A as the "base" manuscript for his edition
of the three—a fact sufficient to shake one's confidence in the supposedly
authoritative X and Y. Munich Bayerische Staatsbibliothek 13582, front
flyleaf (s. xiv in.; Regensburg, St. Blaise, O.F.P.) (S), contains *Sprüche*
95, 94. There are two similarly random fragments in Middle Low German: Berlin Staatsbibliothek Preussischer Kulturbesitz Germ. 4° 795, s.
xiv in. (m), the Möser fragment, comprising three bifolia which contain
Sprüche 221, 52, 34, 35, the end of 100, 40, and the beginning of an
unknown poem; and Leipzig, Ratsbibliothek 421 ff. 91–96, (2 missing
leaves), 97–102, s. xiv ex. (n), containing *Sprüche* 31, 46, 39, 103, 101,
102, 115, 40. One further manuscript, apparently no longer extant, must
be mentioned. By remarkable coincidence, the previously unknown
Spruch (UCLA Strip I, st. 7, beginning "Do ere ir hoves alrerst began . . .")
stood at the head of a codex of songs described in the inventory of the
Electoral Library at Wittenberg, dating from 1434 or 1437: "4. Item alius
liber magnus, qui incipit Do ere ires hoves erst began, etc., et finitur, sus
leret Herman von der Dhame, cum notis."[14]

How do the UCLA roll fragments fit into this picture? Clearly their
text varies markedly from D and C. The most immediately apparent
difference is that of the sequence of stanzas. For a series of five stanzas
the UCLA fragments follow the sequence of D, since UCLA Strip I, 2–6
= D (and presumably X) 35, 36, 38, 40, 51; but the first stanza on Strip
I is out of this sequence (= D 63), and the seventh is otherwise unknown.
The order of the stanzas on Strip II (Roethe nos. 223, 131, 127, 132, 134,
61, 98) has no correlation with the sequence of either D or C.

Of more significance are the textual variants. There are many places
where the text of the UCLA fragments conveys an idea similar to the text
of D or C, but in quite different words. Let us take as an example
Roethe 61 (p. 441), lines 4–5:

> D   dû bleses kalt uñ huches warm
>   ûz eines mannes munde: staeter triuwen bistû arm
>
> C   der kuchet kalt, der blaset warm
>   ûz eines mannes munde: staeter triuwen ist er arm
>
> UCLA   dv hovchest chalt vñ blæsest warm
>   in dinem hertzen. bistv leider gantcer triwen armen

---

[14] E. G. Vogel, "Verzeichnis von Büchern, ehemals in der Schlosscapelle zu Wittenberg
befindlich," *Serapeum* 21 (1860) 229–301; K. Bartsch, "Ein altes Bücherverzeichniss,"
Germania 24 (1879) 16–21; W. Lippert, "Der älteste kursächsische Bibliothekskatalog aus
dem Jahr 1437," *Neues Archiv für sächsische Geschichte und Altertumskunde* 16 (1895)
135–139; this reference was kindly provided by Dr. Gisela Kornrumpf.

In general the strips agree more often with D against C than with C against D. Although the evidence is unfortunately limited, the text of the UCLA fragments shows an affinity with that of the Möser fragments (m), the remains of an early fifteenth-century manuscript in Low German. For the two UCLA stanzas that recur in m, nos. 2 and 5 of Strip I (Roethe 35, 40), the choice and order of the words frequently link m with the UCLA text against D and/or C, despite the difference in dialect. For example, in Roethe 35 line 8 one finds " . . . des ir got selbe bekennet" D; " . . . rehte als si got erkennet" C; " . . . des ir ouch got bechennet" UCLA; " . . . des ir ok god bekennet" m.

There is an important point here that Roethe's edition tends to disguise—not deliberately, for the evidence is all set forth in his notes, but merely through the manner of presentation: That is, D and C *also* differ markedly from one another in stanzaic sequence; D and C *also* differ— sometimes very widely—in the words chosen to express the same thought. On purely commonsense grounds, adding the evidence of the UCLA fragments to that presented by Roethe himself, I question whether there is any such thing as a "DC tradition"; and I question whether Roethe's collection Y ever existed. Rather, I suspect that any stemma for—or any rational consideration of—the transmission of Reinmar's poems would have to be based not on the codex but on the pre-codex, the singer's rolls, and it would have to be constructed stanza by stanza. I am moved to offer several other tentative suggestions: (1) that the collection X, organized by or with Reinmar, was taken from rolls; (2) that what Roethe calls "Y" in fact means X plus whatever of Reinmar's songs were not included in X, which circulated originally as rolls; (3) that the rather "fractured" tradition—in 21 parts—that Roethe himself perceived in the Manesse Codex ("aus vielen Quellen, verschieden an Umfang und Wert") is witness to transmission via rolls; (4) that the UCLA strips are not descended from X and so-called Y, but from rolls—rolls identical with, gemelli of, or descended from those which made up X and the catch-all called Y; and (5) that the text of the Möser fragments, m, likewise descend ultimately from an independent roll tradition, perhaps sharing, for two of its stanzas (UCLA I, 2 & 5), a common roll-ancestor with the UCLA roll.

III

Thus far, I have advanced suggestions concerning the circulation of Middle High German verse on rolls, based primarily on textual evidence drawn solely from the works of Reinmar von Zweter. Now I

should like to consider what external evidence there is to support such a
supposition for MHG verse generally, and what its implications would
be, for the editing of these works.

Surviving *Liederhandschriften* like the Manesse codex are court
books commissioned by noblemen or patricians for their own pleasure,
years after the poets were dead. These splendidly illustrated codices are
of course far removed from the actual circumstances of composition and
performance by the poets themselves; and it would be naive to insist
upon too literal an interpretation of the portrait illustrations in such
manuscripts. Nevertheless, it is striking to observe that the poets depicted
in both the Manesse and the Weingarten manuscripts are almost never
portrayed with a codex; rather, the written form with which they are
associated is a lengthy strip of parchment—draped across a lectern or a
lap, or more frequently with one end held in the hand, the remainder
floating improbably in the air. There are 137 author-portraits in the
Manesse codex, some 35 of which depict the poet accompanied by some
form of written material. In 20 of the 35 cases, the poet is shown with
one of these long parchment strips, and in another 10 cases with a letter
or shorter strip; in 2 cases (3 counting Reinmar, along with a roll) there
is a wax tablet, and in 3 cases a folded sheet or quire representing a
codex. The proportions in the Weingarten codex are similarly one-sided:
15 portraits with a parchment strip, 1 with a wax tablet, none with a
codex. Without insisting too heavily on the realism of these depictions,
it is clear that, in the early fourteenth century, such long parchment
strips were an immediately recognizable symbol that identified a poet.
The first poet portrayed in the Manesse codex, the emperor Henry VI, is
shown with two symbols, indicative of his dual nature—in his right
hand a scepter, symbolizing his *imperium*, and in his left, the lengthy
parchment strip that identifies him as poet.

The disconcerting fact is that the secondary scholarly literature has
basically misinterpreted what these bands represent. Instead of stylized
representations of actual rolls, the ribbons are thought, on the one hand,
to be symbols of writing—i.e., symbols denoting that the personage
with whom they are associated was a writer; or, on the other hand, they
are thought to be banderols on which a few words might be written
along the length of the ribbon, such as those emanating from the angel
Gabriel in miniatures of the Annunciation—a sort of cartoonist's bal-
loon.[15] They are invariably referred to as *Spruchbänder* or *Schriftbänder*,

---

[15] See in particular E. Jammers, *Das königliche Liederbuch des deutschen Minnesangs*
(Heidelberg 1965) 85: "Der heutige Betrachter wird jedenfalls den Text vermissen; er kennt
solche Schriftbänder von der kirchlichen Kunst her; beim Englischen Grusse an die Jungfrau

and never as *Rolle*. The origins of the iconography of the author portraits has been sought in the distant portrait traditions of the Evangelists, rather than in the immediate real world of the thirteenth century.[16]

    I would suggest, rather, that these ribbons represent singers' rolls—
that this was chosen as the pictorial symbol of the poet because people
actually saw such things in poets' hands.[17] That the ribbons are banderols seems farfetched, since they are invariably blank, and the function
of a banderol is after all to convey words to the viewer of the picture.
That they symbolize writing, however, I do not quarrel with; I wish only
to stress the reality that underlies the symbol. Just as the quires and the
wax tablets depicted in the portraits are representations of the real world
of the thirteenth century, so too are the rolls. There is no need to seek
their identity in the rolls that float across the desks of the Evangelists.
Instead, I suggest that this iconography had a basis in fact, and that
Middle High German songs initially circulated on rolls, before their subsequent collection into codices like C and D.

    Support for this suggestion is afforded by the depictions of poets
with rolls found in the manuscripts of other vernaculars, French and
Provençal. For example, the Provençal poet sitting at his desk, pen in
hand, declaiming with a roll draped across the desk, in Morgan MS 819
fol. 63, of North Italian origin in the 1280s; or the portrait of Jean Bodel
reading his congé from a roll, in Arsenal MS 3142 fol. 227, written in
North France at the end of the thirteenth century.[18] Oxford, Bodleian
Library MS Douce 308 contains *inter alia* a late thirteenth-century text
of the illustrated *Bestiaire d'amour* of Richard de Fournival (d. 1260), in
which Richard is twice depicted (fol. 86d r–v), once writing on a roll,
and a second time handing the roll to another person. Guillaume de
Machaut is depicted writing in a roll and again standing before his lady

---

Maria in Nazareth z. B. tragt sehr oft der Erzengel Gabriel ein solches Band mit den
Worten 'Ave Maria gratia plena.' Aber sowohl die Heidelberger wie die Weingartner
Handschrift verzichten bei allen Spruchbändern auf einen Text; somit hatte auch die
gemeinsame Vorlage Vb keinen Text."

  [16] R. Kroos, *Die Weingartner Liederhandschrift*, Textband (Stuttgart 1969) 140: "Der
sitzende, mit seinem Werk (hier als leeres Spruchband abgekürzt) beschäftigte Verfasser als
Titelbild zu seinen Schriften, das Autorenporträt im engsten Sinne also, hat eine aus der
klassischen Antike in die frühchristliche und mittelalterliche Buchillustration führende Tradition, besonders reich in Gestalt des meditierenden, lesenden, schreibenden oder diktierenden
Evangelisten."

  [17] Curiously, one of the few works that recognizes this rather obvious point is the practical handbook by Gero von Wilpert, *Deutsche Literatur in Bildern* (Stuttgart 1965) 23 no.
56, to which Helmut Gneuss kindly referred me.

  [18] Reproduced in K. Langosch et al., *Geschichte der Textüberlieferung* 2 (Zurich 1964)
277.

with a roll in his hand in Paris B.N. fr 1586 which is the oldest illustrated manuscript of his work and was produced during his lifetime probably for someone at the court.[19]

Let us look specifically at what is happening in the portrait of Reinmar (Plate 5).[20] The poet sits composing his verse, his eyes closed to indicate thought. He dictates verses to his notary, who sits below him and records them on wax tablets. It has been said that Reinmar is dictating simultaneously to both the notary with the tablets and the woman who sits opposite the notary, writing on a roll draped across her lap. Reinmar's face, however, is directed toward the notary; and the woman is looking at the notary, who is concentrating on his stylus and tablets. She is more likely transcribing the text in clean form, as it takes shape on the wax tablet. She holds the roll in her left hand, and is clearly writing across, not along, the parchment with her quill. The roll reaches to the floor on either side, and appears to be somewhat longer than her height.

I do not think there is any doubt that the "Spruchband" on which the girl is writing is in fact a roll, just as the wax tablet is a wax tablet; and just as we know that medieval authors composed their works on tablets, so we can see that they circulated their poetry on rolls.

When in the mid-thirteenth century Thomas of Hales tells the *puella* to whom he addressed his *Luve Ron* to *untrende*, i.e., unroll it, there can be little question regarding either what the autograph was written on or what Thomas thought his audience would expect a poem to be written on.[21] Neither this, nor the early fourteenth-century English poem beginning "Of rybaudz Y ryme / and rede o my rolle" in the Harley lyrics, can be said merely to be evoking the image of Evangelists writing

---

[19] Unfortunately, while Guillaume tells us a great deal about the dissemination of his works, he does not evidently refer to rolls; see S. J. Williams, "An Author's Role in 14th c. Book Production: G. de Machaut's *Livre ou je met toutes mes choses,*" *Romania* 90 (1969) 433–454, and idem, "Machaut's Self-Awareness as Author and Producer," in *Machaut's World: Science and Art in the 14th Century* (New York 1978) 189–197, kindly brought to my attention by Mr. Terry Nixon. Regarding B. N. fr 1586 see *Les Fastes du Gothique: le siècle de Charles V* (Paris 1981) n. 271 and bibliography.

[20] Number 97 in the Manesse codex. There is no indication that the iconography is taken from the text itself, as is at times the case, unless the depiction of three writers derives from "Got unt din eben ewikeit mit drin personen under schriben, sit es gelobt, daz unser leit der drier einer hat vertriben, der dir ze kinde ist bi beliben."

[21] No. 66 in C. Brown and R. H. Robbins, *Index of Middle English Verse* (New York 1943) and Supplement (Lexington 1965). See B. Hill, "The 'Luue-Ron' and Thomas de Hales," *Modern Language Review* 59 (1964) 321–330, and R. Woolf, *The English Religious Lyric in the Middle Ages* (Oxford 1968) 57 n. 3. This was brought to my attention by H. Gneuss.

Plate 5. Heidelberg, Universitatsbibliothek MS. Germ. 848 (Manesse Codex)
f. 323, no. 97, from the facsimile Leipzig 1925–27, reduced

on rolls.[22] The barrier to our recognizing the prevalence of this form is
the fact that few literary rolls survive — other than in pictures, where they
abound, or as mentions in texts. Among the references to rolls specifically pertinent to the present discussion[23] are the late twelfth-century
fragment of a French roll containing *Ganymede and Helena*, in Harvard
University Houghton Library 198;[24] the *Carmen de Timone comite et de
miraculo fontis Sancti Corbiniani* in Munich clm 21571, which was transcribed from a roll in the late eleventh century at the abbey of
Weihenstephan in Bavaria according to a marginal note, "in rotula scilicet
antiquitus composita, unde haec sunt transscripta";[25] the oldest German
rhymed love-letter on a mid-fourteenth century roll in Munich Bayerische
Staatsbibliothek Germ. 189[26] and the fragments of a late thirteenth/early
fourteenth-century roll containing the *Wartburg-Krieg*, now in Berlin,
Geheimes Staatsarchiv Preussischer Kulturbesitz xx. HA St. A. Königsberg
33.11;[27] the recently discovered fragments of a late thirteenth-century roll
in the binding of Basle Universitätsbibliothek F IV 12 containing portions of Konrad von Würzburg, Der Kanzler and Der Marner;[28] the lost
late thirteenth- or early fourteenth-century roll containing the *cantigas*
of the Gallician poet Martim Codax;[29] the *Song of the Barons*, written

---

[22] Brown-Robbins *Index* 2649, and Suppl. Printed. R. H. Robbins, *Historical Poems of
the XIVth and XVth Centuries* (New York 1959) 27–29.

[23] The following examples of rolls containing literary texts pertain to Germany and/or
to the period before 1300.

[24] I. Schröbler, "Zur Überlieferung des mittellateinischen Gedichts von 'Ganymede und
Helena,'" in *Unterscheidung und Bewahrung: Festschrift für Herman Kunisch* . . . (Berlin
1961) 321–330.

[25] The poem is edited by E. Dümmler, MGH *Poetae latini aevi carolini* 2 (Berlin 1884)
120–124.

[26] Petzet-Glauning no. LIV.

[27] First noticed by J. Zacher, *Zeitschrift für deutsches Altertum* 12 (1866) 516–525, who
believed the fragments to be leaves from a codex; identified as fragments from a roll by L.
Denecke, ed., *Orendel: Der graue Rock. Facsimileausgabe* (Stuttgart 1972) 13 n. 34. Brought
to my attention by Dr. Gisela Kornrumpf and Dr. Nigel Palmer.

[28] I am grateful to Dr. Martin Steinmann for having brought these fragments to my
attention. Nigel Palmer indicates that they contain the following texts: Konrad von Würzburg
(ed. E. Schröder) 32, 1.2 and 4; Der Kanzler (ed. H. M. S.) II.1, II.2, II.3, II.9, II.4, II.7,
XVI.2, XVI.1; Der Marner (ed. P. Strauch) XIV.1, XIV.9, XIV.8, XIV.2, XIV.18d,
XIV.7, XIV.3, and two hitherto unattested strophes in first and fifth position in the manuscript. For a full study and edition of the Basel fragments, see now Martin Steinmann,
"Das Basler Fragment einer Rolle mit mittelhochdeutscher Spruchdichtung," *Zeitschrift für
deutsches Altertum und deutsche Literatur* 117 (1988) 296–310.

[29] B. Spaggiari, "Il canzoniere di Martim Codax," *Studi medievali* ser. 3, 21 (1980)
367–403. Partially reproduced in M. Pope, "Mediaeval Latin Background of the Thirteenth-
Century Galician Lyric," *Speculum* 9 (1934), following pp. 14 and 15. Kindly referred to me
by Dr. Mirella Ferrari.

shortly after 1263, which was edited in 1839 from a contemporary roll, now British Library Add. 23,986, that bears the *Interludum de clerico et puella* in a later hand on the dorse; Walter of Bibbesworth's thirteenth-century rhyming French vocabulary on British Library Sloane 809 s. xiii ex. — xiv in.; and the Anglo-Norman romance *Amadas et Ydoire* on the dorse of a pictorial history of England described by Thomas Wright.[30] Along with vernacular literature, both liturgy and drama (which is liturgical in origin) particularly lend themselves to roll form, to judge from the surviving rolls noted by Professor Bischoff.[31]

One cannot argue that, if rolls were so numerous, then more of them would exist today. *Beutelbücher*, those little portable books whose bindings permitted them to be looped over one's sash or belt, as seen in fifteenth-century paintings, are barely known to survive.[32] And certainly precious few medieval wax tablets have survived.[33] Rolls, like mimeographed reports or yesterday's newspaper, were ephemeral: once recopied or outmoded as fashions in songs changed, a roll was discarded in favor of new works on a new roll. Rolls cannot be bound up as quires or booklets can; when no longer needed, they could only be discarded, reused, or, as in the present case, cut up and used by binders.

What were these rolls? Were they texts used in performance? Were they repositories of a singer's repertoire, used as a basis for memorization? No answer emerges at present. One can only say that they served as the initial receptacle for new poems, the form in which they were first written down and first circulated. They were probably no more than one or two membranes in length, to judge from both the pictorial and physical evidence. In the portraits mentioned above, however, the rolls are nearly always displayed completely unrolled, which would make them hard to handle if they were of any great length. Physically, to judge from the UCLA fragments, the rolls were narrow, about 5 inches in width; it would be difficult to roll up manageably anything much over six feet in

---

[30] T. Wright, *Feudal Manuals of English History* (1872) xiv–xv. These and other English rolls are referred to by M. T. Clanchy, *From Memory to Written Record* (London 1979) 105–113; Add. 23,986 is still missing. Regarding Bibbesworth, see J. C. Russell, *Dictionary of Writers of Thirteenth-Century England* (London 1936) 175–176.

[31] B. Bischoff, *Paläographie des römischen Altertums und des abendländischen Mittelalters* (Berlin 1979) 48–50. Further references to rolls can be found in L. Santifaller, *Beiträge zur Geschichte der Beschreibstoffe im Mittelalter*, Mitteil. Inst. für Österreichische Geschichtsforschung 16.1 (Graz 1953) 153–162, although this deals basically with Antiquity and early medieval Europe; and W. Wattenbach, *Das Schriftwesen im Mittelalter*, ed. 3 (Leipzig 1896) 150–174, which should be used with caution.

[32] An overlooked example is in the Beinecke Library of Yale University.

[33] See R. Büll, *Vom Wachs*, Höchster Beiträge zur Kenntnis der Wachse 1.9 (Frankfurt 1968) 38; the Reinmar portrait with the wax tablet is reproduced in fig. 605.

length, with such a width. I would suppose that a singer might have had any number of rolls made up of a single membrane, and that at various times groups of these rolls were gathered, organized by theme or by poet, and transcribed into codices like D or C.

Why would a singer be more likely to want the texts of the pieces that he sang on rolls, rather than in a codex? What characteristics of the roll lent themselves to the singer's tasks? The most obvious, I think, were economy and portability. The roll, being nothing more than a strip of rough parchment frequently unruled, without decoration, and not having to be formed into quires or bound, was obviously less expensive than a book, as is seen in a late thirteenth-century English lawsuit printed by Helen Cam and R. M. Wilson, "A lady claims a missal worth twenty shillings, a manual worth 6s. 8d., and two rolls of songs worth sixpence and twopence respectively, which were snatched from her on the king's highway between Boughton and her home at Wereham on Easter day 1282."[34] Whatever their size relative to the two codices the rolls were clearly inexpensive, and doubtless of lighter weight. As far as portability is concerned, the singer was by nature of his profession itinerant, moving from court to court. Rolls even four or five membranes in length could be carried in pouch or satchel more easily than bound codices.[35] The second reason is more tenuous, for it depends on whether the roll was used in actual performance. If it was, as is suggested by a number of the pictures of poets reading or declaiming from rolls, poets used rolls because of the ease of seeing the text: there were no pages to turn, no columns in which to lose the line. Both portability and visibility of text explain why the roll form was used for liturgy and drama.[36] Oxford, Keble College Roll I, of the mid-fifteenth century, contains services and benedictions performed by a bishop in the spiritual administration of his diocese. At its head is a historiated initial, which depicts him reading from a roll held by an attendant while he blesses a kneeling flock.[37] What purports to be a mid-fifteenth-century performance text of the *Dux Moraud* copied on to a thirteenth-century assize roll survives in

---

[34] Cited from H. M. Cam, *The Hundred and the Hundred Rolls* (London 1930) 182, and R. M. Wilson, *The Lost Literature of Medieval England*, ed. 2 (London 1970) 163. Kindly referred to me by H. Gneuss.

[35] I should think this would hold true even for very long rolls, such as the well-known mortuary roll of Abbot Vitalis of Savigny (d. 1122).

[36] Bischoff, *Paläographie* 48 n. 101.

[37] M. B. Parkes, *Medieval Manuscripts of Keble College* (London 1979) 332 Roll 1. Surely, visibility for two audiences is a significant key to understanding the Exultet Rolls of southern Italy.

Oxford, Bodleian Library MS Eng. Poet. fol. 2(12) (SC 30519).[38] Both
the bishop and the player had to move from place to place in performing
their different tasks; and the roll—inexpensive, compact, and lightweight,
with clearly laidout text—was well suited to their needs.

What importance then, if any, attaches to the possibility that the
original written circulation of vernacular songs occurred on rolls? For
one thing, if we postulate that the early surviving codices of poems
descend from still-earlier groups of singers' rolls, that would help to
explain the absence of uniformity in sequence of stanzas—discrepancies
that occur in the two main collections of Reinmar's works, D and C. For
another, acceptance of such a hypothesis has serious implications for
modern editions of medieval vernacular verse: if poems initially circulated on singers' rolls, that would mean that a modern editor must
regard as the basic unit of transmission not the codex or whole collection of a writer's poems, but the roll; or if, as seems likely, an individual
Spruch or stanza might appear on several rolls accompanied by a different group of *Sprüche* in each case, then the largest unit of transmission that editors may consider is the individual *Spruch*. The dilemma is
rather analogous to that of the editor of a thirteenth-century university
text—St. Thomas, for example—where the basic unit of transmission is
not the whole of a summa or of a codex but merely the portion of it that
fills one *pecia* of a university stationer.[39]

By way of summary, it is worth dropping back in time to consider
a passage from one of Reinmar's distant predecessors who is also composing songs. In the prologue to his hymns, written at St. Gall around
900, Notker sets forth for us the place of the roll in the early transmission of his work:

> Quos versiculos cum magistro meo Marcello praesentarem, ille gaudio
> repletus in rotulas eos congessit; et pueris cantandos aliis alios insinuavit.
> Cumque mihi dixisset, ut in libellum compactos alicui primorum illos pro
> munere offerrem, ego pudore retractus numquam ad hoc cogi poteram.
> Nuper autem a fratre meo Othario rogatus, ut aliquid in laude vestra

---

[38] N. Davis, ed., *Non-Cycle Plays and Fragments*, Early English Text Society supp. 1
(Oxford 1970) c–cxi. This and the Keble Roll were kindly brought to my attention by
Malcolm Parkes.

[39] See A. Dondaine, "Apparat critique de l'édition d'un texte universitaire," in
L'Homme et son destin, Actes du premier congrès international de philosophie médiévale
(Louvain 1960) 211–220.

conscribere curarem, et ego . . . ad hoc animatus sum, ut hunc minimum vilissimumque codicellum vestrae celsitudini consecrare praesumerem.[40]

Notker presented his new sequences to his teacher Marcellus—whether orally, on tablets, on quires, or on rolls is not clear. Marcellus, pleased with them, collected them on rolls which he parceled out to the other students to sing. He suggested that Notker gather them together in a small book to present to some important person, but Notker modestly demurred. Now, however, under the persuasion of Brother Othar he has produced this little booklet of his sequences in honor of Liutward, bishop of Vercelli, abbot of Bobbio, and archchaplain to Charles the Fat. In editing the *Liber ymnorum*, von den Steinen demonstrates that the collection of sequences made ca. 950, archetype of the surviving manuscripts, was formed jointly from the texts on rolls used in the performance of the liturgy, and the texts in Notker's *codicellum*.[41] Thus we see that Notker's work, like Reinmar's, was initially disseminated on rolls, and that the collection on which our extant manuscripts depend was compiled at least in part from rolls.

---

[40] W. von den Steinen, ed., *Notker der Dichter und seine geistige Welt* 2 (Bern 1948) 10. I am grateful to Dr. Peter Godman for drawing this reference to my attention.

[41] Von den Steinen, ed., *Notker der Dichter* 192–198.

*Ancient Authors and
Medieval Readers*

2. "Potens in Opere et Sermone": Philip, Bishop of Bayeux, and His Books*

In contrasting the world of monastic learning with that of the cathedral schools, Sir Richard Southern said of the twelfth-century student, "He not only knew where to study, he also knew that his studies would have a market value." The schools, in Southern's words, "brought the idea of . . . order and rationality into every area of human experience." In the early twelfth century, "slowly the ruling households of Europe, at all levels from the papal court to the household of a minor baron, were penetrated by men calling themselves *masters*, or as we should say, university men." This theme, the significant place of the schools in the formation of the twelfth-century state, permeates Southern's study of the period.[1]

The key role of the northern French cathedral schools in the growth of Anglo-Norman administration—civil and ecclesiastic—is a near text-

---

*Written to be published in *The Classics in the Middle Ages*, ed. Aldo Bernardo and Saul Levin (Binghamton, N.Y., forthcoming). The present version incorporates a few changes made on the basis of new evidence. Because of unavoidable delays in the appearance of the Binghamton volume, this revision may paradoxically have an earlier publication date than the original.

We thank Robert L. Benson, John F. Benton, and Margaret T. Gibson, who kindly read an earlier version of this essay and gave sound advice. We are grateful to Terry Nixon for his help over the years with the two Bec booklists, as well as for suggestions on specific aspects of this article. We are indebted to Patricia Stirnemann for generously sharing with us her detailed knowledge of many of the manuscripts mentioned below.

The title derives from epistle 8 of Arnulf of Lisieux (cited in n. 9 below), who says of Philip, "Homo enim consilii et fortitudinis est, potens in opere et sermone, in regalibus consiliis et negotiis ecclesiasticis acceptus et efficax. . . ."

[1] R. W. Southern, *The Making of the Middle Ages* (London 1953) 209, and his *Medieval Humanism and Other Studies* (New York 1970) 175.

book example, which no doubt was very much in Southern's thinking when he wrote these statements. Names come to mind almost unbidden: John of Salisbury, Arnulf of Lisieux, Hugh of Amiens, Rotrou of Rouen, Gilbert Foliot, Gerald of Wales—men whose ascent up the Anglo-Norman ladder depended on schooling as well as (or even instead of) birth. Today we know them—in some instances, know them best—for their writings. Their contemporaries knew and honored (or feared, or disliked) them as well for their positions as, respectively, bishop of Chartres, bishop of Lisieux, archbishop of Rouen, bishop of Evreux who became archbishop of Rouen, bishop of London, and bishop-elect of St. Davids. Although only two of these were major *literati*, all were learned, all had been "schooled."

In the present paper we want to pursue this theme through the life of one such man whose career has been neglected: Philip of Harcourt, bishop of Bayeux from 1142 to 1163.[2] He wrote nothing that survives, which explains why he receives scant notice in surveys of the Twelfth-Century Renaissance. His principal claim to notice has been his library, the 140 volumes that he left to the abbey of Bec.[3] Although the books themselves, with scant exception, are not known today, the contemporary catalog of the collection provides much information.

Philip played a significant role in the transmission of ancient Latin authors. His library included such uncommon works as Cicero's *De academicis, De finibus,* Caesarian orations, and philosophical corpus; Seneca's *Natural History,* the Younger Pliny's letters, and Pomponius Mela's *De chorographia.* We have examined the list of Philip's books many times for what it may reveal about the transmission and dissemination of rare

---

[2] Concerning Philip's life see V. Bourrienne, *Un grand bâtisseur: Philippe de Harcourt, évêque de Bayeux 1142–1163* (Paris 1930), and Sarell Everett Gleason, *An Ecclesiastical Barony of the Middle Ages: The Bishopric of Bayeux, 1066–1204* (Cambridge, Mass. 1936). Bourrienne has amassed an impressive amount of information, but it is inextricably mixed with credulous borrowings from "romantic" earlier histories of the Harcourts and the region. Most recently, Philip's career can be followed as that of a recurring minor character in David Crouch, *The Beaumont Twins: The Roots and Branches of Power in the Twelfth Century* (Cambridge 1986).

[3] The catalog of Philip's books has been edited by Gustav Becker, *Catalogi bibliothecarum antiqui* (Bonn 1885) 199–202; and, with slightly different numbering, by H. Omont, *Catalogue général des manuscrits des bibliothèques publiques* 2 (Paris 1888) 394–398, the edition cited here. The collection is briefly discussed by Geneviève Nortier, *Les bibliothèques médiévales des abbayes bénédictines de Normandie* (Caen 1966) 39–45. R. W. Hunt groups Philip's collection with the 56 volumes that belonged to the near-contemporary Celestine III (d. 1144), and with the libraries of two thirteenth-century churchmen, Cardinal Guala Bicchieri (d. 1227) and Bernard II, archbishop of Santiago de Compostela (1223–1237), whose collections were similar in size to Philip's; see his "Universities and Learning," in *The Flowering of the Middle Ages,* ed. Joan Evans (London 1985) 1645.

texts.[4] Here we propose instead to examine it for the writings of Philip's contemporaries, and to use the books to illuminate the man.

*   *   *

We begin with the biographical information that can be assembled from the records, not a negligible quantity.[5] Philip came from a significant though not princely Anglo-Norman family. His father Robert I fitz Anschetil was lord of Harcourt, a sizable holding midway between Evreux and Lisieux. Philip was one of, apparently, eight sons. In common with many Norman nobles, members of the Harcourt family held land on both sides of the Channel. The maternal side of Philip's ancestry is uncertain, but it seems likely that his mother was a sister of Philip of Briouze, lord of Bramber.[6]

Philip's life was ineluctably shaped by the patronage of Waleran, count of Meulan, who was overlord of Harcourt and (given his consistent fostering of Philip's career) doubtless a kinsman as well.[7] Waleran is reputed to have been a learned man, who not only read Latin but composed Latin verse that was admired by contemporaries. Geoffrey of Monmouth sought his patronage, upon the publication of the *Historia regum Britanniae*. Waleran's twin brother Robert, earl of Leicester, enjoyed a similar reputation for learning.[8] Philip's early formation, then, may have benefited from his association with this literate household.

Philip's library, as we shall see, reveals the schoolman in several specific ways, just as his success as an administrator betokens training in both laws. We have no explicit information about Philip's schooling, no mention in document or letter, and we must rely on a combination of

---

[4] See the index to *Texts and Transmission*, ed. L. Reynolds (Oxford 1983), sub nom. "Philip, Bishop of Bayeux."

[5] Unless otherwise noted, the events of Philip's biography given here are based upon the works cited in n. 2 above.

[6] Crouch, *Twins* 120–127, discusses the evidence for the individual Harcourts and their holdings; for a summary and genealogical table see pp. 220–221. Abbé Bourrienne, pp. 1–3, presents a genealogy that differs in most details, for which he offers nothing in the way of substantiation.

[7] As Crouch recognizes, there is no concrete evidence that Philip is Robert fitz Anschetil's son (*Twins* 220 n. 7)—nor even that Robert and Waleran were cousins, though contemporary Bec historians record an unspecified kinship (ibid. 120–121). Both assumptions are reasonable, and they explain much about Philip's career which would otherwise be perplexing. We are grateful to David Crouch for sharing with us his further thoughts on Philip's family.

[8] See Crouch, *Beaumont Twins* 207–211. Crouch is occasionally more willing than are we, to accept at face value formulas in charters, such as *vidi et legi* or *legi et confirmavi*, as indications that Waleran "made it his business personally to research the archives of his dependent religious communities" (p. 208).

deduction and analogy. Given his geographical location, it is likely that at least a part of his studies were at the cathedral school of Chartres. Philip's friend and contemporary Arnulf of Lisieux studied there in the late 1120s/early 1130s, it is thought,[9] before going to Italy to study law; and Philip's and Arnulf's younger contemporary John of Salisbury later studied at Chartres.[10] Count Waleran's cousin Rotrou, bishop of Evreux, archbishop of Rouen, and perhaps a distant kinsman of Philip's,[11] is known to have studied with Gilbert de la Porrée; probably this also took place at Chartres, where Gilbert was chancellor.[12] At least one of Philip's books seems to have been written by Chartres scribes.[13] Orléans, too, is a good possibility for at least some of his schooling—again, to judge from the fact that some of the rarer texts that he owned were disseminated from twelfth-century Orléans.[14] As the contents of his library suggest, he was trained in the *artes*, including the study of formal composition in speaking and epistolary style based on the models of classical and patristic letters and orations; and he read as well in theology and

[9] Frank Barlow, ed., *The Letters of Arnulf of Lisieux*, Camden Third Series 61 (London 1939) xiii–xv. The facts are three: (1) Arnulf, in letter no. 34, reveals that he had obtained his basic education at the cathedral school of Séez where his older brother John (bishop of Séez from 1124) was archdeacon—hence, before 1124; (2) in the introduction to his *Invectiva in Girardum Engolismensem episcopum* written in the summer of 1133, he notes that he was then in Italy, for the study of law; and (3) the *Invectiva* is dedicated to Geoffrey de Lèves, bishop of Chartres, whose clerk Arnulf had been—again, according to the introduction. Thus, Arnulf clearly spent some years in Chartres, between his earliest education at Séez and his legal studies in Italy; Barlow thinks it likely that those years were spent in schooling.

[10] Such, at least, is the assumption of current study; see Olga Weijers, "The Chronology of John of Salisbury's Studies in France (Metalogicon, II.10)," in *The World of John of Salisbury*, Studies in Church History Subsidia 3, ed. Michael Wilks (Oxford 1984) 109–116, esp. 114–116.

[11] Rotrou was first cousin to Count Waleran de Meulan; see Crouch, *Beaumont Twins* p. 16 fig. 2, etc. Crouch elsewhere (p.45) suggests that Philip was a distant relative of the count.

[12] When Gilbert was examined at Paris in 1147, and again at Reims in 1148, he alluded to his pupil Rotrou as evidence of the soundness of his teaching; see *Histoire littéraire de la France* vol. 14, p. 296. Southern, *Medieval Humanism* 67, argues that Gilbert's most important teaching probably occurred at Paris after he had left Chartres, which may well be correct. Gilbert is first documented at Paris in 1141, however, and by that date Rotrou was well past his school days, having become bishop of Evreux in 1138 or 1139.

[13] The manuscript in question—Paris, B.N. lat. 5802, a collection of ancient historians—and the origins of Philip's library are discussed in T. Maslowski and R. H. Rouse, "Twelfth-Century Extracts from Cicero's *Pro Archia* and *Pro Cluento* in Paris B.N. MS lat. 18104," *Italia medioevale e umanistica* 22 (1979) 97–122.

[14] See chap. 5, "*Florilegia* and Latin Classical Authors in Twelfth- and Thirteenth-Century Orléans."

both civil and canon law, whether or not he had formal schooling in these disciplines.

Philip's first living, the rectory of Sompting in Sussex, derived from his maternal uncle(?), Philip de Briouze, lord of Bramber. Thereafter, his rise in the church was rapid, aided almost entirely by his connection with Count Waleran of Meulan.[15] Before 1131, he became dean of Holy Trinity at Beaumont-le-Roger, burial place of the counts of Meulan and a dependency of Lincoln Cathedral, within the gift of Count Waleran. After that, Philip became archdeacon of Evreux, Waleran's "neighborhood cathedral," and then dean of Lincoln Cathedral, during the episcopacy of Alexander (1123–1148). The precise dates are debatable, but these three steps must have been taken in very short order.[16]

Philip was in England in a time of civil war; and in 1139, as a protege of King Stephen's supporter Count Waleran, he was made chancellor of Stephen's government. In December of that same year Roger, bishop of Salisbury, died; and Philip of Harcourt resigned the chancellorship, to free himself to fill the vacancy—to which, as anticipated, he was named by King Stephen, at Waleran's urging.[17] But support of the royal court was not adequate to overcome the objections of the cathedral chapter at Salisbury, who refused to elect Stephen's nominee Philip. The fact that Bishop Roger had died while imprisoned by King Stephen may have helped to make the Salisbury chapter a bit testy. At any rate, it was likely in the course of this melodrama that Philip became possessed of a reliquary, "an arm, gold plated and adorned with precious stones," from the treasury of Salisbury Cathedral—which he kept until he was persuaded to return it in 1148.[18] This was the arm-reliquary of St. Aldhelm

---

[15] Concerning Philip's relationship with Count Waleran and his twin Robert of Leicester, see Crouch, *Beaumont Twins*, esp. pp. 45 and 220.

[16] For the documentation, such as it is, see Crouch, *Twins* 45 and nn.

[17] See the index sub nom. "Philip de Harcourt" in Crouch, *Beaumont Twins*, for the indications of consistent support from Waleran in the stages of Philip's career.

[18] "Bracium unum, aureis lammis coopertum, et lapidibus preciosis adornatum"; see V. Bourrienne, ed., *Antiquus cartularius ecclesiae Baiocensis (Livre noir)*, 2 vols. (Paris 1902) 1.80–81, documents numbered 61 and 62, which record all that we know about the incident: Hugh archbishop of Rouen (no. 61) notifies the archbishops of Canterbury and York and all the English hierarchy that bishops Philip of Bayeux and Jocelin of Salisbury have reached agreement for return of the arm, along with a "gift"—doubtless some sort of amends—of ten silver marks. In fact, though only the arm is returned, the "quarrel" concerned "certain things [plural] carried off from the treasury of Salisbury Cathedral" (*controversia . . . pro quibusdam absportatis de thesauro Salesburiensis ecclesiae*); perhaps the ten marks are payment for losses. For reasons unknown, an identical charter was addressed to the same recipients presumably at the same time by Rotrou, bishop of Evreux (no. 62). Neither document is dated; in both cases, Bourrienne has named the English archbishops as "Thomas of Canterbury" (1162–1170) and "Henry of York" (Henry Murdac,

that had been given to Salisbury in the eleventh century by St. Osmund.[19]

The setback in Philip's career was only temporary, for within three years he was elected bishop of Bayeux in Normandy, a position he held from 1142 until his death in 1163. With Stephen's capture by Angevin forces in 1141, Philip's patron Waleran had recognized that the future in Normandy lay with the Angevins, and had pragmatically shifted his Continental allegiance to Geoffrey of Anjou in order to safeguard the family's Norman lands. Philip's election to Bayeux must have been part of an overall exchange of tokens between Waleran and Geoffrey. Subsequently, however, Waleran's relations with the Angevins cooled markedly as he flirted too openly with the French Crown.[20] Apparently, Philip successfully distanced himself from Waleran in this matter; his tenure at Bayeux was marked from beginning to end by civil, and ultimately cordial, relations with the House of Anjou.

Normandy during the English anarchy,[21] left largely on its own, had witnessed an upsurge in local autonomy, with the emphasis on survival of the fittest. The church, and especially the bishops, were for the

---

d. 1153), an impossible combination. R. H. C. Davis, *King Stephen, 1135–1154* (Berkeley 1967) 47 and n., sensibly suggests that the manuscript must have said (or meant) "T[heobald]" rather than "Thomas" as archbishop of Canterbury—hence, that the agreement occurred between 1147 and 1153 (the tenure of Henry of York), probably in 1148 at the Council of Reims. This is the date accepted by Thomas G. Waldman, who is preparing an edition of "The *Acta* of Hugh 'of Amiens,' Archbishop of Rouen, 1130–1164" for the Royal Historical Society's Camden Series. We are grateful to Dr. Waldman for this information.

[19] Previous mentions of this incident have not, to our knowledge, identified the relic at the center of the quarrel. The list of Osmund's gifts, ca. 1078–1099, is printed by C. Wordsworth, *Ceremonies and Processions of the Cathedral Church of Salisbury* (Cambridge 1901) 183: "brachium sancti Aldelmi argent' et deaurat'." William of Malmesbury's *Vita* of Aldhelm explains how Osmund was given Aldhelm's left arm by Malmesbury in 1078; lodged in a sumptuous reliquary, it performed miracles of healing at Salisbury: see William of Malmesbury, *De gestis pontificum anglorum*, ed. N.E.S.A. Hamilton, Rolls Series (London 1870) 428–429. The reliquary recurs in the inventory of ornaments found in the treasury at Sarum in 1214; Wordsworth 169: "brachium sancti Aldelmi coopertum argento, cum multis lapidibus, continens alias reliquias." It is curious that Philip should have taken such pains to get, and stubbornly to keep, the relics of an Anglo-Saxon saint.

[20] See Crouch, *Beaumont Twins* 58–79.

[21] Frank Barlow, *The Feudal Kingdom of England*, 2d ed. (New York 1961) provides a useful survey of the political and social history of Philip of Bayeux's lifetime; concerning the disputed succession of Henry I and the civil wars of King Stephen's reign, see pp. 201–234; for Normandy, see esp. 208–209, 210, 221. For more recent bibliography see Davis, *King Stephen*, 1135–1154; W.L. Warren, *Henry II* (Berkeley 1973), esp. chap. 2 (pp. 12–53), "The Pursuit of an Inheritance (1135–54)"; and Marjorie Chibnall, *Anglo-Norman England 1066–1166* (Oxford 1986), and esp. 77–101 concerning civil war and succession.

most part faithful to Stephen. The turning point in the reestablishment of ducal authority in Normandy came, as we have seen, just before Philip took office. Geoffrey of Anjou, secure in his alliance with Robert of Gloucester, by 1141 dominated much of the south and west of Normandy; and by the spring of 1144 he received the submission of Rouen. Philip administered the see of Bayeux under Geoffrey duke of Normandy from 1144 until the spring of 1150, when Geoffrey gave the duchy to his son Henry, future Henry II of England. At that time it was necessary for Philip once again to adapt to the court of a new ruler, though the adjustment was not so difficult as that in the period 1142–1144, no doubt; and for the last fourteen years of his life he worked effectively in and with Henry's court.

The Norman cathedral of Bayeux, consecrated in 1077 under Bishop Odo, had been burnt down in 1105 by Odo's nephew Henry I. Of Odo's cathedral, only the square towers and the crypt remained. The visible devastation of the building's fabric symbolized the financial ruin of the see itself. Philip's immediate predecessors, Bishop Richard II and his nephew Bishop Richard III, could not or would not withstand the encroachments of their assertive kinsman Robert earl of Gloucester, who was the principal lay power in the diocese. This bastard son of Henry I was also the indispensable ally of Geoffrey of Anjou, who was not eager to alienate his supporter in order to benefit the new bishop of Bayeux whose political past was suspect, from an Angevin viewpoint. The great Norman abbeys like Fécamp and Troarn had also helped themselves to rights, privileges, and property at the expense of the bishops of Bayeux—no doubt largely a matter of self-preservation during the breakdown of authority.

Philip set about restoring his diocese. Much of the present cathedral was built or planned by him, with the six bays of the nave having been completed under his episcopacy and the gothic windows and buttresses in the time of his successors.[22] Along with his rebuilding in stone, Philip must have spent even more of his time and energy in rebuilding the episcopal authority, with the estates, rents, rights, and privileges

---

[22] Concerning the architecture of the new cathedral see J. Vallery-Radot, *La Cathédrale de Bayeux*, 2d rev. ed (Paris 1958). It would be interesting to know if the famous bas-reliefs were placed on the walls of the new nave under Philip's direction. We have found no distinct connection between any of the scenes depicted and any of the books in Philip's library. The bas-relief of a chained ape is particularly interesting, in that it is an early depiction of this subject in northern Europe according to H. Janson, *Apes and Ape Lore* (London 1952) 49. E. Lambert, "Les écoinçons de la nef de la Cathédrale de Bayeux," in *Mélanges Henrik Cornell* (Stockholm 1950) 262–271, did not explore potential literary sources.

pertaining to it; this was Philip's major undertaking, begun immediately and pursued relentlessly throughout his episcopacy.[23] All the techniques at his disposal were brought to bear in this matter, his influence with Rome, and with the duke, and his knowledge of law. He was so zealous in this area that Haskins considered him instrumental in the development of the jury of presentment or inquest.[24] Philip traveled back and forth to Rome at least three times to secure the written instruments he needed. He was there in 1144 during the brief pontificate of Lucius II; we know, from the protocol of a trial held at the Curia, that he was present in Rome (still? again?), together with Archbishop Hugh of Sens and bishops Arnulf of Lisieux, Albero of Liège, Benedict of Orléans, and Bernard of Saragossa, on 15 February 1145 (N.S.)—the day when Lucius II died and the day of Eugenius III's election;[25] and he went twice more (in 1146 and in 1150 or 1151) during the term of Eugenius III. Three bulls from Lucius, reissued virtually unchanged by Eugenius, herald the upswing in Bayeux's fortunes.[26] (1) The first confirms to Philip all the possessions of the diocese (including rights and rents, as well as real property), itemized in prosaic detail;[27] Philip had obviously arrived in Rome well briefed, with his claims indisputably documented. (2) The second called upon all the faithful in the diocese—abbots, priors, clergy, laity—to help Philip in his task of recovering his rights, ordering them to hand over any of the bishop's property that they might hold illegally, and nullifying all exchanges, sales, or gifts of Bayeux property by all bishops since Odo— an attempt to roll back the clock forty-five years at one go.[28] (3) The third was addressed to Duke Geoffrey (just as a future one would be addressed to Duke Henry, as soon as he took the reins in Normandy),

---

[23] Concerning Philip's renovation of his diocese, see Bourrienne, *Un grand bâtisseur* pt. 2 "L'évêque" (pp. 9–113); Gleason, *Ecclesiastical Barony* 41–67; and C. H. Haskins, *Norman Institutions*, Harvard Historical Studies 24 (Cambridge, Mass. 1918) 203–216, 222–225.

[24] Haskins, *Norman Institutions* 148–150 and chap. 6, "The Early Norman Jury," pp. 196ff.

[25] See Helmut Gleber, *Papst Eugen III. (1145–1153) unter besonderer Berücksichtigung seiner politischen Tätigkeit,* Beiträge zur mittelalterlichen und neueren Geschichte 6 (Jena 1936) 11, who suggests that this group of northern prelates influenced the election. The protocol is printed by Paul Fridolin Kehr, Abh. Göttingen, N.F. 22.1 p. 345 no. 46. We are grateful to Robert L. Benson for this reference.

[26] The bulls are preserved in the cartulary of Bayeux cathedral, the *Livre noir* edited by Bourrienne.

[27] *Livre noir* nos. 154 (16 May 1144, Lucius II); 155 (18 March 1145) and 156 (3 Feb. 1153, Eugenius III).

[28] *Livre noir* nos. 157 (16 May 1144, Lucius II = Jaffé Löwenfeld #8612) and 173 (18 March ?1145, Eugenius III).

reminding him that Henry I in an earlier day had held inquests (or assizes, or *recognitiones*) to determine the possessions of the see, and asking Geoffrey to order a new *recognitio* to help restore Bayeux as it had been.[29] (The purpose of Henry I's inquests, by contrast, had been to benefit the Crown, a difference that the pope did not dwell on.) Geoffrey, in response, not only ordered *recognitiones* on Philip's behalf (i.e., juries of inquest taking sworn information from people who knew), but he even empowered Philip to order *recognitiones* on his own initiative, and to compel compliance as if the order had come from the duke.

Philip's methods were those of a schoolman: He went after his goals armed with the written word—the right, effective words, written by those (the pope, the duke) whose words had power among lesser lords lay and ecclesiastic. Without an army but simply by knowing how to use the written word and the law courts effectively, Philip persisted until he gradually established in law the see's rights, and secured the observation of those rights. (Actually, he never did quite compel submission from Robert of Goucester, who made many promises but delivered nothing; but Philip outlived him, which had much the same effect.)

Philip's reliance on the power of documentation is visible in the well-known *Livre noir* of Bayeux, the cathedral cartulary that contains documents dating from the early eleventh century until the early fourteenth. As the *Livre noir*'s editor Bourrienne noted, the manuscript begins with a segment written in a single early thirteenth-century hand which has copied the first 213 charters, from the earliest (1035–1037) until 1205; later hands continued to record until the second decade of the fourteenth century.[30] If we look beneath the surface of the opening segment, however, we can recognize a unit within a unit: Almost certainly, its kernel is the archive that Philip assembled to place the privileges, liberties, immunities, and possessions of his diocese on unassailable legal grounds. Roughly 100 of these 213 charters date from the twenty-one years of Philip's episcopate, compared with only 98 for the following forty-two years.[31] More distinctive still is the amount, and especially the nature, of the documentation in this segment that dates from before

---

[29] *Livre noir* no. 206 (16 May 1144, Lucius II); cf. *Livre noir* no. 39 (ca. 1144) for the duke's allusion to the corresponding bull of Eugenius, which evidently does not survive.

[30] *Livre noir* vol. 1 p. xiii, the charters numbered 1–214; nos. 33*bis* and 168, which pertain to the 1260s, are later insertions.

[31] Of the first 213 charters in the *Livre noir* (nos. 1–214, less the inserted no. 168), the following documents probably date from Philip's episcopacy: nos. 7, 9–10, 12–19, 24–28, 30–33, 35–37, 39–44, 52–54, 58–63, 71, 73, 76, 89–90, 99–101, 103–104, 106, 117–118, 127, 138–139, 148–151, 154–159, 161–166, 173–175, 178–179, 181–195, 198–203, 206–207, 210, 213.

Philip's accession. There are only some 15 of these earlier charters. Of them, 9 are grants, or confirmations of grants, that date from Odo's day;[32] this reminds us that papal bulls nullified all sales, gifts, or exchanges "since the time of Bishop Odo." The one still earlier charter, dated 1035–1037, is an inventory of diocesan lands and possessions drawn up by Bishop Hugh II;[33] we recall that Philip's first concession from the papacy, in 1144, was papal confirmation of an inventory of Bayeux's possessions, which was itemized in terms similar to this. Of the only 5 charters in the *Livre noir* that date from the anarchic period between Odo's death and Philip's accession, all but one are *acta* of Henry I of England confirming or restoring rights of Bayeux as they had been at various previous times;[34] and here we recall that, although the papal bulls nullified any loss the diocese had suffered, nothing was said to disqualify any gains enjoyed "since the time of Bishop Odo." It does not stretch the imagination to see in these early charters the documentation that Philip had gathered up to take with him to Rome, when he first set out in 1144 to put his episcopal house back in order.

*　　*　　*

The twelfth-century prelates of Normandy comprised a small interwoven society of familiar faces. For example, two successive deans of Philip's cathedral became his colleagues as successive bishops of Coutances: Richard I de Bohun, seen in 1146 as dean of Bayeux, became bishop of Coutances in 1150; he was succeeded as bishop by William III de Tournebu, seen as dean of Bayeux in 1153 (his bishopric ends before 1183).[35] Philip himself belonged to the inner cadre of four who at midcentury firmly ran that Norman church and served the often absent kingduke in the government of the duchy: Hugh of Amiens, archbishop of Rouen 1130–1164; Rotrou, bishop of Evreux 1139–1165; Arnulf, bishop of Lisieux 1142–1184; and Philip, bishop of Bayeux 1142–1163. The four were colleagues, and perhaps something more, centering on the figure of the archbishop. Hugh of Amiens (b. ca. 1095) was successively prior of St. Martial of Limoges, abbot of Reading, and (during the whole of Philip's episcopacy) archbishop of Rouen. Trained at the cathedral school of Laon, Hugh wrote several works of theology and exegesis, including *Contra hereticos sui temporis, De fide catholica, In laudem memoriae, Questiones theo-*

---

[32] *Livre noir*, nos. 1–6, 22–23, 172.

[33] *Livre noir*, no. 21.

[34] *Livre noir*, nos. 8, 29, 34, 38; no. 102 — confirmation of a gift of land to the cathedral's *succentor*, dated 1135–1142 — is the only charter that does not patently fit the mold.

[35] See Bourrienne, pp. 61, 70, and B. Gams, *Series episcoporum ecclesiae catholicae* (Regensburg 1873–1886; repr. Graz 1957) 542.

logicae (or *Dialogi*), and *Tractatus in hexaemeron* (or *In Genesim 1–3*).[36] It is not only by virtue of his office but by virtue of these writings that Hugh of Amiens links his three suffragans: Two of Hugh's works—the *Dialogi* and *De fide*—appear on the list of books that Rotrou (Hugh's successor as archbishop) left to the cathedral of Rouen.[37] A third work, the Genesis commentary, which was praised by Bernard of Clairvaux,[38] bore a dedication to Hugh's "dearest son, the learned Arnulf, bishop of Lisieux."[39] Philip completes the circle, for he also owned something of Hugh's. We cannot tell which, since the booklist says simply *Liber Hugonis archiepiscopi*; perhaps it was the *Contra hereticos*, the most widely circulated of Hugh's works.[40] Assertive, capable, and learned, these four prelates in addition enjoyed the happy accident of exceptionally long tenures shared concurrently, providing an unexpected bedrock of stability beneath the agitated surface of Norman affairs through the middle of the twelfth century.

Philip was the first bishop at Bayeux since Odo to play an important role in the government of the duchy. He was one of the entourage of Norman bishops who accompanied the duke to England for his coronation as Henry II in 1154. Philip's role in Duke Henry's administration comes to the surface particularly for the period after the duke was crowned,

---

[36] Dom Martène's edition of Hugh's works is printed in Migne's *Patrologia latina* vol. 192; a modern edition of the Genesis commentary (of which Martène knew only a fragment) was produced by Francis Lecomte, "Un commentaire scripturaire du XIIe siècle: Le 'Tractatus in Hexaemeron' de Hugues d'Amiens (archevêque de Rouen 1130–1164)," *Archives d'histoire doctrinale et littéraire du moyen âge* 33 (1958 [1959]) 227–294. For Hugh's biography see the article of E. Vacandard in the *Dictionnaire de théologie catholique*; Lecomte's introduction; and the D.Phil. dissertation of Thomas G. Waldman, "Hugh 'of Amiens,' Archbishop of Rouen 1130–64" (Oxford 1970).

[37] Edited by L. Delisle, "Documents sur les livres et les bibliothèques au moyen âge 1: Bibliothèque de la cathédrale de Rouen au XIIe siècle," *Bibliothèque de l'Ecole des chartes* II (1849) 218: "Liber Hugonis archiepiscopi ad Albanensem episcopum [= *Dialogi*]; libellus ejusdem de expositione fidei catholice et orationis Dominice." The second volume is now Geneva, Bibliothèque publique et universitaire MS lat. 41. Rotrou's list includes in addition Pliny, *Natural History*; Jerome, *Epistolae*; Augustine, *De civitate Dei*; Isidore, *Etymologies*; and Vitruvius, *De architectura*. Evreux Bibliothèque municipale MS 92, containing the *Confessions* and other Augustiniana—but not *De civitate Dei*—also bears Rotrou's *ex libris*, part of a bequest to his first cathedral, Evreux ("Hunc librum dedit dominus Rotrodus Rothomagensis archiepiscopus ecclesie Ebroicensi").

[38] Cf. Lecomte, p. 227 and n. 6.

[39] The letter is printed by Lecomte, 235–236. Arnulf wrote an epitaph on Hugh's death, printed in PL 201.200.

[40] See Nortier, *Les bibliothèques* 346. We are grateful to Thomas G. Waldman for confirming this suggestion.

because English records survive in much greater measure than do Continental ones.

Following the coronation we see Philip attesting royal charters issued from every corner of Henry's sprawling domain, ranging from Périgueux down in Aquitaine to York in the north of England.[41] At least sixty-one of Henry II's *acta* have Philip as witness.[42] Not surprisingly, the largest group of these (fifteen) were issued at Rouen, capital of the duchy and seat of the Norman archdiocese, where both Henry and Philip were apt to find themselves, not necessarily on joint errands. Another three emanated from Bayeux itself. Of the remainder, seventeen were issued from various English sites, and twenty-six from different locales in Henry's Continental domains. Philip was joined as witness by Bishop Arnulf of Lisieux on forty-three occasions, and in nineteen instances by Bishop Rotrou of Evreux.[43] His appearance as witness indicates, of course, that Philip was frequently in attendance upon the king and his itinerant court, and that the king found him reliable — just as, in 1161, the king is said to have entrusted Philip with taking a message to Pope Alexander III during the schism, although age ultimately prevented Philip from making the journey.[44]

Philip seems on occasion to have wielded extensive authority in Normandy, on the duke's behalf. At the same time that Philip was employing the process of the sworn inquest to reestablish and maintain the rights of his see, Henry II was extending the use of this process throughout the duchy; a regularized procedure of ducal justice was especially necessary after the coronation in 1154, when Henry divided his time between the Continent and England. For this purpose he resurrected the post of justiciar of Normandy, to act as chief judicial officer of the duchy in the duke's absence. There were ordinarily two of these at one time, most often the seneschal of Normandy and a Norman bishop, or other combinations, on a rotating basis. Philip's confreres Arnulf, bishop of Lisieux, and Rotrou, then bishop of Evreux, served as justiciars during this period.[45] Not surprisingly, in at least two surviving documents Philip too seems to act in this capacity — once with Robert de Neubourg, seneschal of Normandy, and the second time in tandem with Bishop

---

[41] See L. Delisle, *Recueil des actes de Henri II*, ed. E. Berger, 3 vols. (Paris 1916–1927) 1.80 and 1.180–181.

[42] See Appendix below, for a list of the locations and the dates of the 61.

[43] For a list of these acts, together with the dates and locations, see the Appendix below.

[44] Gleason, *Ecclesiastical Barony* 29.

[45] See Haskins, *Norman Institutions* 165–166.

Rotrou, the seneschal's brother.[46]

Thus, Philip's ecclesiastical career, which crossed over the Channel and back, was paralleled by a career in civil administration on both sides of the water, as Stephen's chancellor in England in young manhood, as a member of Henry II's traveling entourage and witness to his charters in England in ca. 1154–1155 and on the Continent ca. 1156–1163, and perhaps as Henry II's justiciar in Normandy. Arnulf of Lisieux asserted that Philip was, "in the deliberations of the king, as in the affairs of the church, both welcome and effective."[47]

The full extent of his involvement in the Angevin administration can only be surmised, given the paucity of Continental records—which is a pity. To judge from what is known about him, Philip had both the nature and the training of a model civil servant, and was doubtless employed more frequently than the surviving evidence documents.

*   *   *

According to the *Chronicle* of Robert of Torigny (d. 1186), Philip had intended to retire at the end of his life to the abbey of Bec (just as his friend Arnulf of Lisieux was to end his days, and leave his books, with the abbey of St. Victor), but death intervened; however, Robert adds, Philip had already given the abbey 140 books.[48] A copy of the list of Philip's books survives, on the first flyleaf of Avranches Bibliothèque municipale MS 159 (fol. iv), in a hand not much later than the date of his death. Also, beginning on the second flyleaf (fols. 2–3), a different hand of similar date has enrolled a list of books in the Bec library.[49] Avranches 159, written at Mont-St-Michel, is a book of histories that begins with Eusebius and his continuators and ends with the last redaction of Robert of Torigny's *Chronicle*. Robert was a monk at Bec from 1128 until he left in 1154 for Mont-St-Michel, where he was abbot until his death in 1186. He had been an avid builder of Bec's library, and after his move he commissioned books for Mont-St-Michel to be copied from

---

[46] Ibid. 167 and n. 63. Not surprisingly, the seneschal was also a frequent joint witness, with Philip, of royal acts (see above)—20 of the 61 charters witnessed by Philip were also attested by Robert. We note, in passing, that Robert de Neubourg retired to the abbey of Bec (he had funded the building of the abbey's chapter house) at the end of his life in 1159, just as Philip was to do in 1163; ibid. 166 n. 57. Robert de Neubourg and Bishop Rotrou were brothers, first cousins of Waleran of Meulan, and thus probably distant kin of Philip; see Crouch, *Beaumont Twins* p. 16 fig. 2.

[47] Barlow, *Letters* p. 11 ep. 8, "in regalibus consiliis et negotiis ecclesiasticis acceptus et efficax."

[48] L. Delisle, ed., *Chronique de Robert de Torigni*, 2 vols. (Rouen 1872–1873) 1.344–345.

[49] For a reproduction of fol.iv see Nortier, *Les bibliothèques*, facing p. 66.

Bec exemplars.[50] To all appearances, Avranches 159 is Robert's own copy of his *Chronicle*. His interest in securing copies of the books at Bec may explain the presence of the two Bec booklists on the flyleaves, but that point is uncertain.

Philip's list is headed "Tituli librorum quos dedit Philippus episcopus Baiocensis ecclesie Becci" (Titles of the books that Philip bishop of Bayeux gave to Bec). The two opening words are written in display letters and the entire heading is slashed in red, with the next eight lines spaciously arranged. But then the writer decided that he wanted the whole text on one page, and he compressed the remainder of the list into forty-three long lines. Individual volumes (each of which may contain several works) are distinguished by the formula *In alio*, slashed in red. The body of the list appears to have been rapidly copied (presumably from the original at Bec), to judge from the minor slips of the eye. At the end of the list is the note, "Summa volumin a.cxiii. excepti .xxvii. volumina quos dedit episcopus sed nondum habuerunt" (Total number of volumes 113, not counting 27 volumes which the bishop gave but which they [i.e., the Bec monks] do not yet have). The flyleaf list describes the 113 volumes;[51] the missing 27, which would raise the total to the 140 cited by Robert of Torigny, have not been identified.

The second list, headed "Tituli librorum Beccensis almarii" (Titles of the books in the Bec library), is not as straightforward as it looks. It may represent an integration of Philip's books with other books at Bec, to judge from the frequent duplications of one list by the other.[52] In

---

[50] Concerning the library of Mont-St-Michel see Nortier, *Les bibliothèques*; F. Avril, "La décoration des manuscrits du Mont-St-Michel (XIe–XIIe siècles)," in *Millénaire du Mont-St-Michel* 2 (1967); and J. J. G. Alexander, *Norman Illumination at Mont-St-Michel* (Oxford 1970). Scarcely any manuscripts survive from Bec, but a number of the surviving books from Mont-St-Michel correspond closely with descriptions in the Bec catalogs: Avranches Bibl. mun. MSS 83, 92, 93, 96, 104, 113, 116, 157, 159–162, 225–226, 230, 235, 243; Paris, B.N. lat. 5997A; Vendôme 189.

[51] Numbered 115 by Omont's edition, which assigns numbers (69, 76) to two entries written in the margins. Because the text of Becker's edition is inaccurate, being derived from F. Ravaisson's edition of 1841 rather than from the manuscript, we cite Omont's text and numbers here.

[52] This list is printed with Philip's booklist (see n. 3 above): Becker 257–266, Omont 385–394. The possible merger of Philip's manuscripts with other Bec books was examined in some detail by Terry Nixon; we are grateful to him for helpful discussions of the problem. David N. Dumville dates the Bec catalog "from the mid-twelfth century"; see his "An Early Text of Geoffrey of Monmouth's *Historia regum Britanniae* and the Circulation of Some Latin Histories in Twelfth-Century Normandy," *Arthurian Literature* 4 (1985) 1–36 at 7 and n. 26. Unfortunately, the appendix that was to present the evidence for this dating was not published with the article. We thank Dr. Dumville for calling this article to our attention.

some instances, however, it would seem as if Philip's books have been taken apart and rebound with other works at Bec to form new codices, containing the works of a single author or works on a single topic;[53] any search for survivors from Philip of Harcourt's collection must take the possibility of rearrangement into account. The list does not appear to be a complete inventory of the Bec library, however, since a significant number of Philip's books do not reappear here; moreover, it seems to be a composite of an older list and of a partial revision with certain authors grouped together—which results in some duplication.

Unfortunately, history has not lent a helping hand in reconstructing Philip's library; neither he nor Bec's librarian left an *ex libris* mark on the books themselves, although a distinctive table of contents was entered in some of Bec's books before the end of the twelfth century.[54] It is a hopeful sign that the surviving manuscripts thought to have been Philip's, few though they are, have been identified just within the last dozen years or so.[55] For now, however, the two lists contain the bulk of our knowledge of his books.

For Philip, the written word—instrument of the secular schools as represented in the *ars dictaminis* and in legal training, in collections of model letters and law codes—was the basis of his power. The list of his books vividly reflects this attitude.[56] Philip owned the books of the early twelfth century, books embodying the codification of subjects, books

---

[53] For example, no. 95 (Omont, p. 397) on the list of Philip's books reads "In alio [volumine] historia Henrici de Anglia, et liber Bede minor de temporibus et de natura rerum." The Bec catalog suggests that the two Bede works were removed, and added to a manuscript containing Bede's *Ecclesiastical History* and some smaller works: no. 80 (Omont, p. 389), "In alio [volumine] historia Anglorum libri V [= the *Ecclesiastical History*]. De temporibus liber I minor. De naturis rerum liber I. Liber Gilde sapientis de excidio Britannie. Vita sancti Neoti, qui in capite ponitur," with the Henry of Huntingdon was left on its own as Bec no. 132 (Omont, p. 393): "In alio, historia Henrici de gente Anglorum libri X." more likely, though, Bec no. 132 is either the equivalent (with abbreviated title) of Philip's no. 95, or a second copy of the *Historia*.

[54] See, e.g., Leiden BPL 20, *Historia Normannorum* (Bec no. 120); B.N. MS lat. 12211, Augustine (Philip no. 12 = Bec no. 6); and possibly Paris, B.N. MS lat. 1685, Athanasius (Bec no. 113?); Léopold Delisle, in *Bibliothèque de l'Ecole des Chartes* 71 (1910) 506–521, noted this feature of certain Bec manuscripts and suggested that the Bec catalog was compiled from these lists.

[55] These manuscripts belonged, or possibly belonged, to Philip of Bayeux: Paris, B.N. lat. 152 fol. 32, Pomponius Mela (a leaf from no. 66 in the catalog of Philip's books); B.N. lat. 5802, Suetonius etc. (nos. 68 and 79); B.N. lat. 12211, Augustine (no. 12); and Cambridge, University Library MS Gg 2.21, Henry of Huntingdon (no. 95), which Patricia Stirnemann has recently identified as Philip's manuscript; we thank her for this information.

[56] Hunt ("Universities and Learning," 165) observed that Philip's collection was "remarkable for the relatively large number of Latin classical prose writers with not a single poet"—a reflection, surely, of his dictaminal training.

relevant to the professional ecclesiastical administrator: exegetical texts, law codes, dictaminal models, histories. His collections of ancient letters and orations—the Younger Pliny, a very great deal of Cicero, and even Ennodius, a rare find—would have served as models of style for a training in *dictamen*, a discipline of increasing formality though not as yet well served by manuals, and one that led to training in the law.[57] Like later generations, Philip saw books as useful instruments, part of the equipment of his profession; and throughout his life, it seems, he continued to acquire new works as they appeared.

Naturally, much of his library was commonplace. The standard works of the Fathers—Augustine, Jerome, Ambrose, Gregory, and others—comprise about a third of his collection; and he had kept, as one tends to do, a handful of very elementary schoolbooks—rhetoric, geometry, astronomy, arithmetic, and the like. What makes us value the collection, in contrast, is its indication that Philip kept abreast of what was new, and never ceased to acquire the very latest books that were of use. Thus he owned many works written by his contemporaries, both older and younger, such as Gerald of York (d. 1108), Petrus Alfonsus (d. ca. 1115), Gilbert Crispin (d. 1119), Hildebert of Le Mans (d. 1133), Hugh of St. Victor (d. 1141), Adelard of Bath (d. ca. 1146), Bernard of Clairvaux (d. 1153), Gilbert de la Porrée (d. 1154), Zacharias Chrysopolitanus (d. 1156), Gratian (d. ca. 1160), Hugh of Amiens (d. 1164), Simon Chevre d'Or (d. 1170), and perhaps Geoffrey of Monmouth (d. 1155).

The Gospel harmony *Super unum ex quattuor* typifies Philip's acquisition of the up-to-date and the useful.[58] The work of Zacharias Chrysopolitanus, a Laon Premonstratensian who died in 1156, *Unum ex quattuor* was compiled at Laon between 1140 and 1145; thus, it is one of the many works that Philip acquired after he had become bishop. Like the later Bible history of Peter Comestor, which it clearly influenced, Zacharias's *Unum ex quattuor* filled a need for an adequate cross-referenced merging of the Gospel accounts, and its popularity was imme-

---

[57] See the discussion in chap. 6, "*Florilegia* and Latin Classical Authors," passim. For an example of the use of a dictaminal *florilegium* by a late twelfth-century scholar, see A. Goddu and R. H. Rouse, "Gerald of Wales and the *Florilegium Angelicum*," *Speculum* 52 (1977) 488–521.

[58] Cat. #113, "In alio Zacharias super 'Unum ex quatuor.'" This does not reappear in the Bec list. Regarding Zacharias and the composition and circulation of the concordance see B. de Vregille, "Notes sur la vie et l'oeuvre de Zacharie de Besançon," *Analecta Praemonstratensia* 41 (1965) 293–309; and T. J. Gerits, "Notes sur la tradition manuscrite et imprimée du traité 'In unum ex quatuor' de Zacharie de Besançon," *Analecta Praemonstratensia* 42 (1966) 276–303 with brief descriptions of the 102 surviving manuscripts. See also the list in F. Stegmüller, *Repertorium biblicum medii aevi* (Madrid 1940–), nos. 5699 and 8400.

diate. In an era when the bishop was expected to do most of the preaching in his diocese, Philip no doubt found Zacharias's work an indispensable exegetical tool for the making of sermons. The text disseminated rapidly from Laon, with 11 of the 102 surviving manuscripts dating from the twelfth century. As is often the case, we can see that Philip's copy (pre-1164) must have been one of the earliest.

Although one would expect to find law books on Philip's list, given his involvement with legal matters for his diocese and with judicial matters for his duke, nevertheless his collection of law texts both civil and canon exceeds expectation. The study of civil law goes back to the late eleventh century in Bologna, and the influence of Roman law in northern Europe can be seen in the second quarter of the twelfth century; but mid-twelfth-century manuscripts of the whole corpus of civil law are not common. Philip's list represents the earliest documentable appearance in northern Europe of the full array of Roman law, in seven volumes — Codex, *Tres partes,* New Digest, *Inforciatum,* Old Digest, *Liber authenticorum,* and Institutes — in varying combinations and in duplicate.[59] More remarkable still, in the field of canon law, is the fact that (besides the old law, the letters and decretals of Ivo of Chartres and the decretals of Burchard of Worms) Philip owned not one but two copies of Gratian's *Decretum.*[60] Philip's copies of Gratian (nos. 69–70), like his manuscript of Zacharias, attest to the speed with which a new tool could be put to use: Gratian is thought to have finished his compilation only about 1140; and although the *Decretum* was known to the masters and students at Bologna, there is no evidence of its use in the papal chancery itself before 1160.[61] It is reasonable to suppose that Philip acquired both his Roman law manuscripts and his manuscripts of the

---

[59] Nos. 71–77 in the catalog of Philip's books. No. 76, "In alio [volumine] Instituta Justiniani," has been added by the scribe in the margin, presumably correcting an oversight. Concerning the spread of Roman law to the North, see R. C. Van Caenegem, *Royal Writs in England from the Conquest to Glanvill,* Selden Society Publications 77 (London 1959) pt. 3 chap. 2, "Roman and Canon Law Influences on the Early Common Law," pp. 360–390, especially 367–370.

[60] One of these, no. 69, has been added in the margin by the scribe, presumably in correction of an omission.

[61] For the dissemination of Gratian through the Anglo-Norman hierarchy, see the reference to Van Caenegem in the preceding note. Concerning the appearance and early knowledge of Gratian's *Decretum* in northern Europe, see W. Holtzmann, "Die Benutzung Gratians in der päpstlichen Kanzlei im 12. Jahrhundert," *Studia Gratiana* I (1953) 325–349. See also Robert L. Benson, "Barbarossas Rede auf dem Reichstag von Roncaglia (1158): Zur Benutzung kanonischen und römischen Rechtes bei Rahewin," forthcoming; we are grateful to him for allowing us to see the relevant portion of this article in typescript.

Decretum in the course of his trips to Rome (1144, 1146, 1150/1).[62]
Other evidence of early acquaintance with Gratian in the North includes
an unmistakable quotation in a letter of John of Salisbury written at
Canterbury in 1158–1160,[63] and a *Decretum* bequeathed to Lincoln
Cathedral sometime between 1151 and 1158 by Hugh, archdeacon of
Leicester.[64] Philip may well have played a significant role in the early
and rapid dissemination of Roman and canon law among the Anglo-
Norman jurists.

   Like other contemporary princes of church and state — such as Henry
the Liberal, count of Champagne — Philip collected histories.[65] No doubt
he felt that a familiarity with the past was a fitting enlargement of his
horizon — as well as a practical guide for behavior in the political world.
He owned such venerable works as Florus's *Epitome* of Livy, Suetonius's
Lives of the Caesars, a *Gesta Caesarum*, Pseudo-Clement, the *Historia
tripartita*, Orosius, the early medieval historians Gregory of Tours and
Freculf of Lisieux, the Jewish historian Josephus, and Nennius; and he
owned contemporary works like the *Historia Normannorum* of William
of Jumièges, doubtless with the revisions of Robert of Torigny, and
Henry of Huntingdon.[66]

---

   [62] Philip perhaps was the recipient of a decretal from Alexander III addressed simply
"Baiocensi episcopo": see Walther Holtzmann, *Decretales ineditae saeculi XII*, ed. and rev.
Stanley Chodorow and Charles Duggan, Monumenta iuris canonici B: Corpus collectionum
4 (Vatican City 1982) 39, no. 21, which is a reply to a query about penances. Such a
request implies canonistic knowledge, rather than ignorance; we thank Robert L. Benson
for bringing this decretal to our attention.
   [63] See epistle 99 (1158–1160): *The Letters of John of Salisbury* I: *The Early Letters
(1153–1161)*, ed. W. J. Millor and H. E. Butler, rev. C. N. Brooke (London 1955) 153. John
also quotes form the *Decretum* in epistle 100 (ibid., p. 157), which is potentially earlier
(ep. 100 can be dated only to the years 1147–1171, the tenure of its probable addressee).
Like Philip, John had traveled to Italy; see the itinerary in this same volume of his letters,
app. 1, "John of Salisbury at the Papal Curia," pp. 253–256. W. Holtzmann has suggested
that John brought a copy of the *Decretum* to England on his return from Rome in 1153–54;
see his review of S. Kuttner and E. Rathbone's "Anglo-Norman Canonists . . . " (*Traditio*
7 [1949–51] 279–358), in *Savigny Zeitschrift für Rechtsgeschichte, Kan. Abt.* 39 (1953) 466;
cited by Van Caenegem, *Royal Writs* 366 n.
   [64] See Van Caenegem, *Royal Writs* 368.
   [65] For an investigation of the books of twelfth-century French princes, in particular
Henry the Liberal, see P. Stirnemann, "Quelques bibliothèques princières et la production
hors scriptorium au XIIe siècle," *Bulletin archéologique du Comité des travaux historiques
et scientifiques* n.s. 17–18A (Paris 1984) 7–38, and "Les bibliothèques princières et privées
aux XIIe et XIIIe siècles," forthcoming in *L'histoire des bibliothèques françaises* vol. 1
(Paris 1989); we thank her for allowing us to read the latter in typescript. Dr. Stirnemann
has discovered the inventory of Henry's library and is preparing an edition of it.
   [66] It has been said that Leiden BPL 20, a two-part composite manuscript that belonged
to Bec and contains the *Historia Normannorum* of William of Jumièges, Geoffrey of

We should like in the concluding section to consider the information afforded by three particular titles on Philip's booklist. To say they illuminate "Philip's circle" would be an exaggeration. Certainly, however, they provide evidence about Philip's relationships with various contemporaries which is available from no other source.

The first of these is the *Historia* of Henry of Huntingdon, no. 95 in the list of Philip's books. The Bec catalog specifies that the abbey's *Historia* contained ten books;[67] this, potentially Philip's volume, must have been the version that included events to the year 1147.[68] The possible source of Philip's text is a matter of interest, since evidence of knowledge of Henry's *Historia* on the Continent is narrowly limited. We know of only two surviving manuscripts and two mentions of the work that date from Philip's lifetime: respectively, (1) a mid-twelfth-century manuscript, BN lat. 6042, containing the 1147 ten-book edition; (2) another mid-twelfth-century manuscript of the same version, Cambridge University Library Gg 2.21, thought to be Philip's manuscript; (3) quotations in the *Chronicle* of Robert of Torigny, monk of Bec and (after 1154) abbot of Mont-St-Michel, based on a text similar to but not identical with MS lat. 6042; (4) entry no. 95 in the catalog of Philip of Bayeaux, along with what is probably a duplicate record, entry no. 132 in the Bec catalog.[69]

Monmouth's *Historia regum Britanniae*, and an excerpt from Nennius's *Historia Britonum*, as well as some classical Alexander-lore, is a Bec rearrangement of two of Philip's codexes, nos. 43 and 44: "In alio, historia Normannorum. In alio, vita Alexandri et historia Britonum"; see Margaret Gibson, "History at Bec in the Twelfth Century," in *The Writing of History in the Middle Ages*, ed. R. H. C. Davis and J. M. Wallace-Hadrill (Oxford 1981) 183 n. 1, and Crouch, *Twins* 208, following Gibson. Although we should be glad if it were, we think BPL 20 is not Philip's. The Alexander material (Julius Valerius, plus the *Epistola ad Aristotilem*), which in Philip's collection appeared in the same codex with the *Historia Britonum*, in the Leiden manuscript belongs to part 1, with William of Jumièges, rather than to part 2, with Geoffrey of Monmouth and Nennius, a division confirmed by the quire structure, quire signatures, and hands.

[67] *Tituli librorum Beccensis almarii* no. 132: "In alio [volumine] historia Henrici de gente Anglorum, libri X."

[68] See Thomas Arnold, ed., *The History of the English, by Henry, archdeacon of Huntingdon, from A.C. 55 to A.D. 1154* . . . , Rolls Series (London 1879) x–xvi for a discussion of the versions, and xxxvi–xlii for a list of surviving manuscripts both badly out of date. Recently Diana Greenway has taken a major step forward in bringing up to date the study of manuscripts of Henry of Huntingdon ("Henry of Huntingdon and the Manuscripts of His *Historia Anglorum*," *Anglo-Norman Studies 9: Proceedings of the Battle Conference 1986*, ed. R. Allen Brown [Woodbridge, Suffolk 1987], 103–126); her description of the Bec/Mont-St-Michel manuscripts relies on assumptions, not always justified, of Delisle in the nineteenth century; see Greenway 113–114, and esp. nn. 56 and 58.

[69] Concerning B.N. lat. 6042, see Arnold, p. xxxvii n. 2; concerning CUL Gg 2.21 see n. 55 above; Robert of Torigny's use of Henry's *Historia* is discussed below.

Where would Philip have laid hands on an exemplar from which to have his copy written, given the extreme rarity of this text in Normandy? An obvious possible local source is Robert of Torigny. Robert notes, in the prologue to his *Chronicle*, that he has used Henry's *Historia* as a source of information.[70] Moreover, Robert had had occasion to meet Henry of Huntingdon; this information is revealed by the inclusion in Robert's *Chronicle* of a letter from Henry of Huntingdon to an unidentified Warinus Brito, mentioning *inter alia* Henry's stopover at Bec in 1139 on his way to Rome in the entourage of Theobald, the new archbishop of Canterbury (and, until his election, abbot of Bec). Curiously, a passage of the letter as quoted by Robert does not, in fact, occur in the text of this letter in manuscripts of Henry's *Historia*; Robert's version has Henry describing the occasion in these terms: "I met [at Bec] a certain Robert of Torigny, monk of that place, a seeker-out of sacred and secular books and a very learned collector. When he had asked me questions about my history of the English kings, and had eagerly listened to my answers, he brought me a book to read about the British kings who held our island before the English [i.e., Geoffrey of Monmouth]."[71] It is hard to ignore the possibility that Robert inserted this bit of flattery himself.[72] Apparently, this encounter with Henry of Huntingdon impressed Robert, for a miniature that depicts the meeting is included on fol. 174 of Avranches MS 159, Robert's own manuscript of his *Chronicle*.[73]

We think it likely, however, that Philip of Bayeux acquired his text of the *Historia* directly from Henry of Huntingdon. Certainly he did not require Robert of Torigny to serve as his link to Henry, archdeacon of Huntingdon: Huntingdon is an archdeaconry of the see of Lincoln, where Philip was dean in the 1130s. Alexander, bishop of Lincoln throughout Philip's deanship, was likewise Henry's patron who encouraged and supported his historical writing. Philip and Henry were contemporaries who would have known each other at that time. The acquaintance had an opportunity to be revived when Philip's attendance on Henry II in the

---

[70] Robert does not say that Henry sent him a copy of the *Historia*, as Arnold assumed (p. xxxvii n. 2, "copy of the History sent by Henry to Robert de Monte [of Torigny]").

[71] This long version, together with notice of the discrepancy between it and the *Historia* version, appears in Delisle's edition of Robert of Torigny's *Chronicle*, 1.97–98 and n. 2, and in Arnold's edition of the *Historia*, xxi and n. 1. Curiously, Léopold Delisle, Robert of Torigny's editor, ignored the fact that Philip of Bayeux had owned a manuscript of Henry of Huntingdon's *Historia* which was willed to Bec. Delisle supposed that B.N. lat. 6042 was copied, at Mont-St-Michel, from a Bec manuscript that Robert quoted.

[72] Arnold, *History of the English* xxi n. 1 makes this suggestion.

[73] See Avril, *Millénaire* 2 p. 233 (the book Robert gives to Henry of Huntingdon is mistakenly identified as Nennius's *History*), and fig. 124.

months after the coronation led him again to Lincoln, where we see him witnessing royal charters (ca. 1155). The likeliest source of Philip's *Historia* is a text secured from Henry of Huntingdon himself.

The second title we shall discuss, the *Ylias* of Simon Chevre d'Or, has a double-edged interest: Simon's work is the latest datable work on Philip's booklist (no. 112), and Philip's booklist is the earliest datable mention of Simon's work.[74] The *Ylias*, a Latin poem dealing with the Trojan War, was written at the behest of Henry the Liberal, count of Champagne—therefore after 1153, when Henry became count—and its appearance on Philip's list gives it a terminus ante quo of 1163. Not a great deal is known about Simon—that he wrote poetic epitaphs for contemporary figures who died in 1151 (Hugh of Mâcon, bishop of Auxerre), 1152 (Suger of St. Denis, Count Thibaut of Blois), and 1153 (Bernard of Clairvaux, Pope Eugenius III), presumably shortly after the dates of their deaths, and that he became, whether early or late in his life, a canon of St. Victor in Paris. Simon was still alive after 1170, for he wrote a poem on the death of Becket.[75] The appearance of this title on Philip's booklist accomplishes two things at once: it serves, as medieval booklists so often do, to help date the composition; and it documents in striking fashion that Philip, a busy administrator for church and state, could notice and acquire a work of contemporary poetry written for the court of Champagne shortly after it was completed. How it came to Philip's notice is not known—perhaps via Arnulf of Lisieux who, like Simon, had ties with both St. Victor and the comital house of Blois/Champagne; or perhaps Simon himself sent it to Philip in hopes of future patronage.

The booklist reveals that Philip's copy of the *Ylias* was part of a volume (no. 112) that included a number of other works: Seneca's *Natural Questions*, a work that had emerged from obscurity only in Philip's lifetime;[76] the *Natural Questions* of Adelard of Bath, composed in 1111–1116 and dedicated to Richard II, Philip's predecessor in the see of

---

[74] Regarding Simon, see A. Boutemy, "La Geste d'Enée," *Le moyen âge* 52 (1946) 243–256; J. Stohlmann, "Magister Simon Aurea Capra: Zu Person und Werk des späteren Kanonikers von St. Viktor," in *Hommages à A. Boutemy* (Brussels 1976) 343–366. See also M. M. Parrott, "The *Ylias* of Simon Aurea Capra: A Critical Edition," D. Phil. Diss. (University of Toronto 1975), which contains a detailed examination of the manuscripts discussed above. We are grateful to George Rigg, who directed this thesis, for having helped us consult it.

[75] See F. Swietek, "A Metrical Life of Thomas Becket by Simon Aurea Capra," *Mittellateinisches Jahrbuch* 11 (1976) 177–195.

[76] Regarding the transmission of Seneca's *Natural Questions* see Reynolds, *Texts and Transmission* 376–378.

Bayeux;[77] the *Virgilian Cantos* of Proba, a fourth-century Christian poet; and poems and other works by Hildebert of Le Mans (d. 1133).

Philip's manuscript of this collection does not survive—though a fragment of it may exist. It seems, however, to have been the progenitor of a small but important body of manuscripts. Four manuscripts figure in this story, Escorial 0.3.2, Vatican Reg. lat. 585, Avranches 93, and Copenhagen Gl. Kgl. 546 fol. The Escorial manuscript, written in the early fourteenth century, is the only one to preserve the whole sequence of works reported to have comprised Philip's volume. Parrott, the editor of the *Ylias*, has demonstrated that, for that work, the Escorial manuscript is a direct copy of the Vatican manuscript, which was written in the second half of the twelfth century, perhaps late in the century. The Vatican manuscript now is just a fragment, containing only the poetry portions (Proba, Simon, Hildebert) of the collection that was in Philip's codex, the *Natural Questions* portion having been detached to go its own way. Vatican Reg. lat. 585 could possibly be the remains of Philip's own manuscript, but we are doubtful that it is old enough. A third echo of Philip's manuscript appears on the front and back flyleaves of the Avranches manuscript, whose medieval home was Mont-St-Michel: In the late twelfth century, someone at the Mont copied onto these flyleaves a text of Simon's *Ylias* from an exemplar closely related to the Vatican/Escorial version; the most logical source is Philip's manuscript, which by the date was at Bec, the source of a number of Mont-St-Michel texts. The fourth witness to Philip's codex no. 112 is the Copenhagen manuscript, which is a fragment, a quire of eight leaves. The extant quire does not contain either the *Ylias* or Seneca's *Natural Questions*— i.e., the only words in the group that have been sorted out by a modern edition; thus, its affiliation with the rest of the manuscripts is not yet established. It needs to be collated with the Vatican manuscript, for those texts that the two have in common. Until that has been done, one can only say that the Copenhagen fragment dates from the mid-twelfth century and, thus, it could on the basis of date be a fragment of Philip's codex. In any event, the existence of these four manuscripts and fragments, presumably descendants of Philip's codex, indicates that Bec could on occasion serve as a point of dissemination for the interesting texts left by Philip.

---

[77] The manuscripts of Adelard of Bath's *Natural Questions* are discussed by C. Burnett, "The Introduction of Arabic Science into Northern France and Norman Britain: A Catalogue of the Writings of Adelard of Bath and Petrus Alfonsi and Closely Associated Works, Together with the Manuscripts in Which They Occur," unpublished preprint, pp. 25–27.

The last volume to consider (no. 57) contained the works of Ennodius, late fifth-/early sixth-century rhetorician and bishop of Pavia: letters, verses, *dictiones*, epitaphs, epigrams, and panegyrics.[78] His works were prized in Carolingian times primarily as purveyors of a variety of classical verse forms; and the brief flurry of interest produced three surviving ninth-century manuscripts. Thereafter—in a common enough pattern—Ennodius was not again heard from until the middle of the twelfth century. A number of witnesses survive from that time, including two surviving manuscripts, excerpts in the *Florilegium Angelicum*, and a mention in a letter. The record of Philip's Ennodius is as early as any of these, and earlier than most.

The discussion of Ennodius in a letter—the only medieval literary assessment of Ennodius—probably refers directly to Philip's manuscript. In 1160, Philip's colleague Bishop Arnulf of Lisieux wrote to Henry of Pisa, "I am sending you the book of Ennodius. It belongs to someone else, but if you decide that you like it, I shall have a transcript of it sent to you as soon as possible."[79] The indications are that it was Henry of Pisa, cardinal-priest of Sts. Nereus and Achilleus and a papal legate to France, who had inquired about Ennodius; for Arnulf remarks that he himself had never seen the work until Henry mentioned it. (Henry was often in Normandy in the late 1150s and 1160s and knew both Arnulf and Philip.)[80] Arnulf's letter continues with an oft-quoted diatribe on Ennodius's turgid style ("Once having seen the work, I was amazed that an author should have had the gall to publish it, or that anyone else should have been disposed to make copies of it . . . " etc.)—concluding that the perpetrator of such writings should more aptly be called "Innodius" (complicated, tangled) than "Ennodius" (open, plain).

Was this Philip's book that Arnulf had in his hands? As we have mentioned, Arnulf and Philip were contemporaries, colleagues, and friends. By 1160, Philip and Arnulf had been associated with one another in the king's service on numerous occasions, and from one end of Henry's

---

[78] See R. H. Rouse and M. A. Rouse, "Ennodius in the Middle Ages: Adonics, Ps.-Isidore, Cistercians, and the Schools," in *Popes, Teachers, and Canon Law in the Middle Ages: Studies in Honor of Brian Tierney,* ed. J. R. Sweeney and S. Chodorow (Ithaca, 1989) 91–113. Note on p. 92 that the *stemma codicum* should show L as a direct descendant of V.

[79] Barlow, *Letters of Arnulf* 36–38, ep. 27; and F. Vogel, MGH Auct. Ant. 7 (Berlin 1885) lx–lxi. The letter is printed and discussed by P. Von Moos, "Literarkritik im Mittelalter: Arnulf von Lisieux uber Ennodius," in *Mélanges offerts à René Crozet* (Poitiers 1966) 929–935.

[80] Regarding Henry of Pisa see P. Clausen, "Aus der Werkstatt Gerhochs von Reichersberg," *Deutsches Archiv 23* (1967) 47–56.

•

domains to the other—York, Lincoln, Oxford, Westminster, as well as Rouen, Caen, Le Mans, Périgueux, and so on.[81] They had shared common adversaries who had usurped the rights of their respective sees, most notably the Benedictines of Fécamp; and in about 1153 Arnulf had petitioned Eugenius III on Philip's behalf in a strongly supportive letter.[82] Almost certainly, then, Philip of Harcourt was the "someone else" from whom Arnulf borrowed a rare copy of Ennodius to satisfy Henry of Pisa. Henry must thereafter have returned it, for it was included with Philip's gift to Bec.

If Arnulf had not heard specifically of Ennodius before, yet knew a good place to seek out a text when Henry of Pisa asked, the implication is that Arnulf knew Philip had a large and varied library. This in turn raises the intriguing possibility that some of the library which Arnulf left to St. Victor may have been copied from Philip's books, or that the two at least may have shared common sources of supply and common interests.

*   *   *

Medieval booklists have various uses for modern scholars, the most obvious being to date texts and authors, and to document the circulation of this or that work in a given area and time. Here we have seen, as well, that a booklist can add substance to an otherwise shadowy but important figure, and can document the use of codified learning in twelfth-century administration.

Robert of Torigny's epitaph for Philip is more than a little disapproving: "Philip, the bishop of Bayeux . . . was prudent and shrewd both at increasing, and at recovering, the property of his church, and he accomplished much there; but 'the wisdom of this world is foolishness, to God' [1 Cor. 3.19]." Proper, if uncharitable, sentiments for a Benedictine. But Philip's diocese, Philip's king, and Philip himself were well served by his share of the wisdom, and the learning, of this world, as contained in and attested by the books he owned.

---

[81] They jointly witnessed at least 44 *acta*, at 17 different locations; see Appendix.

[82] Barlow, *Letters of Arnulf* 11–12, ep. 8. The purpose and the circumstances of this letter are a mystery: In it Arnulf adds his voice to that of the Bayeux chapter in petitioning the pope to permit Philip to return home.

APPENDIX
Charters of Henry II Witnessed by Philip

Philip attested at least sixty-one *acta* of Henry, count of Anjou, duke of Normandy, and (from 1154) king of England. A selection of Henry's acts were first sorted by Léopold Delisle; they were further edited, after Delisle's death, by Elie Berger, who published them in three volumes (*Recueil des actes de Henri II, roi d'Angleterre et duc de Normandie, concernant les provinces françaises et les affaires de France* [Paris 1916–1927]). They are listed here in the order of the numbers assigned by Berger (occasionally different from Delisle's); numbers with asterisks date from before Henry's accession to the English throne.

Readers should recall that, although the arrangement of the acts in the edition follows the rules of chronology applicable to charters, the result is not necessarily convincing in historical terms. For example, no. 2 is dated March 1155 in London, while the only other London act, no. 231 (near the end of the present list), is dated 1155/1163—which is to say, one can demonstrate with certainty only that the act was written after Henry's accession in 1154 and before Philip's death in 1163; but common sense suggests that Philip affixed his signature to both no. 2 and no. 231 during one and the same sojourn in London, in 1155.

As we have mentioned above, for some twenty-eight of these acts, Arnulf bishop of Lisieux joined Philip as a witness; for another four, Rotrou bishop of Evreux was co-witness; and for fifteen, Philip was joined by both Arnulf and Rotrou. The name of no other signatory, lay or ecclesiastical, is coupled with Philip's with any regularity (save, of course, the name of the king/duke's agents, English chancellor or Norman seneschal, who signed with Philip as without him). Consequently, we have noted those acts that bear the signatures of either or both of these bishops.

20.* Bayeux, 1151.
35.* Rouen, 1151—1153. Arnulf.
45.* Rouen, 1151—1153. Arnulf.
72.* Le Mans, 1154. Arnulf.
74.* Périgueux, 1154. Arnulf.
78.* Fontevrault, 1154. Arnulf.
 2. London, 1155. Arnulf.
25. Sauve-Majeure, abbey of, 1156. Arnulf.
26. Oxford, 1155 or 1157. Arnulf.
32. Chéci (near Orléans), 1156 or 1157. Arnulf.
33. Rouen, 1156—1157.

35. Falaise, 1157. Arnulf, Rotrou.
39. Barfleur, 1157. Arnulf.
40. ? n.p., ca. 1157.
44. Lincoln, 1155—1158. Arnulf.
48. Northampton, 1155—1158. Rotrou.
50. Northampton, 1155—1158.
56. Westminster, 1155—1158. Arnulf.
57. Westminster, 1155—1158. Arnulf.
58. Westminster, 1155—1158. Arnulf.
64. Westminster, 1155—1158. Arnulf.
65. Westminster, 1155—1158. Arnulf.
66. Westminster, 1155—1158. Arnulf.
67. Westminster, 1155—1158. Arnulf.
68. Westminster, 1155—1158. Arnulf.
76. York, 1155—1158. Arnulf.
77. York, 1155—1158. Arnulf.
95. Argentan, 1156—1159.
97. Argentan, 1156—1159.
98. Argentan, 1156—1159. Arnulf.
100. Argentan, 1156—1159. Arnulf.
101. Bayeux, 1156—1159. Arnulf, Rotrou.
104. Caen, 1156—1159.
108. Le Mans, 1156—1159. Arnulf.
112. Rouen, 1156—1159. Arnulf.
113. Rouen, 1156—1159. Arnulf.
116. Rouen, 1156—1159.
117. Rouen, 1156—1159. Arnulf. Rotrou.
122. ? n.p., 1156—1159.
123. Le Mans, 1157—1159. Arnulf.
134. Rouen, 1156—1160. Arnulf, Rotrou.
137. Lions, 1160.
138. Rouen, 1160. Rotrou.
141. ? n.p., 1160. Arnulf, Rotrou.
148. Argentan, 1156—1161. Arnulf, Rotrou.
152. Bayeux, 1156—1161. Arnulf, Rotrou.
153. Caen, 1156—1161. Arnulf, Rotrou.
154. Caen, 1156—1161. Arnulf, Rotrou.
180. Rouen, 1156—1161.
188. Rouen, 1156—1161. Arnulf, Rotrou.
198. Rouen, 1159—1161. Arnulf, Rotrou.
204. Les Andelys, 1156—1162. Rotrou.

205. Les Andelys, 1156—1162. Rotrou.
206. Argentan, 1156—1162.
208. Caen, 1156—1162. Arnulf, Rotrou.
215. Rouen, 1156—1162. Arnulf,
216. Rouen, 1156—1162. Arnulf, Rotrou.
223. Fécamp, 1162. Arnulf, Rotrou.
230. Lincoln, 1155—1163.
231. London, 1155—1163.
236. Rouen, 1157—1163. Arnulf, Rotrou.

3. The Medieval Circulation of Cicero's 'Posterior Academics' and the *De finibus bonorum et malorum*

In the 'Academics' Cicero set forth in dialogue form the philosophy of the 'New Academy', comparing it with other contemporary schools of thought, especially the Stoic and the Epicurean. The hallmark of the New Academy, in contrast with the dogmatism of the Old Academy, was a fundamental skepticism in the matter of epistemology: no form of perception based on the senses is sure, every assertion can be countered, there are no absolutes; the best that a man can do is to hear all sides of a question with an open mind, and then give conditional assent to the more probable view.[1] Having produced a draft of the 'Academics' in two books, Cicero, in response to valid criticisms of Atticus, revised the work, in the process dividing it into four books. For unknown reasons, both versions circulated; and, ironically, neither survives intact.

The 'Academics' is one of those ancient works that survived, insofar as it did survive, only by a slender thread. From the first edition, the 'Prior Academics', only the second of two books is extant, that known from its interlocutor as the *Lucullus*; the text rests on a fair number of manuscripts.[2] From the second version, the 'Posterior Academics', we

---

Originally published in *Medieval Scribes, Manuscripts and Libraries: Essays Presented to N. R. Ker*, ed. M. B. Parkes and A. G. Watson (London 1978) 333–367.

[1] For the content and early history of the 'Posterior Academics' see Cicero, *Academica posteriora*, ed. M. Ruch (Paris 1970) 1–45; A. E. Douglas, "Cicero the Philosopher," *Cicero*, ed. T. A. Dorey (London 1965) 135–170. R. del Re, "Gli 'Accademici' di Cicerone (Questioni e ricerche, studi moderni)," *Cultura e scuola* 42 (1972) 34–39, adds little to the picture.

[2] Interest in the *Lucullus* from the late thirteenth century and particularly in the Renaissance is described by C. Schmitt, *Cicero scepticus*, International Archive of the History of Ideas (The Hague 1972). Information regarding the manuscripts of the text can be gleaned

have only book 1, with its ending lacking; the text is said by its editors to depend upon one medieval manuscript and a group of Renaissance Italian manuscripts. Neither edition enjoyed much popularity in Antiquity; and they were, if anything, even less popular with patristic writers. While Lactantius found the skepticism of the 'Academics' compatible with Christianity, in that it revealed the limitations of human reason unaided by faith,[3] Augustine found its skepticism pernicious and devoted a treatise to refuting the Academic position, his *Contra academicos*. Both Lactantius and Augustine seem to have known one or other edition in its entirety: the disintegration and present form of the two editions lie somewhere in the early Middle Ages.

The surviving portions of the two editions are transmitted by quite separate routes. Book 2 of the 'Prior Academics', the *Lucullus*, survived because at some early state it became attached to the philosophical corpus of Cicero. While the philosophical works never enjoyed a large circulation, they were known to two major Carolingian scholars, Hadoard and Lupus.[4] Linked with one or more of Cicero's other philosophical works, the 'Prior Academics' survives in at least twelve medieval manuscripts, and its stemma is similar to those of the other works, of which that for the *De legibus* has been the most carefully studied.[5] The survival of the 'Posterior Academics' is as yet unaccounted for and largely unexamined. Perhaps the limited popularity—and even the mutilation—of the 'Posterior Academics' in the Middle Ages was the result of the antipathy between skepticism and Christian thought; Douglas hints that it is more than 'mere coincidence that both the *Academica* and the *De natura deorum* survive in versions which lack a large part of the skeptics' case.'[6] On the contrary, given the lack of enthusiasm for the 'Academics' even among the Ancients, one might wonder whether the survival of even a part of the work is not rather the result of a fortunate accident. Moreover, one might question whether or not the admittedly limited knowledge of the 'Posterior Academics' in the Middle Ages was in fact quite so narrowly limited as editors and historians have led us to believe.

from P.L. Schmidt, *Die Überlieferung von Ciceros Schrift 'De legibus'*, Studia et testimonia antiqua 10 (Munich 1974); and A. S. Pease, *M. Tulli Ciceronis de divinatione* (Urbana, Ill. 1920–23, rptd. 1963) 604–619.

   [3] Schmitt, *Cicero scepticus*, 25–28.

   [4] C. H. Beeson, "The *Collectaneum* of Hadoard," *Classical Philology* 40 (1945) 201–222; and "Lupus of Ferrières and Hadoard," *Classical Philology* 43 (1948) 190–191; B. Bischoff, "Hadoard und die klassiker Handschriften aus Corbie," *Mittelalterliche Studien* 1 (Stuttgart 1966) 49–63.

   [5] Schmidt, *Die Überlieferung*.

   [6] Douglas, "Cicero the Philosopher," 150.

Enlightenment on these points can only derive from an investigation of the transmission.

The text of the 'Posterior Academics' is said to survive in only one medieval manuscript, the twelfth-century Paris, Bibl. Nat., MS lat. 6331, and in over fifty manuscripts of the late fourteenth and fifteenth centuries, most of them Italian. The text of the 'Posterior Academics' was studied by Halm and following him by James Reid. The accepted classification of the manuscripts was done in 1908 and 1922 by Otto Plasberg.[7] A new investigation based on a collation of nearly all surviving manuscripts completed by T. J. Hunt in 1967 both confirmed Plasberg's stemma and lent it precision.[8] It is unlikely that an unknown witness to the text will emerge to alter substantially the affiliation of the survivors. All told, in contrast to such texts as Suetonius or Vegetius, a substantial amount of good work has been devoted to the modern text of the 'Posterior Academics'. This effort, however, has been directed largely towards reconstructing the text, rather than towards reconstructing its medieval circulation. The manuscripts involved are dated in only the most general fashion, and their origin and provenance in large part remain to be worked out.

Plasberg and Hunt classify the manuscripts of the 'Posterior Academics' in two families descended from a common archetype. The first of these, Δ, is said to consist of the single medieval manuscript of the text, Paris, Bibl. Nat., MS lat. 6331 (π), three manuscripts (traditionally ascribed to the fifteenth century) that descend from π, and the *deteriores*. The second family, Γ, consists of nine late fourteenth- and fifteenth-century manuscripts of Italian origin, all descended from a common ancestor. In addition, the 'Posterior Academics' appears in three medieval library catalogs, two of the twelfth century and one of the thirteenth: the catalog of Bec, among the books given to the abbey by Philip of Bayeux before 1164; and the late twelfth-century catalog of the Cistercian house at Pontigny; and the mid thirteenth-century *Biblionomia* or

---

[7] M. *Tullii Ciceronis opera*, ed. J. G. Baiter and C. Halm 4 (Zurich 1861); M. *Tulli Ciceronis academica*, ed. J. S. Rein (London 1885); M. *Tulli Ciceronis paradoxa stoicorum, academicorum reliquiae cum Lucullo*, ed. O. Plasberg (Leipzig 1908); and M. *Tulli Ciceronis scripta quae manserunt omnia academicorum reliquiae cum Lucullo* (Leipzig 1922). The most recent edition by Ruch reproduces Plasberg's text. We have cited the 1922 edition throughout.

[8] T. J. Hunt, "The Textual Tradition of Cicero's *Academicus primus*," unpublished M.A. thesis, University of Exeter 1967; and "The Origin of the Deteriores of the *Academicus primus*," *Scriptorium* 27 (1973) 39–42. He has a study of the tradition of the 'Posterior Academics' in progress. We are pleased to acknowledge our debt to Mr. Hunt for his generous permission to use his findings.

catalog of Richard de Fournival. Thus far there has been no successful attempt to relate these catalog references either to the stemma or to the surviving manuscripts.

THE 'POSTERIOR ACADEMICS' AND THE *DE FINIBUS*

T.J. Hunt first noticed a crucial factor in the transmission of the 'Posterior Academics' that had been previously ignored. In the medieval catalog notices and in most of the Γ manuscripts the 'Posterior Academics' follows Cicero's *De finibus bonorum et malorum*, while in the Δ family the former is treated as book 6 of the latter. Indeed, the text can be said to owe its survival to the fact that, at an early stage in the transmission—presumably after the work had become fragmented—someone appended the 'Posterior Academics' to the *De finibus*. Hunt observed that the association of these two works forms a plausible unit. The *De finibus*, likewise in dialogue form, is Cicero's discussion of the definitions of good and evil by the Stoic and Epicurean schools. The structure of the *De finibus* may be summarized as follows: book 1, exposition of Epicurean doctrine; book 2, refutation of Epicureanism; book 3, exposition of Stoic doctrine; book 4, refutation of Stoicism by Antiochus; book 5, ethical system of Antiochus (the Old Academy). Obviously, some early scholar felt that the sequence was completed by the refutation of Antiochus's doctrine in the mutilated first book of the 'Posterior Academics'. Since the surviving portion of the 'Posterior Academics' forms no unit of its own, it might easily have been taken as a hitherto lost concluding book of the *De finibus*.[9] For whatever reason, and whenever and by whomever done, the grafting of the 'Posterior Academics' on to the *De finibus* undeniably took place. Therefore, the *De finibus* holds the key to the circulation of the 'Posterior Academics.'

The *De finibus*, as well, enjoyed a very limited circulation before the fourteenth century. It survives in four medieval manuscripts, and in a large number of fourteenth- and fifteenth-century manuscripts, primarily Italian. Unfortunately we have neither a modern edition of the *De finibus* nor a study of its transmission.[10] While editors agree that the manuscripts descend ultimately from a common archetype, no edition

---

[9] Hunt, "Textual Traditions," 45–49. Curiously, no editor of either the 'Posterior Academics' or the *De finibus* has hitherto remarked on this.

[10] For the *De finibus*, see *De finibus bonorum et malorum*, ed. T. Schiche (Leipzig 1915, rptd. 1961); *Cicéron des termes extrêmes des biens et des maux*, ed. J. Martha (Paris 1928, rptd. 1967).

attempts to present a *stemma codicum*. The manuscripts would appear, however, to represent two families, the older of which circulated in Germany and the younger in France; the 'Posterior Academics' appears as book 6 of the *De finibus* in the latter family.

The German family includes the oldest manuscript of the text, Vatican, MS Pal. lat. 1513 (A), containing the *De finibus* only; according to Bischoff, it was written somewhere in western Germany in the eleventh century and belonged to the abbey of Lorsch in the fifteenth.[11] MS Pal. lat. 1513 breaks off at *De finibus* 4.7.16, leaving the possibility that the manuscript originally contained the 'Academics' as well; but, to judge from the *variae lectiones* recorded in the editions, MS Pal. lat. 1513 is rather far removed stemmatically from the French family which does contain the 'Posterior Academics'. Moreover, its nearest neighbors contain the *De finibus* without the 'Academics'. These are two fifteenth-century copies of another German manuscript, now lost: Erlangen, Universitätsbibl., MS 847 (E), an important collection of Cicero's works written by Bernhard Groschedel and Conrad Haunolt at Heidelberg in 1466; and Vatican, MS Pal. lat. 1525 (B), written in Germany in 1467.[12] There are only two references to the *De finibus* in German medieval library catalogs, both at Bamberg; in the catalog of Michaelsberg (probably made between 1172 and 1201) and again in the catalog of Bamberg Cathedral Library, dated ca. 1200.[13] The *De finibus* even eluded the two great medieval German collections of Ciceroniana, namely, London, Brit. Lib., MS Harley 2682 (s. xi), which once belonged to Cologne Cathedral, and Berlin, Staatsbibl. Preussischer Kulturbesitz, MS lat. Fol. 252 (s. xii), compiled by Wibald of Corvey who drew, in part, on the Harleian volume.[14] After the Bamberg references German catalogs make

---

[11] B. Bischoff, *Lorsch im Spiegel seiner Handschriften*, Münchener Beiträge zur Mediävistik und Renaissance-Forschung, Beiheft (Munich 1974) 117. For facsimile, see E. Châtelain, *Paléographie des classiques latins* 1 (Paris 1884) pl.43.1.

[12] E is described in detail by H. Fischer, *Die lateinischen Papierhandschriften der Universitätsbibliothek Erlangen*, Katalog der Handschriften 2 (Erlangen 1936) 322–324, no. 618. B is described in detail by E. Pellegrin et al., *Les manuscrits classiques latins de la Bibliothèque Vaticane* 4.2 (Paris 1982) 178–181. For facsimile, see Châtelain, pl. 25.

[13] *Mittelalterliche Bibliothekskataloge Deutschlands und der Schweiz*, ed. P. Ruf, iii, pt. 3 (Munich 1939) 367 (Michaelsberg): " . . . Tulii de finibus bonorum II, ad Herennium, de oratore II, Tusculanarum I, officiorum I, de amicitia II" (it is not certain whether these comprise one codex, nor is it clear what is meant by II); pp. 343–344 (Cathedral) " . . . Liber de fide bonorum et malorum. . . ."

[14] L. D. Reynolds and N. G. Wilson, *Scribes and Scholars*, 2d. ed. (Oxford 1974) 96, 100; A. C. Clark, "Excerpts from the Harleian MS 2682," *Journal of Philology* 28 (1890) 69–87; and *Collations from the Harleian MS of Cicero* 2682, Anecdota Oxonienses, Classical Series, pt. 7 (1892).

no mention of the *De finibus* until the fifteenth century when they begin to reflect the influx of texts from the South.

MS LAT. 6331 AND ITS DESCENDANTS

To follow the interest in this text we must turn to the French family of the *De finibus*. Its distinguishing feature is that it treats the 'Posterior Academics' as the sixth book of the *De finibus*. The oldest member of the French family, Paris, Bibl. Nat., MS lat. 6331, is also the oldest surviving manuscript of the 'Posterior Academics'.[15] It dates from the second half of the twelfth century and was written somewhere in France north of the Loire. It contains, fols. 1–85, Cicero, *De finibus*; 85^v–93^v, 'Posterior Academics'; 94–123^v, Seneca, *De beneficiis*; 124–37, *De clementia*; 137–40, *De remediis fortuitorum*; 140^v, *Passio sancti Albani*. Three hands wrote the manuscript: the first wrote the *De finibus* and the 'Posterior Academics', a second contemporary hand the Senecan works and a third, slightly later but still of the twelfth century, added the *Passio*. The manuscript entered the royal library with the books of Pierre and Jacques Dupuy in the seventeenth century, and from then its history is known.[16] At some time before it reached the Dupuys the manuscript had been rebound, and in the process the original order of the contents was inverted, thus disguising its medieval appearance and hence its identity. The original order was: I (fols. 94–140^v), Seneca, *Ben.*, *Clem.*, *Rem. fort.*, and the *Passio* on a blank leaf of the last quire; II (fols. 1–93^v), Cicero, *De finibus*, 'Posterior Academics' (as book 6). The change is evident from the physical appearance of the manuscript: the opening leaf of the *De beneficiis* is more discolored than that of the *De finibus* and, in addition, this leaf (now fol. 94) bears an erased inscription and what seems to be a chain mark. Moreover, the original order of MS lat. 6331 is confirmed by one of its descendants, Amsterdam, Universiteitsbibl., MS 77, which contains the same sequence of works.

Restored to its original state, MS lat. 6331 corresponds to an entry in the late twelfth-century catalog of the Cistercian abbey of Pontigny: 'Volumine uno: Seneca de beneficiis lib. sex, de clementia duobus, de remediis fortuitorum bonorum uno, de finibus bonorum et malorum

---

[15] See Châtelain, *Paléographie des class. lat.*, pl. 43.2. This manuscript was assumed to date from the fifteenth century by Reid, *Ciceronis academica*, 63, 65.

[16] It is no. 146 of their catalog: H. Omont, *Anciens inventaires et catalogues de la Bibliothèque Nationale* 4 (Paris 1911) 200. The erased notes of the thirteenth century on fol. 123^v would probably reward further attention.

vi';[17] the 'Posterior Academics' was clearly contained in the Pontigny manuscript because the *De finibus* is accorded six books. Granted, MS lat. 6331 bears none of the normal Pontigny signs: it did not remain long at Pontigny, as we shall see.[18] Nor does it have the appearance of a Cistercian book: it was not written there. The only troublesome discrepancy is the fact that the *De beneficiis* is said by the catalog to comprise six books, whereas MS lat. 6331 divides it, as it should be, into seven books. This must simply be an error on the part of the cataloger, perhaps an echo of the 'six' books of the *De finibus*. The key to the identification, besides the contents and their order, is the addition of the Cistercian *Passio* of St. Alban, king of Hungary.[19] Pontigny colonized the royal monastery of Egres in Hungary at the request of King Bela III in 1179. MS lat. 6331 may in fact have been taken with the brothers to Egres, as were a number of Pontigny books; at any rate we know that the manuscript left the house, because a contemporary hand has noted 'Vacat' next to this entry in the catalog.[20]

Aspects of the later history of MS lat. 6331 can be glimpsed through its descendants for the text of the 'Posterior Academics', not uninteresting manuscripts in themselves. Plasberg identified four manuscripts which are so close to MS lat. 6331 (π) textually that he treated them as if they were direct copies: Amsterdam, Universiteitsbibl., MS 77 (Plasberg: 80) (ρ); Leiden, Bibl. der Rijksuniversiteit, MS Periz. Fol. 25 (π_1); Vatican, MS Pal. lat. 1511 (π_2); and Paris, Bibl. Nat., MS lat. 14761 (τ). Hunt confirmed the identifications, and identified the source of the *deteriores* of this family, Florence, Biblioteca Medicea Laurenziana, MS conv. sopp. 131 (ω). Hunt's investigations produced the following stemma:

---

[17] The catalog is entered, in a hand of the second half of the twelfth century, at the end of Montpellier, Fac. de Médicine, MS 12, fols. 176–181; see C. Samaran and R. Marichal, *Catalogue des manuscrits en écriture latine portant des indications de date, de lieu ou de copiste* 6 (Paris 1968) 301 and pl. 198 (which is a picture of the original manuscript rather than of the catalog). The catalog is printed in *Catalogue générale des manuscrits des bibliothèques publiques des départements* 1 (Paris 1849) 697–717; this entry is on p. 714.

[18] For the history of the library see C. H. Talbot, "Notes on the Library of Pontigny," *Analecta sacri ordinis Cisterciensis* 10 (1954) 106–168.

[19] *Bibliotheca hagiographica latina* 1 (Paris 1898) no. 203. The *Passio* is ascribed to Transmundus of Clairvaux. Paris, Bibl. Nat., MS lat. 6331 contains a metrical version of an epitome of the full *Passio* found also in Dijon, Bibl. Mun., MS 646 (386), fol. 33 (s. xiii), and Rheims, Bibl. Mun., MS 1400, fol. 48ᵛ.

[20] For those entries marked 'vacat' see Talbot, *Analecta sacri ordinis Cisterciensis* 10, 108–109. For Egres see L. H. Cottineau, *Répertoire topo-bibliographique des abbayes et prieurés* 1 (Macon 1939) 1032.

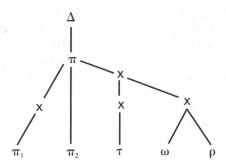

This stemma represents an advance over Plasberg's; by placing the *deteriores* in descent from Bibl. Nat., MS lat. 6331, it demonstrates in effect that $\Delta = \pi$—that is, it establishes MS lat. 6331 as the progenitor of the entire family. But the stemma is in difficulty with respect to the subfamily $\tau\omega\rho$. The problem lies in the treatment of ρ, which Plasberg identified as Amsterdam, Universiteitsbibl., MS 80 and assigned to the fifteenth century. Clearly, no one who has studied the *De finibus* or the 'Posterior Academics' since 1880 has looked at this manuscript afresh. The correct pressmark is Amsterdam, MS 77—not 80—and it dates not from the fifteenth but from the twelfth century.[21] Since Amsterdam, MS 77 is certainly a descendant of MS lat. 6331, these changes do not alter its limited value as a witness to the text; but they do cast doubt on the classification given above. It is most unlikely that two intermediate copies separate π from the near-contemporary ρ—although, by its very existence, Amsterdam, MS 77 suggests that the *De finibus* and the 'Posterior Academics' may have been better known in the second half of the twelfth century than one has assumed.

On closer inspection, Amsterdam MS 77 appears in fact to be an ancestor of Paris, Bibl. Nat., MS lat. 14761 (τ) and of Florence, MS conv. sopp. 131 (ω). The senseless errors which Hunt ascribes to ρ in his collation are not errors at all, but places where ρ has a hole in the parchment (difficult to detect on microfilm) which allows letters from the next leaf to show through. There is nothing included in τ or ω that is omitted from ρ. The actual errors in ρ seemingly reappear in τ and, for the most

---

[21] The mistaken pressmark and date derive from H. Deiter, "Der Amsterdamer Cod. no. 80," *Philologus* 51 (1892) 361–363; "Vergleichung des Amsterdamer Codex no. 80," *Programm Gymnasiums* (Aurich 1892). M. B. Mendes da Costa, *Catalogus der Handschriften* 2 (Amsterdam 1902) 18, called attention to Deiter's error.

part, in ω, which Hunt states to be a contaminated text; ρ is almost certainly a direct copy of π. The more plausible stemma for the Δ family is this:

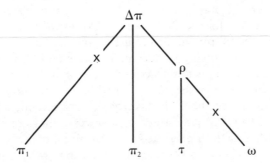

Amsterdam, Universiteitsbibl., MS 77, in contrast to Paris, Bibl. Nat., MS lat. 6331, looks like a twelfth-century Cistercian book. It is large in format, written by one person on thick, somewhat fuzzy cream-colored parchment.[22] The script and the initials are well made without embellishment. It contains Jerome, *De viris illustribus* (on Seneca); Seneca, *Epistolae ad Paulum; Epitaphium Senecae*; Seneca, *Epistolae ad Lucilium, De beneficiis, De clementia, De remediis fortuitorum*; Cicero, *De finibus*, 'Posterior Academics' (as book 6). As we have seen, the last five works correspond to the order of the works in Bibl. Nat., MS lat. 6331 (as restored) and to the description of the latter in the Pontigny catalog. Immediately following the catalog entry for MS 6331 is an entry for Seneca's letters: 'Ejusdem epistole in alio volumine ad Lucilium numero CIII'. It seems likely that Amsterdam, MS 77 is a copy, made at Pontigny, of these two Pontigny codices. Reynolds has suggested that the latter entry be identified with a twelfth-century codex of Seneca's letters, Montpellier, Fac. de Médicine, MS 132, which contains letters 1–24, 66–88, numbered 1–103 — since this tally is unique.[23] Montpellier, MS 132, however, bears no indication that it was ever at Pontigny. Amsterdam, MS 77 has numbered the exchange with Paul and the epitaph I–XV, and

---

[22] Parchment; two cols., thirty-eight lines; quires of ten leaves, catchwords, signed in roman numerals; 246 × 177 mm (338 × 243 mm), ruled in lead point; written by one hand; alternating red and blue initials, plain; 2° fo, [obno]xios vos. Described by Mendes da Costa, *Catalogus*, 17–18, who ascribes it to the fifteenth century. The manuscript was reported for the *De remediis* by M. Bonnet, "*Sénèque De remediis fortuitorum*," *Revue de philologie* 13 (1889) 25–31.

[23] L. D. Reynolds, *The Medieval Tradition of Seneca's Letters* (Oxford 1965) 106.

the subsequent eighty-eight letters (divided into eighty-nine) *Ad Lucilium* are numbered XVI–CIIII. Given its relationship with Paris, MS lat. 6331 and its date, Amsterdam, MS 77 is a strong contender as a representative of the second Pontigny codex as well; the cataloger may well have dropped a minim. If so, the Montpellier codex could not be its parent. At any rate, for the *De beneficiis*–'Posterior Academics', Amsterdam, MS 77 is in all probability a direct copy of Paris, Bibl. Nat., MS lat. 6331, written at Pontigny during the brief period after the catalog was made (since MS 77 is not described there), but before the removal of MS lat. 6331 indicated by the 'Vacat' noted beside the entry for the latter. Nothing is known of the early history of Amsterdam, MS 77 until it appears in the hands of Jan Gruter (1560–1627), librarian at Heidelberg.

Amsterdam, MS 77 produced two descendants in the fifteenth century: Florence, Biblioteca Medicea Laurenziana, MS conv. sopp. 131; and Paris, Bibl. Nat., MS lat. 14761. MS conv. sopp. 131 was finished (probably in Florence) on 30 May 1406, according to its colophon: 'Absolvit autem scriptor postrema manu ad III kal. jun., Verbi anno incarnati MCCCC sexto'.[24] One of the oldest dated manuscripts in humanist script, it belonged to, and was possibly written for, the Florentine scholar Antonio Corbinelli who bequeathed it to the Badia in Florence in 1425; as part of this *fonds* it passed to its present home in the Laurenziana.[25] MS conv. sopp. 131 lacks its first 130 leaves, and now contains only the *De finibus* and the 'Posterior Academics', entitled *Fragmentum de academicis*. Hunt has shown, as regards its text of the 'Academics', that this is a manuscript of the Δ family with a number of Γ readings, as witness its separate rubric for the 'Academics'. It is probably at least one copy removed from Amsterdam, MS 77; thus it tells us nothing about the latter's whereabouts.

---

[24] Its place as progenitor of the *deteriores* was established by Hunt, *Scriptorium* 27 (1973) 39–42; but Vatican, MS Rossi 559 (Italy), containing the *De finibus* in five books followed by the 'Posterior Academics' (expl. *fuit facultate*) and dated s. xiv by the I.R.H.T., remains to be examined.

[25] For the early home and possible origin of the manuscript, as well as bibliography pertaining to it and to Corbinelli, see A. C. de la Mare, "Humanist Script: The First Ten Years," *Das Verhältnis der Humanisten zum Buch*, ed. F. Krafft and D. Wuttke, Deutsche Forschungsgemeinschaft, Kommission für Humanismusforschung, Mitteilung 4 (Boppard 1977) 89–110. According to Dr. de la Mare the same scribe wrote Florence, Laurenziana, MS conv. sopp. 111 (Sallust and Justinus), dated 1405 (which also belonged to Corbinelli and which has corrections and variant readings in Niccolò Niccoli's hand), and Florence, Laurenziana, MS 51.4 (Varro, *De re rustica*) which is the most accurate copy of the lost San Marco manuscript presumed to have belonged to Niccoli.

Paris, Bibl. Nat., MS lat. 14761 is made up of two manuscripts of separate origin.[26] They were already together by the end of the fifteenth century when Claude de Grandrue described the volume in the catalog of St. Victor; the catalog also describes several alchemical texts, now missing, which were then part of the codex (fols. 298–372).[27] MS lat. 14761 now contains as part I, fols. 2–84, 152–241, Cicero, *Ad familiares*; 242–7, table to the letters; 85–151, *De oratore*; written by two people, one Italian (fols. 2–29), one French (fols. 29–247).[28] Part II contains the *De finibus* and the 'Posterior Academics' (as book 6); it was written by the hermit Girolamo da Matelica, who wrote for Vespasiano da Bisticci in Florence.[29] At least some of the paper used in part II is of French origin. Three watermarks are discernible; an anchor surmounted by a cross, similar to Briquet 392; a crossbow and a unicorn; and (on fol. 284 only) three fleurs-de-lys on a shield, Briquet 1680, which was known in Paris in 1451. Girolamo went to Paris to study (he was there by 1457 and had returned to Italy by at latest 1463), and supported himself by copying books in the Faubourg St. Germain-des-Prés.[30] Girolamo could conceivably have carried paper south, and have copied the *De finibus* and the 'Posterior Academics' after his return to Florence; but Paris seems the more likely place.

The text of Paris, Bibl. Nat., MS lat. 14761 is independent of that in Florence, Laurenziana, MS conv. sopp. 131, and each is a separate witness to Amsterdam, MS 77. Although the text of MS lat. 14761 is careless, it could be a direct copy of Amsterdam MS 77, which would locate the latter at Paris in the mid-fifteenth century. Laurenziana, MS

---

[26] Part II: paper; forty to forty-four long lines; 188 × 137 mm (205 × 140 mm), ruled in ink; written by Girolamo da Matelica; five-line opening initials, undecorated.

[27] "Theorica peroptima ad cognitionem totius alkymie veritatis 298. Practica prefate theorice 319. Quedam alia concernentia alkymiam 336. Tabule super predictis de alkymia 349. A scilicet tercii ab omnibus B de aqua forti C 361 et usque 372."

[28] Gilbert Ouy kindly informed us that the French copyist of pt. 1 also wrote Paris, Bibl. Nat., MS lat. 7783 and Montpellier, Fac. de Méd., MS 359. The former bears an erased note of the late fifteenth century: 'Pro Mauricio Maubraines huius libri possessore'. Neither manuscript came to St. Victor.

[29] We are grateful to Dr. A. C. de la Mare for the identification of Girolamo's hand; for a capsule biography, and a list of manuscripts in his hand, see de la Mare, "New Research on Humanistic Scribes in Florence," in *Miniatura fiorentina del Rinascimento 1440–1515: Un primo censimento*, ed. A. Garzelli 1 (Florence 1985) 393–600 at 434 and 498. See also J. Leclercq, "Un Traité de Jérôme de Matelica sur la vie solitaire," *Rivista storica della chiesa in Italia* 18 (1964) 13–22; and "Jérôme de Matelica et Aegidius Ghiselinus," *Rivista storica* 20 (1966) 9–17.

[30] At least two manuscripts which he copied in Paris indicate where he worked: Florence, Laurenziana, MS conv. sopp. 399, 'Parisius suburbio Sancti Germani'; and Oxford, Bodleian Lib., MS Canon. pat. lat. 176, 'In suburbio Sancti Germani de Pratis prope Paris'.

conv. sopp. 131, on the contrary, would seem to derive from a descendant of Amsterdam, MS 77 to which readings from the Γ family had been added. In sum, neither descendant gives any reliable information concerning the location of their common ancestor in the fifteenth century.

In the late fourteenth or early fifteenth century, long after it had left Pontigny, Paris, Bibl. Nat., MS lat. 6331 produced two other descendants quite independent of Amsterdam, MS 77 and its family: Leiden, Bibl. der Rijksuniversiteit, MS Periz. Fol. 25 and Vatican, MS Pal. lat. 1511. The Leiden manuscript is a large collection of Cicero's works: *De officiis, De finibus*, 'Posterior Academics' (as book 6 of the preceding), *Disputationes Tusculanorum, De natura deorum, De divinatione, De fato, De legibus, De senectute, De amicitia, De paradoxa*.[31] T. J. Hunt suggests for the 'Academics' (and thus, undoubtedly, for the *De finibus*) that an intermediate stands between Leiden, Periz. Fol. 25 (π_1) and MS lat. 6331 (π). Certainly its text is more corrupt than those of the other two direct descendants of π, Pal. lat. 1511 (π_2) and Amsterdam, MS 77 (ρ). In its six folios of 'Academics', π_1 omits five words found in the text of π; π_2 omits one, ρ none. Moreover, π_1 has added two words by error; π_2 and ρ, none. Beyond these, π_1 contains twenty-two significant errors (i.e., excluding idiosyncrasies of spelling), compared with sixteen for ρ and nine for π_2. The five marginal *variae lectiones* in π, preserved in both π_2 and ρ, do not appear in π_1—though one of the variants[32] has crept into the text of π_1 (*interdum*: Plasberg ed., 1922, p. 13, line 9). Whether or not all this is sufficient to indicate an intermediate manuscript is debatable. According to Gilbert Ouy, Leiden, MS Periz. Fol. 25 was written in the scriptorium, if not in the very hand, of Pierre d'Ailly. The small dragons in the decoration are typical of manuscripts written for d'Ailly; the hand compares favorably, in Ouy's judgment, with Cambrai, Bibl. Mun., MSA 954, written by d'Ailly himself.[33] Pierre d'Ailly, scholar and ecclesiastical diplomat, resided principally in Paris, and from the time of the Council of Constance was Martin V's legate in

---

[31] The manuscript is described by T. P. Sevensma, *Codices Perizoniani*, Bibliotheca Universitatis Leidensis: Codices manuscripti 4 (Leiden 1946) 27–28, and Schmidt, *Die Überlieferung* 57–58.

[32] Hunt, "Textual Tradition," 184, lists a second, *coherente* (Plasberg, *Ciceronis scripta*, p. 12, line 26); but actually Leiden, MS Periz. Fol. 25 reads *coher/cente* (fol. 119ᵛ, lines 8–9), as in the text of Paris, Bibl. Nat., MS lat. 6331.

[33] Noted by Ouy in the manuscript itself, and kindly confirmed in a personal communication, dated 5 June 1976. See his "Autographes calligraphiés et scriptoria d'humanistes en France vers 1400," *Bulletin philologique et historique année 1963* (1966) 891–898. For facsimile of MS Periz. Fol. 25 see G. I. Lieftinck, *Manuscrits datés conservés dans les Pays Bas* 1 (Amsterdam 1954) 90, no. 209, pl. 237.

Avignon. He must have found Paris, Bibl. Nat., MS lat. 6331 or a copy of it either in Paris or at Avignon.[34] The manuscript contains an armorial device (in the hand of scribe or decorator) that helps to date it.[35] The arms of Pope Benedict XII (1394–1424) appear on fol. 229^v with the word 'hereticus' incorported in the device; this could not have been made before Benedict's deposition at the Council of Pisa in 1409 and again by the Council of Constance in 1417. The manuscript must therefore have been written after 1409 and before d'Ailly's death in 1420. There are other arms (again in the hand of the scribe or decorator) — those of the Philippes de Barac'h, a Breton family (fols. 115^v, 121^v, 178^v, 237, 296^v), and of the dukes of Brittany (fols. 202^v, 205, 223) — and two names 'Sellarii' (fol. 296^v, over the device of the Philippes de Barac'h) and 'Grunelle' (fol. 177). The names are unidentified, and the connection between Pierre d'Ailly and the Philippes de Barac'h is unknown.

Hunt considers the second manuscript, Vatican, MS Pal. lat. 1511, to be probably a direct copy of Paris, Bibl. Nat., MS lat. 6331. MS Pal. lat. 1511 contains only the *De finibus* and the 'Posterior Academics' (as book 6), and dates from the fifteenth century.[36] If we knew where it was written, it would tell us the location of MS lat. 6331 at that time. MS Pal. lat. 1511 is written on parchment prepared in the Mediterranean manner, namely, large white sheets scraped from the flesh side, leaving the hair follicles visible on the hair side; and the frame on the opening page is southern, to judge from its heavy acanthus leaves, gold balls and

---

[34] Wherever he may have been when he produced this manuscript, d'Ailly had access, presumably in that same place, to other significant exemplars. The text of the *De natura deorum, De divinatione*, and *De fato* in MS Periz. Fol. 25 agrees closely with that in Lupus of Ferrières's manuscript, Vienna, Nationalbibl., MS 189; see F. Boesch, "De codice Ciceronis Leidensi Perizoniano in folio N.25," *Schedae philologae Hermanno Usener . . . oblatae* (Bonn 1891) 76–87. For the *De legibus* it is very closely related to three manuscripts that descend from another which apparently belonged in the thirteenth century to Richard de Fournival: Berlin, Deutsche Staatsbibl., MS lat. 201 (Phill.) (s. xii²); Paris, Bibl. Nat., MS lat. 15084 (s. xv¹), St. Victor, which appears to be annotated by Nicholas of Clamanges (see Schmidt, *Die Überlieferung*, pl. 2); and Rouen, Bibl. Mun., MS 1041 (s. xv¹), written ca. 1420 by Guillaume Euvrie, a fellow of the Sorbonne: see Schmidt, *Die Überlieferung*, 57–58, 58–60, 60–67, 201–205.

[35] See K. A. de Meyier, "Les Armoiries et l'histoire d'un Cicéron de Leyde," *Scriptorium* 2 (1948) 121–122.

[36] Parchment; two cols., thirty-three lines; catchwords in boxes; 222 × 158 mm (340 × 250 mm), ruled in brown crayon and ink; one hand, similar to J. Kirchner, *Scriptura gothica libraria* (Munich 1966) pl. 49 (Paris, A.D. 1406), and to S. H. Thomson, *Latin Bookhands of the Later Middle Ages 1100–1500* (Cambridge 1969) pl. 24 (Toulouse, A.D. 1429); bound in parchment; 2° fo, *nostri a nostris*. Armando Petrucci has kindly offered his opinion that the manuscript could date from as late as the third quarter of the fifteenth century.

pastel colors with white highlights and dark outlines. The text, however, is written in a French gothic hand, and the decoration of the minor initials (fols. 13, 35^v, 49, 53, 82^v) is French—gold spiky-leafed vine. The interior of the opening initial in the southern frame (Cicero writing) may also be French. Such a combination of northern and southern elements may indicate that the manuscript was written at Avignon. There is no evidence of ownership, however, until the manuscript appears in the Fugger catalog (1555).[37]

On the basis of its two later descendants, Leiden, MS Periz. Fol. 25 and Vatican, MS Pal. lat. 1511, perhaps Paris, Bibl. Nat., MS lat. 6331 came to rest, for a time, at Avignon in the late fourteenth and early fifteenth centuries; the evidence is less than compelling.

THE SECOND FRENCH FAMILY

There is good reason to postulate the existence of a second French family of the *De finibus* and the 'Posterior Academics', independent of but related to Paris, Bibl. Nat., MS lat. 6331 and its descendants. The pre-fourteenth-century evidence for this family includes: (1) a twelfth- or thirteenth-century manuscript of the *De finibus* without the 'Posterior Academics'; (2) readings from a codex of the *De finibus*, now lost; (3) a catalog description of a codex containing the *De finibus* followed by the 'Posterior Academics'; and (4) a set of late twelfth-century extracts from the *De finibus*.

Leiden, Bibliotheek der Rijksuniversiteit, MS Gronovius 21 (R, for the text of *De finibus*) is a manuscript of the late twelfth or early thirteenth century; its history is unknown until it was found somewhere along the Rhine by Bernard Rottendorf in 1650.[38] MS Gronovius 21 is composed of two manuscripts which had already been joined when the mid-thirteenth-century table of contents was written: I. Cicero, *De finibus, Timaeus*; Aulus Gellius, *Noctes Atticae* lib. 1–7; II. *Theoretica geometria*; Hyginus; commentary on Boethius.[39] The presence of the rare text of the early books of Gellius suggests a French source.[40] For the *De*

---

[37] P. Lehmann, *Eine Geschichte der alten Fuggerbibliotheken* 2 (Tübingen 1960) 110 and 513.

[38] P. Lehmann, "Aus dem Leben, dem Briefwechsel und der Büchersammlung eines Helfers der Philologen," *Erforschung des Mittelalters* 4 (Stuttgart 1961) 107–127.

[39] Part I: parchment; two cols., sixty-three lines; 2° fo, *quod vero securi* (part I), *longitudo* (part II).

[40] For the transmission of the early books of Aulus Gellius, see A. *Gellii Noctes Atticae*, ed. P. K. Marshall 1 (Oxford 1968) v–xiii; also A. C. de la Mare, P. K. Marshall, R. H.

finibus, the readings of MS Gronovius 21 are quite closely related, perhaps as a sister, to those which were recorded in 1545 by the French
scholar-publisher Guillaume Morel from 'an old manuscript'.[41] The manuscript source of Morel's readings has evidently not survived, but what
seems to be a second witness to it survives in the form of selected
extracts.

Extensive twelfth-century extracts from the *De finibus*, hitherto
unnoticed, appear on fol. 164[r-v] of Paris, Bibl. Nat., MS lat. 18104. MS
lat. 18104 is a composite volume consisting of three parts. Part I (Isidore
and Augustine) is written in Tours minuscule of the ninth century, and
part II (Fortunatus) is of the same date.[42] Part III, now fols. 136–95,
containing extracts from patristic and ancient authors written by one
hand, dates from the late twelfth century; the appearance of cedillas,
and absence of biting and the primitive paragraph marks in the gibbet
form suggest a date in the last third of the century. On fol. 226[v] it bears
a note in a late thirteenth-century hand: 'Tertia die post festum sancti
Clementis obiit Maholt, mater Oliveri Mandeguerre'. These people have
not been identified. The signature of Claude Joly and the date December
1666 appear on fol. 227. It is probably through Joly that Part III, if not
the whole manuscript, came to Notre Dame. There is no indication,
however, of the date when the three parts were brought together.

To demonstrate that the *De finibus* extracts in MS lat. 18104 derive
from Morel's source is difficult because the coincidence of passages
excerpted in MS lat. 18104 and those excerpted by Morel is slight; we
shall have to use the text of MS Gronovius 21, sister(?) of Morel's source,
as corroborating evidence. To begin with, the extracts (X) cannot come
from any known manuscript of the *De finibus*. Leaving aside *lacunae*,
we need only say that X never agrees in error with any or all of the
German manuscripts (ABE) against the rest of the tradition. X twice
agrees in error with Bibl. Nat., MS lat. 6331 (P, for the text of *De
finibus*): at 1.7.23 *patrioque: patrio quoque* PX, and at 2.26.85 *igitur
ipsum: ipsum igitur* PX; but X does not follow P in error elsewhere (e.g.,

---

Rouse, "Pietro da Montagnana and the Text of Aulus Gellius in Paris B.N. lat. 13038,"
Scriptorium 30 (1976) 219–225.

[41] For Morel, see J. F. Michaud, *Biographie universelle*, 2d ed., 29 (Paris n.d.) 272–273.
The readings are recorded in G. Morel, *Observationum . . . in M. T. Ciceronis libros
quinque de finibus bonorum et malorum commentarius* (Paris 1545), not seen by us. The
relationship of Morel's readings to the text of MS Gronovius 21 is established by Schiche,
De finibus, v–vii.

[42] Noted by C. H. Beeson, *Isidorstudien*, Quellen und Untersuchungen zur lateinischen
Philologie des Mittelalters, 4.2 (Munich 1913) 40. We thank Joshua Lipton for supplying us
with the result of a preliminary examination of this manuscript.

three times in 1.18.61), and X contains words omitted in P (1.18.57 *vos* om. P, hab. X; 2.30.96 *morbi* om. P, hab. X, *est* om. P, hab. X; etc.). Nor can X come from MS Gronovius 21 (R) itself: X has the passage *ratione — nec* in omitted by R at 3.17.58, and on other occasions X does not agree with R in error — e.g., 1.17.55 *opinemur: opinamur* R; 1.18.59 *exedunt: excedunt* R; 2.30.96 *intelligas: intelligat* R. But the agreement of X with R in error is nonetheless striking: 1.19.63 *ab eo et* om. RX; 1.19.63 *viam* om. RX; 4.27.76 *nil* om. RX; 5.7.18 *prima* om. RX, *primum: primo* RX. Most notably X agrees with R's interpolation at 5.7.19, *possit ut aut non dolendi ita sit [fit X] ut quanta* add. RX. We are dependent upon the collations of Baiter, Schiche and Martha for the readings of the Morelianus; in only three of the extracted passages does the Morelianus give rise to *variae lectiones*: at 1.19.63 *ab eo* om. Morel., *ab eo et* om. RX; at 5.18.48 *scire se: se scire* Morel. X; and earlier in the same paragraph, *recurrant ut aliquid* Morel., *recurrantur aliquid* X, *recurrentur aliquid* R, *requirant ut aliquid* P, *recurrant aliquid* BE. Given that we are comparing, on the one hand, an editor's report of Morel's report of a reading with, on the other, the excerpter's report of what he read, it is likely that Morel and the excerpter are both relying on the same manuscript. It is indisputable that, at very least, they each relied upon a manuscript belonging to the same small family of *De finibus* texts.

The origin of the whole collection of extracts (Bibl. Nat., MS lat. 18104 pt. III) is suggested by the authors represented. The rare works cited, besides the *De finibus*, include the younger Pliny's letters in the ten-book family (and preceded by Apuleius's *De deo Socratis* and *De dogmate Platonis*), and Cicero's 'Philippics', books 1–4 from the Colotiana family of the text. Among the more common are Cicero's 'Tusculan Disputations', Eutropius, Frontinus, Florus's *Epitome* and Petrus Alphonsus's *Disputatio*. The only place in the twelfth century where these specific works are known to have been together is at Bec, among the manuscripts given to the abbey before 1164 by Philip of Harcourt, bishop of Bayeux. Philip's manuscript of the *De finibus* (not extant) is described thus in the Bec catalog: 'In alio [volumine] Pomponius Mela de cosmographia et Tullius de fine boni et mali et de academicis et Timeus Platonis ab ipso Tullio translatus et Tullius de particione oratoria et liber Candidi Ariani ad Victorinum de generatione divina et Hilarius de sinodis et eiusdem liber contra Valentem et Auxencium'.[43]

---

[43] Printed in G. Becker, *Catalogi bibliothecarum antiqui* (Bonn 1885) 199–202 (see p. 201, no. 64); and *Cat. gén. des mss. des bibl. publ. de France: Départements* 2 (Paris 1888) 385–399 (see p. 396, no. 66). For Philip see V. Bourienne, *Un Grand Bâtisseur: Philippe de*

It is possible, therefore, that the extracts in Bibl. Nat., MS lat. 18104 were copied at Bec from the books of Philip of Bayeux. However, there are difficulties with such a localization. For one thing MS lat. 18104 includes extracts from three extremely rare works—Cicero's orations *Pro Archia, Pro Cluentio* and *Post reditum in senatu*—which are not recorded at Bec. A second difficulty lies in the relationship of the extracts with Bibl. Nat., MS lat. 5802, almost certainly to be identified with no. 79 in the Bec list of Philip's books. Superficially, it appears that the compiler of the extracts must have made use of this manuscript: among other things, MS lat. 5802 contains Florus's *Epitome*, Frontinus, Eutropius, the 'Tusculans', and the 'Philippics' in the rare four-book family—all of which are represented in the extracts in MS lat. 18104. However, the recent edition of Florus indicates that the extracts from the *Epitome* do not derive from Bibl. Nat., MS lat. 5802, but rather that both descend from a common parent.[44] (The stemmatic relationship of the extracts to the several other texts contained in MS lat. 5802 has not yet been determined.) MS lat. 5802 is thought to have been written, and hence its exemplars would have been found, at Chartres.[45] Moreover, MS lat. 18104 contains occasional initials that incorporate elements of what is thought to be Chartres decoration. On the one hand, then, the extracts may have been compiled at Chartres, though we lack evidence that all the works represented in the extracts were available there. On the other hand, Bec cannot be ruled out: Philip gave to the abbey another manuscript of Florus (no. 68 in the Bec list) which has not survived and which could have been the missing common parent.

The *De finibus* extracts in MS lat. 18104, therefore, may have been taken from Philip of Bayeux's text—and, in that case, Morel may also have taken his readings from Philip's manuscript. The extracts may, instead, derive from the parent or exemplar of Philip's text. In either

---

Harcourt, *évêque de Bayeux* (Paris 1930); S. E. Gleason, *An Ecclesiastical Barony of the Middle Ages: the Bishopric of Bayeux 1066–1204*, Harvard Monographs 10 (Cambridge, Mass. 1936) 28–29; and G. Nortier, *Les Bibliothéques médiévales des abbayes bénédictines de Normandie* (Caen 1966) 42–45. What seems to be a copy of portions of Philip's manuscript exists in Vendôme, Bibl. Mun., MS 189 (s. xii–xiii) which belonged to Mont St. Michel in the seventeenth century. It contains Hilary, *De sinodis, Contra Constancium, Ad Constancium, Ad eundem, Exemplum blasphemi Auxentii, Adversus Arrianum Auxencium*; Pomponius Mela, *De corographia*; sermons; William of Conches, *Dragmaticon philosophiae*; list of conflicting passages of Scripture. See *Cat. gén. des mss. des bibl. publ. de France: Départements* 3 (Paris 1885) 456.

[44] Florus, *Oeuvres*, ed. and trans. Paul Jal 1 (Paris 1967) cxlvi–cxlvii.

[45] Paris, Bibl. Nat., MS lat. 5802 is one of a group of manuscripts which have been identified by François Avril of the Bibliothèque Nationale as bearing decorative motifs thought to have been employed at Chartres in the middle of the twelfth century.

case, it is probable that Philip's text belonged to the Morel-MS 18104 family, whose only surviving full text is Leiden, MS Gronovius 21. The surprising information afforded by the Bec catalog is the fact that Philip of Bayeux had a codex in which the 'Posterior Academics' followed the *De finibus*, but with a rubric or colophon or some mark of identification of its own. There may also have been a suggestion that the 'Posterior Academics' comprised book 6, which would help to explain the error in the extracts in MS lat. 18104, where passages from book 5 of the *De finibus* are mislabeled (from a colophon in Philip's manuscript?) as book 6;[46] but despite that possibility, it is evident that his manuscript somewhere clearly designated the 'Academics' by name.

This piece of information permits one, with a high degree of probability, to assign to the Bec-lat. 18104-Gronovius family the manuscript of Richard de Fournival (d. 1260).[47] Fournival's *Biblionomia* or catalog of his library contains the following entry: '[75] Ejusdem [Ciceronis] liber achademicarum disputationum, in quo ostendit *quod genus phylozophizandi arbitrandum sit minime et arrogans maximeque et constans et elegans*. Item ejusdem liber de universalitate qui vocatur Thimeus Tullii. In uno volumine. . . .'[48] The words italicized, Cicero's own description of the 'Academics', were either taken directly from *De divinatione* 2.1–7 when the *Biblionomia* was written, or they were taken from the rubric of the manuscript, which, in turn, derived from the *De divinatione*.[49] Since Fournival, in commissioning manuscripts, not infrequently had them supplied with lengthy descriptive rubrics, the latter is more likely the case. On the surface, it looks as if Fournival had a copy of the 'Posterior Academics' and the *Timaeus*, which would make a rather thin volume.

Fortunately, we have evidence other than the *Biblionomia* that describes the contents of Fournival's manuscript. Fournival's library, with the exception of the medical books, passed to the newly founded College de Sorbonne in 1272, *via* the bequest of Gerard of Abbeville, friend of Robert de Sorbon and, like Fournival, canon of Amiens. Fournival's

---

[46] The 'Posterior Academics' is not quoted in Paris, Bibl. Nat., MS lat. 18104, but it is mentioned by name at the end of the extracts from the *De finibus* in a confusing note: 'Liber Tullii qui dicitur de achademicis non est nisi quedam translatio thimei Platonis et idem ordo qui est ibi'.

[47] For bibliography on Fournival and his library, see R. H. Rouse, "Manuscripts belonging to Richard de Fournival," *Revue d'histoire des textes* 3 (1973) 253–269.

[48] Ed. Delisle, *Cabinet des manuscrits*, ii, 529.

[49] Fournival again drew on *De divinatione* for his description of 'Ad Hortensium' (i.e., the *Lucullus*): '[76] Eiusdem liber ad "Hortensium" de "cohortatione ad phylosophie studium" qui inscribitur Lucullus et interdum Hortensius, in uno volumine. . . .'

manuscript is more helpfully described in the subject catalog of the Sorbonne's chained library, compiled ca. 1321–30:

> P.1. Disputationes Tullii vel liber academicorum ejusdem. 'Non eram nescius Brute'
>
> P.1. Thymeus ejusdem de universitate. 'Multa sunt a nobis et in achademicis scripta'[50]

The catalog of the chained library does not list donors' names, but there can be little doubt that we have here Fournival's volume. The incipit of the 'disputations', however, is that of the *De finibus*. Given the incipit, the appearance of the name 'Academics' in the title and the inclusion of the *Timaeus* at the end of the codex, we should venture that Fournival had a copy of the same exemplar that had served Philip of Bayeux, containing *De finibus*, 'Posterior Academics', *Timaeus*. Clearly there was some ambiguity in the titles and/or colophons of the first two in Fournival's manuscript; the name *De finibus* evidently did not appear, although the Bec catalog shows that this title was in Philip's manuscript. Perhaps Fournival's codex contained not only the name 'Academics' but also a suggestion or indication that it belonged to the preceding work. Whatever the appearance of the manuscript, it was such that it allowed Fournival and the Sorbonne catalog of the 1320s to consider the *De finibus* and the 'Posterior Academics' as one work, the *Liber academicorum*.

In addition to the catalog, an early fourteenth-century Sorbonnist, Thomas of Ireland, described part of Fournival's volume in the list of *originalia* appended to his *Manipulus florum*, finished in 1306: '[7] Dispositiones [i.e, Disputationes] eiusdem lib. V. Principium: "Non eram nescius Brute." Finis: "perreximus omnes" '.[51] Thomas evidently gave the manuscript closer scrutiny than did either Fournival or the later Sorbonne cataloger, for he has discerned that the title 'Academics' pertains only to the brief text at the end. Lacking the title *De finibus* for the preceding five-book work, he took the only other title offered by his text, *Disputationes*. Later in the list Thomas describes the *Timaeus*: '[9] De universalitate. Principium: "Multa sunt a nobis." Finis: "neque dabitur," vel non est finis.' The slight and mutilated 'Posterior Academics' he does not list at all; or—a possibility not to be ignored—perhaps Fournival's manuscript did not contain the text of the 'Academics', but only the name.

---

[50] Ed. Delisle, *Cabinet des manuscrits*, iii, 87.

[51] The list of authors and works is edited by R. H. and M. A. Rouse in *Preachers, Florilegia, and Sermons: Studies on the Manipulus florum of Thomas of Ireland*, Pontifical Institute of Medieval Studies, Studies and Texts 47 (Toronto 1979) 251–310.

If we accept Fournival's manuscript as belonging to the group, then we have a significant family of twelfth- and thirteenth-century manuscripts of the *De finibus*—three or four, depending upon whether or not the Bec manuscript is identified with the Morelianus—at least one, and probably two, of them containing the 'Posterior Academics' as well. What we have not so far established is the relationship of this family to the other texts of the *De finibus*, especially to those that incorporate the 'Academics' as book 6. At this point our investigation suffers from the lack of a stemma for the *De finibus*; instead we must approach the problem on the basis of historical evidence and of readings recorded but not pursued by the editors of the *De finibus*, to suggest what such a stemma might look like. The obvious weakness in our evidence for the presence of the 'Posterior Academics' in two manuscripts of this family, Philip of Bayeux's and Fournival's, is that it depends on hearsay, open to alternative interpretations; and the only surviving text, MS Gronovius 21, lacks the 'Academics'. If the interpretation presented here is correct—if, let us say, the 'Academics' were omitted from MS Gronovius 21 simply by choice—then we should at least be able to demonstrate that the *De finibus* text in MS Gronovius 21 is more closely affiliated to the *De finibus* in Paris, Bibl. Nat., MS lat. 6331 and its descendants—manuscripts that contain the 'Posterior Academics' as book 6—than it is to the German manuscripts of the *De finibus* which lack the 'Academics'. Unfortunately, the most widely accepted edition of the *De finibus*, that of T. Schiche, does not even include Bibl. Nat., MS lat. 6331 in its apparatus; and the more recent French-Latin edition of Jules Martha is neither thorough nor reliable in its report of variant readings. Using the two in concert, and verifying in the manuscripts themselves wherever possible, we have taken book 1 of the *De finibus* as a rough sample to test the possibility of an affinity between MS Gronovius 21 (R) and Bibl. Nat., MS lat. 6331 against the German manuscripts ABE. We found no place where either R or P agrees with ABE in error against the other—none, at any rate, that withstood a look at the manuscripts. There are, in contrast, a number of significant RP agreements in error.[52] One major error, the displacement of two passages in R and P, seems sufficient *prima facie* evidence of a common ancestor. Both R and P have inserted 1.9.30 *Etenim quoniam-ipsa iudicari* (P: *Etenim-sensibus* only) out of

---

[52] For example, at 1.3.8, *usu venire* edd., *usui venire* A[1], *venire usu* RP; 1.5.14 *pertinerunt: pertinent* RP; 1.8.26 *quoquo modo: quoquo ut modo* RMorel., *quoque ut id modo* P; 1.11.39 *nec ulla pars*: om. *nec* and *pars* RP; 1.14.47 *eventurum: proventurum* RP; 1.16.50 *non depravata: non* om. RP; 1.16.50 *turbulenta est* (*et.*: codd.) *si: turbulenta non potest fieri: et si* RP; 1.20.67 *atque nostra: ut nostra* RP.

place, near the end of 1.8.26; both also preserved the passage in its proper place in the text at 1.9.30. And both R and P have inserted 1.9.31 *voluptatem-fugiendum* (R: *expetendam-fugiendum* only) each at a different place: R at 1.8.26, following the displaced passage from 1.9.30; and P in 1.9.30 itself, following the same passage (*Etenim-iudicari*) in its true position. The only possible explanation is a common ancestor with marginal corrections supplied with faulty or ambiguous *signes de renvoi*.

This common ancestor must have contained the 'Posterior Academics' with a rubric or colophon of its own, a state preserved in one side of the tradition. If this is the case, then the loss of the separate designation, and the denomination of the 'Posterior Academics' as book 6 of the *De finibus*, may have occurred as late as the twelfth century; the scribe of Paris, Bibl. Nat., MS lat. 6331 could have been the one responsible. The stemma would take the following form:

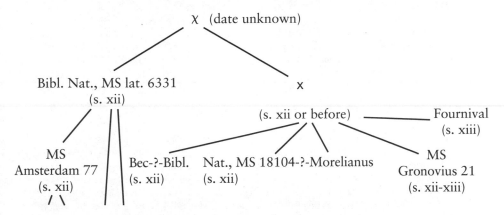

The *De finibus* and the 'Posterior Academics' were copied in the twelfth and thirteenth centuries more frequently than they were cited. William of Malmesbury was aware, from Cicero's list of his writings in the *De divinatione* (2.1–7), that there were four books of the 'Academics' and, from a passage in Augustine's *De civitate Dei*, that the first book had Varro as interlocutor. But he confesses himself unable to find any but the 'third' and 'fourth' books—i.e., the *Lucullus*, divided into two books: 'Hic liber primus Achademicorum in Anglia non inuenitur, sed nec secundus in quo Catulus pro Achademicis disputans introducitur, sicut ex multis que in hiis libris proxime scriptis animaduerti potest. Tertius uero et quartus liber Achademicorum hi duo sunt qui proprie Lucullus appellantur, quia in uno introducitur Lucullus contra Achademicos disputans, in altero Tullius ei pro Achademicis respondet.'[53] C. C. J. Webb notes seven instances in which John of Salisbury echoes a construction or item of vocabulary from the *De finibus* in his *Policraticus*, and another three in the *Metalogicon*.[54] However, several of these were available from alternative sources, and the remainder are commonplaces. John echoes the 'Academics' four times in the *Policraticus*, but each passage derived from Augustine's *Contra academicos*. Thus there is no dependable indication that John knew either the *De finibus* or the 'Posterior Academics' first hand.[55] Both works were evidently known to Vincent of Beauvais, who completed the first edition of his *Speculum historiale* in and around Paris by 1244.[56] The *florilegium* of Ciceroniana in the *Speculum* contains five extracts from the *De finibus*, and one short extract from the 'Academics' labeled as such.[57] While the extracts (as printed) offer no significant variants, the appearance of the *De finibus* in five books and of the 'Posterior Academics'

---

[53] William's discussion of the 'Academics' occurs in notes appended to the *Lucullus* in Cambridge, Univ. Lib., MS Dd. 13.2, a manuscript copied in 1444, complete with William's notes, from an earlier manuscript which goes back to William himself: see R. A. B. Mynors, "A Fifteenth-century Scribe: T. Werken," *Trans. Cambridge Bibl. Soc.* 1 (1953) 97–104; R. M. Thomson, "The Reading of William of Malmesbury," *Revue bénédictine* 85 (1975) 362–402, and esp. 370–382, and the literature cited there.

[54] *Policratici . . . libri VIII*, ed. C. C. J. Webb (Oxford 1909) and *Metalogicon* (Oxford 1929).

[55] In his edition of Walter Burley's *De vita et moribus philosophorum*, Bibliothek des litterarischen Vereins in Stuttgart, 177 (Tübingen 1886), H. Knust conveys the impression that Burley quoted the 'Posterior Academics' and the *De finibus*, each once: see p. 294 ('Register'). Knust's index and his apparatus, however, refer not to sources but to *Parallelstellen*, indiscriminately. Thus Knust's reference to the 'Posterior Academics', a passage in chap. 30 (Knust, p. 110), is taken from *Tusculans* (the parallel in the 'Academics' cannot possibly have been the source); and a passage in chap. 64 (Knust, p. 276), stating the commonplace that 'Epicurus said that pleasure was the greatest good', is obviously no evidence of acquaintance with the *De finibus*.

[56] B. L. Ullman, "A Project for a New Edition of Vincent of Beauvais," *Speculum* 8 (1933) 312–326.

[57] 'Idem de boni et mali lib.I: Nemo voluptatem, quia voluptas sit, aspernatur, neque dolorem, quia dolor est, consectatur [*De fin.* 1.10.32.] Denique aut voluptate omittuntur maiorum voluptatum adipiscendarum causa aut dolores suscipiuntur malorum dolorum effugiendorum gratia [1.10.36]. Idem in secundo *[sic]*: Omnia officia eo referri oportet, ut adipiscamur principiae naturae [3.6.22]. Idem in li. 4: Una voluptas multis obscuratur in vita voluptaria [4.12.31]. Idem in 5 li.: Virtus rationis definitae absolutio definitur [5.14.38]'. (*Speculum historiale* [ed. Venice 1591], bk. 6 chap. 28). 'Idem in libro de Academicis: Inepte quis Minervam docet ['Posterior Academics' 5.18]' (*Speculum historiale*, bk. 6 chap. 29). For the *Speculum* see J. Schneider, "Recherches sur une encyclopédie du xiiie siècle: Le *Speculum majus* de Vincent de Beauvais," *Comptes rendus. Académie des Inscriptions et Belles-Lettres* (1976) 174–189.

under its own name suggests that Vincent constitutes another witness to the Bec-Fournival-Gronovius 21 tradition. Although Vincent did not include much from the *De finibus* and the 'Posterior Academics', he was responsible for disseminating that little far and wide: the impressive-looking *florilegium* of classical quotations in Bern, Burgerbibl., MS 161 (s. xiv)[58] is nothing more than a culling of quotations from the *Speculum historiale*; those from the *De finibus* and the 'Academics' are on fol. 77^v. The extracts from these two works in the well-known Verona *florilegium* of 1329 are likewise Vincent's.[59] Finally, Roger Bacon, who, with Vincent, is one of the earliest writers whose knowledge of the *De finibus* can be accepted with any certainty, knew the text. There is good reason to believe that he knew Fournival's manuscript. Bacon quotes twice from the *De finibus* in his *Moralis philosophia*, composed in Paris in the 1260s, and in each case he calls it the 'Academics':[60] 1.6.11, ' . . . ut Tullius scribit de Aristotile in quinto Academicorum libro [*De finibus* 5.25.73]', and 3, proemium 2, 'Quoniam ipse Tullius, quinto Achademicorum libro, dicit . . . [*De finibus* 5.23.65]'. Bacon was also one of the first scholars in the West to cite Plato's *Phaedo* which, along with the *De finibus*, also came to the Sorbonne with the books of Richard de Fournival.[61]

ORLÉANS

For one part of the French tradition, the lost manuscripts of Philip of Bayeux and Richard de Fournival and the surviving MS Gronovius 21—the family known to Vincent of Beauvais and Roger Bacon—it is possible to suggest a likely center of dissemination.[62] Philip of Bayeux

---

[58] H. Hagen, *Catalogus codicum Bernensium* (Bern 1875). A similar example is Erfurt, Stadtbibl., MS Amplon. Quarto 393 (A.D. 1380); see W. Schum, *Beschreibendes Verzeichniss der amplonianischen Handschriftensammlung zu Erfurt* (Berlin 1887) 655–657; and Schmidt, *Die Überlieferung*, 216–217, n. 10.

[59] See R. Sabbadini, *Le Scoperte dei codici latini e greci ne' secoli XIV e XV*, 2 (Florence 1914) 95–96. He is unaware that Vincent is the source of the extracts.

[60] *Rogeri Baconis moralis philosophia*, ed. E. Massa (Zurich n.d.) 28 and 46.

[61] Delisle, *Cabinet des mss 2, Biblionomia* no. 86. In addition, the Sorbonne owned by 1306 a manuscript of Seneca's 'Dialogues' (described by Thomas of Ireland in the list of authors and works appended to the *Manipulus florum*)—a work which Bacon told the world that he had discovered in Paris; although it does not appear in the *Biblionomia*, the 'Dialogues' also may once have belonged to Richard de Fournival.

[62] The role of Orléans as a center of dissemination for classical texts is discussed in detail in chap. 5 below, "Florilegia and Latin Classical Authors in Twelfth- and Thirteenth-Century Orléans."

was an educated cleric and counsellor to Henry II of England, spending
much of his life at court in Angevin France. Among the books that he
gave to Bec are a number whose transmission leads directly back to
Orléans—among them Pomponius Mela's *Cosmographia* (in the same
codex with Philip's *De finibus* and 'Academics'), the ancestor of which
(Vatican, MS Vat. lat. 4929, s. ix) was at Orléans in the twelfth century;
the younger Pliny's letters preceded by Apuleius as in Florence,
Laurenziana, MS San Marco 284 (s. xi) which, as we have demonstrated
elsewhere, must have been in Orléans in the twelfth century;[63] and the
letters of Ennodius, a difficult and little-read corpus which owed what
circulation it enjoyed to the fact that the letters were read in the main
French twelfth-century school of the *ars dictaminis*, Orléans. Similarly,
Philip's manuscript of Quintilian's 'Institutes', known through the extracts
from it made by Stephen of Rouen, was a close descendant of Bern,
Burgerbibl., MS 351,[64] which belonged to Lupus of Ferrières and which
thereafter went to Fleury. Finally, Philip's manuscript of the 'Philippics',
Paris, Bibl. Nat., MS lat. 5802, was written at Chartres and is a representative of the Colotiana family of this text, comprising only four manuscripts including, apart from Philip's, Berlin, Deutsche Staatsbibl., MS
201, a codex with a Loire background, and Paris, Bibl. Nat., MS lat.
6621, written for Richard de Fournival.[65]

　　Some seventy-five years later there were a number of manuscripts
in Fournival's *Biblionomia* whose texts were closely associated with
Orléans. (Richard himself was a poet and trained in the *auctores*.) Much
of this we have discussed elsewhere, including the complicated but revealing transmission of Fournival's Propertius. All surviving manuscripts of
Tibullus stem from Fournival's manuscript; and the principal medieval
extracts from Tibullus appear in the *Florilegium gallicum*, evidently compiled at Orléans. The *Biblionomia* contains the oldest reference to the
poem on Troy written by Hugh Primas (of Orléans).[66] Fournival's copy

---

[63] R. H. and M. A. Rouse, "The Florilegium Angelicum," *Essays Presented to R. W. Hunt*, 80 no. 1.

[64] M. Winterbottom, *Problems in Quintilian*, Institute of Classical Studies suppl. 25 (London 1970) 22–30.

[65] A. C. Clark, "The Textual Criticism of Cicero's *Philippics*," *Classical Review* 14 (1900) 39–48, and Rouse, *Rev. d'hist. des textes* 3 (1973) 254–255. The medieval provenance of the fourth manuscript in this family is still a mystery: Oxford, Merton College, MS 311, s. xii², sold by Thomas Trillek (bishop of Rochester 1364–72) to William Rede who gave it to Merton. A good description, and an edition of the household list it contains, can be found in *Survival Anc. Lit.*, p. 73 and Appendix to no. 130.

[66] Delisle, *Cabinet des mss*, 2, *Biblionomia* no. 110. Paris, Bibl. Nat., MS lat. 16208, which probably came to the Sorbonne from Fournival (although it does not appear in the *Biblionomia*), contains the oldest text of Hugh's poem (fol. 136ᵛ), beginning 'Dives eram'

of the *De legibus* is derived from Vienna, Nationalbibl., MS 189, another manuscript of Lupus of Ferrières which must have been in the Orléanais in the twelfth century.[67]

Very little is known about the contents of the medieval libraries of Orléans. There are no surviving catalogs; the manuscripts apparently did not bear distinctive pressmarks and, like the books of Notre Dame in Paris, they were dispersed to the four winds. An indication, however, of some of the books that were available at Orléans can be found in the marginalia of an early thirteenth-century manuscript of Papias and Huguccio, Bern, Burgerbibl., MS 276.[68] The margins of the Papias, in particular, are filled with examples of usage from ancient Latin authors. The annotator refers once to St. Columba, once to Fleury and three times to Orléans, where he probably worked. Among the texts that he knew are many of the rarer works in the collections of Philip of Bayeux and Richard de Fournival.[69] Noteworthy in the present context are seven examples from the *De finibus* (actually nine in all: one comes *via* Nonius Marcellus, and one is unidentified): fol. 24, "Bacillus. Unde Nonius in 7^a parte: Cicero in secunde finibus bo. et ma. ut bacillum aliud est inflexum ect. [*De finibus* 2.11.33]'; fol. 42, 'Civitas. Cicero dicit in 5. fi. bo. et ma. quod omnium arcium finis est convivere q. d. regimen civitatis, que dicitur a convivendo, id est simul vivendo. Unde cives quia convives [unidentified]'; fol. 44, 'Colere. Cicero in 5. finium bo. et ma. Cultus animi, id est doctrina, est cibus anime [5.19.54]'; fol. 175, 'Philosophie tres sunt partes. Hanc dictionem ponit Tullius in 5. finium bonorum et malorum. Discipline triplex est via. Altera disserendi, altera vivendi, altera natura [*sic*] [5.4.9]'; fol. 179^v, 'Politicus. Tullius 5. finium bo. et ma. Politicon grece, civile vel populare latine [5.23.66]'; fol. 204, 'Rhetorica civilis [et] philosophica. Tullius in secundo finium bo. et ma. [cf. 2.6.17]'; fol. 207, 'Sacerdos, id est philosophus. Cicero in 5. fi. bo. et ma. [cf. 5.29.87]'; fol. 210, 'Sapientia. Tullius dicit . . . Sapientia est rerum divinarum et humanarum causarumque quibus he res continentur scientia. Idem dicit T. in secundo finium bo. et ma. [2.12.37]'; fol. 210^v, 'Sat, id

---

(H. Walther, *Initia carminum ac versuum medii aevi posteriora latinorum* [Göttingen 1969] no. 4619).

[67] Schmidt, *Die Überlieferung*, 170–172, 216, 228, 414.

[68] The annotations are discussed more fully below, pp. 167–176. A specific example of the use of these annotations in the study of the transmission of a text can be seen in M. Reeve and R. H. Rouse, "New Light on the Transmission of Donatus's *Commentum Terentii*," *Viator* 9 (1978) 235–249.

[69] Among them are Tibullus, Propertius, Seneca's tragedies, Cicero's philosophical works, Plato's *Meno* and *Phaedo*, Pliny's letters, Ennodius, Seneca's 'Dialogues' and the early as well as the later books of Aulus Gellius.

est satis. Cicero in 5. finium bo. et ma. ei que satis est quicquid accesserit nimium est [5.27.81].' These references indicate that the annotator had first-hand knowledge of the *De finibus*. It is worth remarking also that the annotator of Bern, MS 276 quotes at least twenty times from the early books of the *Noctes Atticae*; one of only four surviving pre-fourteenth-century copies of these books is contained in Leiden, MS Gronovius 21. In sum, apart from the assumed affiliation of the *De finibus* manuscripts of Philip of Bayeux, Richard de Fournival, and MS Gronovius 21, there are relationships between the rare works known to Fournival, Philip, the scribe of MS Gronovius 21, and the annotator of Bern, MS 276; and the only apparent point of intersection is Orléans. Therefore, it is not merely plausible but likely that the progenitor of the Bec-Fournival-Gronovius family of the *De finibus* and the 'Posterior Academics' was located at Orléans in the twelfth and thirteenth centuries.

THE 'POSTERIOR ACADEMICS' AND THE *DE FINIBUS* IN ITALY

Thus far we have traced the circulation of the *De finibus* and the 'Posterior Academics' to the end of the thirteenth century. The activity has all been north of the Alps, and, for much of the tradition of the *De finibus* and for all of the 'Posterior Academics', centered on France. And we have endeavoured to suggest how all the surviving information may fit together—codices, catalog descriptions, collected extracts and quotations by medieval writers. The next step—beyond 1300 and south to Italy—brings us into unmapped territory. There are fixed points, consisting not only of references and descriptions but of numerous surviving manuscripts, but the relationships among them have not been sorted out. We shall examine the fourteenth- and fifteenth-century Italian circulation of the *De finibus* and the 'Posterior Academics', conscious that here more than ever we are relying upon conjecture from external evidence, lacking the solid core of stemmatic evidence.

The later, southern, manuscripts of the *De finibus* have not been classified, and very little information is available regarding their readings. The southern manuscripts of the 'Posterior Academics' have been better treated. Plasberg and, with greater precision, Hunt identified a second family of the 'Posterior Academics', termed Notre.3a, represented in nine manuscripts of the late fourteenth and fifteenth centuries, Italian or Mediterranean in origin.[70] Plasberg and Hunt agree that Γ stems

---

[70] Plasberg, *Ciceronis scripta*, xviii–xx; Hunt, "Textual Tradition," 188–217.

from the same archetype as Δ (Bibl. Nat., MS lat. 6331).[71] This still leaves us, however, with a number of unanswered questions. Where does the Γ family come from? Does it represent a long-neglected manuscript discovered in some ecclesiastical library in Italy, like the Verona Catullus or Pliny's letters, or does Γ originate north of the Alps and represent the returning of a text to Italy? If the latter is the case, from which family of the 'Posterior Academics' does it come and when did it move south?

In the majority of Γ manuscripts the 'Posterior Academics' appears in company with the *De finibus* — but never as book 6. This suggests that Γ descends from the Bec-Fournival-Gronovius family.[72] Moreover, the position on the stemma of the 'Posterior Academics' of Γ — separate from Δ (Bibl. Nat., MS lat. 6331), but descending from the same archetype — is identical with the position on the stemma of the *De finibus* which we have suggested above for MS Gronovius 21. The manuscripts, however, are all late; before discussing them in detail, we must consider the earlier evidence for the *De finibus* and the 'Academics' in the south, and see what connection if any this earlier activity may have with the emergence of Γ.

The 'Posterior Academics' appears to have been known in Italy to Dante when he wrote the *Convivio* (ca. 1304–07).[73] No intermediate source has been adduced for lines 125–47; lines 128–30 in particular seem to be a close Italian paraphrase of 'Posterior Academics' 1.4.17. Dante probably planned and composed the *Convivio* while he was in Bologna (1304–06). At this early date, if there was a text of the 'Posterior Academics' available at Bologna it was inevitably in the company of the *De finibus*.[74] Obviously, we cannot say to which family Dante's text belonged, and we have no suggestion of how or when these two works reached Bologna.

---

[71] Plasberg, p. xx; Hunt, 217–222.

[72] If full collation of the *De finibus* in MS Gronovius 21 with the *De finibus* in the Γ manuscripts of the 'Academics' should confirm our conjecture as to their origin, it would simplify matters if editors were to give the progenitor of Bec-Fournival-Gronovius the designation Γ.

[73] Hunt, "Textual Tradition," 42. For the *Convivio* see E. Moore, *Scripture and Classical Authors in Dante*, Studies in Dante (Oxford 1896) 258–273; P. Toynbee, *A Dictionary of Proper Names and Notable Matters in the Works of Dante* (Oxford 1898) 157; P. Renucci, *Dante disciple et juge du monde gréco-latin* (Paris 1954); Dante Alighieri, *Il Convivio*, ed. M. Simonelli (Bologna 1966) 147 and 239.

[74] Note also in this context the codex in the papal library at Avignon written in 'littera Bononnensi'; see below n. 87.

PETRARCH'S MANUSCRIPT AND ITS DESCENDANTS

The first reference to a manuscript of the 'Posterior Academics' comes from Petrarch and, as we might expect, it is in association with the *De finibus*. Petrarch's interest in and knowledge of these two texts was worked out by Billanovich:[75] Petrarch was the first to restore the title of *Lucullus* to the 'Prior Academics' (hitherto thought to be the lost *Hortensius*), and he was the first to state that the *Varro* ('Posterior Academics') formed part of the same work with the *Lucullus*.[76] When Petrarch was in Naples, October-November 1343, his friend Barbato gave him 'parvum Ciceronis librum . . . cuius in fine principium solum erat libri Achademicorum'—a small book of Cicero's, at the end of which was the beginning, only, of the 'Academics'.[77] This, Billanovich feels certain, was the *De finibus* and the 'Posterior Academics'. Petrarch had not known either text when he compiled his list of *desiderata* a few years earlier. In contrast, only a few months after the meeting with Barbato he mentions (4 May 1344) having the *De finibus* as a companion on his sickbed. He used the *De finibus* in his *Rerum memorandarum libri* (written 1343-5), and cited both the 'Posterior Academics' and the 'Prior Academics' therein. He also cites the *De finibus* in the *Rerum familiarium libri* and in glosses to the Ambrosiana Virgil and to Bibl. Nat., MS lat. 2201. While it is frustrating that Petrarch does not explicitly identify the 'parvum Ciceronis librum' it is not surprising; the pas-

---

[75] P. de Nolhac, *Pétrarque et l'humanisme* 1 (Paris 1907) 213–268, and G. Billanovich, "Nella biblioteca del Petrarca," *Italia medioevale e umanistica* 3 (1960) 1–58, esp. 33–39.

[76] Billanovich's claim for Petrarch is true in the respect that he was the first to publicize his discovery, by means of his writings and his network of correspondents. But William of Malmesbury, two centuries earlier, had been aware that the *Lucullus* was in fact part of the 'Academics', and that the *Ad Hortensium*—a text that he regrets having been unable to locate—was a separate and distinct work. See the passage quoted above on p. 81–82, which continues: 'Dicit item Cicero in principio secundi libri De Divinatione se composuisse librum in quo introduxit Hortensium hortantem ad studium philosophie. Dicit etiam ibidem se sex libros De Republica composuisse. Qui libri quia in Anglia non reperiuntur, ego Willelmus Malmesburgensis more meo hic apposui quicquid de materia et intentione eorum in beato Augustino invenire potui'.

[77] Unfortunately little is known about Barbato and less about his interest in manuscripts and his intellectual contacts. Though he was one of Petrarch's close friends, this is the only manuscript which he is known to have found for Petrarch. He held a number of important posts at the court of Naples, in finance and eventually in the royal chancellery, and obviously he had the proper contacts to afford him entry to the libraries of humanists and to those of the Church. For him see R. Weiss, "Some New Correspondence of Petrarch and Barbato da Sulmona," *Modern Language Review* 43 (1948) 60–66; and "The Translators from the Greek of the Angevin Court of Naples," *Rinascimento* I (1950) 195–226; A. Campana, *Dizionario biografico degli italiani* 6 (Rome 1964) 130–134.

sage occurs in Petrarch's description of his difficulties in identifying the surviving parts of the 'Academics'.

What is striking is that there is no suggestion that the 'Academics' formed book 6 of the *De finibus*. Had that been the case, Petrarch would surely have taken pains to sort the matter out. On the contrary, he states that the discovery of 'the begining, only, of the "Academics" ' at once clarified for him the identity of the *Lucullus*; presumably, then, the 'Posterior Academics' had a rubric of its own. He was, therefore, dealing not with a manuscript of the Δ family, but instead with a manuscript related to the Bec-Fournival-Gronovius family. Petrarch's manuscript has not been identified, if it survives. It is perhaps the manuscript described in the 1426 catalog of the Visconti-Sforza library, to which the bulk of Petrarch's collection went after his death: 'Tullius de finibus bonorum et malorum in forma parva et littera antiqua, copertus corio rubeo veteri albicato, cum quo est eiusdem liber Achademicorum non completus. Incipit *Non eram nescius Brute*, et finitur *quadam fuit facultate*. Sig. CCLX.' The manuscript is noted again in the inventory of 1459 (no. B.470), but it is not discernible in the catalog of 1518, made after the collection had passed to the French.[78] There is an important discrepancy here, however, that must be faced. The explicit in the Visconti catalog is that of the Δ family of the 'Academics'; in Γ, *facultate* is followed by the meaningless addition *et to*, very likely a survival from the common Δ Γ archetype. Its absence from the catalog description is open to many interpretations, emphasizing the hazards of attempting to classify manuscripts on the basis merely of descriptions.[79] In addition, *littera antiqua* often means 'humanistic script'; if the manuscript were in humanist script it would be too late to have been Petrarch's.

The *De finibus*, alone, spread quite rapidly, doubtless through the medium of Petrarch's circle of friends, and survives in a fair number of fourteenth-century manuscripts. It is possible also that at some stage representatives of the German family of the *De finibus*, without the 'Academics', made their appearance in Italy.[80]

These texts of the *De finibus* are unclassified, and there is no proof as yet that they form a related family of any sort; we list them here briefly, since they have for the most part been overlooked.

---

[78] E. Pellegrin, *La Bibliothèque des Visconti et des Sforza*, Publications de l'Institut de recherche et d'histoire des textes 5 (Paris 1955) 210, no. 620 and 310, no. 470.

[79] For example: that we are incorrect in the assumption that Petrarch's was a Γ manuscript; that the Visconti codex was not Petrarch's; that the codex, or the cataloger, omitted a meaningless jumble.

[80] None so far has come to light.

Florence, Archivio di Stato, carte Strozziane ser. 3 no. 46 (composite): fols.
11–36 (earlier foliation, 83–108), s. xiv ex., Italy. Paper.
Contents: *De finibus*. Belonged to Coluccio Salutati. For a time bound
with Florence, Bibl. naz., MS Magl. XXXIX.199 (*Lucullus* and *De legibus*
contained *inter alia*, ending at fol. 82), which also belonged to Salutati.
See B. L. Ullman, *The Humanism of Coluccio Salutati* (Padua 1963), 136,
177, 224, 264; Schmidt, *Die Überlieferung*, 239–40, 243 n. 15.

Escorial, MS V.III.6, s. xiv, Italy (Verona, according to Schmidt); 2° fo, *gatas ad*.
Contents: I. *Cicero, Lucullus, De natura deorum, Disputationes Tusculanorum,
Timaeus, De legibus, De finibus, De divinatione, De fato, Pro rege Deiotario,
Pro Marcello, Pro Ligario, Post reditum in senatu, In Catilinam, Philippicae
1–4*; II. Alexander of Aphrodisias, *De anima, De fato*. May have belonged to
Bernardino Maffei. Belonged to Antonio Agustín, archbishop of Tarragona.
See G. Antolín, *Catálogo de los códices . . . del Escorial* 4 (Madrid 1916) 181
et seq.; and Schmidt, *Die Überlieferung*, 229.

Glasgow University, Hunterian Museum, MS T.2.14 (56), s.xiv–xv, France; 2°
fo, *natura*.
Contents: Cicero, *De oratore, De haruspicum responso;* Vegitius, *De re
militari;*[folios excised]; Cicero, *De finibus* 2–5, beg. 'In eo autem
voluptas . . . [2.4.14]', *Lucullus*. Once joined at the end by *Logica
Algazelis* (now MS v.2.17 [397], which was separated off by Hunter.

Milan, Biblioteca Ambrosiana, MS E.15 inf., s.xiv ex.–xv in., north Italy (Padua,
Venice or Bologna); 2° fo, *et ad vite*.
Contents: Cicero, *De officiis, Disputationes Tusculanorum, De natura
deorum, Timaeus, De senectute, De amicitia, De divinatione, De legibus,
De finibus*. R. Cipriani, *Codici miniati dell' Ambrosiana* (Milan 1968),
233, attributes the illumination to Niccolò di Giacomo of Bologna. Written by Marcus de Rephanellis, whom Schmidt (against Sabbadini) identifies as the Venetian notary of that name (fl. 1362–1409); Schmidt, *Die
Überlieferung*, 248 et seq. Belonged to Francesco Ciceri of Milan (1521–96).

Milan, Biblioteca Ambrosiana, MS S.64 sup., s.xiv², north Italy (Venice?); 2°
fo, *quamquam*.
Contents: *De legibus, De finibus, De divinatione, Timaeus, De fato,
Disputationes Tusculanorum, Paradoxa*. Written by Desideratus Lucius,
Venetian lawyer, politician and diplomat (ca. 1320/30–96); see Schmidt,
Die Überlieferung, 232–233.

Paris, Bibl, Nat., MS lat. 6375, s.xiv, Italy; 2° fo, *nosque ipsi*.
Contents: Cicero, *Lucullus, De natura deorum, De finibus*. Belonged to
the library of the Visconti and Sforza; 1424 catalog no. 624 (Pellegrin,
Bibl. des Visconti et des Sforza).

Vatican, MS Arch. S. Pietro H.23, s.xiv ex., Italy; 2° fo, *legimus quam*.
Contents: Cicero, *De finibus*. On fol. 2, note dated 1411 pertaining to

Padua; see E. Pellegrim *et al.*, *Les Manuscrits classiques latins de la Bibliothèque Vaticane, i,* Documents, etudes et repertoires pub. par l'Institut de Recherche et d'Histoire des Textes, 21 (Paris 1975) 49.

Venice, Biblioteca nazionale Marciana, MS VI, 81 (3036), s.xiv med., France; 2° fo, *ut achamorum [sic].*

Contents: Cicero, *De finibus* (extracts), *Timaeus, Lucullus, De divinatione, De fato;* Plato, *Phaedo;* followed by various later works. Bought in 1448 by Joannes Marchanova and bequeathed to St. John in Viridario in 1467.

Wolfenbüttel, Herzog-August-Bibl., MS Gud. lat. 2 (4306), s.xiv med., north Italy; 2° fo, *quid eius.*

Contents: twenty-four works of Cicero (followed by Macrobius, *Comm. in sompnum Scip.* and Boethius, *Comm. in Top.*), including the *De finibus* followed by *Lucullus.* In Paris by the fifteenth century, according to Schmidt. Bears the name (s.xvii) of the Parisian family De Rochefort, fol.1. See Schmidt, *Die Überlieferung,* 177 et seq.[81]

If not all, at least several of the fourteenth-century texts of the *De finibus* must surely derive from Petrarch. This is the most likely source for Salutati's manuscript. The Wolfenbüttel manuscript contains a text

---

[81] We have listed only the fourteenth-century manuscripts. The text proliferates in Italy in the next century and is already moving back to the north in its opening decades. The Councils were a crossroads through which texts passed both north and south. The following is a reasonable example of this movement. Brussels, Bibl. Roy., MSS 10007–10011, s. xv¹, from Louvain, containing Verrines 1–7, Cicero's orations (as in Paris, Bibl. Nat., MS 7794), bears at the end a list of manuscripts copied at the cathedral of Rheims (printed by T. Gottlieb, *Ueber mittelalterliche Bibliotheken* [Leipzig 1890] 338–339), which concludes with 'Timeus Platonis, Phedron de anime immortalitate, Gorgias de rhetorica ad vitam beatam et futuram, Tullius de Tusculanis disputationibus li. 5, Item de finibus bonorum et malorum li. 5 in quibus Stoicorum, Peripateticorum, Epicureorum et Achademicorum sectas varietatesque distinguit. Hunc librum feci conscribi in libraria ecclesie Remensis'. Next to the list is the erased *ex libris*, 'Iste liber pertinent<>bonorum [?] in Leodio'. The exemplar of MSS 10007–10011 is Rheims, Bibl. Mun., MS 1110, written in 1416 for Cardinal William Filastre (1348–1428) at Constance during the Council, doubtless from an exemplar brought north from Italy; MS 1110 fol. I: "Scriptum Constancie, in concilio generali anno Domini millesimo CCCC decimo septimo et dicti concilii tercii. Ego Guillelmus cardinalis Sancti Marci olim decanus Remensis hunc librum dono librarie ecclesie Remensis; scriptum manu propria Constancie in concilio generali, die primo octobris anno suprascripto, G. cardinalis S. Marci.' The exemplar for the codex at the end of the list (*Timeus-De Finibus*) is Rheims, Bibl. Mun., MS 862, which contains this note: (fol. A) 'Hunc librum continentem Thimeum, Gorgiam et Phedonem Platonis, Disputaciones Tusculanarum, Paradoxa et de Finibus bonorum et malorum Tullii, scribi fecit in Ytalia Guillelmus, cardinalis Sancti Marchi, olim decanus Remensis, et illum misit ad bibliothecam ecclesie Remensis, cujus construende ipse decanus curam gesserat'. (Fol. B) 'Hic cathenatur 17 augusti, anno 1416'. For Rheims and Cardinal Filastre see J. Le Braz, "La bibliothèque de Guy de Roye, archévêque de Reims (1390–1409)," *Institut de Recherche et d'Histoire des Textes: Bulletin d'information* 6 (1957) 67–79; Schmidt, *Die Überlieferung,* 31–33.

that is derived from a common ancestor, perhaps from the same exemplar, as is one of Petrarch's copies of the *De legibus*. The text of the *De legibus* also provides a link with Petrarch for three other manuscripts, Escorial, MS V.III.6 and Milan, Ambrosiana, MSS E.15 inf. and S.64 sup. The *De legibus* in all three descends, according to Schmidt, from another of Petrarch's copies of that work. The 'Philippics' i–iv and *Post reditum* in Escorial, MS V.III.6 derive from Bibl. Nat., MS Lat. 5802 and London, Brit. Lib., MS Harley 4927,, both of which belonged to Petrarch. When one such connection is demonstrated, it makes Petrarch the likeliest source for the rare *De finibus* as well.

Granted that several of these fourteenth-century texts of the *De finibus* may come from Petrarch's library, one is faced with the perplexing query: what has become of the 'Posterior Academics'? There is no satisfactory answer. However, Billanovich's description of Petrarch's lengthy wrestle with the 'Academics' — his attempt (which continued to the last year of his life) to impose some logical explanation upon the two mutilated texts that he had, the *Varro* and the *Lucullus*[82] — permits one to speculate that he may have suppressed the 'Posterior Academics' during his lifetime, withholding it from circulation until he had identified it to his own satisfaction, which he never succeeded in doing. Perhaps, rather, he considered it not worth circulating; his final word on the 'Academics' (March 1374, the year of his death) is decidedly unenthusiastic: it is 'a work more subtle than it is necessary or useful'.

The two manuscripts (not identified) of the *De finibus* in the papal library at Avignon may well be considered in this context. Petrarch acquired some of his manuscripts in Avignon, and Avignon perhaps acquired some of its manuscripts from him. The first of these, no. 1344 in the catalog of ca. 1394,[83] contains nearly all of the Ciceroniana found in Escorial, MS V.III.6 and Ambrosiana, MS S.64 sup. (described above).[84] Although the Avignon codex contains much more, and the

---

[82] Billanovich, *Italia med. e umanistica* 3 (1960) 33–39.

[83] This catalog, dated 1375, is edited by F. Ehrle, *Historia bibliotheca Romanorum pontificum* I (Rome 1890); cf. p. 541. For the date 1394 (pontificate of Benedict XIII) see A. Maier, "Die 'Bibliotheca minor' Benedikts XIII," *Archivum historiae pontificiae* 3 (1965) 139–191, esp. 140–142. No. 1344 of the 1394 catalog is to be identified with no. 662 of the 1369 catalog (Ehrle, 339), which provides the second folio reference (*que*) and the penultimate (*experiencia*) according to Schmidt, *Die Überlieferung*, 236; it is no. 828 of the Peniscola catalog, ed. M. Faucon, *La Librairie des papes d'Avignon* 2 (Paris 1887, rptd. 1969) 132.

[84] Ehrle, *Historia bibl. Rom. pont.*, 541, no. 1344: 'Item Tullius ad Ortencium, item idem de natura deorum, item idem de divinacione, item idem de facto, item idem de legibus, item idem in Thimeon Platonis, item idem de finibus bonorum et malorum, item oracio eiusdem pro rege Delotharo, item oracio eiusdem pro Marco Marcello, item alia oracio eiusdem pro Quinto Logario, item congratulacio revocationis eiusdem ad senatum,

order of the works is different, Schmidt suggests on this basis that Petrarch acquired a copy of this manuscript in or just after the middle of the fourteenth century.[85] If Schmidt's conjecture is correct, then Petrarch owned a second copy of the *De finibus*, without the 'Posterior Academics'; and if he obtained it, as Schmidt suggests, pursuant to a letter dated November 1347,[86] then it postdates his acquisition of the Barbato manuscript, which he received in 1343 and referred to in 1344. Perhaps it is this text, of the *De finibus* alone, that Petrarch circulated, and that appears in some or all of the fourteenth-century manuscripts above. A second Avignon manuscript, again containing the *De finibus* without the 'Academics', appears in the 1394 catalog as no. 1345,[87] described as 'in uno volumine de littera Bononnensi'. The fact that the manuscript was written in Bolognese script suggests an importation from northern Italy.

A third papal manuscript appears only in the Peniscola catalog, made after 1411, as no. 827.[88] This manuscript survives, as Escorial, MS

---

item inventiones eiusdem ad Kathelinam, item idem de amicicia, item de senectute, item de paradochiis excoicorum, item de questionibus Tusculanis, item de officiis, item liber veteris rethorice eiusdem, item invectiva eiusdem in Salustium, item cronice Orosii; in uno volumine cooperto de rubeo'.

[85] Schmidt, *Die Überlieferung*, 235–237. Schmidt's evidence is slight, depending as it does upon similarity but not identity of contents, arranged in different sequence. He pushes conjecture even further to postulate, on the basis of the Escorial and Ambrosiana manuscripts, the contents of two entries in the Visconti-Sforza catalogs, possibly referring to the same manuscripts, possibly Petrarch's: catalog of 1426, 'Tullii multi libri simul positi coperti corio rubeo novo cum clavis auricalchi videlicet liber introducens Lucillum loquentem ad Hortensium, liber de natura deorum et alli multi. Incipit: *Magnum ingenium* et finitur *mutandam censuissetis*. sig. CCXLVIIII' (Pellegrin, *Bibl. des Visconti* 120, no. 206); catalog of 1459, 'Cicero ad Hortensium, de legibus, de finibus bonorum et malorum, Tusculanorum et orationes quedam' (Pellegrin, *Bibl. des Visconti*, 311, no. 483). His interpretation of the evidence, however, is plausible, if not wholly convincing.

[86] Schmidt, *Die Überlieferung*, 237 and n. 10, and p. 196.

[87] 1369 catalog, no. 29 (Ehrle, *Hist. bibl. Rom. pont.*, 286); Peniscola catalog, no. 826 (Faucon, *Lib. des papes*, 131). Ehrle, p. 541, no. 1345: 'Item liber rethorice nove Tullii, item liber eiusdem orationum, item oracio eiusdem pro Quinto Ligario, item oracio pro Marco Marcello, item alia oracio eiusdem pro rege Deiotario, item congratulacio revocationis eiusdem ad senatum, item invectiva Salustii contra Tullium, item invectiva Tullii contra Sallustium, item liber eiusdem de finibus bonorum et malorum, item liber eiusdem de tusculanis questionibus, item liber eiusdem de natura deorum, item liber eiusdem de essencia mundi, item liber eiusdem de senectute, item de amicicia, item liber eiusdem de re militari, item liber eiusdem de facto, item liber eiusdem de legibus, item liber eiusdem veteris rethorice, item liber eiusdem de invectiva contra Kathelinam, item liber eiusdem philipicarum, item liber eiusdem ad Hortensium, item liber eiusdem de paradoxis, item liber eiusdem de officiis, item liber eiusdem de divinacione; in uno volumine de littera Bononnensi, cooperto de croceo.' We thank Daniel Williman for references to Cicero in the registers of papal spoils in the Vatican archives.

[88] Faucon, *Lib. des papes*, 131–132.

R.I.2, s. xiv, which contains *Disputationes Tusculanorum, Philippicae 1–4, In Catilinam, Lucullus*, an unidentified work beginning 'Si quando inimicorum', *Pro Marcello, Pro Ligario, Pro rege Deiotario, Invectiva in Sall.*, Sallust, *Invectiva in Tull., De finibus*, beginning 'Incipit liber de achademicarum', *Timaeus, De re militari, In Verrem*. It is tempting to relate this manuscript, or at least some of its contents, to a letter of Gregory XI to Bernard Carit, 11 August 1374, asking for copies of Cicero from the Sorbonne library;[89] several of the texts seem to reflect the books of Richard de Fournival that had passed to the Sorbonne — e.g., the *De finibus*, mislabeled the 'Academics'. Collation should quickly show whether or not the text in this manuscript belongs to the same family as the *De finibus* in Leiden, MS Gronovius 21 — a representative, according to our conjecture, of the family to which Fournival's *De finibus* — 'Academics' belonged. The 'Philippics' in only four books is a sign of the Colotiana family of that text, the family to which Fournival's text belongs. Fournival's text of the 'Verrines', Paris, Bibl. Nat., MS lat. 7775, is now mutilated; but we know, from an early fifteenth-century copy of it (Bibl. Nat., MS lat. 7823), that Fournival's manuscript contained the oration *In Q. Caecilium*, the *Actio prima* and (in five books) the *Actio secunda* — 'three books or, by another way of reckoning, seven', as the Peniscola catalog describes it.[90]

THE Γ FAMILY OF THE 'POSTERIOR ACADEMICS'

The earliest surviving manuscripts of the Γ family of the 'Posterior Academics' (accompanied, in most codices, by the *De finibus*) date only from the very late fourteenth and the fifteenth centuries. During this same time-span there was a proliferation of texts from the Δ family in Italy and elsewhere, including two possibly direct descendants of Paris, Bibl. Nat., MS lat. 6331, the progenitor (ω) of the *deteriores*, and the many descendants of the latter. It is therefore most helpful that Hunt has classified these manuscripts with regard to their texts of the 'Posterior Academics'. We shall merely list the nine Γ manuscripts, relying upon Hunt's demonstration of their affiliations.[91]

---

[89] Ed. Ehrle, *Hist. bibl. Rom. Pont.*, 142.

[90] W. Peterson, "The Manuscripts of the Verrines," *Journal of Philology* 30 (1907) 161–207; Rouse, *Rev. d'hist. des textes* 3 (1973) 254–255. Escorial, MS R.I.2 came to our attention too late to be examined and collated for the purposes of this paper.

[91] Hunt, "Textual Tradition," 188–213; see stemma, p. 213. For a possible fourteenth-century Γ manuscript see *The Public Library of Renaissance Florence*, ed. B. L. Ullman and P. A. Stadter (Padua 1972) p. 229, no. 888: "M. T. Ciceronis de finibus bonorum et

Escorial, MS T.III.18, s.xv med., north Italy, possibly Spain (Plasberg-Hunt ϕ_2);
2° fo, *ut cum*.

Contents: *Orator, Brutus, Topica, De fato*, 'Posterior Academics', *Ad
Herennium*. A sister manuscript for the 'Academics' to Vatican, MS Vat.
lat. 1720 below.

Florence, Biblioteca nazionale centrale, MS Magl. XXI.30, s.xv³/₄, Italy (Florence?)
(Plasberg-Hunt γ_1); 2° fo, *ne ipsos*. Paper (Briquet 11702, made in Pisa ca.
1440).

Contents: *De finibus, De fato*, 'Posterior Academics', *Timaeus, De natura
deorum*. A sister manuscript for the 'Academics' to Gdansk, MS 2388
below.

Florence, Biblioteca Medicea Laurenziana, MS Strozzi 37, s.xv (1410–20), Italy
(Florence) (Plasberg-Hunt ϕ); 2° fo, *commutabilia*.

Contents: *Paradoxa, De amicitia, De senectute, Somnium Scipionis, De
fato*, 'Posterior Academics', *Pro Archia*. A sister manuscript for the
'Academics' to the common parent of Escorial, MS T.III.8 and Vatican,
MS Vat. lat. 1720.

Gdansk, Biblioteka Gdanska Polskiej Akademii Nauk, MS 2388 (IXq.B.11), s.xv
(1450–60), Italy (Florence) (Plasberg-Hunt γ); 2° fo, *nii medeam*.

Contents: *De finibus*, 'Posterior Academics'. Written 'per me Ormannum'.
Belonged to Johannes Bernardinus Bonifacius, marquis of Oria (d. 1597 in
Danzig).

Madrid, Biblioteca nacional, MS 9116, s. xiv²/₄, north Italy (Plasberg-Hunt v_1);
2° fo, *sensu*.

Contents: *De natura deorum, Timaeus, De divinatione, Disputationes Tusculanorum, Paradoxa, De finibus*, 'Posterior Academics'. A sister manuscript for the 'Academics' to Naples, MS IV.G.46 below.

Modena, Biblioteca Estense, MS lat. 213, s. xiv ex.–xv in. (Plasberg: 1393, on
unstated grounds), north Italy (Padua?) (Plasberg-Hunt μ); 2° fo, *cum
inciderit*.

Contents: *De finibus*, 'Posterior Academics', Apuleius's *De magia* (frag.).

Naples, Biblioteca nazionale, MS IV.G.43, s. xv³/₄, north-east(?) Italy (Plasberg-
Hunt σ); 2° fo, *videmur*.

Contents: *De finibus* (to 5.27.79 'ipsa contenta est. Quare', continuing
without interruption), 'Posterior Academics' (from 5.19 'pravumve quid
consentiens'). Note at the change of texts: 'Que sequuntur uno tenore ab
inepto scriba precedentibus adnexa haudquaquam ad istum librum spect-
ant, sed ad primum librum Academicorum qui hic ut in editis deficit'.
Bears notes concerning Ladislas of Hungary, king of Naples (1408–24).

---

malorum, Achademicorum, partitiones, de caelo et mundo, de fata, item Francisci Petrarchae
Florentini de vita solitaria. . . ."

Naples, Biblioteca nazionale, MS IV.G.46, s. xv (1420s?), north
Italy (Schmidt: Padua?) (Plasberg-Hunt v); 2° fo, *ventitarum*. Paper.
Contents: *De legibus, De re militari, Partitiones oratoriae, De optimo
genere oratorum*, 'Posterior Academics', *Timaeus*. The *De legibus* in this
manuscript shares a common parent with that in two fifteenth-century
manuscripts probably written at Padua (Munich, Clm 15958 and
Laurenziana, MS conv. sopp. 224), this common ancestor in turn descending from Petrarch's *De legibus*. It belonged to Ianus Parrhasius of Cosenza
(1470–1522) who bequeathed it to Antonio Seripando from whom it passed
(before 1529) to the Neapolitan Augustinians of S. Giovanni a Carbonara.
See Schmidt, *Die Überlieferung*, 256–257.

Vatican, MS Vat. lat. 1720, s. xv (1425–40), Italy (Florence) (Plasberg-Hunt ϕ_1):
2° fo, *inquit ad*.
Contents: *Brutus, Orator, De oratore, De senectute, De amicitia, De fato*,
'Posterior Academics'.

Hunt's stemma:

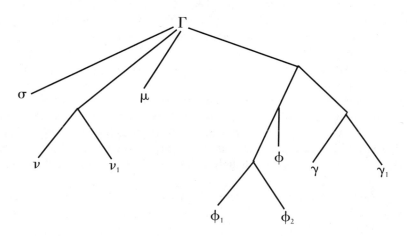

At the beginning of our consideration of the southern manuscripts
we suggested as a working hypothesis that Γ finds its source in the family of *De finibus* — 'Academics' texts represented by the lost manuscripts
of Philip of Bayeux, Richard de Fournival, the Morelianus, and the surviving MS Gronovius 21. Here we may examine in more detail the evidence supporting this conjecture. First of all, it is clear that the archetype of Γ contained the *De finibus*, as well as the 'Posterior Academics'.
The *De finibus* is present in σ, ν, μ, γ and $γ_1$, which represent four

separate witnesses to Γ; it is missing only in ν_{I} and the three φ manuscripts, all of which share common ancestors with manuscripts that do
contain the *De finibus*. Secondly, it is clear that Γ did not concur with
the Δ manuscripts in treating the 'Posterior Academics' as book 6 of the
De finibus. Most of the Γ manuscripts have separate titles for each of
these works, while a few have no inscriptions for either; but in none of
the nine is the 'Posterior Academics' labeled book 6. This proves at any
rate that the archetype of Γ treated the two works in the same fashion as
did Philip of Bayeux's manuscript. But, while the treatment of the texts
is the same, are the texts themselves related? Hunt's full collation of the
'Posterior Academics' in the Γ manuscripts cannot help with this question, since the single known survivor of the Bec-Fournival-Gronovius
family, MS Gronovius 21, contains only the *De finibus*. We come again
to an obstacle that by now is familiar: knowledge of the circulation of
the 'Academics' is dependent upon the stemma of the *De finibus*, which
has not yet been established. However, suggestions of the sort of relationship that we have postulated appear in the apparatus of Schiche's
edition of the *De finibus*.[92] Schiche arbitrarily selected one of these southern manuscripts, Naples, MS IV.G.43 (N for *De finibus*, σ for 'Academics'),
for use in his edition (not reported by Martha). Although he did not
report all of N's variants, there are occasional indications of agreement
between N and MS Gronovius 21 (R) or the Morelianus (D), to which
we can sometimes add the witness of the extracts in Paris, Bibl. Nat.,
MS lat. 18104 (X)—against the reading of the three German texts (ABE)
and the other French family represented by Bibl. Nat., MS lat. 6331 (P,
for *De finibus*). The following are examples: *De finibus* 1.8.26 *quoquo
modo: quoque modo* A, *quoque ut modo* RDN, *quoque ut id modo* P;
2.30.96 *tanti aderant vesicae* A Martha, *tanti autem vesicae* BE, *tanti
autem morti aderat vesicae* P, *tanti autem aderant vesicae* RXN Schiche;
3.20.66 *viles* XN, *eules* R, *cules* A, *civiles* BE, *abiecti* P; (A breaks off at
4.7.16) 4.28.78 *accommodatarum* P, *accommodare* BE, *accommodarum*
RN; 5.7.18 *primum* edd., *prima* BEP, *primo* RXN; 5.18.48 *recurrentur
aliquid* R, *recurreruntur aliquid* N, *recurrantur aliquid* X (so also prob.
D, reported as *recurrant ut aliquid*), *requirant ut aliquid* P, *recurrant
aliquid* BE. These instances, by no means conclusive, certainly permit
the assumption that the text of the *De finibus*—and thus that of the
'Academics'—in the Γ family is derived from the French Bec-Fournival-
Gronovius tradition.

We can offer no evidence for the specific source of the Γ manuscripts—which codex, through what medium, at what date. Perhaps

---

[92] Ed. T. Schiche (Leipzig 1915, rptd. 1961).

they descend from the codex given in 1343 by Barbato to Petrarch, which the latter did not circulate and which only became available after his death. Perhaps, instead, they derive from a text of this family which reached Italy only at the end of the fourteenth century. At any rate, it is evident that the source of Γ was not some long-forgotten Italian text, but that it came instead from France.

While it has not altered the wording of the text, a view of the manuscripts themselves and the traces they have left has provided a clearer picture of the medieval circulation of the 'Posterior Academics'. The catalogs and manuscripts indicate that the 'Academics', rather than surviving in one medieval text, was extant in at least four medieval copies, Philip of Bayeux's, Richard de Fournival's, Bibl. Nat., MS lat. 6331 and Amsterdam, MS 77 (and possibly more, if Morel's codex or the extracts in the *Speculum historiale*, Bern, MS 276 or Bibl. Nat., MS lat. 18104 are independent witnesses). The four manuscripts all appear in the second half of the twelfth century or the early thirteenth, in north central France. Their individual movements and influence can occasionally be glimpsed. The text represented in each makes its way south in the fourteenth and fifteenth centuries to emerge in Avignon and Renaissance Italy. The 'Posterior Academics' is one of that small number of ancient texts that owe their survival not to the ninth century but rather to the twelfth. Its history illustrates again the role of the medieval north as the source for ancient texts on which the Italian Renaissance thrived. And, finally, it exemplifies to perfection the value of examining the transmission of a text in terms of the works with which it circulated: the 'Posterior Academics' has no tradition of its own apart from the *De finibus*; and future editors of the latter text must surely take as a point of departure the extensive work already done on the 'Posterior Academics'.[93]

─────────────

[93] We wish to thank Terence J. Hunt, Pierre Gasnault, and Albinia de la Mare for their generous help with this paper.

Florilegia:
Content and Structure

4. The *Florilegium Angelicum*: Its Origin, Content, and Influence[1]

The *Florilegium Angelicum* is a collection of extracts from ancient and patristic orations and epistles compiled in France during the second half of the twelfth century. It takes its name from Rome, Biblioteca Angelica MS 1895. The *florilegium* contains extensive extracts from a number of rare works, such as the younger Pliny's letters, Cicero's Verrine orations, the works of Ennodius, and the pseudo-Plautine *Querolus*. For these in particular, it was a significant vehicle of dissemination in the twelfth and thirteenth centuries. Surviving wholly or in part in at least seventeen manuscripts the *Florilegium Angelicum* thus achieved a far larger circulation than its more famous contemporary, the *Florilegium Gallicum*. Yet for all practical purposes this book is still unknown. We wish to excavate this *florilegium* in specific, and, in the process, to illustrate through it some aspects of what can be gained from the study of *florilegia* in general.

The whole *florilegium* or substantial portions of it are found in nine manuscripts: Rome, Bibl. Angelica 1895, fols. 1–79^v, s. xii^2, France (A), incomplete; Vatican, Pal. lat. 957, fols. 97–184^v, s. xii^2, France (P), incomplete; Florence, Bibl. Laurenziana, Strozzi 75, s. xii^2, France (F); Vatican, Reg. lat. 1575, fols. 63–100^v, s. xii–xiii, France (R), rearranged;

Originally published in *Medieval Learning and Literature: Essays Presented to R. W. Hunt*, ed. J. J. G. Alexander and M. T. Gibson (Oxford 1975) 66–114.

[1] We are grateful to M.-Th. d'Alverny, Bernhard Bischoff, Élisabeth Pellegrin, and Jean Vezin for their considerate help on numerous details in the preparation of this paper. We wish in particular to thank Birger Munk Olsen for sharing with us his extensive knowledge of pre-13th century MSS of Latin classical authors. Thanks are also due to the curators of Latin MSS at the Bibliothèque Nationale and the staff of the Institut de Recherche et d'histoire des textes, Paris. This study was carried out with the support of the American Council of Learned Societies.

Sydney, University Libr., Nicholson 2, s. xiii[2], France (N), extracts; Vatican, Vat. lat. 3087, fols. 23–68[v], s. xiii[2], S. France or Italy (V); Paris, Bibl. de l'Arsenal 1116 E, fols. 128–142[v], s. xiii[1], France, St. Victor (S), extracts; Évreux, Bibl. Municipale 1 fols. 64–114[v], s. xiii med., France, Lyre (E), incomplete; and London, British Libr. Add. 25104, s. xv, Italy (L). To these should be added the description of a copy now lost, item 84 in the *Biblionomia* of Richard de Fournival (d. 1260).[2] Of them, Angelica 1895 (A), which alone contains a prologue, is the dedication copy. Selections or brief extracts from the *florilegium* are found in six manuscripts: Auxerre, Bibl. Municipale 234, s. xiv[2], France (x); Brussels, Bibl. Royale 10098–10105, s. xiii[1]; France (b), Cicero orations and Jerome only; Leyden, Universiteitsbibl. B.P.L. 191B, s. xii[2] (l); London, Brit. Libr., Royal 11 A.v., s. xii–xiii (r), Jerome only; Paris, Bibl. Nationale, lat. 15172, s. xiii, France, St. Victor (s); and Vatican, Reg. lat. 358, s. xv, France, Tours (v). Complete reorganizations of the *florilegium* in which the extracts are arranged by subject are known in two manuscripts, Rome, Bibl. Angelica 720, s. xiii, France (a) and Paris, Bibl. Nationale, lat. 1860, s. xiii med., S. France (p). Since many of these are uncataloged, a description of each is given in Appendix III.

The manuscripts of the *florilegium* can be grouped as follows, on the basis of a collation of the extracts from Pliny's letters and from Seneca's *De beneficiis* and through a comparison of their contents. The two older manuscripts, A and Pal. lat. 957 (P), are sufficiently similar in physical appearance to have been written in the same scriptorium. This must in fact have been the case, because A is a direct copy of P, scrupulously corrected from the archetype. This is evident from the following readings, in which errors unique to P have been corrected: Pliny's letters, 1.13.5 *desideria* PA, *desidia* A corr., cett.; 4.9.8 *Iugulari* PA, *Iugulat* A corr., cett.; Seneca, *De beneficiis* 1.5.2 *materiam et* PA, *materiam beneficii et* A corr., cett.; 1.7.2 *gravius* PA, *gratius* A corr., cett.; 2.16.1 *amicosa vox* PA, *animosa vox* A corr., cett. The affiliation of P and A is further

---

[2]Published in L. Delisle, *Le Cabinet des manuscrits de la Bibliothèque nationale 2* (Paris 1874) 518–535; item 84, p. 529, and Appendix III below. In addition to Fournival's library, MSS of the *Florilegium Angelicum* were known in two other medieval libraries, Cluny and Notre Dame in Paris: item 224, *Flores philosophorum excerpti ex libri Saturnalium Macrobii*, in a catalog of the books at Cluny made in 1800 (L. Delisle, *Inventaire des manuscrits de la Bibliothèque nationale: Fonds de Cluni* [Paris 1884] 397–404); and item 47, *Flores philosophorum, excerpti de libro Macrobii Saturnaliorum*, among the books left to Notre Dame in 1296 by Pierre de Joigny, canon of Rouen and master of theology in Paris (Delisle, *Cabinet*, 3.5; and P. Glorieux, *Répertoire des Maîtres en théologie de Paris au xiiie siècle* 1 [Paris 1933] no. 183). We are unable to identify either of these among the surviving MSS. For the Cluny reference we are indebted to B. Barker-Benfield, the Bodleian Library, Oxford.

apparent in the errors which they share against the rest of the tradition, which the scribe of A failed to rectify. For example, in Pliny's letters 1.20.11, where the others rightly read *prestare dicentibus brevitas*, both P and A omit *dicentibus*. In the extracts from *De beneficiis* 1.1.7, both P and A place the phrase *Errat qui sperat . . . torsit* before two other phrases from the same paragraph, while the other manuscripts concur in placing this phrase after the others, following the order of Seneca's text. Two extracts from *De ben.* 1.4.3 and 4.4, *Qui referre gratiam debet . . .* and *Honestissima contentio est beneficiis . . .*, found in the others, are lacking in P and A. One cannot postulate that P is a copy of A made before correction, firstly because the corrections are made in the hand of the manuscript and thus without significant time lapse; and secondly, because of the unique readings in A not found in P: Pliny 1.16.8, *floruisset in primis* A, *floruisset in precio* P cett. (wording not in Pliny text); 5.5.4 *finivit* A, *finunt* P, *finiunt* cett. (recte); *De ben.* 1.1.1 *fero* A, *sero* P cett. (recte); 1.6.3 *optime* A, *opime* P cett. (recte). Another indication is found in the extract from *De ben.* 2.11.1; the passage, as rephrased in the *florilegium*, begins *Quidam tibi proscriptione servatus. . . .* In P there is an erasure between the words *tibi* and *proscriptione*, although nothing is missing. (The length of the erasure suggests that it may have been *proscriptione* written twice.) A reproduces the meaningless blank. Finally, there is the fact that P does not present the extracts from Gregory's letters following the extracts from Jerome, a sequence found only in A. P hence emerges as a fair copy of the archetype, almost certainly the compiler's fair copy.

A evidently produced one descendant, that being the collection of extracts from the *florilegium* in Arsenal 1116 E (S). S agrees in error with AP against the rest of the tradition at Pliny 1.20.11, with A and the rest against P in error at 3.3.7, and it includes extracts from Gregory's letters. P produced, apart from A, only the partial text in Auxerre 234 (x). It is obviously related to P because it is the only other manuscript of the *florilegium* to include the extracts from Julius Paris. Three manuscripts which contain the complete *Florilegium Angelicum*, Strozzi 75 (F), Reg. lat. 1575 (R) and Vat. lat. 3087 (V), descend independently from the archetype. While they may be at some remove from it, the three share no errors in common against P and A and hence do not descend from a single intermediate parent. Each of the three contains errors and omissions not reproduced in the others. F, oldest of the three, thus cannot be an ancestor of either of the other two; apart from its unique errors, it has numerous *lacunae* of one or more words. In evidence, one need cite only the most glaring example, its omission of three successive extracts from Pliny's letters, 1.17.2, 17.3, 18.5, which appear in the other two. R cannot be an ancestor of V, not only because of unique errors and *lacunae*, such as the omission of an entire extract from Pliny 1.12.3, but also because R, as we shall see, represents a rearranged order while V presents the original sequence. V is late in date (fourteenth century) and replete with independent errors. Despite the possible distance from the archetype of F, R, and V, there is no pattern of common errors that pair any two against the third, and hence no indication of a common ancestor intermediate between two of them and the archetype. The remaining manuscript of the whole text, London B.L. Add. 25104 (L) of the fifteenth century, seemingly shares a common ancestor (γ) with F, as these readings suggest: Pliny 1.7.3 *qui* FL, *quid* rem.; 2.4.3 *liberalitas* FL, *liberalitas tua* rem.: 2.6.5 *aliquanto* FL, *aliquando* rem.; 3.21.3 *putamus* APFL, *putavimus* RV. Moreover, only F and L conclude with the brief *Alexander Atheniensibus* which must have been in γ. Évreux 1 (E), Leyden B.P.L. 191 B (l), and R constitute another sub-family, descending from a manuscript (β) in which the works were grouped by author, with the Christian authors (Gregory, Jerome, Sidonius, and Ennodius) preceding the classical authors and, among the latter, with the 'proverb' material concluding the collection. This order is reflected in E and R.[3] The extracts in l are few and dispersed among other texts, but shared readings show its affiliation: for example, Pliny 1.3.5 *ipse tibi* REl, *tibi ipse* rem.; 1.20.12 *varie sunt voluntates* REl, *varie voluntates* rem.; 2.3.5 *milicie* REl, *malicie* rem. Although Sydney Nicholson 2 (N) contains selections from virtually every text in the *florilegium*, the extracts are too few and the manuscript too badly effaced to permit a precise affiliation. N does not reflect the *lacunae* of AP (*De ben.* 1.4.4) or F (Pliny 3.9.8), nor the revised order of β, and hence it appears to derive independently from the archetype. The six remaining manuscripts, those which are rearranged topically and those which contain only a handful of extracts from the *florilegium*, we have not attempted to place on the stemma.

Having established the relative authority of the manuscripts of the *Florilegium Angelicum*, we are now equipped to settle a number of problems regarding the arrangement and actual contents of the archetype. The two most authoritative manuscripts, A and P, are both unfortunately incomplete. A breaks at the end of quire 10 in the middle of extracts from Aulus Gellius, indicating that it once contained more, and is now lacking its final quire or quires. P has quires numbered i–x; quire

---

[3] R and E each has errors not found in the other. For example, the extract from Pliny 1.12.3 omitted in R is found in E. And in many instances E differs, in error, from R; for example, Pliny 1.4.4 *dicimus* E, *dominis* R recte; 1.5.17 *etiam verum* E, *verum etiam* R recte; 1.9.8 *Tullius* E, *Attilius* R recte.

x breaks in the midst of extracts from Ennodius, indicating a missing quire or quires. It is followed by a quire numbered i, containing extracts from Gregory's letters and from Julius Paris's Epitome of Valerius Maximus. The text of the Epitome breaks at mid-sentence at the end of the quire, indicating that another quire or more are lacking here as well. One must hence turn to the later copies in order to determine what the *florilegium* actually contained. Where the manuscripts containing the full text or large portions of it, APFNVLRES, concur, we have the contents of the *florilegium*. With the exception of the prologue, which appears in A alone, and of the extracts from Gregory's letters, which are a separate question, the nine agree upon the following content and (saving RE) sequence: Macrobius, *Saturnalia*; *Proverbia philosophorum*; Jerome, epistles; Apuleius, *De deo Socratis*; Pliny the Younger, epistles; Cicero, orations; Sidonius, epistles; Seneca, *De beneficiis*; Seneca, *Epistulae ad Lucilium*; *Sententiae philosophorum*; *Praecepta Pithagorae*; *Ænigmata Aristotilis*; Cicero, Tusculan Disputations; Aulus Gellius, *Noctes Atticae*. At this point A breaks off. But the other manuscripts, including A's exemplar P and its descendant S, continue with extracts from Cicero's Verrine orations and the works of Ennodius. Here the extracts in S cease, and the text in P is broken. However, the remaining manuscripts, including P's descendant x, continue with extracts from Martin of Braga, *De formula honestae vitae; Querolus*; and Censorinus, *De die natali*.

The extracts from Censorinus mark the limit of reliable consensus and thus presumably the end of the archetype. However, there remains one problem concerning the sequence of works in the *florilegium*, the extracts from the letters of Gregory the Great. Extracts from Gregory's letters were clearly a part of the archetype of the *Florilegium Angelicum* since the Gregory extracts in A, copied from the added quire in P, are corrected from the archetype and since they appear in other manuscripts of the *florilegium* — though not in the same place in the order, and not in all manuscripts. The Gregory extracts may have been an afterthought — a tactful addition to a *florilegium* dedicated to a pope. In making his fair copy, the compiler added them on a separate quire numbered i, along with extracts from Julius Paris. In making the presentation copy, he entered the Gregory extracts where they might most appropriately appear, following the extracts from the letters of Jerome. That the Gregory extracts remained unattached to the archetype, perhaps in the form of a loose quire, is also suggested by their treatment in the later manuscripts. The manuscripts which include them follow the suggestion of P, presumably reflecting that of the archetype, that they precede the collection because the quire that contains them bears the signature i. β must have contained the Gregory extracts at the beginning, since both R and E do.

The writer of S placed the extracts from Gregory and those from Jerome as well at the head of the collection. In x the Gregory extracts appear instead as the final section, following the example rather than the precept of P. N, V, γ, and Fournival's manuscript omit the extracts from Gregory's letters entirely and proceed in the order described above.

What disposition the compiler made of the extracts from Julius Paris we cannot know, because of the incomplete state of A. The fact that these extracts appear in only two manuscripts, P and the partial text in P's descendant x, suggests that they were an addition to P which did not exist in the archetype.

Extracts from three other works are found in more than one manuscript. At an early stage in the transmission, extracts from the oration of the Scythian legates to Alexander, from Quintus Curtius 7.8.12–30, were added to the *florilegium* following the extracts from Censorinus. These appear in four manuscripts: FL (γ), N, and V. Moreover, the writer of β included longer extracts from Quintus Curtius, an addition probably inspired by his having seen the *Oratio Scytharum*. Since a sample collation indicates that β, γ, N, and V descend independently from the archetype, the extracts thus must represent an addition to the archetype itself. The absence of these extracts from x indicates that this addition was made after the presentation copy was written; and the description of Fournival's manuscript of the *Florilegium Angelicum* also suggests that the Censorinus extracts, not Quintus Curtius, originally marked the end of the *florilegium*. Extracts called *Alexander Atheniensibus*, three sentences from Julius Valerius (ed. Keubler, p. 46. 20–8), follow the *Oratio ad Alexandrum* in F and L. This represents an individual addition by the writer of γ, one obviously suggested to him by the subject-matter of the preceding extracts. Finally, there are lengthy extracts from Ps.-Quintilian's *Declamationes maiores* in two manuscripts, R and x, and a shorter series from the collection in Paris B.N. lat. 15172 (s). Quotations from Quintilian in the topically arranged Paris B.N. lat. 1860 (p) perhaps derive from this same collection. As with the *Alexander Atheniensibus*, these were obviously not part of the archetype; but their independent addition to the *Florilegium Angelicum*, based on orations and epistles, is wholly understandable.

An examination of the transmission of the more unusual texts included in the *Florilegium Angelicum* has permitted the identification of two manuscripts, Vat. lat. 4929 and Berne 136, from which the compiler drew his extracts. The appearance in the *florilegium* of extracts from the *Querolus*, from Censorinus' *De die natali*, and, in two manuscripts, extracts from Julius Paris's Epitome of Valerius Maximus, reveals the presence of Vat. lat. 4929, assembled by Heiric of Auxerre. Vat. lat.

4929, discovered by Barlow and Billanovich,[4] was probably put together by Heiric toward the mid-ninth century from a number of older books, among which was a collection of three texts which had been edited in the sixth century at Ravenna by Rusticius Helpidius Domnulus: the Epitome of Valerius Maximus, Pomponius Mela's *De chorographia*, and Vibius Sequester's *De fluminibus*. For these it is the sole remaining authority.[5]

Of the texts[6] contained in Vat. lat. 4929, extracts from the *Querolus* and Censorinus follow one another at the end of the *Florilegium Angelicum*; and extracts from Julius Paris appear in the odd last quire of P (fol. 184[rv]), and immediately following the *Querolus* and Censorinus in x (fols. 156[v]–169[v]).[7] While there are other manuscripts of the *Querolus* and Censorinus upon which our compiler might have drawn, Vat. lat. 4929 is the only complete manuscript of the Epitome. That the *Florilegium Angelicum* drew on Vat. lat. 4929 was first noticed inadvertently by Ranstrand; he recognized the influence of readings in Vat. lat. 4929 on the extracts from the *Querolus* in Paris, B.N. lat. 15172 (s) fol. 126[v]. (He and Gagnér, who had also examined it, considered s to be a variant version of the extracts from the *Querolus* in the *Florilegium Gal-*

---

[4] C. Barlow, "Codex Vaticanus latinus 4929," *Memoirs of the American Academy in Rome* 15 (1938) 87–124 and pls. 11–18; G. Billanovich, "Dall'antica Ravenna alle biblioteche umanistiche," *Aevum* 30 (1956) 319–353.

[5] Vat. lat. 4929 (V) was annotated around 1100 by a grammar master who added extensive scholia to the *Querolus*. In the mid-12th century a copy of V was made which included the scholia, but it is now lost. It in turn produced Vatican Reg. lat. 314 pt. VI, fols. 112–16, s. xii[2] (S), which survives in a collection of fragments assembled by Paul Petau. Barlow, p. 100, and G. Ranstrand, *Querolusstudien* (Stockholm 1951) 26–27, assign this MS to Micy St. Mesmin; however, Reg. lat. 314 is made up of eight or nine fragments of varying dates, only the first of which bears the Micy *ex libris*. The lost MS (copy of V, parent of S) moved south at some date and was acquired by Petrarch at Avignon in 1335; a copy, incorporating Petrarch's notes, survives as Milan, Bibl. Ambrosiana H 14 inf. (s. xv). Cf. Billanovich, op. cit.

[6] Vat. lat. 4929 contains, fol. 1[rv], a fragment of the Greek alphabet (s. xi); fols. 2–34, Censorinus, *De die natali*; fol. 34[v], blank; fols. 35–50, an epitome of Augustine's *De musica*; fols. 50[v]–54, four anonymous sermons (s. ix–x); fol. 54[v], blank; fols. 55–77, *Querolus*, with commentary added s. xi ex. or s. xii in.; fol. 77[v], three concentric circles; fol. 78, labyrinth; fols. 78[v]–148, Julius Paris, Epitome of Valerius Maximus; fols. 148[v]–149, blank; fol. 149[v], verses beg. *Septem mira . . .* ; fols. 149[v]–188, Pomponius Mela, *De chorographia*; fols. 188–95, Vibius Sequester, *De fluminibus*; fols. 195[v]–196, blank; fol. 196[v], list of churches (s. xi; Barlow, s. x); fol. 197[rv], blank except for pen trials. Taken from Barlow, 87–88.

[7] The initial survey of the extracts from Vat. lat. 4929 was carried out by Edward Weeden.

licum.[8]) A collation of the extracts from the *Querolus* shows that the text of the *Florilegium Angelicum* shares five readings with Vat. lat. 4929 (V) against the other manuscripts of the *Querolus*; three of these are from the text of V, and two derive from the late-eleventh- or early-twelfth-century glosses on the text. From Ranstrand's edition of the *Querolus,*[9] the five readings are: p. 11.22 *peierat: perierat* V, florilegium; p. 13.12 *dibacchationes: debacchationes* VR, flor.; p. 20.15 *inesse felicem sinunt: esse felicem non sinunt* V, flor.; p. 9.21–2 *satis aliis multis defensorum: satis tibi aliisque multis defensorum* V (*tibi* add. interlin.), flor.; p. 20.12 *corpora videntur quantum animus: corpora videntur sed quantum animus* V (*sed* add. interlin.), flor.

The extracts from the Epitome of Julius Paris in P contain four readings which tie them to Vat. lat. 4929. The most significant is Kempf 476.16,[10] where V and P give the dative singular *Locri*, and the later manuscripts as well as Valerius Maximus offer the correct genitive singular *Locris*. Three readings in P derive from corrections made in the text of V by the above-mentioned glossator: 476.22 *Epidauriae Scolapio*, corr. to *Epidauri Aescolapio*; 476.23 *turpei dei* corr. to *turpe id ei*; [13.15] *ignorares eandi* corr. to *ignorare se an di*. The readings in the Epitome, as well as those in the *Querolus*, which derive from corrections made by the glossator, represent his invention rather than the readings of another manuscript. The two extracts from Censorinus in the *Florilegium Angelicum* contain no significant variants.

The *Florilegium Angelicum* contains, in sequence, extracts from Apuleius called *De deo Socratis* (but including as well his *Asclepius, De Platone,* and *De mundo*); from the younger Pliny's letters; and from the following orations of Cicero: (Pseudo-Cicero) *Pridie quam in exilium iret, Post reditum in senatu, Post reditum ad Quirites, De domo sua, Pro Sestio, In Vatinium, De provinciis consularibus, De haruspicum responsis, Pro Balbo,* and *Pro Caelio.* The last two texts, Pliny's letters and this group of orations, were not easily found in twelfth-century France. Fortunately, the manuscript from which the extracts were taken can be identified as Berne, Burgerbibliothek 136 s. xii[2], which contains Gregory, *In Ezechielem;* Apuleius, *De deo Socratis, Asclepius, De Platone, De mundo;* Pliny's epistles bks. 1.1–5.6; and Cicero's orations (in the num-

---

[8] Ranstrand, op. cit., 69–72; A. Gagnér, *Florilegium Gallicum. Untersuchungen und Texte zur Geschichte der mittellateinischen Florilegienliteratur,* Skrifter utgivna av Vetenskaps-Societeten 18 (Lund 1936) 212.

[9] G. Ranstrand, ed., *Querolus sive Aulularia incerti auctoris comoedia,* Göteborgs Högskolas Årsskrift 57 (1951).

[10] Ed. C. Kempf, *Valerius Maximus* (Stuttgart 1966) 472–591.

ber and order given above). It is a well-known manuscript and has been collated and classified for its texts of Pliny and Cicero.

For its text of Pliny (and Apuleius as well) Berne 136 descends from Florence, Bibl. Laurenziana, S. Marco 284, s. xi (F), of the ten-book family.[11] Berne 136 contains the same works of Apuleius and the same text of the letters as are found in S. Marco 284, i.e., that ending at bk. 5.6. The editors of Pliny's letters have long known of the existence of the extracts in the *Florilegium Angelicum* and that they belong to the ten-book family; but the editors knew them in only five manuscripts, F, R, V, S, and Angelica 720 (a)[12] and, since they contribute nothing toward establishing the text of the letters, they received little attention. It is clear on the basis of the readings that the compiler of the *florilegium* used an F text as his source. However, because Berne 136 is so faithful a copy of F, we cannot prove from readings alone that Berne 136 rather than F is the source of the extracts. The proof rests in the fact that excerpts from Apuleius, Pliny, and Cicero all three appear in the *florilegium* consecutively and in the same order as in Berne 136.

The collection of Cicero's orations in Berne 136 is quite as rare as Pliny's letters.[13] These orations are known in only five manuscripts which date from before 1200, all descending from a common archetype: Paris, Bibl. Nationale, lat. 7794, s. ix, France (P);[14] London, British Libr.,

---

[11] The transmission of the younger Pliny's letters is set forth in R. A. B. Mynors, *C. Plini Caecili Secundi epistularum libri decem* (Oxford 1963) v-xxii. Concerning the direct dependence of Berne 136 on F, see E. T. Merrill, *C. Plinii Caecili Secundi epistolarum libri decem* (Leipzig 1922) xi n. 23. The initial survey of the extracts from Pliny in the *Florilegium Angelicum* was carried out by William Patt.

[12] D. Johnson, "The Manuscripts of Pliny's Letters," *Classical Philology* 7 (1912) 70.

[13] Concerning the transmission of this group of Cicero's orations see A. C. Clark, "The Vetus Cluniacensis of Poggio," *Anecdota Oxoniensia*, Classical Series pt. 10 (Oxford 1905); W. Peterson, "Cicero's *Post reditum* and Other Speeches," *Classical Quarterly* 4 (1910) 167–177; Clark, *The Descent of Manuscripts* (Oxford 1918) 266–280; J. Cousin, ed., *Cicéron: Discours Pour Caelius, Sur les provinces consulaires, Pour Balbus*, Collection Budé (Paris 1962) 58–74; idem, *Cicéron: Discours Pour Sestius, Contre Vatinius*, Collection Budé (Paris 1965) 91–103. The initial survey of the extracts from these orations in the *Florilegium Angelicum* was carried out by Joyce Segor.

[14] The MS, written by several Tour hands, had probably come to Paris by the sixteenth century, for it bears an erased note of that date on fol. 32[v] upper margin: *A frere Joachim Perion estudiant a Montagu a Paris en crestiente*, referring to the Collège de Montagu (1314–1792). On fol. 1 top left, it bears the unidentified pressmark: O. lx. xxix (similar to, but not that of, St. Denis). Few books survive from the college, making it difficult to determine whether or not this is the college pressmark. The MS was part of the Royal Library by 1622 (Rigault CCCVII). The *frere Joachim Perion* is probably the French humanist of that name (ca. 1497/98–1557/59) who became a Benedictine monk at Cormery and studied at Paris for some twenty years. He was editor and translator of classical

Harley 4927, s. xii[2], France (H); Brussels, Bibl. Royale 5345, s. xii, ascribed
to Gembloux (G);[15] Berlin, Staatsbibl. Preussischer Kulturbesitz lat. fol.
252, s. xii, Corvey, presumably assembled by Wibald of Corvey (E); and
Berne 136.[16] For the orations Berne 136 is a direct copy of the ninth-
century P made after the latter was corrected and punctuated in the early
twelfth century, apparently from the parent of G and E. The writer of
Berne 136 followed the system of punctuation and was influenced by the
manner in which P[2] broke the text into sentences by the use of capital
letters.[17] As in the case of Pliny's letters, Berne 136 reads so close to its
exemplar that one cannot tell on the basis of readings alone from which
the extracts in the *Florilegium Angelicum* derive. That the extracts come
from Berne 136 is again proven by the fact that the latter also contains
Apuleius and Pliny's letters.

One wonders, of course, where the compiler of the *Florilegium
Angelicum* found these two important manuscripts. He was obviously
working at a place where interesting classical texts were available, including a number that were rare in twelfth-century Europe. (To those already
mentioned, one would want to add in particular the Verrine orations of
Cicero.) As we shall see later, the compiler's purpose was to provide a
collection of eloquent quotations, from which one might draw apt and
stylish phrases for the composition of public pronouncements and official letters. In the second half of the twelfth century this combination of
interests, in the classical authors and in the *ars dictaminis*, immediately
suggests Orléans as a possible home for the *Florilegium Angelicum*.
While present knowledge of the curriculum at Orléans is slight, its posi-

---

authors, especially Greek. We are grateful to Pierre Gasnault for calling this to our attention.

[15] The ascription stems from the presence of a 12th-century leaf from Gembloux in its
binding.

[16] Besides these five, extracts from this collection of orations appear in the *Florilegium
Gallicum*, compiled in France toward the middle of the 12th century; two leaves of a mid-
9th-century (ca. 860) MS written in the area of the Loire, containing the *Pro Sestio* 41.
88–46. 99 are found in Leyden Voss. lat. F. 67, fols. 1–2[v]; the Ps.-Ciceronian *Pridie* is
known in Rouen MS 1040, fol. 11 (s. xii; Lyre); and Berne, Burgerbibliothek, MS 395, fols.
1–15 (s. xii med.) contains the *Pridie, Post reditum in senatu*, and *Post reditum ad Quirites*.
The 13th-century extracts from the orations in Brussels Bibl. Royale, MS. 10098–10105
(Van den Gheyn 1334) come from the *Florilegium Angelicum*. The 10th-century text in
Paris B.N. nouv. acq. lat. 340, fol. 107 (Cluny), said by Hauréau (*Notices et Extraits* 6
[Paris 1893] 260–261) and Manitius (*Geschichte der lateinischen Literatur* 2 [Munich 1911]
482) to be an introduction to the *De haruspicum responsis*, is a fragment of Grillius on
Cicero's *De inventione*; see E. Courtney, "Ignis fatuus extinguitur," *Scriptorium* 15 (1961)
114–115. Thus far no effort has been made to classify the extracts in the *Florilegium
Angelicum* or the *Florilegium Gallicum*, or the texts in the Leyden MS or Berne 395.

[17] Peterson, op. cit.

tion as the center for classical studies is clearly established in the well-known statements of such contemporaries and near-contemporaries as Matthew of Vendôme, Geoffrey of Vinsauf, Helinand of Froidmont, Alexander Neckham, and John of Garland, and is celebrated posthumously, so to speak, in Henri d'Andeli's *Battle of the Seven Liberal Arts* in the middle of the thirteenth century. And Orléans seems to have been famous across Europe for teaching the *ars dictaminis*.[18] We can, therefore, accept as a hypothesis that the *Florilegium Angelicum* was compiled at Orléans. To make this more than an assumption, one must consider the external evidence.

The information one can glean from Vat. lat. 4929, one of the manuscripts used by the compiler of the *Florilegium Angelicum*, goes far toward confirming our assumption. The transmission of individual works in Vat. lat. 4929 offers supporting evidence at least. For its text of the *Querolus*, one can localize its sister manuscript (Leyden Voss. lat. Qu. 83, s. ix[1]) at Fleury,[19] whence it passed to Pierre Daniel. The *De fluminibus* of Vibius Sequester was copied from Vat. lat. 4929 at least once, producing Vatican MS. Reg. lat. 1561, fols 11^v–15^v, (s. xii[2]);[20] this also belonged to Pierre Daniel. More telling as to its whereabouts in the eleventh and twelfth centuries is the physical evidence in Vat. lat. 4929 itself. The earliest evidence is the appearance on fol. 196^v of a late-tenth- or early-eleventh-century list of thirty-six parishes and the tithes they paid under the administration of one Arnulf. Delisle identified the parishes with villages in the area of Pithiviers, which lies in the diocese of Orléans.[21] Barlow suggested that the writer of the list might be identified with Arnulf, bishop of Orléans 973–1003.[22] This would suggest that

---

[18] Concerning the schools at Orléans see L. Delisle, "Les écoles d'Orléans au xiie et au xiiie siècle", *Annuaire: Bulletin de la Société de l'histoire de France* 7 (1869) 139–154; L. J. Paetow, *The Arts Course at Medieval Universities* . . . , University Studies 3 (Urbana 1910) 503–509, 575–581; E. Faral, *Les Arts poétiques du XIIe et du XIIIe siècle* (Paris 1924); B. Marti, *Arnulfi Aurelianensis Glosule super Lucanum* . . ., Papers and Monographs of the American Academy in Rome 18 (1958), Introduction. Besides the bibliography given in these, see S. Guenée, "Université d'Orléans," *Bibliographie d'histoire des universités françaises des origines à la Révolution*, Institut de Recherches et d'histoire des textes et Commission internationale d'histoire des universités (Paris 1970). The best survey of medieval letter collections with full bibliography is the introduction to *The Letters of Peter the Venerable*, ed. Giles Constable 2 (Cambridge 1967) 1–44.

[19] Ranstrand, op. cit., p. 24, description (incorrectly dated s. x); 37–41, analysis; 59, stemma.

[20] Incorrectly dated s. xiii in *Vibius Sequester*, ed. R. Gelsomino (Leipzig 1967) xx.

[21] The list is printed by L. Delisle, "Notice sur vingt manuscrits du Vatican," *Bibliothèque de l'École des Chartes* 37 (1876) 487–488. It was also published by A. Reifferscheid, *Bibliotheca patrum latinorum italica* 1 (Vienna 1870) 445–446.

[22] Barlow (n. 4 above), 99–100.

Vat. lat. 4929 belonged to the library of the Cathedral of Orléans or to some member of the chapter. It almost certainly remained at Orléans, to judge from the glosses of the late-eleventh- or early-twelfth-century scholar or scholars who annotated the manuscript. Among the glosses and additions are two concerning the Loire. Finding the *De fluminibus* deficient in its knowledge of his home, he adds: *Liger* [Loire], *Gallie, dividens aquitanos et celtas, in oceanum brittannicum evolvitur.*[23] Noting the appearance of *Liger* in the *Querolus* (16.22), he reminds readers that Tibullus knew of his river, with the gloss: *Ligerem] Ligerem dicit a nominativo Liger, quem ponit Albius Tibullus, carnutis et flavi cerula limpha Liger* (Tibullus 1.7.12).[24]

The writer's corrections, glosses, and his commentary on the *Querolus* show that he was learned, and suggest that he was a master at the schools in Orléans. Like Heiric, who had corrected the manuscript before him, he was concerned about correct divisions between words and the proper use of capital letters. He knew Greek well, according to Barlow. In the scholia to the *Querolus* he gives extensive verbatim quotations from Firmicus Maternus, *Mathesis;* Fulgentius, *Mythologia;* and Justinian's *Institutes.*[25] Both Fulgentius and Firmicus, neither of whom was common ca. 1100, were known at Fleury, not twenty miles from Orléans.[26]

Berne 136 bears no *ex libris.* Soon after it was written it was used by the compiler of the *Florilegium Angelicum.* Paris B.N. lat. 14749, fols. 22–121^v, containing Cicero's orations, was copied from Berne 136 in the fifteenth century.[27] It has recently been discovered that B.N. lat. 14749 was in large part written by the French humanist Nicolas de Clémanges;[28] however, we do not know where Clémanges copied Berne 136, save to suppose that—as did the compiler of the *florilegium*—he found it at some center of learning. In the middle of the sixteenth century, Berne 136 belonged to Pierre Daniel, who wrote the table of contents on fol. 1. Daniel crops up yet again, in connection with one of the

---

[23] Ibid., 123, and pl. 18.

[24] Ibid., 106, 109.

[25] See ibid., 105–107.

[26] Fulgentius appears in the 11th-century booklist of the abbey, and Firmicus is cited in the catalog of 1552; G. Becker, *Catalogi bibliothecarum antiqui* (Bonn 1885) 147, item 62. III; *Catalogue général des manuscrits des bibliothèques publiques de France* 7 (Paris 1889) 52.

[27] Peterson (n. 13 above).

[28] The discovery was made by Gilbert Ouy, whose discussion in detail of Nicolas's hand is still awaited; see Ouy's report in the *Annuaire de l'École des Hautes études* (1965–6) 259.

earliest known excerpts from the *Florilegium Angelicum*. At the top of the second column of the last page (fol. 34^v) of Berne 633 (s. xii^2; France), the hand of the manuscript has copied the first of the *florilegium*'s extracts from Aulus Gellius, leaving the rest of the column blank. The reproduction of the passage as it appears in the *Florilegium Angelicum*, in which the wording of the original has been altered in a distinctive fashion, proves that the latter and not a text of Gellius was the writer's source. This manuscript belonged to Daniel in the sixteenth century.

Pierre Daniel was a lawyer at Orléans and sometime *bailli* of the abbey of Fleury. Although he acquired a number of books from other scholars and libraries, notably Pierre Pithou and St. Victor, the greater part of his library was assembled from ecclesiastical collections in and around Orléans. Therefore, when one is faced, as in this case, with a group of manuscripts that belonged to Daniel and that are known to emanate from a common center, it is reasonable to assume that it was in the Orléanais.[29]

In sum, when one considers jointly the nature and purpose of the *Florilegium Angelicum*; the indications of place afforded by Vat. lat. 4929; and the omnipresence of Pierre Daniel in the later life of manuscripts related to the *florilegium*, one has a strong case for Orléans as the home of the *Florilegium Angelicum*.

Although one has references to Orléans as a center of classical studies, and one knows the names of a few individuals associated with the schools there, actual physical remains are few — works known to have been composed there, texts known to have been available there, manuscripts with an undisputed Orléans provenance. Therefore, to establish Orléans as the probable home of the *Florilegium Angelicum* has implications extending beyond the work itself. It is self-evident that if the *florilegium* was compiled at Orléans, the texts used by its compiler must also have been available there. Let us examine briefly some specific applications of this fact. MS Berne 136 was used above to provide evidence of a possible home for the *Florilegium Angelicum*; one can now, with greater justification, use the cumulative evidence concerning the latter to localize Berne 136 at Orléans. Moreover, since Berne 136 was itself written only shortly before our compiler used it, one is provided as well with a strong suggestion that the two important older codices from which it was copied — the eleventh-century S. Marco 284 (Pliny's letters

---

[29]Regarding Daniel see É. Pellegrin, "Membra disiecta floriacensia," *Bibliothèque de l'École des Chartes* 117 (1959) 1–56, esp. 1–9; and A. Vidier, *L'Historiographie à Saint-Benoît-sur-Loire et les miracles de saint Benoît* (Paris 1965) 30–33.

and Apuleius) and the ninth-century Paris B.N. lat. 7794 (Cicero's orations)—were both in Orléans in the mid-twelfth century.[30]

The *Florilegium Angelicum* contains extracts from many works that were widely available, and there is no point in laboring the fact that a text of each was probably at Orléans. But the localization is important as it applies to two rare texts, Cicero's Verrine orations and the works of Ennodius. The northern or X family of the Verrines[31] emerged in the late eighth century among the books of the palace library of Charlemagne, as described in Berlin Diez B. Sant. 66;[32] and the text dispersed in the course of the ninth century from Tours. The oldest manuscript, British Libr. Add. 47678 (formerly Holkham Hall 387) s. ix[1] (C), containing 2 Act. II-III, was written in the script of Tours and passed to Cluny, where it is described in the twelfth-century catalog of the abbey's books.[33] (A single leaf from this mutilated manuscript is now Geneva, Bibliothèque

---

[30] While B.N. lat. 7794 produced no descendants save Berne 136, S. Marco 284 apparently produced a family of MSS presumably disseminating from Orléans. Among these was a MS of the letters and Apuleius given to Bec by Philip of Bayeux in 1164, which may in turn have been the parent of Rouen 1111 (s. xiii; Lyre OSB), containing the F text, and of a MS now lost but once at Mont-Saint-Michel; and Leyden Universiteitsbibl. B.P.L. 199 (s. xiii; N. France) which also contains the F text, as do a group of hitherto unnoticed extracts in Paris B.N. lat. 18104, pt. III fols. 160ᵛ–161 (s. xiii). The letters and Apuleius are also found together in a codex described in the late-12th-century catalog of St. Martial of Limoges by Bernard Itier. The letters alone appear in the 12th-century catalog of St. Aubin at Angers, but there is no way of telling its parentage. See the appropriate sections of G. Nortier, *Les Bibliothèques médiévales des abbayes bénédictines de Normandie*, 2d ed. (Caen 1971) and M. Manitius, "Handschriften antiker Autoren in mittelalterlichen Bibliothekskatalogen," *Zentralblatt für Bibliothekswesen*, Beiheft 67 (Leipzig 1935) 141. The MS of the letters of St. Martial is incorrectly entered in Manitius (121) under Pliny the elder.

[31] At the head of the Italian or Y family stand Paris B.N. lat 7776, s. xi; Paris B.N. lat. 4588A fols. 66–91, s. xiii; Florence, Laurenziana, pl. 48. 29, s. xv; British Libr. Harley 2687, s. xv; and a bi-folium of the 12th century written in a Caroline hand, in Monte Cassino 361 P, pp. 219–222. Paris B.N. lat. 7776, written in Italy, bears the following notes of ownership: fol. 174ᵛ: *In reversione mea de curia. Ego istud proposui facere et ducere ad effectum et firmavi cum (sten?). In dominica ii de mense septembri. In segnoria. Ingh. de (manga ponti?)* 1226 [The date may be a later addition]. fol. 1 bottom, erased (s. xiv–xv): *per Stephanum presbiterum de ecclesia . . . Jacobi monachi remisi Solinum.* Center partially covered by arms of the Cittadini family of Siena. MS bears notes by Celso Cittadini, 1553–1627—concerning his books, see M. Cl. Di Franco Lilli, *La biblioteca manoscritta di Celso Cittadini* (Studi e Testi, cclix, 1970). Sent to Paris with other MSS for the Royal Library by Mabillon, 8 July 1686; see P. Gasnault, "Manuscrits envoyés d'Italie à la Bibliothèque du roi par Mabillon," *Bibliothèque de l'École des Chartes* 129 (1971) 411–420.

[32] B. Bischoff, "Die Hofbibliothek Karls des Grossen," in *Karl der Grosse 2 Das geistige Leben* (Düsseldorf 1965) 42–62.

[33] Ed. Delisle (n. 2 above), 458–481, item 498.

publique et universitaire MS lat. 169.[34]) From the Cluny catalog one can see that C once contained the same works as the codex described from the palace library. Another spur from Tours appears at Cologne in the form of the extracts from the Verrines in British Libr. Harley 2682 s. xi (H) and the direct copy of these in Berlin lat. fol. 252 s. xii, Corvey (E), made by Wibald of Corvey.[35] A third line is seen in Paris B.N. lat. 7774A (2 Act. IV-V) s. ix^1 (R), also written at Tours. This manuscript may have passed to Lupus of Ferrières, since he is known to have had a manuscript of the Verrines and since he annotated the second manuscript now in MS lat. 7774A (fols. 103–184^v), Cicero's *De inventione*.[36] A second witness to the parent of R survives in Paris B.N. lat. 7775 (2 Act. I paragraphs 90–111, IV, V) s. xii (S), which belonged to Richard de Fournival in the first half of the thirteenth century and passed with his books via Gerard of Abbeville to the Sorbonne library.[37] Both R and S are incomplete today, but fortunately a copy was made of S by Nicolas de Clémanges in the early fifteenth century when it was still whole. The latter volume is Paris B.N. lat. 7823 (D), which was left to St. Victor (pressmark HHH 8) by Simon de Plumetot.[38]

It requires no stretch of the imagination to assume that the Verrines, disseminated from Tours, might find their way to Orléans. However, on the basis of the quite limited amount of text we have to deal with, it is difficult to ascertain whether the *florilegium*'s source was one of the surviving manuscripts, or another no longer extant. The *Florilegium Angelicum* contains eighteen extracts from Actio II, books IV and V of the Verrines. One would naturally assume that they come from a text of the northern European family. The reading at V.71 *inducte* with R and S against *indictae*, of the Italian or Y family, indicates as much; but at IV.105, the extracts read *perstringere* with the Y

---

[34] G. Vaucher, "Un fragment de MS. de Cicéron aux Archives de Genève," *Bulletin du Musée de Genève* (1931) 120–124. The identification with London, B.L. Add. 47678 we owe to Professor Bischoff.

[35] A. C. Clark, "Excerpts from the Verrines in the Harleian MS. 2682 . . . ," *Journal of Philology* 18 (1890) 69–87.

[36] Lupus requests (ca. 856–8) a MS of the Verrines in ep. 101 to Reg.; ed. and trans. G. W. Regenos, *The Letters of Lupus of Ferrières* (The Hague 1966). There is of course no way of telling how long the two parts of Paris B.N. Lat. 7774A have been together.

[37] See R. H. Rouse, "Manuscripts belonging to Richard de Fournival," *Revue d'histoire des textes* 3 (1973) 259.

[38] The hand of Nicolas de Clémanges and the donation of Simon de Plumetot were kindly confirmed by Gilbert Ouy, who has long studied these two individuals; see his *Le catalogue de la bibliothèque de l'abbaye de Saint-Victor de Paris de Claude Grandrue*, 1514, with V. Gerz-von Buren (Paris 1983); and "Les manuscrits autographes du chancelier Gerson," *Scriptorium* 16 (1962) 293–297.

family against R, *praestringere*. S reads *perstringere*, corrected to *prestringere*. The correction cannot be dated, save to say that it appears to be medieval; if it occurred after the *Florilegium Angelicum* was compiled, then S could have been the source of the extracts. Henceforth, in dealing with Paris B.N. lat. 7775, one should at least consider the possibility that it was either written at Orléans or carried there within a relatively short time after it was written.

Of the Christian authors represented in the *florilegium*, Ennodius is surely the rarest. Vogel knew of eighteen manuscripts, only four of which antedate the *Florilegium Angelicum*—and two of these are English.[39] He noticed none of the twelve manuscripts of the *florilegium* which contain extracts from Ennodius.[40] The manuscripts of Ennodius emerge in northern Europe in two classes. The first of these is represented by a single manuscript from Lorsch,[41] now Brussels Bibl. Royale, 9845–8 (Van den Gheyn 1218), s. ix^1 (B); it produced no known descendants. The surviving manuscripts of the second class disseminate from Corbie. Ennodius was known to Radbert of Corbie (d. ca. 850).[42] The oldest manuscript of the second class, Vat. lat. 3803 s. ix^2 (V), is written in a good Corbie hand of the second half of the ninth century, and is probably to be identified with the Ennodius in the twelfth-century catalog of the abbey.[43] A direct copy of this manuscript, Lambeth Palace 325 s. ix^2 (L), also written in Corbie script,[44] was taken to England and came to rest at Durham Cathedral, where it was copied in the twelfth century producing Berlin, Deutsche Staatsbibl. Phill. MS. 1715 (Rose 172), Fountains Abbey, O. Cist. Ennodius continued to circulate through English houses, but our concern is with the continental circulation.

Of the surviving continental manuscripts, even the oldest of V's descendants is too late to have served as source for the *Florilegium Angelicum*; this is the late-twelfth- or early-thirteenth-century text contained in Troyes MSS. 658, 461, 469 (Clairvaux E. 45, I, 22, I, 23). Vogel

---

[39] The transmission of the Ennodius corpus is set forth by F. Vogel, *Magni Felicis Ennodi Opera*, M. G. H. *Auct. ant.*, vol. vii (Berlin 1885) xxix-xlviii.

[40] Brussels B. R. 10098–10105, the Ennodius *florilegium* cited by Vogel, does not come from the *Florilegium Angelicum*, despite the fact that portions of two selections (Jerome and Cicero's orations) form the latter appear in 10098–10105.

[41] B. Bischoff, *Lorsch im Spiegel seiner Handschriften*, Münchener Beiträge zur Mediävistik und Renaissance-Forschung, Beiheft (Munich 1974) 39, 67, 85.

[42] Manitius (n. 16 above) 407, 411.

[43] Ed. Delisle (n. 2 above), 239, item 343 *Ennodius, Exameron Basilii*, and p. 430, item 128 *Ennodii liber*.

[44] We are grateful to Professor Bischoff for identifying the script of V and L.

thought that the Clairvaux text derived from a now-missing apograph of V, and this manuscript is of course a potential source of our extracts. The Pseudo-Isidorian *Decretals*, written ca. 850 perhaps at Reims,[45] afford evidence of yet another potential source. They contain (under specious attributions) four works of Ennodius, taken from a text of the second class older than V, ancestor or sister of the latter.[46] In addition, Philip of Bayeux owned a manuscript of Ennodius which passed with his books to Bec in 1164.[47] The twelfth century witnessed an effort to produce a compendium or abbreviation of Ennodius, since the whole text was long and cumbersome. This abbreviation is found in two manuscripts, Bourges 400, fols. 126^v–133, (s. xii^2; St. Sulpice) and British Libr. Royal 8 E. iv (ca. 1200; Rievaulx?). Vogel presumed the first of these to have been lost and did not know of the second. There is no way to determine whether or not the manuscript from Bourges was written in that area. But it permits the supposition that a manuscript of the second class no longer extant was available in the Loire region in the twelfth century, to be copied for Philip of Bayeux and to be used both in the making of the abbreviation and in the compilation of the *Florilegium Angelicum*.

The localization at Orléans of the *Florilegium Angelicum* and Vat. lat. 4929 has wider implications concerning Orléans as a crossroads in the dissemination of classical texts in central France. The *Florilegium Gallicum* also drew on Vat. lat. 4929,[48] and hence its contents probably also reflect the libraries of mid-twelfth-century Orléans. Of the two oldest surviving manuscripts of the *Florilegium Gallicum*, Paris, Bibl. de l'Arsenal 711 (s. xii; St. Victor) once concluded with extracts from Pomponius Mela,[49] of which Vat. lat. 4929 contains the archetype; and

---

[45] W. Goffart, *The Le Mans Forgeries*, Harvard Historical Studies 77 (Cambridge, Mass. 1966) 66–67: and H. Fuhrmann, *Einfluss und Verbreitung der pseudoisidorischen Fälschungen*, Schriften der M.G.H. 24.1 (Stuttgart 1972) 191–194.

[46] There is no way of comparing the text of Ennodius used for the *Florilegium Angelicum* with that used by Pseudo-Isidore. For the four works which the *Decretals* reproduce, there are no extracts from XLVIII or CLXXIV; and there are no variant readings recorded from the *Decretals* for those passages in the *Florilegium Angelicum* which comprise the two extracts from CCXIV and the sixteen from IL.

[47] Becker (n. 26 above), 201, item 86: 55.

[48] The *Florilegium Gallicum's Querolus* extracts contain readings which derive from glosses in Vat. lat. 4929; see Ranstrand (n. 5 above) 67–69. Concerning the *Florilegium Gallicum* see Gagnér (n. 8 above), and the bibliography in R. H. Rouse, "The A Text of Seneca's Tragedies . . . ," *Revue d'histoire des textes I (1971) 103 n. 1*.

[49] The later folios of the MS are now missing save for fols. 244–7, which R. Rouse recently identified with Hamburg Staats- und Universitätsbibl. MS 53c in scrin. (formerly

Paris, Bibl. Nationale, lat. 7647 was evidently owned by Pierre Daniel.[50] Similarly, portions of the library of Richard de Fournival may have come from Orléans. Fournival, the *Florilegium Gallicum*, and the twelfth-century annotator of Vat. lat. 4929 probably drew on a common source of their knowledge of Tibullus: the annotator quotes Tibullus in glossing the word 'Loire', the *Florilegium Gallicum* contains lengthy extracts from Tibullus, and Fournival owned the manuscript of the whole text from which all surviving copies of Tibullus descend.[51] Fournival also owned a manuscript of the Verrines, possibly that used by the compiler of the *Florilegium Angelicum*,[52] as well as a manuscript of the *florilegium* itself. Finally, four rare texts connected with the *Florilegium Angelicum* or

---

belonging to Friedrich Lindenbrog [1573–1648] who had business offices in Paris). However, the original contents of MS 711 were recorded by Claude de Grandrue; see H. Martin, ed., *Catalogue des manuscrits de la Bibliothèque de l'Arsenal* 2 (Paris 1886) 52. The *De chorographia* of Pomponius Mela moved in the 12th century to three important French libraries. It appears among the books which Philip of Bayeux left to Bec in 1164, *Pomponius Mela de cosmographia et Tullius . . . et Hilarius de sinodis et eiusdem liber contra Valentem et Auxencium*; Becker (n. 26 above) 201, item 86: 64. A brief portion of the *De chorographia* (lib. I cc. 1–7) appears in a 12th-century MS of the works of St. Hilary of Poitiers, following Hilary's *Adversus Arrianum Auxencium*; the MS, bearing the 17th-century *ex libris* of Mont-Saint-Michel, is now Vendôme MS 189, fols. 65–9. The volume is almost certainly a copy of that which belonged to Philip of Bayeux; besides the association with Hilary, a substantial number of Mont-Saint-Michel's books were copied from Bec exemplars (see Nortier [n. 30 above] 45, 69). Another copy is recorded in the late 12th-century catalog of St. Martial of Limoges by Bernard Itier; ed. Delisle (n. 2 above) 497, item 3: 48. Significantly, this is the same dissemination one has for the younger Pliny's letters which, starting from the Orléanais, are owned by Philip of Bayeux, Mont-Saint-Michel, and St. Martial of Limoges; see above, n. 30.

[50] Two leaves from the first part of Paris B.N. lat. 7647 containing the *Distinctiones monasticae* were recently found in Leyden Voss. lat. Qu. 2, fols. 57–8 (Paul Petau), by É. Pellegrin (n. 29 above) 52. It should also be remembered that Gagnér (n. 8 above) 211–212, noted that one of four variant readings recorded by Daniel from a MS at Saints-Gervais-et-Protais compared favorably with MS 7647. Ranstrand (n. 5 above) 75, however, disagreed and concluded that the *Florilegium Gallicum* from Saints-Gervais-et-Protais is now lost.

[51] The extracts in the *Florilegium Gallicum* are discussed in B. L. Ullman, "Tibullus in Medieval *Florilegia*," *Classical Philology* 23 (1928) 128–74. Barlow (n. 4 above) 106, felt that the line from Tibullus in Vat. lat. 4929 came from a *florilegium*, and pointed to its existence in Clm 6929 as evidence. In 1100, however, that *florilegium* was at Freising, and the only other contemporary collection of Tibullus extracts was at Monte Cassino; see F. Newton, "Tibullus in Two Grammatical *Florilegia* of the Middle Ages," *Transactions of the American Philological Association* 93 (1962) 253–286. The fact that the compiler of the *Florilegium Gallicum* drew on a complete MS of Tibullus suggests instead that the Orléans annotator may have known a MS of the whole text.

[52] Paris B.N. lat. 7775; see above.

with Vat. lat. 4929—the Ps.-Ciceronian oration *Pridie quam in exilium iret*, Pliny's letters, Ennodius, and Pomponius Mela—appear in the collection left to Bec by Philip of Bayeux in 1164, suggesting that the libraries of Orléans also supplied him with books.[53]

Having localized the *Florilegium Angelicum*, we may now take up the question of its date and authorship. To judge from the hand and the decoration of P and A, the *florilegium* was compiled in the third quarter of the twelfth century. Neither manuscript contains letter unions, save for pp. Ampersands, the tironian seven uncrossed and *et* written out are used interchangeably. The cedilla is still found frequently, and A preserves an occasional *æ*, but as an archaism, as is the occasional appearance of the *NT* ligature in P. These features tend to date the manuscripts toward the middle rather than toward the end of the century. On the other hand, the appearance of the *œ* ligature in P would not permit the manuscript to date earlier than the middle of the century; here, paleographic evidence is confirmed by the compiler's reliance upon Berne 136, written at or after mid-century. The decoration of the two manuscripts, in particular of A which, as the presentation copy, is the more elaborate, also merits attention (see Plates 6–7). The section initials contain a stylized stem-and-leaf design, geometric and two-dimensional. Red, purple, yellow, green, and blue are used. The backs of upright letters are outlined with thick line or tendril, scalloped at times but never extending beyond the end of the letter as tendrils will begin to do toward the end of the century. A good example of decoration of this style is seen in Brussels, Bibl. Royale, MS. II 1635, dated 1156.[54]

The prologue in A dedicates the *Florilegium Angelicum* to a pope, who, 'enmeshed in the business of the world, with a ready response judges the intricacies of causes [*involucra causarum determines*] in such fashion that all marvel' at his eloquence. The approximate dates of P and A exclude Innocent III (1198–1215) as too late. The hands of the two are not sufficiently early for Eugene III (1145–53), nor would the inflated language of the prologue very likely have been addressed to the protégé of Saint Bernard. This leaves Adrian IV (1154–9), Alexander III (1159–81), and the five popes whose brief tenures bring one to the end of the century. Of them, the canon lawyer Alexander III best fits the

---

[53] Concerning Philip of Bayeux, see V. Bourrienne, *Un Grand Bâtisseur: Philippe de Harcourt, évêque de Bayeux* (Paris 1930); S. E. Gleason, *An Ecclesiastical Barony of the Middle Ages. The Bishopric of Bayeux 1066–1204*, Harvard Historical Monographs 10 (Cambridge, Mass. 1936) 28–29; and Nortier (n. 30 above) 42–45.

[54] See M. Wittek, ed., *Manuscrits datés conservés en Belgique*, i. 819–1400 (Brussels 1968) 20, item 7, pls. 27–9.

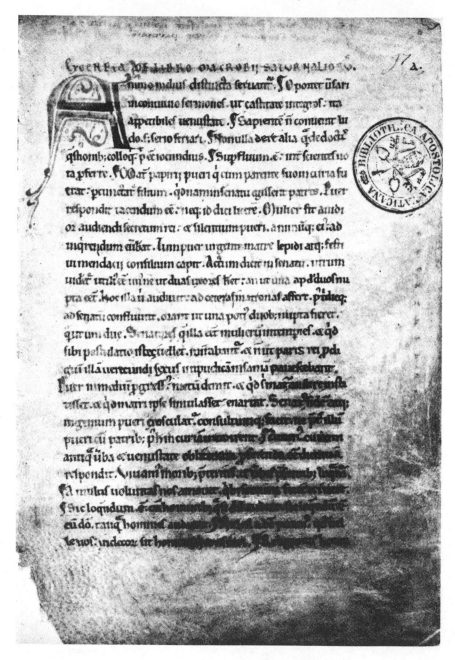

Plate 6. Vatican City, Biblioteca Apostolica Vaticana, Pal. lat. 957, fol. 97.

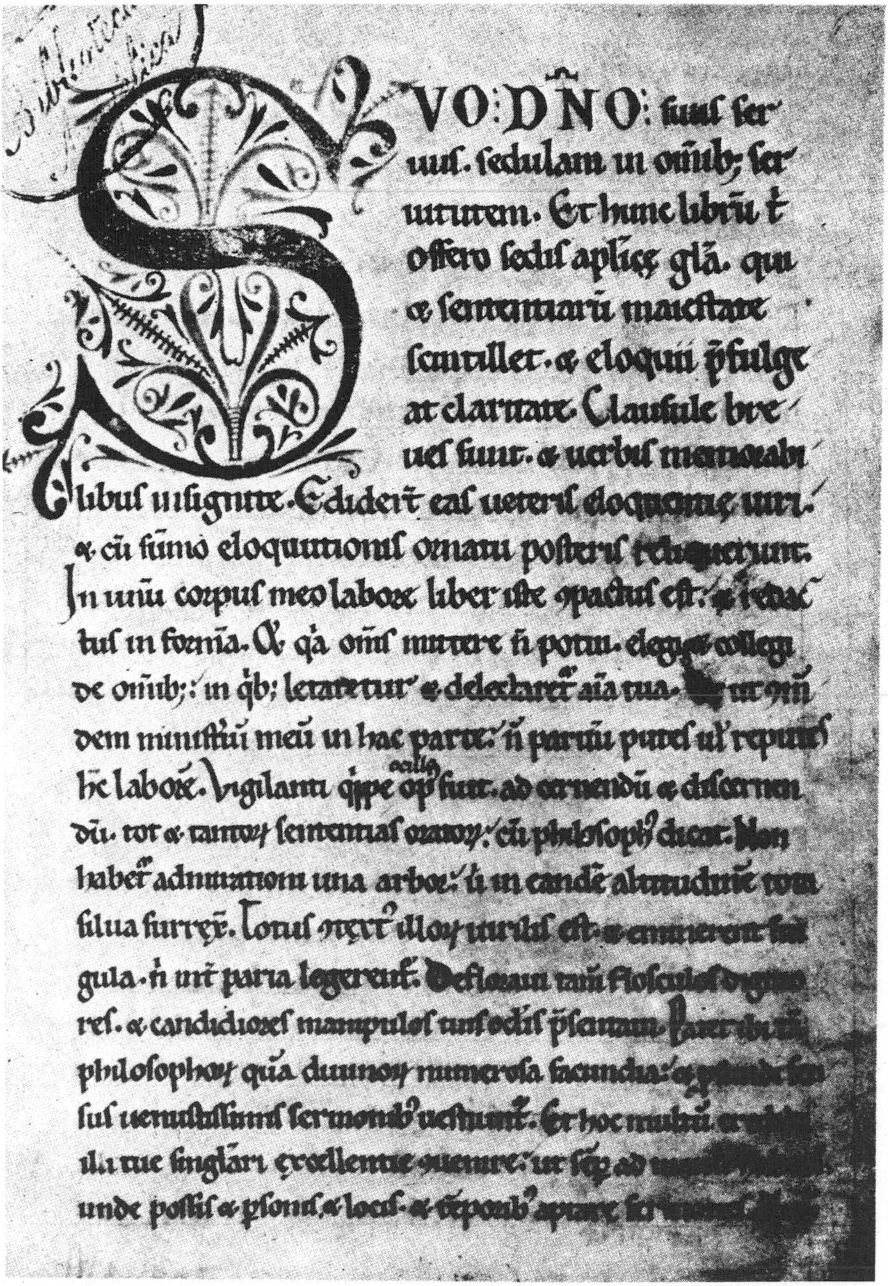

Plate 7. Rome, Biblioteca Angelica, MS. 1895, fol. 1. (Natural size)

dedicatee of the prologue and the dates of P and A. Moreover, Alexander III (as well as his successor) employed masters from Orléans in the papal chancery.[55]

Nothing can be said about the author of the *Florilegium Angelicum*, save that he was someone at Orléans in the third quarter of the twelfth century who was interested in epistolary style, knowledgeable in the classics and, no doubt, desirous of papal preferment. One can, however, lay to rest a troublesome ghost, emanating from the attribution of the *florilegium* to Censorinus in the *Biblionomia* of Richard de Fournival. Manitius, Beeson, and Ullman, in their efforts to identify the Censorinus mentioned by Hadoard in the poem prefaced to his *florilegium*, seized upon the *florilegium* attributed to Censorinus in the *Biblionomia* and noticed other similarities, real or presumed, between the two *florilegia*, namely, that each quoted from Sidonius' letters and from the *Sententiae philosophorum*; they also found it significant that Fournival's manuscripts of Cicero's philosophical works (*Biblionomia* 73–6) were arranged in the rare order of the Leyden corpus, as were the extracts in Hadoard's *florilegium*. They concluded that Fournival's *florilegium*—i.e., the *Florilegium Angelicum*—must therefore have already been in existence in the ninth century.[56] Because of Fournival's attribution, Censorinus not only became the author of the *florilegium* but was also made the author of an anonymous collection of aphorisms called *Sententiae philosophorum*, since it appears in both Hadoard's and Fournival's *florilegia* associated with the name Censorinus.

In actuality there is no connection between the two *florilegia*. They do not contain extracts from the same collection of *sententiae philosophorum*. Hadoard's are drawn from Publilius Syrus,[57] and those in Fournival's *florilegium* are the anonymous collection erroneously attributed to Caecilius Balbus.[58] The attribution to Censorinus in the *Biblionomia* is the result of an easily understandable muddle. In the *Florile-*

---

[55] John, Robert, and William, see letters 65 and 85 of Stephen of Tournai, *P.L.* ccxi. 356–7, 380–1. It is interesting to note that in 1177 John of Cornwall also praises Alexander III for his ability to see through intricate language, 'que contra obici possunt dissoluuntur et Iohannis Damasceni involucrum enodatur'; *Eulogium ad Alexandrum papam III,* ed. N. M. Haring, *Mediaeval Studies* 13 (1951) 276. Concerning the meaning and use of the esoteric term *involucrum* see M.D. Chenu, "*Involucrum*: le mythe selon les théologiens médiévaux," *Archives,* 22 (1955) 75–79.

[56] Manitius (n. 16 above) 480; C. H. Beeson, "The Collectaneum of Hadoard," *Classical Philology* 11 (1945) 205–206; B. L. Ullman, "A List of Classical Manuscripts perhaps from Corbie," *Scriptorium* 8 (1954) 24–37.

[57] W. Meyer, ed., *Pubilii Syri Mimi Sententiae* (Leipzig 1880).

[58] E. Woelfflin, ed., *Caecilii Balbi De nugis philosophorum quae supersunt* (Basle 1855) 37–43.

gium Angelicum, the extracts from the *Querolus* are followed by extracts from Censorinus' *De die natali*. The change is marked by the rubric, *Explicit. Censorinus.*, meaning *Explicit Querolus. Incipit Censorinus.* The description in the *Biblionomia* shows that Fournival's manuscript ended with the *Querolus*, doubtless concluding with the ambiguously worded rubric. On that basis, Fournival simply took the little-known author of the *De die natali* and made him author of the twelfth-century *Florilegium Angelicum*. In our ignorance of the actual compiler's identity, we must take what comfort we can from the elimination of one well-known but ill-suited candidate.

The compiler, while preserving his anonymity, at least displays his literary style for us in the prologue or dedicatory epistle contained in A.[59] At the same time, he reveals his concept of the purpose and value of the *florilegium*. The prologue falls into three parts: (1) a commendation of the book, calling attention to its merit and to the labor involved in its creation; (2) a flattering statement of the book's appropriateness to its papal dedicatee; and (3) a request for (continued?) papal favor and protection. The writer briefly indulges in an initial flourish of rhymed pairs of parallel verbs ('compactus et redactus . . .', 'elegi et collegi . . .', etc.), then abandons the device. Under the circumstances, his classical quotations are quite restrained in number, though aptly chosen—a snippet from Quintilian, a longer segment from one letter of Seneca. The vast majority of his quotations are scriptural; these include allusions, which may or may not be conscious (such as the echo of Matthew 4:4, 'in verbis gratie que procedent de ore tuo'). Although one should allow for the role played by convention, it is also probable that intentional flattery is implied by his application to the pope of language which, in its biblical context, referred to God (such passages as 'quid a te volui . . .', 'O custos hominum . . .', 'Sub umbra alarum tuarum . . .', and so on).

The *Florilegium Angelicum* is a book of maxims or aphorisms, sententious statements of universal truths eloquently expressed. However, it is quite evident, from the emphasis of the prologue, that the compiler gave greater consideration to beauty of expression than to ethical content. The book contains 'brief passages remarkable for their memorable words, . . . profound meaning clad in the most attractive language'. He tells his recipient that, unable to include everything, he has rather 'chosen and collected together those passages in which your spirit might delight and take pleasure'. There is no hint of a pious hope that the contents might lead to salvation or even to edification. As the compiler

---

[59] Edited by B. Munk Olsen, "Note sur quelques préfaces de florilèges latins du xiie siècle," *Revue romane* 8 (1973) 185–91; and below, Appendix I.

makes clear in the prologue, the *florilegium* is a reference book for discourse, for the writers of business letters. He has written the work, he tells the pope, 'so that you may have always at hand [a source] from which to fit your speech appropriately to person and place and occasion'. The *florilegium* permits one to give advice, support arguments, state conclusions, in the eloquent language of famous men of letters.

The compiler's manner of working is easy to discern. He normally selects brief passages, often mere parts of sentences in his exemplar. He alters them as much as is necessary to make a coherent free-standing statement out of context. In order to do this, (1) he changes verb-forms and cases of nouns so as to have the proper grammatical components to form a sentence; (2) as frequently as possible he eliminates references to specific persons, substituting a noun of general or universal application; (3) he naturally omits words and phrases that refer by implication to preceding or subsequent passages which are not included in his extract; (4) when the meaning of a passage is obscure without its context, he supplies his own word or phrase which epitomizes the author's meaning. Two examples from Pliny's letters will illustrate the changes:

> *Pliny, Ep.* 1.6.2 Iam undique siluae et solitudo ipsumque illud silentium
>   quod uenationi datur, magna cogitationis incitamenta sunt.
> *Florilegium Angelicum.* Silentium maximum cogitationis incitamentum est.
> *Pliny, Ep.* 3.16.6 (Describing the admirable behaviour of Arria, a Roman
>   matron): Sed tamen ista facienti, ista dicenti, gloria et aeternitas
>   ante oculos erant.
> *Florilegium Angelicum.* Quicquid facias, gloria sit tibi ante oculos et eternitas.

Amusingly enough, as the latter example shows, the compiler was not averse to an occasional slight improvement of the word order found in his models of eloquence. The total effect of his method is that scarecely a passage escapes without some mark of its having gone through his hands.

Normally, it is not easy to trace the use made of a *florilegium*, because of the difficulty of determining with certainty the immediate source of classical quotations which float freely about, entirely detached from their matrix. We can show, however, in this case that the *Florilegium Angelicum* was extensively used by Gerald of Wales in the later years of his life.[60] He used it in a number of works written after

---

[60] Gerald's quotations from ancient Latin prose texts are identified and extracted in Edward E. Best Jr., "Classical Latin Prose Writers quoted by Giraldus Cambrensis," unpubl. Ph.D. diss. (University of North Carolina 1957). For his citations from verse see G. J. E.

1198, the most important of which are the *De principis instructione* and the collection of letters included in the *Symbolum electorum*.[61] The latter work provides a good example of how such a *florilegium* might be used. Take for example epistle 24, addressed to Walter Map. Gerald's theme is that the mature man turns his intellectual efforts to study of the divine, and abandons the frivolous classical literary studies of his youth. In support of this he cites not only the story of Saint Jerome's fear of being judged 'Ciceronianus, non Christianus', but also a passage from Cicero himself. The irony is more apparent than real, for Gerald's view is the traditional Christian attitude toward the pagan past: studying the pagans for one's own enjoyment is a misuse of time and effort, but it is legitimate and even laudable to 'spoil the Egyptians', taking truth where one finds it from the 'dicta poetarum moralia et philosophorum'. He adduces a lengthy string of patristic and scriptural quotations intertwined to prove that one should devote oneself to serious study and abhor the frivolous, and adds, 'Hear the concurring testimony of the Gentiles.' Thereupon he produces eight successive passages from the ancients, six of which are taken from the *Florilegium Angelicum*, namely four extracts from Pliny's letters and one each from Cicero's Tusculans and Sidonius' letters. Proof that these quotations are drawn from the *florilegium* rather than from the respective whole texts is provided by the wording of the quotations, which in each case agrees with the revised form imposed by the florilegist.

For example, Gerald's epistle 24 and the *Florilegium Angelicum* read, 'Dulce honestumque ocium ac pene omni negotio pulchrius est studere', for Pliny 1.9.6, 'O dulce otium honestumque ac paene omni negotio pulchrius!' Epistle 24 includes consecutively two sentences which are treated as one extract in the *florilegium* (i.e., the second has no paragraph mark of its own): 'Nulla tibi temporis asperitas studii tempus eripiat. Nam perit omne tempus quod studiis non impertitur.' These come from two paragraphs in Pliny, 3.5.15, 16, with some twenty words intervening: '. . . ut ne caeli quidem asperitas ullum studii tempus eriperet . . . Nam perire omne tempus arbitrabatur, quod studiis non impenderetur.' And in his *De principis instructione* 1.15 Gerald repeats, with only one variant, the *florilegium*'s extract from Pliny 3.16.6 noted

Sullivan, "Pagan Latin Poets in Giraldus Cambrensis," unpubl. Ph.D. diss. (University of Cincinnati 1950).

    [61] Gerald's works are published in the Rolls Series: *Symbolus electorum*, ed. J. S. Brewer 1 (1861) 199–395; *De principis instructione*, ed. G. F. Warner, 8 (1891). Concerning the latter work see K. Schnith, "Betrachtungen zum Spätwerk des Giraldus Cambrensis: De principis instructione," *Festiva Lanx, Festgabe Johannes Spörl* (Munich 1966) 53–66.

above, beginning 'Quicquid agas [facias: *Florilegium Angelicum*] gloria
sit. . .'. In all, the *Florilegium Angelicum* accounts for the whole of
Gerald's knowledge of Pliny's letters and of Cicero's orations and the
Tusculans, and for at least a portion of his quotations from Seneca's letters, the *De beneficiis*, Macrobius, Aulus Gellius bks. 10–20, and the
letters of Sidonius.[62]

Gerald probably used a manuscript of the β family of the *Florilegium Angelicum*. This is suggested by the fact that he quotes four passages from the letters of Symmachus. He is again using a collection of
extracts,[63] one that was popular in France in the twelfth century, rather
than the letters themselves; he shares the reading 'supervacanei' (*Vita
Remigii* 27) with the Symmachus *florilegium*, against 'superforanei' in
the text of the letters (ep. 3.48). The Symmachus *florilegium* precedes
the *Florilegium Angelicum*, written in the hand of the latter, in R. The
Symmachus collection also appears in E, but in a different hand and in a
separate manuscript bound with the text of the *Florilegium Angelicum*.
Unlike E, R is perhaps old enough to have been the manuscript which
Gerald used. However, the presence of Symmachus in E, even as an
addition, raises the possibility that the Symmachus *florilegium* appeared
in β, common parent of R and E. The most one can say is that Gerald of
Wales probably used the *Florilegium Angelicum* in R, in β, or in some
late-twelfth-century copy of the latter now lost. Gerald used the
Florilegium Angelicum only in works written after 1198, indicating that
he did not know of it in England or in his earlier school-days in Paris.

---

[62] Gerald was an avid user of intermediate sources, among them Petrus Cantor's
Verbum abbreviatum and perhaps the *Moralium dogma philosophorum*; see E. M. Sanford,
"Giraldus Cambrensis' Debt to Petrus Cantor," *Medievalia et Humanistica* 3 (1945) 16–32;
and W. Berges, *Die Fürstenspiegel des hohen und späten Mittelalters*, Schriften des
Reichsinstituts für ältere deutsche Geschichtskunde 2 (Leipzig 1938) 145. To these one
should also add the *Florilegium Gallicum*. It is, for example, the source for most of
Gerald's knowledge of Seneca's *De clementia*, cited seven times in the *De principis
instructione* and elsewhere. In two instances Gerald and the *Florilegium Gallicum* (cited
from Paris B.N. lat. 17903, fol. 128ᵛ) agree in readings against the established text: *De
clem.* 1.1.7, *conplectuntur: amplectuntur* Flor. Gal., Prin. inst. 1.7, Symbolum ep. 31,
Spec. eccles. intro.; and *De clem.* 1.9.11, *advocatum: advotum* Flor. Gal., Prin. inst. 1.7,
Top. Hib. 3.48. Nothdurft, unaware of his use of a *florilegium*, remarks that Gerald was
the only person besides Hildebert at the beginning of the century to draw on the *De
clementia* in any substantial fashion; see K. D. Nothdurft, *Studien zum Einfluss Senecas
auf die Philosophie und Theologie des zwölften Jahrhunderts* (Leyden 1963) 119–20.

[63] Best (n. 60 above) 131–132, 141. Thirty-eight collections of extracts from the letters of
Symmachus are listed by J. P. Callu, *Symmaque: Lettres, Livres I-II*, Collection Budé
(Paris 1972).

He probably found the *florilegium* in the course of his trips to Rome, ca. 1197–1214, to argue his claim to St. Davids.[64]

As a witness to changing interests in classical authors, it is instructive to observe how long into the thirteenth century the *Florilegium Angelicum* continued to be copied, and what happened to it toward the middle of the century. At most, four of the seventeen surviving manuscripts date from the twelfth century. The thirteenth century saw ten copies of this collection or parts of it written in France. The last copy was made in the mid-fifteenth century, when the winds blew from the south. A similar pattern is seen in the *Florilegium Gallicum* of which two manuscripts were written in the twelfth century and eight in the thirteenth, fourteenth, and fifteenth centuries. These texts well indicate by their survival that the interest of twelfth-century humanists in classical authors did not pass away with Peter of Blois, Gerald of Wales, and Walter Map.[65] The *florilegia* of the twelfth century did not disappear; instead, they were appropriated, absorbed, and eventually recast as preachers' tools.

We can see both the *Florilegium Angelicum* and the *Florilegium Gallicum* changing form before our eyes. In Brussels, Bibl. Royale, 10030–2 (Van den Gheyn 1508), the greater part of the *Florilegium Gallicum* has been absorbed into the *Flores paradysi* B, a Cistercian *florilegium* compiled at the abbey of Villers-en-Brabant in the second quarter of the thirteenth century. The *florilegium* is equipped with an extensive subject index of twenty-three folios and was intended, according to its compiler, to aid in the composition of sermons.[66] On two different occasions in the mid-thirteenth century the *Florilegium Angelicum* was totally rearranged by broad topic. The first rearrangement survives in Rome, Bibl. Angelica 720 (a), a small handbook of the thirteenth century. In it the extracts have been arranged under subject headings, often virtues and

---

[64] Concerning Gerald see D. Knowles, *The Monastic Order in England* (Cambridge 1950) 662–677; R. B. C. Huygens, "Une lettre de Giraud le Cambrien à propos de ses ouvrages historiques," *Latomus* 24 (1965) 90–100.

[65] Concerning this question see Paetow (n. 18 above); E. K. Rand, "The Classics in the Thirteenth Century," *Speculum* 4 (1929) 249–269; H. Wieruszowski, "Arezzo as a Center of Learning and Letters in the Thirteenth Century," *Traditio* 9 (1953) 321–391, and in particular her "Rhetoric and the Classics in Italian Education of the Thirteenth Century," *Studia Gratiana* 11 (1967) 169–208; these two articles are conveniently found in Wieruszowski's collected studies *Politics and Culture in Medieval Spand and Italy*, Storia e letteratura, Studi e Testi 121 (Rome 1971) 387–474, 589–627.

[66] Concerning the *Flores paradysi*, see R. H. and M. A. Rouse, *Preachers, Florilegia, and Sermons: Studies on the Manipulus florum of Thomas of Ireland*, Pontifical Institute of Mediaeval Studies, Studies and Texts 47 (Toronto 1979) 126–139.

vices: *De commendatione ieiunii, De iusticia, De humilitate quod non debet esse nimia*, and so on. A far more elaborate example of such restructuring is seen in Paris B.N. lat. 1860, fols. 75–153ᵛ (p), of the mid-thirteenth century. In p, the text of the *Florilegium Angelicum* has been supplemented with additional material from Terence, Sallust, Cicero (*De officiis, De senectute, De paradoxis, De amicitia*), and Boethius. The extracts from Christian authors Gregory, Jerome, and Ennodius have been dropped. The *florilegium* is arranged under 299 chapter-headings. At the head of the text stands a subject index of ca. 330 entries in triple columns, referring to the 299 chapters. Attention is called to the *exempla* occurring in the text itself by marginal rubrics. This is only the prose portion of the new *florilegium*; it is followed on fols. 153ᵛ–216 by a parallel collection of verse extracts from the poets, namely the authors of the *Liber Catonis* (Cato, Avian, Theophilus, Claudian, Statius, Maximianus, Pamphilianus), Horace, Virgil, Persius, Juvenal, and Prudentius. The extracts are again arranged by subject, under 231 chapter-headings, but without a subject index. Finally, in the opening years of the fourteenth-century portions of the *Florilegium Angelicum*, taken from Fournival's copy, were absorbed into the *Manipulus florum* written by Thomas of Ireland at the Sorbonne. This *florilegium* is topically organized and alphabetically arranged. In the *Manipulus*, which survives in some 200 copies, classical aphorisms from the *Florilegium Angelicum* were given renewed currency among preachers and writers of the fourteenth and succeeding centuries.

The *Florilegium Angelicum* is a window through which we can observe a stage in the transmission of several classical texts. It documents the influence of ninth-century Carolingian libraries on a twelfth-century cathedral school. It illustrates how certain twelfth-century humanists' *florilegia* were transformed into thirteenth-century preachers' tools. It accounts in part for at least one medieval author's glittering knowledge of classical texts. And it reminds us once again of the significant role played by *florilegia* in the medieval dissemination of ancient thought and letters.

APPENDIX I

Dedicatory epistle affixed to the *Florilegium Angelicum* (Rome, Bibl. Angelica MS 1895, fol. 1ʳᵛ)

Suo domino suus servus sedulam in omnibus servitutem. Et hunc librum tibi offero, sedis apostolice gloria, qui et sentenciarum maiestate scintillet et eloquii prefulgeat claritate. Clausule breves sunt et verbis memorabilibus insignite. Ediderunt eas veteris eloquencie viri et cum summo eloquutionis ornatu posteris reliquerunt. In unum corpus meo labore liber iste compactus est et redactus in formam. Et quia omnes mittere non potui, elegi et collegi de omnibus in quibus letaretur et delectaretur anima tua. Et ut commendem ministerium meum in hac parte, non parvum putes vel reputes hunc laborem. Vigilanti quippe oculo[67] opus fuit ad cernendum et discernendum tot et tantorum sentencias oratorum. Cum philosophus dicat, Non habetur admirationi una arbor ubi in eandem altitudinem tota silva surrexit. Totus contextus illorum virilis est et eminerent singula nisi inter paria legerentur.[68] Defloravi tamen flosculos digniores et candidiores manipulos tuis oculis presentavi. Patet ibi tam philosophorum quam divinorum numerosa facundia et profundi sensus venustissimis sermonibus vestiuntur. Et hoc multum credidi illi tue singulari excellencie convenire ut semper ad manum habeas unde possis et personis et locis et temporibus aptare[69] sermones. Nichil [fol. 1ᵛ] quippe tam cognatum sapiencie, nichil eloquencie tam innatum, quam singula verba suis librare ponderibus et quid cuique conveniat invenire. Accedit ad hec quod iuxta prophetam dedit tibi dominus linguam eruditam[70] ut noveris quando debeas proferre sermonem, eruditam plane et lucidissimo sermonum flore vernantem que speciali dulcedine mulceat auditores. In miraculum vertitur et stuporem quod tocius mundi negociis intricatus repentinis responsionibus involucra causarum determines ut mirentur omnes in verbis gracie que procedunt de ore tuo.[71] Ego, ut verum fatear, sepius admiratus sum et plerumque nichil aliud timebam nisi ne desineres cum cepisses. Sed parco verbis ne adulationis notam incurram. Testes michi sunt qui audierunt verba oris tui, si tamen intelligere potuerunt. Et nunc, domine pater, quid a te volui super terram[72] nisi dignantissimam graciam tuam que me prevenit in benedictionibus

---

[67] *oculo*: superscript, in original hand.
[68] Seneca, *ep.* 33.1, 4.
[69] Quintilian, *Institutiones* 6.5.11.
[70] Is. 50: 4.
[71] Cf. Matth. 4: 4.
[72] Ps. 72: 25.

dulcedinis.[73] O custos hominum,[74] illa michi custos sit et custodem alium non requiro. Ecce non dormit neque dormitat[75] invidia, virtutum virus, caritatis exclusio, tinea sanctitatis. Sub umbra alarum tuarum protege me[76] ne quando dicat inimicus meus, Prevalui adversus eum.[77] Scio, dulcissime pater, quia in me perficies quod cepisti et quem recepisti ad graciam in graciam conservabis, ut tibi semper illum versiculum et memoriter teneam et ore decantem,[78] Quoniam ex omni tribulatione eripuisti me et super inimicos meos d[espexit] o[culus] meus.[79] Filius virginis qui te fecit sacerdotem magnum et excelsum in verbo glorie incolumem te conservet ecclesie sue, sibi ad honorem, tibi ad virtutem, orbi ad salutem in longitudinem dierum.

---

[73] Ps. 20: 4.
[74] Job 7: 20.
[75] Cf. Ps. 120: 4.
[76] Ps. 16: 8.
[77] Ps. 12: 5.
[78] Cf. Deut. 31: 19.
[79] Ps. 53: 9.

APPENDIX II
Contents of the *Florilegium Angelicum*

Dedicatory epistle
In Rome, Bibl. Angelica MS 1895, fol. 1^{rv}, only.
Beg. *Suo domino suus servus sedulam in omnibus servitutem. Et hunc librum tibi offero sedis* . . . , ends . . . *tibi ad virtutem orbi ad salutem in longitudinem dierum.*

Macrobius, *Saturnalia*
Extracts from books I–II only.
Beg. *Animo melius distincta servantur* (Praef. 6). ¶*Oportet versari* . . . , ends . . . *ibi saltem timeat.* ¶*Vivebat enim in eo excedens iocus et seria mordacitas* (II. 3.13).

Versus *Ciceronis* (among the extracts from Macrobius)
Anthologia Latina 268 (Riese).
> *Crede ratem ventis animum ne crede puellis*
> *Namque est feminea tutior unda fide*
> *Femina nulla bona vel si bona contigit ulla*
> *Nescio quo fato res mala facta bona est.*

Proverbia philosophorum
Corresponds to the text edited by Woelfflin under the name of Caecilius Balbus (Basle 1855), 18–35, items I. 1–XLVIII. 3.
Beg. *Cum quidam stolidus audiente Pitagora* . . . ¶*Socrates: Que facere turpe* . . ., ends . . . *cotidie se punit consciencia.* ¶*Verbosa lingua indicium est malicie.*

Jerome, epistles
Beg. *Studio legendi quasi cotidiano cibo alitur et pinguescit oratio* (ep. 35.1). ¶*Libenter accipitur ab* . . ., ends . . . *libidinosa coinquinacione violarint.* ¶*Cuius corpus integrum est sit et inviolabilis conversacio.* Continues without rubric:
¶[*Adversus Jovinianum*] Beg. *Difficile est ab experte quondam voluptatis illecebras abstinere* (I. 3). ¶*Quando minora maioribus* . . ., ends . . . *libidinem quam excercent.* ¶*Virtus excelsum te faciat, non voluptas humilem* (II. 38).

Gregory the Great, epistles
Extracts from the first nine books only.
Beg. *Ubi presentes esse non possumus nostra per eum cui precipimus* . . . (I. 1), ends . . . *Opinionem male agentium ex indiscrete defensionis ausu in nos nullo modo transferamus* (IX. 79).

Apuleius

Taken from Berne, Burgerbibl. MS 136, fols. 7–23.

    De deo Socratis. Beg. *Quorumdam imperitorum hominum turba vana* . . . (III). ¶*Plerique se incuria discipline* . . . , ends . . . *indoctus et incultus existit.* ¶*In emendis equis* . . . *parentes pepererunt et fortuna largita est* (XXIII). Continues without rubric:

    [*Asclepius*]. Beg. *Tractatum numinis maiestate plenissimum* . . . (I). ¶*A divine cognacionis partibus* . . . , ends . . . *et agitacione vegetatur.* ¶*Summe incensiones dei sunt cum gracie referuntur a mortalibus* (XLI). Continues without rubric:

    [*De Platone*]. Beg. *Egritudo mentis est stulticia cuius partes* . . . (I. xviii). ¶*Insania ex pessima consuetudine* . . . , ends . . . *turbidi violentique sunt.* ¶*Confunditur dignitas cum regendi potestatem non mores boni sed opulencia consecuta est* (II. xxviii). Continues without rubric:

    [*De mundo*]. Beg. *Phylosophya est virtutis indagatrix expultrix* . . . (I). ¶*Nebula constat aut* . . . , ends . . . *posteriora videtur ostendere.* ¶*Deum ultrix necessitas* . . . *se totum dedit atque permisit* (XXXVIII).

Pliny the Younger, epistles

Taken from Berne, Burgerbibl. MS 136, fols. 42–73, of the ten-book family.

Beg. *Numquam te obsequii peniteat* (I. 1.2). ¶*Humiles et sordidas* . . . , ends . . . *causas cotidie finiunt.* ¶*Acerba semper et immatura mors eorum qui immortale aliquid parant* (5.5.4).

Cicero, orations

Taken from Berne, Burgerbibl. MS 136, fols. 74–154ᵛ.

Extracts from the following orations:

    Ps.-Cicero, *Pridie quam in exilium iret.* Beg. *Liberale officium est serere beneficium* (I. 2). ¶*Ut metere possis* . . . , ends . . . *fortune poscit libido.* ¶*Nemo generis antiquitate sed virtutis ornamentis summam laudem consequitur.*

    Cum senatui gracias egit. Beg. *Numquam in nobis beneficiorum memoria moriatur* (3). ¶*Quis ullam ulli* . . . , ends . . . *improbos bonos excites.* ¶*Cui amicissimus* . . . *necessarios tuos amicos reddere elabora* (29).

    Cum populo gracias egit. Beg. *Nichil est in presenti magis* . . . (2). ¶*Nichil dulcius hominum* . . . , ends . . . *et qui habet solvit.* ¶*Memoriam beneficii* . . . *eius monimenta in te permaneant ad graciam referendam* (24).

    De domo sua. Beg. *Exercitacionem mali et petulancia* . . . (3). ¶*In imperita multitudine* . . . , ends . . . *ante quam ipse didicerit.* ¶*Virtutis ingenii fortune* . . . *et carendo impaciencia* (146).

Pro P. Sestio. Beg. *Plus miramur hoc tempore siquem* . . . (1). ¶*Pio dolori et iuste* . . ., ends . . . *acciderit feramus.* ¶*Cogitemus corpus esse mortale animi vero motus et virtutis gloriam sempiternam* (143).

In P. Vatinium testem. Beg. *Melius est plerumque scelus et* . . . (6). ¶*Quid quisque nostrum* . . ., ends . . . *non suo defendat.* ¶*Quos crimine coniungis testimonio disiungere non potes* (41).

In senatum de provinciis consularibus. Beg. *In sentencia dicenda non pareas dolori* . . . (2). ¶*Indignissimum est ut scelus* . . ., ends . . . *perditis non exquirant.* ¶*Cum sedate fuerint* . . . *numquam beneficio sit extincta* (47).

De haruspicum responsis. Beg. *Nichil facias iratus nichil impotenti* . . . (3). ¶*Iniquum valde est* . . ., ends . . . *concordia retinere possumus.* ¶*Faciles sunt apud eos* . . . *unam salutis ostendunt* (63).

Pro Cornelio Balbo. Beg. *Patronorum auctoritates multum in iudiciis valent* (1). ¶*Cum maximis rei publice negociis* . . ., ends . . . *particeps et commodorum.* ¶*Perversum est cum non de viciorum pena sed de virtutis premio in iudicium quis vocatur* (65).

Pro Caelio. Beg. *Multis etiam in communi ocio esse* . . . (1). ¶*Aliud est maledicere aliud accusare* . . . ends, . . . *industrie sint future.* ¶*Conservande* [sic] *sunt cives bonarum artium, bonarum partium, bonorum hominum* (77).

Sidonius, epistles

Extracts from books 1–9

Beg. *Audias plurima pauca respondeas* (1.2.4). ¶*In convivio aut nulla* . . ., ends . . . *est durius agitur.* ¶*Res in scribendo discrepantissime sunt maturitas et celeritas* (9.16.3).

Seneca, *De beneficiis*

Extracts from books 1–2 only.

Beg. *Beneficia male collata male debentur de quibus non redditis sero querimur* (1.1.1). ¶*Inter plurima maximaque* . . ., ends . . . *relicta eloquencia.* ¶*Ac inter alia hoc quoque* . . . *sed non patitur aviditas quemquam esse gratum* (2.27.3).

Seneca, *Epistulae ad Lucilium*

Extracts from letters 1–52 only.

The coincidence in the number of letters suggests that the compiler drew on a manuscript of the Beta family.

Beg. *Turpissima est iactura que per negligenciam fit* (ep. 1.1). ¶*Omnes horas complectere* . . . ¶*Non puto pauperem* . . . , ends . . . *quemadmodum laudet aspexeris.* ¶*Dampnum facere philosophiam non dubium erit postquam prostituta est* (ep. 52.15).

Sententiae philosophorum

Corresponds to the text edited by Woelfflin under the name of Caecilius Balbus (Basle 1855) 37–43, items 1–83.

Beg. *Nulle sunt occultiores insidie quam hee . . .*, ends . . . *Hactenus preteriti temporis infamia migrat.*

Praecepta Pithagorae

Items 144–5 of Ps.-Seneca *Liber de moribus*; ed. Haase, Seneca *Opera*, suppl. (Leipzig 1869).

Beg. *Fugienda sunt omnibus modis et abscidenda igni ac ferro . . .*, ends . . . *veritas colenda est que sola homines proximos deo facit.*

Ænigmata Aristotilis

Ed. B. Hauréau, *Notices et Extraits des manuscrits de la Bibliothèque nationale* 33.1 (Paris 1890), 227–228. In manuscripts of the *Florilegium Angelicum* the sentence beg. *Nemo alieno peccato punitur . . .* is frequently given the rubric 'Galienus'.

Beg. *Stateram ne transilias id est ne pretergrediaris iusticiam. ¶Ignem gladio . . .*, ends . . . *excesserit vicium est. ¶Nichil facias quod fecisse peniteat.*

Cicero, Tusculan disputations

Extracts from books I-V.

Beg. *Honos alit artes omnesque inceduntur ad studia gloria* (1. 2.4) *¶Iacent ea semper que . . .*, ends . . . *Epitaphium Sardanapalli regis Sirie: Hec habeo que edi queque exsaturata libido hausit at illa iacent multa et preclara relicta* (V.35.101).

Aulus Gellius

Extracts from books IX-XX only.

Beg. *Herodes consularis Atticus vir ingenio ameno et greca facundia . . .* (IX.2.1). *¶Video inquit Herodes . . .*, ends . . . *vivendi disciplina est. ¶Ne imperium sit . . . si qua scimus omnibus aliis fient communia* (XX.5.8).

Cicero, Verrine orations

Extracts from Actio II books iv-v only.

Beg. *Abducuntur non numquam a iure homines et ab institutis suis magnitudine pecunie* (II.iv.12). *¶In rebus venalibus . . .*, ends . . . *et inclinacio temporum. ¶Tacite magis et occulte inimicicie sunt timende quam inducte atque aperte* (II. v.182).

Ennodius

Extracts from nearly all Ennodius' works, save the *carmina*.

Beg. *Usu rerum inter homines evenit ut quantum . . .* (1) *¶Superflua scribere res . . .*, ends . . . *morbis prestat obsequia. ¶Debit humiliare potentissimos optata sublimitas* (468).

Martin of Braga, Formula honestae vitae

Extracts from paragraphs 2–5.

Beg. *Prudentis animi est examinare consilia et non* . . . (2) ¶*Crebo speciem* . . ., ends . . . *prodesse nulli nocere.* ¶*Nichil tibi intersit an iures an firmes* (5).

Querolus (rubr.: *Plautus in Aulularia*)

Taken from MS Vat. lat. 4929, fols. 55–77.

Beg. *Pecunia est rerum ac sollicitudinum causa et caput* (prologue). ¶*Quod pro meritis* . . ., ends . . . *totum ille qui potest.* ¶*Tres edaces domus una non capit* (V.4).

Censorinus, *De die natali*

Two sentences taken from MS Vat. lat. 4929, fols. 2–34.

> *Non quanto quisque plura possidet sed quanto pauciora optat tanto est locupletior. Nichil egere deorum est quam minime autem proximum a diis* (1.4). Followed without rubric by four unidentified sentences:

> *Ea est consuetudinis vis ut ea invetereta etsi falsa opinione genita est nichil inimicius sit veritati. Pudet imbecillitatis cum rationis et veritatis auctoritate. Quem profecto homine melior est nichil prestantius esse deberet. Quicquid difficile est in precepto leve est amanti.*

Addenda to the *Florilegium Angelicum*

Quintus Curtius Rufus, *Oratio Scytharum ad Alexandrum*

Ed. E. Hedicke, *Historiae Alexandri Magni* (Leipzig 1908), 7.8.12–30. Found in F, L, N, V.

Beg. *Si dii habitum corporis tui aviditati animi parem esse* . . . ¶*Quid tu ignoras* . . ., ends . . . *benivolencia dubites.* ¶*Imperio tuo hostes an amicos nos velis esse considera.*

Alexander Atheniensibus

Ed. B. Keubler, Julius Valerius' *Res gestae Alexandri* (Leipzig 1888) 46, lines 20–8.

Found in F, L.

Beg. *Imperiale siquidem videbatur cum armis et iusticia me vestre urbi* . . ., ends . . . *Non enim valebitis si in his perseveratis.*

Ps. Quintilian, *Declamationes maiores*

Extracts from Bks. 2, 1, 3–8, 11–19.

Found in s (partial), x, R.

Beg. *Non est simplicis innocencie negare facinus* (2.4). ¶*Uxor est quam iungit* . . ., ends . . . *cui potest credi.* ¶*Quisquis in tormentis occiditur ideo tortus est ut occideretur* (19.12).

Julius Paris, Epitome of Valerius Maximus' *Factorum ac dictorum memorabilium libri* IX.

Found in P, x.

Beg. *Decem principum filii senatus auctoritate* . . . (1.1) ¶*E mille virginis vestalis* . . . , ends . . . *se canum vallavit.* ¶*Dyonisius tyrannus metu tonsorum* . . . *barbaros et servos habebat* (9 Ext. 2.4).

CONTENTS BY MANUSCRIPT*

	P	A	F	N	V	L	Fournival	R	E	S	x	a	p	s	l	v	b	r
Dedicatory epistle		0																
Macrobius	1	1	1	1	1	1	1	16		3		x	x					
Proverbia philosophorum	2	2	2	2	2	2	2	17		4		x	x			3		
Jerome	3	3	3	3		3	3	2	2	1		x					1	1
Gregory	17	4						1	1	2	14	x						
Apuleius	4	5	4	4	3	4	4	12		5		x	x					
Pliny	5	6	5	5	4	5	5	5	5	6		x	x		3	2		
Cicero, orations	6	7	6	6	5	6	6	9	9	7		x	x				2	
Sidonius	7	8	7	7	6	7	7	3	3	8		x	x		4	4		
Seneca, *De beneficiis*	8	9	8	9	7	8	8	7	7	9		x	x		2			
Seneca, epistles	9	10	9	8	8	9	9	6	6	10	8		x	5	1			
Sententiae philosophorum	10	11	10	10	9	10	10	18		11	1	?	?	1		1		
Praecepta Pithagorae	11	12	11	?	10	11	?	19		12	2	?	?	2				
Ænigmata Aristotilis	12	13	12	?	11	12	?	20		13	3	x	?	3				
Cicero, Tusculans	13	14	13	11	12	13	11	8	8	14	4	x	x					
Aulus Gellius	14	15	14	12	13	14	12	13		15	5	x						
Cicero, Verrines	15		15	13	14	15		10		16	6	?	x					
Ennodius	16		16	14	15	16		4	4	17	7	x		5	5			
Martin of Braga			17	15	16	17		11			9		x	7				
Querolus			18	16	17	18	13	14			10		x	4				
Censorinus			19	17	18	19	14	15			11		x	6				
Quintus Curtius			20	18	19	20		22										
Alexander Atheniensibus			21			21												
Quintilian								21			13		?	8				
Julius Paris	18										12							

*The numbers represent the relative order of a given work within each manuscript. (Manuscripts a and p are arranged by topic rather than by author.)

APPENDIX III
The Manuscripts

The following manuscripts contain the text of the *Florilegium Angelicum*; selections (i.e., entire sections) from it; and extracts (i.e., excerpts from sections) from the *florilegium*. Titles in square brackets indicate that the manuscript has no rubric nor other physical indication to mark the beginning of a given section. An asterisk denotes material which is not part of the *Florilegium Angelicum*.

x Auxerre, Bibl. Municipale, 234 (s. xiv²; France). Selections from the *Florilegium Angelicum*.

*fols. 1–140	Giles of Rome, *De regimine principum*; beginning lacking.
fols. 141–142	*Sententiae philosophorum.*
fol. 142	*Praecepta Pithagorae.*
fol. 142	*Ænigmata Aristotilis.*
fols. 142–146	Cicero, Tusculans.
fols. 146–148ᵛ	Aulus Gellius.
fols. 148ᵛ–149	Cicero, Verrine orations.
fols. 149–152	Ennodius.
fols. 152–156	Seneca, *Epistulae ad Lucilium.*
fol. 156	Martin of Braga, *Formula honestae vitae.*
fol. 156ʳᵛ	*Querolus.*
fol. 156ᵛ	Censorinus, *De die natali.*
fols. 156ᵛ–169ᵛ	Julius Paris.
fols. 169ᵛ–173	Quintilian, *Declamationes.*
*fols. 173–174	Jerome, epistles; extracts from epp. 64, 55, 123, 54, beg. *Quod pectore concepimus ore probemus . . .*, ends . . . *Quod luxurie parabatur virtus insumat.*
fols. 174–178	Gregory, epistles.
*fols. 178–179	Ps.-Hegesippus, extracts from books 1–4 of the Histories, beg. *Nemo clarior sit splendore generis quam munere religionis . . .*, ends . . . *potuerunt cavere quod divinitus decernebatur.*
*fols. 180–242	Praises of the Virgin, beg. *Sicud sol oriens mundo in altissimis dei . . .*; text breaks, incomplete, at the end of the quire.

Written by one or two hands in two columns of 41–3 lines each, on parchment and paper. Parchment ruled with lead point; paper not ruled. Sexterns. 292 × 205 mm (215 × 150). Belonged to Pontigny in 1778, no. 276 in catalog of that date; not in the revolutionary commission's list of 1794; cf. Talbot, "Notes on the Library of Pontigny," *Analecta sacri ordinis Cisterciensis* 10 (1954) 165.

Described in *Catalogue général des manuscrits des Bibliothèques publiques de France* 6 (Paris 1887) 81. Manuscript seen.

b Brussels, Bibl. Royale MS 10098–10105 (Van den Gheyn 1334) (s. xiii[1]; France). Selections (Jerome and Cicero's orations) from the *Florilegium Angelicum.*

I.	*fols. 1–9	Solinus, *Collectanea rerum memorabilium*; extracts.
	*fols. 10–15	Fulgentius, extracts.
	fols. 15–18	Jerome, epistles; extracts. Only the extracts on fol. 15 are taken from the *Florilegium Angelicum.*
	*fols. 19–20	Cicero, *De senectute*; extracts.
	*fol. 20[v]	Cicero, *De amicitia*; extracts.
	*fols. 21–28[v]	Cicero, *De officiis*; extracts.
	fol. 28[v]	Cicero, orations (*De domo, [Pro Sestio], In Vat., De prov. cons., De harusp., Pro Balbo, Pro Caelio*); added in a different hand.
	*fols. 29–37	Ennodius.
	fol. 37[v]	Cicero, orations (*Pridie, Cum senatui gracias egit, Cum populi gracias egit*); added in a different hand.
	*fols. 38–41	Claudian. Brief extracts from the following in this order: *Panegyricus de tertio consulatu Honorii Augusti; Pan. de quarto cons. H. A.; Pan. dictus Manlio Theodoro consuli; De consulatu Stilichonis; Pan. de sexto cons. H. A.; De bello Getico; Carmina minora; In Rufinum; De bello Gildonico; In Eutropium; Fescennina de nuptiis Honorii; Epithalamium de nupt. Hon.; Carmina minora xxxii.*
	*fols. 41–42[v]	Horace, *Carmina* and *De arte poetica*; extracts.
II.	*fols. 43–88[v]	Isidore, *Quaestiones in Vetus Testamentum.*

Two manuscripts, already bound together by the fifteenth century.
I. Written by several hands in two columns (fols. 38–42, 3 cols.) of 40–50 lines each. Ruled with ink and lead point 220 × 145 mm. Modern binding. fol. 1 (s. xv), *Liber carthusiensium prope Leodium* (Carthusians of Liège, est. 1390); fol. 1 (s. xvii), *Coll. societatis Iesus Lovanii* (repeated). The manuscript passed to the Bibl. Royale in 1838. According to the fifteenth-century table of contents describing I and II on fol. 1, portions of the manuscript are missing. Described in J. Van den Gheyn, *Catalogue des manuscrits de la Bibliothèque royale de Belgique* 2 (Brussels 1902) 280–281; and P. Thomas, *Catalogue des manuscrits de classiques latins de la Bibliothèque royale de Bruxelles* (Ghent 1896) 63, nos. 198–201. Manuscript seen on film.

E Évreux, Bibl. Municipale, 1 (s. xiii med.; France). *Florilegium Angelicum.*

*I.	fol. 1	lacking.
	fols. 2–31	Seneca, *De beneficiis*, epitome. fol. 2 beg. . . . *bene posito beneficio multorum amissorum dampna solatur* . . ., ends . . . *dare et perdere. Hoc est magni animi perdere et dare.*
	fols. 31ᵛ–32ᵛ	blank.
*II.	fols. 33–62	Symmachus, epistles; extracts. Beg. *Frivolis meis litterata potius curiositate quam iusta* . . ., ends . . . *mundum epistolis saltem nuntiis erigatur.*
	fols. 62ᵛ–63ᵛ	blank.
III.	fols. 64–69ᵛ	Gregory, epistles.
	fols. 69ᵛ–79ᵛ	Jerome, epistles, *[Adversus Jovinianum]* End of quire ii. fol. 79ᵛ bottom, note: *Tercius quaternus et proximus sequens debent hic intrare..ii.* [catchword:] *pulchrum et affirmare.* [Cf. fol. 98 below.]
	fols. 80–81ᵛ	Ennodius.
	fols. 81ᵛ–85ᵛ	Pliny, epistles.
	fols. 85ᵛ–90ᵛ	Seneca, *Epistulae ad Lucilium.*
	fols. 90ᵛ–93ᵛ	Seneca, *De beneficiis.*
	fols. 93ᵛ–97	Cicero, Tusculans.
	fol. 97ʳᵛ	Cicero, orations. Text breaks, incomplete, with end of quire; catchword, *delectionem que versari*, indicates a missing quire or quires. fols 98–114ᵛ, comprising two quires, are misplaced and should follow fol. 79ᵛ.
	fols. 98–104	Jerome (concluded).
	fols. 104ᵛ–112	Sidonius, epistles.
	fols. 112–114ᵛ	Ennodius; completed fols. 80–81ᵛ above.
*IV.	fols. 115–119ᵛ	Cyprian, epistles; moral extracts. Beg. *Ne eloquium nostrum arbiter prophanus inpediat aut clamor* . . ., ends . . . *munimentum spei tutela fidei medela peccati.*
	fols. 119ᵛ–122ᵛ	Cassiodorus, epistles; moral extracts. Beg. *Dictio semper agrestis est que aut* . . ., ends . . . *iudicem dehonestat cum more vestium verba suspensa venduntur.* Quire ends here without catchword; text may be incomplete.
*V.	fols. 123–138ᵛ	Jerome, epistles; moral extracts. Beg. *In epistola prima Damasus papa Jeronimo. Capitulo, Dormientum te* etc. *Lectione veluti cotidiano cibo aliter et* [ep. 35] . . ., ends . . . *quis iste dolor qui nec tempore ratione curatur* [ep. 97]. Quire ends here; text may be incomplete.
*VI.	fols. 139–157	Solinus, extracts. Beg. *Cum et aurum clementia et optimarum artium* . . ., ends . . . *non obscure iam pridem lacedemoniorum fedo exitu.*

fols. 157ᵛ–158ᵛ	blank save for *ex libris.*
*VII. fols. 159–168	*Moralium dogma philosophorum.*
fol. 168	Publilius Syrus, *Sententiae* A - F.
fol. 168ᵛ	Ten legal formulas (see Évreux catalog for bibliography).
fol. 169	pastedown. Hymn to St. Nicolas and various brief notes by different hands.

Seven individual manuscripts already bound together by the fifteenth century. III: Written in long lines, 28–32 per page. Ruled with lead point. 1⁸ sig. i, 2⁸ sig. ii. (at end in a contemporary hand: *Tercius quaternus et proximus sequens debent hic intrare*), 3¹⁰, 4⁸, 5⁸ sig. iii (misplaced), 6⁸⁺¹. 176 × 130 mm (127 × 97). Plain initials in green, blue, red. Original binding, oak board, bevelled edges, bare; front cover lacking. fol. 158ᵛ, *Iste unus librorum est cenobii Lirensis ordinis sancti Benedicti Ebroicensis dyoceseos. Alecis* (and monogram, s. xv) = Lyre OSB. Described in *Catalogue général des manuscrits des Bibliothèques publiques de France* 2 (Paris 1888) 401–402. Manuscript seen.

F Florence, Bibl. Laurenziana, Strozzi 75 (s. xii²; France). *Florilegium Angelicum.*

*fol. iʳᵛ	Notes in French hand, s. xiv-xv.
fols. 1–5ᵛ	Macrobius, *Saturnalia*; with *Versus Ciceronis.*
fols. 5ᵛ–8ᵛ	*Proverbia philosophorum.*
fols. 8ᵛ–23	Jerome, epistles, *[Adversus Jovinianum].*
fols. 23–25ᵛ	Apuleius, *De deo Socratis, [Asclepius, De Platone, De mundo].*
fols. 25ᵛ–28ᵛ	Pliny, epistles.
fols. 28ᵛ–33ᵛ	Cicero, orations.
fols. 33ᵛ–40ᵛ	Sidonius, epistles.
fols. 40ᵛ–43ᵛ	Seneca, *De beneficiis.*
fols. 43ᵛ–48	Seneca, *Epistulae ad Lucilium.*
fols. 48–49ᵛ	*Sententiae philosophorum.*
fol. 49ᵛ	*Praecepta Pithagorae.*
fols. 49ᵛ–50	*Ænigmata Aristotilis.*
fols. 50–54ᵛ	Cicero, Tusculans.
fols. 54ᵛ–57ᵛ	Aulus Gellius.
fols. 57ᵛ–58	Cicero, Verrine orations.
fols. 58–62	Ennodius.
fol. 62ʳᵛ	Martin of Braga, *Formula honestae vitae.*
fols. 62ᵛ–63	*Querolus.*
fol. 63	Censorinus, *De die natali.*
fol. 63ʳᵛ	Quintus Curtius, *Oratio Scytharum.*
fol. 63ᵛ	*Alexander Atheniensibus.*
*fols. 63ᵛ–72ᵛ	Valerius Maximus, *Facta et dicta memorabilia*; extracts. Beg. *Sulpicio sacerdoti inter sacrificandum . . .,* ends . . . *taurus ad amorem Enee vacce immugiit.*
*fols. 72ᵛ–74	Notes by various Italian hands, s. xvi.

Written by one hand in long lines, 32 per page. Quaternions, signed in Roman numerals; catchwords. First initial decorated, vine stems in gold, short tendrils terminating in scallops outline major letters. Front pastedown: *Comprato da me Carlo di Tommaso Strozzi l'anno 1616 in Spoleto.* Described in A. M. Bandini, *Biblioteca Leopoldina Laurentiana* . . ., 2 (Florence 1792), cols. 408–9. Manuscript seen on film.

---

l Leyden, Universiteitsbibl., B.P.L. 191 B (s. XIII²). Extracts from Seneca's letters and *De beneficiis*, Pliny, Sidonius, and Ennodius, taken from the *Florilegium Angelicum*.

*I. fols. 1–42ᵛ	Augustine, *De catechizandis rudibus*.
*II. fols. 43–135ᵛ	A collection of texts on the monastic life: *Instructio pie vivendi et superna meditandi*; Hugh of St. Victor, *De institutione noviciorum*; Martin of Braga, *Formula honestae vitae*; Arnulfus, *Speculum monachorum* (*P.L.* clxxxiv. 1175); *Sermo de b. Arsenio anachoreta* (*Acta Sanctorum, Iulii*, IV, p. 617).
III. fols. 136–142ᵛ	Seneca, *Epistulae ad Lucilium*; extracts from epp. 1–88; only the extracts on fols. 141ᵛᵇ–142ᵛ are taken from the *Florilegium Angelicum*.
fols. 142ᵛ–144	Seneca, *De beneficiis*.
*fols. 144ᵛ–145ᵛ	Seneca, *De remediis fortuitorum*; extracts.
*fols. 145ᵛ	Jerome, *De viris illustribus* c. 12, *Seneca*.
*fols. 146–148ᵛ	Martin of Braga, *Formula honestae vitae*.
*fols. 149–153ᵛ	Seneca, *Epistulae ad Lucilium*; extracts from epp. 1–47.
*fols. 153ᵛ–155	Correspondence of 'Seneca' and 'Paul'; followed, bottom of the page, by *Epithaphium Senece*.
*fols. 155–159	Seneca, tragedies; extracts.
fols. 159ᵛ–161	Pliny, epistles.
fols. 161–163	Sidonius, epistles.
fol. 163ʳᵛ	Ennodius.
*fols. 163ᵛ–167	Cicero, *De senectute*; extracts.
*fol. 167ʳᵛ	Sallust, *Bellum Catilinae*, cc. 1–4; text breaks incomplete with the end of the quire.
*IV. fols. 168–183	Guillelmus de Boldensele, *Peregrinatio ad terram sanctam*.

A composite manuscript in four parts. They were bound together in the fourteenth or early fifteenth century (after 1351) when the volume was foliated in Roman numerals and described on a slip of parchment now bound in the volume. It belonged to the abbey of St. James OSB in Liège.

I. fols. 1–42ᵛ (s. XII); II. fols. 43–135ᵛ (s. XIV); IV. fols. 168–183ᵛ (A.D. 1351). III. fols. 136–167ᵛ (s. XIII²): Written by one hand in two columns of 31 lines each. 1–4⁸, catchwords. (150 × 115 mm). fol. 136, *Liber sancti Iacobi in Leodio*. Described in *Bibliotheca Universitatis Leidensis, Codices manuscripti*, iii,

Codices Bibliothecae Publicae Latini (Leyden 1912) 94–95; and G. I. Lieftinck, *Manuscrits datés conservés dans les Pays-Bas* i (Amsterdam 1964) 81, and ii, pl. 144 (of fol. 170). Manuscript seen.

r London, British Libr., Royal 11 A.v (s. XII-XIII; Merton Priory, Surrey). Extracts from Jerome's epistles, taken from the *Florilegium Angelicum* (fols. 69–72ᵛ).

*fols. 1–3	Notes headed *De ecclesiastica correctione.*
*fols. 3–30	Collection of anonymous *sententiae* arranged by subject. Beg. *De divina natura. Principium et causa omnium deus . . .*
*fols. 30–32ᵛ	Additional *sententiae* arranged by subject. Beg. *Ecclesia dicitur fidelium conventus . . .*
*fols. 33–68ᵛ	Isidore, *Expositio in Genesim et Exodum.*
fols. 69–72ᵛ	Jerome, epistles. Beg. *Studio legendi . . .*, ends incomplete, *. . . quod si negaverit terra consumptum est.*
*fols. 73–98ᵛ	Abelard, *Sic et non*; mutilated.
*fols. 99–109ᵛ	*Dialogue inter philosophum Iudaeum et Christianum*; fragment.
*fols. 110–112ᵛ	Fourteen excerpts primarily on religious life attributed in the rubric to St. Bernard.

Written by one hand in two columns (fols. 1–98). *ex libris, Liber sancte Marie Merton.* Described in G. F. Warner and J. P. Gilson, *Catalogue of Western Manuscripts in the Old Royal and Kings Collections* i (London 1921) 337.

L London, British Libr., Add. 25104 (s. xv, Italy). *Florilegium Angelicum.*

fols. 1–8	Macrobius, *Saturnalia*; with *Versus Ciceronis.*
fols. 8–14	*Proverbia philosophorum.*
fols. 14–40ᵛ	Jerome, epistles, *[Adversus Jovinianum].*
fols. 40ᵛ–44	Apuleius, *De deo Socratis, [Asclepius, De Platone, De mundo].*
fols. 44–50	Pliny, epistles.
fols. 50–58ᵛ	Cicero, orations.
fols. 58ᵛ–70	Sidonius, epistles.
fols. 70–75ᵛ	Seneca, *De beneficiis.*
fols. 75ᵛ–83ᵛ	Seneca, *Epistulae ad Lucilium.*
fols. 83ᵛ–85ᵛ	*Sententiae philosophorum.*
fols. 85ᵛ–86	*Praecepta Pithagorae.*
fol. 86ʳᵛ	*Ænigmata Aristotilis.*
fols. 86ᵛ–94ᵛ	Cicero, Tusculans.
fols. 94ᵛ–101ᵛ	Aulus Gellius.
fols. 101ᵛ–102	Cicero, Verrine orations.
fols. 102–109	Ennodius.
fols. 109–110	Martin of Braga, *Formula honestae vitae.*
fols. 110–111	*Querolus.*

fol. 111	Censorinus, *De die natali.*
fols. 111–112	Quintus Curtius, *Oratio Scytharum.*
fol. 112^rv	*Alexander Atheniensibus.*

Written by one hand in long lines, 28 per page. Parchment ruled in ink. Eleven alternating sexternions and quaternions, 180 × 114 mm (134 × 68). Humanist hand, titles and paragraph marks in red. Described briefly in *Catalogue of Additions to the Manuscripts in the British Museum in the Years 1854–1875* 2 (London 1877) 155. Manuscript seen.

S Paris, Bibl. de l'Arsenal, 1116E (fols. 128–142^v) (s. XIII^1; France; St. Victor). Extracts from the *Florilegium Angelicum.*

fols. 128–133	Jerome, epistles, *[Adversus Jovinianum].*
fols. 133–135	Gregory, epistles.
fol. 135^rv	Macrobius, *Saturnalia*; with *Versus Ciceronis.*
fol. 135^v–136	*Proverbia philosophorum.*
fol. 136^rv	Apuleius, *De deo Socratis, [Asclepius, De Platone, De mundo].*
fols. 136^v–137	Pliny, epistles.
fol. 137^rv	Cicero, orations.
fols. 137^v–138^v	Sidonius, epistles.
fols. 138^v–139	Seneca, *De beneficiis.*
fols. 139–140	Seneca, *Epistulae ad Lucilium.*
fol. 140^rv	*Sententiae philosophorum.*
fol. 140^v	*Praecepta Pithagorae.*
fol. 140^v	*Ænigmata Aristotilis.*
fols. 140^v–141^v	Cicero, Tusculans.
fol. 141^v	Aulus Gellius.
fol. 141^v	Cicero, Verrine orations.
fols. 141^v–142	Ennodius.
*fol. 142	*Sententiae* from Gregory, Jerome, Augustine, Seneca, Rabanus, Ambrose, and the Scriptures. Beg. *Pollutus nigritie viciorum non cessat . . .*, ends *. . . non solum non proficit sed etiam lapsum incurrit.*
fol. 142^v	blank.

Written by one hand in two columns of ca. 50 lines each. Parchment pricked but not ruled. 1^8, 2^8(^-1); catchwords. 206 × 150 mm (148 × 115). Capitals in red; rubricated. Arsenal 1116 is a composite manuscript in 12 parts dating from the twelfth to the fifteenth centuries. They appear as one volume with the pressmark PP 14 in the catalog of St. Victor by Claude de Grandrue (A.D. 1514). Described in H. Martin, *Catalogue des manuscrits de la Bibliothèque de l'Arsenal* 2 (Paris 1886) 286–289. Manuscript seen.[80]

---

[80] A manuscript of excerpts from the *Florilegium Angelicum* belonged to Cardinal Guala Bichieri (d. 1227), briefly noted as no. 73 in the catalog of Bichieri's books: 'Item

p Paris, Bibl. Nationale, lat. 1860 (s. XIII med.; S. France). *Florilegium Angelicum* arranged by subject.

I. *fols. 1–56ᵛ	*Interpretationes nominum hebraicorum.*
*fols. 57–59	Alan of Lille, *De sex alis cherubim*; lacks beginning.
*fols. 59–60	Brief extracts from patristic texts on penitence.
*fols. 60ᵛ–72ᵛ	*Moralium dogma philosophorum.*
*fols. 72ᵛ–74ᵛ	Martin of Braga, *Formula honestae vitae.*
fols. 75–153ᵛ	*Florilegium* of classical prose, being the classical texts (only) from the *Florilegium Angelicum*, enlarged and arranged by subject under 290 headings, and preceded by a subject index A–V on fols. 75–7. Beg. fol. 77, *c. I. De proposito et deliberatione alicuius rei faciende. Tullius de officiis primo. Efficiendum est ut rationi appetitus obediant eamque neque . . .*, ends *c.* CCXC. *Quorum virtus est placitis abstinere vel modum tenere . . . Ennodius in epistola: Gravius est calcasse degustata dulcia quam intacta.*
*fols. 153ᵛ–216	*Florilegium* of classical verse arranged in 231 chapters, preceded by a table of chapters, fols. 153ᵛ–155. Beg. fol. 155, *c. I. De novo inceptore alicuius rei . . . Et labor est unus tempora prima pati . . .*, ends *c.* CCXXXI. *De consumacione alicuius operis . . . Anchora de prora iacitur stant littore puppes.*
fol. 216ᵛ	blank.
*II. fols. 217–246ᵛ	Summary of the O.T., with marginal concordance. Beg. *Inter varia nature et gratie dona . . . Quattuor sunt regule scripture, istoria . . .*, ends *. . . fiant opera sicut Cornelius faciebat.*

Comprises two manuscripts.

I. (s. XIII med., S. France). Written by one hand in two columns of ca. 50 lines each. Ruled with lead point. 1–27⁸; catchwords. 335 × 220 mm (210 × 97). Initials orange-red, occasionally blue; short single tendrils terminating in scallops.

---

excerpta epistolarum b. Ieronimi cum variis excerptionibus doctorum et philosophorum'; see A. Hessel and W. Bulst, "Kardinal Guala Bichieri und seine Bibliothek," *Historische Vierteljahrschrift* 27 (1932) 784. Probably Bichieri's manuscript was either MS S, or the exemplar from which S derived. The cardinal had close and well-documented associations with St. Victor. In late 1213 he broke his journey there, on his return to Italy from a three-year stay as papal legate in England; and the following year when Bichieri founded S. Andrea, a house of canons in his native Vercelli, he brought canons from St. Victor to set up his foundation, with the Victorine Thomas Gallus as first abbot. Bichieri bequeathed his library to San Andrea; but either his manuscript of excerpts from the *Florilegium Angelicum* or a copy made from it found its way to St. Victor in Paris.

II. (s. xiii in., N. France). Written in two columns of 55 lines each. fol. 246ᵛ (s. xv): *Liber sancti Marie de Mortuimaris* (Abbey of Mortemer OSB in the diocese of Rouen).

The whole is identified with item 15 in the catalog of books taken by M. de Mareste from the Abbey of Mortemer in 1677; ed. L. Delisle, *Cabinet des manuscrits* 1 (Paris 1868) p. 525. Colbert 959, Regius 3758[10]. Described in Ph. Lauer, *Catalogue général des manuscrits latins* 2 (Paris 1940) 200–201. Manuscript seen.

s Paris, Bibl. Nationale, lat. 15172, fols. 122–40 (s. xiii[1]; France; St. Victor). Selections from the *Florilegium Angelicum*.

*fols. 122ᵛ–125ᵛ	Ps. Seneca, Proverbs. Beg. *Alienum est omne quicquid . . .*, ends *. . . zelum autem hominibus viciosum est.*
fols. 125ᵛ–126	*Sententiae philosophorum.*
fol. 126ʳᵛ	*Praecepta Pithagorae.*
fol. 126ᵛ	*Ænigmata Aristotilis.*
fol. 126ᵛ	*Querolus.*
fols. 127–130ᵛ	Seneca, *Epistulae ad Lucilium.*
fol. 130ᵛ	Censorinus, *De die natali.*
fol. 131	Martin of Braga, *Formula honestae vitae.*
fols. 131–134ᵛ	Quintilian, *Declamationes*, beg. *Incipit mathematicus. Mors est laudanda . . .* , ends incomplete, *. . . Affirmationem sumit ex veritate quicquid non habet ex homine. Ex hoc iniquissimum.*
*fol. 134ᵛ	Sequence, beg. *In affectu cordis puri assurgamus . . .*, ends *. . . mente loco imitari petrum tot . . .* [illeg.].
*fols. 135–137ᵛ	(misnumbered 131–133ᵛ) Jerome, epistles; extracts. Beg. *Libenter accipio ab offerente . . .*, ends *. . . Vinctum me tenet affectio tui. Verba concessi.*
*fol. 137ᵛ (133ᵛ)	Vegetius, *De re militari*; extracts. Beg., *Nemo metuit facere . . .*, ends *. . . etiam si honerosa gestaverit.*
*fol. 138ʳᵛ (134ʳᵛ)	Unidentified extracts, beg. *Sancta et apostolica romana ecclesia que tanquam pia mater ad sublevandos gemitus et labores . . .*
*fol. 138ᵛ (134ᵛ)	Unidentified extracts, beg. *Bone mentis intentio semper in opere pietatis elucet et in religionis amore atque defensione iusticie . . .*
fols. 139–140ᵛ	(135–136ᵛ) blank, except for pen essays and the note: *Obiit frater Andreas.*

Two quires written by one hand in two columns of 35 lines each. Ruled with dry point and lead point. 1⁸⁺², 2⁶⁺³. 175 × 120 mm (140 × 90). fol. 122 s. xiii, *ex libris* and anathema of St. Victor. By the end of the fifteenth century the two quires had been bound together with a number of twelfth- and thirteenth-century manuscripts and formed item FFF 22 in the catalog of St. Victor by Claude de Grandrue (A.D. 1514). Manuscript seen.

a Rome, Bibl. Angelica 720 (s. XIII; France). *Florilegium Angelicum* arranged by subject.

fols. 1–106^v	*Florilegium* in 105 chapters. Mutilated. The first 10 chapters are missing; the text begins in the middle of chapter 11. A quire containing chapters 73–86 is missing between fols. 86^v and 87, and another containing chapters 102–3 is lacking between fols. 103^v and 104. Beg. . . . *sed secundum famem restringere. Idem. Ubi aqua et panis est ibi nature satisfactum* . . . [ch. 12] *De commendatione ieiunii* . . ., ends [ch. 105] *De ingratitudine et inuriis irrogatis . . . Iniurias vero dilatat atque auget quod autem et amplius.*
fol. 107^{rv}	Miscellaneous notes; s. XIV–XV, Italy.
fol. 108^{rv}	Subject index, letters A–E; s. XIV–XV.

Written by one hand in long lines, 17–19 per page. Ruled with lead point. 1^{8+1}, 2^8, 3^{8+1}, 4^{8+1}, 5–8^{10}, 9^{10+1}, quire missing, 11^8, 12^{8+1}, quire missing, 14^5; catchwords. 147 × 105 mm (111 × 70). Initial letters slashed in red. Described briefly in H. Narducci, *Catalogus codicum manuscriptorum . . . in Bibliotheca Angelica . . .* (Rome 1893) 301–302. Manuscript seen.

A Rome, Bibl. Angelica, 1895 (s. XII^2; France). *Florilegium Angelicum.*

I. fol. i	blank.
fol. 1^{rv}	Dedicatory epistle.
fols. 2–8	Macrobius, *Saturnalia*, with *Versus Ciceronis*.
fols. 8–12^v	*Proverbia philosophorum*.
fols. 12^v–31	Jerome, epistles, *[Adversus Jovinianum]*.
fols. 31–37	Gregory, epistles.
fols. 37–40	Apuleius, *De deo Socratis, [Asclepius, De Platone, De mundo]*.
fols. 40–44^v	Pliny, epistles.
fols. 44^v–51	Cicero, orations.
fols. 51–59	Sidonius, epistles.
fols. 59–63	Seneca, *De beneficiis*.
fols. 63–69	Seneca, *Epistulae ad Lucilium*.
fols. 69–70^v	*Sententiae philosophorum*.
fol. 70^v	*Praecepta Pithagorae*.
fol. 71^{rv}	*Ænigmata Aristotilis*.
fols. 71^v–77	Cicero, Tusculans.
fols. 77–79^v	Aulus Gellius; text breaks, incomplete, with the end of quire ten.

*II. fols. 80–81	Grammatical rules.
*III. fols. 81ᵛ–96	Prudentius, *Psychomachia*.
*IV. fols. 97–105	Horace, *Epistola ad Pisones*.
*V. fols. 105–133	Horace, *Epistolarum libri duo*.
*VI. fols. 133ᵛ–137	Grammatical rules and a Latin-Italian glossary.

A composite manuscript in six parts.

I. Written by one hand in long lines, 27 per page. Ruled with lead point. 1–10⁸, 185 × 117 mm (143 × 94). Large section initials colored dusty blue, red, and gold. Described in A. Sorbelli, *Inventari dei manoscritti delle biblioteche d'Italia* 56 (Florence 1934) 82–83. Manuscript seen.

N Sydney, University Lib., Nicholson 2 (s. XIIIˡ; France). Extracts from the *Florilegium Angelicum*.

fols. 1–2	Macrobius, *Saturnalia*; with *Versus Ciceronis*.
fols. 2–3ᵛ	[*Proverbia philosophorum*].
fols. 3ᵛ–11ᵛ	Jerome, epistles [*Adversus Jovinianum*].
fols. 11ᵛ–13	Apuleius, *De deo Socratis*, [*Asclepius, De Platone, De mundo*].
fols. 13–15ᵛ	[Pliny, epistles.]
fols. 15ᵛ–22	Cicero, orations.
fol. 22	Seneca, *Epistulae ad Lucilium*.
*fols. 22ᵛ–24	Boethius, *De consolatione philosophiae*, extracts.
fols. 24ᵛ–25	Seneca, *De beneficiis*.
*fols. 25–26	Unidentified extracts, illegible.
fols. 26–27	*Sententiae philosophorum*.
fol. 27	Cicero, Tusculans.
fol. 27ʳᵛ	[Aulus Gellius.]
fol. 27ᵛ	[Cicero, Verrine orations.]
fols. 27ᵛ–29ᵛ	[Ennodius.]
fols. 29ᵛ–30	Martin of Braga, *Formula honestae vitae*.
fol. 30	[*Querolus.*]
fol. 30	[Censorinus, *De die natali*.]
fol. 30	[Quintus Curtius, *Oration Scytharum*.]
*fols. 30–31ᵛ	Unidentified extracts, beg. *Qui descendet a superis sola hymnorum licet mercede . . .*
*fol. 31ᵛ	In lower margin, verses beg. *In coitu sex dampna luo nam denarium do . . .* (Walther no. 8864).
*fols. 31ᵛ–32ᵛ	Brief extracts from Seneca, Jerome, Ambrose, Aristotle, and the Scriptures, beg. *Fastidientis stomachi est multa degustare . . .*

Written by one hand in long lines, 28 per page. Ruled in ink. 1–8⁴, 158 × 130 mm. First and second initials blue and red, with red and blue penwork; remaining ten initials in red. Fol. 32ᵛ erased: *Iste liber est ad usum fratris Laurentii*;

given to the University of Sydney from the estate of Sir Charles Nicholson in 1924. Described in K. V. Sinclair, *Descriptive Catalogue of Medieval and Renaissance Western Manuscripts in Australia* (Sydney 1969) 175–178. Manuscript seen on film.

P Vatican City, Bibl. Apostolica, Pal. lat. 957 (s. XII²; France). *Florilegium Angelicum.*

*I.	fols. 1–60	Walter Burleigh, *De vita et moribus philosophorum.*
	fols. 61–84ᵛ	Theobald, *Pharetra fidei contra iudeos.*
	fols. 85–92	Guido Aretinus (?), *Regulae rhythmicae.*
	fols. 92ᵛ–95	Thomas Colete, *Ars notaria.*
	fols. 95ᵛ–96ᵛ	*Obiectiones contra iudeos,* beg. *Mota dicit dominus in evangelio* . . .
II.	fols. 97–102	Macrobius, *Saturnalia;* with *Versus Ciceronis.*
	fols. 102–107	*Proverbia philosophorum.*
	fols. 107–125ᵛ	Jerome, epistles *[Adversus Jovinianum].*
	fols. 125ᵛ–128ᵛ	Apuleius, *De deo Socratis, [Asclepius, De Platone, De mundo.]*
	fols. 128ᵛ–132ᵛ	Pliny, epistles.
	fols. 132ᵛ–139	Cicero, orations.
	fols. 139–147ᵛ	Sidonius, epistles.
	fols. 147ᵛ–151ᵛ	Seneca, *De beneficiis.*
	fols. 151ᵛ–158	Seneca, *Epistulae ad Lucilium.*
	fols. 158–159ᵛ	*Sententiae philosophorum.*
	fol. 159ᵛ	*Praecepta Pithagorae.*
	fols. 159ᵛ–160ᵛ	*Ænigmata Aristotilis.*
	fols. 160ᵛ–166ᵛ	Cicero, Tusculans.
	fols. 166ᵛ–171ᵛ	Aulus Gellius.
	fols. 171ᵛ–172	Cicero, Verrine orations.
	fols. 172–176ᵛ	Ennodius. Text breaks incomplete with the end of quire ten, . . . *dampna sermonis. Mater bonorum*
	fols. 177–184	. . . Gregory, epistles.
	fol. 184ʳᵛ	Julius Paris. Text breaks incomplete with the end of the quire, . . . *trahebat ab ea se que nam aut agenda aut intan* . . .

Composed of two manuscripts probably joined in Heidelberg.

I. (s. XIV) fol. 92, *Explicit summa magistri Gwidonis anno domini 1368 in octava epiphanie domini.*

II. Written by two hands: (1) fols. 97–176ᵛ, (2) fols. 177–184ᵛ, in long lines, 28 per page. Ruled with lead point. 1–10⁸ (sig. i-x), 11⁸ (sig. i). 207 × 133 mm (160 × 90). Initials colored red, yellow, and blue; titles in semi-rustic capitals. Manuscript seen.

v Vatican City, Bibl. Apostolica, Reg. lat. 358 (s. xv; France; Tours). Extracts from the *Florilegium Angelicum*.

fols. 1–108[v]	A collection of extracts from Scripture and from medieval and ancient authors; beg. *Incipit hic series descripta parabolarum Flosculus* . . . [Proverbia Salomonis:] *Audiens sapiens sapiencior erit* . . ., ends [John of Salisbury, *Policraticus*:] . . . *dampnum nobis in curia detur. Liber ad eos etc.* The collection includes a block of extracts from the *Florilegium Angelicum*:
fols. 74–75	*Sententiae philosophorum*; twenty-four sentences.
fol. 75	Pliny, epistles; seven sentences.
fol. 75[rv]	*Proverbia philosophorum*; twenty-seven sentences.
fol. 75[v]	Sidonius, epistles; eleven sentences.
fols. 75[v]–76	Ennodius; seventeen sentences.

Parchment. *ex libris* note, s. xvi: *Ce livre est a Lucas Fumee chanoine de Tours.* Paul and Alexander Petau. There is no reason to repeat a description of the whole manuscript since it is fully described in A. Wilmart, *Codices Reginenses Latini* 2 (Vatican 1945) 331–340. Manuscript seen.

R Vatican City, Bibl. Apostolica, Reg. lat. 1575 (s. xii/xiii; France). *Florilegium Angelicum*.

*fols. 1–24[v]	Council of Aachen 816, *Regula canonicorum*.
*fols. 34–40[v]	*Epistola beati Jeronimi de vita et exitu sancti Pauli.*
*fols. 41–59	Symmachus, epistles; extracts. Beg. *Ne michi vicio vertatur intermissio litterarum* . . ., ends . . . *studium meum incitamento religionis acuetur.*
*fol. 59[v]–61[v]	Epistles of 'Alexander and Dindimus'.
*fol. 62	Sermon, beg. *Miserere mei deus* . . . *Triplex est divina misericordia, parva, mediocris et magna* . . .
*fol. 62[v]	Augustine, *Sermo de trinitate*, beg. *Audio fratres quod quidam inter se disputant* . . . , followed by a fragment of a poem: . . . *pauperibus placuit pro condicione/* . . . *pro sola po–itate chorus/* . . . *humili paupertas provida passu/* . . . *piti copia rapta gradu/* . . . *gri terrici/* . . . *ius cognomine non quia durus/* . . . *lor ferebat honus/* . . . *francie ludovici/* . . . *ut rex hec loca regi/* . . . *homo deteriore domo.*
fols. 63–65[v]	Gregory, epistles.
fols. 65[v]–72[v]	[Jerome, epistles, *Adversus Jovinianum*.]
fols. 72[v]–75[v]	Sidonius, epistles.
fols. 76–78	Ennodius.
fols. 78–79[v]	Pliny, epistles.
fols. 79[v]–82	Seneca, *Epistulae ad Lucilium*.

fols. 82–83ᵛ	Seneca, *De beneficiis.*
*fols.83ᵛ–85	Seneca, *De remediis fortuitorum.*
fols. 85–87	Cicero, Tusculans.
fols. 87–89ᵛ	Cicero, orations.
fol. 89ᵛ	Cicero, Verrine orations.
fol. 90	Martin of Braga, *Formula honestae vitae.*
fols. 90–91	Apuleius, *De deo Socratis, [Asclepius, De Platone, De mundo].*
fols. 91–92ᵛ	Aulus Gellius.
fols. 92ᵛ–93	*Querolus.*
fol. 93	Censorinus, *De die natali.*
fols. 93–94ᵛ	Macrobius, *Saturnalia;* with *Versus Ciceronis.*
fols. 94ᵛ–96ᵛ	*Proverbia philosophorum.*
fols. 96ᵛ–97	*[Sententiae philosophorum.]*
fol. 97	*Praecepta Pithagore.*
fol. 97	*Ænigmata Aristotilis.*
fols. 97–99ᵛ	Quintilian, *Declamationes.*
fols. 99ᵛ–100ᵛ	Quintus Curtius, *Historiae Alexandri;* extracts, including the *Oratio Scytharum.* Beg. *Ingenium plerumque et naturam fortuna corrumpit . . .,* ends *. . . moribus quam insignibus estimari.*
*fol. 101	Jerome, *De viris illustribus* c. 80, *Methodius.*
*fols. 101–105	Methodius, *De consummatione seculi.*
*fols. 105ᵛ–106	Ivo of Chartres, ep. 63, beg. *Post multam oblivionem . . .*

Written in three hands in two columns of 46–50 lines each. Ruled with lead point. Quires of 4 leaves signed vi, vii, viii, viiii, x, xxii, xxv, mutilated quire of 3 leaves, quire of 4 leaves unsigned, xxviii, xxviiii, xxx, quire of 4 leaves signed xxxii; inserts on slips of parchment. 230 × 153 mm. Plain initials without tendrils. fol. 40ᵛ (s. xiii–xiv), *Universis presentes litteras visuris, dominus Guillelmus miles de Villañ.* Fol. 106ᵛ, medieval *ex libris* note erased: *Iste . . .* Fol. i, table of contents by Alexander Petau. Manuscript seen.

V Vatican City, Bibl. Apostolica, Vat. lat. 3087 (s. xiii[2]; S. France or Italy). *Florilegium Angelicum.*

I. *fols. 1–18ᵛ	Moral exempla drawn largely from Scripture and arranged by subject (*De caritate, De patientia, De dilectione seu amore . . .*). Table of chapters, f. 1. Text, f. 1ᵛ, beg. *De caritate. Dominus dicit in evangelio, Maiorem caritatem nemo habet . . .,* ends *. . . ut non cum hoc mundo damnemur cui est honor et gloria in secula seculorum amen.*

*fols. 19–22ᵛ	Sixteen *carmina* in honor of the Virgin, among which are two by Adam of St. Victor and one by Peter Abelard.
fols. 23–27	Macrobius, *Saturnalia*; with *Versus Ciceronis*.
fols. 27–31	*Proverbia philosophorum.*
fols. 31–33	Apuleius, *De deo Socratis, [Asclepius, De Platone, De mundo].*
fols. 33–36ᵛ	Pliny, epistles.
fols. 36ᵛ–41ᵛ	Cicero, orations.
fols. 41ᵛ–48	Sidonius, epistles.
fols. 48–51	Seneca, *De beneficiis.*
fols. 51–55	Seneca, *Epistulae ad Lucilium.*
fols. 55–56	*Sententiae philosophorum.*
fol. 56	*Praecepta Pithagorae.*
fol. 56ʳᵛ	*Ænigmata Aristotilis.*
fols. 56ᵛ–60	Cicero, Tusculans.
fols. 60–63ᵛ	Aulus Gellius.
fol. 63ᵛ	Cicero, Verrine orations.
fols. 63ᵛ–67	Ennodius.
fols. 67ᵛ–68	Martin of Braga, *Formula honestae vitae.*
fol. 68	*[Querolus].*
fol. 68	Censorinus, *De die natali.*
fol. 68ʳᵛ	Quintus Curtius, *Oratio Scytharum.*
*II fols. 69–85	Seneca, *De beneficiis*; extracts.
fols. 85–87	Martin of Braga, *Formula honestae vitae.*
fols. 87–88ᵛ	Seneca, *De remediis fortuitorum.*
fols. 88ᵛ–89ᵛ	Ps.-Seneca, *De moribus.*
fols. 89ᵛ–90ᵛ	Seneca, *De clementia*; extracts.
fols. 90ᵛ–91ᵛ	Seneca, *Epistulae ad Lucilium*; extracts.
fol. 92ʳᵛ	Johannes Belvantessis, *Summa grammaticalis.* Beg. *Multis modis dicitur sciencia, una plurimum . . .*; followed by a song in praise of the Virgin, beg. *Salve mater salvatoris, missus Gabriel de celis . . .*
fol. 93	table of contents, *ex libris* note, erased.

In two parts which were together soon after pt. I was completed, since a hand of pt. I reappears in a song added to pt. II, fol. 92ᵛ.

I. Written by three hands: (1) fols. 1–18ᵛ, (2) fols. 19–22ᵛ, (3) fols. 23–68ᵛ, in long lines, 35 per page. Ruled with lead point. 1¹², 2–3¹⁰, 4–5⁸, 6–7¹⁰; catchwords. 222 × 158 mm (168 × 100).

II. fols. 69–91ᵛ, s. XIII¹, France; fol. 92ʳᵛ, s. XIII/XIV. Manuscript seen.

Richard de Fournival, *Biblionomia*, item 84.
> Taken from L. Delisle, *Le Cabinet des manuscrits de la Bibliothèque nationale* 2 (Paris 1874) 529.
> Censorini exceptiones florum ex operibus quorumdam sanctorum et phylosophorum moralium: primo quidem de libro Machrobii Saturnariorum vel Saturnarium. Secundo proverbia quorumdam philosophorum. Tercio de epystolis beati Jheronimi. Quarto de libro Epuleii Madaurensis de Deo Socratis. Quinto de epystolis Plinii secundi. Sexto de harenga Tullii pridie quam in exilium iret. Septimo cum senatui gratias egit. Octavo de epystolis Sidonii. Nono de libro Senece de beneficiis. Decimo de epystolis eiusdem ad Lucilium. Undecimo sententie quorumdam philosophorum. Duodecimo de libro Tullii Tusculanarum. Tercio decimo de libro Agellii noctium Atticarum. Quarto decimo de comedia Plauti que dicitur Allularia. In uno volumine cuius signum est littera [K].

In addition to those manuscripts and references discussed above, extracts or selections from the *Florilegium Angelicum* also appear in the following:

Cambridge, St. John's College MS 97, fols. 214–229v (s. xiv; John of London, fl. 1364; St. Augustine's, Canterbury). Apuleius, Pliny, Cicero Orat., Sidonius, Seneca De ben., Cicero Tusc., A. Gellius, Ennodius.

Oxford, Trinity College MS 18, fols. 181–185v (s. xiv; Bonshommes of BMV, Ashridge, s. xv). Ennodius, Pliny, Seneca epp., *Proverbia*, Cicero Tusc.

Vatican City, Bibl. Apostolica, Vat. lat. 5994, fols., 75–79 (s. xiv; Italy). Macrobius, Jerome, Apuleius, Pliny, Cicero Orat., Sidonius, Seneca De ben. and epp., *Sententiae philosophorum*, Cicero Tusc., A. Gellius, Cato, Ennodius.

Venice, Biblioteca Nazionale Marciana MS lat. cl. II, 40 (coll. 2195), fols. 1–12v (s. xiv; Italy). Gregory, Jerome, Macrobius, Seneca De ben., Martin of Braga, Sidonius, Ennodius, Q. Curtius, Seneca epp.

Catalog of the papal library at Pensicola, ed. M. Faucon, *La librairie des papes d'Avignon* 2 (Paris 1882) 140 no 933. Macrobius, Apuleius, Pliny, Ennodius, Seneca.

5. *Florilegia* and Latin Classical Authors in Twelfth- and Thirteenth-Century Orléans*

I would like to examine some aspects of two general questions in this essay. First, what role did Orléans play in the dissemination of classical Latin literature in the twelfth century? And, second, what happened to the study of Latin classical authors in the thirteenth century? The sources, largely unexamined in this context, that will shed some light on these questions are two large *florilegia* of the twelfth century, a large private library and a body of marginalia of the thirteenth, namely, the *Florilegium Angelicum*, the *Florilegium Gallicum*, the library of Richard de Fournival, and the annotations of an anonymous lexicographer.

The preeminence of Orléans as a school for the study of Latin classical authors is reiterated as a *topos* or as reality by numerous late twelfth- and early thirteenth-century writers, such as Matthew of Vendôme, Alexander Neckham, Geoffrey of Vinsauf, Eberhard of Béthune, John of Garland and Henry of Andely. "Let Paris be proud of her logic and Orléans her authors . . .," or as Neckham said, "I think that in no other city the songs of the Muses, watched over with so much zeal, are better interpreted." Clerks went to Paris for the liberal arts, to Bologna for law, to Salerno for medicine, to Toledo for demons, according to Helinand; but for the authors, they went to Orléans.[1]

*I am grateful to my wife Mary for her precise and generous help in preparing this essay.

[1] These comments which are frequently cited are conveniently pulled together in the following publications regarding Orléans: L. Delisle, "Les écoles d'Orléans au XIIᵉ et au XIIIᵉ siècle," *Annuaire: Bulletin de la Société de l'histoire de France* 7 (1869) 139–154; L. J. Paetow, "The Arts Course at Medieval Universities," *University of Illinois Studies in Language and Literature* 3 (Urbana 1910) 503–509, 575–581; E. Faral, *Les arts poétiques du XIIᵉ et du XIIIᵉ siècle* (Paris 1924); B. Marti, *Arnulfi Aurelianensis Glosule super*

It is puzzling then, in light of these contemporary opinions, that Orléans is virtually unmentioned in the discussions of the transmission of ancient authors such as Hall's *Companion to Classical Texts* or Reynolds and Wilson's *Scribes and Scholars*.[2] This inconsistency raises two questions: First, why has Orléans been overlooked in modern discussions? Second, what authors were known at Orléans and what role did Orléans play in their transmission? The answer to the first question is relatively easy, namely, that we have no idea what texts were in Orléans libraries. Not a single surviving manuscript of a classical author can be firmly assigned to Orléans on the basis of script, decoration, colophon or *ex libris*. No medieval booklist or library catalog survives for any monastic or collegiate institution in Orléans through which we might form a picture of what was once there. In contrast to Saint Victor or Clairvaux, whose libraries can be reconstructed with remarkable accuracy because of distinctive pressmarks and detailed fifteenth-century catalogs,[3] Orléans's books were dispersed without trace, like those of Notre Dame and Sainte Geneviève in Paris. Hall's *Companion* and *Scribes and Scholars* are based largely on manuscripts used in Teubner, Oxford and Budé editions. None of these manuscripts, however—even if they were once in Orléans— can be firmly ascribed to Orléans today. The role played by the twelfth-century schools of Orléans in the transmission of Latin classical authors has vanished with the dispersal of their libraries.

In view of these facts, the answer to the second question is obviously more difficult: What ancient authors were to be found at Orléans, and what role did Orléans play in their transmission? Part of what was to be found in Orléans libraries of the twelfth century can be seen, I believe, in two large collections of extracts from ancient authors, namely, the *Florilegium Angelicum* and the *Florilegium Gallicum*. I want in this paper to present evidence suggesting that these two collections were compiled in Orléans; and then I want to associate with them and with Orléans, first, several authors in the library of Richard de Fournival, as

---

Lucanum . . ., Papers and Monographs of the American Academy in Rome 18 (1958), introduction. Besides the bibliography given in these, see S. Gueneé, "Université d'Orléans," *Bibliographie d'histoire des universités françaises des origines à la Révolution,* Institut de recherche et d'histoire des textes et Commission internationale d'histoire des universités (Paris 1970).

[2] F. W. Hall, *A Companion to Classical Texts* (Oxford 1913) 81; Leighton D. Reynolds and Nigel G. Wilson, *Scribes and Scholars,* 2d ed. rev. (Oxford 1974) 97.

[3] I refer to the catalog of Claude de Grandrue edited by Gilbert Ouy, with V. Gerz-von Buren, *Le catalogue de la bibliothèque de l'abbaye de Saint-Victor de Paris de Claude Grandrue, 1514* (Paris 1983), and Grandrue's distinctive foliation of the St. Victor books; and to the catalogs of Clairvaux edited by André Vernet et al., *La bibliothèque de l'abbaye de Clairvaux du XIIᵉ au XVIIIᵉ siècle* 1 (Paris 1979).

described in his *Biblionomia*,[4] and secondly, the books used by a mid-thirteenth-century grammarian, as represented by the authors cited in the margins of Bern, Burgerbibliothek MS 276. While the *Florilegium Angelicum* and the *Florilegium Gallicum* have been studied with regard to the individual texts contained in them, few have treated these *florilegia* as real books, written by someone who drew upon other books, and asked whether one can determine where they were compiled on the basis of the medieval circulation of the texts that they contain. On the one hand, the *Florilegium Angelicum*, the *Florilegium Gallicum*, the *Biblionomia* and the marginalia of Bern 276 each contain extracts from individual texts whose transmission is associated with the Loire Valley; on the other, the appearance of extracts from one or more of the same group of relatively rare authors—the Pseudo-Plautine *Querolus*, Cicero's orations (the *Post reditum* etc. and the *Verrines*), Calpurnius, Nemesianus, Gellius books 1–7, Tibullus and Propertius—ties the four sources together and suggests that they have to one degree or another ultimately drawn on the same collection of books and are products of the same intellectual interests. I should like to consider each in turn, and then to examine the texts common to two or more of them.

Let us turn first to the *Florilegium Angelicum* (FA).[5] It is a collection of extracts from ancient and patristic epistles and orations for use in the composition of letters, which was compiled sometime in the third quarter of the twelfth century and dedicated to a pope, probably Alexander III. The *Florilegium Angelicum* survives wholly or in part in twenty-one manuscripts, among them the dedication copy (from which it derives its name: Rome, Biblioteca Angelica MS 1895 fols. 1–79v) and that copy's exemplar, Vatican MS Pal. lat. 957 fols. 97–184. It contains extracts from the following authors and texts: Macrobius, *Saturnalia*; the *Proverbia philosophorum*; Jerome, letters; Gregory, letters; Apuleius, *De deo Socratis*; the younger Pliny, letters; Cicero, *Post reditum* etc.; Sidonius, letters; Seneca, *De beneficiis* and letters; the *Sententiae philosophorum*; Cicero, *Tusculans*; Aulus Gellius, books 9–20; Cicero, *Verrines*; Ennodius; Martin of Braga; the *Querolus*; and Censorinus.

The origin of the *Florilegium Angelicum* can be discerned through a study of its sources. Two manuscripts from which its compiler drew material can be identified. The first of these (Bern, Burgerbibliothek MS

---

[4] The *Biblionomia* will be cited from the edition of L. Delisle, *Le cabinet des manuscrits de la Bibliothèque nationale* 2 (Paris 1874) 518–535.

[5] Regarding the *FlorilegiumAngelicum* see chap. 4 above, "The *Florilegium Angelicum*: Its Origin, Content and Influence"; and B. Munk-Olsen, "Note sur quelques préfaces de florilèges latins du XIIᵉ siècle," *Revue Romane* 8 (1973) 190–191. I am grateful to Professor Munk-Olsen for his help in preparing this essay.

136, s. xii) was the immediate source of the extracts from Apuleius, Pliny's letters, and Cicero's orations. The extracts in the *Florilegium Angelicum* follow in the same order and preserve the same variant readings. For its text of Apuleius and of Pliny's letters Bern 136, in turn, is a direct copy of Florence, Biblioteca Medicea Laurenziana MS San Marco 284, s. xi (F), a manuscript which produced several offspring in France.[6] For its text of Cicero's orations Bern 136 is, according to Petersen, a direct copy of Paris, Bibliothèque MS lat. 7794, s. ix (P), the oldest and most important witness to this group of orations.[7] Apparently, at some point in the mid-twelfth century all three manuscripts — San Marco 284, lat. 7794, Bern 136 — were in the same place. We know nothing more of Bern 136's origin or provenance save that it was used by Nicholas of Clemanges in the early fifteenth century[8] and that it belonged to the Orléans lawyer Pierre Daniel in the mid-sixteenth century.

The second, a far more famous manuscript, Vatican MS Vat. lat. 4929, s. ix, supplied the text of Censorinus, the Pseudo-Plautine *Querolus*, and Julius Paris's *Epitome* of Valerius Maximus. Vat. lat. 4929 was first studied in depth by Claude Barlow, and was subsequently shown by Billanovich to have belonged to Lupus's pupil, Heiric of Auxerre.[9] Besides the *Querolus* and Censorinus it contains three geographical texts edited in Ravenna in the sixth century by Rusticius Helpidius Domnulus, Julius Paris's *Epitome* of Valerius, Pomponius Mela's *Chorographia*, and Vibius Sequester's *De fluminibus*; for these last three texts Vatican lat. 4929 is the ancestor of all surviving copies. Of the texts in Vat. lat. 4929, extracts from the *Querolus* and Censorinus follow one another at the end of the *Florilegium Angelicum*; and extracts from

---

[6] Besides Bern 136, the surviving manuscripts descendent from F are Leiden, Rijksbibliotheek MS B.P.L. 199, s. xiii, France; Rouen, Bibl. mun. MS 1111 (s. xiii, Lyre OSB); and a group of hitherto unnoticed extracts in Paris, B.N. MS lat. 18104 pt. III fols. 160v–161, s. xiii. The letters and Apuleius are also found together in the late twelfth-century catalog of St. Martial of Limoges, and in the list of books left to Bec by Philip of Harcourt in 1164. See R. A. B. Mynors, *C. Plini Secundi epistularum libri decem* (Oxford 1963) v-xxii; and see below.

[7] W. Peterson, "Cicero's *Post reditum* and Other Speeches," *The Classical Quarterly* 4 (1910) 167–177; and A. C. Clark, *The Descent of Manuscripts* (Oxford 1918) 266–280.

[8] Peterson op. cit. demonstrated that the text of these orations in Paris, B.N. MS lat. 14749 (Σ), s. xv, derive from Bern MS 136 rather than from its parent, B.N. MS lat. 7794; and Gilbert Ouy has identified the writer of MS 14749 as Nicholas of Clemanges. Ouy's discovery was announced in the *Annuaire de l'École des hautes études* (1965–1966) 259. A full study of Clemange's hand is still awaited.

[9] C. Barlow, "Codex Vaticanus latinus 4929," *Memoirs of the American Academy in Rome* 15 (1938) 87–124 and plates 11–18; and G. Billanovich, "Dall'antica Ravenna alle biblioteche umanistiche," *Aevum* 30 (1956) 319–353.

Julius Paris's *Epitome* appear in the last quire of Pal. lat. 957, oldest surviving copy of the *florilegium*. Vat. lat. 4929 is the only complete manuscript of the *Epitome*. A collation of the extracts from the *Querolus* shows that the text of the *Florilegium Angelicum* shares five readings with Vat. lat. 4929 against the other manuscripts of the *Querolus*; three of these are from the text of Vat. lat. 4929, and two derive from the late eleventh- or early twelfth-century glosses on the text, unique to Vat. lat. 4929.[10] The extracts from Julius Paris's *Epitome* in Pal. lat. 957 contain four readings which tie them to Vat. lat. 4929; again three of these derive from specific corrections made to the text of Vat. lat. 4929 by the glossator.[11] There can be little question that the compiler of the *Florilegium Angelicum* had this manuscript in his hands sometime in the second half of the twelfth century.

Where was Heiric's manuscript at that time? Its sister manuscript for the text of the *Querolus*, Leiden, Bibliotheek der Rijksuniversiteit MS Voss. lat. Q. 83, s. ix[1], belonged to Fleury and then in the mid-sixteenth century to Pierre Daniel. Its text of the *De fluminibus* was copied at least once, producing Vatican MS Reg. lat. 1561, s. xii[2]; this also later belonged to Daniel.[12] Vat. lat. 4929 itself contains on fol. 196v a late tenth- or early eleventh-century list of parishes and their tithes under the administration of a certain Arnulf. The parishes have been localized in the diocese of Orléans, and the writer of the list is probably to be identified with Arnulf, bishop of Orléans 973–1003.[13] Thus, Heiric's manuscript was almost certainly at Orléans at the end of the tenth century. And it remained there, to judge from the glosses of the late eleventh- or early twelfth-century scholar or scholars who annotated the manuscript. Among the glosses and additions are two concerning the Loire,[14] one of them being a line from Tibullus.[15] The writer's corrections, glosses and commentary on the *Querolus* show that he was learned. Like Heiric before him, he corrected the manuscript and was concerned with correct separation of words and the proper use of capital letters. He also knew

---

[10] Regarding the transmission of the *Querolus* see G. Ranstrand, *Querolusstudien* (Stockholm 1951). His edition is used above: *Querolus sive Aulularia*, Acta universitatis Gotoburgensis 57 (Göteborg 1951). The readings are quoted above, p. 108.

[11] The *Epitome* is cited from C. Kempf, *Valerius Maximus* (Stuttgart 1966) 472–591. The readings are quoted above, p. 108.

[12] Regarding the *De fluminibus* see R. Gelsomino, ed., *Vibius Sequester* (Leipzig 1967) xx; MS Reg. lat. 1561 is incorrectly dated s. xiii.

[13] Barlow (n. 9 above) 99–100. The list is printed by L. Delisle, "Notices sur vingt manuscrits du Vatican," *Bibliothèque de l'École des chartes* 37 (1876) 487–488.

[14] Barlow 123 and plate 18.

[15] See below at n. 107.

Greek, according to Barlow, suggesting that he may have been a master at the schools in Orléans.[16]

Lesser evidence corroborates that of Vat. lat. 4929. The persistent appearance of manuscripts connected with the *Florilegium Angelicum*, such as Bern 136, in the library of the Orléans jurist and sometime *bailli* of Fleury Pierre Daniel, many of whose books came from Fleury and Orléans, is a tell-tale circumstance.[17] In addition to those already mentioned, the manuscript containing the earliest extract from the *Florilegium*, namely, two *sententiae* from the *Attic Nights*, now Bern MS 633 fol. 34v (s. xii[2]) also belonged to Daniel. Moreover, whereas one commonly thinks of *florilegia* as collections of moral *sententiae*, the quotations in the *Florilegium Angelicum* were selected strictly for their eloquence and tailored for use in public pronouncements and in letters; and the preeminence of Orléans as a school of *ars dictaminis* is well known. Alexander III, for example, employed three masters from Orléans in his chancery.[18]

Over all, then, when one considers both the indications and the implications, the evidence strongly suggests that Orléans was the home of the *Florilegium Angelicum* and the resting place, at least temporarily, of the compiler's manuscript sources.

The second collection of extracts that sheds some light on our questions is the *Florilegium Gallicum* (FG). Studied by Ullman and Gagnér, it was considered, until the discovery of the *Florilegium Angelicum*, the most important twelfth-century collection of extracts from Latin classical authors.[19] The *Florilegium Gallicum* dates from the mid-twelfth century; it was used, as Gagnér has shown, by the compiler of the *Moralium dogma philosophorum*. Considerably larger than the *Florilegium Angelicum*, it contains extracts from thirty-six verse texts and thirty-four prose texts. Among these are a number of very rare works, for some of which the extracts in the *Florilegium Gallicum* figure prom-

---

[16] Barlow 105–107.

[17] A full study of Daniel's library is still awaited. Good introductions are provided by E. Pellegrin, "Membra disiecta floriacensia," *Bibliothèque de l'École des chartes* 117 (1959) 1–56, esp. 1–9; and A. Vidier, *L'historiographie à Saint-Benoît-sur-Loire et les miracles de saint Benoît* (Paris 1965) 30–33.

[18] Noted in letters 65 and 85 of Stephen of Tournai, PL 211.356–357, 380–381.

[19] The *Florilegium Gallicum* is the subject of a series of articles by B. L. Ullman on classical authors in medieval *florilegia*, in *Classical Philology* 23 (1928) 128–174; 24 (1929) 109–132; 25 (1930) 11–21 and 128–154; 26 (1931) 21–30; 27 (1932) 1–42; and of A. Gagnér, *Florilegium Gallicum*, Skrifter utgivna av Vetenskaps-societeten i Lund 18 (1936), and Jakob Hamacher, *Florilegium Gallicum: Prolegomena und Edition der Exzerpte von Petron bis Cicero de oratore* (Frankfurt 1975). *Addendum:* See now also Rosemary Burton, *Classical Poets in the "Florilegium Gallicum"* (Frankfurt 1983).

inently in the stemma—works such as Valerius Flaccus, Ovid's Epistle of Sappho in the *Heroides*, Tibullus, Petronius—and the *Laus Pisonis*, for which FG is the only surviving text. Like the *Florilegium Angelicum*, the *Florilegium Gallicum* existed in more than one copy. It survives wholly or in part in at least twelve manuscripts.[20] The number of unusual authors and texts represented in these two *florilegia* and the relatively large circulation that each enjoyed suggest that they were compiled in an area which was a crossroads: a place to which books were brought, at which they were copied, from which they were carried away. As with the *Florilegium Angelicum*, we shall look for the origin of the *Florilegium Gallicum* through a study of its sources.

The extracts from Cicero's *De oratore* provide some indication of the area in which the *Florilegium Gallicum* originated. Surviving manuscripts of the *De oratore* descend from two ancestors, the one complete, the other mutilated.[21] The complete manuscript, containing the *De oratore*, the *Brutus* and the *Orator*, was discovered at the cathedral of Lodi in 1421 by Gerardo Landriani and was copied a number of times before it vanished.[22] The extracts in the *Florilegium Gallicum* stem from the mutilated family, whose archetype was situated somewhere in northern Europe in the early ninth century. From it descend the copy written by Lupus of Ferrières in the mid-ninth century (now British Library MS Harley 2736 [H]),[23] presumably from a text supplied by Einhard from Fulda; and a sister manuscript no longer extant which produced Avranches, Bibliothèque municipale MS 238, s. ix (A), which belonged to Mont-St-Michel,[24] and a postulated sister of MS 238, from which Hadoard, librarian of Corbie, drew sentences for his *florilegium* (Vatican MS Reg. lat. 1762) and from which Erlangen MS 848 fols. 80–146, s. x (E), descends. Leiden, Universiteitsbibliotheek MS Voss. O. 26, s. xii, of French origin and descended from E, contains substantial extracts from the *De*

[20] Arras, Bibliothèque municipale MSS 64, s. xiii, and 305 fols. 1–63v, s. xiv[1]; Berlin, Deutsche Staatsbibliothek MS Diez. B. Sant. 60, s. xiii; Escorial, Real biblioteca MS Q. I 14 fols. 1–216v; Heidelberg, Universitätsbibliothek MS Sal. 9.62, s. xiii; Paris, Bibliothèque de l'Arsenal MS 711 fols. 182–243, s. xii; Paris, B.N. MSS lat. 7647 fols. 34–185v, s. xii[2], 8089, s. xv, 15172, s. xiii, and 17903 fols. 1–160v, s. xiii; Salamanca, Biblioteca universitaria MS 2306, s. xvi; Tortosa, Biblioteca de la catedral MS 80 fols. 1–98, s. xiii[2].

[21] See K. F. Kumaniecki, ed., *De oratore* (Leipzig 1969) v–xl, and the studies cited there.

[22] Given that fact, it is startling to notice that these three texts were known to Richard de Fournival; *Biblionomia* item 28, "Ejusdem orator libri tres, et quartus Brutus, et quintus orator, in uno volumine."

[23] C. H. Beeson, *Lupus of Ferrières as Scribe and Critic* (Cambridge, Mass. 1930).

[24] The first flyleaf in Avranches MS 162 is two leaves of a copy of this manuscript, containing 3.28–30, 3.30–48.

oratore. One other early manuscript exists but has not been reported: Berlin, Deutsche Staatsbibliothek lat. fol. MS 252, containing the collection of Cicero texts brought together by Wibald of Corvey in the mid-twelfth century.[25] The extracts from the *De oratore* in the *Florilegium Gallicum* seem most closely related to Lupus's manuscript, H, which contains all of the passages extracted, while A, E and the Leiden codex do not. Moreover, E, which contains nearly all of the extracts, is full of errors that do not recur in the *florilegium*: for example, ed. Kumaniecki 1.30 *paucis* E: *perpaucis* H, flor. (recte); 1.31 *exornata* E: *ornata* H, flor. (recte); 2.62 *in dicendo scribendo* E: *in scribendo* H, flor. (recte). We lack the acid test of filiation, agreement of H and the *florilegium* in error, because H has none in these passages. Given the paucity of manuscripts, this at least suggests that it would be sensible to look for a Loire home for the *Florilegium Gallicum*.

   With that in mind, it comes as less of a surprise to note that the extracts in the *Florilegium Gallicum* from Cicero's orations and from the *Querolus* are closely related textually to those in the *Florilegium Angelicum*. The *Florilegium Gallicum* contains extracts from the orations and other Ciceronian texts in this order: *Pro Marcello, Pro Ligario, Pro rege Deiotaro, Pridie quam in exilium iret, Pro Sestio, Pro Caelio*, Catilinarians, *Post reditum ad quirites, In Vatinium, De domo sua, De provinciis consularibus, De haruspicum reponsis, Pro Balbo*, Ps.-Sallust *In Ciceronem*, Ps.-Cicero *In Sallustium*, Philippics. With the exception of the *Post reditum in senatu*, the compiler of the *Florilegium Gallicum* has drawn on the whole group of orations cited in the *Florilegium Angelicum*, that typified by B.N. MS lat. 7794, s. ix (P). The *Florilegium Angelicum* took its extracts from Bern MS 136, which Clark and Petersen agree is a direct copy of P made in the mid-twelfth century. Where did the extracts in the *Florilegium Gallicum* come from? Chronologically, Bern 136 is probably too late to have served as the source. Textually, the extracts in the *Florilegium Gallicum* are closer to P than to any other surviving medieval manuscript. Significant variants eliminate the other three surviving pre-thirteenth-century manuscripts.[26] There are two instances, however, in which the text in the *Florilegium Gallicum* agrees

---

[25] This manuscript figures in a number of stemmas discussed in this essay. The evidence that associates it with Wibald of Corvey is ably pulled together by R. G. M. Nisbet, ed., *M. Tulli Ciceronis in L. Calpurnium Pisonem oratio* (Oxford 1961) xxiii–xxiv; and by P. Lehmann, "Corveyer Studien," in his *Erforschung des Mittelalters* 5 (Stuttgart 1962) 111–112, 131–133.

[26] Berlin, Deutsche Staatsbibliothek MS 252, s. xii, Wibald of Corvey (E); Brussels, Bibliothèque royale MS 5345, s. xi, Gembloux (G); and London, British Library MS Harley 4927, s. xii, France, Petrarch (H).

with the rest of the tradition, against an error in P: *Pro Caelio* 8, *a veorum* P^1: *ab eorum* P^2: *a verborum* GEH, flor.; *Pro Balbo* 45, *arte* P: *artem* GEH, flor. While these might conceivably represent learned corrections, more likely the extracts in the *Florilegium Gallicum* derive from a manuscript no longer extant, a parent or sister of P. In Leiden, MS Voss. lat. F. 67, a composite manuscript, fols. 1–2 comprise a fragment of the *Pro Sestio* (41.88–46.99), which Bischoff says was written around 860 in the area of the Loire.[27] Collation dissociates this text from the other surviving manuscripts and affiliates it closely with P. On the one hand, two readings seem to link the Leiden fragment (L) with the ancestor of G: ed. Peterson 42.91 line 1, *disputatos* L^1G^1: *disparatos* G^2: *dissupatos* L^2i.m., P, ed.; and 44.95 line 21, *diem* om. LG, add. L^2i.m., hab P. On the other hand, this reading at 42.91 line 1 seems significant: *eosque aut ex haec feritate* L: *eosque . . . ex ecferitate* P: *eosque ex feritate* GH, ed. And one has also these five: 41.89 lines 1–2, *id eumquam* L^1P^1: *id umquam* L^2P^2 cett.: *id eum umquam* ed.; 43.94 line 14, *hoc* LP^1: *hos* P^2 cett.: *ilios* ed.; 43.94 line 17, *quisque illas* L: *quisque ilias* L^1 (L^2?): *quisqueilas* P^1: *quisquilias* P^2 cett., ed.; 43.95 line 23, *adduceretur* LP: *adducere* G: *adducetur* H, ed.; 43.95 lines 29–30, *facinorosorum* LP: *facinerosorum* ed. (cett.?). L is neither ancestor nor descendant of P, but it is possibly P's sister.[28] Such a small portion of the text survives that only one of the passages excerpted for the *Florilegium Gallicum* occurs, one with no *variae lectiones*. However, this sentence (and no other, in four pages) is singled out with a paragraph mark in the margin. This, along with its position as sister to P, makes the Leiden fragment—or, rather, the lost whole text—the prime candidate as source for the extracts from the orations in the *Florilegium Gallicum*. We assume that the ninth-century P was still in or around Orléans in the mid-twelfth century when it was copied into Bern 136. Was its sister, written in the Loire valley, still in the region in the mid-twelfth century, to be used by the *Florilegium Gallicum*?

When we turn to the *Florilegium Gallicum*'s text of the *Querolus*, we are on firm and familiar ground. In this instance the compiler of the *Florilegium Gallicum* has used the very manuscript, Heiric of Auxerre's volume (Vat. lat. 4929), that was drawn upon by the *Florilegium Angelicum*. Moreover, the compiler of the *Florilegium Gallicum* used

---

[27] K. A. de Meyier, *Codices Vossiani Latini* 1 (Leiden 1973) 130.

[28] Concerning the medieval circulation of these orations, see T. Maslowski and R. H. Rouse, "The Manuscript Tradition of Cicero's Post-Exile Orations: Pt. 1., The Medieval History," *Philologus* 128 (1984) 60–104; and R. H. Rouse and M. D. Reeve, "Cicero: Speeches," in *Texts and Transmission: A Survey of Latin Classics*, ed. L. D. Reynolds (Oxford 1983) 54–98.

Vat. lat. 4929 independently: while there is some overlap in the extracts included in each collection, neither can derive from the other. As was the case with the extracts in the *Florilegium Angelicum*, those in the *Florilegium Gallicum* agree with Vat. lat. 4929 against the other whole texts of the *Querolus*. The interlinear glosses in Vat. lat. 4929 have also dropped into the text of the *Florilegium Gallicum*: ed. Ranstrand 20.15, *esse felicem non sinunt* V (*esse felicem non* V^3 in ras.), flor.: *inesse felicem sinunt* cett.; 23.15, *fugaces feras vel pugnaces* V (V^3 in ras.), flor.: *pugnaces feras vel fugaces* cett.; 9.21, *satis* (*tibi* spscr. V^3) *aliisque* V: *tibi aliisque* flor.: *satis aliisque* cett. In other words, within a rather short time of one another, the compilers of the *Florilegium Gallicum* and the *Florilegium Angelicum* each had in his hands Heiric's manuscript. Given that both *florilegia* drew on Vat. lat. 4929, which was associated with Orléans above, it is not surprising to find that the oldest complete manuscript of the *Florilegium Gallicum*, B.N. MS lat. 7647, belonged to Pierre Daniel in the mid-sixteenth century,[29] and that the oldest partial copy, Bibliothèque de l'Arsenal MS 711, once contained extracts from Pomponius Mela.[30]

The private library of interest to this study is that of Richard de Fournival, author of the *Bestiaire d'amour* and, probably, the *De vetula*, who died in 1260 as chancellor of the cathedral of Amiens.[31] During his lifetime Fournival amassed a collection of some three hundred books, certainly one of the largest and, in terms of content, one of the most interesting medieval libraries.[32] A catalog of a substantial portion of the collection, the *Biblionomia*, survives. The library—with the exception of the medical books, which were sold—passed to the recently founded

---

[29] Two leaves from the first part of MS 7647, containing the *Distinctiones monasticae*, were recently found in Leiden Voss. lat. Q. 2 fols. 57–58 (Paul Petau); see Pellegrin (n. 17 above) 52.

[30] Arsenal MS 711 has lost folios 244–282; fortunately their contents were recorded on the flyleaf of the manuscript and in the fifteenth-century catalog of St. Victor by Claude de Grandrue. Fols. 244–248 are now Hamburg, Staats- und Universitätsbibliothek MS 53c in scrin.; see T. Brandis and W. W. Ehlers, "Zu den Petronexzerpten des *Florilegium Gallicum*," *Philologus* 118 (1974) 85–112.

[31] Regarding Richard see R. H. Rouse, "Manuscripts belonging to Richard de Fournival," *Revue d'histoire des textes* 3 (1973) 253–269. The following have been discovered since the appearance of the article: *Biblionomia* 27 = Leiden Voss. lat. Q. 103 (s. xii[2]; G. of Abbeville; Sorbonne 1338 cat. LI:11), Cicero *De inventione; Biblionomia* 161 = New York Academy of Medicine MS Safe, s. xiii, Medica. This latter is the first of Fournival's medical books to have reappeared. It belonged to St. Augustine's, Canterbury, and is no. 1274 in the catalog as edited by M. R. James, *The Ancient Libraries of Canterbury and Dover* (Cambridge 1903) 347.

[32] Of equivalent interest in terms of their classical content, only those of Philip of Harcourt and Petrarch come to mind.

Collège de Sorbonne through the agency of Gerard of Abbeville, canon of Amiens and a friend of Robert de Sorbon, to become the nucleus of the college library.[33] The Sorbonne produced a sequence of catalogs of its books, culminating with the catalog of 1338 in which the contents, the donor, and the opening words of the second and penultimate folios are given for each book in the unchained library, thus permitting precise identification of the manuscripts which once belonged to Fournival. Because of the interest of the Sorbonne in its books, thirty-eight manuscripts, corresponding to forty-four entries in the *Biblionomia*, have thus far been identified.

Fournival's manuscripts came from a number of places. The works of the Amiens poet Richard of Gerberoy (*Biblionomia* 114) and of Nicholas of Amiens (*Bibl.* 103–104) he probably acquired at Amiens itself. A number of other works—the *Astronomy of Nimrod* (*Bibl.* 53), the commentary of Grillius on Cicero's *De inventione* (*Bibl.* 32), Fournival's copy of Abu Ma'shar's *Introductorium*—lead to Saint Victor in Paris.[34] For other works in the *Biblionomia*, Orléans would seem to be the likeliest source; such, for example, is Fournival's *Florilegium Angelicum* (*Bibl.* 84), discussed above. Let us consider two other examples, of texts that seem to have been disseminated wholly or principally from the Loire schools.

The first is Cicero's *Epistulae ad familiares*.[35] From Fournival's *Biblionomia* one cannot tell whether his copy contained these, or the letters to Atticus: "29. *Eiusdem [Ciceronis] liber epistolarum*." However, one can see from the opening words of the second and penultimate folios, recorded in the Sorbonne catalog of 1338, that Fournival's manuscript was the *Ad familiares*, and that it was a manuscript of the X family, since it contained only books 1–8.[36] The manuscripts of this family were disseminated from the Loire. Lupus of Ferrières owned a manuscript of the letters, and in 847 wrote to Ansbold of Prum saying that he would collate it with the copy that Ansbold had sent him.[37] That the

---

[33] Regarding the college library see chap. 9 below, "The Early Library of the Sorbonne."

[34] A fuller discussion of the St. Victor background of these three works is given by R. H. Rouse, "The A Text of Seneca's Tragedies in the Thirteenth Century," *Revue d'histoire des textes* 1 (1971) 108–111.

[35] L. Mendelssohn, M. *Tulli Ciceronis epistularum libri XVI* (Leipzig 1893); K. Weyssenhoff, "Les manuscrits des lettres de Cicerón dans les bibliothèques médiévales," *Eos* 56 (1966) 281–287; L. A. Constans, ed., *Cicerón: Correspondance* 1, Collection Budé (Paris 1969) 14–26.

[36] "Epistole Tullii ex legato eiusdem [G. de Abbatisvilla]. Incipit in 2° folio *Pompeius* [1.2.1], in pen. *te iubet* [8.6.5 (que iubet)]"; Delisle (n. 4 above) 3 (1881) 61.

[37] *The Letters of Lupus of Ferrières*, ed. and trans. G. W. Regenos (The Hague 1966) 81.

manuscript referred to contained books 1–8 is suggested by the fact that Lupus shows a knowledge of *Ad fam.* 5.12.3 and 1.9.23, in his letters 49 and 56.[38] In addition, his pupil Heiric of Auxerre cites 5.16.5.[39] Lupus's books remained on the Loire; among those that left Ferrières some passed to Fleury, others to Tours.[40] It is not surprising to see the *Ad familiares* at Tours and Cluny, which were closely associated with Fleury.

The X family of these letters is represented by three medieval manuscripts. British Library MS Harley 2773 fols. 32–60, s. xi–xii (G), was part of the J. G. Graevius library, some of which came from Cologne;[41] and this family of the letters may have passed to Cologne from Tours, as did Cicero's Verrines. Tours Bibliothèque municipale MS 688 fols. 30v–63v, s. xii–xiii (St. Martin of Marmoutiers near Tours), is a direct copy of the letters in Paris, B.N. MS lat. 17812, s. xii (R), suggesting that the latter was in the area of Tours. We shall meet B.N. lat. 17812 again, in discussing Fournival's copy of the Philippics; and for its text of *De natura deorum*, according to van den Bruwaene, MS 17812 "est copié incontestablement sur V"[42]—Vienna, Nationalbibliothek MS lat. 189, s. ix, Lupus of Ferrières. In short, although Fournival's text itself does not survive to be collated, it seems likely that any X-family manuscript at this date must have come from the Loire valley, most probably from Orléans.

To round out our consideration of Fournival's manuscript of the *Ad familiares*, we might note that Nicholas of Clemanges knew books 1–8 of these letters, as did his colleague and correspondent Jean de Montreuil. Nicholas refers to the letters and cites *Ad fam.* 1.1, 5.7, and perhaps 7.5, in a letter written to Jean de Montreuil about 1407.[43] He was presumably drawing on a French manuscript, because he had not come into contact with Salutati in Florence. Clemanges found his copies of Cicero's Verrines and *De legibus* among Fournival's books at the Sorbonne; was that not also the source of his knowledge of Cicero's letters?[44]

---

[38] Ibid. 67–68, 71–72.

[39] MGH *Poetae latini aevi Carolini* 3.431.27.

[40] E. Pellegrin, "Les manuscrits de Loup de Ferrières . . . ," *Bibliothèque de l'École des chartes* 115 (1957) 5–31.

[41] A. C. Clark, "The Library of J. G. Graevius," *The Classical Review* 5 (1891) 370.

[42] M. van den Bruwaene, *Cicerón de natura deorum*, Collection Latomus 107 (Brussels 1970) 37–38.

[43] Weyssenhoff (n. 35 above) 283; *Nicolai de Clemangiis Catalaunensis Opera omnia,* Epp. (Leiden 1613) 86, 95; E. Ornato, *Jean de Montreuil: Opera* 1 (Turin 1963) 84, 203, where he cites epp. 1.9 and 5.13.5, and refers to having his copy bound.

[44] The thirteenth-century catalogs of St. Victor at Marseilles and Rolduc near Liège also refer to copies of the letters, but it is impossible to determine if these are the *Ad*

The second example is Cicero's Philippic orations. Fournival's manuscript of the Philippics was recently identified as Paris, B.N. MS lat. 6602. For its text of the Philippics MS 6602 belongs to the *familia Colotiana*, a group of four manuscripts identified by A. C. Clark that descended from a manuscript which was written in insular script and which belonged to Angelo Colocci in the sixteenth century.[45] We now know substantially more about the origins of the four manuscripts than was known when Clark identified the family at the turn of the century. The first, Paris B.N. MS lat. 5802, which Clark suggested was written in Italy in the thirteenth century (perhaps because it later belonged to Petrarch), was actually written in France before 1164, by which date it had been given to the abbey of Bec in Normandy with the books of Philip of Harcourt, bishop of Bayeux, who died in that year. It can be identified as item 79 in the twelfth-century catalog of the abbey.[46] The manuscript itself is decorated in a style which flourished at Chartres, and was almost certainly written at the cathedral or at the abbey of Saint Pierre.[47] B.N. MS lat. 6602, which Clark says, on the authority of Omont, was written in the Ile de France in the thirteenth century, is, more precisely, one of a group of small manuscripts written for Fournival; it can thus be dated to the period 1230–1260.[48] The third manuscript is presently in two parts; but it was written by one hand and, hence, was a unit in origin. The first part, Berlin Deutsche Staatsbibliothek MS Phillipps 1794 (Rose 201) fols. 3–25v, s. xii, contains, in addition to the Philippics, poems ascribed to Rivallon, archdeacon of Nantes; Cicero's *De legibus* 1–2; and the *De divinatione* 1–2.[49] Part two, now Paris B.N. MS lat. 8049, contains the remainder of the *De divinatione*, Petronius's *Satyricon*, and Calpurnius's *Eclogues*. For Petronius it is one of four surviving pre-fourteenth-century manuscripts, among which are included

familiares; M. Manitius, *Handschriften antiker Autoren in mittelalterlichen Bibliothekskatalogen*, Zentralblatt für Bibliothekswesen suppl. 67 (Leipzig 1935) 22, 28.

[45] A. C. Clark, "The Textual Criticism of Cicero's Philippics," *Classical Review* 14 (1900) 39–48.

[46] Item 79: "In alio Suetonius, et Julius Frontinus, et Eutropius, et Tullius Tusculane et Philippica ejusdem"; H. Omont, ed., *Catalogue général des manuscrits des Bibliothèques publiques de France: Départements* 2 (Paris 1888) 397. The position of the Tusculans and the Philippics is transposed, but this cannot invalidate the identification.

[47] The decoration found in manuscripts written in Chartres during the mid-twelfth century has recently been identified by François Avril, *conservateur* in the Département des manuscrits, Bibliothèque nationale, Paris, to whom I am grateful for this information.

[48] See Rouse (n. 31 above) 254–255, 259–260.

[49] Besides the description of Valentin Rose, there is a good discussion of the provenance of this manuscript in P. L. Schmidt, *Die Überlieferung von Ciceros Schrift De legibus in Mittelalter und Renaissance*, Studia et testimonia 10 (Munich 1974) 201–205 and pl. V.

the Petronius extracts in the *Florilegium Gallicum*. The poems attributed
to the archdeacon of Nantes have been shown by Wilmart to be the
work of Hildebert of Le Mans and to derive from the *Florilegium Saint-
Gratien*.[50] Pease established that the text of the *De divinatione* (divided
between Berlin 1794 and Paris 8049) descended from Vienna Österreichische Nationalbibliothek MS 189, s. ix, which once belonged to
Lupus of Ferrières.[51] For its text of the *De legibus*, Schmidt has shown
that Berlin 1794 descends at one remove from Fournival's manuscript of
the *De legibus* (*Biblionomia* 26).[52] This manuscript, now lost, was copied twice in the fifteenth century, once by Guillaume d'Euvrie (Rouen,
Bibliothèque municipale MS 1041)[53] and a second time in a manuscript
annotated by Nicholas of Clemanges which belonged to Saint Victor
(Paris, B.N. MS lat. 15084).[54] Fournival's lost *De legibus* also descended
from Lupus's volume, Vienna MS 189, when the latter was complete.
Finally, the text of the Philippics in Berlin MS 1794 contains scholia very
similar to those in Fournival's manuscript, B.N. lat. 6602. According to
Schmidt, MS 1794/lat. 8049 belonged to John, duke of Berry (1340–1416).
The fourth manuscript, Oxford, Merton College MS 311, s. xii, is part
of the *familia Colotiana* for only books 1 and 2 of the Philippics.[55] It is
written in one hand, which Clark thought to be English, of the twelfth
century. Nothing is known of its actual origin or provenance before it
appeared among the books of Thomas Tryllek, bishop of Rochester (d.
1372); but a French background is suggested by the other works that
Merton 311 contains. Besides the Philippics, it contains the *De officiis*,
for which its text is not significant, and the first two works of Cicero's
philosophical corpus, namely, the *De natura deorum* and the *De fato*.
For these van den Bruwaene has established that Merton 311 was one of
three manuscripts (along with B.N. lat. 17812 and Tours 688) which are

---

[50] A. Wilmart, "Le florilège de Saint-Gratien," *Revue bénédictine* 48 (1936) 3–40, 147–181,
235–258; idem, "Un nouveau poème de Marbode, Hildebert et Rivallon," *Revue bénédictine* 51 (1939) 169–181.

[51] A. S. Pease, *M. Tulli Ciceronis de divinatione*, University of Illinois Studies in Language and Literature 8, nos. 2–3 (Urbana 1923).

[52] Schmidt (n. 49 above).

[53] Regarding Euvrie, the writer of Rouen MS 1041, who copied other Sorbonne books,
see Schmidt 60–61.

[54] Regarding B.N. MS lat. 15084 see Schmidt 58–69 and pl. II.

[55] F. M. Powicke, *The Medieval Books of Merton College* (Oxford 1931) 29, 31, 180.
Fol. 100 contains the household of an unidentified fourteenth-century ecclesiastical figure,
edited in R. W. Hunt et al., *The Survival of Ancient Literature: Catalogue of an Exhibition . . .* (Oxford 1975), app. to no. 130 (B. Barker Benfield). Concerning Tryllek and
Reed see A. B. Emden, *A Biographical Register of the University of Oxford to A. D. 1500*
3 (Oxford 1959) 1906–1908, 1556–1560.

copied directly from Lupus's manuscript, Vienna 189.[56] For Fournival's Philippics, then, as for the *Ad familiares*, the evidence pretty consistently points to the Loire valley as the center of dissemination.

Finally, in addition to these two examples, one might mention that the joint transmission of two other rare texts owned by Fournival, Cicero's *De finibus* and *Posterior Academics*, is probably also to be traced back to Orléans. The complex tradition of these two has been dealt with at length elsewhere; and while the evidence is not conclusive, it strongly suggests that *De finibus-Academics*, together as a unit, were disseminated from the Loire region.[57]

The fourth and last key to the authors and texts available at Orléans which I want to examine in this essay are the marginalia left by a mid-thirteenth-century grammarian in his books, particularly in his manuscript of Papias, now Bern MS 276.[58] The marginalia consist of extensive citations of usage of rare words by ancient authors. They are written, over a period of time, in a tall spiky hand, and frequently fill up all the space available on the page. To date I have found the hand at work in five manuscripts; there are surely others to be found, one of which may reveal the annotator's identity. The five manuscripts provide indications as to where the annotator worked, and hence should be examined in some detail:

(1) Paris, Bibliothèque nationale MS lat. 8213, a late twelfth-century manuscript of Horace designated V by Holder, and said by him to descend from the ninth-century Horace in Paris, B.N. MS lat. 7973 (U),[59] which latter has been identified with the Horace in the eleventh-century catalog often attributed to Fleury and which was later owned by Pierre Daniel.[60] MS 8213 concludes with twenty verses bearing the mar-

---

[56] Van den Bruwaene (n. 42 above) 37–38.

[57] See chap. 3 above, "The Medieval Circulation of Cicero's 'Posterior Academics' and the *De finibus bonorum et malorum*."

[58] I am grateful to Professor Munk-Olsen for having alerted me to the appearance of this hand in Bern manuscripts, and to Dr. Ch. von Steiger for having allowed me to search the Bern manuscripts for its appearance and for having answered a number of queries about Bern MS 276. Regarding the annotator see M. D. Reeve and R. H. Rouse, "New Light on the Transmission of Donatus's *Commentum Terentii*," *Viator* 9 (1978) 235–249; and P. K. Marshall, Janet Martin and R. H. Rouse, "Clare College MS 26 and the Circulation of Aulus Gellius 1–7 in Medieval England and France," *Mediaeval Studies* 42 (1980) 353–394.

[59] Regarding the two, see O. Keller and A. Holder, *Q. Horatii Flacci Opera* 1 (Leipzig 1899) lxxiv; and J. Wagner, "Collation einer Horazhandschrift aus dem 12. Jahrhundert," *Jahresberichte des philologischen Vereins zu Berlin* 25 (1899).

[60] Delisle (n. 4 above) 2.365; E. Chatelain, "Un nouveau manuscrit des lettres de Sénèque," *Revue de philologie* n.s. 21 (1897) 53 n. 5; G. Becker, *Catalogi bibliothecarum antiqui*

ginal rubric, "Oratio R. Aurelianensis facta dum tercianis gravaretur."[61] It was copied once in the late twelfth century, according to Holder, to produce Basel, Universitätsbibliothek MS F. IV 26, the early history of which is unfortunately lost.[62] MS 8213 itself does not emerge again until it appears in the possession of the French classical scholar Denys Lambin (1520–1572), from whom it passed to Cardinal Mazarin.

(2) Bern, Burgerbibliothek MS 276, an early thirteenth-century volume containing the dictionaries of Papias and Huguccio. The Papias is the most heavily annotated of the manuscripts identified to date. In the fourteenth century it belonged to John of Guignecourt.[63] As I have described elsewhere, the manuscript in the second half of the sixteenth century belonged to Pierre Daniel; and, surprisingly enough, Daniel seems to say that he acquired MS 276 from Fleury.[64] How it came to Fleury is not known. The manuscript passed with Daniel's books to the library of Jacques Bongars, and thence to the Burgerbibliothek, Bern.

(3) Bern, Burgerbibliothek MS C 219 pt. I fols. 1–8v (J. Bongars) is a late tenth- or early eleventh-century fragment of Cicero's *Topica*, and figures in A. S. Wilkin's Oxford edition as β.[65] MS C 219 is a composite manuscript containing four fragments of disparate origin; there is no indication when the four were brought together.

(4) Bern, Burgerbibliothek MS 291 (J. Bongars), an early thirteenth-century manuscript of Isidore's *Etymologiae* and Bede's *De orthographia*; like MS C 219, its origin and medieval provenance are unknown.

(5) Vatican, MS Palat. lat. 1514, Cicero's *Tusculan Disputations*. Folios 1–95 (*Tusc.* to 4.4) are of mid-eleventh-century central Italian origin, according to Lehmann. The manuscript was completed in the late twelfth (Lehmann: the thirteenth) century, and folios 96–97 are restored in an early fourteenth-century hand. The early portion figures as P in the

---

(Bonn 1885) 45 no. 15. The catalog was most recently published by Vidier (n. 17 above) 216, from Bern MS 433 fol. 79v. The latter, however, does not have a proven Fleury background.

[61] M. T. Vernet, "Notes de Dom André Wilmart sur quelques manuscrits latins anciens de la Bibliothèque nationale de Paris," *Bulletin d'information de l'Institut de recherche et d'histoire des textes* 8 (1959) 37–38; Vidier (n. 17 above) 56 n. 195. The oration was published from this manuscript by A. Holder in the *Neues Archiv der Gesellschaft für ältere deutsche Geschichtskunde* 1 (1876) 416.

[62] A reproduction of the manuscript can be seen in C. Kirchner, *Novae quaestiones Horatianae* (Nuremberg 1847) 5–7 plate 3 n. 14. I am grateful to Dr. Martin Steinmann for allowing me to see a copy of the forthcoming catalog description of this manuscript.

[63] Fol. 2, "Iste liber Papie et sequens liber Ugutionis vel Ugucii sunt ad usum fratris Johannis de Guignicuria pro conventu Belvacensi."

[64] Reeve and Rouse (n. 58 above) 235–236.

[65] Cicero, *Topica*, ed. A. S. Wilkins (Oxford 1935) iii and sigla.

editions.[66] MS Palat. lat. 1514 first reappears in the 1555 catalog of the Fugger Library.[67]

The margins of these books, particularly the Bern Papias, are filled with grammatical and rhetorical annotations, the most common being examples of usage in ancient Latin authors. The annotator is familiar with the body of ancient grammarians read in the ninth century, namely, Diomede, Aper, Nonius Marcellus, Festus Pompeius, Servius, and Virgilius Grammaticus. Particularly striking for us is the fact that he cites every text that has been or will be examined in this study in connection with the other three collections, namely, Apuleius, *De deo Socratis* (FA); Pliny's letters (FA); Cicero's orations (FA, FG); *Querolus* (FA, FG); Censorinus (FA); Cicero, *De oratore* (FG, Fournival), *Epistulae ad familiares* (Fournival), Philippics (FG, Fournival), *De legibus* (Fournival), *De finibus bonorum et malorum* (Fournival), Verrines (FA, Fournival); Aulus Gellius, books 1–7 (FG, Fournival), books 9–20 (FA, FG, Fournival); Ennodius (FA); Petronius (FG); Calpurnius (FG); Nemesianus (FG); Tibullus (FG, Fournival); Propertius (Fournival); Seneca's *Tragedies* (Fournival); Plato, *Phaedo* (Fournival); and Seneca's *Dialogues*.

It is likely that the annotator cites a few of these authors wholly or at least in part from intermediate sources such as Nonius Marcellus, Servius, and Virgil the grammarian. He seems, however, to have known at first hand many if not most of the works cited. For example, insofar as I can determine, the annotator had first-hand knowledge of Plato's *Phaedo*, Seneca's *Dialogues*, Tibullus, Propertius, Gellius 1–7 and 9–20, Petronius, Calpurnius and Ennodius, each of which is important in the context of this essay.

The annotator tells us himself where he worked, in a long marginal gloss on the name *Donatus* in Bern MS 276 fol. 64, in which he tries to sort out five or six different Romans named Donatus. He cites there the "antiquum commentum Romani Donati armarii Sancte Crucis Aurelianensis IX," and refers also to a "commentum Virgilii quod est apud Sanctam χολῦβαμ σενον [Columbam, Senon']."[68] The annotator

[66] Ed. M. Pohlenz (Leipzig 1918) xv, xxiii; ed. T. W. Dougan 1 (Cambridge 1905) xxviii, xxxiv.

[67] P. Lehmann, *Eine Geschichte der alten Fuggerbibliothek* 2 (Tubingen 1960) 357 and 514.

[68] See Reeve and Rouse (n. 58 above) 237–238. At the head of the list of Donati the annotator has added, "Item Donatus praetorius, de quo dicit Donatus [= Virgilius] in libro epythomes"; see *Virgilii Maronis grammatici opera*, ed. J. Huemer (Leipzig 1886) 73.14–15. P. Daniel noticed this passage in a manuscript of Virgil the Grammarian, now Bern MS 123 fol. 29v (it omits *praetorius*), and observed in the margin, "In altero vet. cod. sic habetur: Donatus praetorius in apologetico sic fatus est [etc.]," quoted in H. Hagen,

obviously used a manuscript of a commentary of Aelius Donatus in the Chapter Library of the cathedral of Sainte Croix, Orléans, for which he gives as well the number of book chest in which it lay. He also knew that the monastery of Saint Columba in nearby Sens had a manuscript of Tib. Claudius Donatus on Virgil; this knowledge may have been only second hand, for he does not quote Donatus on Virgil. In Bern 276 he refers twice more to books that he has seen at Orléans cathedral: "Remigius in commento Martiani . . . ςιχ εςτ ιν λιβρω ςχη χρυχις αυρελ" (fol. 119), and "Littera dicitur quasi legit iter(?), ut dicit . . . [liber?] Sancte Crucis Aurelianensis" (fol. 123v). And on fol. 94v he refers to the specific chest in which a manuscript of the Pseudo-Boethian *De disciplina scholarium* is kept at nearby Fleury: "Is liber est apud Sanctum Benedictum Floriacensem in arhca (!) Boetii."[69] This fits nicely with the references to and connections with Orléans and the Orléanais in the other books annotated by this hand—the oration by Master R. of Orléans in B.N. MS lat. 8213 and the fact that the latter is a descendant of a manuscript from Fleury, or the *nota* mark beside "Liger" in the annotator's manuscript of Isidore's *Etymologiae*, Bern 291 (fol. 70), not to mention the Bongars, and hence possibly Daniel and Orléans, background for the latter manuscript and for Bern C 219.

The annotator's notes, in quantity and quality, reveal him to have been an active lexicographer. He was obviously collecting material, and his notes refer on several occasions to what I presume are his notebooks: Bern, MS 276 fol. 159, "*Orthinus*: Vide quid de orthino notavi in magno cartapello ca. h." and fol. 162, "*Pala*: Dicta sunt super hoc in parvo cartapello." The authors and works that he cites in his marginalia indicate that he worked, probably over several years, in the middle of the thirteenth century.[70] Very likely he was a master in the arts faculty at Orléans.

That the annotator worked in the same geographical area as the compilers of the *Florilegium Angelicum* and the *Florilegium Gallicum* and as Richard de Fournival is indicated by the frequency with which he draws on the same group of authors that they were using, a group of texts whose circulation in the twelfth and thirteenth centuries was centered on the Loire.

With regard to the books used by the compiler of the *Florilegium Angelicum* the annotator cites, fol. 176, *Querolus* (ed. Ranstrand 9.11),

---

Anecdota Helvetica (Leipzig 1870) 201 n. 8. This suggests the possibility that Daniel and the annotator saw the same manuscript of Virgil the Grammarian.

[69] I have not been able to identify the Fleury manuscript of this text.

[70] See Reeve and Rouse (n. 58 above) 238–239.

"Plautus in Aulularia. tu de pistrinis"; and Censorinus *De die natali*, fol. 89v, "Genus. Censorinus de die natali: unde genialis, id est, voluptuosus," and fol. 142, "Censorinus in libro de die natali ad Quintum Cerellium sic ait: mundus est organum dei secundum Dorilaum [ed. Hultsch, ca. 13.5], id est, celum. unde idem dicit ante omnia igitur dicunt actum vitamque nostram stellis tam vagis quam errantibus (!) esse subiectam earumque vario multiplicique cursu genus humanum gubernari etc. [ca. 8.2]." These suggest the presence of MS Vat. lat. 4929. Among the rarer authors in the *Florilegium Angelicum* he cites Cicero's *Oratio cum senatui gratias egit* once, the letters of the younger Pliny at least nineteen times from the ten-book family of the letters, and Ennodius's letters in at least twenty-three instances. Among the more common authors drawn on by the *Florilegium Angelicum* the annotator cites Macrobius *Saturnalia*, Apuleius *De deo Socratis*, Jerome's letters, Sidonius's letters, Seneca's letters and *De beneficiis*, Cicero's *Tusculan Disputations* (doubtless from Vat. Pal. lat. 1514), and the later books of Gellius.

The extensive use of the letters of Ennodius provides the strongest link with the *Florilegium Angelicum*, on the basis of what is known about the circulation of Ennodius.[71] The surviving manuscripts, which number no more than seven, divide into two families, the oldest being represented by a single manuscript, Brussels 9845–48, s. ix, which belonged to Lorsch.[72] The second family descends from Vatican MS Vat. lat. 3803 (V), a Corbie manuscript of the ninth century.[73] From it come two regional families, the first headed by Lambeth Palace MS 325, written in a Corbie script of the later ninth century, which went to Durham and there produced Berlin MS lat. 1715, s. xii (Fountains Abbey) and several later manuscripts.[74] The second regional family circulated on the Continent and in all probability originated in a copy of Vat. lat. MS 3803 which was taken to Orléans. It is represented by the copy of Ennodius which belonged to Philip of Bayeux, several of whose manuscripts (e.g.,

---

[71] The stemma for Ennodius is that worked out by F. Vogel, *Magni F. Ennodi Opera*, MGH Auct. ant. 7 (Berlin 1885). To the manuscript listed therein should be added Léon Cathedral MS 33 (s. xii-xiii). Concerning the medieval circulation of Ennodius, see R. H. Rouse and M. A. Rouse, "Ennodius in the Middle Ages: Adonics, Pseudo-Isidore, Cistercians, and the Schools," in *Popes, Teachers, and Canon Law in the Middle Ages,* ed. S. Choderow and J. Sweeney (Ithaca 1989), 91–113.

[72] See B. Bischoff, *Lorsch im Spiegel seiner Handschriften* (Munich 1974) 66–67.

[73] Ennodius appears in the twelfth century catalogs of Corbie, ed. Delisle (n. 4 above) 2.518–535; Catalog ii, no. 128, catalog iii, no. 243; and he is quoted by Radbert of Corbie in the prologue to his exposition on Matthew, MGM Epp. 6 (Berlin 1925) 147.33.

[74] R. A. B. Mynors, *Durham Cathedral Manuscripts to the End of the Twelfth Century* (Oxford 1939) 26.

Pliny's letters and Pomponius Mela) emanate from Orléans;[75] by the extensive extracts from a V-family manuscript in the *Florilegium Angelicum*, and by the twenty-three citations of Ennodius in Bern 276. The Ennodius at Clairvaux (now Troyes MSS 658, 461 and 469) is also of this family, as was the lost parent of two fourteenth-century manuscripts, Vatican MS Reg. lat. 129 and Vienna MS 745.[76] Ennodius clearly owes his survival to two important Carolingian abbeys, to twelfth-century Cistercian interest in the Latin Christian fathers, and to the interest in epistolary style which flourished at the school of *ars dictaminis* in Orléans.

With regard to the rarer authors known to the compiler of the *Florilegium Gallicum*, besides the *Querolus* the annotator cites Tibullus, fol. 207, "*Sacerdos* id est vates unde Tibullus in 2^{ndo} elegiarum: Phebe fave novus ingraditur" (ed. Lenz II 5.1), and fol. 229, "*Stragula*. Tibullus in primo elegiarum: nec stragula picta soporem." Neither of these lines comes from the *Florilegium Gallicum* or an intermediate source, so far as I can determine; and hence, like the *Florilegium Gallicum*, they are an independent witness to the text. Equally remarkable is the appearance of citations from Petronius; fol. 180, "*Pondo* id est librum idem asinarum vel de assis. Petronius in libro Satyrarum ipse senatus recti bonique preceptorum mille pondo auri capitolio promittere solet" (ed. Müller 88.9); fol. 231v, "*Suffragia*. Petronius in libro Satyrarum ad predam strepitumque lucri suffragia vertunt" (ed. Müller 119.40); fol. 256, "*Uva passa*. Petronius in primo libro Satyrarum: et tymbre veteres et passis uva racemis" (ed. Müller 135.14). While the first two appear also among the extracts from Petronius in the *Florilegium Gallicum* (ed. Hammacher pp. 122–138), the appearance of a variant (*vertunt* Bern 276, Müller: *vertit* FG) and the absence of the third citation make it evident that the annotator is not borrowing from the *Florilegium Gallicum* but rather from a manuscript of the *Satyricon*.

Where Petronius is, it is not surprising to find Calpurnius and Nemesianus, both of course cited as Calpurnius; fol. 203, "*Renident*, unde Calpurnius in bucolica: mille renidenti dabimus tibi cortice chyas castaneas" (ed. Verdiere 2.81); fol. 220v, "Calpurnius in bucolica: pacis opus docuit iussitque silentibus armis" (ed. Verdiere 1.76); fol. 40v,

---

[75] Becker (n. 60 above) 86.55. Philip's manuscript is very likely the one which Arnulf of Lisieux offered to copy in 1160 for Henry, cardinal priest of Sts. Nereus and Achilles; see F. Barlow, ed., *Letters of Arnulf of Lisieux* (London 1939) 36–38 ep. 27, also printed in Vogel (n. 71 above) lx-lxi, and in P. von Moos, "Literarkritik im Mittelalter: Arnulf von Lisieux über Ennodius," in *Mélanges offerts à René Crozet* (Poitiers 1966) 929–935.

[76] Vienna MS 745 belonged to Adalbertus Ranconis de Ercino, rector of Prague in the mid-fourteenth century, who acquired many of his manuscripts in trips to Paris and Avignon.

"*Cimbia*. Calpurnius in bucolica: Scillenas cymbia musto" (Nemesianus, ed. Schenkl 3.59); fol. 41v, "*Cisbium*. Cymbium . . . de quo dicit Virgilius et Calpurnius in bucolica" (Nemesianus, ed. Schenkl 1.68, 3.59); fol. 143, "Calpurnius in bucolica: Sed quia tu nostra musam de poscis avene" (Nemesianus, ed. Schenkl 1.27). Again, none of the passages appears in the extracts from Calpurnius in the *Florilegium Gallicum*, suggesting that the annotator drew on the text directly. Finally, for the rare authors it should be noted that the annotator cites the early books (1–7) of Aulus Gellius more than twenty times in Bern MS 276. Of the slightly better-known ancient authors excerpted in the *Florilegium Gallicum*, the annotator cites Cicero *De oratore*, then Philippics, the philosophical corpus (*De natura deorum, De divinatione, Timaeus, De fato, Topica, Paradoxa, Lucullus, De legibus*), as well as Martial, Sallust, Quintilian (*Inst., Declam.*) and Suetonius.

Only Calpurnius will bring one closer to the *Florilegium Gallicum* than Tibullus; hence the annotator's knowledge of the *Bucolics* and their transmission merit some comment here.[77] The surviving witnesses to the *Bucolics* group into two families. The first consists of three independent witnesses: the exemplar used by the *Florilegium Gallicum*; Paris B.N. MS lat. 8049, s. xii; and the ancestor of the twenty-six recentiores. The second family consists of readings from an old German codex, preserved by Thadeus Ugolinus, and two fifteenth-century manuscripts, Naples MS V A 8 and Florence, Biblioteca Medicea Laurenziana MS Plut. 90.12 infra, which descend from a common parent. It is interesting, in light of the paucity of older manuscripts of Calpurnius, that B.N. MS lat. 8049 (which is completed by Berlin MS Phillipps 1794, Rose 201) contains Petronius and Calpurnius, as well as Cicero's Philippics (Colotiana family) and *De legibus*, which are closely related to Fournival's manuscripts of these two works.[78] Again, we find ourselves dealing with the geographical area in which the texts of Petronius and Calpurnius emerged.

It is with the library of Richard de Fournival that a common source drawn upon by both individuals is most clearly seen. This is perhaps because the annotator and Fournival were contemporaries, whereas the two florilegists antedate the annotator by almost a century. We have seen that he knew the Verrines (as did the compiler of the *Florilegium*

---

[77] Regarding the transmission of Calpurnius see C. Giarratano, *Calpurnii et Nemesiani Bucolica* (Pavia 1924) and R. Verdiere, *T. Calpurnii Siculi de laude Pisonis et Bucolica . . .*, Collection Latomus 19 (Brussels 1954).

[78] The annotator, however, was not using B.N. lat. 8049 (P), which reads *redempti* and *cymas* at 2.81 and which did not contain Nemesianus. In the latter, the annotator's *musam* with the interpolated codices (V) against *laudem* at 1.27 places his manuscript with the ancestor of the recentiores.

Angelicum) and that (in common also with the compiler of the *Flori-legium Gallicum*) he cites the early books of Gellius, Cicero's *De oratore* and Philippics, and Tibullus, all works which appear in Richard de Fournival's library. Among the other rare works which Fournival owned, the annotator cites Cicero's *De finibus bonorum et malorum* nine times;[79] and he gives nineteen citations from the Latin translation of Plato's *Phaedo*, of which Fournival's manuscript, B.N. MS lat. 16581, s. xiii, is the oldest survivor. Last and perhaps most interesting is the appearance of five citations from Propertius, and one from Seneca's *Tragedies*. From Propertius he cites, fol. 25v, "*Berillus.* Propertius in quarto elegiarum: et solitum digito berillon adederat ignis" (ed. Barber 4.7.9); fol. 97v, "*Historia.* Unde Propertius secundo elegiarum: maxima de nichilo nascitur hystoria" (2.1.16); fol. 106v, "*Insanus.* Item Propertius in secundo elegiarum: scilicet insano nemo in amore videt" (2.14.18); fol. 170, "*Peierat.* Propertius in 4⁰ elegiarum: peierat hiberni temporum esse moras" (4.3.42); and fol. 235, "*Tegula.* Iuvenalis et Propertius pᵃhabent a theca quod est repositio vel regimen" (cf. 4.7.26).[80] Only two of the passages (those on fols. 97v and 106v) appear in the thirteenth-century extracts from Propertius, Vatican MS Reg. lat. 2120 (once a part of B.N. MS lat. 15155; see below); nor do the remaining three come from any other known intermediate source. Since they apparently represent a knowledge of the whole text, it is noteworthy that they agree (at 4.7.9) with Fournival's manuscript, Leiden Voss. lat. O. 38, against the errone-ous *beryllos* in Wolfenbüttel MS Gud. 224. The annotator cites from the Tragedies, fol. 139v, "Seneca in tragedia a qua dicitur: quidquid excessit modum pendet instabili loco" (ed. Giardina, *Oedipus* 909–910). Both of these texts are just emerging in late twelfth- and early thirteenth-century northern Europe. Fournival owned one of the two oldest surviving manu-scripts of each, the Leiden Propertius and the Paris *Tragedies* (B.N. MS lat. 8260); they were both written for him, by the same scribe.

Two works might be singled out for further comment, Plato's *Phaedo* and Seneca's *Dialogues*, because of the role played by Fournival and the Sorbonne in their transmission.[81] Plato's *Phaedo* and *Meno* were translated into Latin by Henricus Aristippus in South Italy in 1156, but they were apparently not read until the middle of the thirteenth century when the earliest surviving manuscript and quotations began to appear.

---

[79] The annotator's citations are printed in "Medieval Circulation of Cicero's 'Posterior Academics,'" above, chapter 3.

[80] Three of these citations were kindly given me by James Butrica, who has recently completed a doctoral dissertation at the University of Toronto on the transmission of Propertius.

[81] Rouse (n. 34 above).

Paris, B.N. MS lat. 16851 fols. 94–162 containing the *Phaedo* was written for Richard de Fournival, and was probably available at the Sorbonne shortly after Fournival's death in 1260, though it did not officially become part of the Sorbonne collection until the death of Gerard of Abbeville in 1272. It is not unlikely that the first school men of the thirteenth century to know the text, Roger Bacon and John of Wales, used Fournival's manuscript at the Sorbonne, just as they seem to have used other of his books. Bacon, for example, refers to Cicero's *De finibus* as the "Academic Disputations," the same title that is used in Fournival's *Biblionomia* and in the subject catalog (ca. 1320) of the Sorbonne.[82] Again, as with Tibullus, Propertius, and Seneca's *Tragedies*, the annotator has a remarkably early knowledge of a work which is just emerging in the north.

This is precisely the case as well with the *Dialogues* of Seneca, which the annotator cites at least twelve times. While they owe their survival to Monte Cassino in the eleventh century, the *Dialogues* are unknown north of the Alps before 1200.[83] John of Garland cites one line from the *Dialogues* in his *Epithalamium B. Mariae Virginis* completed about 1220–1221, but they are not really known until Roger Bacon announces their discovery in 1266 and sends Pope Clement IV an epitome of the text in his *Moralis philosophia*. Both Bacon and John of Wales are clearly familiar with the whole text of the *Dialogues*. The *Dialogues* are not included in either the *Biblionomia* or the 1338 catalog of the Sorbonne. But the Sorbonne obviously did have a copy around 1300–1306, for they are cited seven times in the *Manipulus florum* of Thomas of Ireland and described in detail in the list of books appended to it, a list that is in effect a select catalog of Sorbonne books and, for the most part, books that came from Fournival's collection.[84] The fact that the *Dialogues*

---

[82] See E. Massa, ed., *Rogeri Baconis Moralis philosophia* (Zurich 1953). Regarding the transmission of the *Phaedo* see R. Klibansky, *The Continuity of the Platonic Tradition during the Middle Ages* (London 1939) 29–31; and L. Minio-Paluello, ed., *Phaedo*, Plato Latinus 2 (London 1950).

[83] Regarding the transmission of the *Dialogues* see L. Reynolds, "The Medieval Tradition of Seneca's Dialogues," *The Classical Quarterly* 18 (1968) 353–371, whom I follow here with the exception of the suggestion regarding Thomas of Ireland and the Sorbonne.

[84] See R. H. and M. A. Rouse, *Preachers, Florilegia and Sermons: Studies on the Manipulus florum of Thomas of Ireland*, Pontifical Institute of Medieval Studies, Studies and Texts 47 (Toronto 1979) 156–160 and esp. 299 no. 9; and n. 98 below. In the *Manipulus Florum* there are quotations from "De ira": *Consideratio* al ("lib. ii ante finem"), *Consilium* x. *Ira* bc, bd; and from "De tranquilitate anime": *Ingenium* k, *Prosperitas* ar ("circa medium"), as. The quotations are corrupt and unfortunately cannot be identified with any surviving manuscript. Aside from the eleventh-century Monte Cassino manuscripts there are four thirteenth-century codices: Vatican, MS Chigi H V 153, s. xiii¹, Italy (C); Paris, B.N. MS lat. 15086, s. xiii¹, Italy, Paris, St. Victor (P); Berlin, MS lat. fol. 47,

while still very rare were known both at Orléans and at the Sorbonne, and that the first northerners to cite them at length seem to have drawn upon other texts from the Fournival collection when it was in Gerard of Abbeville's hands, suggests that it was Fournival who brought this text as well to Paris. There are, after all, others of Fournival's books which, either because they were acquired too late or for some other reason, are not included in the *Biblionomia*.[85] Perhaps the *Dialogues* were one of these.

Having examined the relationships between the Bern 276 annotations and the works cited by the other three witnesses, let us now return to three texts which not only have a demonstrable Loire background but which also serve to tie together these three witnesses—the *Florilegium Angelicum*, the *Florilegium Gallicum*, and the library of Richard de Fournival—by appearing in any two of them.

Richard de Fournival's text of Cicero's Verrine orations is closely tied to, and perhaps the source of, the extracts from the Verrines in the *Florilegium Angelicum*.[86] As I have described elsewhere,[87] the text of the Verrines, found at the palace library of Charlemagne in the late eighth century,[88] was apparently dispersed from Tours during the ninth. The oldest manuscript, the "Vetus Cluniacensis" (British Library MS Add. 47678, s. ix[1] [C]), was written in the script of Tours and passed to Cluny.[89] Aside from the manuscript of the Verrines that passed to Cologne and produced the extracts in Harley 2682, s. xi, and Berlin 252, s. xii (Wibald of Corvey),[90] there are only two other pre-thirteenth-century manuscripts of the X family: Paris, B.N. lat. 7774A s. ix (R), also written at Tours, which may once have belonged to Lupus of Ferrières;[91]

---

s. xiii, Italy (B), which Reynolds says is almost certainly a direct copy of C; Paris, B.N. MS lat. 6379, s. xiii ex., France; and Rome, Biblioteca Angelica MS 505, frag., s. xiii ex. Reynolds kindly allowed me to examine microfilms of these, but none bears notes by the annotator of Bern 276.

[85] See Rouse (n. 31 above) 257.

[86] Regarding the transmission of the Verrines see W. Peterson, "The Manuscripts of the Verrines," *Journal of Philology* 30 (1907): 161–207, and Clark (n. 102 below).

[87] See "*Florilegium Angelicum*," above, pp. 114–115.

[88] See B. Bischoff, "Die Hofbibliothek Karls des Grossen," in his *Karl der Grosse* 2. *Das geistige Leben* (Dusseldorf 1965) 42–62; and *idem, Sammelhandschrift Diez B. Sant. 66: Grammatici latini et catalogus librorum,* Codices selecti 42 (Graz 1973) 21–23, 38–39.

[89] Ed. Delisle (n. 4 above) 2.478 no. 498.

[90] The Harleian extracts are discussed by A. C. Clark who shows that the extracts in Berlin 252 descend directly from them; see A. C. Clark, "Excerpts from the Harleian MS 2682 . . . ," *Journal of Philology* 18 (1890) 69–87.

[91] Lupus knew the Verrines; and the second part of B.N. MS lat. 7774A, Cicerto *De inventione*, belonged to him and bears his annotations (Pellegrin [n. 40 above] 11–12).

and B.N. lat. 7775 (S) of the twelfth century, which in the thirteenth belonged to Richard de Fournival.[92]

It is easy to see how the Verrines, disseminated from Tours, might find their way to Orléans. But it is difficult, on the basis of only eighteen extracts, to ascertain the relationship of the *Florilegium Angelicum*'s source to the surviving manuscripts. It is reasonable to suppose that the extracts come from a text of the northern European family. The readings indicate as much, save at Actio 2 book 4.105, where the extracts read *perstringere* with the Italian or Y family against R, *praestringere*. S read *perstringere*, but has been corrected to *prestringere*. The correction appears to be medieval, but is otherwise undatable; if the correction was not made until after the compilation of the *florilegium*, then S could well have been the source. In other words, B.N. MS lat. 7775 may have been employed at Orléans by the compiler of the *Florilegium Angelicum* in the second half of the twelfth century, and acquired at Orléans in the first half of the thirteenth by Fournival.

Richard de Fournival owned two texts whose transmission is closely connected with the *Florilegium Gallicum*, namely, the first seven books of Aulus Gellius and the *Elegies* of Tibullus. Books 1–7 (book 8 is known only by its chapter headings) of the *Attic Nights* circulated separately from the later books (9–20).[93] The first seven books are used in two Continental *florilegia*. In the older of the two, the Gellius extracts alternate with extracts from Valerius Maximus. This collection, known in six manuscripts, was probably made somewhere in France north of the Loire, and antedates the surviving whole manuscripts of the first half of the *Attic Nights*.[94] The other collection of extracts, that in the *Florilegium Gallicum*, has gone unnoticed. It is independent of the Valerius/Gellius anthology, and does not descend from the surviving manuscripts. While the text of books 1–7 survives in numerous manuscripts, only four antedate the fifteenth century — Leiden, Gronovius 21 fols. 21–40v, s. xii² France (R), which Bernard Rottendorf acquired from a Rhineland house in 1650;[95] Paris, B.N. MS lat. 5765 fols. 61v–111v, s. xii, France (P), in which Aulus Gellius is preceded, as in the *Florilegium Gallicum*, by Caesar's *Gallic Wars*; Vatican MS Vat. lat. 3452

There is no firm evidence, however, to show that the Verrines in that codex belonged to him, or to show when the two manuscripts were joined.

[92] Rouse (n. 31 above) 255, 259.

[93] See P.K. Marshall, ed., *A. Gellii Noctes atticae* 1 (Oxford 1968) v–xxi.

[94] Discussed by D. Schullian, "The Anthology of Valerius Maximus and A. Gellius," *Classical Philology* 32 (1937) 70–72.

[95] P. Lehmann, "Aus dem Leben, dem Briefwechsel und der Büchersammlung eines Helfers der Philologen," in *Erforschung* (n. 25 above) 4.115–116, 119.

fols. 1–56, s. xiii, France (V); and Cambridge, Clare College MS 26 fols. 59–93v, s. xiii[1], England (C), given to the college by John Heaver, in which Gellius is preceded by a text of Quintilian's *Institutio* that belongs to a family disseminated from the Loire region.[96]

The extracts in the *Florilegium Gallicum* read first with one, then another of the manuscripts: ed. Marshall 1.17.1 line 8, *irarumque* V[2], ed.: *rarumque* V[1]R: *rerumque* PC, flor.; 2.29.7 line 27, *crastini* VR, ed.: *crastina* P, flor.; 2.29.9 line 7, *otioso animo* A(palimpsest), ed.: *amino otioso* P: *a motu* (*metu*: C) *ociosos* CVR, flor.; 2.29.14 line 23, *primo luci* P, ed.: *prima luce* CVR, flor.; 5.10.6 lines 18–19, *Protagorae* P, ed.: *Prothagorae* VR, flor.; 5.10.14 line 15, *si* PC, flor., ed.: *sic* VR. And in two instances the *florilegium* provides the correct reading against all surviving contemporary manuscripts: 5.10.7 line 24, *et* flor., om. PVR; and, from the later books, 10.23.1 line 25, *deprehendendi*. The extracts, hence, represent an independent tradition. Equally interesting is the fact that the *Florilegium Gallicum* cites the later books, 9–20, as well, raising the possibility that the compiler used a manuscript, no longer known, which contained the earlier and later books together.

The annotator of Bern MS 276, as we have seen, was clearly familiar with both the early and the later books of Gellius. He cites the early books some twenty-three times, the later thirteen times.[97] From the passages cited one can see that he is not drawing on the Valerius/Gellius anthology or on the *Florilegium Gallicum*. Instead, he very likely had access to a manuscript containing both parts of the *Attic Nights*.

A fifth pre-fifteenth century manuscript, apparently no longer extant, belonged to Richard de Fournival. It is *Biblionomia* 89, "Agelii liber noctium Atticarum." Unfortunately this manuscript was not described in the 1338 catalog of the Sorbonne; therefore, one cannot discover its contents on the basis of the opening words of the second and penultimate folios, as one could for Fournival's codex of Cicero's general letters. Books 1–7, however, as well as the later books, are quoted at some length in the *Manipulus florum* which was compiled by Thomas of Ireland at the Sorbonne and published in 1306. Thomas almost certainly was using Fournival's manuscript.[98] He quotes the *Attic Nights* seven times, five quotations from the early books and two from the

---

[96] This manuscript was recently discovered by P.K. Marshall; its place in the stemma is discussed in Marshall et al. (n. 58 above).

[97] The citations are printed, ibid., app. A.

[98] Regarding Thomas's use of Fournival's manuscripts in the bibliography appended to the *Manipulus* see R. H. Rouse, "The List of Authorities Appended to the *Manipulus florum*," *Archives d'histoire doctrinale et littérarie du Moyen âge* (1965 [1966]): 243–250; and Rouse and Rouse (n. 84 above).

later.[99] These extracts do not derive from P or R or a copy of them, but are close to V (for the early books). The small circle of those who knew the early books of Aulus Gellius now includes the compiler of the *Florilegium Gallicum*, Richard de Fournival, and the annotator of Bern 276; and there is a possibility that each knew a manuscript of the full text, including both early and later books.

Tibullus provides the clearest example of the tie between the *Florilegium Gallicum* and the library of Richard de Fournival, because of the very limited circulation of the *Elegies*.[100] The *Elegies* are mentioned in the late eighth–century list of books at the Carolingian court.[101] They are known in two eleventh-century collections of extracts, one from Freising and the other from Monte Cassino, both of which have been studied by Newton.[102] Long extracts from Tibullus appear in the *Florilegium Gallicum* in the mid-twelfth century, and short extracts appear in a group of thirteenth-century school books.[103] The surviving manuscripts of the whole text descend, as Ullman has shown, from Richard de Fournival's manuscript, which was discovered by Petrarch at the Sorbonne in 1333.[104] One can see from these traces that the Tibullus codex from the Palace School or a descendant of it must have come to rest somewhere in central France, and that a single manuscript could account for this transmission. Let us consider the possibility, as a working hypothesis, that this manuscript was at Fleury and, with the growth of the schools, passed to Orléans.

The existence of a manuscript of Tibullus at Fleury could account for the appearance of the extracts made at Monte Cassino in the eleventh century by Lawrence of Amalfi, in the absence of an Italian tradition for Tibullus and in light of the close connections between Fleury

---

[99] Thomas's quotations from the *Noctes atticae* are printed in Marshall et al. (n. 58 above), app. B. One can see from the Gellius texts represented that Thomas's source could not have been the Valerius/Gellius *florilegium* nor John of Salisbury's *Policraticus*, nor the collection that John used.

[100] See F. W. Lenz, ed., *Albii Tibulli aliorumque carminum libri tres* (Leiden 1964) 1–41. For the most recent discussion of the transmission of Tibullus, see *Texts and Transmission: A Survey of the Latin Classics*, ed. L. D. Reynolds (Oxford 1983) 420–425. I am grateful to Francis Newton, Duke University, for his help.

[101] Edited by Bischoff, *Sammelhandschrift* (n. 88 above).

[102] F. Newton, "Tibullus in Two Grammatical *Florilegia* of the Middle Ages," *Transactions and Proceedings of the American Philological Association* 93 (1962) 253–286.

[103] B. L. Ullman, "Classical Authors in Certain Medieval *Florilegia*," *Classical Philology* 27 (1932) 22–25.

[104] B. L. Ullman, "The Manuscripts of Propertius," *Classical Philology* 6 (1911) 282–301; idem, "The Library of the Sorbonne in the Fourteenth Century," in his *Studies in the Italian Renaissance* (Rome 1955) 41–53.

and Monte Cassino over the relics of Saint Benedict. The fact that this *florilegium* was probably compiled in southern Italy need not mean that it drew on a manuscript of Italian origin. The Cassino *florilegium* contains a number of northern authors, Bede, Alcuin, Rabanus and Remigius; and the anonymous *Poema ad coniugem* — selections of which accompany two of the three sets of Tibullus extracts in the Cassino *florilegium* — was known at Fleury.[105] The extracts from Tibullus in the eleventh-century *florilegium* from Freising, now Clm 6292 fol. 117, appear to descend from the codex formerly at the Carolingian court, since the works of Claudian in MS 6292 follow the virtually unique order of the Claudian described in the Carolingian booklist in Berlin Diez. B Sant. 66.[106] The Freising extracts, thus, also do not reflect an independent tradition.

At some point the text of Tibullus apparently migrated to Orléans, where it was quoted by a twelfth-century master who noticed that Tibullus knew of the Loire. In the text of the *Querolus* in Vat. lat. 4929, at the word *Ligerem*, he adds the gloss, "Ligerem dicit a nominativo Liger, quem ponit Albius Tibullus, carnutis et flavi cerula limpha Liger" (Tibullus 1.7.12).[107] Interest in elegiac poetry at the schools produced two groups of extracts from Tibullus in the course of the twelfth and thirteenth centuries. Of these, the first is that in the *Florilegium Gallicum* of the mid-twelfth century. It constitutes the largest medieval collection of extracts from Tibullus. As we have seen, the compiler of the *Florilegium Gallicum* also knew and read Vat. lat. 4929, and thus must have been working in and around Orléans. The compiler, the slightly earlier annotator of MS 4929, and the later annotator of Bern MS 276, may all three have found and used there the same manuscript of Tibullus.

The shorter collection of extracts appears in one form or another in a number of *libri manuales* used in the teaching of grammar and meter.[108] The Tibullus extracts in the manuals derive from a single set of extracts made sometime in the early thirteenth century, probably at Orléans; they are added to or mixed with Tibullus excerpts taken from the *Florilegium Gallicum*. The thirteenth-century manuscripts contain-

---

[105] Newton (n. 102 above) 266.

[106] Ibid. 280.

[107] Barlow (n. 9 above) 106, 109.

[108] Concerning the development of these manuals in general see M. Boas, "De librorum Catonianorum historia atque compositione," *Mnemosyne* 42 (1914) 17–46; S. Tafel, *Die Überlieferungsgeschichte von Ovids Carmina amatoria verfolgt bis zum 11. Jahrhundert* (Tübingen 1910); E. M. Sanford, "The Use of Classical Latin Authors in the *Libri manuales,*" *Transactions of the American Philological Association* 55 (1924) 190–248; Ullman (n. 103 above) 37–40.

ing these Tibullus extracts were identified by Ullman and, more recently, Hamacher, as Laon MS 193 (s. xiii; Premonstratensians, Cuissy); Leiden, MS Vulcan. lat. 48 (s. xiii; Celestines, Paris); London, British Library MS Harley 2745 (s. xiii^2; France); Munich, Clm 29110a (s. xiii; Buxheim); Oxford, Bodleian Library MS Add. 208 (s. xiii^1; France); Paris, B.N. MSS lat. 13582 (s. xiii; St-Maur-des-Fosses) and 15155 (s. xiii; St-Victor).[109] Another manual, Laon MS 461 (s. xiii), which, Ullman noted, contained a similar collection of texts though not Tibullus, was written by Jean de Nemours, a student at Orléans about 1220.[110] Five of the manuscripts which do contain the Tibullus extracts—Vulcan. 48, Harley 2745, Clm 29110a, B.N. lat. 15155 and the later Berlin Diez. B. Sant. 60—contain as well extracts from *Orestes*, of which the only known pre-fifteenth-century manuscript, Bern MS 45 fols. 52v–59 (s. ix), evidently originated at Fleury; and it was acquired by Pierre Daniel in 1564.[111] Hence, there are ties of subject matter and of content with the Orléanais.

The close ties between the school collection and the *Florilegium Gallicum* have been well established by Ullman and Hamacher. The latter lists eleven thirteenth-century manuscripts of this sort which have borrowed portions, usually substantial, from the *Florilegium Gallicum*.[112] In addition to those that contain Tibullus extracts named above, four others—Heidelberg, Universitätsbibliothek MS Sal. 9.62 (s. xiii), Basel, Universitätsbibliothek MS D. IV.4 (s. xiii; Dominicans, Basel), East Berlin, Deutsche Staatsbibliothek MS Phillipps 1813 (s. xiii) and Vatican, MS Reg. lat. 1625 (s. xiii^1; France)—contain extracts that derive ultimately from the *Florilegium Gallicum*; and in Berlin Diez. B. Sant. 60 the school collection is combined with the *Florilegium Gallicum*, in a single program of study proceeding from elementary to advanced texts.[113]

Of the manuscripts of these school books, B.N. lat. 15155 is particularly interesting because of its contents and provenance.[114] It contains

[109] B. L. Ullman, "Tibullus . . .," *Classical Philology* 23 (1928) 162–171; and Hamacher (n. 19 above) 59–86.

[110] Ullman (n. 103 above) 40. I am grateful to the Abbé B. Merlette for the identification of Jean de Nemours. The manuscript contains extracts from Seneca, Boethius, Petrus Alfonsus, Ovid, Claudian, Maximian, Geta, Cato, Virgil, Statius, Lucan, Juvenal, *Alexandreis*, Aesop, Horace, Prudentius and other texts religious and profane including Cicero's Tusculan Disputations.

[111] O. Homburger, *Die illustrierten Handschriften der Burgerbibliothek* (Bern 1962) 99–100 pl. 7 and xxxvi.

[112] Hamacher (n. 19 above) 59–86.

[113] Described by Ullman (n. 103 above) 39 and Gagnér (n. 19 above) 38.

[114] Portions of MS 15155 are now in Vatican MS Reg. lat. 2120 fols. 11–35; see D. M. Robathan, "The Missing Folios of the Paris *Florilegium* 15155," *Classical Philology* 33

extracts from Ovid's *Heroides*, including those from the letter of Sappho, which is otherwise known only in the *Florilegium Gallicum* and in Frankfurt, Stadt- and Universitätsbibliothek MS Barth. 110 (s. xii ex.; France). A portion of these are taken from the *Florilegium Gallicum*; but the majority are new extracts, which must, for the letter of Sappho at least, come from the same source as that used by the compiler of the *Florilegium Gallicum*.[115] Besides a selection of the shorter extracts from Tibullus, MS 15155 also contained extracts from Propertius. These extracts evidently derive from the nonextant exemplar of Fournival's Propertius, now Leiden MS Voss. lat. O. 38, s. xiii (L).[116] If MS 15155 is an Orléans manuscript, as Novati has suggested,[117] and if Fournival acquired his Propertius, as well as his Tibullus, in Orléans, then this common parent of L and of its sister, Wolfenbüttel MS Gud. 224 s. xii^2 (N), would have to have been in Orléans as well. The fact that the annotator of Bern MS 276 cites five lines of Propertius derived either from L or its parent serves to strengthen the case. It may also be noted that MS 15155 contained extracts from the *De vetula*, attributed to Richard de Fournival. Since there is only one manuscript of the *De vetula* which antedates the fourteenth century, these extracts are the oldest witnesses to the text.[118] While MS 15155 had come to rest at Saint Victor by the fifteenth century, it did not originate there; for in the fourteenth century it was sold to a Rouen master by one Henri François of Orléans.

In its day Orléans was a crossroads, as was the imperial court at Aix-la-Chapelle in the ninth century or the papal court at Avignon in the fourteenth. It was a city to which books such as B.N. MSS lat. 7794 and 7973, Medicea Laurenziana MS San Marco 284 and Vatican MS lat. 4929 were brought, at which they were quoted, extracted and copied, and from which they were carried away by a community of scholars as they moved from one place to another. Only a cosmopolitan center of literary study could account for the variety and number of rare authors

---

(1938) 188–197. The remainder was found in Bern MS 327 fols. 15–28; see E. Pellegrin, "Manuscrits de l'abbaye de Saint-Victor et d'anciens collèges de Paris . . .," *Bibliothèque de l'École des chartes* 103 (1942) 74–96.

[115] Hamacher (n. 19 above) 65, 92–94. See also H. Dörrie, *Untersuchungen zur Überlieferungsgeschichte von Ovids Epistulae Heroidum*, Nachrichten der Akademie der Wissenschaften zur Göttingen, phil.-hist. Kl. (Göttingen 1960) 364–365.

[116] I am grateful to James Butrica and Francis Newton for information regarding the place of these extracts in the tradition of Propertius.

[117] See F. Novati, "Un poème inconnu de Gautier de Chatillon," *Mélanges Paul Fabre* (Paris 1902) 267.

[118] P. Klopsch, *Pseudo-Ovidius De vetula: Untersuchungen und Text,* Mittellateinische Studien 2 (Leiden 1967); and D. M. Robathan, *The Ps.-Ovidian De vetula* (Amsterdam 1968).

found in the two *florilegia*, in the lexicographer's marginalia, and in Fournival's library, and for the widespread dispersal of these works.

* * *

In the foregoing I have attempted to add some reality to the *topos* that Orléans was a center for classical studies in the twelfth century, by proposing the names of specific ancient authors, texts, and manuscripts that were to be found there. But what happened to this study of classical authors in the next century? Again according to the *topos*, the thirteenth century witnesses the quick demise of twelfth-century humanism. Philology and her handmaidens Grammar and Rhetoric are driven from the field by Dialectic and Logic, in the *Battle of the Seven Liberal Arts*. Scholasticism reigns supreme in Paris and Oxford for the next two hundred years. Study of the authors, composition and poetry give way to the professional aspect of the *ars dictaminis,* and Orléans becomes a law school in the thirteenth century. Contemporary commentary such as Henry of Andely's poem, and the direction in which the university developed at Paris and Orléans, caused Louis John Paetow to say that the interest in humane letters which characterized the twelfth century was destroyed by the growth of scholasticism.[119] He was led to polarize these two disciplines and to pit them one against the other as mutually exclusive opposites. This was in part the result also of reading back into the thirteenth century the repugnance expressed by fifteenth-century humanists for scholastic argument.

Paetow's characterization of the fate of classical letters is still prevalent.[120] Neither the existence of figures familiar with ancient authors such as Fournival and the cataloger of the library of Saint Pons, nor the extensive number of scholastics who cite ancient Latin authors, has substantially shaken Paetow's assessment.[121] They have been all too often regarded as isolated figures, solitary throwbacks to the twelfth-century renaissance or lonely precursors of Petrarch, assuredly quite unrelated to the world of thirteenth-century scholasticism in which they lived. Instead, it is only sensible to examine those who cite the classics in the context of their own time, by asking how and to what purpose ancient authors were used in the thirteenth century. What happened, for example, to the

---

[119] See Louis J. Paetow, *Two Medieval Satires on the University of Paris: La bataille des VII ars of Henri d'Andeli and the Morale scolarium of John of Garland*, Memoirs of the University of California 4.1–2 (Berkeley 1927) 13–30.

[120] Its main purveyor is C. H. Haskins, *The Renaissance of the Twelfth Century* (Cambridge, Mass. 1927) 98f., 356; and it is from him, of course, that Paetow learned it.

[121] I am referring here in part to E. K. Rand, "The Classics in the Thirteenth Century," *Speculum* 4 (1929) 249–269.

Florilegium Angelicum and the *Florilegium Gallicum* in the thirteenth and fourteenth centuries?

Interest in both *florilegia* remains strong, to judge from the surviving manuscripts. The *Florilegium Angelicum* survives in three copies of the twelfth century, twelve manuscripts of the thirteenth century, four of the fourteenth and two of the fifteenth. The *Florilegium Gallicum* is known in two manuscripts datable to the twelfth century, five manuscripts of the thirteenth century, two of the fourteenth and two of the fifteenth. Both collections of classical extracts achieve their maximum interest in the thirteenth century, and continue to be copied into the fifteenth century. Interest in them, therefore, persists long after the "demise" of Orléans.

A major aspect of this thirteenth-century interest, however, is quite new and different from anything that we have seen in the twelfth century. It is an interest generated by the new community of preachers who combat heresy and sustain orthodoxy from the pulpit, emanating first from Cistercian houses and then from the universities in the thirteenth century. We can watch them appropriate these older collections and re- cast the very same work as preachers' tools.

Both the *Florilegium Gallicum* and the *Florilegium Angelicum* are absorbed into a large indexed Cistercian *florilegium* of the early thir- teenth century known as the *Flores paradysi.*[122] The *Flores paradysi* was compiled at the abbey of Villers-en-Brabant in the early thirteenth cen- tury. It exists in three states, represented by Brussels, Bibliothèque royale MS 4785 (Van den Gheyn 970) fols. 1–133v, s. xiii[1], Villers (A); Brussels, Bibliothéque royale MS 20030–32 (Van den Gheyn 1508), s. xiii[1], Villers (B); and Paris, Bibliothèque nationale MS lat. 15982, s. xiii[2], Sorbonne (C). The enlarged or B version contains substantial portions of the *Florilegium Gallicum*, and smaller portions of the *Florilegium Angel- icum*. According to its prologue, the *Flores paradysi* was compiled for use in the composition of sermons. To provide easier access to the texts that it contains, its compiler has equipped it with a large subject index of approximately 1000 entries, referring back to sequences of letters of the alphabet placed in the margins of the manuscripts. Such indexed Cistercian *florilegia* are also seen at Clairvaux, where the *Liber excep- tionum ex libris viginti trium auctorum* (Troyes, Bibl. mun. MS 186, Clairvaux L. 50) compiled before 1246 by Abbot William Montague is a fine example. The contents of both the *Liber exceptionum* and the *Flores paradysi* are absorbed in turn by another preachers' tool, the

---

[122] Regarding the *Flores paradysi* and several related works see R. H. Rouse, "Cister- cian Aids to Study in the Thirteenth Century," *Studies in Medieval Cistercian History* 2 (1976) 123–134.

alphabetical *Manipulus florum* compiled by Thomas of Ireland at the Sorbonne and finished by 1306. Thomas himself drew heavily on Fournival's copy of the *Florilegium Angelicum*. By accident, hence, extracts from the *Florilegium Angelicum* entered the foremost collection of extracts for preachers via two different routes.

By being absorbed into the *Flores paradysi* and provided with a detailed subject index the *Florilegium Gallicum*, in particular, was transformed into a preaching tool. In similar fashion and in response to the same demands the *Florilegium Angelicum* was at two different times restructured according to topic and, in one of these instances, provided with a subject index. In Rome, Biblioteca Angelica MS 720, a small handbook of the mid-thirteenth century, the extracts from the Christian authors in the *Florilegium Angelicum*—Gregory, Jerome, Sidonius, Martin of Braga, Ennodius, and the "proto-Christian" Seneca—are arranged by subject, for example, *De commendatione ieiunii*, *De iusticia*, *De humilitate quod non debet esse nimia*, and so on. A considerably more extensive ˌestructuring of the *Florilegium Angelicum* is seen in Paris, B.N. Mˢ lat. 1860 fols. 75–153v, of the mid-thirteenth century. Here the text of the *Florilegium Angelicum* has been enhanced with quotations from Terence, Sallust, Cicero (*De officiis*, *De senectute*, *De paradoxis*, *De amicitia*) and Boethius. The extracts from patristic authors Jerome, Ennodius and Gregory have been omitted. The new collection of extracts is arranged under 290 chapter headings and begins with an extensive subject index of some 330 entries written in triple columns, referring back to the chapters. *Exempla* included in the extracts are noted in the margins for easy identification. The prose portion of the *florilegium* is followed on fols. 153v–216 by a parallel collection of extracts from the ancient poets: the authors of the *Liber Catonis* (Cato, Avian, Theophilus, Claudian, Statius, Maximianus, Pamphilius), Horace, Virgil, Persius, Juvenal and Prudentius. These extracts also are arranged by subject, under 231 chapter headings; but they lack a subject index.

Perhaps the best-known example of such reordering is the absorption of the *Florilegium Gallicum* into the *Speculum historiale* by Vincent of Beauvais of the Order of Preachers. Though the fact is not always recognized, the *Speculum* too belongs in the milieu of aids for preachers. In setting forth the usefulness of his work, completed in 1244, Vincent of course mentions first of all that it will lead to the knowledge and the love of God; but he notes as well a number of mundane tasks for which the *Speculum* will be of use. Preaching is given first place on his list.[123]

---

[123] Vincent of Beauvais, *Speculum maius*, in the "Generalis prologus" which is affixed in the edition (Venice 1591) to the *Speculum naturale*. Fol. 1va: "Certus sum . . . hoc ipsum

The *Florilegium Gallicum* is almost entirely absorbed by Vincent, to emerge author by author in the *Speculum historiale*. One even knows, thanks to the painstaking studies of Berthold Ullman, which manuscript of the *Florilegium* Vincent used, Paris B.N. MS lat. 17903.[124] Once they were available in the *Speculum*, the dicta of the ancient Latin authorities were extracted again to form new collections. That in Bern MS 160 fols. 70v-94 (s. xiv[1]) is a good example. In it one can find appropriate texts for citation from Cicero, Sallust, Varro, Aesop, Seneca, Persius and Juvenal, all carved out of the *Speculum historiale* and not a few of them traceable ultimately to the *Florilegium Gallicum* of the mid-twelfth century.

Twelfth-century classical *florilegia* were thus both absorbed into thirteenth-century preachers' tools, and themselves recast as preachers' tools. They not only provided the authoritative *sententiae* beloved of scholastic preachers, but also served as a quarry for *exempla*. We saw, for example, how each of the *exempla* in the *Florilegium Angelicum* was marked in the margins of B.N. lat. 1860. A good case in point is the story of the oration of the Scythians to Alexander, which appears in a number of thirteenth- and fourteenth-century manuals written for the use of preachers and moralists, among them Jacobus de Cessolis's *De ludo scacchorum*, Arnold of Liège's *Alphabetum narrationum*, Walter Burley's *De vita ac moribus philosophorum*, the *Dialogus creaturarum*, John of Ferrara and perhaps the *Speculum laicorum*.[125] In this story the Scythians send a delegation to Alexander, who is about to attack their city, to dissuade him by reminding him of the fickleness of fortune and the futility of greed. It is a good lesson on the transitoriness of glory and the falsity of material gain, a theme plied by both ancient and medieval moralists. The ultimate source of the story is Quintus Curtius's *History of Alexander* 7.8.12–30. There, however, the oration is fuller, and it clearly has no effect: Alexander responds, as might be expected, by brushing these warnings aside. Alexander's response is naturally not included in the *exemplum* as it appears in the manuals noted above. The earliest appearance of this story in its abridged form as an *exemplum* is

---

opus non solum mihi, sed omni studiose legenti non parum utilitatis afferre, non solum ad Deum . . . cognoscendum, ac per hoc diligendum . . ., verum ad praedicandum, ad legendum, ad disputandum, ad soluendum, necnon et generaliter ad unumquemque fere modum et genus artis . . . explicandum."

[124] See the articles listed in n. 19 above.

[125] See G. Cary, *The Medieval Alexander*, ed. D. J. A. Ross (Cambridge 1956) 149, 298–299.

in the *Florilegium Angelicum*.[126] The English classicizing friar Thomas Ringstead (d. 1365) quotes the *exemplum* in his popular lectures on Proverbs, and doubtless drew it directly from the *Florilegium Angelicum*, since the latter was known in England and since he quotes it in the form that it assumes in the *exemplum*.[127]

Ringstead might have used the *Florilegium Angelicum* in a manuscript like Cambridge, Saint John's College MS 97, s. xiv, where it appears in the company of William of Malmesbury's collection of extracts from classical authors.[128] But parish priests more likely knew the *Florilegium Angelicum* in a different setting, in a collection similar to that in Oxford, Trinity College MS 18, s. xiv. This manuscript, to judge from its contents, is a handbook of parish theology. Besides extracts from various portions of the *florilegium* (Sidonius, Ennodius, Pliny, Seneca letters and *De ben., Proverbia philosophorum,* Cicero *Tusc.*), it contains the main English manual of pastoral care, William of Pagula's *Oculus sacerdotis*, complete with a subject index; Johannes de Deo's *Flos decretorum* and his *Liber pastoralis*; Innocent's *De miseria humanae conditionis*; Grosseteste's *Templum Domini*; and an extract on confession from John de Burgh's *Pupilla*, written about 1380–1385, which allows one to date the manuscript in the late fourteenth century. Leonard Boyle, O.P., has identified in this manuscript a list of tithes due to the church of Dunsby, Lincolnshire, in 1388, indicating that the volume might have belonged to a Lincolnshire parish priest.[129] In the fifteenth century it belonged to the house of Bonhommes at Ashridge, Buckinghamshire.[130]

A similar example is found in the description of a manuscript in the papal library at Pensicola, item 933: "Item excerpta ex libris qui sequuntur: Salustius in Catilinario . . . Macrobius in saturnalibus, proverbia philosophorum, Apuleyus, Plinius secundus in epistolas, multa notabilia, Ennodius . . ." This manuscript, a collection of extracts from a large number of ancient authors including recognizable chunks of the

---

[126] The story from Quintus Curtius also appears in Walter of Chatillon's *Alexandreis* (PL 209.548–552). The wording, however, does not allow the *Alexandreis* to have been the source of the *exemplum*.

[127] Concerning Ringstead see Beryl Smalley, *The English Friars and Antiquity in the Early Fourteenth Century* (Oxford 1960) 217, where his use of the *exemplum* is noted, though without a knowledge of its source.

[128] Unfortunately, though, St. John's MS 97 does not itself include the Alexander *exemplum*.

[129] The pastoral portions of the manuscript are described in L. E. Boyle's Oxford D. Phil. dissertation on William of Pagula and English manuals of pastoral care; and I am grateful to him for the details regarding its date, place of origin and provenance.

[130] Concerning the manuscripts of this house see H. C. Schulz, "The Monastic Library and Scriptorium at Ashridge," *Huntington Library Quarterly* 1 (1937–1938) 305.

Florilegium Angelicum, concludes with ". . . modi dictandi sermones, de arte predicandi, tractatus Galleni, item de arte sermocinandi, alius tractatus de modo componendi sermones, sermones ad status."[131] It is as good an example as Trinity MS 18 of the use to which these older collections were put in the fourteenth century. This is not humanism in any Renaissance sense; but neither does it substantiate the notion of a rejection of or disinterest in classical authors and the eloquence of classical Latin on the part of the scholastic era. For preachers, a moral could be driven home with authorities and *exempla* from the ancients as well as with biblical and patristic authorities, and books such as the *Florilegium Angelicum* and the *Florilegium Gallicum* supplied preachers with these.

✣   ✣   ✣

This article has argued for continuity, and for an effort to discern the links to this continuity in the transmission of ancient authors, through the study of *florilegia* and marginalia along with surviving manuscripts. In so doing it has suggested the role played by Orléans in linking together Lupus of Ferrières, Heiric of Auxerre, Philip of Bayeux, Richard de Fournival, Petrarch and Nicholas of Clemanges as perceptible stages in the transmission of certain ancient authors. And it has described a tangible continuity between twelfth-century humanist and thirteenth-century preacher.

---

[131] The catalog is printed in M. Faucon, *La librarie des papes d'Avignon . . . 1316–1420* 2 (Paris 1887) 140. The manuscript described has not been identified.

Alphabetical Tools

6. *Statim invenire:*
Schools, Preachers, and New Attitudes
to the Page

Twelfth-century scholarship is characterized by the effort to gather, organize, and harmonize the legacy of the Christian past as it pertained to jurisprudence, theological doctrine, and Scripture. The products of this effort, the *Decretum*, the *Sentences*, and the Ordinary Gloss to the Bible, were in existence by about 1150. In a certain sense the "twelfth century" can be said to close with the achievement of these goals and the emergence of a new mode of scholarship characterized by efforts to penetrate these great mosaics of the twelfth century, to gain access to the whole works of authority, and to ask fresh questions of them.[1] Major products of the second effort, the verbal concordance to the Scriptures and the theological summas, were in existence by about 1250.[2] While the *Glossa ordinaria* and the verbal concordance are the most important tools of biblical scholarship devised in the Middle Ages, these two works embody strikingly different approaches to written authority, each created in response to the needs of its own time.[3] The change in approach represented by the contrast between the Gloss and the concordance has hitherto been attributed to the coming of the mendicant orders, the

Originally published in *The Renaissance of the Twelfth Century*, ed. R. L. Benson and G. Constable with C. D. Lanham (Cambridge, Mass. 1982) 201–225.

[1] See Richard W. Hunt, "Manuscripts Containing the Indexing Symbols of Robert Grosseteste," *Bodleian Library Record* 4 (1953) 241–255 at 249–250.

[2] Thirteenth-century scholarly apparatus was the subject of the A. S. W. Rosenbach Lectures in Bibliography given by Richard H. Rouse at the University of Pennsylvania in 1975. See chap. 7 below, "The Development of Research Tools in the Thirteenth Century."

[3] See Richard H. and Mary A. Rouse, "The Verbal Concordance to the Scriptures," *Archivum Fratrum Praedicatorum* 44 (1974) 5–30.

institutionalization of the university, and the introduction of the new Aristotle. This explanation has never satisfactorily come to grips with the problem of the transition from one mode of thought to another, shaped by events taking place in the decades before Francis and Dominic. We should like to investigate the transitional period that lies between the completion of the Gloss and the making of the verbal concordance, using as evidence changes in the apparatus that scholars created to serve their needs.

     This study will deal, then, with the evolution of scholarly apparatus in the second half of the twelfth century: the forms that such instruments took, and the causes of their creation. The explanation of both forms and causes has much to do, of course, with the twelfth-century growth of the schools and the needs of formalized instruction. It has probably more to do with the growing need — or, rather, a growing perception of the need — for a pastoral ministry of preaching, in the service of a new, rootless urban society and in the face of the most widespread and successful challenges to orthodoxy that the Church had faced in many centuries. The explanation also has to do with the emergence of a new form of sermon. Throughout, it was the needs of the intellectual community that determined the shape of their scholarly tools. By identifying these needs, we hope to illuminate as well the changes in society that gave rise to them.

     We shall discuss the transition from memory to page layout, as a means of locating material in the codex; the impetus for this change came, at least initially, from the needs of the schoolroom. And we shall examine the background to the first works that are alphabetically organized for searchability, the "distinction" collections; the force that underlay their creation was a newly aggressive preaching ministry, which used that new device the *distinctio* to preach in a new way. Finally, we shall observe that the interrelationships between classroom and pulpit led to combining the best techniques of both, to produce a new generation of tools for a new generation of scholar-preachers.

FROM MEMORY TO ARTIFICIAL FINDING DEVICES

     Before the idea of searchability came the idea of putting into order. Order is not a twelfth-century creation, but it certainly was reemphasized in the first half of that century. This includes not only such obvious examples as the Lombard's *Sentences* and Gratian's *Decretum*, but also such works as Peter Abelard's *Sic et non*, and the Gloss — the "ordering" of patristic exegesis according to the order of Scripture; the makers of the Gloss were referred to as *ordinatores glose*.[4] One of the most explicit advocates of order was Hugh of St. Victor. The *Didascalicon* is much concerned not only with why and what and how one studies, but equally with the order of study. Of course, if one's study is logically ordered, one may use one's recall as a finding device, rather than "thumb the pages of books to hunt for rules and reasons" (*Didascalicon* 3.3). "We ought, therefore, in all that we learn, to gather brief and dependable abstracts to be stored in the little chest of memory" (*Didascalicon* 3.11). Hugh's *De tribus maximis circumstantiis gestorum*[5] discusses mnemonic devices, and includes historical tables to be memorized. Hugh of St. Victor seems to be the last major figure to propose memory as the sole or principal means of retrieving information.[6]

Hugh stands in the tradition of memory training or "artificial memory" that reaches back to Antiquity.[7] Yet there were various sporadic attempts, throughout the era in which one literally searched one's memory, to provide artificial devices as a supplement, not so much to aid the memory as to perform tasks for which the memory was unsuited. Let us examine three such devices, beginning with the mid-eleventh century: those of Papias, Deusdedit, and Gilbert of Poitiers.

Papias's dictionary, the *Elementarium doctrinae erudimentum* (saec. XI med.), was a milestone in itself, as the first alphabetically arranged work of any magnitude.[8] Moreover, in order to help readers find their way through his complicated lexicon, Papias describes in the prologue a system of signposts that would appear in the manuscript. The breaks of the alphabet were to be marked by three sizes of letters: the first word beginning with a given letter was to be marked by a large A, B, C, etc. in the text; each successive change in second letter (words beginning Ab— — —, Ac— — —, etc.) was to be marked in the margin by a middle-sized B, C, etc., and each change in third letter (Aba— — —, Abb— — —, etc.) by a small marginal *a, b*, etc. Genders of nouns were

[4] Beryl Smalley, *The Study of the Bible in the Middle Ages*, 2d ed. (Oxford 1952) 225.

[5] Discussed by William M. Green, "Hugo of St. Victor, *De tribus maximis circumstantiis gestorum*," *Speculum* 18 (1943) 484–493. The *Didascalicon* is cited from Jerome Taylor, trans., *The Didascalicon of Hugh of St. Victor: A Medieval Guide to the Arts*, Columbia University Records of Civilization 64 (New York 1961).

[6] This is not to say that memory training as such ceased to be of interest; but from this time forward, memory was aided by artificial finding devices.

[7] Concerning artificial memory, see Frances A. Yates, *The Art of Memory* (Chicago and London 1966).

[8] Concerning this dictionary see Lloyd W. and Betty A. Daly, "Some Techniques in Mediaeval Latin Lexicography," *Speculum* 39 (1964) 229–239; and Lloyd W. Daly, *Contributions to a History of Alphabetization in Antiquity and the Middle Ages*, Collection Latomus 90 (Brussels 1967) 71–72.

to be designated (m., f., n.); and the names of authors cited were to be given in abbreviated form—he lists the abbreviations—in the proper place in the margin (Hisidorus, *hi*; Augustinus, *aug*; and so forth). Papias's apparatus, with its use of letter size and marginalia, was far ahead of its time; and contemporary copyists, to whom such features were unknown and, presumably, of no interest, disregarded the instructions of the prologue. Papias's instructions began to be honored in practice largely in copies of the dictionary made after the twelfth century (see, for example, Paris, BN lat 17162, saec. XIII[1]), when scribes were familiar with, and readers appreciated the value of, such signposts. Papias's major innovation, that of organizing a large work alphabetically, inspired no emulation among his contemporaries.

The technique for searching devised by Cardinal Deusdedit for his collection of canonical texts (1083–87)[9] points up a curious problem. Beginning with the Gregorian Reform, when the first great canon law compendia were assembled, the canon lawyers faced the same need to search through written authority that would confront the school of theology over a century later; why did not the former, as did the latter, produce elaborate reference tools? Perhaps the difference lies in the fact that canon law as a field of study evolved before, and outside of, the universities. For whatever reason, the canonists depended upon rational classification by subject, with little apparatus to aid in searching before the late thirteenth century. Deusdedit was an exception: he compiled a subject index, in rational rather than alphabetical order, as an aid to searching his collection of 1,173 canonical texts, divided into four books. Deusdedit explained his motives in a preface: he did not arrange the material itself according to subject, because this would have required him to violate the integrity of the documents, recording portions under one heading, other portions under other headings; therefore, to enable one to find information concerning a specific topic, he provided a list of subjects for each of the four books (a total of roughly 800), with reference by number to the appropriate chapters, or books and chapters. What looks, at first glance, like a chapter list at the head of each book is in fact a primitive subject index. In the early thirteenth century, similar subject indexes in rational order would appear at the schools where they were part of the rapidly increasing and evolving body of searchable

---

[9] Edited by Victor Wolf von Glanvell, *Die Kanonessammlung des Kardinals Deusdedit* (Paderborn 1905); see the discussion of Paul Fournier and Gabriel LeBras, *Histoire des collections canoniques en Occident*, 2 vols. (Paris 1931–32) 2.37–54. We are grateful to Robert Somerville, Columbia University, for drawing our attention to Deusdedit's index.

tools; Cardinal Deusdedit's index, in contrast, occurred in isolation, and it was neither imitated nor improved upon by other canonists.[10]

The third example dates from the first half of the twelfth century. The manuscripts of Gilbert of Poitiers's Commentary on the Psalms contain marginal indexing symbols—twelve different ones, each occurring a varying number of times, and employed to group the psalms by theme. Gilbert's classification of the psalms is derived from Cassiodorus; and it is possible that he found there as well the notion of marginal symbols, although Cassiodorus uses quite different symbols, applied for different purposes.[11] Gilbert's symbols consist of Greek letters, conventional signs and the like—for example, 8, $\sim$, Ψ, Φ, ζ. The symbol 8 refers to the two natures of Christ, $\sim$ to the Passion and Resurrection, Ψ identifies the penitential psalms, and so on. To take as an example an early dated manuscript of the Commentary, Oxford, Balliol College MS 36 (saec. XII; written before 1166, when it was given to Lincoln Cathedral by Robert de Chesney):[12] on fol. 3, beside the beginning of Gilbert's gloss on Psalm 2, there is the marginal symbol $\overset{i}{8}$. This tells one that Psalm 2 is the first psalm that treats *De duabus naturis in Christo*, and that the next psalm with the same theme is Psalm 8. On fol. 8v, beside the beginning of Psalm 8, is the symbol $\overset{ii}{8}$; and it goes on—at Psalm 20 we find $\overset{iii}{8}_{xx}$; at Psalm 71, $\overset{iiii}{8}_{lxxi}$; and so on to the last, at Psalm 138, $\overset{viii}{8}_{lxxxi}$; which has no figure at the bottom, thus indicating that it is the last. Gilbert has devised a finding system in chain fashion—that is, one is referred not to all the psalms on a given theme, but merely to the next "link," which will direct one in turn to the next. The principal drawback is obvious: this is a one-way chain, that leads forward only. Therefore, if one were reading Psalm 138, for example, the symbol $\overset{viii}{8}$ tells one only that there are seven other psalms concerning the dual nature of Christ, without identifying any of them. These symbols were used in twelfth-century manuscripts of Gilbert's Commentary, but even by the end of that century new manuscripts ceased to include them, or included them only sporadically; copyists evidently found them of no use, and quite likely had forgotten their

---

[10] Not until the time of Martinus Polonus (d. ca. 1279) do we have a subject index to the *Decretum*.

[11] See Cassiodorus, *Expositio psalmorum*, CCL 97 (Turnhout 1958) 3; Cassiodorus's notes or symbols are on this model: GEO (= hoc in geometrica), M (= hoc in musica), (= hoc in astronomia), etc.

[12] The volume was kindly brought to our attention by Malcolm Parkes. It is described by R. A. B. Mynorts, *Catalogue of the Manuscripts of Balliol College Oxford* (Oxford 1963) 26. MS 36 can be identified with no. 60 in the twelfth-century catalog of the cathedral; ed. Reginald M. Woolley, *Catalogue of the Manuscripts of Lincoln Cathedral Chapter Library* (London 1927) vii.

significance. We have seen the symbols (including the top and bottom numerals) in the margin of the psalms in one early thirteenth-century manuscript (Oriel College MS 77), and others may turn up. But Gilbert's indexing method was too eccentric for acceptance by any significant number of people, and at the time of its creation, there was insufficient interest for anyone to imitate and improve upon it. The use of marginal symbols for indexing was not tried again until the independent development of indexing symbols or "concordantial signs" by Grosseteste and his circle at Oxford, in the middle of the thirteenth century.[13]

LAYOUT AS A FINDING DEVICE OF THE SCHOOLS

The devices of Papias, Deusdedit, and Gilbert of Poitiers failed to inspire emulation principally because they were created at the wrong time and place, where need or demand for them was lacking. The insufficiency of memory as a finding device—and, hence, the need for artificial devices—became crucial only with the growth of the schools and, especially, with the emerging prominence of theology at Paris in the course of the twelfth century. The number of students to be instructed was large, in comparison for example with the number at such cathedral schools as Laon. The time for instruction was limited, in comparison with the lifelong immersion in prayerful reading that distinguished monastic learning. And the very subject matter of theology was itself in the process of being defined and redefined, with the *Glossa ordinaria* and Peter Lombard's *Sentences* standing out as towering landmarks. In this context, the deficiency of memory as the principal means for finding was glaringly apparent: one cannot remember what one has not read, and one may well wish to find a part without reading the whole.

The major collections of the twelfth century—the Gloss, the *Decretum*, the *Sentences*— were in effect "finding devices" in themselves. For example, one did not need to search all the literature, both patristic and canonical, on a given question of law, because Gratian had already done the job. Peter Lombard is explicit on this point: he has compiled

---

[13] S. Harrison Thomson, "Grosseteste's Topical Concordance of the Bible and the Fathers," *Speculum* 9 (1934) 139–144; idem, "Grosseteste's Concordantial Signs," *Medievalia et humanistica* 9 (1955) 39–53; Hunt (n. 1 above). We have identified two additional MSS containing versions of the Grossetestian symbols: San Marino, California, Huntington Library MS HM 26061, kindly shown us by Jean Preston in 1972; and BN n.a.l. 540, kindly brought to our attention by François Avril in 1977. The latter is a concordance to the Fathers and a key to the symbols different from that in Lyon MS 414.

the *Sentences* "so that it will not be necessary for the seeker to turn through numerous books; for the brevity [of the *Sentences*] offers him, without effort, what he seeks" ("ut non sit necesse quaerenti librorum numerositatem evolvere, cui brevitas quod quaeritur offert sine labore").[14] These compilations were a new kind of literature in many ways, not the least of which is that they are designed, not for reflective reading, but for seeking out specific information.

This leaves, of course, the problem of how to locate a given sort of information within the compilations themselves. As we have implied above, the original impetus was the needs of the schools, where teaching took the form of commentary on a text, with the written page as its point of departure. The original response was well tailored to these needs: scholars of the mid- and late twelfth century employed the physical arrangement and appearance of the manuscript book and page as an aid to finding. Many of the devices used were not new; the change lay in their systematic and increasingly sophisticated application.

The simplest finding device was the list of chapter headings prefaced to a work. Tables of chapters can be found in earlier books. But with the mid-twelfth century such tables in new works become the norm, rather than the exception; and at this date we may safely assume that chapter lists are intended not only as an overview or summary of the contents but also as a device to facilitate searching. Peter Lombard, in the prologue to the *Sentences*, puts the implicit into words: "Ut autem quod quaeritur facilius occurrat, titulos quibus singulorum librorum capitula distinguuntur praemisimus."[15] Here the compiler himself makes provision for a finding device. It is instructive to contrast the Lombard's language with the words of another "prologue," the first of Bernard's *Sermones in Cantica canticorum*, only a few years earlier in time but far removed in spirit. Bernard hopes that his auditors or readers will delight in the hard work of difficult inquiry: "Ut quod in ea latet, delectet etiam cum labore investigare, nec fatiget inquirendi forte difficultas."[16] The Lombard's hopes are quite other: "Quod quaeritur offert sine labore . . ., ut quod quaeritur facilius occurrat." Peter Lombard's is the language of the new *instruments de travail*, reiterated in virtually every twelfth- to fourteenth-century aid to study that has a prologue—expressions like *sine labore, facilius occurrere, presto habere,* and *citius* or even *statim invenire.*

---

[14] *Magistri Petri Lombardi Parisiensis episcopi Sententiae in IV libris distinctae,* ed. Ignatius Brady, Spicilegium Bonaventurianum 4 (Grottaferrata 1971) 4 (= PL 192.522).

[15] Ibid.

[16] *Sancti Bernardi opera,* ed. Leclercq, 1.5.13–15 (= PL 183.787).

While a list of chapters could help one to single out the chapter that contained the information sought, the actual locating of information in the text was facilitated by the layout of the page.[17] Innovations in layout of the manuscript page are surely the most highly visible of all the twelfth-century aids to study — such techniques as running headlines, chapter titles in red, alternating red and blue initials and gradation in the size of initials, paragraph marks, cross-references, and citation of authors quoted. One cannot give a precise *terminus ante quem* for general acceptance of the individual elements, save to say that by about 1220 they were all standard; most can be seen on the pages of any late twelfth-century glossed Bible or manuscript of the *Sentences*. Twelfth-century manuscripts of the *Sentences*, for example, have the chapter titles in red, and a two-line majuscule begins the first word of each chapter. Subdivisions of the chapter's topic (*prima causa, secunda, tertia*) are entered as marginal rubrics. Authors quoted in the text have their names in red in the margin, tied neatly to the precise words of the text, beginning and end, by *puncti* — usually two dots (..) above the words at the beginning, and two vertical dots (:) above the end. These functioned like quotation marks, accompanied by rudimentary footnotes.

In biblical study the great product of the twelfth-century schools was the development of the commentaries to be applied to the Scriptures, the *Glossa ordinaria*, and its corollary in the book — namely, the layout of the glossed page. If the Gloss became the main vehicle for the accumulation and transfer of thought, clearly the book would have to undergo a marked alteration in the process of being adapted, first to accommodate, and then to focus on, the commentary. The exegesis of earlier centuries had been continuous works, physically independent of the text of the Bible. Adaptation of exegesis to the biblical text was worked out probably in Paris in the course of the twelfth century, a change that is currently being reconstructed by Christopher de Hamel.[18] His researches have identified several successive steps in the developing layout of the Gloss. By mid-century or slightly after, it had reached the stage in which the text of the Scriptures shrank in width from the two columns of an unglossed Bible to a single column in the center of the page, written on widely separated lines in a bold or enlarged script. The glosses were entered on either side in separately ruled sections, written in

---

[17] See Malcolm B. Parkes, "The Influence of the Concepts of *Ordinatio* and *Compilatio* on the Development of the Book," *Medieval Learning and Literature: Essays presented to Richard William Hunt*, ed. J. J. G. Alexander and M. T. Gibson (Oxford 1976) 115–141.

[18] See his unpublished D.Phil. diss. (Oxford 1979) on the layout of the glossed Bible in the twelfth century. We are grateful to him for having shared with us his firsthand knowledge of these books.

smaller script with two lines of gloss for every line of text. The connection between gloss and text was made precise by the inclusion of lemmata (usually underlined in red) in the gloss; and tie marks either linked gloss to text or, more commonly, linked a gloss that was incomplete at the end of one column to its continuation (in the next column, or on the next page). This three-column format became standard by the middle of the century, with Gilbert of Poitiers's commentary on the Psalms and Peter Lombard's commentary on Psalms and the Pauline epistles. It is seen in hundreds of surviving glossed books of the Bible.[19]

At a later stage, Gilbert's and the Lombard's commentaries, initially written continuous in columns flanking a column of Scripture, were presented on the page as two columns of commentary interspersed with, and virtually engulfing, the text of the Scripture written in large letters. This stage, in existence by 1166, is marked by the appearance of several techniques important to locating material, in particular the marginal citation of authorities that were quoted. Herbert of Bosham produced an "edition" or restructuring of the layout of the Lombard's *Magna glosatura* about 1170–76, which is a splendid example of the techniques available by the last quarter of the century to assist the reader in finding his way about a glossed text.[20]

Let us take as an example Bosham's edition of the Lombard on Psalms. Each "quinquagena" or group of fifty psalms is preceded by a chapter list, that is, the number of each psalm followed by a four-to-six-line summary of its content. The work is written in two columns per page. In each column, in large script, is a passage from the Gallican Psalter; to its left, in half-size script, is the same passage from the Hebrew Psalter; and to its right and above and below, again at half size, is the Lombard's commentary. In the outside margins (that is, to the left of the left-hand, to the right of the right-hand column of glossed text) are three columns of marginal apparatus. In the first or inner column are cross-references within the book of Psalms, written in very small script, on this model: "S. i. super fructum suum," meaning "See above, Psalm 1, at

[19] A good example is plate 43 in R. A. B. Mynors, *Durham Cathedral Manuscripts to the End of the Twelfth Century* (Oxford 1939), fol. 4v of MS A.III.4 (3rd quarter of the twelfth century) containing I-IV Kings. Cf. Smalley, *Study* pl. 1.

[20] See Ignatius Brady, "The Rubrics of Peter Lombard's Sentences," *Pier Lombardo* 6 (1962) 5–25. Our description of Bosham's edition is based on Oxford, Bodleian Library MS Auct. E infra 6 (S.C. 2051) and Cambridge, Trinity College MSS 150, 152–153, which were given by Bosham to Christ Church, Canterbury; see Montague Rhodes James, *The Ancient Libraries of Canterbury and Dover* (Cambridge 1903) 85 nos. 855–57, and Beryl Smalley, *The Becket Conflict and the Schools* (Oxford 1973) 81–83.

the passage *fructum suum*." In the second column are the author citations in red, with both *puncti* (corresponding to identical *puncti* in the
text) and, where necessary, an inclusive vertical line marking the beginning and end. This device is the Lombard's own, but it is Herbert who
explains the necessity of these quotation marks: he wishes to distinguish
clearly the words of the glossator (the Lombard) from those of the expos-
itors (the patristic commentators) and to distinguish the latter one from
another, "lest you be led to mistake Cassiodorus for Augustine or Jerome,
or the glossator for an expositor, a matter in which we have seen, not
just the unlettered, but very learned readers fall into error."[21] (Compilers
must have given much thought to the matter of how and where to cite
their sources; some seventy years later, Vincent of Beauvais stated that
he had decided to cite his sources in the text, as Gratian had done, rather
than in the margins in the style of the *Magna glosatura*, because marginalia
tended to be lost in copying.)[22] The third or outside column contains
cross-references to books of the Bible other than the Psalms. At the top
of the page is a running headline, in alternating red and blue, giving the
number of the psalm contained on that page; the running headline changes
over the proper column, where the text of a new psalm begins. Herbert's
manuscripts of the revised *Magna glosatura* are the earliest we know
that employ cross-references and running headlines in a deliberate and
consistent fashion. Bosham's layout, *mutatis mutandis*, is typical of that
employed for glossed Scripture in the course of the 1170s and 1180s.[23]
De Hamel has recorded a great many examples of this format, demonstrating that it spread across Europe with great speed.

The utility of the devices of layout worked out in the twelfth century is evident: we still use virtually all of them today, save that we have
moved the marginalia to the foot of the page.[24] And whenever one has
occasion to turn directly from use of a well-laid-out twelfth- or thirteenth-
century manuscript to look for something in the exceptional modern

---

[21] "Verba expositorum inter se et etiam a verbis glosatoris distinxi, ne Cassiodorum pro
Augustino sive Ieronimo, vel glosatorem inducas pro expositore, in quo interdum non
simplices sed eruditiores etiam vidimus lectores erasse"; quoted by Brady (n. 20 above)
10–11.

[22] "Nequaquam in margine sicut sit in psalterio glossato et epistolis Pauli vel in sentenciis,
sed inter lineas ipsas sicut in decretis ea inserui"; cited and discussed by Parkes (n. 17
above) 133.

[23] A number of fine examples appear among the books acquired in Paris, probably in
the 1180s, and left to Durham cathedral by Robert of Adington; see Mynors (n. 19 above)
78–82 and pl. 48, showing fol. 4v of MS A.III.17 (glossed Isaiah).

[24] The word "footnote" seems to date only from the nineteenth century; the earliest
citation for the word in the *Oxford English Dictionary* is "1841. Savage, *Dictionary of
Printing* p. 88: *Bottom notes* . . . are also termed *Foot Notes*."

printed text that does *not* have, for example, running headlines or clear paragraph divisions, one has an annoying sense of lost ground. By the end of the twelfth century, then, we might assume that the needs for a "finding technique" for classroom use were being met by the development of the clearly displayed text, with its chapter lists, running headlines, and marginal apparatus. With the teaching of the *sacra pagina* wedded to the order of the text, why should artificial tools for retrievability be developed?

ALPHABETIZATION AS A FINDING DEVICE FOR PREACHERS

And yet, the limitations of layout as a finding device are obvious: they are imposed by the physical limits of the page. This will be true of any work in any age; for the glossed Bible, the limits had been reached by the end of the twelfth century. Although we sometimes overlook the fact, the late twelfth-century masters who lectured on the Gloss were themselves aware of its insufficiencies and of the need to go beyond it.[25] It was therefore inevitable that alternative methods of retrieving information must eventually be devised, methods that would require different notions of order, as opposed to ordering information according to the text. Such a change was bound to be difficult, for it involved not merely creating a new ordering of ideas, but also consenting to break with an already established order. It is perhaps for this reason that canon law, with its early and carefully ordered body of topics, produced no artificial tools (until the late thirteenth century, when the notion was borrowed from others). For theologians, the order of topics was defined by the order of the Scriptures; as new information accumulated, the natural inclination was to force it into the mold of the Gloss, so that the Gloss, and glosses on the Gloss, swelled to unwieldy proportions. Despite the strains, it seemed impossible to conceive of any other method of making accessible to students the information necessary to the study of the sacred page.

Therefore the need, already apparent in the twelfth century, to create tools for teaching purposes was initially held back by the barrier of tradition. Instead, the first tools that successfully employed artificial order as a finding device, in contrast to reliance on layout, emerged in response to a different need, in a field unencumbered with established conventions. These were the late twelfth-century collections of biblical "distinctions," created in response to the need for sermon material. This

---

[25] See below at n. 62.

innovation illustrates how need shapes response: for the very same masters who, in their teaching, were glossing the Gloss in traditional fashion—such men as Peter the Chanter, Peter of Poitiers, Prepositinus, Alan of Lille, Peter of Capua—felt free to create new structures when responding to the needs of preaching. Before we go on to discuss the what and the why of distinction collections, therefore, we must consider structure and arrangement.

One immediately striking aspect of these new tools, and surely the most influential in the long view, is the fact that certain of the late twelfth-century distinction collections, as well as all significant thirteenth-century ones, were arranged in alphabetical order to facilitate searching. They were the first tools so organized;[26] and they were, insofar as we have been able to determine, the direct ancestor of all later alphabetical and searchable tools—beginning with the alphabetical verbal concordances to the Scriptures and the first alphabetical subject indexes before the middle of the thirteenth century, and continuing through the thirteenth and fourteenth centuries with alphabetical indexes to the Fathers and Aristotle, collections of *exempla* and *florilegia* alphabetized by topic, tenant and tax rolls alphabetized by name, and so on. The adoption of the alphabet to order ideas, by a handful of men in the late twelfth century, implies on their part a major change in attitude toward the written word. "The Middle Ages did not care much for alphabetical order," because they were committed instead to rational order.[27] The universe is a harmonious whole, whose parts are related to one another. It was the responsibility of the author or scholar to discern these rational relationships—of hierarchy, or of chronology, or of similarities and differences, and so forth—and to reflect them in his writing.[28]

---

[26] Alphabetical order was of course used before the distinction collection; the main medieval example is the glossary, in particular Papias's dictionary. It belongs to a separate tradition, however, akin both to older glossarial works and to the later works of Huguccio, Alexander of Villedieu, the *Graecismus*, and Brito, the composition and use of which were narrowly confined to the *artes*. Alphabetical apparatus, at least for the faculty of theology, began with alphabetized distinction collections.

[27] C. H. Haskins, *The Renaissance of the Twelfth Century* (Cambridge, Mass. 1927) 78: "The Middle Ages did not care much for alphabetical order, at least beyond the initial letter, and they would have faced a telephone directory with the consternation of an American office boy." Haskins made this statement merely as an aside, and it would be unjust to fault him for it; however, it typifies the assumptions of many historians, of his day and of our own. Moreover, one can still take only minor exception to the statement as it applies to the Middle Ages up to the second half of the twelfth century.

[28] Possibly the nicest example of the conflict between the two sorts of order, and of the scholastic's estimate of alphabetical order, comes from Albertus Magnus, who, in his commentary on the *De animalibus*, apologizes for using alphabetical order after having said

Given this predisposition, therefore, the acceptance of alphabetical order was reluctant and proceeded at an uneven pace, even within the confines of a single literary form. Peter the Chanter (about 1190) and Alan of Lille (before 1195), for example, arranged their distinction collections alphabetically; but the contemporary collections of Peter of Poitiers (about 1190) and Prepositinus (1196–98) were arranged in the order of the Psalter, while others, such as Peter of Cornwall (about 1189–1200) and Peter of Capua (before 1214), combined alphabetical with rational order. Complete alphabetization (alphabetization throughout the word) never became *de rigueur* in distinction collections. Moreover, the adoption of alphabetical order in one set of circumstances obviously influenced but by no means ensured its acceptance in another where, from our viewpoint, it would seem to have been equally applicable. Thus, for example, while the Chanter alphabetized his distinctions, it would not have occurred to him to equip his *Verbum abbreviatum* with an index. In the thirteenth century the earliest subject indexes, and a good many later ones, were arranged in rational rather than alphabetical order. At a time (just after mid-century) when Robert Kilwardby was making alphabetical indexes to the works of the Fathers, Grosseteste's intellectual heirs were still compiling a concordance to the Fathers arranged in rational order. And shortly after the Dominicans under Hugh of St. Cher had compiled a massive alphabetical concordance of the words in the Bible, other Dominicans were compiling biblical subject indexes or "real" (as opposed to "verbal") concordances in rational order; in some of these— for example, the *Concordantiae morales bibliorum* mistakenly attributed to Anthony of Padua—the order is so well thought out, with rational subdivision of books into parts further subdivided into chapters, that they are not difficult to use as finding devices.[29]

"hunc modum non proprium philosophie esse"—but he uses it nonetheless, for the benefit of the unlearned reader; *Opera omnia*, ed. Auguste Borgnet (38 vols. in 90 Paris 1890–99) 12.433. We are grateful to Lynn White, jr., for this reference.

[29] Concerning the development of distinction collections see Richard H. and Mary A. Rouse, "Biblical Distinctions in the Thirteenth Century," *Archives d'histoire doctrinale et littéraire du moyen âge* 41 (1974) 27–37, and in the text below; concerning Kilwardby's indexes see D. A. Callus, "The 'Tabulae super Originalia Patrum' of Robert Kilwardby O.P.," in *Studia mediaevalia in honorem . . . Raymundi Josephi Martin* (Bruges 1948) 243–270; idem, "New Manuscripts of Kilwardby's 'Tabulae super originalia patrum'," *Dominican Studies* 2 (1949) 38–45; idem, "The Contribution to the Study of the Fathers made by the Thirteenth-Century Oxford Schools," *Journal of Ecclesiastical History* 5 (1954) 139–148; concerning Grosseteste's concordance see n. 13 above; concerning the *Concordantiae morales bibliorum* see Arduinus Kleinhans, "De concordantiis Biblicis S. Antonio Patavino aliisque fratribus minoribus saec. XIII attributis," *Antonianum* 6 (1931) 273–326.

The use of alphabetical order, then, was not inevitable; once introduced, its acceptance was neither immediate nor widespread; and it never, during the Middle Ages, succeeded in supplanting the use of rational order, even for those tasks for which alphabetical order would have been more efficient. Nevertheless, in the subsequent discussion we emphasize the alphabetical aspect, for two reasons. First is the obvious one, that the alphabetical principle eventually won out, as the device for making information retrievable. The second is that such tools document the emergence of a different attitude to written tradition. Prior to this time, alphabetization had been largely restricted to lists of things which had no known or discernible rational relationship: one alphabetized lapidaries, for instance, because no classification of stones existed. For the alphabetized distinction collections, such a rule did not hold: one was in no sense compelled to use alphabetical order, as witness those collections organized according to the order of the Scriptures or some other rational order. Rather, the use of alphabetical order was a tacit recognition of the fact that each user of a work will bring to it his own preconceived rational order, which may differ from those of other users and from that of the writer himself. Applied to distinction collections, this notion meant recognition that, while one might teach in the order of the text of the Bible, one did not preach thus. Applied, for example, to the Bible itself, this notion produced the verbal concordance. Alphabetization was not simply a handy new device; it was also the manifestation of a different way of thinking.

Biblical Distinction Collections

It is ironic that, of all the useful alphabetical tools descendent from the burgeoning "need to find" of the twelfth-century schools, the collection of biblical distinctions has the role of progenitor. The distinction is an oddity, of quickly passing importance, one of those ideas whose time has come and, long since, gone. In discussing layout we were content merely to say "the *Sentences*" or "the Gloss," confident that these names would be immediately recognized and understood. Here, we must consider what distinctions were, why and when collections of them were compiled, and what function the distinction performed that made it, however briefly, a matter of importance.[30]

---

[30] The term *distinctio*, "distinction," has many other meanings in the language of the twelfth century (as in the twentieth). For example, *distinctiones* as employed in the organization of legal compendia have a quite separate history, which does not concern us here; and *distinctiones* meaning "chapter divisions" is mentioned below, following n. 66.

A biblical *distinctio* distinguishes (hence the name) the various figurative meanings of a word in the Bible, supplying for each meaning a text of Scripture in which the word is used with that meaning. Let us take as an example a late twelfth-century *distinctio* on the word *nubes*:[31]

> Tres sunt nubes: obscuritas in prophetis, profunditas in divinis consiliis, occulta et inaudita fecunditas virginitatis. De nube prophetarum scriptum est, "Tenebrosa aqua in nubibus aeris" [Ps. 17:12 = AV 18:11]; de nube consiliorum Dei legitur, "Rorate, celi, desuper, et nubes pluant justum" [Isa. 45:8]; de nube virginitatis et fecunditatis absconditae dicit propheta, "Super nubem levem et candidam ingredietur Dominus Aegyptum" [Isa. 19:1].

Clearly, the *distinctio* is stated in highly compressed language; for most of us, this "explanation" of the meaning of *nubes* is no explanation at all. One would need to know in advance, for example, the standard (or a standard) interpretation of "tenebrosa aqua in nubibus aeris" as a reference to prophetic ambiguity. As stated in a distinction collection, the language was likely to be more compressed still; in the early collections (some of the oldest manuscripts of the Chanter's, for example) distinctions were often displayed schematically, so that our distinction would have looked like this:

obscuritas in prophetis. Unde, Tenebrosa aqua in nubibus aeris.
nubes profunditas in divinis consiliis. Unde, Rorate celi desuper et nubes pluant justum.
occulta et inaudita fecunditas virginitatis. Unde, Super nubem levem etc.

Within the compass of a decade, beginning around 1189 or 1190, the twelfth century produced at least five major collections of distinctions, containing up to 1,500 biblical terms and distinguishing as many as six or eight meanings for each: the *Pantheologus* of Peter of Cornwall, Peter the Chanter's *Summa Abel*, the collection of Alan of Lille, and the distinctions on the Psalms of Peter of Poitiers and Prepositinus. Distinction collections continued to be produced, with undiminished enthusiasm, through most of the thirteenth century.

Such instant and continued popularity demonstrates that these collections met a need. It has sometimes been assumed that the source of this demand lay in the field of exegesis—that these were tools for teach-

---

[31] From Peter of Blois, Sermon 2, PL 207.565. Other examples, and a discussion of the thirteenth-century evolution of the *distinctio*, are found in Rouse and Rouse, "Biblical Distinctions" (n. 29 above).

ing, or tools for composing works of theology.[32] The collections of Peter of Poitiers and Prepositinus, arranged in the order of the biblical text, could have served as the basis for classroom lectures (though the *distinctiones* of Prepositinus may have been delivered as a series of sermons).[33] Also, one certainly finds distinctions being used in commentaries of the late twelfth century: in the Chanter's *Verbum abbreviatum*, for example, or in Gilbert Foliot's commentary on Canticles, which opens with a detailed consideration of several interpretations of the word *osculetur*.

The major demand for a ready supply of distinctions, however, arose from the making of sermons. More specifically, one can say both that the demand originated with preachers, and that the preponderant use of the distinction, throughout its brief but busy life, was for the composition of sermons. We have traced elsewhere how, subsequent to the appearance of the first distinction collections, the *distinctio* became a standard device used in sermons throughout the thirteenth century and beyond. But actually, as we shall see, the employment of distinctions in sermons precedes by perhaps twenty-five years and more the compilation of the earliest collections — although the *distinctio* could not be called a commonplace in sermons until the turn of the century. Such a pattern of development is reflected in all the searchable tools of the thirteenth century: the needs of users motivate the making of the tool which, by virtue of its accessibility, increases the use. Others have said that *distinctiones* appeared in the generation following the death of the Lombard; and the single case of Gilbert Foliot has been cited repeatedly.[34] A few specific examples will provide a clearer idea of who and when and, eventually, why.

There are rare *distinctiones* in the sermons of Peter Lombard himself (d. 1160), surely among the earliest uses of this device; see, for

---

[32] See, for example, Joseph de Ghellinck; *L'essor de la littérature latine au XIIe siècle* (2nd ed. Brussels 1955) 81: "Instruments de travail, qui nous font entrer de plus près dans l'atelier de composition des oeuvres théologiques de cette fin du XIIe siècle: *la Summa quae dicitur Abel . . .*"; cf. also 232–234.

[33] Georges Lacombe, *La vie et les oeuvres de Prévostin*, Bibliothèque thomiste 11, sect. historique 10 (Le Saulchoir 1927) 112–130. Concerning the collection of Peter of Poitiers and its use, see Philip S. Moore, *The Works of Peter of Poitiers, Master in Theology and Chancellor of Paris* (1193–1205) (Washington D.C. 1936) 79–81.

[34] Richard W. Hunt, "English Learning in the Late Twelfth Century," *Transactions of the Royal Historical Society* 4th ser. 19 (1936) 19–42 at 33–34, 40–41. Hunt's example of Peter of Cornwall's enthusiastic description of Gilbert's use of distinctions is also cited by Smalley, *Study* 248; by Hugh MacKinnon, "William de Montibus: A Medieval Teacher," *Essays in Medieval History presented to Bertie Wilkinson*, ed. T. A. Sandquist and M. R. Powicke (Toronto 1969) 32–45 at 38 n. 16; and, obliquely, by ourselves (n. 29 above) 30 n. 10.

example, in an Advent sermon on the text "Aspiciebam ego in visione noctis . . ." (Dan. 7:13), the distinction of *visio*: "Est enim triplex visio, scilicet visio noctis, visio diei, visio lucis . . .," which goes on to expound each sort of vision, with a biblical quotation supporting each one.[35] Peter Comestor (d. 1179) was an early large-scale user of *distinctiones*, with much amplification of each meaning; see, for example, in a sermon on the text "Convertit me ad viam portae sanctuarii exterioris . . ." (Ezek. 44:1), the detailed *distinctio* on the word *via*: "Quatuor enim sunt viae hominis: via infirmitatis, . . . via necessitatis, . . . via vanitatis, . . . via veritatis." He explains each *via*, supporting each with a biblical quotation (*via necessitatis* with a quotation from Horace!); and he tells whether it leads north, south, east, or west, and why.[36] The Comestor is the first preacher for whom one can say that the *distinctio* was a favorite rhetorical device.[37] Peter of Blois (ca. 1135 to after 1204) used *distinctiones* in preaching: the example "Tres sunt nubes" cited above is his. Marie-Thérèse d'Alverny has documented the use of *distinctiones* in the sermons of Alan of Lille (d. 1203).[38] And we know that Gilbert Foliot, bishop of London, was using *distinctiones* to great effect in his preaching by the 1170s, for Peter of Cornwall describes his "exhilaration" at hearing Gilbert preach according to this new form, when Peter was but a *novus canonicus* (he is thought to have joined the Austin Canons of Aldgate about 1170).[39] There is no need to give further names—not that the list would be endless, but that it would be imprecise; we lack both accurate dating and printed editions for so many twelfth-century sermons. The examples cited will suffice as evidence that twelfth-century preachers, from before 1160, had begun to employ *distinctiones* in their sermons.

This new fashion created a need for preachers to have available a body of distinctions from which to choose, a need that was met by the creation of the new tools. Circumstantial evidence clearly indicates as much; and, fortunately, Peter of Cornwall explicitly describes the progression, from the use of distinctions in preaching to the making of a

---

[35] PL 171.373–74, under Hildebert's name.

[36] Sermon 2, PL 198.1725–28.

[37] On this point, see the blunt assessment of Jean Longère, *Oeuvres oratoires de maîtres parisiens au XIIe siècle: Etude historique et doctrinale* (2 vols. Paris 1975) 1.55: "Pierre Comestor est parmi ceux qui ont le plus usé et abusé des distinctions."

[38] Marie-Thérèse d'Alverny, ed., *Alain de Lille: Textes inédits,* Etudes de philosophie médiévale 52 (Paris 1965), esp. 242–245 and nn., 270 and nn., 276–277 and nn.

[39] For the details of Peter's career see Richard W. Hunt, "The Disputation of Peter of Cornwall Against Symon the Jew," *Studies in Medieval History presented to Frederick Maurice Powicke,* ed. Richard W. Hunt et al. (Oxford 1948) 143–156, esp. 143–145.

distinction collection for further preaching. He states, on the one hand, that he was inspired to compile his *Pantheologus* by hearing Foliot's use of distinctions in a sermon; and, on the other, he explains that his collection was fashioned so that sermon-makers (*sermonem facientes*) need not so much make sermons, as to form sermons already made for them ("non tam sermonem facere quam iam factum formare").[40]

The *Pantheologus* illustrates, as well, the reluctant but steady shift from rational to alphabetical order, in response to the preachers' demand for quickly accessible sermon material. The distinctions in the *Pantheologus* were divided into four parts, according to the text of the Bible: part one contained distinctions of words in the Psalms, and in other books "tam veteris quam novi testamenti"; part two, distinctions of words in the four sapiential books; part three, distinctions of words in the major and minor prophets; and part four, a catchall in rational order (beginning with *Deus*) "from all the books of both Old and New Testament," containing distinctions of words "which the other parts omitted." Peter of Cornwall completed the *Pantheologus* about 1189, relying on his *capitula* or lists of words being distinguished, at the head of each part, to make the work searchable ("Capitula . . . disposuimus ut . . . sine difficultatis mora que querit inveniat,"[41] language reminiscent of the Lombard's in similar circumstances). But not long after the work was completed, he realized that the *capitula* were not adequate, particularly for the collection in part four, to enable one to find immediately (*statim invenire*) what was wanted. Therefore, he made a second list, containing the same *capitula* rearranged in first-letter alphabetical order, with a brief prefatory paragraph explaining "how to find quite easily what is sought, according to a new method, alphabetical order."[42] The surviving copy of this alphabetical list is dated about 1200. Peter's list may be regarded as a proto-index. More important, it documents with clear and datable evidence one man's conscious shift, within some ten years' time,

---

[40] From the prologue to part 4, as seen in Oxford, Lincoln College MS lat. 83 fol. 1r-v; we thank Richard Hunt for making available to us his transcript of this prologue. Virtually the same words occur in the prologue to part 1, edited by Hunt (n. 34 above) 38–42, esp. 40.72–76 ("sermones facientem").

[41] Ibid. 42.131–34.

[42] Oxford, St. John's College MS 31 fol. 2: "Explanatio qualiter facillime inveniuntur que queruntur in quarta parte Pantheologi secundum novum modum scilicet per litteras alphabeti. Quia per capitula que primitus ante initium quarte partis Pantheologi apposuimus non potest qui vis statim invenire que in libro illo invenire desiderat . . . ideo hic eadem capitula, sed non eodem ordine quo ibi, disposuimus. Hic enim eadem secundum ordinem alphabeti disposuimus. . . . "

from rational to alphabetical order to make his work searchable for preachers.

We should like to be able to describe the procedures by which Peter of Cornwall and his fellows compiled their collections of distinctions — the sources of their interpretations, and the means by which they located multiple biblical usages for each of several hundred words. But the present state of research does not provide any certain indications, and the compilers themselves do not say. At any rate, the problem of how to find a variety of passages that use the same word was eventually solved, in the thirteenth century, by the alphabetical verbal concordance, and it seems likely that the continuing demand for distinctions was no small factor among the needs that produced the concordance: the flyleaf of the oldest datable copy of the concordance contains distinctions, employing the concordance reference system and written in the hand of the manuscript's original owner.[43]

The Thematic Sermon

Whatever may have been the mechanics of compiling twelfth-century distinction collections, the cause was the use of distinctions in preaching. But why did distinctions begin to be used in sermons? Lacking a thorough survey of the evolution of sermon form during the twelfth and thirteenth centuries, we offer a tentative conclusion: the origin of the distinction seems to be closely linked with the emergence of the thematic sermon.

By the fourteenth century the form of the scholastic sermon, the so-called thematic sermon, had become pretty well standardized: theme, protheme, statement of divisions of the theme, confirmation of the divisions, amplifications of the divisions.[44] In a group of Parisian sermons for the academic year 1230–31,[45] the majority already incorporate the principal elements of this structure; that is, most of them take a "theme" — meaning, not a topic, but a verse of Scripture — which is then divided, usually into three but also into two or four or more components, each of which divisions is then amplified to produce a three-part (or two- or four-part) sermon. Frequently, in these sermons of 1230–31, the divisions of the theme consisted of a *distinctio* on a key word in the biblical

---

[43] Rouse and Rouse (n. 3 above) 23.

[44] Concerning the elements of the full-blown thematic sermon, see Thomas-Marie Charland, *Artes praedicandi: Contributions à l'histoire de la rhétorique au moyen âge*, Publications de l'Institut d'études médiévales d'Ottawa 7 (Paris 1936) 107–226.

[45] Marie-Madeleine Davy, ed., *Les sermons universitaires parisiens de 1230–1231*, Etudes de philosophie médiévale 15 (Paris 1931).

quotation, with each meaning, duly amplified, serving as one part of the sermon.

The use of *distinctiones* in earlier sermons, in the last half of the twelfth century and on into the early thirteenth, coincides with the origin of what would later become the thematic sermon. The form of the sermon was not yet systematized: one does not find in the twelfth century a division, stated or implicit, of the sermon into an imposed number of parts.[46] But one does begin to find sermons with a true "theme," that is, one selected scriptural passage, usually brief enough to be reiterated from time to time by the preacher and to be retained by his auditors. In the established sermon form — the form eventually displaced (at least among school-trained preachers) by the thematic sermon — there appear to have been two main methods of procedure: either (1) the preacher took a selected passage of Scripture, and used its subject matter as a springboard or topic for discourse; or (2) he took a lengthy passage, perhaps from the *lectio* for that Sunday or feastday, and commented upon its symbolic meaning, a word or phrase at a time.[47] In the newly emerging thematic sermons, the preacher stayed with his brief selected passage, giving, not one symbolic meaning, but rather an investigation of the layered wealth of meanings to be found there. The usefulness, the near inevitability, of the *distinctio* in such a procedure is obvious. Moreover, as the thematic sermon evolved, the *distinctio* served as a nascent structure. See, for example, the sermon of Innocent III on the same theme cited above for the Lombard, "Aspiciebam in visione noctis, et ecce cum nubibus celi quasi filius hominis veniebat" (Dan. 7:13); the entire sermon consists of a distinction on the word *nox* ("in scriptura divina septem modis intelligitur"), followed by a brief distinction of *nubes* (five meanings).[48] This is not yet a formal *divisio thematis*, but we can sense its presence just over the horizon.[49]

---

[46] However, see Longère (n. 37 above) 1.55, who assumes that Peter of Poitiers's fourfold explanation of his theme is meant as a statement of divisions — although, as Longère adds, Peter's sermon does not adhere to the stated plan.

[47] For purposes of comparison see J.-P. Bonnes, "Un des plus grands prédicateurs du XIIe siècle: Geoffroy du Loroux, dit Geoffroy Babion," *Revue bénédictine* 56 (1945–46) 174–215; he prints two sermons based on the same biblical text: the one, by Babion, is discursive in style; the other, by Peter the Chanter, is quasi-thematic and uses distinctions.

[48] PL 217.323–28.

[49] See also Longère (n. 37 above) 1.57: "Les sens de l'Ecriture peuvent fournir le cadre autour duquel s'organise le déploiement d'un thème."

THE THIRTEENTH-CENTURY FUSION

The thematic sermon's need for material motivated the creation of the first tools in searchable order, rational and alphabetical. The needs of teaching from the page motivated the development of the techniques of layout. But the distinction between preaching and classroom, though indispensable to a theoretical discussion, is largely artificial. The masters who taught also preached, and made preaching tools; the students they taught were being prepared to spend much of their time in the pulpit.[50] Therefore it is not surprising to see that the makers of distinction collections utilized the techniques created in the development of the great glossed page.

The distinction collection of Peter of Capua[51] reveals, as clearly as any work could, the close interrelationship between classroom lectern and pulpit, between theology lecture and sermon, between university preparation and parish application—however one cares to put it; Peter calls them respectively the contemplative and the active life (a novel use of this terminology), and likens them to Rachel and Leah, two wives of one man. Peter of Capua himself embodies the interrelationship: he was first a master of theology, presumably at Paris, and thereafter papal legate, cardinal-deacon of S. Maria in via lata (1193), and cardinal-priest

---

[50] Good descriptions of the relationship of preaching and teaching as seen by the Chanter and Stephen Langton are found in John W. Baldwin, *Masters, Princes, and Merchants: The Social Views of Peter the Chanter and His Circle*, 2 vols. (Princeton 1970) 1.110–111, and Smalley, *Study* 207–209.

[51] The description of Peter of Capua's *Alphabetum* is based on an examination of fourteen manuscripts, all but one (Trier) written in the thirteenth century: Bruges, Bibl. mun. MS 253 (Ter Duinen, O.Cist.); Chalon-sur-Saône, Bibl. mun. MS 15 (La Ferté-sur-Grosne, O.Cist.); Charleville, Bibl. mun. MS 230 (Signy, O.Cist.); Douai, Bibl. mun. MS 433 (Marchiennes, O.S.B.); Hereford Cathedral MS P.VI.6; Paris, Bibl. Maz. MSS 1007 (Royaumont, O.Cist.) and 1008 (Paris Carmelites, 1550/1); Paris, BN MSS lat 16894 (St-Germain-des-Prés, O.S.B.) and lat 16896 (St-Jacques, O.P.); St-Omer, Bibl. mun. MS 217 (Clairmarais, O.Cist.); Toulouse, Bibl. mun. MS 211 (Toulouse, O.F.M.); Trier, Stadtbibl. MS 721 (saec. XIV-XV; Germany); Troyes, Bibl. mun. MS 114 (Clairvaux, O.Cist.); Vienna, Öst. Nat.-bibl. MS 1380. There are at least two other surviving MSS not seen by us: Monte Cassino MS 355 (O.S.B.) and Vatican, MS Vat lat 4304. Virtually all of these look to have been written in the first half of the century, many if not most of them in Italy. *Addendum:* Since this article was written a study of Peter of Capua has appeared: Werner Maleczek, *Petrus Capuanus, Kardinal, Legat am vierten Kreuzzug, Theologe* (Vienna 1988); he lists fifteen further manuscripts of Peter's *Alphabetum*, pp. 239–242. To these can be added two more: Duke University MS 104 (s. xiii[1], Italy), and Yale University, Beinecke Library MS Marston (s. xiii in., Spain), a curious revision of Peter's *Alphabetum* attributed to Durand of Huesca. We are preparing an edition of Durand's verse prologue.

of S. Marcello (1201) until his death in 1242.[52] He began his collection of distinctions—some of which had originated as classroom lectures ("operis principium in scolarium audientium curavimus inchoare")—at the insistence of his students in Paris, and completed it after he was named cardinal: "a magistro Petro in scholis inchoatum et post modum ab eodem sancte romane ecclesie cardinali licet indigno, correcto ipso principio, consumatum."[53] Perhaps he completed the work not long after changing positions, for the wording of the prologue implies that he was nagged by the responsibility of this unfinished task, and pressed on to get it done.[54] He addressed the work jointly to the clergy of Rome and his former students, and expressed the hope that it would be useful to both, the former in their preaching, the latter in their studies.[55]

It is evident, however, that the work was principally designed for the composition of sermons, a task already incumbent upon the *venerandus clerus romanus* and soon to be so for most of Peter's *viri scolastici*. Peter entitled the collection "Alphabetum in artem sermocinandi"; and his explanation of its use is headed, "Qualiter debet quis de hoc opere texere sermonem." From this explanation we can see that Peter had in mind some form of thematic sermon: "When one wishes to make a sermon, he should lay as his foundation some scriptural passage, since . . . one builds more suitably on a stable foundation. He should then consider carefully how many key words are contained in the passage," look them up in Peter's collection, and construct a sermon from them "according to his own discretion."[56]

---

[52] *Addendum:* Regarding Peter's life, see now Maleczek; passim. Maleczek's evidence indicates that the author of the *Alphabetum* was the Cardinal Peter of Capua who died in 1214, and not—as we have said formerly—his nephew, the Cardinal Peter of Capua who died in 1242; see esp. Maleczek pp. 236–245.

[53] Another rubric speaks of his "responsio . . . facta scolaribus in ipsis scolis insistentibus pro presenti opere inchoando."

[54] "Curavimus tamen contra negotiorum importunitatem luctando . . . illud opus ipsum correcto primo principio prosequi, ne forte illud de nobis irrisorie diceretur quia hic homo cepit edificare et non potuit consumare."

[55] "Dilectis plurimum et diligendis semper in visceribus Ihesu Christi venerando clero romano, et viris scolasticis prophetarum filiis . . .," the opening words of the prologue. And later, ". . . in quo et venerandus clerus exercitetur facilius ad loquendum, et sollicitudo scolastica presto et ad manum pleniorem habet copiam ad scrutandum."

[56] Cum ergo placuerit alicui sermonem proponere, auctoritatem [*scil.* sancte scripture] aliquam iaciat in fundamento, ut basis sub columpna firma subsistat et super stabile fundamentum commodius valeat edificare. Consideret etiam diligenter quot dictiones in ipsa auctoritate ponuntur, et a quibus litteris ipse dictiones incipiunt, quibus etiam rebus conveniant proprie dictiones ipse; quo diligenter prenotato, secundum premissam duplicem ordinem de facili poterit in hoc opere de singulis dictionibus tractatus singulos invenire,

To make his work searchable, Peter of Capua first of all combined two techniques used in earlier collections of distinctions, that is, alphabetical and rational order. His words are arranged alphabetically by first letter; but internally, among those beginning with a given letter, the words are arranged in a descending hierarchy, according as they deal with nine topics: God, angels, the firmament, the air, man, beasts, the earth, the waters under the earth, and the abyss. To take an example of how this nonalphabetical hierarchy works: under the first letter *Altissimus* comes before *Aer, Avis* before *Adam*, and *Abissus* comes eighty-first and last of the words that begin with A.

Along with the techniques of searchable order derived from the tradition of preaching tools, Peter added the techniques of layout developed in the classroom for teaching from and commenting upon the written page. Peter calls each alphabetical section simply *littera*, and refers to the sections by number — *littera iii* (= C), *littera v* (= E), and so on. Running headlines across both pages of the opening read like this: left-hand page, "F L[ittera]," right-hand page, "VI." At the head of each *littera* is a numbered list of *capitula*, the words that are distinguished; the list for each successive *littera* recommences with the number *i*. The number of each chapter is written in the margin beside its beginning, in large Roman numerals with heavy red and blue paragraph marks. In the text at the head of each chapter is a tally of the distinctions, in red: *Altissimus vi modis in bono, uno in malo; Altitudo viii modis in bono, tribus in malo*; and so on. The initial of the opening word in chapter one of each *littera* is very large (sometimes the whole first word is in twelve-line capitals), with the initials of subsequent chapters two lines in height, alternating red and blue. Marginal rubrics, marked with smaller paragraph marks, indicate subtopics within a distinction; for example, in the chapter *Altitudo* are these marginal rubrics: "Qualis sit quelibet altitudo," "Unde sit altitudo," "Quid agitur per altitudinem." Finally, in the margin just below each chapter number is a list, in small and highly abbreviated script, of from two to ten cross-references to similar or contrasting chapters; Peter notes in his prologue that, when preaching on the word *rosa*, one might also want to use the material on *flos* or *lilium*; or when preaching on "fasting" (*ieiunium*), one might use the material against "gluttony" (*gula*). Not only the idea, but the physical appearance of these cross-reference notes is patterned on the notes in Bosham's edition of the *Magna glosatura*. Take for example the cross-references for the first chapter, *Alpha*:

---

quibus inventis, facile erit lectori ipsos coniungere et ex ipsis sermonem texere iuxta suam discretionem." We discuss this "duplex ordo" below.

I. lit. iii. C. lxx co^a
I. lit. v. C. xxxviii
I. lit. vi. C. xxxiii 7 xxxviii co^a
I. lit. xi. C. xii
I. lit. xv. C. xxxii

These are to be interpreted as follows: "Infra, littera iii (= C), capitulum lxx (=*Cauda*), contra," with the others referring respectively to *Elementa, Fimbrie, Festinatio (contra), Littera,* and *Primogenitus.* Later chapters will, of course, have cross-references that begin "S." (*supra*) as well.

Peter of Capua's *Alphabetum* was a response to the needs of those who composed thematic sermons. His biblical distinctions were arranged alphabetically and subdivided rationally, to make them easier to find. The searchability of his work was enhanced by his use of the devices of layout—numbered chapter lists, running headlines, marginal rubrics, color, graduated letter size, paragraph marks, and extensive cross-references. And all of this, both the intricate and sophisticated form of his response and the need itself, Peter inherited from his twelfth-century predecessors.

We have, thus far, investigated the twelfth-century origins of the effort to make information accessible in the layout of the glossed Bible and in the alphabetical collections of biblical distinctions. Let us now look ahead, to examine how this effort would affect the Bible of the twelfth century and transform the very attitude to written texts that was prevalent then.

The Bible, which in the twelfth century had invariably been in multiple volumes (one each for the Pentateuch, Psalter, Gospels and Epistles, and so on), in the early thirteenth century was reduced to a single thick but portable volume, via compression of letter form and layout, and the preparation of thinner parchment.[57] It descended from the communal altar to become the private property of the priest, a personal possession of the friar; few priests of the twelfth century owned a whole Bible, we should think. The numerous and varying chapter structures found in twelfth-century Bibles gave way slowly to a single standard structure, when Stephen Langton's divisions (before 1203)[58] were adopted by and popularized through the verbal concordance and other Dominican tools in the 1230s. Eusebius's canon tables and the marginal concor-

---

[57] This subject has not to our knowledge been studied in print. The art-historical aspects of it are examined by Robert Branner, *Manuscript Painting in Paris during the Reign of St. Louis*, California Studies in the History of Art 18 (Berkeley 1977).
[58] Smalley, *Study* 222–224.

dances in the Gospels, common to Bibles from late Antiquity on, disappeared in the early thirteenth century when they were made redundant
by the concordance. Conversely, Jerome's *Interpretations of Hebrew
Names*, which had enjoyed only a limited circulation before 1200, was
thoroughly revised around the turn of the century to become part of the
biblical canon, appearing in virtually all Bibles thereafter.[59] Whereas
Jerome's *Interpretations* go through the Bible book by book, the revised
versions integrate the names into a single list alphabetized by the first
two letters, to make them searchable; their purpose quite clearly was to
serve preachers, with the interpretations being used in sermons very
much as distinctions were. Early thirteenth-century Bibles not infrequently
contain, as well, brief indexes, in rational or alphabetical order, of biblical "themes" for preachers—for example, the index of texts useful for
preaching against the Manichees (that is, the Cathars) that is found in
early Dominican pocket Bibles.[60]

By mid-century two concordances, one in alphabetical order, the
other in rational order, existed in numerous copies to serve as an apparatus to the Scriptures.[61] Concording, relegated to the gloss in the twelfth
century, now had a book of its own. At this juncture we have come to
the type of book that can only be searched, for it cannot be read.

What transformation in attitude to written authority do these new
Bibles and concordances reflect? Or to put it another way: What route
has one traveled, starting with the snippets of Augustine contained in the
twelfth-century Gloss, to reach the massive alphabetical indexes to
Augustine's major works compiled by Robert Kilwardby in the middle of
the thirteenth century?

---

[59] For example, of some 91 whole Bibles of the thirteenth century described in the
Bibliothèque Nationale's *Catalogue général des manuscrits latins* 1 (Paris 1939), 81 contain
one or more versions of the revised *Interpretations*.

[60] For example, BN lat 174 (saec. XIII) fols. 181v–203, and University of California,
Los Angeles, Research Library MS 170/348 fols. 383v–385v, a French or English Dominican Bible of the second quarter of the thirteenth century. The index begins, "*I° quod pater
et filius et spiritus sanctus una substantia et unus Deus. Io. ca. i. In principio et vidimus
gloriam eius; Io. ca. i . . . ,*" and ends, "*Explicit summa breviata contra Manicheos et
Paterinos, et contra Passaginos et circumcisos, et contra multos alios hereticos qui nituntur
subvertere veritatem quorum dampnatio iam olim non cessat et eorum perditio non dormitat
de qua dampnatione ille custodiat suos qui ad dexteram maiestatis residet in excelsis super
novem ordines angelorum. Amen.*" It is followed in this manuscript 170/348 by a second
subject index with additional scriptural citations, fols. 385v–386v.

[61] Concerning the great alphabetical verbal concordance see Rouse and Rouse (n. 3
above); regarding the real concordance see Kleinhans (n. 29 above), and Friedrich Stegmüller,
Repertorium biblicum medii aevi 2 (Madrid 1950) 119–120 no. 1382.

One inescapable "product" of the Gloss, if we may call it that, was a keen awareness of its inadequacies. Masters "accepted [the Gloss] as a necessary evil";[62] basic instruction often requires a textbook. The glossed Bible was the major effort of the schools to order the legacy of the past, biblical and patristic, via juxtaposition; but it was insufficient, and the masters knew this. On the one hand, they decried the superfluity of glosses that tended to obscure, rather than to illuminate, the biblical text. On the other, they realized that the Gloss inadequately represented patristic thought. This latter concern was no mere matter of logistics, of squeezing more and longer extracts onto the page. Rather, it was a fundamental discontent with extracts as such.

One can see, before mid-century, an acknowledgment of the higher authority of the full text, as opposed to that of extracts taken out of context. Geoffrey of Auxerre describes how Gilbert of Poitiers, in his defense at the consistory of Reims in 1148, arrived armed with the *codices integri*, to the consternation of Bernard and his other accusers who had brought with them only a sheet of extracts as their documentation; and the accusers returned, the next day, equipped with their own whole texts.[63]

The emphasis on the authority of the whole work, and on the necessity of reading statements in context, grew during the second half of the century, to the point of generating a significant change in terminology. Geoffrey used the expected term, *integri*, to designate the full texts; the new term, or rather an old one put to new use, was *originalia*.[64] Previously, one had used phrases such as *originalia rescripta, originalia documenta*, to refer to the original documents, that is, those with signature and seal, issued by an official. By 1191 Ralph Niger was using the phrase *originalia scripta* in a new sense, meaning the whole work of an author in contrast to extracts from the work. Niger says that, from the very brevity of the gloss, his students must understand the necessity of turning to the whole works, "intelligant ad originalia scripta fore recurrendum."[65] In the contemporary usage of Stephen Langton the word was a noun, *originale* or *originalia*—as when he contrasts *glosa*

---

[62] Smalley, *Study* 226.

[63] See Nikolas M. Häring, "Notes on the Council and the Consistory of Rheims (1148)," *Mediaeval Studies* 28 (1966) 39–59, esp. 48–49.

[64] Joseph de Ghellinck, " 'Originale' et 'Originalia,' " *Archivum latinitatis medii aevi (Bulletin Du Cange)* 14 (1939) 95–105.

[65] Cited from Smalley, *Study* 226 and n. 4; regarding Niger see G. B. Flahiff, "Ralph Niger: An Introduction to His Life and Works," *Mediaeval Studies* 2 (1940) 104–126 and Ludwig Schmugge's introduction to his edition of *De re militari et triplici via peregrinationis Ierosolimitane* (Berlin 1977) esp. 3–14.

Ieronimi with *Ieronimus in originali*, or simply *in glosa* with *in originali*. Niger and Langton are the earliest that we have found to use *originale* in this sense; and in both instances, the word is used in a context indicating the insufficiency of the Gloss. In their choice of *originalia* rather than *integri*, moreover, there is a deliberate implication that the whole works possess the authority or authenticity of the originals, lacking in mere excerpts. The noun forms, *originale* and *originalia*, were universally accepted by the middle of the thirteenth century; and accepted along with them was the idea they represent, that the intent of a writer is best grasped through reading his words in context. This is not by any means to imply that one dispensed with the Gloss, but rather that one went beyond, to search out the *originalia*.

The emergence of a concept of whole work in contrast to extracts was accompanied by a parallel interest in the proper division of the whole work into its components — parts, books, chapters, *distinctiones, quaestiones*, and the like. Such divisions and subdivisions had to constitute coherent units, so that the process of division would aid the reader to understand the organization of the whole work and the intent of its author; and the units had to be small enough to serve for reference purposes. Not surprisingly, the Bible was the first text to receive such attentions; as we noted above, the standard capitulation of the Bible has been ascribed to Langton, on the basis of slender but suggestive evidence. And one sees elsewhere Langton's interest in the matter of chapter divisions, "which are very necessary for finding what you want and for remembering"; in an early Langton gloss on Jerome's prologue to the book of Joshua, he observes, "Here you have authority for chapter division."[66] In the early thirteenth century, the chapters of the Lombard's *Sentences* were further broken down by Alexander of Hales into subdivisions, called *distinctiones*, of more manageable length; and during the course of the thirteenth century other scholars provided chapter structures for *originalia* that lacked them, such as *Gregory's Moralia*.[67]

---

[66] " . . . que valde necessaria sunt ad inveniendum quod volueris et ad tenendum memoriter. Hic habes auctoritatem distinguendi capitula"; cited from Smalley, *Study* 224 and n. 1.

[67] Concerning Hales see Brady ed. 1.1 (n. 14 above) 143*–44*; concerning Gregory see Neil R. Ker, "The English Manuscripts of the *Moralia* of Gregory the Great," *Kunsthistorische Forschungen: Otto Pächt zu seinem 70. Geburtstag,* ed. Artur Rosenauer and Gerold Weber (Salzburg 1972) 77–89. The famous manuscript of Lactantius, Bodleian Library MS Canon. pat. lat. 131, written in France probably in the third quarter of the twelfth century, has chapter divisions added by an early thirteenth-century writer. The text of Glanvill, written ca. 1187–89 in continuous sequence, undergoes several restructurings in the next generation to render it more usable; see George D. G. Hall, ed. and trans., *The*

Fairly early on, just as with the shift from *libri integri* to *originalia*, a change in attitude is manifest in a change of terminology. By about 1220 one has explicit acknowledgment of the importance of division and subdivision of works: Jordanus of Saxony, in the introduction to his Priscian commentary, states (for the first time, in the tradition of *accessus* literature) that the form of a work includes both its *forma tractandi* (the way in which a book treats its subject matter) and the *forma tractatus*, "the separation into books and chapters, and their order."[68] Not long before Peter of Capua, in the prologue to the *Alphabetum*, describes in the same sequence these two aspects of his own work, *De modo tractandi* and *De ordine tractatus*. Attention to a fixed, and meaningful, division of the whole into manageable units had rapidly become an accepted part of scholarship, in the *artes*, in biblical study, in patristics, in preaching tools.

The concept of whole work permitted, and the emphasis on use of the whole works required, the creation of tools with which to search the *originalia*. In the thirteenth century, indexes to the *originalia* were compiled, borrowing the devices of alphabetical or rational order created for the twelfth-century preaching tools and utilizing the divisions into chapters as their reference system. Even before the mid-thirteenth-century *tabulae originalium*, this fruitful conjunction of ideas—notion of the whole work, sensible division into chapters, alphabetical arrangement—produced the finest achievement of thirteenth-century toolmaking, the verbal concordance of the Bible.

* * *

Scholars in the early twelfth century did not need the devices used by thirteenth-century preachers to organize their materials. The learned community was small in numbers, and its methods of instruction not yet formalized; the legacy of Antiquity and of the monastic church sufficed: rote familiarity with a finite body of authority, arranged according to rational principles and retained by memory. Little more was needed, given the lack of institutionalized procedures of instruction for clergy or for lay Christians. It is the supplying of these procedures that accounts for the transformation in scholarship discussed here. The Church, faced with diversity (both heterodoxy and heresy), accepted the need actively

---

Treatise on the Laws and Customs of the Realm of England commonly called Glanvill (London 1965) xl-lvi.

[68] The passage is discussed by Martin Grabmann, *Mittelalterliches Geistesleben: Abhandlungen zur Geschichte der Scholastik und Mystik* 3 vols. (Munich 1926–56) 3.234; and Jan Pinborg, *Die Entwicklung der Sprachtheorie im Mittelalter*, Beiträge zur Geschichte der Philosophie und Theologie des Mittelalters 42.2 (Munster 1967) 25–26.

to present and interpret a common faith to Western Christendom; this resulted in the attention paid to the schools for the instruction of clergy, in an emphasis upon the instruction of the laity through preaching, and in the eventual nurturing of the Mendicant Orders. This is the context in which the emergence of an apparatus to scholarship is to be seen.

Chenu states, in an oft-quoted passage introducing the evangelical return to the Gospel, "What interests us more than the actual results of these ventures, however, is the spirit that animated the men who undertook them, their taste for quenching their thirst at original sources, and also their anxious faith-inspired search for appropriate tools."[69] Unquestionably, it was the thirteenth century, not the twelfth, that produced, developed, adapted, and continually improved the tools for mining the patristic and biblical heritage. But it owed no small debt, in spirit and in sheer technology, to the intellectual and scholarly ferment of the twelfth century.

---

[69] Marie-Dominique Chenu, *Toward Understanding Saint Thomas*, trans. A.-M. Landry and D. Hughes (Chicago 1964) 46.

7. The Development of Research Tools in the Thirteenth Century*

In the course of the thirteenth century a flood of texts appeared that belonged to a genre virtually unknown before, works such as the alphabetical collections of biblical *distinctiones*, the great verbal concordances to the scriptures, alphabetical subject indexes to the writings of Aristotle and the Fathers, and location lists of books. These are works designed to be used, rather than read. Moreover, in many cases—for example, the concordance, or a subject index to the works of Augustine—these new tools helped one to use, rather than to read, the texts to which they were devoted. Tools such as these are unknown in classical antiquity. They are alien to the Hebrew and Byzantine traditions until imported from the Latins. And they emerge with striking suddenness in the West, to the point that one may say that before the 1190s such tools did not exist, and that by 1290 the dissemination and new creation of such tools were commonplace.

The appearance of such devices indicates a significant change in attitude toward written authority. The major works of the twelfth century, the *Ordinary Gloss* to the Bible, the *Sentences* of Peter Lombard, and Gratian's *Decretum*, represent efforts to assimilate and organize inherited written authority in systematic form. In contrast, the tools of the thirteenth century represent efforts to search written authority afresh, to get at, to locate, to retrieve information. They are the visible and

---

*This essay is essentially a retranslation into English of "La diffusion en Occident au XIIIe siècle des outils de travail facilitant l'accès aux textes autoritatifs," *Revue des études islamiques* 44 (1976) 114–147 (repr. as "L'évolution des attitudes envers l'autorité écrite: Le développement des instruments de travail au XIIIe siècle," in *Culture et travail intellectual dans l'Occident médiéval* [Paris 1978] 115–144); it was subsequently expanded as *Preachers, Florilegia and Sermons: Studies on the "Manipulus florum" of Thomas of Ireland*, PIMS Studies and Texts 47 (Toronto 1979) 3–90.

tangible manifestation of a new mode of thought which distinguishes the thirteenth century from preceding centuries. The spirit, the attitude toward authority embodied in these texts was more assertive, even aggressive, than that of the twelfth century. As Dom Wilmart remarked, "[at the beginning of the thirteenth century] patristic antiquity is not rejected; to the contrary, it is employed with fervor, if not with the same superstitious respect. . . . But it is no longer merely reproduced: it is pressed into the service of a mode of thought which is in the process of self-renewal."[1]

Often it is said that three factors in particular shaped the development of the intellectual life of the thirteenth century: the rapid growth of the universities, the predominant influence of the mendicant orders, and the impact of Aristotle on Western thought. To these should be added, as a fourth factor or as a concomitant of each of the others, the attitude of the age toward its written heritage—practical, utilitarian, active rather than passive.

Why did this change in attitude produce research tools? Why at this particular time? In what circumstances did man begin to produce such tools, and what was their influence on his work? Before one could address such general questions about causes and effects, one would need more precise information about the tools themselves. Both their nature and their number are not well known; their very existence has, in general, been overlooked. We shall consider, as examples, three different types of tools, each the result of a desire to facilitate access to sources: biblical concordances, alphabetical subject indexes, and catalogs of books. On the basis of these three types of tools, we shall then consider three of the most important technical innovations that went into their construction: arrangement in alphabetical order, use of arabic numerals, and division into chapters. Finally, we shall suggest some answers to two questions: Why did these research tools appear so suddenly, and what was the result of their invention?

A. THE TOOLS

1. Biblical Concordances

The development of the concordance should be examined in the context of the methods used to "distinguish" words found in the text of

---

[1] A. Wilmart, "Les allégories sur l'écriture attribuées à Raban Maur," *Revue bénédictine* 32 (1920) 56.

the Bible.[2] The collections of biblical *distinctiones* that abound in western Europe from the end of the twelfth century are the earliest of alphabetical tools save the dictionaries. Distinction collections provide one with the various figurative and symbolic meanings of a noun that is found in Scripture, illustrating each meaning with a scriptural passage.

Let us take as an example a thirteenth-century distinction on the word *equus*, horse.[3]

> Horse = preacher. Job 39[.19]: "Wilt thou give strength to the horse, or clothe his neck with neighing?" Gregory's gloss on this passage says that the horse signifies the preacher, to whom God first gives strength, to master his own vices, and then a whinny, that is, a voice to preach to others. Horse = temporal dignity, as in Ecclesiastes 10[.7]: "I have seen servants upon horses. . . ." Horse = the easy life; thus in the Psalm [31(32 AV).9]: "Do not become like the horse and the mule, who have no understanding." Horse = the present age; Genesis 49[.17]: "Let Dan be . . . a serpent in the path, that biteth the horse's heels that his rider may fall backward."

Some collections give as many as fifteen or more different meanings, for several hundred or even thousands of different biblical terms. Previously, distinctions have been regarded as tools for scholarly exegesis, and have been described in static terms. But their usefulness in the classroom must have been secondary. Moreover, the notion of what constituted a *distinctio* changed considerably with the years, as we shall see.

This device appears toward the end of the twelfth century in sermons and in theology lectures — it is hard to determine which of the two was the source. But alphabetically arranged collections of such distinctions were, from the very beginning, a biblical tool for preachers. One can discern two types of collections, on the basis of audience: those which were made privately for personal use, normally surviving in a single copy; and those intended for public circulation. The former type — the earlier, and by far the more numerous — includes for example the Cistercians' *Distinctiones monasticae*. The latter, fewer in examples but many times more numerous in copies, include the better-known collections such as the *Summa Abel* of Petrus Cantor (d. 1197) and the distinction collections of Alan of Lille (d. 1202) and Warner of Langres (d. 1202), and that of Peter of Capua (d. 1214) written expressly for the use of the clergy of Rome and equipped with a system of cross-references. During the second half of the century the most popular collections were

---

[2] See R. H. Rouse and M. A. Rouse, "Biblical *Distinctiones* in the Thirteenth Century," *Archives d'histoire doctrinale et littéraire du moyen âge* 41 (1975, for 1974) 27–37.

[3] On the flyleaf of Rouen, Bibl. mun. MS 109 (before 1249; Jumièges).

mendicant in origin, including the collections of Maurice of Provins, Nicholas Gorran, and Nicholas Biard, which were widely diffused by the university stationers.

If we examine contemporary sermons, we can see how preachers made use of collections of *distinctiones*. At the beginning of the century, preachers would select two or three senses of each word that occurred, in turn, in the biblical passage on which a sermon was based, and recite these distinctions without elaboration to illustrate the "theme." By about mid-century, preachers tended to choose from the collection three "distinguished" meanings of just the principal word in the sermon's theme, and use these individually as the bases for a sermon divided into three parts. Distinction collections themselves evolved in the same sense. The earlier ones were very laconic, often presented on the manuscript page in schematic or diagrammatic form. Progressively, the individual distinction grows longer and is accompanied by subdivisions and moralizations, becoming in essence the broad outline and scriptural basis for an entire sermon. Distinction collections of the end of the thirteenth century place their emphasis on moral subjects useful for sermons—in these later collections one would be less likely to find *equus* than *equitas*. By the early fourteenth century, new collections of "distinctions" in actuality include *exempla*, patristic *auctoritates* or extracts, and the like; they have evolved into miscellaneous alphabetical collections of generalized *materia praedicabilis*. By contrast, the thirteenth-century collections continued to be frequently copied throughout the first third of the following century.

The verbal concordance to Scripture is very closely related to this process of distinction. It is an important reference tool, literally invented in order to facilitate comparison and distinction of words in the Bible. Once created, it became the basis for the compiling of further collections of *distinctiones*. Quétif and Echard were the first to study the history of the verbal concordance.[4] During the succeeding 250 years, scholars contented themselves with quoting this study, more or less faithfully. An examination of the concordance manuscripts themselves reveals a story rather different from that proposed by Quétif and Echard and their successors.[5]

The first concordance (Saint Jacques I), which was compiled at Saint Jacques in Paris under the direction of Hugh of Saint Cher, was

---

[4] J. Quétif and J. Echard, *Scriptores ordinis praedicatorum* 1 (Paris 1719) 203–210, 466–467, 610–611, 632.

[5] R. H. and M. A. Rouse, "The Verbal Concordance to the Scriptures," *Archivum fratrum praedicatorum* 44 (1974) 5–30.

probably already in existence by 1239. This pioneering work originated the reference system used thereafter: each appearance of a word was noted according to book of the Bible, chapter of the book (following the chapter divisions attributed to Stephen Langton), and relative location within the chapter, indicated by means of one of the first seven letters of the alphabet A—G. The production of this major work over a period of time required an impressive organization of man-power. There survive, in the fifteenth-century bindings of manuscripts from Saint Jacques, four quires of what must be the penultimate draft of this concordance, revealing something of their methods: each quire was written by a different copyist responsible only for a fixed portion of the alphabet, as one can see from the blank space each left when he had finished his assigned task. Corrections were then noted, so that it would be ready for the final copy. A drawback of Saint Jacques I is the fact that its words are not cited in context. This version survives in eighteen manuscripts, thirteen of which date from the thirteenth century.

A second concordance (Saint Jacques II), the work of Richard of Stavensby and perhaps other English Dominicans at Saint Jacques, was the first version to present the words in context, i.e., words along with the passage in which they occur. Known in the older literature under the name *Concordanciae anglicanae*, this has for inexplicable reasons been considered to be the most important version of the medieval concordance. In reality, however, the context-passages were too long, the added apparatus (indicating various points of grammar, etc.) too intricate, and this concordance suffocated in its own complexity. Only some seven manuscripts of Saint Jacques II survive, and it seems that no two of these contain exactly the same text.

It was the third concordance of Saint Jacques, already in circulation by 1286, which at last responded to the need for a verbal concordance of words-in-context, providing a brief context of (usually) four to seven words for each *lemma*. Saint Jacques III was published by the university stationers at Paris, and survives in some eighty copies. Although trial and error began in the 1230s, then, it is only in the 1280s that medieval Europe has a satisfactory verbal concordance to the Bible. The erroneous attribution of Saint Jacques III to Conrad of Halberstadt originated, it seems, with Johannes Trithemius at the end of the fifteenth century.

During the course of the thirteenth century the concordance became the primary tool for the compilation of biblical distinctions. Indeed, one of the two oldest datable copies of the Saint Jacques I concordance (bequeathed to the abbey of Jumièges in 1249) had belonged to a priest who had covered its flyleaves with *distinctiones*, one of which was the distinction on the word *equus* cited above. By the fourteenth century, the various *artes praedicandi* and other preaching manuals took it for granted that a preacher would have access to a concordance.

2. Alphabetical Subject Indexes

Parallel with the development of the concordances, the alphabetical subject index made its appearance. Numerous indexes employing a variety of techniques seem to have emerged spontaneously across Europe. It is impossible to discuss these indexes either chronologically or developmentally, since very few can be dated with sufficient precision. We can at least make the general observation that, as with the distinction collections, one encounters indexes first of all among the Cistercian preachers, then later among the mendicants. Let us examine three institutions where alphabetical subject indexes were developed—the Cistercian abbeys of France and the Low Countries, the University of Paris, and the University of Oxford—always with the understanding that this three-part discussion is not so much a matter of chronological progression as of near-simultaneous responses to similar needs.

The Cistercians displayed a remarkable ingenuity in the creation of reference systems for texts that defied alphabetical arrangement.[6] At Clairvaux and its daughter house Villers-en-Brabant, a sensible means of indexing *florilegia* was in use before 1246. Two such *florilegia*, the *Liber exceptionum ex libris viginti trium auctorum* and a *Flores Bernardi*, are attributed to William of Montague, ninth abbot of Clairvaux (d. 1246).[7] Montague divided his *florilegia* into numbered *distinctiones* (in this context meaning simply "divisions"), and further subdivided each *distinctio* by means of letters of the alphabet, with both letters and numbers written out in the margin for visibility. These arbitrary divisions, with no particular relation to divisions in the text, serve only one purpose, to permit an index to be made. The index to the *Liber exceptionum*, for example, which fills twenty-three folios, contains some 2200 subjects, for each one of which there are up to twenty-five references or more. The reference consists of *distinctio*-number, subdivision-letter, and the

---

[6] See R. H. Rouse, "Cistercian Aids to Study in the Thirteenth Century," *Studies in Medieval Cistercian History* 2 (1976) 123–134.

[7] The *Liber exceptionum* survives in eight manuscripts, the oldest of which is Troyes, Bibl. mun. MS 186 (s. XIII[1]; Clairvaux L.50). The *Flores Bernardi* survive in two manuscripts, of which the older is Troyes, Bibl. mun. 497 (s. XIII[1]; Clairvaux H.49). Concerning William of Montague, see *Histoire littéraire de la France* 18 (Paris 1835) 149–152, 338–346.

lemma—for example, "Abducere: XIX.a *magni*," meaning that in the part of the text numbered nineteen, within subdivision A of that part, there is an excerpt beginning with the word *magni* that pertains to the subject *Abducere*. Toward the end of the thirteenth century or the beginning of the fourteenth, this system (with an added third sequence of sub-subdivision) was applied at Clairvaux to a *florilegium* of extracts from the Bible, in a manuscript (Troyes, Bibl. mun. 1037) with a text of 151 folios accompanied by an index of 23 folios. The other principal example of this "Cistercian system" occurs in the *Flores paradysi* compiled at Villers-en-Brabant during the first half of the thirteenth century. The earliest version of the text (in Brussels, Bibl. roy. MS 4785–4793), which must date from about 1216–1230, contains an artificial reference system in which each "opening" or pair of facing pages is designated by letters of the alphabet (Aa, Ab, Ac, . . . Ba, Bb, etc.) and each extract on the two-page opening is designated by a single letter. The index (450 subjects or keywords) refers to opening and extract, for example, "Ac.g" (= third opening, seventh extract). In the enlarged version of the *Flores paradysi*, three series of "concentric" alphabets referring to segments, and subdivisions of segments, of the text replaced the sequences that referred to a physical part of the specific manuscript (the openings).[8] The index of this version contained some 900 subjects/keywords which, according to the work's prologue, were chosen because of their usefulness for the preparation of sermons. Although they were naturally intended for the benefit of the abbeys where they were made, texts of both the *Liber exceptionum* and the *Flores paradysi* soon appeared at the universities, Paris and (the latter work only) Oxford. These tools are especially revealing because, as indexes to *florilegia*, their creation cannot be explained in terms of an "evangelical return to the whole works of the Fathers," which is the traditionally proposed explanation for the origin of medieval indexes. Rather, it was the new emphasis on preaching which inspired the invention of these particular reference tools.

Farther north, the Cistercian house of Ter Duinen and its daughter house Ter Doest, near Bruges, developed their own system of indexing.[9] The scriptorium of Ter Duinen, which served both houses, invented a method of foliation composed of sequences of letters and dots—from *a* to *z*, followed by dot-*a* to dot-*z*, then *a*-dot to *z*-dot, double-dot-*a* to

---

[8] Brussels, Bibl. roy. MS 20030–20032, Van den Gheyn 1508 (s. XIII[1], Villers).

[9] G. I. Lieftinck, *De Librijen en scriptoria der Westvlaamse Cistercienserabdijen Ter Duinen en Ter Doest in de 12e en 13e Eeuw* . . . , Mededelingen van de koninklijke Vlaamse Academie voor Wetenschappen, Letteren en schone Kunsten van Belgie, Kl. der Let. 15 no. 2 (Brussels 1953).

double-dot-z, and so on, through seventeen permutations. Even though it was awkward, the system was methodically applied to the books produced by this scriptorium through the course of the first half of the thirteenth century. Lieftinck offered the perceptive suggestion that the system of letters-with-dots was devised and employed because the monks did not yet have at their disposal a numbering system with a decimal base. At least five surviving manuscripts from these abbeys are equipped with subject indexes to their contents, employing a reference system that specifies the folio by letter and dot, followed in addition by one of the seven letters A—G to indicate the vertical location on the page, this latter being an unusual adaptation of the A—G system used by the Dominicans in their concordances.

A device employed by thirteenth-century readers who used the Ter Duinen/Ter Doest indexes still survives, a strip of parchment about eight inches long which served as a bookmark. One side of this strip preserves, as a reminder, a key to the alphabets: "Ut memoriter teneatur alphabetum taliter ordinatur: a .a a. :a a: [etc.]." The other side is divided into equal portions by the seven letters A through G; by placing the marker along any quarto-size folio, one could find the passage to which the index referred. Moreover, at one end of the strip there survives a parchment disk inside a sleeve that leaves one-quarter of the disk visible. The disk is marked, at the four points of the compass, "I prima, II secunda, III tertia, IIII quarta," which refer to the columns left-to-right on a two-page opening. When the parchment strip was used as a bookmark, one turned the disk so that the correct column number was visible.[10] Destrez considered disks of this sort to be a copyist's tool; given the elaborate reference system, one would in the present case, at least, be more justified in regarding it as a reader's tool.

Paris was of course a major center of the devising and use of alphabetical tools in the thirteenth century. The several motive forces that created the various indexing tools, devices, and procedures flowed into and out from Paris. By the middle of the thirteenth century, it in fact becomes

---

[10] A. Schmidt, "Mittelalterliche Lesezeichnen," *Zeitschrift für Bücherfreunde* 2 (1898–1899) 213–215; J. Destrez, "L'outillage des copistes du XIIIe et du XIVe siècle," in *Aus der Geisteswelt des Mittelalters,* Beiträge zur Geschichte der Philosophie und Theologie des Mittelalters, Texte und Untersuchungen suppl. 3 pt. 1 (Munster 1935) 19–34; H. Schreiber, "Drehbare mittelalterliche Lesezeichnen," *Zentralblatt für Bibliothekswesen* 56 (1939) 281–293; P. Lehmann, "Blätter, Seiten, Spalten, Zeilen," in his *Erforschung des Mittelalters* 3 (Stuttgart 1960) 55; A. C. de la Mare, *Catalogue of the Collection of Medieval Manuscripts Bequeathed to the Bodleian Library, Oxford, by James P.R. Lyell* (Oxford 1971), pl. XXXIa; and R. B. Marks, *The Medieval Manuscript Library of the Charterhouse of St. Barbara in Cologne,* Analecta Carthusiana 21 (Salzburg 1974) 40–42, and 61, pls. 1–3.

pointless to try to distinguish between Cistercian tools and university tools. The two communities shared at least one activity in common, that of preaching to the laity. After the foundation of a Cistercian house of studies at Paris, the Collège Saint-Bernard, the two institutions shared personnel as well. The indexing method that had been peculiarly Cistercian, the use of marginal letters and changing alphabets as reference systems, was picked up and used by the schools; the A—G reference system, developed by the Paris Dominicans for the concordances, was adapted for their particular needs by the Cistercians of Bruges. Books from the Paris schools invaded Cistercian (as well as Benedictine) libraries, to the point of eclipsing the monastic *scriptoria*, while indexed Cistercian *florilegia* from Villers and Clairvaux made their way into the studies of the masters, and the shops of the stationers, in Paris and Oxford.

One of the archetypical contributions of the University of Paris in this field is the application of indexing techniques to the works of Aristotle. *Distinctiones*, biblical concordances, and Cistercian indexes were, as we have seen, devoted to those works which constitute the very core of the Christian tradition. At the Paris schools, however, we see for the first time the development of reference works designed to facilitate access to texts for strictly scholarly purposes, without the remotest connection to sermon-preparation.[11] By mid-century, there were alphabetical indexes to the majority of works in the Latin Aristotelian corpus, Old Logic, New Logic, the *Ethica*, the *Libri naturales*.[12] Since these reference tools are anonymous, it is obviously impossible to prove that they originate at Paris; but the combination of the two activities, Aristotelian studies and creation of indexes, can point nowhere else at this period.

The oldest manuscript of Aristotle indexes (now MS 124 of the Biblioteca seminario, Pisa) exemplifies the handbook or collection of tools that belonged to an individual scholar in the middle of the thirteenth century. The volume begins with a list of the chapter-incipits of the *Ethics*, followed by an alphabetical index of the work. Next are the chapter-incipits and alphabetical indexes to the Old Logic (Porphyry's *Isagoge*, the *Categories*, the *Periermeneias*, the *Liber sex principiorum*) and to Boethius's *De divisionibus* and *De differentiis topicis*, incipits and

---

[11] But see, all the same, U. Berlière, "Jean Bernier de Fayt, abbé de Saint-Bavon de Gand 1350–1395," *Annales de la Société d'émulation de Bruges* 56 (1906) 359–381, and ibid. 57 (1907) 5–43; and R.H. Rouse and M.A. Rouse, "The Texts called *Lumen anime*," *Archivum fratrum praedicatorum* 41 (1971) 5–113.

[12] M. Grabmann, *Methoden und Hilfsmittel des Aristotelesstudiums im Mittelalter*, Sitzungsberichte der Bayerischen Akademie der Wissenschaft, Phil.-hist. Abt. 5 (Munich 1939) 139–149; C.H. Lohr, "Medieval Latin Aristotle Commentaries," *Traditio* 26 (1970) 156–157.

alphabetical indexes to the *Prior Analytics* and the *Posterior Analytics*, to Plato's *Timaeus*, and to six works of Boethius including the *De consolatione philosophiae*. Next is the alphabetical index (without the list of incipits) to the *De animalibus* in the translation of Michael Scott. The final item is the list of chapter-incipits and the alphabetical index to Aristotle's *Libri naturales*.[13] This manuscript's index to the *Ethics* is based on the old partial translations of the *Ethica nova* and the *Ethica vetus*, rather than the more recent translation from the Greek of the whole *Nicomachean Ethics*. According to Grabmann, one may deduce from the index to the *Opera naturalia*, based on a mixture of translations from Greek and Arabic which antedate Moerbeke's, that the indexes in this volume date "from the middle, or more likely from the beginning, of the thirteenth century."[14] The reference system employed by these indexes is clearly Parisian: For each topic, the reference gives the name of the text, the number of book and chapter, and a letter of the alphabet for relative placement within the chapter. This system, of course, is the one developed at Paris for the first Saint Jacques concordance to the Bible.

Rather than attempting to describe one by one the other indexes created or employed at Paris toward mid-century—most indexes being anonymous and undated—let us examine a random cross-section of these tools, as represented by the reference works that were included in the private library of a single Paris master, Gerard of Abbeville (d. 1272).[15] Among his books one finds first of all those basic reference tools that one might almost call "standard" by this date: an alphabetical dictionary of terms beginning with *Abyssus*,[16] an alphabetized biblical concordance (Saint Jacques I),[17] and two collections of biblical *distinctiones*.[18] In addition, among the indexes or indexed works from Gerard's library one finds the enormous alphabetical index to the works of the Fathers by Kilwardby,[19] as well as a copy of Kilwardby's *Intentiones* of the works of Augustine;[20] an alphabetical index to the works of Augustine com-

---

[13] Described by Grabmann 124–155.

[14] Ibid. 129.

[15] Concerning Gerard, see chap. 9 below, "The Early Library of the Sorbonne."

[16] Paris, BN MS lat. 15983 fols. 204–208.

[17] Recorded in the 1338 catalog of the Sorbonne as no. XXI.4; ed. L. Delisle, *Le cabinet des manuscrits de la Bibliothèque nationale* 3 (Paris 1881) 23.

[18] Paris, BN MS lat. 15569, and Sorbonne 1338 catalog no. XLI.4 *Distinctiones Philippi cancellarii.*

[19] BN lat. 15984; concerning Kilwardby, see further below at n. 31.

[20] BN lat. 15983 fols. 164–204.

piled in 1256 by a certain Robert of Paris;[21] a patristic *florilegium* with an alphabetical index (the Cistercian *Liber exceptionum*);[22] and a composite alphabetical index to Aristotle's *Physica, Meteorica, Parva naturalia* and *Metaphysica*.[23] Moreover, Gerard owned a copy of Fishacre's commentary on the *Sentences*;[24] one can see that this manuscript came from Oxford, because the lines of each page are numbered (to facilitate indexing, as we shall see in a moment). Gerard's manuscript of Fishacre does indeed contain an index, eight folios in length; but the maker of the index has paid no attention to the ready-made reference system, that is, the line-numbering, since that method was foreign to him. Instead, he has made a proper Paris index in this Oxford book, using the standard Parisian method of marginal letters of the alphabet for reference. Gerard's private collection of reference works encompasses a wide choice of texts, extending from the Bible to contemporary works, by way of Aristotle and the Fathers.

Gerard's indexes (as well as his other reference works, like the concordance) were ready-made works, developed by "professionals," so to speak. By the date of Gerard's death, and more and more toward the end of the century, one began to employ at Paris a different order of alphabetical index. This was the personal index, drafted by the owner of a manuscript for his own individual use. Scholars had come to handle with ease the flexible reference system which one may justifiably qualify as "Parisian," the system based on a combination of numbered two-page openings and marginal letters. The owner-indexer would note in the margins as many or as few letters as his interests required, then draw up a list of topics that, in breadth and character, reflected his specific needs. For each topic he would then note the location (number of opening, letter in the margin) of passages dealing with the subject. Free-standing indexes such as those in Gerard of Abbeville's library permitted scholars access to the texts hallowed by tradition, such as the works of the Fathers or the works of Aristotle. Owner-produced indexes, by contrast, were employed above all to facilitate access to contemporary works, such as the writings of contemporary university masters or the collected sermons of the preachers of the day—for example, Gerard of Abbeville's index (either owner-produced or owner-commissioned) to the commentary of his contemporary Richard Fishacre. The Paris masters Godfrey of Fontaines

---

[21] BN lat. 16334; cf. C. Samaran and R. Marichal, *Catalogue des manuscrits en écriture latine portant des indications de date* . . . 3 (Paris 1974) 521, pl. 47.

[22] BN lat. 15983 fols. 1–163v.

[23] BN lat. 16147.

[24] BN lat. 15754.

(d. 1306) and Peter of Limoges (d. 1307) both left, among the books they bequeathed to the Sorbonne, manuscripts with indexes of this sort drafted in their own hands. Peter of Limoges seems to have sketched in some sort of index, at times extremely brief, in each of his manuscripts of collected sermons. An unusually systematic example of this occurs in a two-volume sermon collection (Paris, BN lat. 16492–16493) for which Peter drew up an index six folios long; the manuscript's folio numbers and the marginal letters are both, like the index, in his well-known hand.[25] Indexes in the hand of Godfrey of Fontaines, found in Godfrey's manuscripts of the works of contemporary theologians such as Thomas Aquinas and Henry of Ghent, have often been set down casually wherever there was white space available in the volume, even across the bottom margins of the pages. J. J. Duin has described Godfrey's indexes that survive in BN MSS lat. 15350, 15811, and 15819; to these we can add those in lat. 15848 (fols. 54, 190) and 16906 (fol. 257).[26] The indexes created by these two university masters have attracted our attention because both men are known and dated, and their hands identifiable; but we must recognize that they are not unusual in this activity. Rather, we must regard them as representative of the efforts of numerous students and masters at the University of Paris, whose personal indexes remain anonymous.

Let us turn now to Oxford. There, the effort was focused on the works of the Fathers, under the dominating influence of the Oxford Franciscans. At its earliest stage, the work seems to have been the domain of a small group struggling to find a practical solution to a difficult problem, how to find one's way through the large patristic corpus. Under the guidance of Robert Grosseteste they devised a mechanism for indexing patristic texts: They created a complicated series of symbols (Greek letters, mathematical and conventional signs, and so on) which a scholar could jot down in the margin of a work in the appropriate place while he was reading—with the ultimate goal of incorporating all the references into one integrated central index. The key to the meaning of the symbols, and the beginnings of a master index to patristic and biblical texts, was discovered by Harrison Thomson in the pages of a Bible (now Lyon, Bibl. mun. 414).[27] The heading reads, *Tabula magistri Roberti*

---

[25] M. Mabille, "Pierre de Limoges, copiste de manuscrits," *Scriptorium* 24 (1970) 45–47 and pls. 10–13.

[26] J. J. Duin, "La bibliothèque philosophique de Godefroid de Fontaines," *Estudios Lullianos* 3 (1959) 24, 26, 29.

[27] S. H. Thomson, "Grosseteste's Topical Concordance of the Bible and the Fathers," *Speculum* 9 (1934) 139–144; idem, "Grosseteste's Concordantial Signs," *Medievalia et*

Lincolniensis episcopi cum addicione fratris Ade de Marisco . . . ("The index of Master Robert, bishop of Lincoln, with the addition of [Oxford Franciscan] Friar Adam Marsh"). Thomson dated this to the period 1235–1250. The Grosseteste/Marsh master index is organized in logical, rather than alphabetical, order according to nine categories (*De Deo, De Verbo,* etc.), each with a vast number of subdivisions. A similar concordance of patristic texts has recently been identified,[28] in a small collection of excerpts from the Fathers (BN nouv. acq. lat. 514) that dates from the mid-thirteenth century and that is English, probably Franciscan, in origin. In the center of this *florilegium* is the index, ten folios written three columns to the page, containing a list of symbols, each of which is followed by references to the patristic texts that deal with the subject. Rather than being a different version of the index found by Thomson, this second seems to be a separate creation, parallel in method and intent, and no doubt produced by the same milieu. Both reflect a centrally organized system, centered at Oxford. The Grosseteste symbols continued in use throughout the second half of the thirteenth century. They appear in the margins of at least seventeen surviving manuscripts. The most recently discovered is a mid-thirteenth-century Bible, identified at the Huntington Library in 1972.

The Oxford Franciscans, a generation or so after Adam Marsh, were responsible as well for compiling the *Tabula septem custodiarum super Bibliam.*[29] This is an index to the incidental comments on scriptural passages in the writings of the Fathers, arranged in the order of the text of the Bible. With this *Tabula,* it was possible to look up any verse in the Old or New Testament, to find exactly where any or all of a dozen of the most important Fathers of the Church had commented on its meaning. This enormous work, sometimes filling two volumes, permitted scholars to examine the Bible verse by verse, from Genesis to the Apocalypse. The *Tabula* survives in nine copies of English origin, but

---

humanistica 9 (1955) 39–53; R. W. Hunt, "Manuscripts Containing the Indexing Symbols of Robert Grosseteste," *Bodleian Library Record* 4 (1953) 241–255.

[28] We thank F. Avril for having brought this manuscript to our attention.

[29] There is no study of the *Tabula* in print. Surviving manuscripts include the following: Cambridge, Peterhouse 169 (s. XV); London, British Library Harley 3858, NT only (s. XIVex., Durham); BL Royal 3 D.i (A.D. 1452), copy of Peterhouse 169; Oxford, Balliol College 216 and 217 (s. XV, ex dono William Grey 1478); Bodleian Library Bodl. 685 = SC 2499 (A.D. 1339, Oxford); Magdalen College 78, NT only (s. XIV); Magdalen College 150 (A.D. 1449); Merton College 205 (s. XIV); and New College 315, Genesis to Job only (s. XV). The work is recorded in the catalog (A.D. 1372) of the Austin Friars of York; ed. M. R. James, in *Fasciculus Joanni Willis Clark dicatus* (Cambridge 1909) 2–96, no. 57.

never circulated on the Continent.[30]

The work of the Dominican Robert Kilwardby parallels that of the Franciscans in Oxford.[31] During the five years that he spent at Oxford as his order's regent master in theology from 1256 to 1261, Kilwardby produced a three-level system of access to the core of Christian written authority: (1) *intentiones*, which are summaries chapter by chapter of various patristic (especially Augustinian) works—sixty-one works of Augustine, John Chrysostom's *Quod nemo laeditur nisi a seipso*, the *Hexameron* of Ambrose, Hugh of Saint Victor's *Didascalicon*, and the *Sentences* of Peter Lombard; (2) individual *tabulae* or alphabetical indexes, for each of forty-six works of Augustine, four works of Anselm, the *De fide* of Damascenus, and the *Sentences*; and (3) a combined master alphabetical index, with references to the principal works of Augustine, Ambrose, Boethius, Isidore, and Anselm, and with occasional references as well to the *Historia scholastica* and the *Sentences*. In all his reference tools, Kilwardby employed as the smallest unit of reference the A—G system devised by his fellow Dominicans at Saint Jacques, doubtless a souvenir of years spent in study at Paris. Kilwardby's prodigious output comprises a wide-ranging introduction to the Fathers of the Church; the some thirty manuscripts that survive attest his influence on both sides of the channel.

Like the Cistercians and the Paris masters on the Continent, the masters and students at Oxford devised their own individual indexing technique which they took back home with them to Evesham or Worcester or elsewhere. The system was based on line-numberings on the manuscript page, to facilitate accuracy of reference.[32] Pelster, Richard Hunt, Neil Ker, and Graham Pollard among them discovered more than sixty manuscripts whose lines are numbered in this fashion, and we feel cer-

---

[30] The *Tabula septem custodiarum* will be described in detail in the forthcoming edition of its companion work the *Registrum Anglie de libris doctorum et auctorum ueterum*, discussed below.

[31] D. A. Callus, "The *Tabulae super originalia patrum* of Robert Kilwardby O.P.," in *Studia medievalia in honorem . . . R. J. Martin* (Bruges 1948) 85–112; idem, "New Manuscripts of Kilwardby's *Tabulae super originalia patrum,*" *Dominican Studies* 2 (1949) 38–45; idem, "The Contribution to the Study of the Fathers Made by the Thirteenth-Century Oxford Schools," *Journal of Ecclesiastical History* 5 (1954) 139–148.

[32] F. Pelster, "Das Leben und die Schriften des Oxford Dominikanerlehrers Richard Fishacre (+1248)," *Zeitschrift für katholische Theologie* 54 (1930) 517–553; A. G. Little and F. Pelster, *Oxford Theology and Theologians* (Oxford 1934) 61–62; Lehmann, "Blätter, Seiten . . . " (n. 10 above) 58–59. See also N. R. Ker, *Fragments of Medieval Manuscripts Used as Pastedowns in Oxford Bindings*, Oxford Bibliographical Society Publications 5 (Oxford 1954) nos. 210, 372, 1644b, 1722, 1902a, 1943. We are grateful to the late Graham Pollard for having shared with us his unpublished notes on line-numbering.

tain there are others. The two facing pages of a manuscript "opening" are divided into four columns tagged *a, b, c, d* (from left to right), and the lines are numbered in arabic numerals, usually by fives, down the center between the two columns. This method was employed in Oxford, and in centers influenced by Oxford, during more than 150 years. It appeared first in manuscripts of the *Commentary on the Sentences* by Richard Fishacre (d. 1248);[33] the latest known example of such line-numbering is found in a manuscript written about 1412.[34] In addition to those manuscripts in which line-numbering was an integral part of the copying of the text, there are manuscripts whose first or early owners added the line-numbers after the fact, to make reference easier. In at least two instances, line-numbers have been added to twelfth-century manuscripts, an example of the fourteenth-century adaptation of thirteenth-century techniques to an older book for practical purposes.[35]

Use of this system of line-numbering did not remain confined to Oxford, as Pelster had thought. Instead, as we have implied, Oxford students in returning home to their livings took the system with them and continued to apply the technique in their professional lives. It is hardly surprising to see that many of the line-numbered books are texts used in the administration of a diocese, deanery, or parish — for example, two manuscripts of the *Summa* of Raymond of Pennafort bear line-numbers.[36] The purpose of the line-numbering was to enable the owner of a book to create his own index if he wished, or simply to be able to note down references to parts of the book with precision. Sixteen of the surviving manuscripts, at least, contain an index that makes use of the line-numbers for reference; one of them contains as well a thirteenth-century explanation of how the index operates.[37] This reference system, still widely used today for classical texts and poetry, in the Middle Ages

---

[33] The following Fishacre manuscripts contain line-numbers: Bologna, Univ. 1546 (s. XIII); Cambridge, Gonville and Caius College 329 (s. XIII); London, British Library Royal 10 B.viii; Oxford, New College 112 (s. XIII), with index, fol. 322ff. (the index alone appears in New College 31); Oxford, Oriel College 43 (s. XIII); Paris, BN lat. 15754 (before 1272); Vatican Library Ottob. lat. 294. There are more surviving manuscripts of this work with line-numbers than without.

[34] Oxford, Bodleian Library Hatton 11 = SC 4132, a *Regimen animarum* in the hand of a Johannes de Clyra or Clyua; regarding the date, see M. B. Parkes, *English Cursive Book Hands*, 1250–1500 (Oxford 1969) no. 23.ii.

[35] London, British Library Royal 6 C.ix (s. XII), works of St. Bernard; London, Lambeth Palace 347 (s. XII), works of St. Jerome.

[36] Oxford, Bodleian Library Selden supra 48 = SC 3436 (s. XIII²), with an index on pp. 418–435; and Oxford, University College 21 (s. XIII).

[37] Oxford, New College 112 (s. XIII), Fishacre on the *Sentences*; explanation of the index on fol. 322.

did not cross the Channel, despite the fact that a certain number of English line-numbered manuscripts themselves (like Gerard of Abbeville's Fishacre) were carried to the university centers of Paris and Bologna well before the end of the thirteenth century.

At Oxford, at Paris, and among the Cistercians, the use of subject indexes grew in response to the needs of each community. The indexes produced by these groups, at first idiosyncratic and hesitant, improved progressively and employed increasingly sophisticated techniques in the course of the thirteenth century. By the century's end, the usefulness of indexes was taken as a matter of course by the literate West, not only for the needs of preachers but also in the fields of theology, philosophy, and law. One can see the point demonstrated in the works of the Dominican John of Freiburg (d. 1314), written during the 1280s and 1290s. It is of course no surprise, by this date, to find John compiling an alphabetical table that encompasses jointly Raymond of Pennafort's *Summa* and William of Rennes's gloss on the *Summa*. But it is indeed striking to see John of Freiburg adding an alphabetical index to his own book, the *Summa confessorum* (written 1297–1298), in order to facilitate access to the book's content.[38] Here we see the first known example of an index made by the author to be an integral part of the structure of a newly written work. The index, by this action, has clearly been accepted as worth its weight in parchment.

3. Library Catalogs

The biblical concordance, as well as the various types of indexes, was a new tool filling a new function, that of aiding research. The library catalog, on the contrary, was a well-established genre; but in the thirteenth century, an inventive turn of mind enabled scholars to give the old genre new direction. The majority of booklists and catalogs in the Middle Ages, especially prior to the thirteenth century, were strictly inventories of property which one checked off, from time to time, against the volumes on hand, just as one checked off the linens in the press and the candles in the box. Beginning with the thirteenth century, one starts to see the first catalogs that had as a principal function to enable one to locate a book, within a given library or within a region.

Location lists in fact precede the appearance of in-house subject catalogs, no doubt because readers were reasonably familiar with the con-

---

[38] Leonard E. Boyle, "The *Summa confessorum* of John of Freiburg and the Popularization of the Moral Teaching of St. Thomas . . .," in *St. Thomas Aquinas 1274–1974: Commemorative Studies* 2 (Toronto 1974) 245–268, esp. 248–249.

tents of their own libraries. Du Molinet in 1678 and Bellaise in 1687 described a collection of catalogs of the books of Norman abbeys (Savigny, Mont-Saint-Michel, Saint-Etienne of Caen, Bec, Jumièges, and others), which they dated in the first half of the thirteenth century and which they suggested may have been assembled at Savigny.[39] The volume itself has disappeared, but Bellaise's description allows one to infer that it was simply a collection of independent catalogs and not one single integrated catalog.

Toward the end of the thirteenth century a similar collection of individual booklists, this time of Parisian libraries, was assembled in tabular form at the Sorbonne.[40] Only a fragment survives, the part containing the end of the booklist from Sainte-Geneviève and the beginning of that from Saint-Germain-des-Prés. (The fragment that pertains to Sainte-Geneviève preserves information from a lost catalog dating from the 1230s or 1240s.) Evidently the booklists of the different abbeys in the city were copied, on just one side of large pieces of parchment, sheets that could then be posted on the wall or on a door for common use in order to help Sorbonnists find in other local institutions books that were not available at the Sorbonne.

The earliest integrated location list, and the most remarkable, is the *Registrum Anglie de libris doctorum et auctorum ueterum*.[41] This is a list of some 1400 works (often further identified with their incipits) of some ninety-eight patristic and other authors. The titles in the list are followed by indications of their location in a certain number (as many as 30 or more) of the ecclesiastical institutions of England, Scotland, and Wales. These indications consist of arabic numerals which refer to a key, a numbered list of 189 monastic or cathedral libraries which is placed at the head of the *Registrum*. Although none of these libraries is Franciscan, the master list is organized geographically according to the division of Great Britain into the *custodiae* of the Franciscan Order. The three surviving manuscripts of the *Registrum* date from the beginning of the

---

[39] Noted by Delisle, *Cabinet* (n. 17 above) 1 (1868) 527–528.

[40] See "Early Library," below pp. 373–375.

[41] An edition by R. A. B. Mynors, R. H. Rouse, and M. A. Rouse is forthcoming. Meanwhile, see the valuable study of M. R. James, "The List of Libraries Prefixed to the Catalogue of John Boston and the Kindred Documents," *Collectanea franciscana* 2 (1922) 37–60. Rather wide of the mark is the study of E. A. Savage, "Notes on the Early Monastic Libraries of Scotland with an Account of the *Registrum librorum Angliae* and of the *Catalogus scriptorum ecclesiae* of John Boston of the Abbey of Bury St. Edmunds," *Edinburgh Bibliographical Society* 14 (1930) 1–46, reprinted as "Co-operative Bibliography in the Thirteenth and Fifteenth Centuries," in his *Special Librarianship in General Libraries* (London 1939) 285–310.

fifteenth century;[42] it is nevertheless possible to establish from external evidence that the *Registrum* must date from the first or second decade of the fourteenth century.

Although there is no concrete evidence on the matter, it seems obvious that such an impressive English Franciscan project from this date must have originated at the house of the Greyfriars at Oxford, the work of the same group of scholars who compiled the *Tabula septem custodiarum* described previously. One of the two surviving witnesses to the *Registrum* contains the text of the *Tabula* as well. Perhaps the compilation of the *Tabula* inspired, or even necessitated, the creation of the *Registrum*; for, while the *Tabula* refers one, for each verse of the Bible, to passages in the works of "twelve doctors" of the Church, the *Tabula* does not itself quote the authoritative passages. This causes a dilemma; as one scribe noted sardonically, "If you possess the works of these twelve doctors, or even some of them, this present book [the *Tabula*] will be very useful to you for preaching; but if not, I do not know what good it will do you."[43] Perhaps it was for this reason, to begin with, that the Oxford Greyfriars conceived the idea of drawing up a catalog of the places where an itinerant friar might find these books. However that may be, the finished project grew beyond any such limits to become a location list of a very large number of works written by a series of Christian (and a few ancient) authors much more extensive than the dozen authors included in the *Tabula*. The essential goal remained the same: to permit the individual friar to find what he needed to carry out the mission of his order.

The *Registrum*'s information about the contents of the various monastic and other book collections across Britain was gathered in person by visiting Franciscans. The number of people involved in the enterprise is not known, but this must necessarily have been a community effort of the Oxford Franciscans, comparable to that required by the Paris Dominicans in making the concordances. Once the information had been gathered and the reports brought back, the integrated list—the *Registrum*—was put together at Oxford. The whole was a triumph of energy and organization.

The arrangement and cataloging of books within the individual colleges and other university institutions were also influenced by the changes

---

[42] Oxford, Bodleian Library Tanner 165; Cambridge, Peterhouse 169; and a copy of the latter, London, British Library Royal 3 D.i.

[43] London, British Library Harley 3858, fol. 62: "Si hos duodecim doctores aut aliquos ex his habueris, valde utilis ad predicandum presens liber tibi sit; sin autem, nescio quid tibi valebit."

in book usage reflected in the union catalogs and location lists. In monastic institutions, book collections had traditionally been kept in book chests or *armaria*—though the individual volumes themselves doubtless were, for much of the time, parceled out among the members of the house. We find, however, in the writings of the Dominican Humbert of Romans, about 1270, instructions that books in the *armaria* should be physically arranged by subject matter, and that certain ones of them should be chained at lecterns for the common use of all, rather than being either locked away in a chest or loaned out for the use of only one person.[44] Before the end of the thirteenth century, both the Collège de Sorbonne in Paris and University College in Oxford had such a collection of chained books attached to reading benches. Early in the next century, about 1320, a member of the Sorbonne compiled a subject catalog of the hundreds of individual texts bound together in the some three hundred chained codexes of his college.[45] This development—arrangement of manuscripts by subject matter, affixing chains to selected books, an index of the content of a whole collection—corresponds in its way, in both purpose and ingenuity, to the making of concordances, distinction collections, subject indexes, and union catalogs; and it is in such a context that it should be considered. The common goal of all these devices was to facilitate access to desired information.

B. THREE TECHNIQUES OF RESEARCH TOOLS

Using as our basis the foregoing eclectic sample of the tools themselves, we can now examine certain aspects of the phenomenon in general. Even though, in the thirteenth century, the various reference tools emerged in many milieus simultaneously, independently of one another and among communities quite different superficially, they all bear a certain family resemblance. These tools embody the concept of utility, of plain practical usefulness. They are made to be used, as the humble word "tool" implies and as these devices themselves repeat time and again in their prologues: "ad utilitatem predicandi," "ad utilitatem simplicium maxime, quosdam casus utiles," "valde utilis ad predicandum," "utilem et salutarem scientiam apprehenderis," and so on. But there is a further level, a second tier of utility, so to speak: These tools are intended, as well, to help the reader use the texts to which they are keys. The

---

[44] Humbert of Romans, *Instructiones de officiis ordinis*, in his *Opera*, ed. J. J. Berthier, 2 (1888–1889; rptd. Turin 1956) 263.
[45] See "Early Library," below pp. 381ff.

notion that the text of the Bible, or the works of the Fathers of the Church, should be *useful* would have been strange, and likely repugnant, to monastic thought. But a preacher composing sermon after sermon, a teacher looking for the authoritative quotation that would support his argument, a writer seeking an appropriate phrase, would feel very much at home with the utilitarian attitude inherent in reference tools. For example, Robert Kilwardby explains that his index pertains not merely to the text of Augustine's *De Trinitate* but to Augustine's chapter-prologues as well, "because they contain many useful things" (*quoniam utilia plura continent*). Tools were both conceived and used for practical purposes.

In order to render the tools both useful and usable, their creators devised new techniques and applied old techniques in new ways, often in quite individualistic and idiosyncratic fashion. For that reason, in examining the techniques of tool-making we must remember that this is less a question of technical evolution than an untidy mix of adoption, adaptation, and innovation of techniques. We have noted in passing the technical achievements peculiar to particular tools. Now, we should like to consider three techniques that pertain to tool-making in general: alphabetization, arabic numbering, and chapter division or capitulation.

1. Alphabetization

Alphabetical order is the organizing principle of almost all the reference tools considered here. Theoretically, the adoption of alphabetical order entailed nothing more than the application of an existing technique. In practice, though, the matter was more complicated than that. First-letter alphabetization of lists of words was a part of the Greco-Roman inheritance, as Lloyd Daly has shown; and in the Middle Ages the technique was employed by, among others, the dictionary-makers Papias, Huguccio, and Brito. Nevertheless, we notice that each of these in turn took the trouble to explain alphabetical arrangement, as if taking it for granted that the process would be unfamiliar to his readers.[46] Scholars in the Middle Ages found it more natural to organize things in accord with their logical interrelationships: God had created a harmonious universe, and thus its parts must logically and harmoniously relate to one another. An author who arranged materials on the illogical, or rather nonlogical, basis of the alphabet seemed either to deny the logical relationships, or to confess himself incapable of perceiving them. And of

---

[46] Lloyd Daly, *Contributions to a History of Alphabetization in Antiquity and the Middle Ages*, Collection Latomus 90 (Brussels 1967).

course we recognize that alphabetical arrangement would be ridiculous for numerous literary genres. The point is that, even in cases where alphabetization would have been advantageous, it was rejected, or, more accurately, it was not considered as a possibility. For example: It was thoroughly acceptable to arrange a list of stones in alphabetical order, since there was no set of logical relationships among stones; but to the contrary, for a *florilegium* to place the section of quotations on the subject of *Filius* before that on *Pater*, or *Angelus* before *Deus*, simply because the alphabet required it, would have seemed completely absurd. Alphabetical order was in fact disparaged. Albert the Great apologizes, in his *De animalibus*, for discussing a series of animals in alphabetical order after having said initially that this method is not appropriate to learned matters (*hunc modum non proprium philosophiae esse*); he has done so nonetheless, he says, for the benefit of the reader with little learning.[47] Aside from wordlists, such as dictionaries, lexicons, herbals, lapidaries, medical recipes, mnemonic verses (all items that defied logical classification), it was logical arrangement that dominated the field. As keys to the contents, or "finding devices," in logically organized works, one had lists of chapter-titles; to find the meaning of biblical language, one searched the gloss for cross-reference, after having first found the word in the text of the scriptures. These two procedures were practical if one were reading or browsing through a text, but they do not lend themselves to searching. Relatively suddenly, the idea took hold that alphabetical order could be usefully applied to tools for searching, in many fields; and alphabetized concordances and the like appeared in large numbers by mid-century or shortly thereafter. It was not, however, until alphabetical arrangement had proven successful for *distinctiones* collections, biblical concordances, and subject indexes—all of them, in essence, just enlarged wordlists—that this principle was cautiously accepted for application to more complex tools such as encyclopedias, *exempla* collections, *florilegia*, and similar compendia, beginning with the *Alphabetum narrationum* in 1297 and in particular the widely circulated *Manipulus florum* in 1306.[48] In the course of the fourteenth century, preachers gradually had at their disposal as many alphabetically arranged handbooks as logically ordered ones.

---

[47] Albertus Magnus, *Opera omnia*, ed. A. Borgnet, 12 (Paris 1891) 433.

[48] Concerning the *Alphabetum narrationum*, see J.-Th. Welter, *L'exemplum dans la littérature religieuse et didactique du moyen âge* (Paris 1927) 304–319; concerning the *Manipulus florum*, see R. H. Rouse and M. A. Rouse, *Preachers, Florilegia and Sermons* (cited above).

2. Arabic Numbering

Reference works require a system of reference symbols, by means of which one can designate either a portion of the text (book, chapter) or a physical portion of a manuscript (folio, two-page opening, column, line). The creators of reference tools were near-unanimous in rejecting roman numerals as too clumsy to handle. Before there was widespread acquaintance with arabic numerals, the absence of a practicable and universally recognized set of symbols posed a knotty problem for toolmakers. The commonest solution was to employ letters of the alphabet; for a sequence of more than twenty-three items (folios, *distinctiones*, etc.), one could repeat the alphabet with a modification for each repetition—e.g., one could double, then triple, the letters (aa, bb, . . . aaa, bbb)—or even resort to the curious letters-and-dots symbols created by the Bruges Cistericans.

This need for a system that permitted one to locate and refer to information in a text contributed materially to the introduction of arabic numerals in the West. Sarton, in explaining the West's slow acceptance of arabic numerals, remarked that they were "not actually needed by business . . . no social need. . . nor . . . for a long time any scientific need, because hardly anyone realized the implications of the new symbolism."[49] In contrast, those who compiled the indexes and those who systematically marked divisions in manuscripts had great need for arabic numerals. In fact, the Cistercian sequence of dotted letters was clearly a homemade place-value system, employing letters rather than numbers, that was created to meet specific needs. Saving the concordances, virtually all reference tools of the thirteenth century used arabic numerals. The so-called arabic numbers had been known among specialists in western Europe since the early or mid-twelfth century, in translations of arabic mathematical and astronomical treatises, but it was only in the course of the thirteenth century that arabic numerals began to supplant roman numerals for purposes of numbering manuscript folios; and, curiously enough, it was the Oxford University scholars' line-numbering in manuscripts before the middle of the thirteenth century that constitutes the first casual, matter-of-fact employment of arabic numerals by an entire community. While historians of science may wax regretful that the West was so tardy in accepting the "radically new [arabic] arithmetic" with its revolutionary concept of zero,[50] we can observe to the contrary that the index-makers, indifferent to the ramifications of

---

[49] George Sarton, *Introduction to the History of Science* 2.1 (Baltimore 1931) 5.
[50] Ibid.

the arithmetic, adopted the numerals eagerly, for the down-to-earth reason that these provided an unmatched means of marking one's place.

The technical key to concordances and indexes was the reference-system, which depended upon the way a text was divided. There were three basic methods: First is reference to preexisting divisions of the text, usually book and chapter, sometimes made more specific by incorporating the *lemma*, the exact word within the book and chapter where the pertinent passage begins. A second method is division of the text, by means of letters of the alphabet written in the margin, into artificial sections more or less equal in length, for reference. This type of division was especially appropriate for *florilegia*, which lack the natural divisions of book and chapter that one would find in a treatise or summa. A related type of artificial reference division for *florilegia* consists of bestowing a marginal letter of the alphabet (in order) upon each excerpt or quotation, to facilitate access and cross-reference. The *Manipulus florum* (1306), despite the fact that its 260-plus subject-headings are alphabetically arranged and, thus, have no use for an alphabetical subject index, nevertheless identifies each quotation with a marginal letter, for the sole purpose of permitting cross-reference; thus, for example, at the end of the quotations under the heading *Amicitia* one is cross-referred, as well, to the specific quotation *Amor d*. The third reference system consists of dividing up the physical manuscript itself according to numbered folios or numbered two-page openings, so that one may refer to page, column, even line. In discussing this method, one should first of all note that, rather than numbering the folio (the two pages that, back to back, comprise one leaf), thirteenth-century copyists more often designated the opening, the two pages that face one another when one opens a book; in this latter circumstance, the number occurs in the upper left-hand corner of the verso, and the four columns of the facing pages are counted from left to right (sometimes, not always, overtly labeled with the letters A, B, C, D).[51] One should note, as well, that the practice of foliating manuscripts and of numbering lines and columns is not a chance occurrence *in vacuo*, but a direct response to the desire of readers and users of manuscripts to be able to refer precisely to any given passage in a text. Although arabic numerals were used with increasing frequency for foliation in the second half of the thirteenth century, we must not conclude from this that it was the availability of arabic numerals which

---

[51] Regarding this system see C. A. Robson, *Maurice de Sully and the Medieval Vernacular Homily* (Oxford 1952) 14–24, and idem, "The Pecia of the Twelfth-Century School," *Dominican Studies* 2 (1949) 267–279.

caused the increase in foliation (if anything, the causation ran the opposite direction, with foliation and line-numbering hastening familiarity with the new numerals). Rather, the practice of foliating manuscripts, which was venerable but rare, suddenly increased in the thirteenth century because there was demand.

In addition to the three principal methods of division for reference there was a process that could be applied in conjunction with any of the three, namely, the system of mentally dividing a passage into sevenths, designated by the first seven letters of the alphabet A – G, to serve as the smallest and most specific unit of reference. This technique, which was first used in the Dominican biblical concordances, could be used for example in conjunction with a chapter-reference; Etienne de Bourbon, Robert Kilwardby, and most of their successors employed this system. One might also combine this system, as the Bruges Cistercians did, with reference to a folio and column, to delimit the portion of the column intended.

3. Division into Chapters

The elements that moved scholars to adopt arabic numerals and alphabetical arrangement led also to certain changes in the basic structure of texts, and of the manuscripts that contained the texts. The introduction of alternating red and blue initials in order to distinguish sections or paragraphs, hallmark of books associated with the schools, is an example. Often, more fundamental changes were made. Texts were subdivided, running titles were added to every page, chapter numbers were inscribed in the margins. The best, and best-known, instance is the new chapter-division for the text of the Bible, often attributed to Stephen Langton. In existence by 1203, this new and more sensible capitulation was widely and rapidly disseminated via the research tools produced by the Dominicans, especially the concordances, thus ensuring that the previous hodge-podge of competing divisions of Scripture would be supplanted by a single standard. The same spirit motivated the division of the Lombard's *Sentences* into distinctions (a multi-purpose word meaning, in this context, "subdivisions"), a task that we know to have been accomplished by Alexander Hales between 1223 and 1227.[52] The Hales subdivisions, accepted as quasi-standard, were often added to the margins of older manuscripts of the *Sentences*, and were rapidly adopted as

---

[52] Established by Ignatius Brady, "The Rubrics of Peter Lombard's *Sentences*," *Pier Lombardo* 6 (1962) 5–25.

necessary apparatus in new copies.[53]

Gregory the Great's *Moralia in Job* is a good example of what happened in the thirteenth century to a cumbersome work from previous ages.[54] The lengthy *Moralia*, comprising six volumes divided into thirty-five books without further division into chapters or paragraphs, was a difficult mass in which to find one's way about. Toward the end of the twelfth century, running headlines began to be added to the manuscripts, to distinguish the books one from another. The ubiquitous quotations from the Book of Job are slashed with yellow, underlined, or denoted by some kind of mark in the margins. By the mid-thirteenth century, a fairly uniform chapter-structure has evolved, to be incorporated in new copies of the work, and one begins to find lists of chapters at the beginning of the thirty-five books. Moreover, the new chapter-divisions are often noted after the fact in the margins of older manuscripts of the *Moralia*, "so that a careful reader, by using these, may find more quickly the passages with which he wishes to be instructed," or as we should say, may find what he is looking for (*ut per ea diligens lector citius invenire possit sentencias quibus edificari desirat*)—as the writer of Eton College MS 13 (s. XIII) noted at the end of the chapter-list. Finally, since the *Moralia* is a commentary on Job, it became customary to note consecutively at the appropriate place in the margin (separate from the chapter-numbers of the *Moralia* itself) the numbers of the forty-two chapters of the Book of Job. We might mention that the text of Job in the Huntington Bible mentioned above, in connection with Grosseteste's indexing symbols, presents the reverse of this, with cross-references in the margins of the biblical text to the text of the *Moralia*. Although the *Moralia* never circulated in pocket format as did the Scripture in the thirteenth century, the work was generally confined to a single codex (rather than the earlier norm of two or three) from this time onward.

The effect of new modes of use on the structure of older texts is easily demonstrated for Gregory's *Moralia* because of Neil Ker's perceptive and thorough study of the surviving manuscripts. But one might profitably examine a fair number of other early texts to see how the new

---

[53] There were a number of similar cases. Concerning the division of Augustine's *De Trinitate*, see R. W. Hunt, "Chapter Headings of Augustine *De Trinitate* Ascribed to Adam Marsh," *Bodleian Library Record* 5 (1954) 63–68. Kilwardby divided the *City of God* into chapters "to make the book easier to read" (*ut libri huius lectioni faciliorem redderet*), according to Nicholas Trevet; see B. Smalley, *English Friars and Antiquity in the Fourteenth Century* (Oxford 1960) 62.

[54] N. R. Ker, "The English Manuscripts of the *Moralia* of Gregory the Great," in *Kunsthistorische Forschungen Otto Pächt* (Salzburg 1972) 77–89.

thirteenth-century attitudes toward and use of the written heritage influenced the format of manuscripts and the structures of the texts themselves.[55]

C. REASONS FOR THE CREATION OF TOOLS

Why should it be, when Western religiosity and Western instruction had thus far been content with the minimum of technical apparatus, that the thirteenth century saw the creation of a multitude of reference tools and aids to searching? Three factors in particular should be singled out: the church's renewed emphasis on preaching; an increased interest in the whole text (in contrast to extracts); and a growth in professionalism and professional training.

1. The Needs of Preachers

Initially, the creation of tools was almost entirely a response to the newly felt needs of preachers in composing sermons. The church in the later years of the twelfth century began to focus increasing attention upon preaching to the laity, partly in response to widespread and successful heresies, partly in response to a perceived lay desire to hear sermons, a desire which itself had in a real sense contributed to the flourishing of heresy. Historically, the sermon had been employed by missionary preachers in the process of conversion. Once western Europe had been converted, the sermon — save in exceptional circumstances such as preaching the crusades — withdrew into the monasteries, where the monastic homily was the abbot's principal means of instructing his community. Of all the priests with cure of souls, only the bishops were under obligation to preach, and they only once a week. Even this slender obligation was often neglected.

We know very little about popular preaching outside the monastery at the end of the twelfth century and beginning of the thirteenth, orthodox or heterodox. Who was the Brother Albert of Mantua who preached

---

[55] For example, the *Institutiones divinae* of Lactantius, or the legal treatise of Glanvill; see *The Treatise on the Laws and Customs of the Realm of England Commonly Called Glanvill*, ed. G. D. G. Hall (London 1965) xl-lvi. See especially M. B. Parkes, "The Influence of the Concepts of *Ordinatio* and *Compilatio* on the Development of the Book," in *Medieval Learning and Literature: Essays Presented to R. W. Hunt*, ed. J. J. G. Alexander and M. T. Gibson (Oxford 1976) 115–141. *Addendum:* See now R. H. Rouse and M. A. Rouse, "*Ordinatio* and *Compilatio* Revisited," in *Ad litteram: Authoritative Texts and Their Medieval Readers*, ed. K. Emory and M. Jordan (Notre Dame, Ind. forthcoming).

at Bologna during six weeks in the year 1204 and by whom, it is said, "many were converted"?[56] Were there many wandering preachers like the fellow who, in Salimbene's description, bore a long black beard and announced his presence by blasts on his trumpet? Member of no order, he preached in the streets of Parma in the 1240s.[57] Among the obviously orthodox, it was the Cistercians who first experienced the need to train preachers and to compose sermons, for they were the ones initially charged by the papacy with combatting heresy on its own ground in the south of France and elsewhere; and the schools, especially Paris, reflected this activity well before the end of the twelfth century. Warner of Langres, Alan of Lille, and perhaps Prévostin each wrote both an antiheretical treatise and a collection of *distinctiones* for preachers.[58] Masters such as Stephen Langton, Peter the Chanter, and William de Montibus were conscious that they were training students whose primary task in life would be to preach, and to do it intelligently. The urgent need for preachers to propagate the faith in the "mission fields" of western Europe had been grasped by Innocent III as early as 1198 when he charged the Cistercians with preaching to the Cathar regions, and this same notion was codified by the Fourth Lateran Council. By the 1240s, when certain preachers in southern France were authorized to accord twenty days' indulgence to anyone who came to hear their sermons, it is obvious that the church has wholeheartedly accepted its responsibility to preach to the laity as a central part of the church's ministry.[59]

Although it is clear, from the prologues and colophons of countless reference tools, that they were created as aids to preachers, we should like to make a few precisions. First of all, we should note that the need for preaching tools was not limited to, nor did it originate with, the mendicant orders. The notion of an evangelical return to the original sources and a faith-inspired search for appropriate tools, phrases that M. D. Chenu applied to the mendicants,[60] in fact pertains to most of the literate West after about 1175, including the Cistercians, Augustinian canons, and secular clerics, as well as the later Dominicans and Franciscans.

---

[56] *Corpus chronicorum Bononiensium*, ed. A. Sorbelli, 2 (Città di Castello 1906–1907) 68–69; R. W. Southern, *Western Society and the Church in the Middle Ages*, Pelican History of the Church 2 (1970) 273–274.

[57] Salimbene de Adam, *Cronica* 1, ed. F. Bernini, Scrittori d'Italia 187 (Bari 1942) 98–100.

[58] See the work cited in n. 2 above.

[59] N. Paulus, *Geschichte des Ablasses im Mittelalter* 2 (Paderborn 1923) 43–44.

[60] M. D. Chenu, *Introduction à l'étude de saint Thomas d'Aquin* (Montréal 1950) 40–41.

Further, we note that with the passing of the sermon from cloister to parish, the form and content of the sermon underwent certain transformations that increased the necessity for the new reference tools. In the thirteenth and fourteenth centuries, the older sermon style of phrase-by-phrase exegesis on a passage of Scripture was gradually replaced by discussion of a fixed topic, organized with a logical structure and "justified" by means of exegesis, *exempla*, and quotations from authorities. Subjects having to do with the sacraments, ethics, and morals replaced the questions of doctrine and dogma that dominate the structure of the *Sentences*. To compose sermons that ranged in topic from *abstinentia* to *ambitio*, from *amor* to *mors*, the preachers had as a resource, among other things, the classical *florilegia* of ethical and moral philosophy compiled in the twelfth-century renaissance. The two most important classical *florilegia* of the twelfth century, the *Florilegium Gallicum* and the *Florilegium Angelicum*, were in fact rearranged by subject and equipped with subject indexes by the middle of the thirteenth, as an aid for preachers.[61]

One more precision: The needs of sermon-writers, the earliest and probably the most important motivation in the creation of tools, continued to provoke the creation of further reference tools well into the fifteenth century; by this time, of course, tools were being created for many other specialized purposes, but preaching tools still continued to grow in numbers and variety and to adapt in form. As an illustration of the continuing evolution, we might mention that, although compilers began to produce large collections of *exempla* (moral stories useful for preachers) from the beginning of the thirteenth century, these collections had neither an alphabetized topical arrangement nor an alphabetical subject index that would permit the collections to be searched, before the end of the century.[62] In similar fashion, the Dominicans began work on the verbal concordance to the Bible (Saint Jacques I) by the 1230s, but the definitive version (Saint Jacques III) did not circulate in Paris until around the 1280s. Alphabetized collections of biblical distinctions as a genre appeared, flourished, and then ceased to be compiled, all in the course of the thirteenth century. For these reasons one must not envisage either the reference tools or the sermons and other works for which the

---

[61] The indexed Cistercian *Flores paradysi b* (i.e., the second recension, as found in Brussels, Bibliothèque royale MS 20030–32, s. XIII) incorporates large chunks of the *Florilegium Gallicum*, as well as smaller excerpts form the *Florilegium Angelicum*; indexed or alphabetized reorderings of the *Florilegium Angelicum* appear in Paris, BN MS lat. 1860 fols. 75–153v, and Rome, Bibliotheca Angelica MS 720 fols. 1–108v.

[62] Welter, *L'exemplum* (n. 48 above) 290–334; Callus, "Contribution" (n. 31 above) 145–146.

tools were used, as static and unchanging texts. There was a reciprocity between tools and the materials they served, which affected the transformations in both.

2. Renewed Interest in Whole Texts

A second factor that influenced the development and evolution of reference tools was a renewed concern with the whole text, as opposed to excerpts or quotations or summaries. At the universities it was recognized that in order to carry out effectively the newly emphasized preaching mission of the church, preachers should be well grounded in Holy Scripture and the writings of the Fathers. Scholars as a result began to focus their attention on treating the text as an integral whole, even to the extent of valuing the integrity of an author's *oeuvre*: thus, while in manuscripts written in the twelfth century one would commonly find one or perhaps two of a patristic writer's works, in the thirteenth century one can see obvious deliberate attempts to collect (if possible) all the texts of a writer within a single codex. The catalog of Richard of Fournival's thirteenth-century library records many examples. Paris, Bibliothèque nationale MS lat. 15641, for instance, contains thirty-four separate works by Saint Ambrose, clearly the result of an attempt to reunite the Ambrosian *Opera omnia* in a single volume.

The growing importance, and generally higher esteem, accorded to the whole work in contrast to extracts can be seen in a quite revealing thirteenth-century change of terminology, with roots which one can trace back to the middle of the twelfth. Geoffrey of Auxerre describes how, on the occasion of Gilbert of Poitiers's defense at the consistory of Reims in 1148, Gilbert and his colleagues arrive bearing *codices integri*, to the confusion of Bernard and his other accusers who are armed only with a selection of patristic *auctoritates* or excerpts on a single sheet.[63] Toward 1160, Peter of Blois blames the emergence of dialectic upon a reliance on extracts instead of whole works: he complains that his nephew William has been captured by the logic masters, with whom he learns dialectic not through the usual medium of reading whole works, but by reading extracts on leaves and separate quires (*non in libris sicut solet . . . sed in schedulis et quaternis*).[64] As we see here, Geoffrey of Auxerre uses the phrase *codex integer* to mean "the entire work," and later in the century

---

[63] N. M. Haring, "Notes on the Council and Consistory of Rheims (1148)," *Mediaeval Studies* 28 (1966) 39–59, esp. 48–49.

[64] Peter of Blois, ep. 101; PL 207.312.

Peter in similar context employs the simple word *liber*, book. Both implicitly compare the whole work to extracts, to the disadvantage of the latter.

Ten or twenty years later, the theologians at the schools are emphasizing the distinction between reading extracts and immersing oneself into the whole text; and eventually they consider the latter to be so important that they endow the whole texts with something of the authority of the author's originals, by giving whole texts the new name *originalia*. Earlier in the Middle Ages, one had used the expressions *originalia rescripta* and *originalia documenta* to designate original documents, that is, instruments with signature and seal, issued by officials whether religious or lay.[65] By 1191, we see Ralph Niger employing the phrase *originalia scripta* in a changed sense, to indicate not the original or autograph text, but to signify the work in its entirety in contrast to extracts from it: Niger tells his students that the very brevity of the extracts in the gloss should be enough to warn readers that they must turn, instead, to the whole works (*intelligant ad originalia scripta fore recurrendum*).[66] With Niger's contemporary Stephen Langton the word becomes a noun, *originale* or *originalia*, for example when he contrasts the *glosa Ieronimi* with *Ieronimus in originali*, or simply *in glosa* with *in originali*.[67] Langton and Niger are perhaps the first to employ *originale* in this sense. This meaningful change rapidly gained wide acceptance, however; and by 1250 phrases like *compilatio originalium, ad originalia inquirenda, legit in originali* are commonplace. We note that *originalia*, explicitly or implicitly, means not just "whole texts," but "whole texts in contradistinction to excerpts." Moreover, the choice of *originale* (rather than *integrum* or the like) clearly and, we think, consciously implies that the whole work possesses an intrinsic authority absent from a mere extract. Once the importance of the *originale* is accepted, of course, the way is clear for the appearance of its concomitant, the *tabula originalium* or index. We are not playing on words; here, at least, the thing (*tabula originalium*) did not appear until after the adoption of the word (*originale*). These two together, the new meaning for the word *originale* and the creation of subject indexes for *originalia*, are visible signs of the new importance accorded the whole text. Indeed, by the beginning of the fourteenth century, an alphabetically arranged *flori-*

---

[65] J. de Ghellinck, "*Originale et originalia*," *Archivum latinitatis medii aevi* (Bulletin DuCange) 14 (1939) 95–105.

[66] B. Smalley, *The Study of the Bible in the Middle Ages*, 2d ed. (Oxford 1952) 226 n. 4. Concerning Niger, see G. B. Flahiff, "Ralph Niger: An Introduction to His Life and Works," *Mediaeval Studies* 2 (1940) 104–126.

[67] Smalley, op. cit. 227 and n. 3, 228 and n. 1.

legium or collection of excerpts, the *Manipulus florum* of Thomas of Ireland, attempts to take advantage of the change by presenting itself as an introduction to the *originalia patrum*.[68]

3. The Growth of Professions

Along with the other factors, the creation of reference tools was clearly encouraged by the growth of professionalism and the development of specialized training in the course of the thirteenth century, above all at the universities. More than simply the increased importance of preaching, it was the training of preachers in the schools that created an "audience" for tools—and that created the tools themselves. Much the most impressive scholarly tool of the thirteenth century was the verbal concordance to the Bible, created by the Order of Preachers at the University of Paris. In the schools of theology as in the Cistercian abbeys, the new genre of tools, indexes, and other alphabetical instruments, were at first produced by traditionalists with conservative aims. Learned prelates like Grosseteste and Kilwardby perceived, in the concordance or the subject index, a means of penetrating as deeply as possible into the core of the Christian tradition. For such as them, the index was not designed to help one cope with an ever-increasing flood of newly composed contemporary works, but rather to focus upon the authoritative texts (mostly patristic) necessary to the training of preachers and theologians, and to provide access to this corpus. Other scholars, however, quickly recognized both the value and the flexibility of the index—creating such tools, for example, to facilitate access to newly preached sermons of Fishacre, or to newly translated works of Aristotle. The schools of law and of medicine borrowed the theologians' invention to create indexes and other alphabetical reference tools adapted to the needs of their own professions.[69]

A neglected aspect of this growing professionalism is professional book-production at the universities. When one wonders why it should be that certain of these alphabetical tools were so widely used, one should recall the important role played by the university stationer in their diffusion. If a work was available at Paris in the form of *peciae*

---

[68] R. H. Rouse, "The List of Authorities Appended to the *Manipulus florum* of Thomas of Ireland," *Archives d'histoire doctrinale et littéraire du moyen âge* (1965) 243–250.

[69] L. MacKinney, "Medieval Medical Glossaries and Dictionaries," in *Medieval and Historiographical Essays in Honor of James Westfall Thompson* (Chicago 1938); J. F. von Schulte, *Die Geschichte der Quellen und Literatur des canonischen Rechts* 2 (Stuttgart 1877) 485–506; E. Seckel, *Beiträge zur Geschichte beider Rechte im Mittelalter* 1 (Tübingen 1898).

(quires for rent), it could of course be copied by numerous copyists simultaneously, thus increasing geometrically the number of copies of the text in circulation and, as a result, increasing the text's influence.[70] For example: The first verbal concordance (Saint Jacques I), which was circulated by traditional methods of manuscript production, survives in only some twenty-five copies; the version (Saint Jacques III) published some forty years later via the university stationers survives in more than eighty copies. The *Manipulus florum*, an alphabetized collection of extracts for preachers, survives in some one hundred eighty copies; slightly less than ten percent of these derive from the private recension, while all the rest are descendants of a Paris stationer's editions. In addition to the concordance and the *Manipulus florum*, works distributed via the Paris stationers include the alphabetical distinction collections of Maurice of Provins, Nicholas Gorran, and Nicholas Biard, subject indexes to the Lombard's *Sentences* and to Aristotle's *Ethics*, such preachers' *florilegia* as the *Liber pharetrae* and the *Alphabetum narrationum*, and others, all of them indebted to the university system of book production for much of the popularity they enjoyed.

D. THE INFLUENCE OF MEDIEVAL REFERENCE TOOLS

What effect had the various research tools and scholarly aids of the thirteenth century on contemporary writing? De Ghellinck assumed that such devices had distanced preachers and writers from the *originalia* and, ultimately, had supplanted the reading of and familiarity with the whole texts; thus, such tools were in large part responsible for what he saw as the declining vitality of expression that marked the late Middle Ages.[71]

Certainly, the influence of these devices depends almost entirely upon the fashion in which they were employed. If a writer used such tools mechanically, the results were predictably insipid. But if tools were used to find a sought-for item of information, they instead represented a positive factor, in the sense that they afforded a writer greater flexibility and freer expression. Fourteenth-century preachers, for example, had at their disposal not only a battery of preachers' aids, but also detailed

---

[70] See now the collected articles edited by L. J. Bataillon et al., *La production du livre universitaire au moyen âge* (Paris 1988).

[71] De Ghellinck, *"Originale"* (n. 65 above); interestingly, the "fact" that the quality of expression did indeed diminish in the late Middle Ages was, in de Ghellinck's view, sufficiently self-evident not to require argument.

directions for their use. The preachers' handbook or *ars praedicandi* of Jean de Chalons (ca. 1372) details no fewer than fourteen different modes of developing a sermon, and the majority of these make use of reference tools.[72] In his explanation of Expansion by Opposition, for example, Jean says, "In the theme-passage *Ero humilis in oculis meis*, the principal subject is *humilitas* and its opposite *superbia*. Search, therefore, in the concordance under the word *superbia*, or in the *Manipulus florum* under the same word, or in [the *Distinctiones* of] Maurice or in the Dictionary [of Brito], to find the conditions and properties of *superbia*, and choose several of them to form a proposition with several members, which holds the '*Superbia* is such-and-such.'" (We note in passing that each of the tools alluded to here had been published by university stationers at Paris.) A skillful preacher like John of Schoonhoven, for example—one of Ruysbroeck's disciples—knew how to use a tool like the *Manipulus florum* to advantage, finding by means of it the words and quotations that he wanted.[73] Able writers made judicious use of such tools, rather than allowing the tools to prescribe how and what they wrote. Let us take an example from vernacular literature, the *Epistre d'Othea* of Christine de Pisan.[74] In writing this work, Christine was free to choose, on the basis of her literary judgment, an arbitrary structure comprising one hundred chapters, each devoted to a single moral topic (virtues, vices, etc.) and each constructed on virtually the same model: The theme is set forth in verse, a prose anecdote (mostly stories from antiquity) illustrates the theme, and an "allegory" expounds the moral, rounded off with two appropriate quotations, one from the Bible and one from patristic literature. Christine knew securely in advance that she would be able to lay hands on the building blocks to fill her structure: Bersuire's *Ovide moralisé* provided the ancient stories, and for the rest she had at her disposal two standard alphabetized reference tools, the concordance to help her find biblical quotations and the *Manipulus florum* to find quotations from the Fathers.

---

[72] Jean de Chalon's *ars praedicandi* is found, for example, in Paris, BN MSS lat. 14580 fols. 152–160, 14909 fols. 126–128, and 15173 fols. 12–24v. See T.M. Charland, *Artes praedicandi: Contribution à l'étude de la rhétorique du moyen âge* (Paris 1936) 53; P.Glorieux, *Répertoire des maîtres en théologie de Paris au XIIIe siècle* 2, Etudes de philosophie médiévale 18 (Paris 1934) 261–262.

[73] Albert Gruijs, *Jean de Schoonhoven . . . De contemptu huius mundi: Textes et études*, Thèse de doctorat du 3 e cycle . . . Université de Paris (Nijmegen 1967); John of Schoonhoven's use of the *Manipulus florum* is documented there.

[74] The work is not edited. See P. G. C. Campbell, *L'Epitre d'Othea: Etude sur les sources de Christine de Pisan* (Paris 1924) 160–169; and the notes of C. F. Bühler in his edition of the translation of *L'Epistre* into English by Stephen Scrope, Early English Text Society 264 (London 1970).

The importance of reference tools to fourteenth- and fifteenth-century writers has a corollary for the modern historian of the literature of this period. When a scholar examines a late medieval author's thought, or edits a text composed in this period, he must attempt not only to identify the ultimate source of an extract or allusion, but also to seek out the intermediate source from which the quotation may have come. One must, in other words, study not only an author's thought but his working methods. Too often, it is the unsuspected reference tool that has, in fact, set the literary horizons of an author. We can illustrate this by once again taking Christine de Pisan as an example. The fifth chapter of the *Epistre d'Othea* describes the rescue of Andromeda by Perseus. Perseus, says Christine (following Bersuire), signifies Renown; and she quotes, "Saint Augustine says that two things are necessary to a good life: a good conscience and a good reputation, the conscience for one's own good and the reputation for the benefit of one's neighbor. And whoever relies solely on his conscience and despises reputation is cruel." Christine has borrowed this quotation (which she employs as well in her *Livre des trois vertus*) from the chapter *Fama* in the *Manipulus florum*. This same citation from Augustine appears in Geoffrey Chaucer's *Tale of Melibee*;[75] the author of Chaucer's French source for this tale, Renaud de Louens, like Christine, had borrowed the quotation from the *Manipulus florum*. The author of the *Manipulus*, Thomas of Ireland, in turn had borrowed this excerpt (and many others) from the thirteenth-century *Flores paradysi*, an alphabetically indexed *florilegium* discussed above. Clearly, if Christine de Pisan or Chaucer's source had not found this excerpt, they would each simply have used another, without great loss to Western literature. But since both of them did, in the event, borrow it, we should be aware of the fact that the use of this quotation by two important late medieval vernacular authors depends, in unbroken succession, upon the choice made by an anonymous Cistercian florilegist at the beginning of the thirteenth century when he created his reference tool.

* * *

The entirety of these thirteenth-century scholarly tools comprises the foundation of all later attempts to provide access to the written heritage. Historians of printing and psychologists of communication generally attribute the appearance of indexes and the introduction of alphabetical arrangement to the invention of the printing press. The press, by

---

[75] J. B. Severs, in W. F. Bryan and G. Dempster, eds., *Sources and Analogues of Chaucer's Canterbury Tales* (Chicago 1941) 560–614, esp. 604, to lines 927–929.

producing 500 or more uniform copies of a single text, enabled one to join a uniform apparatus to the text. Thus, Walter Ong said in 1977, "Once a fixed order is established in print, it can be multiplied with little effort almost withouᵗ limit. This makes it more worthwhile to do the arduous work of elaborating serviceable arrangements and—what is all-important—of devising complex, visually serviceable indexes. A hundred dictated handwritten copies of a work would normally require a hundred indexes, . . . whereas five thousand or more printed copies of an edition of a given work would all be served by one and the same index."[76] The logic of this argument is sound; literate society certainly complicated things by inventing the subject index over two hundred years before inventing the press. The fact remains that indexes and other finding tools were invented because there was need for them—not because it was easy, or practical, to make them at a certain time. In devising these tools, medieval man pushed the manuscript book to the very limits of precision; and in the final analysis the uniformity and much greater precision of the printed book were essential before the reference tool could advance further. It is certainly true, as well, that many works were alphabetically indexed for the first time upon first printing. Both the methods and the motives, however, were inherited from the Middle Ages. The chapter summaries and subject indexes to the works of Saint Augustine in the early modern Maurist edition (reprinted in Migne's *Patrologia*) are those devised in the thirteenth century by Robert Kilwardby, because the Benedictines of Saint Maur considered them the best available.

---

[76] W. Ong, *Interface of the Word* (Ithaca 1977) 163.

Book Production:
Stationers and Peciae

8. The Book Trade at the University of Paris, ca. 1250–ca. 1350[*]

In the old days—by which we mean, before Jean Destrez—institutional historians studied, and attempted to explain, the book trade at the medieval University of Paris on the basis of the official documents left by the university. As we now know, they missed the point almost entirely. Destrez, working instead from the manuscripts produced by that book trade, was able to deduce the mechanisms of stationer-production, a process to which the most detailed scrutiny of the archives would never have provided the key. Since Destrez's time, most study of the Paris book trade, and virtually all such study of significant value, has been based as was his upon examination of stationer-produced manuscripts.

It therefore occurred to us that it might prove fruitful to return once again to the published archives and other printed sources—armed, as our predecessors were not, with a knowledge of what was really taking place—and to see if the documents will now give up a bit more information than they yielded in the past. We are fortunate, of course, that by now the printed sources include meticulous studies of numerous pecia-disseminated works of St. Thomas produced by the Leonine Commission, to set alongside the printed charters, regulations, oaths, and tax records. Once begun, however, our study inevitably spread again to touch the manuscripts, incorporating further discoveries of our own and information generously contributed by friends.

Originally published in *La production du livre universitaire au moyen âge: Exemplar et pecia*, ed. L. J. Bataillon, B. G. Guyot, and R. H. Rouse (Paris 1988) 41–114.

[*]This article could not have been written without the generosity of numerous scholars, whose contributions on special topics are acknowledged throughout. Here we wish to thank especially Louis Bataillon, O.P., and Hugues Shooner, who graciously shared with us their knowledge of the subject as a whole.

We have organized our information around two broad topics—the university bookmen, and the books they produced. Our observations are confined to Paris, and largely to the century from 1250 to 1350.

I. THE UNIVERSITY BOOKMEN

A. *Librarii and Stationarii*

First, let us consider the meaning of the word *stationarius*, and specifically in what respects it differs from *librarius*. The surviving university documents are not only sparse but ambiguous in their references to the book trade, and the early ones especially are casually imprecise in terminology. For example, the oldest surviving Paris book provision (1275) regulates the "*stationarii*, who are commonly called *librarii*"—and thereafter consistently refers to the stationers as "the aforementioned *librarii*."[1] Modern scholars have too often misinterpreted this evidence, with a perverse twist of logic: If stationers are still called *librarii* in 1275 (they seem to say), then we may justifiably equate *librarii* with stationers—in 1250, or 1225, or as early as we please. Art historians have been particular, though unintentional, culprits; for they refer in passing to secondary studies, simply to document the fact that a book trade existed, before getting down to the matter of importance for themselves, the physical evidence for professional illuminators. Thus, one study notes that "the oldest mention of *librarii* and *stationarii* goes back to the last third of the twelfth century at Paris, the time when the new system of book production [by peciae] was initiated"; and another states that, "[in the 1170s] mention is made for the first time of the existence of *stationarii*." In both cases the ultimate source is a letter (ca. 1175) of Peter of Blois that alludes to a scoundrelly secondhand-book monger (*mango librorum*), with never a mention of the words *librarius, stationarius,* or *pecia*. Robert Branner's excellent study of *Manuscript Painting in Paris during the Reign of St. Louis* likewise speaks in the text of "students who earned their keep by copying texts for the booksellers"; in the index, "bookseller" is defined as *librarius*, but the footnote to this passage refers to Destrez's *La pecia* (in toto, not to a specific page). Still more recently, in 1982, the distinction between *librarii* and *stationarii* has been posed as a sharp dichotomy of old books/new books: "Books . . . were to be purchased from *libraires*, who acted as agents

---

[1] *Chartularium Universitatis Parisiensis*, ed. H. Denifle and E. Chatelain, 4 vols. (Paris 1889–1897) no. 462 (vol. 1 pp. 532–534); hereafter cited as CUP.

selling volumes placed on deposit with them. New manuscripts were commissioned from *stationnaires*, . . . who hired calligraphers and other craftsmen"—whereas, in fact, both sorts of bookmen acted as agents for book sales, and both produced new books on commission. (Although this author cites Jules [*sic*] Destrez, he doubtless derived this characterization of *librarii* and *stationarii* from his other source, the nineteenth-century work of Paul Delalain.)[2] Now, in none of these instances does the imprecision have any bearing at all on the validity of the art-historical arguments being advanced; but such careless language adds unnecessary confusion to an already blurred picture.

It is clear from most contemporary contexts that the two terms were not synonymous—that *librarius* is the general term, and that *stationarius* refers to one specific kind of *librarius*. From at least 1316, university book provisions are always careful to name both groups, *librarii et stationarii*. Moreover, among the thirty-seven bookmen (including two bookwomen) whose individual oaths survive (from a forty-year period, 1314–1354), many are called *librarius* (or *clericus et librarius, librarius et illuminator, librarius juratus*) without the designation *stationarius*; but every *stationarius* bears the double title: *stationarius et librarius*.[3]

The term *librarius* as a noun exists in antiquity, and its use extends uninterrupted, from then through the period we are considering and beyond. Its meaning, however, is unhelpfully elastic, including (not exhaustively) scribe, bookseller, and librarian. On the contrary, at Paris the term *stationarius* originates as a university phenomenon. The word is not attested at Paris before the last third of the thirteenth century (see below); at that time, and without interruption through the fourteenth century at least, this term occurs only and specifically in a university context. We are probably nearer the truth, then, if we consider that stationers were not merely regulated, but created, by the university community.

---

[2] See Paul Delalain, *Etude sur le libraire parisien du XIIIe au XVe siècle* (Paris 1891) xvii-xxii, esp. xviii-xix; François Avril, "A quand remontent les premiers ateliers d'enlumineurs laïcs à Paris?" in *Les dossiers de l'archéologie: Enluminure gothique*, no. 16 (1975) 37 n. 3; Walter Cahn, "St. Albans and the Channel Style in England," in *The Year 1200: A Symposium* (New York 1975) 199 and n. 75; R. Branner, *Manuscript Painting* . . . (Berkeley 1977) 2 and n. 6; and Patrick M. de Winter, "The *Grandes Heures* of Philip the Bold, Duke of Burgundy; The Copyist Jean l'Avenant and His Patrons at the French Court," *Speculum* 57 (1982) 786 and n. 1. De Winter also mistakenly assumes that "both *libraires* and *stationnaires* . . . lent, against a set fee, controlled and approved *exemplaria* from which copies could be made" (ibid.).

[3] Concerning the nature of these oaths, see Appendix 1 below, "A Note on the Sources."

A *stationarius* is someone who has a *statio*. *Statio* can mean "a fixed place of business, a shop,"[4] and scholars have singled this out as the characteristic distinguishing a *stationarius* from the supposedly itinerant *librarius*.[5] This is clearly wrong, as witness university regulations that distinguish ordinary *librarii* from those marginal figures who operate out of stalls. The street-by-street Paris tax records of the 1290s also imply a fixed location for *librarii*. Or to take specific examples: Geoffroy de St. Léger, Thomas de Maubeuge, and Richard de Montbaston were important producers of decorated books for the luxury trade, not itinerants working out of a barrow; yet all three are known, through their individual oaths, as "mere" *librarii* and not *stationarii*.[6] Regardless of etymology, at the University of Paris a different connotation of the word applied. A useful analogy is the *stationarius* of late antiquity: a minor official, military or governmental, who holds a *statio*, i.e., an office or position. Indeed, by the beginning of the fourteenth century (before 1313) the university's records employ the words "the office of stationer."[7] In the world of Paris booksellers, therefore, a *stationarius* is not merely one who "owns a shop" but one who fills a post.

What was unique about that post? In answering that question, let us first clear the underbrush by noting the things that are *not* distinctive: both the *stationarii* and the other *librarii* were regulated by the university; both were heavily involved in the secondhand trade; both produced new books; and both (as we shall see) were roundly damned by the university as frauds, cheats, and thieving rascals—but without any distinction between one group of bandits and the other. The sole distinguishing

---

[4] The word "shop" here, and throughout this paper, means merely "place of business" and does not imply "workshop": *boutique*, not *atelier*.

[5] See, for example, Delalain, *Etude* xvii and nn. 2, 3. Concerning the permutations of the word *stationarius*, see Olga Weijers, *Terminologie des universités au XIIIe siècle*, Lessico intellettuale europeo 39 (Rome 1987) 240–260, "Stationarius, Librarius, Peciarius, Exemplator(-arius), Scriptor, etc." Her work clearly shows that the term was used differently at the Southern universities from the use at Paris. We thank her for permitting us to consult her work in typescript.

[6] See CUP 2.191: "nullus non juratus habeat aliquem librum venalem altra valorem decem solidorum, nec sub tecto sedeat." Four (of the surviving seven) *taille* books of Paris have been published: H. Géraud, ed., *Paris sous Philippe-le-Bel . . . Le rôle de la taille . . . 1292* (Paris 1837); Karl Michaëlsson, *Le livre de la taille de Paris . . . 1296*, Göteborgs Universitets Årsskrift 64 no. 4 (Göteborg 1958); idem, *Le livre de la taille de Paris . . . 1297*, ibid. 67 no. 3 (Göteborg 1962); and idem, *Le livre de la taille de Paris . . . 1313*, ibid. 57 no. 3 (Göteborg 1951). Concerning Geoffroy, Thomas, and Richard, see pt. I-C below.

[7] CUP 2.98: regulations "circa officia stacionariorum," with a threat that should any stationer contravene them, "ex tunc *a suo officio* sit ille qui hoc fecerit alienus" (italics ours). Concerning the date of these regulations, added to the oath of 1302, see below. The term continued to be used regularly; see CUP 2.189, at the end of the editors' lengthy note.

factor is that those *librarii* who were stationers rented out peciae, and those *librarii* who were not stationers did not. The stationer did not have a different function, but rather an additional one.

1. What did stationers do that was new?

As Destrez was aware, parcelling out the quires of a manuscript to several scribes at once for rapid reproduction was a time-honored procedure, one that antedated, and eventually coexisted with, stationer production. The system was employed as early as the ninth century—in the production of Bibles at Tours, for example: Destrez himself cites examples from the thirteenth and fourteenth centuries; and Doyle and Parkes have shown the same process in operation in the late fourteenth and early fifteenth centuries, among commercial London scribes reproducing works of Chaucer and Gower.[8]

The procedure as adapted for stationer-production, however, presents several distinctive additions: (1) The notion of the exemplar, i.e., the production of a text whose sole *raison d'être* was the production of further copies. (2) The intent to produce many copies simultaneously, rather than a single copy rapidly; thus, the peciae were not divided up among several scribes at once, but rather each scribe copied each pecia in turn, with other copyists following in stages behind him, doing likewise. (3) The publicized offer of peciae, for a fixed rental fee. (4) Most distinctive of all, the regulation and supervision of this process by the university, backed by its authority and power of monopoly.

2. When did stationer production begin?

Destrez singled out the period 1225–1235 as the time when "le fonctionnement de la pecia est *déjà une institution régulière et normale*"—which he qualified in the next sentence with "plus probablement." Later he summarizes, "C'est probablement à l'Université de Paris, vers 1225–1235, que cette institution de la pecia fait son apparition." Destrez's datespan was based on a single manuscript of Philip the Chancellor's *Quaestiones*, B.N. lat. 16387, which he thought to have been copied not long after the work was composed, 1225–35.[9] Destrez's uneasiness, reflected in the repeated "probably," undoubtedly stemmed from the fact that, of the hundreds of other Paris manuscripts

---

[8] E. K. Rand, *A Survey of the Manuscripts of Tours* (Cambridge, Mass. 1929) vol. 1 pp. 22–23, 31, 135–136, no. 77; J. Destrez, *La pecia* (Paris 1935) 21 and n. 1; and A. I. Doyle and M. B. Parkes, "The Production of Copies of the *Canterbury Tales* and the *Confessio amantis* in the Early Fifteenth Century," in *Medieval Scribes, Manuscripts and Libraries: Essays Presented to N. R. Ker,* ed. M. B. Parkes and A. G. Watson (London 1978) 163–210.

[9] Destrez, *La pecia* 23, 42.

with pecia marks that he had found, all clearly date from the second half of the thirteenth century or later. Historians have sometimes seized upon Destrez's date, while ignoring Destrez's reservations, and have cited the university stationers in connection with the production of books in Paris from ca. 1220 or before.

This date seems too early, in that the university did not have suffi-cient structure to regulate the trade and impose an oath by 1225. The fact that the university was capable of concerted boycott, in the face of student-townsmen riots, does not in any sense imply the capacity for continuing and continuous regulation of details. While the individual faculties were capable of enforcing internal regulations of curriculum, for example, and of attempting to wrest from the chancellor the right to regulate the license to teach, it seems most unlikely that the faculties at that date could have acted in concert to stipulate and enforce detailed regulation of booksellers.[10] Compare the later practices with this period: the only recorded delegation of *taxatores* (those who set rates for pecia rental), in 1304, consisted of the rector, the proctors of the nations, and representative masters of the higher faculties;[11] the assembling of such a group—and especially the implicit assumption that the rector of the Arts Faculty was the leader—simply does not fit what we know of the Uni-versity of Paris in the second quarter of the century. The earliest surviv-ing book provisions at Paris, those of 1275, are authenticated with the seal of the university: the university did not have a corporate seal until 1246.[12] In 1275 the university did not even have a customary meeting place for its general congregations; it conducted corporate business in various borrowed halls, such as the College de St.-Bernard or, most fre-quently, the church of St-Julien-le-Pauvre, before settling on the cen-trally located hall of the Mathurins as its quasi-official congregation house. The book provisions of 1275 were adopted at a university session held—uniquely, it seems—in the chapter house of the Dominicans of St. Jacques.[13]

---

[10] Surviving records of individual faculties' exercising the right to enforce their own statutes date only from the 1270s at Paris; see Pearl Kibre, *Scholarly Privileges in the Mid-dle Ages* (Cambridge, Mass. 1962) 251 n. 1.

[11] CUP no. 642 = vol. 2 p. 107.

[12] Kibre, *Privileges* 99.

[13] CUP 1.534: "Acta ex deliberacione et statuta sunt hec in congregatione generali Parisius in capitulo fratrum predicatorum et sigillo Universitatis sigillata." All the later book provisions discussed in this article were issued from the Mathurins. For the Collège de St-Bernard, see CUP 1.539 (1276); for St-Julien-le-Pauvre, see CUP 1.257 (1254), 1.589, 1.590, 1.591 (all 1281); and cf. 1.542 (1277, law faculty) and 1.570 (arts faculty).

What hard evidence do we have of stationer production at Paris in the first half of the thirteenth century? (1) First, there is Destrez's example, the manuscript of Philip the Chancellor with pecia marks. We have not seen this manuscript, but to judge from Destrez's plate, a date before 1250 is not necessarily indicated. The fact that the text is written below, rather than above, the top line of ruling would, on the contrary, tend to date it post 1240.[14] (2) A second matter pertains to Paris only by inference. Graham Pollard notes the Vercelli contract of 1228, which promises the students two *exemplatores* if they will settle in this city; and he makes a plausible case for tracing back the existence of *exemplatores*, via Padua, to Bologna ca. 1200.[15] One may certainly assume that, if pecia-production were in full bloom at Bologna by 1200, it would not have taken fifty years for the University of Paris to recognize the obvious advantages of the system and to adopt it for themselves. The problem with this evidence is the unanswered question: Where are the manuscripts? Why do we not have ten, twenty, fifty Italian law-books with pecia marks surviving from the first decades of the thirteenth century? We do not know the answer; but we suggest that the interpretation of the word *exemplator* is not, in fact, as straightforward as Pollard assumed, and that the service performed by an Italian *exemplator* in 1300 was not the same as that which his namesake had performed in the year 1200.

The earliest datable pecia mark was thought by Pollard to be in a Parisian manuscript of Hugh of St-Cher's postills on the Pauline epistles, which was bequeathed to Durham Cathedral by Bertram of Middleton, who died in 1258.[16] To judge from its good quality, however, this manuscript is clearly not a pecia manuscript of the type produced by the trade which Destrez is describing. It may reflect a method of producing books internal to St-Jacques of Paris, in which a writer is simply keeping a record of the number of quires he has transcribed. The earliest use (known to us) of the word *stationarius* at Paris occurs in Roger Bacon's *Opus minus* (1267).[17] (We should mention that Bacon, in 1267, speaks of *stationarii librorum* of some forty years earlier, on whose corrupt exemplars he blames the corrupt text of the scriptures; but his assumption was surely an anachronism: a thoroughgoing survey of thirteenth-century Paris Bibles has revealed none with pecia-marks

[14] Destrez, *La pecia*, pl. 1; N. R. Ker, "From 'Above Top Line' to 'Below Top Line': A Change in Scribal Practice," *Celtica* 5 (1960) 13-16.

[15] Graham Pollard, "The *Pecia* System in the Medieval Universities," in *Medieval Scribes, Manuscripts and Libraries* 145-161, esp. 146-148.

[16] Ibid., 146.

[17] Roger Bacon, *Opus minus,* in his *Opera*, ed. J. S. Brewer, Rolls Series 15 (London 1859) 333.

written before the 1260s or 1270s.) The word occurs again in 1270, in a Notre Dame record of a piece of property sold by a *stationarius librorum*.[18]

We may mention in addition two arguments *ex silentio* — significant silence, in our estimate. First, Destrez cites an exemplum from a sermon of Robert de Sorbon, to document the continuing vitality of the old practice of reproducing a manuscript by distributing its quires, quite outside the university pecia system. The exemplum tells of a beguine who bought at Paris a *Summa de vitiis et virtutibus*; subsequently, while living in a cathedral city, she used to provide the priests who came to town with quires of the *Summa* for copying, with the result that the text was multiplied throughout the whole region. Robert died in 1274. The "significant silence" is the fact that he does not, as one might have expected, explain the beguine's activities to his Parisian audience by likening them to the procedure of the stationers.[19]

The second item is the oldest surviving book provision of the University of Paris, dated 1275. It is too long to quote in extenso, but we note the following: (1) It makes no distinction between the terms *stationarii* and *librarii* ("stationarii, qui vulgo librarii appellantur"). (2) The document fills 50 lines of print, in the *Chartularium*; of these, a total of only 5 lines are concerned with the exemplars of "said booksellers" (*dicti librarii*). (3) The entire obligation of these "booksellers" with respect to exemplars is expressed in one sentence: "Because great harm ensues from corrupt and faulty exemplars, we order that the said booksellers swear that they will display care and efficiency, diligence and effort, to see that their exemplars are true and correct, and that they will charge for these no more than a just and moderate salary or payment — or whatever rate has been set by the university or its delegates." The simplicity of this document, set alongside the detailed provisions of later ones, suggests the probability that it is not only the earliest to survive, but the earliest that ever existed, at Paris.[20]

---

[18] B. Guérard, *Cartulaire de Notre-Dame* 3 (Paris 1850) 73–74. Concerning this stationer, William of Sens, see below, pt. I-D.

[19] Destrez, *La pecia* 21 and n. 2.

[20] CUP no. 462 = vol. 1 pp. 532–534. Although we are considering in this article only the University of Paris, we note that it is instructive as well to compare the simplicity of that university's book provisions of 1275 with the more detailed regulations found in the earliest surviving book provisions of Bologna, edited by Miroslav Boháček, "Zur Geschichte der Stationarii von Bologna," *Eos* 48 pt. 2 (1956) 258. Contemporary with the Paris document (Boháček offers the date 1274–1276), the wording of the Bolognese statutes seems to imply that university had begun to regulate booksellers and stationers slightly earlier, on the one hand. On the other hand, marked similarities — both Paris and Bologna are primarily concerned with regulating the secondhand book trade, not the rental of pecia; and

We do not imply, obviously, that the complex system of pecia-production sprang into instant existence, ex nihilo, in 1275. The following explanation seems more likely: The system had developed in the 1250s and 1260s, gradually evolving its own practices, procedures, and customs. By 1275, the transactions of pecia-rental had increased greatly, in number, in usefulness to the university, and in instances of abuse such as over-charging and circulation of faulty texts. At that point, the university both felt the responsibility and had the corporate capacity to attempt to regulate the procedure.

Even in 1275, the university's control of—and interest in—the operation of the stationers was just beginning to take shape. As late as 1302 we find that the university book provisions do not distinguish by nomenclature (although there is distinction of function) between stationers and other *librarii*. While the statute of 1275 casually refers to all bookmen as *librarii*, the oath of 1302 just as casually calls them stationers: "In A.D. 1302 . . . the stationers, in general assembly at the Mathurins, swore the following articles. . . ." The subsequent oath, however, like the 1275 document, begins with the rules for selling books on behalf of a third party, a matter that concerned all *librarii* and not just the stationers. The assembled bookmen swore to observe seven detailed articles that regulated their actions as agents for sale, followed by three brief articles concerning *exemplaria*—that (1) the exemplars should be true and correct, and that the charge for them would be (2) no more than the university's assessed rates, or (3) no more than a just and moderate sum, for exemplars that had not been assessed.[21] In other words, the university was scarcely more sophisticated or specific in its dealings with the stationers in 1302 than it had been in 1275.

This state of affairs was to change, and in fairly short order. An addendum to the oath of 1302 provides three further, and detailed, regulations for stationers; the date of the addition is unknown, but it probably fell within the first decade of the century, surely before 1313.[22] By

---

the two universities allow booksellers exactly the same commission, on sales made as agents for third parties—confirm that the two were each well aware of the other's practices. Such a useful practice as book-production via pecia-rental, in other words, would have been transmitted almost at once from one university to the other. In weighing such subjective matters as "wording" and "tone" of these documents, we must also recognize that, in 1274–76 and later regulations, the language at Bologna tends to be precise and legalistic, whereas at Paris, in 1275 and later, book provisions are apt to read like sermons calling sinners to repentance.

[21] CUP no. 628 = vol. 2 pp. 97–98.

[22] CUP no. 628, addendum = vol. 2 p. 98. The original of this document does not survive. The addendum was made "tempore Johannis de Briquebec," presumably the rector, but his dates are not known. The only surviving full copy of the oath and its adden-

1316 at latest, regulation of stationers is still more detailed, the university clearly distinguishes between *stationarii* and *librarii* as groups, and the surviving written oaths distinguish precisely the status of individuals in the book trade.

We should be very much surprised, in sum, if there were pecia-produced manuscripts at Paris as early as 1225. More important, we feel that it is very misleading to assume that the nascent pecia-production of the 1250s and 1260s came under the sort of detailed university regulation which is first implied by the book provisions of the early fourteenth century.

B. University Control over Bookmen

Did the university control all members of the Paris booktrade? While it is true that a royal *ordonnance* of 1370 speaks of "the *librarii* of the university" (*librarii universitatis*)[23] — from which one might infer the existence of *librarii* who were *not* attached to the university — it is clear from other evidence that the university claimed and, by 1313 at latest, exercised jurisdiction over the entire trade: *librarii* (including stationers), illuminators, parchmenters. A surviving individual oath from 1316 contains an escape clause, to the effect that the oath-taker was not bound if the university failed to compel "all the other *librarii* of Paris" to abide by the same oath — a clear implication that the university had jurisdiction over every single bookdealer, or ought to. (In later oaths, from 1335 onward, the university prudently dropped this clause.) In addition, the royal privilege for the *librarii universitatis* (discussed below) was, in practice, applied to all the *librarii* (and illuminators and parchmenters) of Paris. The university regulations of December 1316 are quite explicit: Any *librarius* who had not sworn an oath was limited to the sale of books valued at ten *solidi* or less (= two quires? perhaps three?) and was forbidden to "sit under a roof," i.e., to own a shop.[24]

---

dum is contained in Vatican Library MS Reg. lat. 406, a collection of (largely) thirteenth-century university material made evidently for the Picard Nation. The collection was written by a single hand at the beginning of the fourteenth century, the latest dated document being the *taxatio* of 1304; see A. Wilmart, *Codices Reginenses latini* 2 (Vatican City 1945) 477–482. The addendum must in any case antedate the taille of 1313; see below.

[23] CUP no. 661 = vol. 2 p. 123.

[24] CUP no. 732 = vol. 2 pp. 188–189, esp. the editors' note at the end; CUP no. 733 (1316) = vol. 2 p. 191.

1. Limited extent of university control

A necessary distinction must be made, however, when we speak of university "control" of the booktrade. All members of the trade received privileges (legal and financial) from the university, in return for swearing to observe rules that prescribed their dealings with the masters and scholars. But it would be far wrong to assume that all of an individual *libraire*'s work—or even, necessarily, the most lucrative portion of it— had to do with the university. Provided they met their university obligations, *librarii* (including *librarii* who were stationers) were otherwise free to produce and sell books, illuminators to illuminate, scribes to write, for anyone else they pleased: the Court, the cathedral, the wealthy laymen of the capital and the provinces. This part of their trade, for many the most substantial part, did not fall under university regulation.[25] Major producers of books for the luxury trade—men such as Thomas de Maubeuge, Geoffroy de St. Léger, Richard de Montbaston (see pt. I–C below)—were free to charge whatever the market would bear and to organize production and sales as they wished, in their dealings with outsiders. The external trade of "university" *librarii* needs to be emphasized, because too often the university's regulations of the internal trade are cited in the context of production of elaborately decorated deluxe items for king and nobles. The distinction must be borne in mind, as we consider the university's relations with "its" *librarii*.

2. Resistance to university control

Relations between university and bookmen at Paris were normally adversarial, and often stormy. And in between the outbreaks that were turbulent enough to have left a record, the attitude must have been continually one of justified suspicion on the part of the university, and justified resentment on the part of the booksellers. An examination of the university book provisions, the oaths required of *librarii* and *stationarii* in the thirteenth and fourteenth centuries, shows part of the reason why:

---

[25] Only one sort of regulation consistently mentions "outsiders" (*extranei*), namely, the agent's fee that a bookseller might add to the cost of a secondhand book sold for a third party: the charge to nonuniversity purchasers was 50 percent higher. Such regulations always forbade the *librarius* to demand a fee from the seller also, *if* that seller was "magister vel scolar" (see CUP no. 628 [1302] = vol. 2 p. 97; CUP no. 1064 [1342] = vol. 2 p. 531). Moreover, stationers were forbidden to exceed the university's set rental rates, *if* they were renting to masters or scholars (ibid.). Pointedly in these cases, tacitly in others, the university regulated the booktrade strictly for the good of the university; *caveat extraneus*!

A very large concern, and perhaps the foremost concern, of the university was not with the regulation of pecia-rental, which seems so significant to us, but with what strikes us as a minor matter: the sale of secondhand books. Regulation of this procedure is the first matter dealt with, and it is dealt with at greatest length, in the surviving book-provisions of 1275, 1302, and 1342, and is a major point of contention as well in the only others that survive for our period (1316, repeated verbatim in 1323). The booksellers had to swear, and to deposit a bond to keep the oath, that they would not buy secondhand books and resell them, but would rather merely act as intermediaries between seller and buyer: the *libraires* were required to give a professional assessment of the likely price of books submitted to them, to display those books prominently in their shops, to put would-be buyers into direct contact with the seller — and to take profit limited to four pence in the pound! — an enormous amount of bother for a profit (*if* the book was sold) of 1.7 percent, which can scarcely have paid for the time and the "shelf-space" required.[26] The booksellers must have found this not merely irritating but well-nigh insupportable; and they cheated with regularity. The university *knew* the bookmen were cheating, and repeatedly tried to compel compliance. We see that the oaths drawn up by the university for the *librarii* almost never begin simply "you do solemnly swear that. . . ." Instead, there is an acrimonious prologue saying something like "Given that certain of the booksellers, out of insatiable greed, have seriously inconvenienced the students and have even prevented them from acquiring the absolutely essential books, by buying from them below market price and selling to them at inflated rates, and by engaging in underhanded maneuvers to inflate prices artificially . . . they must hereby swear that" etc.[27] In a record from June 1316, when tempers were especially high, even the salutation is menacing: "To whom it may concern, greeting *in the name of Him who does not allow the misdeeds of the wicked to go unpunished.* Since impunity for evil deeds can only encourage them, . . . since the *librarii* and *stationarii*, subordinates of the university that protects and enriches them, have repeatedly been guilty of

---

[26] If the buyer was an *extraneus*, the fee rose to six pence in the pound, or 2.5 percent — still quite small. At Bologna in 1274–76; (see n. 20 above), the agency fee was expressed differently: twelve pence for a book sold at three pounds *or less* — thus, the same 1.7 percent for a sale at three pounds; but the percentage increased proportionately on cheaper books. The most notable difference from the Parisian regulations is the sharply graduated decrease in the percentage of the commission, as prices rose; thus, the stipulated commission at Bologna on a book sold for forty pounds was only five *solidi*, a microscopic 0.625 percent.

[27] CUP no. 462 (1275) = vol. 1 p. 533.

actions prejudicial to the well-being of the whole university," therefore the university, for their good as well as its own, orders them to swear that. . . .[28] And although there are a few scoldings concerning corrupt exemplars, much the greater part of the vituperation, and of the meticulously regulated procedures that the *librarii* and *stationarii* must swear to observe, refers to the unprofitable business of serving as agents in the secondhand trade.

The documents show, time and again, that the bookmen were reluctant to swear the oath drawn up and imposed by the university. In one instance, the *stationarii* and *librarii* yielded only after winning a few concessions. The story of this confrontation is preserved in two documents from 1316. In June of that year, the university record refers to an (undated) earlier contest, in which the *librarii et stationarii* had taken the oath only with great reluctance. Now, says the document, it is time — indeed, it is well past time — for the oath to be sworn anew. But when they had been summoned in a body before the university officials, the greater part of the bookmen refused to take the oath, saying that they would rather lose their posts than swear to observe such regulations. Therefore, the university blacklists by name twenty-two men, who will no longer receive university privileges and with whom every member of the university is strictly forbidden, under penalty, to do business. In December of 1316, a second document records that the body of *librarii et stationarii* again appeared before the university officials, and swore to obey the regulations; the names of fourteen men are listed.[29]

On the surface, this looks like abject surrender. In reality, faced with a concerted strike, the university had made concessions — although they are not acknowledged as such in the record which, of course, was drafted by the university. The extent of the concessions is unclear, since we do not have the wording of the immediately preceding regulations for comparison. One change that stands out, however, concerns the *librarii* as agents for the sale of secondhand books. A comparison with the regulations of 1302 shows what is new: In 1316, the *librarius* is no longer required to run and fetch the vendor, put the latter in direct touch with the buyer, and stand humbly by while the money changes hands. The *librarius* himself is empowered to sell, as agent for the vendor, with the sole proviso that he shall name (or even produce) the buyer *if the vendor demands it*, after the sale. Even so, the tight restriction on the *libraire*'s profit remains unchanged. A second and more significant concession concerns the *taxatio*; henceforth, the *taxatores*, the assessors of rates,

---

[28] CUP no. 724 = vol. 2 p. 179.
[29] Ibid. (June 1316); and CUP no. 733 (December 1316) = vol. 2 p. 190ff.

will be four of the *librarii* themselves, chosen by the university — a matter considered at greater length below.[30]

3. A major instrument of control: exemption from the taille

The university, then, could give ground, on rare occasions, in order to secure the allegiance of the bookmen. In most cases, though, the university had by the early fourteenth century a sufficiently compelling argument, in the form of an important new privilege: In 1307, a royal *ordonnance* of Philip the Fair exempted all the *librarii universitatis* from paying the commercial tax, the taille, a privilege that remained in force through subsequent reigns. The reverse of the coin, obviously, was a threat: no oath, no tax-exemption.

The university was aware of the power of this weapon, and brandished it openly: Thus, the document of June 1316, which summarizes the undated earlier confrontation between university and bookmen, recalls with relish that, while some of the booksellers were willing to swear, many others objected, *until* "with the passage of time they were forced by necessity, namely, the taille of the lord king of the French, from which they enjoy immunity solely under protection of the university" — and they swore.

This undated previous controversy must have occurred between 1307, date of the royal exemption, and the extraordinary taille of 1313.[31] For the university's account goes on to say that all swore the oath except Thomas of Sens. In the taille book for 1313, only three of the *librarii* of Paris are taxed (all with a second source of income, which probably accounts for their having been taxed), and one of these is Thomas of Sens. In no time at all, Thomas capitulated: His individual oath survives, dated May 1314; and since, in actuality, the so-called "taille of 1313" was collected in Paris between December 1313 and June 1314, his timely oath may have been a last-minute attempt to avoid paying taxes. In his individual oath, we should note, Thomas is revealed as a stationer.[32]

---

[30] See below, at n. 132.

[31] Concerning the tailles, and taille records, see Appendix 1 below.

[32] The other two (cited from Michaëlsson, *1313*) are "Mestre Thomas de mante, libraire, et sa fame, ferpiere" (p. 219) and "Nicolas l'anglois, librere et tavernier" (p. 250). Thomas, also, lists a second occupation: "Thomas de Senz, libraire et tavernier" (p. 234). His individual oath is printed as CUP no. 711 (10 May 1314) = vol. 2 p. 171. Whether because he left it too late, or because he had a second business, the taille book records that Thomas did in fact pay his tax.

C. University Bookmen Found on the Taille Rolls and Other Records

Exemption from the taille was a cherished privilege for members of the booktrade. It is less than a blessing for modern scholarship, however. For the earliest university lists of names of *librarii* and *stationarii*—between twenty-two and twenty-seven names, allowing for possible duplication—date from 1316; and the shop-by-shop taille records nearest in time are those of 1313 from which, as we have seen, virtually all bookmen are exempted. (For example, the Rue Erembourc de Brie, known from earlier taille books to have been thickly settled with booksellers, binders, and especially illuminators, bears a terse notice in 1313: "La rue Erembourc de Brie: nichil."[33] Consequently, we are forced to go back, if we wish to see such things as the location or the comparative economic standing of *libraires*, to the printed tax rolls of 1296 and 1297; and it is too much to expect that any large number of those who were university *librarii* in 1316 would have owned a taxable business twenty years earlier. Fortunately, the oath of December 1316 provides street-names for those who swore, which affords a picture of the geography of the university booktrade in that year (see Map); and a surprising number of these men appear on the taille lists or other records:[34]

(1) Gaufridus Lotharingus, Rue Erembourc de Brie.
(2) Guillelmus de Curia, Rue de Clos-Brunel. At first he was located in or around the cloister of St-Benoît, west of the Rue St-Jacques (1296 taille), but by the time of the 1297 taille he had moved to Clos-Brunel where he still is located in 1316.
(3) Guillelmus le Grant, anglicus, Rue des Noyers.
(4) Jacobus de Troanco, Rue neuve Notre Dame. By 1323 he has been succeeded as a sworn *librarius* by his widow Margareta, doubtless at the same location.
(5) Johannes Brito alias de Sancto Paulo, Rue neuve Notre Dame. He is probably kinsman and successor of Thomas de St. Pol, a *librere* on the Rue neuve Notre Dame who appears in the taille lists for 1296–1300.
(6) Johannes de Garlandia, Rue des Parcheminiers, also known as the Rue aus Escrivains. He appears on the taille lists for 1296–1300.

---

[33] Michaëlsson, *1313*, p. 228.

[34] Unless otherwise specified, the following names and street addresses are taken from CUP 2.191–192, no. 733, the corporate oath of 4 December 1316. To avoid repetition we have not cited here the various appearances in university and tax records of the eighteen men listed below. All are included, with bibliographic references, in App. 2 below, listed alphabetically by first name.

PARIS, CA. 1250-1350:
ÎLE AND LEFT BANK
(adapted from the map
"Paris vers la fin du XIVe
siècle" produced by the
S.D.C.G.-Laboratoire de
Cartographie thématique,
C.N.R.S. 1975): **1**. Palais;
2. Petit-Pont; **3**. Notre-
Dame; **4**. St-Julien-le-
Pauvre; **5**. St-Severin; **6**.
Cordeliers (Franciscans);
7. Cluny (Thermes); **8**.
Mathurins; **9**. Hôpital de
St-Jean; **10**. St-Benoît; **11**.
Sorbonne; **12**. St-Jacques
(Dominicans); **13**. Porte St-
Jacques; **14**. Ste-Geneviève;
15. Porte Ste-Geneviève
(Porte Bordelle); **16**. Porte
St-Victor; **17**. Bernardins
(Cistercians)

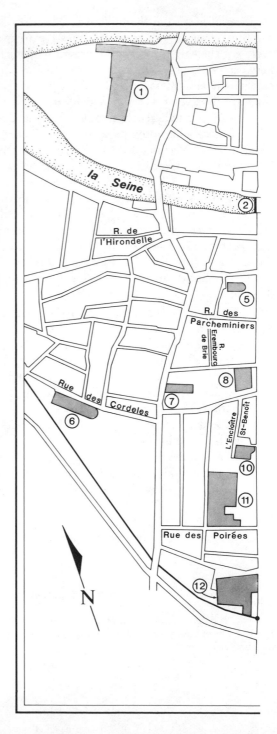

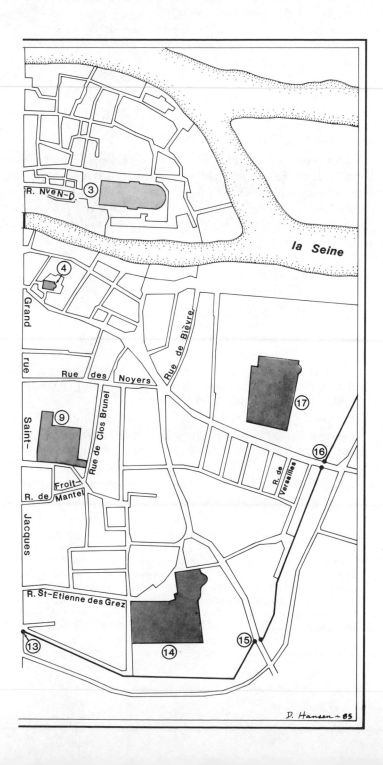

R. Nve N-D.

la Seine

Grand

rue

Rue des Noyers

Rue de Bièvre

Rue de Clos Brunel

Saint-

Froit-

R. de Mantel

Jacques

R. St-Etienne des Grez

R. de Versailles

D. Hansen - 85

(7) Nicolaus dictus Petit-clerc, Rue St-Jacques. He appears (as "Nicolas l'anglois") in the taille list of 1313.

(8) Stephanus dictus Sauvage, Rue Erembourc de Brie.

(9) Thomas Normannus, Rue neuve Notre Dame. He appears on the taille list for 1297–1300; he is possibly succeeded by Gaufridus dictus le Normant, who is succeeded in turn by Johannes dictus le Normant. Thomas was a stationer in 1316.

(10) Thomas de Senonis, Rue St-Jacques. He appears on the taille list for 1313. This Thomas also was a stationer, as we have seen. He is discussed further below, pt. I-D.

Besides these, a few names from the university's lists of *librarii* in the first half of the fourteenth century appear in surviving manuscripts. Three of these appear as scribes of manuscripts written before the dates of their earliest (surviving) oaths as *librarii*, raising the possibility that they entered the booktrade as simple wage-earners and later advanced to the status of shop-owners:

(11) Petrus dictus Bonenfant, who in the oath of December 1316 is a *librarius* located on the Rue de Bièvre. Almost eight years earlier, he appears as scribe of Arnold of Liège's *Alphabetum narrationum* in Vendôme Bibl. mun. 181, fol. 147: "Anno Domini millesimo ccc° viii° [N.S. 1309] . . . in mense januarii fuerunt complete scripte iste pecie a Petro Bonopuero."[35]

(12) Thomas de Wymonduswold (garbled as "Wymondlkold" in the oath of 1323), anglicus. He wrote, and left his name in, a manuscript of Gratian's *Decretum*, Paris, B.N. lat. 3893 (AD 1314), and a Bible, Paris, Bibl. univ. 9.[36]

(13) Johannes de Pointona (also Ponton, Ponitron), anglicus. He swore his individual oath to the university as a *librarius* in 1335; but, given the persistent garbling of his name in the university records, he is probably to be identified with the scribe of a glossed Gratian, Paris, B.N. lat. 14318, written a dozen years earlier, according to its colophon: "Hoc opus complevit Johannes Anglicus de Duntonia AD MCCCXXII." He is probably a kinsman of Guillelmus dictus de Pointona who swears an oath in 1343.

---

[35] The meaning of the colophon of this and a series of related manuscripts is discussed by G. Fink-Errera; see Jean Destrez and G. Fink-Errera, "Des manuscrits apparemment datés," *Scriptorium* 12 (1958) 83–86. The use in the colophon of the word "pecia," by this date, implies that Pierre Bonenfant was working for a stationer (as opposed to the possibility that *pecia* merely means "quire"). The wording does not suggest that Bonenfant himself was the stationer, however.

[36] See François Avril, "Manuscrits," in *Les fastes du gothique: Le siècle de Charles V*, exhibition catalog of the Ministère de la Culture (Paris 1981) 288 no. 233.

Two other *librarii* from the university records appear in surviving manuscripts as booksellers, aptly enough:

(14) Johannes de Remis, who took the corporate oath in 1323, is probably the man referred to in an undated note that appears in a thirteenth-century glossed Pauline epistles, now Munich Clm 3743, fol. 149: "Johannes de Sacrofonte emit hunc librum a Johanne de Remis, librario Parisiensi."

(15) Matheus Vavassor, who swore his individual oath in 1342, had a shop on the Rue neuve Notre Dame, according to the purchase note in a manuscript of the Fens of Avicenna (Paris, Bibl. univ. 130) bought in 1352 "ab uxore et executoribus Mathei Vavassoris, defuncti, quondam librarii in vico novo Beate Marie commorantis." Given the sequence of dates, we may suppose Matheus to have died of the plague.[37]

The last three names open the door for us to a quite different world. All are the producers of de luxe illustrated vernacular texts, with two of them certainly, and the third possibly, illuminators as well as *librarii*. They are striking examples of the double life of Paris booksellers: On the one hand, as sworn university *librarii*, they submit to being berated like naughty children by "our mother, the University"[38] over a minuscule profit of four pence in the pound on sales of scruffy used books to students and masters; and on the other, as participants in the luxury trade outside the university, they are paid as much as a hundred pounds per book by the nobility. While these are the only three names known to us, there must surely have been other *librarii* in like situation, whose names with luck will be uncovered:

(16) Gaufridus de Sancto Leodegario, Rue neuve Notre Dame. Geoffroy de St. Léger appears in the university records in 1316: on the blacklist of June (as "Gaufridus de vico novo"), in his individual oath of November (as *librarius juratus*), and in the corporate oath of December, which gives his full name and street address; he also

---

[37] The note is printed in CUP 2.189, n. 2. It has also been tentatively suggested that Matheus Vavassor might be the illuminator known only as Mahiet (some twenty manuscripts dated ca. 1330–ca. 1350 attach to his name), a collaborator of Pucelle; Avril, "Manuscrits" 300 no. 247.

[38] CUP 2.190 no. 733 (the corporate oath of December 1316), "ad ipsius Universitatis nostre matris honorem." Cf. "Universitas nostra . . . tanquam pia mater," in the highly colored prose of the university's blacklist of the booktrade (CUP 2.179, June 1316)—both Geoffroy of St. Léger and Thomas de Maubeuge, discussed below, were blacklisted at that time; and cf. Geoffroy's individual oath (CUP 2.188, November 1316), in which he places himself "sub protectione matris sue universitatis." It is interesting to see the metaphor of University-as-mother applied to booksellers as well as to students.

takes the corporate oath that survives from 1323, but not that of 1342, the next to survive. He is probably kinsman and successor to Johannes de Sancto Leodegario, who likewise appears on the blacklist of 1316 but who is not mentioned thereafter.

Since 1884 it has been remarked on that Geoffroy's name ("C'est Geufroi de S. Ligier") or the initial G. appears numerous times in a manuscript of Guiart de Moulins' *Bible historiale* (Paris, Bibl. Ste. Geneviève 22), with reference to the illustrations in this codex.[39] François Avril has identified at least thirty-six manuscripts in which the artist of Ste. Geneviève 22 figures, either alone or in collaboration;[40] and Avril argues convincingly that the artist is the *libraire* Geoffroy de St. Léger, which means that Geoffroy headed an important shop at the heart of the Paris booktrade. Between the years ca. 1316 and 1337[41] he also worked in tandem with other illuminators, including both of his neighbors listed below. His patrons included the chancellor of France, nobles such as Louis I duc de Bourbon, and two queens: Clemence of Hungary, second wife of Louis X, and Jeanne of Burgundy, wife of Philip VI. Geoffroy's most frequent products were chivalric romances, Guiart de Moulins's *Bible historiale*, and the *Grandes chroniques de France*. For a list of the manuscripts thus far attributed to him, see Avril's introduction to the facsimile edition of the most lavishly illustrated *Roman de Fauvel* (Paris, B.N. fr. 146), likewise attributed to Geoffroy.

(17) Thomas de Malbodio, Rue neuve Notre Dame. Like his neighbor Geoffroy, Thomas de Maubeuge also appears on three university records for 1316: the blacklist, his individual oath as *librarius* (sworn on the same day as Geoffroy's oath), and the corporate oath; he, too, swore the corporate oath of 1323 but not that of 1342.

One of Thomas's steadiest nonuniversity patrons, it seems, was Mahaut, countess of Artois and Burgundy (1302–1329).[42] The earliest record dates from 1313, when Mahaut purchased two books in French from Thomas for eight pounds Parisian, the *Voeux de Paon* and a *Vie*

---

[39] Samuel Berger, *La Bible française au moyen âge* (Paris 1884) 288, 376–377.

[40] See François Avril's introduction to the forthcoming facsimile edition of Paris, B.N. fr. 146, *Roman de Fauvel*. We are grateful to M. Avril for generously permitting us to consult his work in typescript. For an overview of the vernacular trade at the turn of the century, see Joan Diamond, "Manufacture and Market in Parisian Book Illumination around 1300," *Europäische Kunst um 1300*, ed. E. Liskar (Vienna 1986) 101–110.

[41] The last firm date in Geoffroy's career is taken from a manuscript that was made in collaboration with Richard de Montbaston, discussed below (no. 18).

[42] J.-M. Richard, *Une petite-nièce de saint Louis: Mahaut, comtesse d'Artois et de Bourgogne* (Paris 1887) 99–106, chap. 8: "Les livres." We thank John Benton for referring us to Mahaut and the information about her.

des sains.[43] In 1316, insurgents broke into Mahaut's castle of Hesdin, destroying or carrying off objects of value including 200 pounds' worth of books, which she listed in a claim presented to parlement; Thomas's *Vie des sains* was one of them.[44] In January 1327 (N.S. 1328), the Hesdin accounts note substantial payments to Thomas de Maubeuge of 80 pounds Parisian for a collection of edifying stories in French—saints' lives (a replacement?), miracles of the Virgin, and the like—and 100 pounds for a French Bible. Thomas was also paid during that year for repairing or replacing missals and breviaries of the chapel at Hesdin.[45]

Thomas provided books for other northern nobles. It is recorded in 1323 that he sold a "rommanch de Lorehens" to the count of Hainaut for thirteen pounds Parisian—almost twice the price of the horse purchased for the trip from Hainaut to Paris.[46] Perhaps it is also our Thomas de Maubeuge who in 1349 sold a "rommant de moralite sur la Bible" (doubtless Guiart de Moulins) to the future King John the Good:[47] the date is surprisingly late, however, given that Thomas's name does not appear on the oath of 1342.

One surviving manuscript, an illustrated *Grandes chroniques de France* dated 1318 (now Paris, B.N. fr. 10,132), is securely attributed to Thomas by its elaborate opening rubric, which also did service as an advertisement: "Ci commencent les chroniques des roys de France . . . lesquelles Pierres Honnorez du Nuef Chastel en Normandie fist escrire et ordener en la maniere que elles sont, selonc l'ordenance des croniques de Saint Denis, a mestre Thomas de Maubeuge, demorant en rue nueve Nostre Dame de Paris, l'an de grace Nostre Seingneur MCCCXVIII."[48] It is a large volume containing at least thirty-one miniatures, the first of which occupies the upper half of the opening of the text; save where they have been cropped, instructions to the artists survive in the margins. As a whole, the caliber is second-rate or worse, in comparison with the work of artists such as Master Honoré or Pucelle, or even with the early work of Geoffroy de St. Léger. We do not know whether Thomas himself was the illuminator of this manuscript, as well as its producer,

---

[43] Thomas's receipt of payment is printed, ibid. 102 n. 3.

[44] Le Roux de Lincy, "Inventaires des biens meubles et immeubles de la comtesse Mahaut d'Artois . . . ," *Bibliothèque de l'Ecole des Chartes* 3e sér. 3 (1852) 53–79; booklist on 63 (no. 56).

[45] See Richard 104 and n. 4.

[46] Godefroy Ménilglaise, "Etat des bijoux et joyaux achetés à Paris pour Marguerite et Jeanne de Hainaut en 1323," *Annuaire-Bulletin de la Société de l'histoire de France* 6 (1868) 126–147, at 143–144; cf. 143 n. 4.

[47] L. Delisle, *Cabinet des manuscrits* 2 (Paris 1868) 15–16 and n. 9; Richard 105.

[48] We are grateful to Walter Cahn, who referred us to this manuscript.

although this seems to have been a fairly common situation. What is known, however, is that this illuminator collaborated with Thomas's neighbor and contemporary, Geoffroy de St. Léger, in the production of two other illustrated manuscripts, a *Roman de Graal* (Paris, B.N. fr. 9123), and the *Grandes chroniques* that now belongs to the Musée de Castre.[49] Whether Thomas or Geoffroy was the titular "producer" of these two is unknown.

(18) Richard de Montbaston, Rue neuve Notre Dame. For unexplained reasons, Richard swore an individual oath twice in 1338, in August and again in October, as *librarius et illuminator*. His name appears also on the corporate oath of 1342; he died (a victim of the plague?) before 1353, when Johanna, "widow of the deceased Richard de Montbaston," took an oath as *libraria et illuminatrix*.

One manuscript securely attributed to Richard is an illustrated *Légende dorée* dated 1348 (now B.N. fr. 241), which contains an advertisement on the back pastedown similar to that of Thomas de Maubeuge: "Richart de Monbaston libraire demourant a Paris en la rue neuve Nostre Dame fist escrire ceste legende en francois, l'an de grace Nostre Nostre [sic] Seigneur mil.CCC.XLVIII." This French translation of the *Legenda aurea* was made by Jean de Vignay (d. bef. 1350), whose patron was Jeanne of Burgundy—wife of Philip VI, mother of John the Good.[50] MS fr. 241 is textually closer to the archetype than virtually any other surviving copy.[51] It is not known for whom Richard made this book; but it is part of the French royal library when that collection first appears in 1518, suggesting that the copy was commissioned by a member of the court circle.

The illustrations of MS fr. 241—like those in Maubeuge's *Chroniques*—are workmanlike and nothing more. In the present case, we are doubtless justified in attributing the illustrations as well as the overall production to Montbaston, since he is specifically called an illuminator in his university oath. In three other surviving manuscripts, he can be seen working in collaboration with his neighbor Geoffroy de St. Léger: Paris, Arsenal 3481, *Lancelot*; B.N. fr. 60, *Roman de Thèbes* and *Histoire de Troie*; and B.N. fr. 22,495, *Roman de Godefroi de Bouillon*

---

[49] See Avril, intro. to *Roman de Fauvel*, cited above.

[50] Concerning Jean de Vignay, see the article by Christine Knowles in the *Dictionnaire des lettres françaises* 4 (Paris 1954) 431–433.

[51] We are grateful to Richard Hamer for having referred us to this manuscript, and for sharing with us his findings regarding the place of this manuscript on the stemma of the *Légende dorée*.

et de Saladin, dated 1337, the latest fixed date in Geoffroy's life.[52] Given that Geoffroy would seem to have been the older of the two by roughly a generation — and that Richard himself was not a *libraire* until 1338 — one would suspect that for these three manuscripts Geoffroy was the contractor, so to speak, who engaged Richard to help out with the illustration.

We should like to emphasize that these three — Geoffroy de St. Léger, Thomas de Maubeuge, and Richard de Montbaston — and doubtless many others as yet unidentified, were sworn university *librarii* (as all booksellers in Paris were required to be), but evidently not *stationarii*. Their near-assemblyline production of fancy books for the wealthy — royalty, nobility, prelates, *haute bourgeoisie* — had no relationship at all with the sort of production that stationers were engaged in, the production of exemplar-peciae for rental which, by 1304 if not before, was regulated by the University of Paris. Rather, these men were the spiritual descendants of Herneis *le romanceeur*, who as much as a half-century earlier was producing books in the vernacular (hence his sobriquet) for the newly literate upper classes from his shop on the *parvis* where the Rue neuve Notre Dame opens out in front of the cathedral. In a manuscript of Justinian's *Code* translated into French[53] (now Giessen, Universitätsbibliothek MS 945, ca. 1250), Herneis wrote, as a colophon (fol. 269v), an advertisement of the same sort as that of Thomas de Maubeuge in 1318 or that of Richard de Montbaston in 1348: "Ici faut Code en romanz, et toutes les lois del code i sont. Explicit. Herneis le romanceeur le vendi, Et qui voudra avoir autel livre, si viegne a lui, il en aidera bien a conseillier, et de toz autres. Et si meint a Paris devant Nostre Dame."[54] The historiated initials in this manuscript, according to Robert Branner, were produced by the Bari atelier in Paris in the 1250s.[55] Whether Herneis himself was the artist (and, hence, a part of this atelier) we do not know;[56] but he was clearly both producer and seller of the

---

[52] See Avril, intro. to *Roman de Fauvel*, cited above.

[53] Regarding the translation of Roman law into Old French see R. Bossuat, *Manuel bibliographique de la littérature française du moyen âge* (Melun 1951) nos. 2958–2960; and, in particular, H. Suchier, *Die Handschriften der castilianischen: Übersetzung des Codi* (Halle 1900) and F. Olivier-Martin, *Les Institutes de Justinien en français* (Paris 1935). We are grateful to Terry Nixon for these references.

[54] The colophon is printed by J. Valentino Adrian, *Catalogus codicum manuscriptorum Bibliothecae Academicae Gissensis* (Frankfurt a.M. 1840) 278, from which it has been cited in the secondary literature. See, e.g., W. Wattenbach, *Des Schriftwesen im Mittelalter* (Leipzig 1896) 560; Branner, *Manuscript Painting* p. 2; etc.

[55] Branner, *Manuscript Painting* pp. 1, 103, 229–230 (pl. 285b), assigns nineteen manuscripts to this atelier, and lists another five that are related.

[56] Of the manuscripts attributed to the Bari atelier, two others (besides the Justinian) are in Old French, a Bible (Paris, B.N. fr. 899, s. XIII²) and the famous *Roman de Poire*

manuscript, since the colophon-advertisement is written in the hand of
the text. The principal difference between a man like Herneis and the
three men just discussed is the fact that, working in the 1250s and 1260s,
Herneis likely was not required to take an oath to the University of
Paris. In the fourteenth century Geoffroy, Thomas, and Richard were
required to swear such an oath; but it had little bearing on the types of
books they produced, and no bearing whatsoever on their methods of
production or the prices they charged. For them, swearing the university
oath was little more than a formality, an unavoidable one whose occasional minor inconveniences were easily outweighed by the advantages
of the privileges that it conferred, and one that had little to do with the
way they made a living.

In the realm of Latin manuscripts for the wealthy, Branner and De
Hamel mention Nicolaus Lombardus as an earlier publisher whose product is known. Nicolaus appears on the mid-century tax lists of Ste-
Geneviève-la-Grande, and in 1254 stands surety for Odelina the widow
of Nicolaus the parchmenter in the sale of her house. A note in B.N. lat.
9085 records the details of his commission to provide Gui de la Tour,
bishop of Clermont (1250–1286), with a multi-volume glossed Bible;
Nicolaus *venditor librorum* was to provide the scribe and to receive the
payment (40 lb. par., and two second-hand books). Like Herneis, Nicolaus
likely was not required to take an oath to the University.

D. A Family of Stationers, ca. 1270–ca. 1342

Our search through the taille[57] and other records produced an unexpected dividend, in that it permitted us to identify four successive owners of a single bookshop, three (if not all four) of them stationers, and
surely members of one family. Moreover, to our good fortune, this is the
shop for which one or, more likely, two *taxatio*-lists survive—the only
such lists from Paris.

The taille book for 1292 records, on the west side of the Rue St-
Jacques, the name of "Dame Marguerite, de Sanz, marcheande de
livres."[58] In this year, the assessors used as their starting point for this
segment "la meson mestre Jehan de Meun" outside the Porte St-Jacques
without indicating which names on the list represented tenements out-

---

(B.N. fr. 2186, s. XIII^2). One wonders if Herneis, singled out as *le romanceeur*, was
involved in their production.

[57] We refer in this section to the editions of the taille books of Géraud and Michaëlsson
cited in n. 6 above.

[58] 1292 taille, p. 160.

side, and which inside, the walls, information that might have helped to locate Margaret more precisely. But at least one may note that next to hers on the list is the name of "Gefroi, l'escrivain." No other bookseller was taxed on this street in 1292.

Dame Margaret does not reappear in the next surviving taille records, those of 1296: instead, on the same side of the street one finds "Andri de sens, librere: 36s";[59] this is the Andrew of Sens, stationer, whose list of exemplars and their rental rates survives from 1304. (We shall have more to say about the contents of his list below.) The starting point for the assessors in 1296 reads "A commencier au bout par devers Saint-Jacques, en venant tout contreval," with Andrew's name second on the list. Only one other bookseller, "Raoul le librere," was taxed on the Rue St-Jacques this year, and he is located on the east side of the street.[60] Geoffrey does not appear on the 1296 records; but he was taxed again in 1297, and next to his is the name of "Andri l'englois, libraire: 36s"—surely, despite the discrepancy in the cognomen, the same Andrew of Sens.[61] No other bookseller was taxed, on either side of the street, in 1297. In this year the assessors again used the end of the street as their landmark, "De la Porte Saint-Jacque . . .", with Geoffrey's name first and Andrew's second, on the west side of the street. As a further indication of Andrew's proximity to the Porte St-Jacques one might note the number of names farther north, toward the Mathurins (the end of this segment for the assessors in both 1296 and 1297): while only one taxable establishment stands between Andrew and the *porte*, there are fourteen (1296) or fifteen (1297) between Andrew and the Mathurins (see Map). Andrew (as "Andri de sens") continues to appear at this location, paying the same tax of thirty-six sous, through the remaining years of the taille (completed in 1300).[62]

Finally, in the records of the special taille of 1313 we find, thanks to his refusal to take the university oath, "Thomas de senz, libraire et tavernier" (perhaps he added the second trade because of the university ban).[63] This time, the assessors worked the west side of the Rue St-Jacques from north to south, "from the *hôtel* of Robert Roussel to the

---

[59] 1296 taille, p. 234.

[60] 1296 taille, p. 236, "Du cymetire Saint-Beneoit, jusques a la porte Saint-Jaque"—an assessment, according to the rubric on p. 235, of the east side of the street, "le coste de la Grant-Rue devers Saint-Ylaire."

[61] 1297 taille, p. 217. As we explain below (Appendix 1), the taille book is at best a copy, and possibly a copy of a copy, of the original returns, a fact that leaves room for copyists' errors. See also pt. I-E below, however.

[62] Paris, Arch. nat. KK.283 fol. 221 (1299), fol. 293 (1300).

[63] 1313 taille, p. 234.

well in front of Master Jean de Meun's house outside the gate"; but the
location is assured by the fact that the name on the list following Thomas's
is again that of "Geoffroy l'escrivein." Thomas of Sens, as we have seen,
swore an individual oath as a *stationarius* in May 1314; he (alone) is
mentioned by name, as an example *in malo*, in the preamble to the university blacklist of June 1316; and his name appears, in lists that do not
distinguish between *stationarii* and other *librarii*, appended to the corporate oaths of (December) 1316, 1323, and 1342.[64]

Thomas of Sens is also connected, in some unexplained way, with
that curious manuscript, Paris, Bibl. Mazarine 37.[65] Mazarine 37, which
bears the *ex libris* of the Dominicans of St-Jacques, contains the books
of the Bible from Genesis to the end of the Psalms; a scant majority of
the quires come from a single Bible, and the numerous lapses and losses
have been made up by the insertion of quires from at least three other
Bibles of similar size, with a concomitant overlapping of text. For the
most part the quires, like peciae, are numbered and are signed by a corrector; and numerous copyists have left their marks in the margins, to
remind them of how far they had gone.[66] In addition, there is a series of
notes that mark the places, in this text, where the "small peciae" of
another text end ("pecia de minoribus" or "pecia parvarum").

At the bottom of fol. 178v, the end of a quire in the text of 2
Paralipomenon, someone has noted in large letters "Tomas de sans qui
habitat." Neither its appearance nor its phrasing suggest that this is a
mark of ownership. And, in fact, there is little tangible evidence, in the
form of surviving manuscripts, that Bibles were produced via the pecia
method. Nevertheless, despite the dearth of copies, a Bible does appear
on the list of the Sens shop's exemplars, when the shop belonged to
Thomas's predecessor (father?) Andrew in 1304; even by that date the
exemplar was imperfect, comprised of "120 peciae, 2 of them missing"
(*In textu Biblie, cxx pecias, ii demptis*).[67] There is no plausible relationship of these 120 peciae with the 39 quires (whether or not one calls
them peciae) of Mazarine 37; and the number of "small" peciae (small,
presumably, in physical size but not in amount of text contained) referred
to is 32. It is unlikely, then, that Mazarine 37 is the exemplar from

---

[64] See CUP 2.171, 179, 180, 192, 273n, 531.

[65] To add to the results of our own examination of this manuscript and to the detailed
dossier of Destrez (40 handwritten pages), we have benefited form the advice of Louis
Bataillon, who first drew our attention to the appearance in it of Thomas of Sens's name.

[66] For an illustrated description of the signs by which scribes marked, in exemplars, the
place where they finished one session of copying, see P.M. Gils's study of Pamplona MS 51
(cited in n. 77 below)—an exemplar from the Sens shop.

[67] CUP 2.109.

Thomas's shop. But it is possible that among the heterogeneous quires that constitute Mazarine 37 there are parts of the old Sens exemplar, particularly since Mazarine 37 wound up in the hands of Thomas of Sens's neighbors at St-Jacques. The marginal note, likely a pen trial, is perhaps an idle copy of the heading of one of Thomas's peciae, one which began with Psalm 90 ("Qui habitat in adiutorio Altissimi . . .").[68]

To this sequence of Margaret, Andrew, and Thomas "of Sens," circumstantial evidence reveals that a fourth name should be added, at the head of the list: William of Sens. There is no record of William's location; but certainly he was a university stationer, by 1270 at latest. In that year, according to the cartulary of Notre Dame, "Guillelmus dictus de Senonis, clericus, stacionarius librorum," sold to the bishop of Paris a grange situated just outside the Porte St-Jacques.[69] Moreover, accidents of survival have preserved several collections of exemplar peciae that were rented out by the stationer William of Sens, who entered his mark of ownership across the upper margin of the first folio recto of each pecia in a form like this:

xxxviii   tercii thom'   G. Senon. est

i.e., the pecia number, an abbreviated title of the work, and the statement of ownership. Normally, when a work ceased to be in demand for rental and the exemplar-peciae were bound up together as a codex and sold, these marks seldom survived: they were either trimmed off by the binder or were deliberately effaced by the book's new owner. (Also, there is no reason to assume that William carried out this practice consistently.) Nevertheless, there are at least four surviving collections of (bound) peciae that preserve one or more of William's marks: Pamplona Cathedral 51, Thomas Aquinas *In Tertio Sententiarum*; Paris, Bibliothèque de la Mazarine 333, William Brito *Expositiones vocabulorum Bibliae*; Troyes, Bibliothèque municipale 546, G. de Militona *Postillae super Ecclesiasticum*, and 667 pt. I, Jean de Varzy *Postillae super librum Proverbiorum*. In two other manuscripts, copied from university exemplars, the scribe whether idly or by design reproduced the exemplar's marginal annotation "Guillelmi Senonensis est": Vatican Library Borgh. lat. 134, Albertus Magnus *De sensu et sensato*; and Paris, Bibliothèque de la Mazarine 281 (top of fol. 26), which contains the biblical concor-

---

[68] It was the practice of William of Sens to write his name and a short running title at the head of exemplar peciae; see below.

[69] Cited above, n. 18. This William is to be distinguished from Master William of Sens, who also disposed of a grange, to the Sorbonne in 1254. CUP 1.270–271; cf. CUP 1.222.

dance in 108 peciae.[70]

The concordance to the Bible in 108 peciae appears on the list of the exemplars of Andrew of Sens in 1304;[71] we should expect as much, if Andrew were William's successor and heir to his stock as stationer. We note, moreover, that the concordance in 108 peciae had appeared as well on the anonymous *taxatio* of ca. 1275.[72] It is a reasonable assumption that this earlier *taxatio* in fact pertains to the same stationer's shop, some thirty years earlier, when it belonged to William. Certainly there is great variation between the bodies of works contained in the two lists, as one might expect with the passing of three decades: more than two-thirds of the works priced in 1275 are absent from the 1304 list, which latter introduces an even larger number of new titles not to be found on the former. Given the time-interval, however, one cannot fail to be impressed instead by the number of exact correspondences (saving the rates, which have nearly all risen) between the two. If we restrict our examples to those works that do not qualify as set texts for the class-room (texts, potentially, widely on offer), we see that both lists of exemplars contain the *De principiis rerum* of Johannes de Siccavilla in 14 peciae, the sermon-collection beginning "Precinxisti" in 47 peciae, the collection of distinctions of Maurice of Provins in 84 peciae, the sermons *de dominicis* and *de festis* of Nicholas Biard in 69 peciae, and so on. The lists likewise share in common eleven works of canon law, though the 1275 list neglects to specify the number of peciae in these.[73] The most notable correspondence occurs in the list of exemplars of St. Thomas's works: Each of the nineteen titles on the list of 1275 reappears on the list of 1304, with the identical number of peciae in most cases (and one suspects the discrepancies of being slips of some sort—e.g., a simple inversion in the number of peciae, lxvi and xlvi respectively, that are recorded for the *Quaestiones de veritate*).[74]

We accept, then, as a working hypothesis that the *taxatio* of ca. 1275 lists the exemplars of William of Sens. Minor corroborative evidence is provided by Peter of Limoges (d. 1306). On a blank folio of his

---

[70] For references to and information about these manuscripts, we are grateful to Louis Bataillon, O.P., J.-G. Bougerol, O.F.M., B.-G. Guyot, O.P., and Hugues Shooner. Concerning the two Troyes manuscripts, see Fr. Bougerol's *Les manuscrits franciscains de la Bibliothèque de Troyes*, Spicilegium Bonaventurianum 23 (Grottaferrata 1982) 21–22, 29.

[71] CUP 2.109, no. 642.

[72] CUP 1.645, no. 530. For the sake of brevity, we occasionally refer to this as "the list of 1275."

[73] Concerning the canon law texts in the 1275 list, see Appendix 1. I[N]-A below.

[74] CUP 1.646 and 2.108. Concerning the surviving copies of the *taxationes*, see Appendix 1 below.

manuscript of John of Hauteville's *Architrenus* (Vatican Reg. lat. 1554 fol. 166v), Peter has jotted down informal accounts, almost all to do with the copying of books. Among these is a note, "I paid William of Sens for the *De proprietatibus rerum*, part 2 of Thomas's *Summa*, and the *Contra Gentiles*" (*Solui Willelmo sen. pro proprietatibus rerum, 2. parte summe thome et contra gentiles*).[75] All three of these works appear on the *taxatio* of 1275 (and on Andrew's list of 1304). One might dismiss the appearance of the Thomistic works as coincidence, on the assumption that any stationer at the time would have offered these (a dubious assumption; see below); but the *De proprietatibus rerum* of Bartholomaeus Anglicus is not an automatic nor obvious candidate for reproduction by university stationers. (Peter's manuscript of the *De proprietatibus*, left to the Sorbonne, survives as Paris, B.N. lat. 16099.)

'Finally, we note that the two *taxationes*, of ca. 1275 and 1304, follow one after the other in the surviving archives. The probable explanation for the fact that these two alone survive, and that they survive together, is that they represent the same shop.

Was this shop, even in William's day, at the same location where the taille books later place Margaret, Andrew, and Thomas, i.e., very near the southern end of the west side of the rue St-Jacques? There is every reason to think so. As the perceptive reader will have recognized, the importance attached to the particular location of Margaret, Andrew, and Thomas of Sens lies in its proximity, not to the *porte*, but to the Dominican convent of St-Jacques — located on the west side of the street, and bounded on the south by the gate, to which it gave its name. It must have been quite advantageous, for a Paris stationer at the end of the thirteenth century, to sit virtually on the Dominicans' doorstep, with no competitor in the neighborhood. One can see that Andrew, at any rate, exploited this advantage, for his rental list in 1304 offered an impressive catalog of Dominican writers: some thirty works of St. Thomas, some twenty works of St. Albert, eight works of Nicholas of Gorham, two lengthy works — a complete cycle of sermons for the year and a collection of biblical *distinctiones* (a total of 129 peciae) — of Nicholas Biard, and numerous individual items: the Dominican biblical concordance,[76]

---

[75] We thank Louis Bataillon, O.P., who brought this note to our attention. Inter alia, the same page records payments to scribes, with the rate of payment (sometimes per quire produced, sometimes per pecia copied); one scribe's name is written in Hebrew characters, probably to be associated with the codex of excerpts from the Talmud (B.N. lat. 16558) left by Peter of Limoges to the Sorbonne. See Bataillon's discussion and transcription of these accounts in *La production du livre universitaire au moyen âge: Exemplar et pecia*, ed. L. Bataillon, B. Guyot, and R. Rouse (Paris 1988) 265–273.

[76] But see below, at n. 125, for a curious anomaly.

and works of Robert Kilwardby, William *de Malliaco*, James of Voragine, etc.

We have already mentioned evidence which shows that William of Sens, also, had at least some Dominican works on offer—namely, his surviving exemplar of Thomas on the Sentences, references to his exemplars of Albert's *De sensu et sensato* and the concordance, and Pierre de Limoges's note of payment to him for two other works of Aquinas. If, as we believe, the rental list of ca. 1275 is his, its lengthy list of the works of Aquinas strengthens the impression that William's shop was associated with the Dominicans (although the works of Albert the Great are curiously absent).

The strongest case, however, rests on Pamplona Cathedral MS 51, William of Sens's exemplar of St. Thomas on book 3 of the Sentences. The careful work of P.M. Gils reveals several pertinent facts.[77] For one thing, Pamplona 51 is not merely the earliest surviving stationer's exemplar of this work, but it is the earliest, and possibly the only, one for whose existence there is any evidence. It was demonstrably in circulation before 1272 (B.N. lat. 15773, a direct copy of William's exemplar, was bequeathed to the Sorbonne by Gerard of Abbeville, who died in that year)—that is, during Thomas's lifetime and before the end of his final stay at St-Jacques. The commentary on the Sentences, we should note, was probably the earliest of Thomas's surviving works (1254–1256), and it is thought to have been later revised. Copious revisions are visible, literally, in William's exemplar, in the form of original text lined through and replaced with marginal revisions, or of folios and even several whole peciae that have been replaced. Because Pamplona 51 remained in circulation for a long time and engendered numerous surviving descendants, one can see the text both as it was originally, in the earlier copies, and as it became after the revisions, in the later ones. Clearly someone, whether or not St. Thomas himself, was able to introduce revisions into the exemplar after, perhaps long after, William had put it into circulation.[78] In sum, while Pamplona 51 is not so obliging as to give us William's address, as the first and long-enduring exemplar of a major work of St.

---

[77] P.-M. Gils O.P., "Codicologie et critique textuelle: Pour une étude du ms. Pamplona, Catedral 51," *Scriptorium* 32 (1978) 221–230 and pls. 17–19. We are grateful to Fr. Gils, and to F. F. Hinnebusch, O.P., for sharing with us their knowledge of *Thomas In tertium Sententiarum*.

[78] Gils (pp. 226–227) makes the logical and probably correct assumption that the revisions were Aquinas's own, but this remains to be demonstrated. As he points out (227 n. 15), we shall not know either the extent or the sense of the textual revisions until the publication of the Leonine Commission's edition of this work. For an example of the disastrous effect of these revisions on one scribe, see below at n. 143.

Thomas it singles William out as the "official stationer" of the Dominicans of St-Jacques.[79] And if, as Gils suggests, the revisions are Thomas's own, one could even assume a quasi-partnership, between stationer and convent.

There is, perhaps, one further reference to William, dated 1264; but the identification is not certain, and the meaning of the reference is difficult to interpret. A William of Sens is recorded as the scribe of a four- (formerly five-) volume illuminated Bible that belonged to the Cistercians of Loos near Lille (now Lille, Bibl. mun. MSS 835–838). The colophon of the last volume (MS 838 fol. 265v) reads, "Anno domini MCC sexagesimo quarto scripta fuit hec biblia a Guillermo Senonensi et diligenter correcta secundum hebreos et antiquos libros a fratre Michahele de Novirella tunc priore fratrum predicatorum Insulensium et capellano domini pape, expertissimo in biblia."[80] At present we cannot explain why the statement is framed as if it referred to events of the past ("scripta fuit" instead of "scripta est," "tunc priore" and not simply "priore"); it may have no significance at all, but the anomaly is unsettling.

Is this William of Sens, scribe, the same man as the Parisian stationer William of Sens?[81] There is good reason to think so. The date in the colophon, 1264, is appropriate for a man who was a stationer by 1270. More important is the fact that, like William the stationer, the William

---

[79] For an example of the advantage to St-Jacques of this association, see below at nn. 126–127.

[80] The colophon has been the subject of considerable interest to art historians studying a group of late thirteenth-century Bibles with related programs of illustration. Like the Lille Bible, others in this group are probably associated with Flanders and Artois, but their origin is as yet undetermined. See especially E. J. Beer, "Liller Bibelcodices, Tournai und die Scriptorien der Stadt Arras," *Aachener Kunstblätter* 43 (1972) 190–226; see also W. B. Clark, "A Re-United Bible and Thirteenth-Century Illumination in Northern France," *Speculum* 50 (1975) 33–47; A. von Euw and J. M. Plotzek, *Die Handschriften der Sammlung Ludwig* 1 (Cologne 1979) 85–103; and the bibliography cited in all three studies.

[81] Beer (193 and n. 26) and others after her (e.g., von Euw and Plotzek 88) identify the William of the colophon with a Dominican mentioned in the *Vitae fratrum ordinis Praedicatorum necnon Cronica ordinis ab anno MCCII usque ad MCCLIV* of Gerardus de Fracheto, ed. B. M. Reichert (Louvain 1896). Fracheto tells an edifying tale of a certain William, former *officialis curiae* of Sens, who received extreme unction at the convent in Orléans and died a good death: "Frater Guillelmus quondam officialis curie Senonensis dum in conventu Aurelianensi esset inunctus . . . paulo post . . . in domino quievit" (pp. 251–252). Given the facts that Fracheto himself was dead in 1271, that his chronicle extends only to 1254, and that the William of whom Fracheto writes was already dead at the time of writing, chronology makes it most unlikely that this William was the writer of the Lille Bible in 1264. Moreover, the *vita* associates the Dominican William with the bishop of Sens and the Dominicans of Orléans, but not with either Paris or the environs of Lille, the two places associated with Michael de Novirella (see below).

of the colophon is associated with the Dominicans of Paris, in the person of Michael de Novirella.

Michael came from Neuvirelle in Flanders. Through his mother Beatrix he was the beneficiary of support from Jeanne and Marguerite of Flanders and Hainaut, as well as from Mahaut of Béthune; and he figures as an executor in the wills of Jeanne (1244) and Mahaut (1258).[82] Inevitably, he must have studied at St-Jacques in Paris, where he became "expertissimus in biblia." No doubt he was there during the period when, under the leadership of Hugh of St. Cher, the Paris Dominicans were scrutinizing the text of the scriptures via comparison with Hebrew and early authoritative Latin versions ("secundum hebreos et antiquos libros") for the compilation of the earliest *correctoria* in the 1240s. It was probably through the good offices, certainly with the approval, of Hugh of St-Cher, Provincial of the order in France and (from 1244) cardinal[83] that Michael was named prior of the Dominican convent of St-Jacques in Lille (by 1264, and perhaps, to judge from the testament of Jeanne of Flanders, as early as 1244) and chaplain of Pope Urban IV (d. 1264). Michael's successor as prior is mentioned in 1275, and Michael is specifically referred to as no longer living in a document of 1276.[84]

William the stationer was in Paris, evidently next door to the Dominican house and certainly producing books for Paris Dominicans, by ca. 1270. Michael of Neuvirelle had no doubt studied at the Paris convent, probably in the 1240s, before going to head the convent in Lille. How are these facts to be accommodated with the colophon of a Bible that belonged to the Cistercians of Loos? In the first place, it is unlikely that Michael, as prior of a large convent, was this five-volume Bible's "corrector," in the technical sense that word has in the medieval book trade; we assume the colophon is an allusion to his having been part of the Dominican team that corrected the text from which the text of the Lille Bible derives. It is plausible that Michael, in 1264 as prior of Lille, commissioned William of Sens in Paris to copy the corrected Dominican Bible from an authoritative exemplar at St-Jacques of Paris for use at St-Jacques at Lille, and that the Bible was eventually transferred to the

---

[82] See M.-D. Chapotin, *Histoire des Dominicains de la Province de France* (Rouen 1898) 346–347. He prints the wills of Jeanne (346 n. 1) and Mahaut (347 n. 2).

[83] The most recent summary of the career of Hugh of St. Cher is that of Robert E. Lerner, "Poverty, Preaching, and Eschatology in the Revelation Commentaries of 'Hugh of St-Cher'," in *The Bible in the Medieval World: Essays in Memory of Beryl Smalley*, ed. K. Walsh and D. Wood (Oxford 1985) 157–189.

[84] Beer 193 and nn.; Chapotin 635–636. Chapotin (636 n. 2) prints the charter of Michael's successor Hellin de Comines (1276) which refers to "frater Michael . . . dum viveret . . . ."

Cistercians. Equally plausible is the possibility that the Cistercians of Loos went to Michael and asked him, as a Dominican with Parisian connections, to arrange for the copying of a "corrected text" for their use. This second possibility would fit with the fact that the writing figure, in the first historiated initial of the Lille Bible, is manifestly a monk (Cistercian?), rather than the Dominican friar depicted in the corresponding place in the so-called Dominican "exemplar" (Paris, B.N. lat. 16719, ca. 1250).[85] If either of these explanations is correct, then the William of Sens who became a stationer was evidently in 1264 earning his living in part, if not entirely, as a scribe, probably for the Paris Dominicans. We might note that the stationer's rental list of ca. 1275, undoubtedly William's, offers a text of the Bible,[86] although Bibles produced via the pecia method are virtually unknown.[87] The notion of a pecia-produced Bible, however, is far removed from the reality of the Lille Bible.

The Lille Bible is one of a group of lavishly illuminated multi-volume Bibles with similar and obviously related iconographic programs, dating from the 1260s and 1270s; those that are localized were owned (though not necessarily written or decorated) in the region of Flanders and the Artois. They are all said to have textual affinities with the Dominican "exemplar" (Paris B.N. lat. 16719–16722), but the extent and significance of the correspondence has not been demonstrated as yet. Art historians are still working out the center of production, with Arras, Tournai, Cambrai, perhaps Liège, and Paris as possible candidates. Until the origin of these Bibles is established—and perhaps even then—the identification of the scribe of the Lille Bible will remain problematic. If he was indeed the stationer William of Sens, this would be the only known example of William's involvement in the production of large illuminated books for the luxury trade.

Presumably William of Sens was dead by 1292, since his name is absent from the tax rolls and since a Dame Margaret of Sens—his widow, we presume—now appears as the only *libraire* close to the Dominican house. While the bookshop evidently survived him, one wonders how the university (and, especially, how the Dominicans) would have dealt

---

[85] See Beer's comparative table of illustrations, 195–197. Beer (191 and n. 18) treats with justifiable caution the proposed identification of B.N. lat. 16719–16722 as supposed "exemplar" for this group of Bibles; see below.

[86] CUP 1.647 (rental list of ca. 1275), without note of the number of peciae; it is probably the same exemplar, now in imperfect state, that we noted on the rental list of Andrew of Sens in 1304.

[87] We are grateful to Laura Light for sharing with us her unique knowledge of the manuscripts of thirteenth-century Parisian Bibles.

with the loss of the most important stationer in this part of town. Would
the university have accepted a woman in this office?[88] There are no contemporary documents to answer the question. Analogies from the next
century, however, are suggestive. We know that both man and wife were
occasionally sworn as *librarii et stationarii*: we have the oaths of "Petrus
de Perona, clericus et Petronilla uxor ejus, stationarii et librarii," a.
1323; and of "Nicholaus de Zelanda, alias Martel, et Margareta ejus
uxor. . . . librarii et stationarii," a. 1350.[89] We also have examples of
widows succeeding their husbands as sworn *librarii* of the university—
such as "Margareta uxor quondam Jacobi de Troanco" (Jacobus de
Troanco or Troancio or Troencio appears as a *librarius* in 1316), a.
1323; "Agnes relicta defuncti Guillelmi Aurelianensis, libraria" (William
appears as a *librarius* in 1342), a. 1350; and "Johanna relicta defuncti
Richardi de Monte baculo, illuminatrix, libraria jurata" (Richard de
Montbaston appears as *librarius*, or *librarius et illuminator*, in 1338 and
1342), a. 1353.[90] In light of later practice—and particularly in light of
this bookshop's importance to Dominican masters and scholars—we
think it likely that Margaret succeeded not only to the ownership of the
shop but also to William's function as stationer.

To summarize: These are the demonstrable facts about William of
Sens, Margaret of Sens, Andrew of Sens, and Thomas of Sens: We
know, from separate pieces of evidence, that three of the four (all but
Margaret) were stationers. Again, information from different sources
reveals that three of the four (all but William) occupied the same location, at successive times. We know that the *taxatio* of 1304 belonged to
Andrew, and that the earlier *taxatio* is more closely bound to it than
mere coincidence would account for. We know that the stationer William is explicitly named on surviving exemplars of editions that recur on
both lists. Moreover, William appears as the sole disseminator of at least
one Dominican work, and he may have been on such terms (friendship?
subordination? partnership?) with the order as to alter an existing exemplar, at the order's request.

With the foregoing established, the following may be assumed:
that William of Sens, stationer, had a shop near the Porte St-Jacques
from at least 1270 and probably before; that the *taxatio* of ca. 1275 was
his; that Dame Margaret (probably also a stationer), Andrew the stationer, and Thomas the stationer were William's successors, surely his

---

[88] As we have noted above, however, it is not certain that the university had clearly
defined and distinguished the office of stationer by this date.

[89] CUP 2.189 and 2.658n.

[90] CUP 2.273n and 2.658n.

kinsmen, doubtless his widow and, probably, his son and grandson; and, therefore, that this single family, working at the same location, served the University of Paris in general, and the studium of St. Jacques in particular, as stationers for some three-quarters of a century, from 1270 at the latest until at least 1342.

The Sens family through its several generations was regarded by Paris scholars as the "authorized" or at least authoritative publisher of the works of St. Thomas, to judge from a fascinating note entered in the margin of an early fourteenth-century manuscript of Aquinas's *De potentia Dei*, now Vienna, Nationalbibliothek 1536 fols. 98–191.[91] The ten *quaestiones De potentia*, written when Thomas was in Italy 1259–1268, appear to have been taken straight to William of Sens on Thomas's return to Paris and edited there, 1269–1270. The work is included both in the exemplar list of William of Sens (ca. 1275) and in that of Andrew of Sens (1304).[92]

It was perhaps some fifty years after William first made an exemplar of the *De potentia* that the copyist of Vienna 1536 wrote the following note on the bottom of fol. 137 (in the arguments to *quaestio* 4): "Frater Antoni: Non inveni soluciones argumentatorum istius questionis in peciis Roberti. Surrexi itaque et adivi pecias illas antiquas priores Senonensis. Et cum in gravi difficultate inveneram peciam in qua erat hec questio, nichil ibi plus erat, quia pecia erat noviter scripta, sed erat spacium foliorum duorum relictum ad solucionem argumentorum. Et dixit [. . . erasure] quod querem residuum quia pecia antiqua est perdita." The scribe was using the peciae (pirated?) of a certain Robert; two Roberts are mentioned in fourteenth-century university records of bookmen, Robert of Worcester (1316) and Robert Scoti (1342), but the context does not permit one to say whether or not either of these was a stationer.[93] When he found that a portion of the text was missing from Robert's exemplar, he sought out what he knew to be the more authoritative peciae—they are called not only *antiquae* but *priores*—that belonged to "Senonensis," which at this date must mean Thomas of Sens. Having gone to the trouble ("in gravi difficultate") to locate the corresponding pecia at Thomas's shop, the scribe was dismayed to discover that it also

---

[91] We are indebted to Hugues Shooner for bringing this manuscript to our attention and for sending us a reproduction of the pertinent folio. For further discussion of this manuscript see his "La production du livre par la pecia," in *Production du livre* (n. 75 above) 17–37.

[92] CUP 1.646 and CUP 2.108, respectively.

[93] Also, four other Roberts are called *librere* in the taille books from the end of the thirteenth century: Robert a l'ange, Robert de Craen, Robert d'Estampes, Robert de l'Ille-Adam. For references to all the Roberts, see App. 2 below.

lacked the solutions to this *quaestio*; all the Sens pecia had was a space of two folios left blank for the missing text. "He said" (i.e., Thomas, no doubt) that the scribe must search elsewhere for the rest. Therefore the scribe left this explanatory note (as well as three-and-a-half blank columns) for Friar Antony, his patron.

The note also "explains" why the Sens pecia lacked the crucial text: it was a remade pecia, and the original had been lost. This is no surprise, after the passage of so many decades; but it is not the whole story. For the missing portion was not subsequently located by the scribe, nor by Friar Antony, nor has it been seen to this day. Very likely, then, either the original pecia had been lost almost immediately, before any (surviving) copies of the complete text could be made; or, more likely still, these *solutiones* had never been part of the Sens exemplar—perhaps due to a fault in the text from which William had made his exemplar, since the stationer was well aware (witness the two blank folios) that part of the text was lacking.

The subsequent history of this lacuna serves to validate the scribe's estimate of the "priority" of the Sens exemplars of St. Thomas. In early days, their shop had a virtual monopoly on the circulation of his works. As a result, if the Sens exemplar lacked a portion of the text, then—for this, as for a number of other works of Aquinas—that portion simply ceased to exist.

E. Henricus Anglicus: Stationer?

We cannot in good conscience relinquish the Sens clan without considering the relationship to this family of a certain Henricus Anglicus: kinsman/business associate? or rival? The point of conjunction is the Paris exemplar of Aquinas's *Summa contra gentiles* in fifty-seven peciae, which appears on both the surviving rental lists, William's (ca. 1275) and Andrew's (1304); this missing exemplar, called α by the Leonine editors of *Contra gentiles*, was the common ancestor of about 80 percent of the surviving texts of that work.[94] A text of *Contra gentiles* in fifty-seven peciae, now bound together as Paris B.N. lat. 3107, bears the name "h. englici" (fols. 81, 85 erased, 89) or "henr. anglici" (fol. 121) at the head of four peciae. Moreover, these notations are set out in the same form as, and are surely modeled after, the stationer's mark of William of Sens that we have described above; e.g., on fol. 81 recto across the top margin is written "xxi^a pe^a contra gentiles h.englici." On the basis of these

---

[94] St. Thomas Aquinas, *Opera omnia iussu edita Leonix XIII* 13 (Rome 1918) intro., esp. p. xxix.

externals, one might wonder if Henricus Anglicus were not a kinsman—perhaps on Margaret's side of the family—responsible for (at least) four peciae in the Sens exemplar to which he signed his name. Andrew of Sens, we remember, was called "Andri l'englois" in the taille book of 1297.[95]

Several puzzling aspects of B.N. lat. 3107, however, preclude such a facile assumption. The manuscript, true enough, bears some of the physical signs that characterize a set of exemplar-peciae: there are pecia numbers at the head of each quire; most of the peciae have been signed by a corrector; and one can see that many of the quires have been folded in two lengthwise, a common fate of exemplar-peciae that were carried to and fro. Also, the number of peciae matches the number on the Sens lists—the number, as well, that the editors have found in the margins of pecia-produced manuscripts of the *Contra gentiles*. But both the date of the manuscript and its state of preservation look wrong. From the appearance of the hands (there are at least two), one would date this manuscript between 1300 and 1320 or 1330, not 1270; and, while some peciae show more signs of use than others, none of B.N. lat. 3107 looks as if it belonged to an exemplar that was in service for some thirty years (1275 to 1304). The deciding evidence, however, is not physical but textual. According to the editors of the *Contra gentiles* this cannot possibly be the missing exemplar α.[96] There are countless errors, including serious lacunae, in the text that are not reflected in α's descendants; and the fifty-seven peciae of B.N. lat. 3107 do not even divide at the same places in the text that are marked in the descendants of α. The latter discrepancy is all the more curious in view of the fact that the writers of B.N. lat. 3107 have taken pains to make each pecia end at a desired point in the text, either by leaving blank the final line or lines of a pecia's last column (e.g., in peciae 7, 8, 15, 16, 18, 20, 21, etc.) or conversely by adding an extra line or lines to the last column (e.g., in peciae 3, 9, 14, 17, etc.).[97] The editors state explicitly, then, that looks are deceiving: Anyone who wishes to consider B.N. lat. 3107 as an exemplar (at Paris, or anywhere else) of *Contra gentiles*, they conclude, will have to treat it either as an exemplar that was never copied, or an exemplar whose copies have all vanished.[98] The assessment of B.N. lat. 3107 was published

---

[95] We thank Louis Bataillon for bringing this manuscript to our attention, and for suggesting the possible connection with "Andri l'englois."

[96] St. Thomas Aquinas, *Opera omnia iussu edita Leonis XIII* 15 (Rome 1930) xv-xx.

[97] Ibid. xvii n. 2.

[98] Ibid. xxi: "Si quis ms. Par. 3107 exemplar dicere velit, aut erit exemplar sine exemplatis aut si mavis exemplar exemplatorum quae exsulaverunt omnia a traditione manuscripta superstite!"

by the Leonine Commission in 1930, and one may suppose that, at that
early date, they did not understand the possible vagaries and permutations of dissemination via exemplar-pecia as thoroughly as did their successors. Nevertheless, they seem to have asked the right questions of this
manuscript.

Perhaps Henricus Anglicus was indeed a kinsman (uncle? younger
brother?) of "Andri l'englois" alias Andrew of Sens, one who was involved
in a belated attempt in the early fourteenth century to recreate the shop's
lost exemplar from a derivative text. Perhaps, instead, Henricus Anglicus
was a would-be rival, and B.N. lat. 3107 was a pirated exemplar, written in fifty-seven peciae to give it a superficial resemblance to the authoritative exemplar of the Sens shop. In either case, despite the editors' findings, B.N. lat. 3107 was clearly intended to serve as an exemplar; but it
was manifestly an unsuccessful one. And the editors' suggestion, offered
ironically, is probably correct: that copies of this exemplar, which must
have been very few indeed, have not survived. Regardless of how one
interprets the facts, it is likely that there was at some time in the early
years of the fourteenth century a Paris stationer named Henricus
Anglicus—a negligible member of the ubiquitous Sens family, or their
inept and unsuccessful rival—whose existence thus far is witnessed only
by the appearance of his name in B.N. lat. 3107.[99]

F. The Number of Stationarii at a Given Time

Some studies, including fairly recent ones, speak of "the" university
stationer. Others, while less explicit as to the actual number, are obviously based on the contrary assumption that Paris was teeming with stationers, from quite an early date. How many stationers did operate
simultaneously? While it is impossible to answer this question precisely,
one can at least examine objectively the surviving evidence that any reasonable estimate must accommodate.

To begin with, one must remember that the total number of *librarii*
(including stationers) was quite modest. Thus, for example, the docu-

---

[99] This Henricus Anglicus, ca. 1300–1330, is not to be identified with the stationer of
the same name who is mentioned near the end of the century in a manuscript of Holcot on
the Sentences, Paris B.N. lat. 16399 (s. XIV²): "Emptus Parisiis a Henrico Anglico stationario
anno 1374." By 1374—to judge from the absence of pecia-produced manuscripts—a "stationer"
performed some different function from that of the earlier Parisian stationers discussed in
this article. Perhaps the Henricus Anglicus of 1374 is to be identified with either "Henricus
dictus de Neuham, Anglicus" or "Henricus de Lechlade, Anglicus," both of whom we
know from their individual oaths (1342 and 1350, respectively) to have been stationers. We
thank Louis Bataillon for referring us to this manuscript.

ment of 12 June 1316 reports that "most" (*maior pars*) of the bookmen refused the university's oath, and it goes on to blacklist only twenty-two people by name.[100] When an agreement was reached in the following December, the names of only thirteen oath-taking *librarii* are listed;[101] if this number constituted the *maior pars* (an implicit but perhaps mistaken assumption), the full complement should have numbered no more than twenty-six. The oath of 1323 repeats eleven of those names and adds seventeen more, eighteen, with the wife of one man, for a total of twenty-eight. The only other oath that survives from the fourteenth century, that of 1342, again bears twenty-eight names.[102]

The recurrence of the figure twenty-eight looks suspiciously as if the university had a fixed quota, and that may in fact have been the case. If true, this might raise a further question: Were the university's sworn *librarii* merely a select group, chosen from the larger community comprising the *librarii* of Paris? But as we have already said, the evidence indicates instead that the *librarii universitatis* consisted of all the *librarii* in Paris.[103] As further illustration of that point, we note that the taille book of 1297 lists only some seventeen *libraires* in all of Paris: one on the Right Bank, eight along the Rue neuve Notre Dame on the Ile, and eight more on the Left Bank. The 1297 taille book is unfortunately not uniform in recording the occupation of every taxpayer (though it outdoes the two earlier books);[104] but its evidence obviously would not support the notion of a sizable community of *libraires* more numerous than the university's (later) twenty-eight.

A second set of numbers survives, but it is difficult to know what to make of it. From the years 1314–1354, thirty-five individual oaths survive (thirty-seven, if one includes two oaths by married couples, but each double oath undoubtedly represents a single shop).[105] From these, the

---

[100] CUP 2.179–180.

[101] CUP 2.191–192; concerning Gaufridus Brito, who also took the oath at this time, see Appendix 2 below *sub nom.*

[102] CUP 2.273 n and 2.531–532.

[103] See above, at nn. 23–24.

[104] Although the taille book of 1296 is equally consistent, its entire section recording the "Menuz," those who paid 5s or less, has been lost. The oldest, that of 1292, is quite haphazard in recording occupations. None of these three, as edited, has an index by *métier*, so that the figures given here are based on a page-by-page search.

[105] CUP nos. 711, 732 and n., 1179 and n. = vol. 2 pp. 171, 188 f., 657 f. Included in this total is a possible duplicate, the "Henricus le Franc de Venna Anglicus . . . librarius" named in the text of CUP no. 1179 (see Appendix 2). No individual oaths survive from before 1314, and the next in date after 1354 is a series extending from 1367 to 1394, which exceeds the chronological limits of this paper. Concerning the distinction between written individual oaths and the *viva voce* oaths sworn by a group, see the Appendix below.

only documents that explicitly distinguish stationers from other *librarii*, we see that roughly a quarter of the total were stationers—eight of the thirty-five oaths (23%), or ten of the thirty-seven names (27%). These oaths are chance survivals, only thirty-five in forty-one years. There is little statistical validity in assuming, on this basis, that one may merely calculate that one-fourth of twenty-eight (the usual number of *librarii*, perhaps) means seven stationers at any given moment. We are on firmer ground if we look at the years in which the (surviving) oaths were taken, and observe that Thomas of Sens took a stationer's oath in 1314,[106] Thomas the Norman did the same in 1316, John of "Meilac" or "Meillar" (in Brittany) in 1323, and Peter of Peronne and his wife Petronilla a bit later in the same year[107]—and that all five stationers (in four shops) were still in operation, simultaneously, when they took the oath en masse on 26 September 1323.[108] While one cannot be certain that there were no more, therefore, one can at least document that there were no fewer, than four stationer's shops at that specific date.

Even earlier in the century, the language of the university's surviving book provisions gives a sense that there were several stationers. As we have noted, the wording of the earliest (1275, 1302) does not even distinguish between stationers and other *librarii*. The addendum to the oath of 1302 (written between 1302 and 1313, probably closer to the earlier date), however, speaks as if to a group, in three stipulations concerned solely with production and circulation of exemplars: (1) "that each stationer (*quilibet stacionarius*) shall post in his window" a list, with their assessed rates, of those exemplars "which he himself has (*que ipse habet*)"; (2) that he shall not circulate exemplars that have not been assessed, or at least offered to the university for assessing; and (3) "that these stationers (*ipsi stacionarii*)" procure good exemplars quickly for the convenience of the students "and the use of stationers (*et [ad] stacionariorum utilitatem*)." A fourth provision contemplates singling out for punishment any one of the group who might break his faith: if stationers (*stacionarii*) contravene the sworn articles, "a suo officio sit ille qui hoc fecerit alienus penitus atque privatus . . ." By December 1316, the university regulations take for granted the existence of multiple stationers, in a sequence of articles beginning *Nullus stacionarius . . .* —"No stationer shall . . ."—instead of "The stationer shall not . . ." (These provisions are followed by admonitions to the *librarii*, beginning similarly *Nullus librarius. . . .*) The simultaneous existence of compet-

---

[106] CUP no. 711 = vol. 2 p. 171.
[107] These last four are recorded in the note to CUP no. 732 = vol. 2 p. 189.
[108] CUP no. 825 = vol. 2 p. 273.

ing stationers is further implicit in the stipulation, in this same document, that no stationer shall refuse to rent his exemplar to someone wishing to make a competing exemplar from it, so long as the customer leaves the standard pledge and pays the fixed fee.[109]

Evidence shows several stationers operating at once, then, by 1316 at latest and perhaps a decade or more prior to that date. But how many are "several"? Further evidence inclines us to suggest a very low figure, with the possibility that the earlier in time, the smaller the figure should be.

The following hard fact, in particular, must somehow be made to fit with the preceding: When, in 1304, university officials formally set the rental rates for the exemplars of Andrew of Sens, the surviving record shows that this one stationer had a total of 156 different works on offer.[110] To be sure, many of these works were brief, the shortest filling only 2 peciae and the majority requiring fewer than 40. Over a dozen of Andrew's exemplars, however, required 100 or more peciae, with 270 for the longest. This *taxatio* is a chance survival, the only one from fourteenth-century Paris; and thus one has scant basis for judging whether the length of Andrew's list of exemplars was fairly typical or, to the contrary, was so unusual as to be virtually useless as an example.[111] *If* one assumes that Andrew's shop was at all comparable to other fourteenth-century stationers', that in itself would tend to ensure that stationers were few in number. Consider the implications: If all four shops in 1323 had an inventory of rental *peciae* equivalent to Andrew's in 1304, that would total some 600 works that the booktrade had gone to the expense of producing but was prohibited from selling, for the moment. Eventually, when the university agreed that they were no longer in demand, the used *peciae* could be bound and sold, doubtless very cheaply. In the meanwhile, however, the stationer's capital was frozen in his exemplars, his income dependent upon rentals.

It happens that a contemporary record survives, which documents the sharp contrast between rental price and the cost of producing a book. In the scribbled accounts of Pierre de Limoges, mentioned previously,[112] he usually records not only his payments but the agreed rate for the copyist — either so much per page or folio, or so much per quatern or

---

[109] CUP nos. 462 (1275), 628 (1302 and after), and 733 (Dec. 1316) = vol. 1 p. 532 ff., vol. 2 p. 97 f., and p. 190 ff.

[110] CUP no. 642 = vol. 2 p. 107 ff.

[111] The only other surviving Parisian *taxatio*, from thirty years earlier, is nearly as long, listing 138 exemplars; CUP no. 530 = vol. 1 p. 644 ff.

[112] See above at n. 75.

sextern. The smallest figure named seems to be 2s. per quatern;[113] but
there are other records of 2s. 6d. per quatern, 10d. per folio (= 3s. 4d.
per quatern), 5s. per sextern (again, 3s. 4d. per quatern), and even 5s.
per quatern. Of particular interest are two lines of writing; their placement on the page implies a tie between them. The first is the line we have
quoted above, "Solui Willelmo Senonensis pro proprietatibus rerum . . ."
etc.; the next begins, "Laurencius pro suo quaterno [*this last word is
glossed, to forestall cheating, with the added words* de exemplare] habens
5 sol.," followed by the usual sequence of gradually increasing numbers
that comprised Pierre's running total of payments made. A look at the
taxatio of ca. 1275 — probably William of Sens's; if not, competition
and/or the university would have ensured that his for this item was
near-identical — reveals that the *De proprietatibus rerum* contained 102
peciae (100 is the figure on Andrew of Sens's *taxatio* of 1304). It seems,
therefore, that Pierre paid the scribe Laurence 5s. for each pecia copied,
a total for this work of over 500 solidi. Let us be prudent, however —
perhaps Laurence was hired to copy something else entirely — and let us
take, as a figure from the lower range of Pierre's rates, the price 2s. per
pecia; we should still reach a total of 200 solidi, as the price of the copying alone, not counting the additional cost of the parchment. Compare
with this the stationer's rental income — 4s. (6s., in 1304) for the whole
work — and we see that a stationer would have been financially unable to
retain on his list of offerings any exemplars that did not encounter a
constant demand and thus, a rapid turnover, to provide sufficient rental
income.

Such a situation produces its own limitations, almost automatically.
The size of the "pie" in the form of the number of students, and the
amount of money each had for the purpose of renting peciae — did not
increase dramatically. As a result, each additional stationer's shop entailed
carving the "pie" into ever smaller portions for each. Perhaps, in 1323,
the rental market at Paris was large enough, and thus lucrative enough,
that four stationers could afford temporarily to immobilize the capital
needed for the production of 600 exemplar manuscripts. Would it have
been large enough to repay six stationers to produce 900 exemplars, or
that hypothetical seven stationers to produce 1050? or eight? nine? As
one can see, in no time at all, by postulating a larger number of statio-

---

[113] The rate for the scribe Gregorius says cryptically, "p.5.d." If this is rate per folio
rather than the rate per page (= one-half folio), that would equal only 1s.8d. per quatern.
Gregorius copied five works for Pierre, more than any other scribe on this record; perhaps
he was so frequently employed because he worked cheaply. He is also the first on the page,
however; and it may be that he was indeed inexpensive, but that prices — or Pierre's standards — went up as time passed.

ners one would at the same time be postulating the existence of a huge
"library" of manuscripts produced (but not sold) by the commercial
booktrade, far exceeding in size the largest contemporary institutional
libraries.

A second indication that stationers were few is provided by the
reconstructed pecia-history of those works of Aquinas that have been
edited by the Leonine Commission. These studies frequently document
the existence of duplicate sets of peciae, but there is no situation that
could, even hypothetically, be interpreted as evidence for more than two
stationers' shops renting a work of St. Thomas at one time. To the contrary, it is usually a safe assumption that the duplicate sets of peciae
were produced by a single stationer (one of the Sens tribe, doubtless),
either to cope with heavy demand or to replace, gradually, worn-out
peciae. Our own study of the pecia-history of Thomas of Ireland's
Manipulus florum, published by a stationer in 1306, reveals a similar
situation: at most two exemplars, clearly from a single stationer.[114]

Studies of the pecia-history of other works may in future modify the
picture; but the implication of what is presently known seems to be that,
as a rule, only one stationer disseminated a given work. In effect, the
university confirms this implication, in 1316, by forbidding stationers to
withhold their exemplars from would-be competitors: as always, the
prohibition implies the offense. It is a reasonable assumption, therefore,
that the works offered for rental on Andrew of Sens's list of 1304, and
perhaps on William's list of ca. 1275, were available from no other stationer, barring the rare "pirated" edition. Andrew's list contains the
cream of the crop, of those works in demand by students and masters of
theology and canon law at the turn of the century. If his list is exclusive,
it would leave no room for major competitors in supplying these faculties. One should note, as well, that surviving evidence of pecia-production
for the arts and medical faculties suggests a truly small-scale operation.

A third indication that stationers were few lies not in any one fact,
but rather in our skepticism over the "coincidental" omnipresence of the
operators of a single shop, who—alone—turn up in a surprising variety
of records: William of Sens appears in the cartulary of Notre Dame in
1270, the first individual at Paris to be called a stationer; his name is
recorded on surviving exemplar-peciae, including an important exemplar of Aquinas that may well antedate 1270; and his name is associated
with three works from the earlier of the two Parisian *taxationes*, that of

---

[114] R. H. and M. A. Rouse, *Preachers, Florilegia and Sermons: Studies on the Manipulus
florum of Thomas of Ireland*, P.I.M.S. Studies and Texts 47 (Toronto 1979) 162–181, esp.
180.

ca. 1275, by contemporary scratch notes on a flyleaf. Margaret of Sens appears, as the only bookshop on the Rue St-Jacques, in the taille book of 1292. Andrew of Sens appears on the taille lists of 1296 and 1297, and is named on the *taxatio* of 1304—the second earliest person (after William) who can be securely identified as a stationer at Paris. Thomas of Sens appears on the taille list of 1313; his individual oath of 1314, the earliest to survive for any bookseller, calls him a stationer, only the third person (after William and Andrew) to be so designated at Paris; and he, alone, is singled out in the text of the university's angry preamble to the blacklist of June 1316, as the only bookman who had defied the university on the occasion of an earlier confrontation (undated but pre-1313, and yet it still rankled). We should also look more closely at the manner in which the texts of the two *taxationes*, Andrew's and, we believe, William's, are transmitted. We have previously referred to these somewhat imprecisely as "chance survivals." So they are, but in a peculiar sense. Copies of both are preserved, one immediately following the other, in two compendia of thirteenth- and fourteenth-century university documents—papals letters, charters, regulations, etc.[115] Though the compendia are eclectic, and not entirely identical in content, they assume a quasi-official status in that neither is copied (in whole or part) from the other but they are instead separate witnesses to a larger collection taken to be authoritative by the copyists. Yet these compendia, with documents that date from the 1240s to 1304 or after, contain only two stationers' *taxationes*.

We do not believe in fairy tales; no more do we believe that, in the period extending from the mid-thirteenth century through the early years of the fourteenth, there were many stationers in operation, of whom chance has decreed that only a single family should leave clear and numerous footprints. There is no way to document an answer to the question "How many stationers operated simultaneously" save by saying that, in 1323, there was demonstrably a minimum of four shops. However, it seems not only permissible but useful that we go further and record our speculations, on the basis of present information. Let us take them in reverse chronological order:

We feel that the hard economic fact of diminishing returns must have ensured, in 1323 and later, that stationers were few, perhaps no more than the four on record. Even as late as 1316, we think that Thomas of Sens must have been recognizably the most important of the university's (three? four?) stationers, in part because he had been confident enough before 1313 to run the risk of a university-ordered boycott, perhaps feel-

---

[115] Concerning these collections, see Appendix 1 below.

ing that he filled too essential a need for the boycott to be observed. Around the turn of the century, largely in consideration of the length and the strength of his list of exemplars, we feel that Andrew of Sens must have had very little competition at all, and certainly none that approached him in importance. As for William of Sens, we suggest the possibility that, at least in the early years, he was unique at Paris.

II. THE EXEMPLARS

A. *The Selection of Exemplars*

How did stationers decide which works to rent, and where did they acquire their exemplars? Destrez, in his exposition of the workings of the pecia process, visualized an orderly procedure: Masters of the university who completed a new work—say, a summa, a series of lectures, even a florilegium—were to edit and correct the *reportatio* in the case of lectures, or to correct carefully the copy of their autograph for other types of composition, and submit this authentic text to a stationer; he in turn copied from it an exemplar in peciae, corrected these against the author's text with utmost care, and submitted them to the inspection of the university's delegates for approval and for the setting of a rental price. Only after this were peciae available for rental.[116]

The half-century since Destrez's pioneering efforts has shown that in practice the procedure was not at all orderly, at least in Paris. While our clearest evidence of this fact has come from the editions of individual works of St. Thomas, the wording of the regulations itself suggests that the process was rather haphazard. The onus of procuring exemplars— and the very selection of which particular works might be "useful to the studies of the various faculties"[117] (the university's only prescription)— fell entirely upon the stationers.

This was not necessarily a bad system, and it may have worked better than some more cumbersome mechanism; it was obviously to the stationers' own best interests to ferret out and offer for rental those works for which there would be a heavy demand, i.e., the very ones that any sort of university selection commission would have hoped to choose.

---

[116] Destrez, *La pecia*, esp. 26–29. Destrez's description, however, was merely an attempt to "resumer *grosso modo* ce qui . . . se trouve être commun à toutes les Universités," and he was quite well aware that further study would lead to revision of his broad sketch.

[117] "Libri utiles pro studio cujuscunque facultatis": CUP no. 628 (between 1302 and 1313) = vol. 2 p. 98, repeated verbatim in 1342 (CUP no. 1064).

A comparison of the two surviving *taxationes* suggests the forces of the marketplace at work.[118] The earlier, that of ca. 1275, contains a body of some thirty exemplars of works of the Fathers and of such eleventh- and twelfth-century theologians as Anselm, Bernard, and the Victorines, including some fifteen exemplars (most of them containing two or more works) devoted to St. Augustine alone. The stationer whose list this was, probably William of Sens, evidently misjudged his market: for most of these works there is no evidence at all in the surviving manuscripts that they were copied from exemplars. This lack of a market, for various reasons (some obvious, others doubtless more complex), probably explains the absence of patristica and spiritualia from the *taxatio* of Andrew of Sens in 1304.

Inherent in such a laissez-faire system, however, was a factor that unavoidably worked to the detriment of the texts. In leaving the initiative to the stationers, the university further enjoined them to acquire exemplars "in as good a state and in as short a time as possible" (*prout melius et citius poterunt*).[119] Given that theirs was, after all, a commercial enterprise, it is small wonder that the stationers put more emphasis on *citius* than on *melius*. The prefaces to the various Leonine editions of St. Thomas give ample evidence of over-hasty production of exemplars— for example, the *Expositio super Isaiam*, whose editors (H.-F. Dondaine, L. Reid) observe that, while the stationer's exemplar "is doubtless the first in date of the representatives" of St. Thomas's apograph, it is "everywhere mediocre . . . hastily produced . . . [with] a good number of misreadings and omissions," and they record, in a long list of the latter, omissions of 53, 35, 35, 21, 19, and 13 words in length.[120]—Or the notorious example of the *Quaestiones disputatae de veritate*, where the exemplar has been brutally and, it seems, deliberately shortened.[121]

This impression of carelessness (or worse) must be adjusted, however, to make room for the procedure of correction. It is not merely that the university prescribed that exemplars be correct (e.g., in 1275)—one knows, of course, the frequently cited passage (1316) in which the university decrees that stationers whose exemplars prove to be corrupt shall

---

[118] CUP nos. 530, 641 = vol. 1 p. 644 ff., vol. 2 p. 107 ff.

[119] Cited in n. 117 above; in CUP no. 628, the complete regulation (third, in a list headed "Universitas ordinavit que sequuntur"), reads, "Quod ipsi stacionarii librorum utilium pro studio cujuscunque facultatis exemplaria prout melius et citius procurabunt ad commodum studentium et stacionariorum utilitatem."

[120] *Sancti Thomae de Aquino Opera omnia iussu Leonis XIII P.M. edita* (hereafter cited as "Leonine edition") vol. 28, ed. H.-F. Dondaine and L. Reid (Rome 1974), introduction; see esp. pp. 38* and 69*.

[121] Leonine edition, vol. 22.1, ed. A. Dondaine (Rome 1975) 61*–113*.

have to recompense those scholars who have suffered as a result.[122] In addition to the regulations, however—which one might suspect of being simply a dead letter—there is the fact that surviving exemplar peciae bear visible correctors' marks, along with unmistakable examples of their corrections.

We receive a self-contradictory message from the manuscripts, therefore: By and large, exemplars were thoroughly corrected copies of miserable texts. Although no single explanation will resolve this paradox, it is such a standard state of affairs that there must surely be a common element, whatever it may be, inherent in the whole process. For the moment, we may take it that the stationers consistently interpreted the injunction *prout melius et citius poterunt* to mean, "Do the best you can, under the circumstances"—and the circumstances always placed the greater premium on speed of production. When a certain work looked like a "best-seller," a stationer would make a copy of the best text *immediately available*, and would have his exemplar-peciae corrected *as well as time permitted*.

At times the stationer sought out a text; at other times, an author offered his newly completed work to the stationer. The one place where, it seems, initiative never resided was with the university as a formal body.[123] In other words, the notion of some sort of assigned reading list, implied in the heading prefixed by a later hand to the earlier *taxatio*— "The price set by the University of Paris on those books of theology, philosophy, and law that *librarii* are supposed to have"[124])—is clearly off the mark.

B. *The Source of Exemplars*

It is possible that in the early years of pecia-rental, before the practice of producing exemplars for the sole purpose of rental had been worked out, booksellers simply dismembered into their component quires some secondhand books in stock, and offered them for rent to anyone who wished to make his own copy. Such a source for "exemplars" may explain, for example, the presence of the extended list of patristics and

---

[122] CUP no. 462 (1275) = vol. 1 p. 533, "quod exemplaria vera habeant et correcta"; CUP no. 733 (Dec. 1316) = vol. 2 p. 191, "stationarii qui talia [scil. exemplaria corrupta] locant, judicio Universitatis puniantur et scolaribus emendare cogantur."

[123] This refers to Paris only. Some southern universities, in contrast, seem to have required masters to publish and to have specified how it was to be done. There is no indication, however, in the form either of surviving regulations or of surviving manuscripts, that this was the case at Paris in the period considered here.

[124] CUP no. 530 = vol. 1 p. 644.

of pre-scholastic theology on the *taxatio* of ca. 1275; perhaps these titles are relics from a time when pecia-rental was primarily a bookseller's attempt to garner at least some income, however modest, from slow- or non-sellers in his inventory of books.

As it quickly became apparent, however, that the rental market was focused strictly on contemporary and near-contemporary works and on the set texts used in the classroom, a stationer would find it commercially advantageous to acquire in a hurry a good text that he might copy to create an exemplar specifically for rental. The source of his text "in as good a state as possible" occasionally surprises us, however. As we have seen, there was a stationer's shop next-door to St-Jacques, continuously from the lifetime of St. Thomas. This stationer demonstrably had access to Dominican texts. It would appear, however, that neither the stationer nor the members of the order had, or took, the responsibility of seeing that the most authoritative text was the one that was published. Moreover, there is the curious item on the earlier *taxatio*, "Concordancie de Valle Lucenti, c pecias et viij." This refers to the third version of the St-Jacques concordance to the Bible, as one knows from surviving manuscripts with pecia-marks; but it looks, from the description, as if the stationer in fact acquired his exemplar from the Cistercians of Vauluisant:[125] We cannot, of course, prove our assumption that this was the *taxatio* of William of Sens, quasi— in-house publisher of St-Jacques; but in 1304 the concordance in 108 peciae, surely the same exemplar or a copy of it, appears on the list of Andrew of Sens, St-Jacques's next-door neighbor. From these examples, it seems that the source of a stationer's exemplar was not always logically selected.

One must counterbalance this impression, however, with the previously mentioned case of William of Sens's exemplar of St. Thomas on the third book of the Sentences—an exemplar revised, perhaps on the initiative of the Dominicans, if not of Thomas himself, to accommodate revisions. Common sense suggests that a stationer's means of acquiring texts from which to produce an exemplar must have included, among others, the very procedure envisaged by Destrez: that the author of a work, or someone acting for him offered a text of it to a stationer. Certain evidence would be difficult to explain otherwise. For example, there are four independent witnesses to the text of the *Manipulus florum* (1306) of Thomas of Ireland: two manuscripts written for or by Thomas as gifts, a third private family of manuscripts, and the manuscripts of the stationer's tradition. These last, only, contain an additional passage near the end of the prologue, "I wish, however, to suppress the compiler's

---

[125] Ibid. p. 645 line 5.

name, lest the collection be despised should its collector be known."
Thomas of Ireland himself must have inserted this modest disclaimer, a
venerable *topos* in florilegia prologues, into the public edition of his
work when he handed it over to a stationer for dissemination.[126]

A striking instance of an author's use of a stationer as his "publisher"
is the dissemination of Aquinas's *De perfectione spiritualis vitae*, which
is listed, in seven peciae, on both *taxationes*. Both the completion and
the initial dissemination of this work, an important contribution to the
debate between Seculars and Mendicants at the university, can be dated
more narrowly than most. Aquinas began his work in the course of the
year 1269, at Paris; but before he completed it, his chief opponent Gerard
of Abbeville attacked Thomas's position, in his Quodlibet XIV at
Christmastime, 1269. In his concluding chapters, therefore, Thomas took
up Gerard's arguments, often verbatim, and replied to them, completing
the *De perfectione* probably before Easter 1270. The work must have
been handed almost immediately, and directly, to the stationer (William
of Sens, surely) for peciae to be made and rented out. The manuscript of
the *De perfectione* that belonged to Gerard of Abbeville (d. 1272) survives, a descendant of exemplar-peciae; and even earlier, by mid-1270,
Nicholas of Lisieux wrote a reply on behalf of the Seculars, in which he
mentions that "there has come into our hands a little book called *De
perfectione vite spiritualis*, written by some Friar Preacher and transmitted by public exemplar [or: committed to a public exemplar]" (. . . *a
quodam fratre predicatore editus et publico traditus exemplari*). The
editor of the *De perfectione* has shown that there are only three independent witnesses to the archetype, two of which (ϕ^1 and ϕ^2) are stationer's
editions; and, since various descendants of exemplar-peciae contain a
mixed text, i.e., partly ϕ^1 and partly ϕ^2, it is clear that both exemplars
belonged to a single shop and circulated simultaneously.[127] The logical
conclusion is that the Dominicans presented Thomas's apograph to William of Sens immediately upon its completion, and that William was
moved (whether by his own commercial sense or by the express request
of the Dominicans) to make not one but two copies of exemplar-peciae.

This, surely, is a clear case of publication on the author's initiative.
It is an example, too, of the ability of the pecia system to fill sudden
demands for new texts. It gives a signal demonstration of the importance
to the Dominicans (or to anyone else similarly privileged) of having a
quasi-official stationer of their own: Thomas's *De perfectione* survives

---

[126] Rouse and Rouse, *Preachers, Florilegia and Sermons*, 173.
[127] See Leonine edition, vol. 41B, ed. H.-F. Dondaine (Rome 1969), introduction, esp.
pp. 85–9 and 831–37.

today in 118 manuscripts, while Gerard's Quodlibet XIV (privately circulated) survives in 3, and the response of Nicholas of Lisieux in 1 manuscript only.[128]

The sources of a stationer's exemplars, in sum, were varied, and no single rule obtains. The history of each text must be considered individually.

C. Did Stationers Specialize?

The criteria by which a stationer chose the works he would offer are unknown, save that he was guided by his own commercial sense, which doubtless relied partly on the demand of would-be renters and partly on the offers of authors that he knew. But was he also guided—or restricted—by some sort of specialization, or perhaps by a division of the field among stationers? Some such division, whether formal or informal, was inevitable. It would have been impossible for any other stationer to compete on equal terms with the shop run successively by William, Margaret, Andrew and Thomas of Sens, in acquiring for publication the works of Dominican masters. Unfortunately, we do not know the locations and have the *taxatio*-lists of any other stationers, for the sake of comparison. (It takes both elements. Thus, while we know that Thomas Normannus had a stationer's shop on the Rue neuve Notre Dame in 1316, we have no list of his exemplars.)

The gaps in Andrew of Sens's list, however, are almost as revealing as its inclusions. It (and the ca. 1275 list) contains theology, philosophy, and canon law (along with a good sprinkling of preachers' handbooks)—with virtually no other faculty represented. Where are the *artes*? Was teaching in the trivium and quadrivium at Paris in the pre-stationer era so well provided with books that the second-hand trade sufficed thereafter to satisfy the student population? Certainly, such works are noticeably rare, in Destrez's list of surviving exemplar-peciae published by Chenu.[129] (Perhaps this explains the university's emphasis on regulation of the second-hand trade.) It is difficult to believe, however, that there was not, at any given time, at least one Parisian stationer renting peciae for the Arts Faculty—in which case, Andrew of Sens's list is specialized to the extent that he offers almost none. Moreover, the men who are named as members of the university delegation that set the rates for Andrew's exemplars include, along with rector, proctors, and two rep-

---

[128] Ibid. p. 86 n. 2, p. 89.

[129] Jean Destrez, "*Exemplaria* universitaires des XIIIe et XIVe siècles," with intro. by M.-D. Chenu, *Scriptorium* 7 (1953) 68–80.

resentatives of the Faculty of Theology, a representative also of the Faculty of Medicine—yet no medical books appear on the list. The implication is that another stationer was renting out medical books, and that Andrew of Sens was (deliberately?) not. A dozen years later, we are given a hint as to why a *de facto* division of the field among stationers might have been effected: As we have seen, in 1316 stationers must swear not to refuse rental even to someone who wishes to make an exemplar of his own to rent out. Evidently, each stationer attempted to retain a monopoly on his own exemplars, and such attempts were very often successful—else why the regulation?

D. Assessment of the Rental Price

Once a stationer had selected a work, found an accessible text of that work, had a copy made in peciae, and had a corrector go through the exemplar, there remained one more step before rental: the assessment of the rental price. The wording of the various university regulations is obscure on this matter. In 1275, stationers are required to charge "no more than a just and reasonable payment *or* no more than the price set by the university." In 1302, stationers swear that they will not ask more from scholars and masters than the price set by the university, *or* for exemplars not assessed by the university, "no more than a just and moderate price"; and the undated addendum (before 1313) specifies that unassessed (i.e., new) exemplars shall not be circulated "until they have been offered to *or* assessed by the university." The regulations of December 1316, on the contrary, say flatly, "No stationer shall rent out an exemplar before it has been corrected and its rate set by the university."[130]

Should one infer that, at least until 1316, the university distinguished between two types of books, ones essential to the university for which the university assigned rates, and others less important to the university which the stationer might rent, if he chose, without a fixed rate? We cannot say. Unfortunately, the wording of the two still-later fourteenth-century book provisions gives no help.[131] The regulations of 1323 are simply a verbatim copy of those of December 1316, the only change occurring in the names of those who swore the oath. And the regulations of 1342 are a thorough grab-bag of articles quoted from earlier documents—of 1302, of the addendum to 1302, and of 1316 (1323)—with no attempt to reconcile mutually contradictory statements. Thus this

---

[130] CUP nos. 462 (1275), 628 (1302 and after), 733 (Dec. 1316) = vol. 1 p. 533, vol. 2 pp. 98, 190.
[131] CUP nos. 825 (1325), 1064 (1342) = vol. 2 pp. 273, 530 ff.

document says that unassessed exemplars must be rented at a just price (1302), that new exemplars must be offered to *or* assessed by the university (1302 addendum), and that no exemplar may be circulated before the university has fixed its rental rate (1316). It is almost as if the exact wording were irrelevant, provided the *stationarii et librarii* were willing to swear obedience.

We do see, at any rate, in those book provisions that survive, the university beginning in 1316 to take care each time to appoint the *taxatores* for the ensuing term. It is unfortunate in this respect (as in so many others) that there are no other surviving lists like Andrew of Sens's, preserving not only the books, the price, and the number of peciae, but also the names and positions of the assessors and the date of the assessment. We assume, however, that such lists can never have been numerous. Ordinarily, the assessors must (either periodically or on demand) have set a price only for the new exemplars, and a reassessment of the whole inventory would occur on necessary occasions—to take account of inflation, or perhaps to mark the establishment of a new shop or changing proprietorship of an existing one.

Nevertheless, the composition of this committee of assessors was, or eventually became, a matter of importance. The regulations say in 1275 that "the university or its delegates," and in 1302 simply "the university," shall set the rates. Probably the composition of the delegation that assessed Andrew of Sens in 1304 was typical: the university rector, the proctors, and three masters representing the higher faculties. In 1316, however, there was a change. We have previously mentioned the minor relaxation of the rules concerning the sale of second-hand books.[132] The concerted action of the bookmen in 1316 effected at least one other significant change, this one pertaining especially to the stationers. Beginning in December 1316, the assessment of peciae-rentals is no longer to be done by university officials, but instead by four men appointed by the university from among the sworn *librarii et stationarii*. It is they, members of the trade, who henceforth set the rates. These *librarii deputati* (1316) or *principales librarii taxatores* (1342) have other charges as well. They are to seek out any bookmen operating without university license and to collect from these the required surety deposit (100 pounds), for delivery to the university at its next general convocation.[133] The *librarii deputati* receive an unspecified salary for their services; and before the end of the century (by 1376 at latest), the four who hold this office are required to post a bond twice that of the rest of the trade (i.e., 200 pounds), which

---

[132] See above, at nn. 29–30.
[133] CUP no. 733 = vol. 2 pp. 191–192.

suggests that their positions had become powerful, lucrative, and, no doubt, open to abuse (such as bribery and embezzlement).[134] Moreover, the wording of the 1316 regulations implies that these *taxatores*, besides pricing peciae, likewise set the price on all book sales—sales, that is, to masters and scholars, not to the lay public. In sum, the assembled *librarii et stationarii* took important steps in 1316 toward gaining some control even of the university portion of their trade—including control over the price of pecia-rental.[135]

E. The Mechanics of Pecia Rental

The actual procedure of renting out peciae is one on which the university regulations and other documents are obstinately silent. We must therefore be content to read between the lines. For example, a passage (1316) previously mentioned stipulates that "no stationer shall refuse to rent exemplars to anyone—even to someone who wishes to make another exemplar—provided he gives for it the sufficient pledge and pays the established fee"; this must mean that it was standard practice to deposit a pledge as security when renting peciae. The next sentence but one states, "If pledges engaged to the stationer are not redeemed within a year, the stationer may then sell them."[136] Though, admittedly, these might be semi-pawnshop transactions, the fact that the document specifies *stationarii* and not the general term *librarii* is by this date significant. Moreover, it implies that the pledge was in the form of a book—the sort of object a stationer could readily sell; this is not unexpected, since books served as the commonest pledged items in student communities.

Having wrung this much from the documents, we look for any possible manuscript verification to support our interpretation of the words— and one turns up immediately. Delisle transcribes a series of notes, a running account, that appears at the end of a manuscript of Peter of Poitiers's *Commentary on the Sentences* which belonged to the Sorbonnist, Master Jean de Gonesse. The notes are cryptic and (at least in

---

[134] CUP no. 1407 and n. = vol. 3 pp. 227–228; the wording of the oath taken by a *librarius superior* implies some of the abuses that the university anticipated from holders of this office. The size of the bond for ordinary *librarii* varied, in the second half of the century, but the sum is reported to have been "40 or 50 pounds, or sometimes more"; see CUP 1335 and nn. = vol. 3 pp. 161–163 (individual oaths from the years 1367–1394).

[135] It would seem that the university again changed its mind on this issue, shortly thereafter; for in both 1323 and 1342 (the only later surviving corporate oaths of bookmen), one of the four annual *taxatores* is a university agent of some sort. (See Appendix 2, *sub nom.* Alanus Brito.) If this is the case, the change is not recorded in the surviving regulations.

[136] CUP 2.190.

transcription) not always intelligible, but they mean something like this: "Master Jean de Gonesse, *clericus*, paid 18 denarii and still owes 2 solidi for the exemplar of the *Historia* [*scholastica*]. He does not have a pecia [at present]. He needs to have the third pecia again. Master Jean de Gonesse owes for the Histories [a total of] 3 solidi and 6 denarii, of which he has paid 18 denarii and later another 12 denarii. He has finished the twelfth pecia. He does not have pecia 13. At present he owes 6 denarii. He is lacking four peciae, and does not have a pecia [at present]. He has a pecia. He has paid ?? (36 d.?). He still owes 6 denarii."[137] This manuscript of the *Commentary* must be the book that Master John left in pledge, while he copied or caused to be copied the stationer's exemplar of the *Historia scholastica*; and the stationer kept a running account on the flyleaf of John's pledge. The *Historia scholastica* appears (without the number of peciae) on the stationer's list from ca. 1275, with an overall rental of 3 solidi,[138] whereas John (d. 1288) is paying 3s. 6d., a not unreasonable rise in price given the increase (averaging about 30%) in charges of the 1304 list over the ca. 1275 list. Having found one likely example, we suggest that there are other such notes, less readily recognizable unless one is looking for them, which have hitherto been regarded as straightforward pawnbrokers' records.[139]

The foregoing notes have the further implication that one paid a fixed rental fee (though it need not be in one lump sum) for the whole work, rather than an amount for each pecia. This assumption is confirmed by the two surviving *taxationes*. Although these documents do not state explicitly that the assigned sums are rates per exemplar and not per pecia, the rates themselves make the fact obvious, since they vary up or down in rough proportion to the number of peciae contained.

We catch another glimpse of the process, as it functioned in 1316, from one of the university's standard injunctions that stationers are to charge no more for rental than the university allows—to which is casually added, "unless the pecia is kept for more than a week."[140] This tells us that the ordinary length of rental was one week, maximum, and that the ordinary quantity was one pecia at a time. Common sense says as much, since it is the whole point of the process to have the exemplar available for simultaneous copying by as many people as possible. The

---

[137] Delisle, *Cabinet des manuscrits* 2.157–158.

[138] CUP 1.645 line 6.

[139] In at least one instance records of some sort were kept on the exemplar itself, which is perplexing. In Troyes B.M. 546 (see n. 70 above) on fol. 24 is a note "Magister G. de mortuo mari habet iii pecias" and on fol. 96, "Magister G. de mortuo mari habet ii p."; there are no payments recorded, and this may be a scribe's notes to himself.

[140] CUP 2.190.

note about John of Gonesse's rental, from the late thirteenth century, likewise speaks of only one pecia at a time, "Debet rehabere terciam," and the repeated "Habet (*or* Non habet) peciam." The manuscripts of St. Thomas also suggest as much. For example, the editor of the *Expositio super Job* singles out two (of the four) manuscripts with pecia marks whose texts reveal that one pecia (a different one in each) was not accessible at the proper time, so that space had to be left for its later insertion;[141] and R. Gauthier mentions the note of a corrector, in a manuscript of the *Sententia libri Ethicorum*, "These four folios are not corrected because we were unable to get the pecia, which was out, or lost, or in any event unfindable."[142]

Yale University, Beinecke MS 207, St. Thomas on book three of the Sentences, provides an exceptionally interesting insight into the practical difficulties that a scribe might encounter in producing a text from exemplar peciae. Beinecke 207 was copied from the exemplar rented out by the stationer William of Sens, most of which survives as Pamplona Cathedral MS 51.[143]

As we have mentioned, Pamplona 51 was in use over a long period, and at some point it was revised. Eventually these revisions obliged William of Sens to discard four successive peciae, nos. 16–19, and replace them with four others (designated 16*–19*) containing revised text; two at least—18 and 19—were replaced en bloc. A comparison of numerous progeny of Pamplona 51 shows that this change occurred after the exemplar had begun to circulate; these descendants likewise verify the fact that, in replacing the successive peciae—provided only that the text at the beginning of pecia 18* followed directly upon the final words of pecia 17*, and that the text at the end of 19* led without omission to the opening words of pecia 20—William was under no compunction to see to it that the bloc's internal division (end of 18*/beginning of 19*) occurred at exactly the same spot in the text as the former divisions had done. In the event, the location of this internal division in the remade bloc of Pamplona 51 did vary, markedly, from the original.

With this as background, let us turn now to the unlucky scribe of Beinecke 207, who had the misfortune to encounter two difficulties simultaneously.[144] The first was not uncommon: a pecia he needed was

[141] Leonine edition vol. 26, ed. A. Dondaine (Rome 1965) 108*.

[142] Leonine edition vol. 47, ed. René Gauthier (Rome 1969) 80*–81*.

[143] See above at n. 77.

[144] This manuscript is discussed by Gils, "Codicologie et critique textuelle" 228. A fuller description appears in B. A. Shailor, *Catalogue of Medieval and Renaissance Manuscripts in the Beinecke Rare Book and Manuscript Library, Yale University*, vol. 1, Medieval and Renaissance Texts & Studies 34 (Binghamton, N.Y. 1984) 282–283. We are grate-

unavailable, and so he was obliged to leave blank the amount of space that he thought adequate for the missing text, and to continue on with the next available pecia, returning later to fill in the gap. The second difficulty, however, was a rarity: the time at which he was copying peciae 18–19 just happened to coincide with the time at which they were in the process of being replaced by the revised pecia 18*–19*. The result is a mess, esthetically and textually.

The sequence of the mishaps that befell this scribe is fairly clear. He had copied peciae 16 and 17, but 18 was unavailable when he wanted it. He therefore left blank what he estimated to be a sufficient number of columns, and continued on. What he copied next, however, was not the original, but the new pecia 19*, which he began (as scribes tended to do) with the beginning of a fresh page, fol. 46va top. Later—perhaps immediately thereafter—he found that the omitted pecia was now available. What he cannot, at least initially, have realized is that William of Sens was supplying him with the old pecia 18, not the new one. Unluckily for the scribe, old and new did not contain identical portions of the text; in fact, the end of remade 18*—and thus the beginning of 19*, which he had already copied—occurred a full column farther along in St. Thomas's text than the end of old 18, the pecia he now began to copy. As if this were not enough of a problem, it turned out that he had not, in fact, left quite enough room even for the text of old pecia 18 to fit in; and he failed to anticipate the problem soon enough to absorb the excess text by compressing or abbreviating his script over the course of the last two or three columns. As a result, when he had filled all the lined space on fol. 46r, he was left with some five lines of the text of pecia 18 still to copy and with nowhere to put them—since fol. 46v had already been filled, in advance.

The several steps in the scribe's attempt to solve his dilemma are likewise fairly clear, but the explanation for them is elusive. First, he added the remaining text on fol. 46rb, as five lines extending into the bottom margin directly beneath the second column. Then, he changed his mind and scraped away what he had just written. Turning the page, he effaced as well the first eleven lines on fol. 46va (the beginning of pecia 19*); into the space thus created, he attempted to squeeze both the left-over five lines of pecia 18 and the beginning (eleven lines, formerly) of pecia 19*, by quite noticeably compressing his script. The attempt was unsuccessful, however, and he was compelled to write in the margin after all—although, in this final state, it is the left-hand margin on fol.

---

ful to Hugues Shooner for locating for us the exact juncture between pecia 18 and pecia 19*. For further discussion of this manuscript see Shooner (n. 91 above), esp. 17f.

46v instead of the bottom margin of 46r; and the marginal text is not the end of pecia 18, but the end of that portion of pecia 19* which he had rewritten. Finally, he turned back to fol. 46rb and added at the bottom below the scrape-marks, in a small but formal script, "Note: Cursed be the stationer who made me ruin the book of a worthy man."[145]

Why the double, and doubly unsuccessful, attempt at overcoming his lack of space? And in particular, why this vehement condemnation of the stationer (William of Sens)?[146] There are at least two plausible explanations, neither of which flatters the candor and probity of the scribe.

(1) One may suppose, as one possibility, that the problem of old pecia/new pecia, and the resultant loss of a column's worth of text, had nothing to do with the scribe's dilemma at all. Scribes were expected merely to make a swift, accurate, and legible copy of whatever was presented to them, not to read critically for content. Therefore, the scribe of Beinecke 207 may well have completely failed to notice that the juncture of the text at the end of his eighteenth pecia and the beginning of his nineteenth reads like nonsense.[147] In that case, we must expect a purely physical and esthetic explanation. Taken as a whole, Beinecke 207 is a well-presented text, with modest but attractive colored initials; the scribe's pecia marks were deliberately written at the very edge of the page, where they would for the most part disappear when the finished book was trimmed, and most of those which survived the trimming have been carefully scraped away; and all four margins are spacious. It would seem, in other words, that appearances mattered, to the "worthy man" for whom the book was written. After the scribe had first attempted to accommodate in the lower margin the "excess" text at the end of pecia 18, therefore, he may have felt that the resulting extra lines, destroying the symmetry of the page and calling attention to themselves, would surely displease his patron. His attempt to rectify the situation only made matters worse, however; for he still was unable to avoid writing in the margin, and he had made, as well, rather a mess of effacing his first attempt. Therefore, he added a note cursing the stationer, to imply that someone else was responsible for what was, in fact, the result of his own miscalculation.

---

[145] "Nota. Confundatur stacionarius qui me fecit deturpari librum aliculius probi viri"; Yale, Beinecke MS 207 fol. 46rb.

[146] This is the only such note Destrez came across, in the course of surveying thousands of manuscripts; see Shooner (n. 91 above), 17f.

[147] This is Gils's tentative conclusion (n. 144 above): "Il ne l'a peut-être jamais su." Gils was unaware, however, that the scribe of Beinecke 207 had also rewritten the beginning of pecia 19*, as well as the end of pecia 18, a fact that may have influenced his judgment.

(2) Or one may suppose, instead, that the scribe was eventually quite conscious of the fact that the text at the end of his pecia 18 did not "fit" with the beginning of 19*. In that case, the sequence of events would have been something like this: The scribe found, when he reached the end of fol. 46rb, that there were five more lines to copy and no proper space for them, so he added them neatly in the bottom margin; the result would have been a noticeable but not unsightly (nor unusual) correction. He would only at this point have recognized that the text he had just managed with difficulty to complete (pecia 18) did not, in fact, attach directly to the text he had previously written on the verso (pecia 19*). For, while he was likely giving little or no notice to the sense of what he copied, there was one small item at the very end of pecia 18 that caught his attention: the catchword. (So far as we know, every exemplar-pecia that survives bears a catchword at the end, for obvious reasons.) The catchword at the end of pecia 18 did not at all match the opening words of pecia 19*, and the scribe at last realized that his problems extended beyond mere lack of space. What to do? On the one hand, his patron would not be pleased to pay for an incomplete text; and, because of his having to extend the last five lines of pecia 18 into the margin, the scribe had unintentionally called attention to the very place in the text where something—he probably did not know how much—was missing. On the other hand, the fault truly was not his. He had asked the stationer for pecia 19, and had dutifully copied what he was given; then he did the same for pecia 18. Although he now recognized that there was some sort of anomaly, it was not clear—to the scribe, at any rate—that he was obliged to spend the extra time, for which he would receive no extra pay, to straighten the matter out. He had fulfilled the letter, if not the spirit, of his contract; but even so, he must have doubted that his patron would be tolerant enough to share this viewpoint. So he cunningly covered his tracks: he effaced not only the added lines at the bottom of 46rb but also the first few lines of 46va, and rewrote both passages together, at the top of 46v. The previously eye-catching division between peciae, inviting detection of the loss of text, was thus thoroughly disguised; it now occurs about halfway through the fifth line of an eleven-line segment that was unmistakably written all at one sitting. This explanation of the facts, while it implies more serious deceit on the scribe's part than the alternative, at least has the advantage of providing a satisfying reason for the scribe's bitterness, in the note added to fol. 46r. It was in fact the stationer, William of Sens, who was guilty of continuing to circulate the old pecia 18 after it had been superseded, and who therefore created the scribe's dilemma. Perhaps as one final line of defense, should his deception after all be discovered—or, more likely, as a heart-

felt expression of frustration—the scribe called down curses on the stationer's head.

*   *   *

With this observation, we reach the end of the information we have thus far quarried out of the printed sources. But we are optimistic that it is by no means a dead end, just a temporary halt. It seems to us that future knowledge of the mechanism of stationer-production will emerge from a cross-fertilization between textual studies of specific university books, on the one hand, and reexamination—or rather reinterpretation—of the documents and regulations, on the other.

Of the myriad unsolved questions, we feel certain that several will soon be answerable, once a bit more evidence is added to the common pool. For example: Did one pay for the exemplar as a whole? Or could one rent merely a selection of peciae, if one wanted only part of a book? Our study of the university texts of the *Manipulus florum* suggested that many renters failed, seemingly deliberately, to copy the last pecia, which comprised a booklist unessential to the usefulness of the body of the florilegium.[148] Yet the two *taxatio* lists give the rental price per work, not per pecia. And Master John of Gonesse's account, previously mentioned, states the price as a single total; although he reached that total through, it seems, four separate payments, they were obviously not payments by the pecia. Evidence to illuminate this point will surely turn up in time.

Or to take another example, there is the matter of correction: Was the corrector invariably someone other than the scribe—a second pair of eyes, as it were? Many peciae of the surviving exemplar of the *Manipulus florum* bear two separate correctors' marks, including one who leaves his name ("Matt."). Was "correcting" a specialized skill in any sense? The taille rolls list, on the Rue aus Porees in the heart of the university, an "Adam, corrigeeur" in 1292;[149] his name survives, "Ade correctoris," in a thirteenth-century Parisian exemplar of Aristotle *De natura animalium*, now Cesena, Malat. sin. XXIV 4.[150] In the taille books for 1296 and 1297, we find that Adam has been succeeded in the same location (next door to "Robert de Craonne/Craen, libraire") by "Jehannot le corrigeeur."[151] Gauthier, on the basis of the corrector's

---

[148] Rouse and Rouse, *Preachers, Florilegia and Sermons*, 179.

[149] Géraud, 1292, 161.

[150] We thank Louis Bataillon, O.P., for this information about the Cesena manuscript.

[151] Michaëlsson, *1296* p. 234 and *1297* p. 216. For Jehannot as *librere*, see Appendix 2 below.

note cited above, speculated that it was a common practice for individual scholars to rent exemplar-peciae for the purpose of correcting existing texts (whether texts copied from those same peciae, or texts of an independant tradition); and he cites the statutes from other universities — Bologna, Padua, Montpellier, Toulouse — which stipulate a reduced rate for peciae rented for this purpose;[152] but no such statute survives from Paris. Surely, future studies will help to clarify the role of correctors and corrections.

Larger questions will doubtless remain a matter of controversy for some time to come. One of the most perplexing is this: Why did the pecia system disappear at Paris, after the middle of the fourteenth century? The date naturally suggests the Black Death as a contributing cause, but that cannot be the whole explanation. Masters continued to write, and students to read; why was it no longer the practice to disseminate new texts via the pecia-rental method that had served so well in the past? Men (and women) continue to be called stationers, in oaths to the University of Paris or in notes of sale in manuscripts. Yet there is no evidence — in the form of surviving manuscripts copied from exemplar-peciae — that these later stationers functioned as their predecessors had done in the first half of the century. It is to be hoped that the study of the texts produced after the mid-fourteenth century will eventually shed light on the changed mechanics of dissemination.

One major question that remains unanswered is perhaps unanswerable: What were the specific origins of the pecia system? To be sure, reproduction of texts by the use of exemplar-peciae was "merely" an innovative adaptation of a known procedure,[153] but what a brilliant and hugely successful innovation it was! It would be most illuminating to know where, when, why, how, and by whom the process was first devised. We have no evidence on this matter beyond what has been set forth in this paper; but we should like to conclude by suggesting the direction in which, it seems to us, that evidence points.

We suggest that the Parisian form of pecia publication was devised by the Dominicans of St. Jacques, probably in the 1240s. Much of the reason for our conclusion will be apparent to readers of this paper: the evidence for the very close connections between the Dominicans and the stationer's shop of the Sens family, combined with the variety of indications that the shop of William of Sens was very important, very early, and originally without commercial competition. Moreover, it seems — as a subjective judgment — that Dominican authors on the whole benefited

---

[152] Gauthier, loc. cit. (n. 142 above).
[153] See above, at n. 8.

most, and earliest, from the possibilities offered by the pecia system. This impression may well be illusory, based less upon thirteenth-century reality than upon the concentration of twentieth-century editors on St. Thomas. There is also the early (pre-1258) Parisian manuscript of Hugh of St-Cher's postills that contains a pecia mark, though the manuscript does not appear to be a product of the stationer's trade; this may reflect a style of in-house book production at St-Jacques.[154] We recall, as well, that the earliest university book provisions to survive, and probably the earliest that were promulgated at Paris, were adopted at a general session held in 1275 at St-Jacques.

Our principal reason, however, for supposing the Dominicans of St-Jacques and not some member of the book trade to have devised the Parisian system lies in the fact that the Dominicans of Paris, from ca. 1230 on, were demonstrably masters of innovation in the devising of aids to scholarship. The creation of the St-Jacques verbal concordance to the Bible is by no means the sum total of their efforts,[155] but it offers, unaided, a clear enough analogy to illustrate our point. Like the pecia system, the making of the concordance involved intelligent and trail-blazing solutions to problems of technique; it utilized the notion of division of labor among many scholar-writers working simultaneously; and it had as its purpose a vast increase in the availability of information to scholars and preachers.[156] We shall not force the analogy any further, nor consider by name other thirteenth-century Dominican enterprises of similar intent, for in the final analysis this does not constitute evidence. It simply contributes to our sense that there is no other explanation so likely as this—that the Dominicans devised the version of pecia publication as it was known at Paris.

If so, the system would doubtless have remained for a time completely internal to the convent of St-Jacques. The relationship with William of Sens and ultimately with his heirs—whatever its nature: partnership? employer/employee? patron/tradesman?—would have occurred somewhat later (1260s?), when the usefulness of the system necessitated professional help. The rapid importation of the process from Bologna, evidently its place of origin, and its speedy adaptation to the specific needs of the University of Paris, would be explicable in terms of wandering Dominican scholars.

---

[154] See above, at n. 16.

[155] See Rouse and Rouse, *Preachers, Florilegia and Sermons*, index s.v. Dominicans.

[156] Concerning the making of the concordance, see ibid., 9–11; and R. H. and M. A. Rouse, "The Verbal Concordance to the Scriptures," *Archivum Fratrum Praedicatorum* 44 (1974) 5–30.

La pecia dans le monde universitaire leaves its readers with a sense of security, because of the precision and clarity with which Destrez sets forth his evidence. The research of scholars since Destrez has made it possible to examine the production of university books with even greater precision and breadth, but at the expense of the sense of security. Their work has raised questions that had not previously been asked, leaving one with a profound sense of how much still remains to be learned about the university book trade in Paris.

APPENDIX 1

A NOTE ON THE SOURCES

In the course of this article, and especially in our attempts at prosopography, we have had occasion to mention a variety of printed documents, some cited from Denifle and Chatelain's *Chartularium* of the University of Paris and others from the editions, by Géraud and Michaëlsson, of taille books of the city of Paris.[157] Anyone who wishes to investigate the nature of these documents in depth is referred to their editors' introductions, and to the substantial subsequent literature. It is useful, however, to give here a brief description of the documents we have cited and to draw attention to the particular implications pertinent to our argument.

I. UNIVERSITY DOCUMENTS

A. *Taxationes*

The two extant *taxationes* from the University of Paris do not survive in the original but only in copies, included in two roughly similar collections of university documents compiled in the fourteenth century, Vatican Reg. lat. 406 and London B.L. Add. 17304.[158] Reg. lat. 406, written ca. 1304 evidently for the use of the Picard Nation, has been well cataloged by Dom Wilmart.[159] B.L. Add. 17304, also, is a formal collection, written by a single hand in littera textualis, with the latest documents dated in the 1380s; it is thought to have been made for the use of the English Nation.[160] The fact that they are copies has serious implications for the trustworthiness of the *taxationes*; for these lists are replete with roman numerals (numbers of peciae, prices of rental), which are notoriously susceptible to errors in copying. Unlike copyists' errors in prose, for which one at least has grammar and sense as guides, errors in lists of numbers are difficult even to detect, let alone correct. When their

---

[157] These works are cited in nn. 1 and 6 above.

[158] A third collection, formerly Phillipps no. 876, omits copies of the *taxationes*.

[159] Cited in n. 22 above.

[160] B.L. Add. 17304 continued in use long after the collection of documents was written. Later additions include a calendar (ca. 1520s?), and signatures of successive rectors upon taking office (to 1673).

two sources disagreed, the editors of the *taxationes*, working long before the revelations of Destrez, were compelled simply to rely upon the reading of the manuscript which had proved more faithful in other contexts; and, as we now know, this sometimes led them to the wrong choice.[161]

There are countless anomalies in both *taxationes* that await explanation. It has been suggested, for example, that the list of legal texts printed at the end of the ca. 1275 *taxatio* (CUP 1.648–649) may be a separate item, perhaps pertaining to a different stationer: it bears a separate heading, "Hec est taxatio exemplarium," and it repeats, with a rental of "iiii s.," the glossed Raymond of Peñafort mentioned toward the beginning of the 1275 list (CUP 1.645) with a rental of "iii s."[162] We note, however, that the heading for this final section does not differ much from other internal headings—e.g., "Ista sunt exemplaria super theologiam"; one would merely have to suppose the loss of a single word, "Hec est taxatio exemplarium [legum]." There seems little logic in the headings throughout. The list as a whole has no (contemporary) heading at all. And the section of "exemplaria super theologiam" in fact contains only works of Augustine, while the works of Gregory, Isidore, Anselm, Bernard, and Hugh of St-Victor all appear in a previous and untitled section of the list. For the moment, the strongest evidence for the integrity of the *taxationes* as printed is the fact that the fourteenth-century scribes of the surviving copies clearly considered each to be a unit.

B. Bookmen's Oaths, Corporate and Individual

Beginning with its earliest (surviving) book provision in 1275, and in all subsequent ones, the University of Paris prescribed that the *librarii et stationarii* must swear an oath of observance. No names of bookmen are appended to the early documents, however—even though one still has the (an?) original, complete with seal, of the 1275 oath. Either the signatures were recorded elsewhere, on something now lost, or, more likely, the bookmen swore *viva voce* in assemblage before the university's officials.

The first list of bookmen's names in the university records, in fact, appears not on an oath but in a blacklist, dated 12 June 1316. When the dispute was settled on 4 December 1316, the *librarii et stationarii* who took the oath in a body were listed by name, along with the street on

---

[161] See A. Dondaine's edition of St. Thomas's *Quaestiones de veritate*, Leonine edition vol. 22.1, p. 6*.

[162] We thank Hugues Shooner for this suggestion.

which each was located. The two other surviving oaths from this century (1323, 1342) likewise record the names (but not the addresses) of those who swore as a group before the university's officials.

In addition to these four lists of bookmen as a group, Denifle and Chatelain give brief notice of some 35–37 individual oaths from the years 1314–1354, the originals of which survive in the Archives Nationales. These are records of the oath by a single bookman (or, on two occasions, man and wife) who swore—before the *officialis curiae*, surprisingly enough: a reminder of the complex lines of authority still connecting university and cathedral—to observe the regulations of the University of Paris, simultaneously posting a bond to indemnify the university in case of malfeasance. These oaths are chance survivals, and there must originally have been many times this number, as witness the many names on the university's corporate oaths for which the individual oaths do not survive. We suspect that, normally, a *libraire* or stationer swore an individual oath and formally posted his bond only once, upon taking possession of his shop by purchase or inheritance—or as soon thereafter as it became either prudent or inescapable that he do so—and that the requisite annual (?)[163] renewal of the oath before the assembled university masters was done *vive voce*, by the bookmen in a body. Two individual oaths survive, however, for Richard de Montbaston (August and October 1338) and Henricus Guilloti (1351 and 1353), which shows that, if a single written oath was the norm, there were exceptions.[164] The especial usefulness of the individual oaths for our purposes lies in the fact that they distinguish, as the other records do not, between ordinary *librarii* and those who held the offices (the plural *officia* is often used; see CUP 2.189n) of *stationarius et librarius*.

As we have noted in the course of this article, the only university bookmen whose appearance in university records antedates 1316 belong to the Sens family: (1) Thomas of Sens, whose individual oath of May 1314 is said to have been sworn, not before the *officialis curiae* like all the others of which we have a record, but "at the Mathurins, in the presence of the university's representatives, namely, Master Thomas Anglicus, doctor of theology, and Master Hugh of Macon, doctor of canon law, and of numerous other masters there present";[165] and (2)

---

[163] In 1275 the oath is prescribed to be sworn "annis singulis vel de biennio in biennium" (CUP 1.533), and in 1342 "anno quolibet" (CUP 2.530), with an addition in both cases, "or as often as the university may wish."

[164] For references, see these names in Appendix 2 below.

[165] The original does not survive. One has only the copy in B.L. Add. 17304 (see above), which seems to be a summary rather than a verbatim reproduction; thus, for example, it says merely that "he swore the things stationers are required to swear"

Andrew of Sens, whose name as stationer appears, along with those of the university's assessors, on the *taxatio* of 1304. (William of Sens does not appear in any university record, but he is called stationer by a charter of Notre Dame in 1270).

II. THE BOOKS OF THE TAILLE

Taille books survive for part of the sequence 1292–1300, and for the extraordinary taille (feudal dues for the knighting of Philip the Fair's eldest son) of 1313. The records for 1292, 1296, 1297, and 1313 have been edited, while those for 1298–1300 are extant in manuscript at Paris, Arch. nat. KK.283. The taille books of 1292–1300 record the payment, in annual increments, of a fixed sum levied in lieu of Philip the Fair's tax (*maltote*) on commercial transactions, since the latter would have been a nuisance to collect; therefore, one may assume that the rates in those years, if not in 1313 as well, provide a rough comparison of commercial income (rather than, say, a comparison of the worth of real property or of inherited wealth). Two aspects of these records make them less helpful than one might wish, for the purposes of this article.

First is the fact that what survives is not the original report of the individual assessors, but a formal copy made for deposit; indeed, Michaëlsson, the most recent editor of taille books, demonstrated that at least two, and more likely three, formal copies of the taille book were made in 1313, and he assumed that the same was true of the earlier books. Therefore, there is a strong possibility that scribal error and/or misinterpretation of the assessors' returns has crept undetected into the only surviving copy for any given year.

The second problem is the date of the tailles. As we have noted, the earliest list of bookmen in the university records dates from 1316. The taille nearest in date is that of 1313; but, by royal *ordonnance* of 1307, the university's sworn bookmen were exempted from taxation, and they are nearly all absent from the taille book of 1313. This has left us in the position of trying to compare names of university bookmen from 1316 and later with the printed taille records of 1297 and before. As one might expect, the results have been slender.

Finally, we should mention that the taille books make no distinctions between *stationarii* and the other *librarii*, but simply use the general designation *librere* for them all.

("juravit . . . articulos quos tenetur jurare stationarii"). We assume that he posted a bond, but the record does not say so. See CUP 2.171.

APPENDIX 2

LIBRARII AND *STATIONARII* AT PARIS, 1292–1354

We list here all those men and women who are designated as *librarii* (or *librarii et stationarii*) by records of the University of Paris, from the earliest through 1354, or who appear on the street-by-street tax or *taille* records of the City of Paris, 1292–1313, designated as *libreres*. The datespan has been determined for us by the records: 1292 is the date of the first taille book; since the earliest university oath (without names of those who swore, unfortunately) dates from 1275, we assume that all booksellers who appear in the taille books of the 1290s came under the university's jurisdiction, in theory, and doubtless the vast majority in practice. At the other end of the span, 1354 is the date of the last surviving individual oath, in a series of oaths that stretches virtually uninterrupted from 1314. After 1354, there is a gap of thirteen years in the surviving oaths; and those who swore their oaths at the end of the century (from 1367 onward) belong to a rather different world—certainly a different set of circumstances—from the university book trade described in this paper. We have made only one exception to our chronological limits, to incorporate William of Sens; although he antedates both the taille records and the university's oaths-with-names, we know from other evidence that he served university masters and scholars as a stationer.

Within these limits, the list is as complete as we can make it. The manuscript taille records for the three years 1298, 1299, and 1300 obviously cannot be rechecked and cross-checked as can the printed volumes, and that for 1298 in particular is in a poor physical state that makes it impossible to read in places. Nevertheless, in examining this manuscript in 1985 we made a good effort to find everyone specifically called *librere* in the taille for 1298–1300. Our list does not include other aspects of the book trade—illuminators, scribes, correctors, parchmenters, binders, or ink-makers—except for the occasional man or woman who appears in the taille with such a designation in one year and the designation *librere* in another, or those who appear with a double designation (e.g., *librere et enlumineeur*). Our list is intended to complement, but not to duplicate, those of Baron for thirteenth- through fifteenth-century illuminators (but not booksellers),[166] and de Winter's for several

---

[166] F. Baron, "Enlumineurs, peintres et sculpteurs parisiens des XIIIe et XIVe siècles, d'après les rôles de la taille," *Bulletin archéologique du Comité des travaux historiques et scientifiques*, n.s. 4 (1969) 37–121; idem, "Enlumineurs, peintres et sculpteurs parisiens des

aspects of the book trade, but at the end of the fourteenth century.[167]

The taille books of 1292 and 1296–1300 provide a cross-section of the location of the book trade; so, too, does the corporate university oath of December 1316, which gives the street address for each man who swears the oath. For this quarter-century, then, we can see clearly the double focus of the trade: one group centered on the Rue neuve Notre Dame, on the Ile de la Cité; and a second clustered around the university on the Left Bank, in the tangle of little streets bounded roughly by St. Sevrin on the north, the Sorbonne on the west, St. Jacques to the south, and Ste. Geneviève on the east (see Map). Chance survivals of the addresses of *librarii* after this date (1317–1323)—mentions in surviving manuscripts, or (very rarely) records of location in individual oaths—do nothing to alter this picture, although they cannot be regarded as representative. (De Winter's people from the end of the century also seem to reflect the same pattern of distribution.) Among the some 125 names on our list, the known exceptions are 5: Guillaume d'Auvergne, *librere*, on the Rue de Hirondelle 1292–1297 (north and west of St. Sevrin); Henri le petit, *librere*, 1296, and (his successor?) Guillaume *le librere*, *enlumineeur*, 1297, on the Rue des Cordeles (the eastern end, beside the Franciscan house); to the east, Jehan *le librere* on the Rue de Versailles (near the Collège de St. Bernard and the Porte St. Victor) in 1297; and a mention, in the year 1297, of another Jehan *le librere*, the only *librere* recorded on the Right Bank during the years covered by the list (just outside the Porte St. Honoré and, not incidentally, near the Louvre palace).

Having compiled this list permits us one further general observation: that the book trade was a family business, one which often passed from a man to his widow and from father or mother to son or son-in-law. This is not unexpected, but it is pleasing to be able to document the process, in a few cases at least. The time-period covered by the list coincides with the gradual establishment of family names, which exist side-by-side with nicknames and names that designate a place of origin. Thus, one may find in the taille (cf. 1292 taille p. 118) a man called "Jehan le blont" in order to distinguish him from his next-door neighbor "Jehan le fort"; and it would be ludicrous to suggest that this Jehan must, or even might, be kin to everyone else in Paris called "blont." At

---

XIVe et XVe siècles, d'après les archives de l'hôpital Saint-Jacques-aux-Pèlerins," ibid. n.s. 6 (1970–1971) 77–115.

[167]P.M. de Winter, "Copistes, éditeurs et enlumineurs de la fin du XIVe siècle: La production à Paris de manuscrits à miniatures," *Actes du 100e Congrès national des Sociétés savantes* (Paris 1978) 173–198; see especially Appendice, 185–198, "Copistes (écrivains) et éditeurs (stationnaires) parisiens de la période 1375–1405: Travaux pour lesquels ils sont connus."

the same time, one has groups like the Sens family. William and Margaret may indeed have come to Paris from Sens—though even that is not necessarily the case. But when, in the same shop, one later comes to Andrew "of Sens," and still later to Thomas "called 'of Sens'" (*dictus de Zenonis*, as his individual oath puts it), the reference clearly is not to their native town but to their parentage. We have been cautious in suggesting kinship for *librarii* with similar names; but when there is a sequence of two or three such people, following one another chronologically and filling the same office, it is a near-certainty that we are seeing a family business handed on from one member to the next.

It is our hope in presenting this list that in the future many of the names will be identified in manuscripts, accounts, and charters, thereby serving on the one hand to enlarge present knowledge of the Paris book trade and, on the other, to provide a context—of date, place, and circumstances—for anyone studying those manuscripts and other documents.

Organization of the List

Alphabetization

The list is alphabetized by first name and then by cognomen. While we have attempted to record significant variants in the Old French and Latin renderings of a person's name, we have alphabetized them all according to the Latin form. Thus, for *Alain* (or any variations thereof), see *Alanus*; for *Etienne* (etc.), *Stephanus*; for *Geoffroy, Gaufridus*; for *Giles, Egidius*; for *Guillaume, Guillelmus*; for *Henri, Henricus*; for *Jean* or *Jehan, Johannes*; for *Nicole, Nicolaus*; for *Pierre, Petrus*; for *Raoul, Radulfus*.

Arrangement of the entries

Entries are arranged in the following order: (1) Name, with any significant variants; (2) designation of métier as given by the sources; (3) the first and last date at which he/she is known; (4) street address, if known; (5) sources in which the name appears; (6) any other pertinent information, including cross-references to other members of the same family.

Sources

Bibliographic reference to CUP appears in n. 1 above, and to the printed taille books (for 1292, 1296, 1297, 1313) in n. 6 above. Citations of the 1298, 1299, and 1300 taille books refer by folio number to Paris, Arch. nat. KK.283. For a discussion of the comparative advantages and shortcomings of the different sources, see App. 1 above.

† A dagger to the left of a name is meant to allow readers to locate rapidly those who are specifically said to have been stationers. (Distinction between stationers and ordinary *librarii* is made only in individual oaths; see app. 1).

Aaliz a lescurel/de lescurel [*librere?*]. See Fortin de lescurel.

Adam le corrigeeur [*librere?*]. See Jehan le corrigeeur.

Agnes [de Aurelianis], *libraria*. 1350. (CUP 2.658n, individual oath). Widow and successor of *Guillelmus de Aurelianus.

?Alanus Brito, *principalis serviens facultatis decretorum*. 1342. (CUP 2.543, corporate oath?) Alanus Brito, although his name is not among those who took the oath in 1342, crops up at the end of the document as one of the four *taxatores librorum* for 1342. It is not said that he was himself a *librarius*. Probably the university had reclaimed the right to appoint one of its own employees or officers (*serviens* is rather an all-purpose designation) to the group that set the rates for pecia-rental and other book sales (see above, pt. II-D), likely as early as 1323. See *Gaufridus Brito and *Johannes de Guyendale.

Alain le jeune/le genne [*librere*]. 1292. Rue neuve Notre Dame. (1292 taille, p. 149). No occupation is listed for him, but his widow *Julienne is called "la fame Alain le genne librere," in 1296.

†Andreas dictus de Senonis/Andri de Sens/Andri l'englois, *librarius et stationarius*. 1296–1304. Rue St-Jacques. (1296 taille, p. 234; 1297 taille, p. 217; 1299 taille, fol. 221; 1300 taille, fol. 293; CUP 2.107, *taxatio*). Concerning Andreas and the other members of his family *Guillelmus, *Marguerite, and *Thomas of Sens, see above, pt. I-D.

Cristoforus de Ravenelo, *scriptor et librarius juratus*. 1350. (CUP 2.658n, individual oath).

Colin le *librere*. 1300. Rue Erembourc de Brie. (1300 taille, fol. 291v).

Colin de la chastelet (?), *librere*. 1298. Rue neuve Notre Dame. (1298 taille, fol. 144). Possibly the same as *Colin de la lande.

Colin de la lande, *librere*. 1300. Rue neuve Notre Dame. (1300 taille, fol. 288). Possibly the same as *Colin de la chastelet.

Colinus Trenchemer, *librarius* or *stationarius*. 1316. (CUP 2.180, blacklist). Possibly the same as any of the preceding.

Conerardus/Corrardus Alemanus, *librarius* or *stationarius*. 1342. (CUP 2.532, corporate oath).

Daniel de Loctey, *librarius*. 1354. (CUP 2.658n, individual oath).

[Egidius] Gile de Soisson/de Sessons, *lieeur de livres, librere*. 1292–1300. Rue neuve Notre Dame. (1292 taille, p. 148; 1296 taille, p. 214; 1297 taille, p. 198; 1300 taille, fol. 288v). Gile is called *librere* only in 1300.

Egidius de Vivariis, *librarius* or *stationarius*. 1323. (CUP 2.273n, corporate oath).
   Perhaps the successor, and doubtless the kinsman, of *Michael de Vivariis.
Fortin/Sire Fortin de lescurel, *librere*. 1292–1299. Rue neuve Notre Dame. (1292
   taille, p. 148; 1299 taille, fol. 214v). Son of the Dame Aaliz de lescurel who
   is mentioned not only in 1292 and 1299 but in the taille books for 1296 (p.
   214) and 1297 (p. 199) as well. Her occupation is not named; but in the
   earlier records it is she who is taxed, with only a passing mention (1292)
   of "Fortin, son fuiz." Only in 1299 does his name take precedence ("Sire
   Fortin de lescurel librere . . . Dame Aaliz de lescurel sa mere"). Probably
   Aaliz was also a *libraire*, and her son took charge of the business in 1298
   or 1299.
[Gaufridus] Gefroi/Giefroi de biauvez, *librere*. 1292–1299. In 1292 and 1299 he
   is recorded as if on the "Rue de Froit-Mantel," but other tailles locate him
   more specifically on the little "Rue sanz chief encontre l'ospital [de St.
   Jean]," which branches off from Froit-Mantel. (1292 taille, p. 163; 1296
   taille, p. 237; 1297 taille, p. 219; 1299 taille, fol. 222).
?Gaufridus Brito, *notarius publicus*. 1316. Rue neuve Notre Dame. (CUP 2.191,
   corporate oath). Although he took the oath with the *librarii* and
   stationarii in 1316, there is no reason to think that he was himself a book-
   seller. See the similar cases of *Alanus Brito and *Johannes de Guyendale.
Gaufridus Burgondus, *librarius* or *stationarius*. 1316. (CUP 2.180, blacklist).
   Possibly to be identified with *Gaufridus Lotharingus; G. Burg. (but not
   G. Lothar.) is on the blacklist of June 1316, while G. Lothar. (but not G.
   Burg.) swears the oath, in the settlement of Dec. 1316. Gaufridus Burgondus
   is possibly kinsman and predecessor of *Guillelmus dictus le Bourgignon.
Gaufridus le Cauchois, *librarius* or *stationarius*. 1342. (CUP 2.532, corporate
   oath).
Gaufridus de Evillane, *librarius*. 1338. (CUP 2.189n, individual oath).
Gaufridus Lotharingus, *librarius* or *stationarius*. 1316–1323. Rue Erembourc de
   Brie. (CUP 2.192, CUP 2.273n, corporate oaths). Possibly the same as
   *Gaufridus Burgondus (q.v. for discussion).
Gaufridus dictus le Normant, *librarius* or *stationarius*. 1323. (CUP 2.273n).
   Probably related to the later *Johannes dictus le Normant, and perhaps to
   the earlier *Thomas Normannus—despite the fact that Gaufridus and
   Thomas took the oath simultaneously in 1323, which is somewhat unusual
   for members of the same shop/family.
Gaufridus de Sancto Leodegario/Gaufridus de vico novo, *clericus, librarius
   juratus*. 1316–1323. Rue neuve Notre Dame. (CUP 2.180, blacklist; CUP
   2.188–189, individual oath; CUP 2.192 and 2.273n, corporate oaths). Geoffrey of St-Léger is better known as an illuminator; see discussion above,
   pt. I-C. He is probably a kinsman and successor of *Johannes de Sancto
   Leodegario.

Gilbertus de Hollendia, Anglicus, *clericus, librarius*. 1342. (CUP 2.189n, individual oath; CUP 2.532, corporate oath).

Gude (?) de biaune, *librere*. 1299. Rue neuve Notre Dame. (1299 taille, fol. 214v).

Guerin l'englois, *librere*. 1292–1300. At first he is recorded on "La ruele aus Coulons," a tiny street that ran into the Rue neuve Notre Dame; from 1296, he is simply reported as being on the Rue neuve. (1292 taille, p. 149; 1296 taille, p. 212; 1297 taille, p. 197; 1299 taille, fol. 214; 1300 taille, fol. 288).

Guidomarus de Cuomeneuc (?), *clericus, librarius*. 1350. (CUP 2.658n, individual oath; the editors note that the name is almost illegible).

Guillaume, *librere, enlumineeur*. 1297. Rue des Cordeles. (1297 taille, p. 215). He is perhaps successor to *Henri le petit, the only *librere* on this street in 1296, as Guillaume is the only one in 1297. Guillaume may, instead, have taken over the shop of Jehan d'orli, l'enlumineeur (on this street in 1296; taille, p. 232), whose tax of 10 sous in 1296 is identical with Guillaume's in 1297.

Guillelmus de Aurelianus, *librarius* or *stationarius*. 1342, d. bef. 1350. (CUP 2.532, corporate oath). Succeeded by his widow *Agnes.

Guillaume d'Auvergne/l'avergnaz, *librere*. 1292–1297. Rue de Hirondelle, parish of St-André-des-Arts. (1292 taille, p. 159; 1296 taille, p. 231; 1297 taille, p. 213).

Guillelmus dictus le Bourgignon, *librarius* or *stationarius*. 1342. (CUP 2.532, corporate oath). Possibly kinsman and successor of *Gaufridus Burgondus.

Guillelmus de Caprosia, *librarius*. 1342. (CUP 2.189n, individual oath; CUP 2.532, corporate oath).

Guillelmus dictus Cumbaculo, *librarius* or *stationarius*. 1323. (CUP 2.273n, corporate oath).

Guillelmus de Curia/Guillaume de la court, *librarius* or *stationarius*. 1296–1316, prob. d. before 1323. At first he was situated in or around the cloister of St-Benoît, west of the Rue St-Jacques, but by 1297 (still in 1316) he had moved to the Rue de Clos-Brunel, east of the Rue St-Jacques. (1296 taille, p. 235; 1297 taille, p. 220; CUP 2.180, blacklist; CUP 2.192, corporate oath; cf. CUP 2.273n, corporate oath).

[Guillelmus de Garlandia (?) CUP 2.273n, says that the takers of the corporate oath of 1323 included the same names as in 1316 with three exceptions, one of whom is "Guillelmus de Garlandia." There is no such name on the 1316 list. Probably an error for *Johannes de Garlandia].

Guillelmus le Grant, Anglicus, *librarius* or *stationarius*. 1316–1323. Rue des Noyers. (CUP 2.192, CUP 2.273n, both corporate oaths).

Guillelmus Herberti, *librarius* or *stationarius*. 1342. (CUP 2.532, corporate oath).

Guillelmus dictus de Pointona, *librarius*. 1343. (CUP 2.189n, individual oath). Probably kinsman and successor of *Johannes de Pointona.

†Guillelmus Senonensis/dictus de Senonis, *clericus, stationarius librorum*. [1264?] 1270, prob. d. before 1292. [Rue St-Jacques]. Concerning William and other members of his family, *Andreas, *Marguerite, and *Thomas of Sens, see above, pt. I-D.

†Henricus Anglicus/Englicus: His name occurs in Paris, BN lat. 3107 (St. Thomas, *Contra gentiles*). Concerning this stationer (?), see the discussion above, pt. I-E.

Henricus de Cornubia, *clericus, librarius*. 1338–1342 [–1350?]. (CUP 2.189n, individual oath; CUP 2.532, corporate oath). This may be the same as the man with the confusing name, *Henricus le Franc de Venna Anglicus, burgensis Parisiensis (q.v. for discussion).

Henricus le Franc de Venna Anglicus, burgensis Parisiensis, *librarius*. 1350. (CUP 2.658). He pledged his property in 1350 to guarantee the bond posted by the stationer *Henricus de Lechlade. Denifle and Chatelain suggest that "Venna" may perhaps refer to Venn-Ottery in Cornwall (CUP 2.658 n. 1); if so, Henricus le Franc de Venna is probably the same as *Henricus de Cornubia. It is equally likely that this is yet another variant of the name *Henricus dictus de Neuham alias Henricus de Nevanne. Both Henry of Cornwall and Henry of Newham are attested in the years 1338 and 1342, which means that both are likely to have been still living in 1350 and to have been by then in a financial position that would permit them to extend a hand to a fellow countryman.

Henricus Guilloti, *librarius*. 1351–1353. (CUP 2.658n, individual oaths). For unknown reasons, Henricus swore two individual oaths, two years apart.

†Henricus de Lechlade, Anglicus, *librarius et stationarius*. 1350. (CUP 2.657–658, individual oath). His bond of office was guaranteed by *Henricus le Franc de Venna, which implies that Lechlade's own property (also pledged) was not thought valuable enough to serve as collateral for the bond.

†Henricus dictus de Neuham/de Nevanne, Anglicus, *librarius et stationarius*. 1338–1342 [–1350?]. (CUP 2.189n, individual oath; CUP 2.532, corporate oath). Perhaps the same as *Henricus le Franc de Venna Anglicus, burgensis Parisiensis (q.v. for discussion).

Henri le petit, *librere*. 1296. Rue des Cordeles. (1296 taille, p. 232). His shop may have passed to *Guillaume, *librere, enlumineur*.

Herbertus dictus de Martray, *librarius* or *stationarius*. 1342. (CUP 2.532, corporate oath).

[Herneis le *romanceeur*. 1250s? "Devant Nostre Dame" (probably on the parvis). Probably not, at this date, a sworn *librarius* of the university. For a surviving manuscript of his, see pt. I-C above].

Jacobus Blancheti (Blanchetus?), *clericus, librarius.* 1343. (CUP 2.189n, individual oath).

Jacobus de Treciis, *librarius* or *stationarius.* 1316. (CUP 2.180, blacklist).

Jacobus de Troencio/de Troanco/de Troancio, *librarius* or *stationarius.* 1316, d. by 1323. Rue neuve Notre Dame. (CUP 2.180, blacklist; CUP 2.192, corporate oath; cf. CUP 2.273n). He is succeeded by his widow *Margareta.

Johanna, relicta defuncti *Richardi de Montebaculo, *illuminatrix, libraria jurata.* 1353. (CUP 2.658n, individual oath).

Jehan, le *librere.* 1297. In the parish of St. Eustache, "de la Porte St-Honore jusque devant les avugles." (1297 taille, p. 267).

Jehan, le *librere,* regratier. 1297. Rue de Versailles, in the parish of Ste-Geneviève "la Grant." (1297 taille, p. 224).

Johannes de Anglia, *librarius* or *stationarius.* 1316. (CUP 2.180, blacklist). Perhaps he is identical with another Johannes on this list, excluding those whose names appear on the blacklist with him, namely, Johannes de vico novo (= *Johannes Brito de Sancto Paulo), *Johannes de Garlandia, *Johannes de Sancto Leodegario.

Johannes de Belvaco, *librarius.* 1353. (CUP 2.658n, individual oath).

Jehan aus beus/bues. See Jehan de St-Pere-aus-bues.

Jehan Blondel, *librere.* 1292. Rue neuve Notre Dame. (1292 taille, p. 147).

Johannes Brito juvenis, *librarius* or *stationarius.* 1323. (CUP 2.273n, corporate oath). He, along with *Johannes Brito alias de Sancto Paulo, was named one of the four *taxatores* in 1323, which makes it unlikely that they were kinsmen.

Johannes Brito alias de Sancto Paulo, *librarius* or *stationarius.* 1316–1323. Rue neuve Notre Dame. (CUP 2.191–192, CUP 2.273n, corporate oaths). Probably not kin to *Johannes Brito juvenis (q.v. for discussion). Probably kinsman and successor of *Thomas de St-Pol. Possibly to be identified with *Johannes de vico Novo.

Jehan (Jehannot) le corrigeeur/Jehan courageus, *librere.* 1296–1300. Rue aus Porees. (1296 taille, p. 234; 1297 taille, p. 216; 1299 taille, fol. 221: 1300 taille, fol. 293). Jehan is identified as a *librere* only in the last two sources; to judge from the tax that he paid (18 sous, more than the librere *Robert de Craen next door to him), he was not a simple corrector by occupation but rather "le corrigeeur" either pointed out one aspect of his services, or acted as a quasi-cognomen. He replaces at the same address *Adam le corrigeeur, known in 1292 (taille, p. 161). Likely Adam also was a *librere*; and the tax of 58 sous reported for Adam is probably a misreading for 18 (lviii for xviii). For Adam in his role as corrector, see p. 317 above.

Johannes de Fonte, *librarius* or *stationarius.* 1342. (CUP 2.532, corporate oath).

Johannes de Garlandia/Jehan de garlande (guellande), *librarius* or *stationarius.* 1296–1316, probably d. before 1323. Rue des Parcheminiers alias rue aus

Escrivains. (1296 taille, p. 229; 1297 taille, p. 211; 1299 taille, fol. 219, as "Jehan l'englais, librere"; 1300 taille, fol. 290v; CUP 2.180, blacklist; CUP 2.192, corporate oath). Denifle and Chatelain (CUP 2.273n) note that the name of *Guillelmus de Garlandia is one of three that swear in 1316 but not in 1323; since Guillelmus is not recorded on the oath of 1316, this is probably a slip for "Johannes. . . ."

?Johannes de Guyendale, Anglicus, *serviens Universitatis*. 1323. (CUP 2.273n, corporate oath). Although Johannes de Guyendale swore the oath along with the assembled *librarii et stationarii*, he (alone) is given this special designation. He is one of the four *taxatores librorum* for 1323. It is not certain that he was a bookseller. See *Alanus Brito for discussion.

Johannes Magni, *librarius* or *stationarius*. 1342. (CUP 2.532, corporate oath). The sobriquet (in the genitive, acc. to the edition) is evidently employed to distinguish him from *Johannes Parvi Anglicus, recorded in the same document; and it is possible that neither man used these nicknames (?) in other contexts. Either of them, then, may be the same as some other Johannes on our list, saving those who are named with them in the same document of 1342: *Johannes de Fonte, *Johannes dictus le Normant, *Johannes Pointona, *Johannes dictus Prestre-Jehan, and *Johannes Vachet.

†Johannes de Meillac/de Meillar, *clericus, stationarius et librarius*. 1323. (CUP 2.189n, individual oath; CUP 2.273n, corporate oath).

Johannes dictus le Normant, *librarius* or *stationarius*. 1342. (CUP 2.532, corporate oath). Probably related to the earlier *Gaufridus dictus le Normant, and perhaps to the still earlier *Thomas Normannus.

Johannes de vico Novo, *librarius* or *stationarius*. 1316. (CUP 2.180, blacklist). This is probably either the last record of *Jehan de St-Pere-aus-bues, attested 1292–1300, or the first of *Johannes Brito alias de Sancto Paulo, attested from the end of 1316 to 1323; both lived on the Rue neuve Notre Dame.

Johannes Parvi Anglicus, *librarius* or *stationarius*. 1342. (CUP 2.532, corporate oath). The nickname (if such it is) "Parvi" distinguishes him from *Johannes Magni, and he may not have used it in other circumstances.

Johannes dictus Persenal, *scriptor et librarius juratus*. 1350. (CUP 2.658n, individual oath).

Johannes de Pointona/Poniton/Ponton, Anglicus, *clericus, librarius juratus*. [1322–] 1335–1342. (CUP 2.189n, individual oath; CUP 2.532, corporate oath). Probably kinsman and predecessor of *Guillelmus dictus de Pointona. Concerning his surviving manuscript see pt. I-C above.

Johannes Pouchet, *librarius* or *stationarius*. 1323. (CUP 2.273n, corporate oath). If the final letter in Pouchet is in fact the scribal misreading of a slashed *l* (= Pouchelle), this entry may disguise Jean Pucelle; the earliest fixed point in his career is his appearance in accounts covering the years 1319–1324, with a suggested date of late 1323 for the item that mentions Pucelle (Kathleen Morand, *Jean Pucelle* [Oxford 1962] 39 no. 1).

Johannes dictus Prestre-Jehan/Johannes Presbyter, *librarius*. 1335–1342. (CUP 2.189n, individual oath; CUP 2.532, corporate oath).

Johannes de Remis, *librarius* or *stationarius*. 1323. (CUP 2.273n, corporate oath). Concerning his surviving manuscript see pt. I-C above.

Jehan de St Pere aus bues/Jehan aus bues (beus), *librere*. 1292–1300 [–1316?]. Rue neuve Notre Dame. (1292 taille, p. 149; 1296 taille, p. 214; 1297 taille, p. 199; 1299 taille, fol. 214v: 1300 taille, fol. 288v). Possibly to be identified with *Johannes de vico Novo, known in 1316.

Johannes de Sancto Leodegario, *librarius* or *stationarius*. 1316. (CUP 2.180, blacklist). Probably kinsman and predecessor of *Gaufridus de Sancto Leodegario.

†Johannes de Semer, Anglicus, *stationarius et librarius*. 1338. (CUP 2.189n, individual oath).

Johannes Vachet, *librarius* or *stationarius*. 1342. (CUP 2.531, corporate oath).

Julienne, fame Alain le joenne (genne, jenne)/Juliane la normande, *librere*. 1296–1300. Rue neuve Notre Dame. (1296 taille, p. 214; 1297 taille, p. 199; 1298 taille, fol. 143v). Widow and successor of *Alain le jenne. By 1300 she is situated outside the Porte St-Victor, evidently living with (a kinsman?) Thomas le normant, mason (1300 taille, fol. 222).

Margareta uxor quondam Jacobi de Troancio, *libraria* or *stationaria*. 1323. (CUP 2.273n, corporate oath). Widow and successor of *Jacobus de Troancio.

†Margareta [uxor Nicolai de Zelanda], *libraria et stationaria*. 1350. (CUP 2.658n, individual oath). Margaret is not the widow, but the partner, of *Nicolaus de Zelanda; the two take the oath jointly.

Dame Marguerite de Sanz, *marcheande de livres*. 1292. Rue St-Jacques. (1292 taille, p. 160). Concerning Margaret and the other members of her family, *Andreas, *Guillelmus, and *Thomas de Sens, see above, pt. I-D.

Matheus de Attrebato, *clericus, librarius*. 1316–1323. (CUP 2.180, blacklist; CUP 2.189n, individual oath; CUP 2.273n, corporate oath).

Matheus Vavassor/Matheus le Vauvasseur, *clericus, librarius*. 1342, d. by 1352. Rue neuve Notre Dame. (CUP 2.189n, individual oath; CUP 2.532, corporate oath). His address, and the date by which he was dead, are provided by his surviving manuscript; see above pt. I-C.

Michiel de Vacqueria, *librarius* or *stationarius*. 1342. (CUP 2.532, corporate oath).

Michael de Vivariis, *librarius* or *stationarius*. 1316. (CUP 2.180, blacklist). Probably a kinsman, and perhaps the predecessor, of *Egidius de Vivariis.

Nicholas le *librere*/le *lieeur*/Nicolas l'englois, *lieeur de livres*. 1292–1299. Rue neuve Notre Dame, in the parish of St-Christofle. (1292 taille, p. 147; 1297 taille, p. 197; 1299 taille, fol. 214). This Nicolas is called *librere* only in 1299; binding must have been his principal occupation. He is to be distinguished from the contemporary *Nicolas d'Estampes (also on the rue neuve) and the slightly later *Nicolaus dictus Petit-clerc alias l'englois (rue St-Jacques).

Nicole le *librere*. 1326–1327. Rue neuve Notre Dame. Mahaut d'Artois bought books from Nicole in these years. (J.-M. Richard, *Mahaut comtesse d'Artois et de Bourgogne* [Paris 1887] p. 104).

Nicolas l'anglois/l'englois. See Nicolas le *librere*, Nicolaus dictus Petit-clerc.

Nicolaus de Branchis, *librarius* or *stationarius*. 1342. (CUP 2.531, corporate oath).

Nicolas d'Estampes, *librere*. 1292–1296. Rue neuve Notre Dame, parish of Ste-Geneviève-la-petite. (1292 taille, p. 149; 1296 taille, p. 214). Not to be identified with *Nicolas le *librere* (= le *lieeur*) situated elsewhere on the Rue neuve (parish of St-Christofle). In 1296, Nicolas is partnered with *Robert d'Estampes.

Nicolaus de Ybernia [Hibernia], *librarius* or *stationarius*. 1323. (CUP 2.273n, corporate oath). Perhaps kinsman of *Stephanus Hibernicus.

[Nicolaus Lombardus *venditor librorum*. 1250s–1260s? Probably not, at this date, a sworn *librarius* of the university. See R. Branner, "Manuscript-Makers in Mid-Thirteenth Century Paris," *The Art Bulletin* 48 (1966) 65, and C. De Hamel, *A History of Illuminated Manuscripts* (Boston 1986) 117. For a surviving manuscript of his, see pt. I-C above].

Nicolaus Martel. See Nicolaus de Zelanda.

Nicolaus dictus Petit-clerc/Nicolaus Peneler (= Peticler)/Nicolas l'anglois, *librarius* or *stationarius*. 1313–1323. Rue St-Jacques, east side. (1313 taille, p. 250; CUP 2.180, blacklist; CUP 2.192, CUP 2.273n, corporate oaths). Nicolaus was one of only three *libreres* (*Thomas de Sens and *Thomas de Mante were the others) who appear on the tax rolls in 1313, where he is listed (Nicolas l'anglois) as *librere et tavernier*; he was taxed either because he had not taken the university oath (like Thomas de Sens) or because he had a second source of income (the case, probably, of Thomas de Mante, q.v.). In Dec. 1316 Nicolaus is named as one of the four *taxatores* for the year.

Nicolaus de Scotia, *librarius* or *stationarius*. 1323. (CUP 2.273n, corporate oath). Possibly kinsman and predecessor of *Robertus Scoti.

Nicolaus Tirel, *clericus, librarius*. 1335–1342. (CUP 2.189n, individual oath; CUP 2.532, corporate oath).

†Nicolaus de Zelanda alias Martel, *librarius et stationarius*. 1350. Rue St-Jacques. (CUP 2.658n, individual oath). Partnered with his wife *Margareta.

Oudin de biauvez, *librere*. 1296. Rue St-Etienne-des-Grés. (1296 taille, p. 237).

Oudin le breton, *librere*. 1298. Rue Erembourc de Brie. (1298 taille, fol. 145v).

†Petronilla, uxor [*Petri de Perona, *stationaria et libraria*]. 1323. (CUP 2.189n, individual oath; CUP 2.273n, corporate oath). She takes both oaths with her husband.

Petrus Boneffant/dictus Bonenfant/Bonuspuer, *librarius* or *stationarius*. [1309-] 1323. Rue de Bièvre. (CUP 2.180, blacklist; CUP 2.192, CUP 2.273n, corporate oaths). Concerning a manuscript written by him, see pt. I-C above.

†Petrus de Perona, *clericus, stationarius et librarius*. 1323. (CUP 2.189n, individual oath; CUP 2.273n, corporate oath). His wife, *Petronilla, takes both oaths with him.

Poncet/Ponce/Poince le *librere*. 1292–1300. Rue neuve Notre Dame. (1292 taille, p. 147; 1297 taille, p. 196; 1299 taille, fol. 214v; 1300 taille, fol. 288).

Poncius Gilbosus de Noblans, *clericus et librarius*. 1323. (CUP 2.189n, individual oath; CUP 2.273n, corporate oath).

Raoul le *librere*. 1296–1300. Rue St-Jacques, east side. (1296 taille, p. 236; 1300 taille, fol. 293).

Radulfus Abbatis, *librarius* or *stationarius*. 1316 (CUP 2.180, blacklist).

Mestre Raoul le Breton/Raoul le vieil Breton, *librere*. 1292–1300. Rue neuve Notre Dame. (1292 taille, p. 149; 1296 taille, p. 214; 1297 taille, p. 199; 1299 taille, fol. 214v; 1300 taille, fol. 288v). Possibly kinsman to *Raoul le genne Breton, whose shop was on the opposite side of the rue neuve; the distinction Raoul le vieil and Raoul le genne would suggest father and son. It is not typical, however, for family members to set up in competition with one another—and to pay tax on two establishments, instead of one.

Raoul le genne Breton, *librere*. 1296–1299. Rue neuve Notre Dame. (1296 taille, p. 214; 1297 taille, p. 198; 1299 taille, fol. 214v). See *Raoul le vieil Breton.

Radulfus de Varedis, *librarius* or *stationarius*. 1323. (CUP 2.273n, corporate oath).

Richardus dictus Challamannio, *librarius* or *stationarius*. 1323. (CUP 2.273n, corporate oath).

Richardus de Monbaston [*sic*]/dictus de Montbaston/de Monte baculo, *clericus, librarius et illuminator*. 1338–1348, d. by 1353. Rue neuve Notre Dame. (CUP 2.189n, two individual oaths; CUP 2.532, corporate oath). For unknown reasons, Montbaston swore two individual oaths in 1338. He is referred to as "defunctus" in the 1353 oath of his widow *Johanna. Concerning Montbaston's manuscripts, including one dated 1348, see pt. I-C above.

Mestre Robert a l'ange, *parcheminier, librere*. 1292–1300. Rue des Escrivains alias des Parcheminiers. (1292 taille, p. 157; 1296 taille, p. 229; 1297 taille, p. 211; 1300 taille, fol. 291v). Robert's occupation is listed as parchmenter in 1296, as *librere* in 1300.

Robert de Craen/Robert de Craonne/Robert l'englais, *librere*. 1292–1300. Rue aus Porees. (1292 taille, p. 161; 1296 taille p. 234; 1297 taille, p. 216; 1299 taille, fol. 221; 1300 taille, fol. 293). In 1300, he has become "Sire Robert le librere."

Robert d'Estampes, *librere*. 1296–1297. Rue neuve Notre Dame. (1296 taille, p. 214; 1297 taille, p. 199). He is partnered with *Nicolas d'Estampes (a kinsman?) in 1296; his name alone is attached to the shop in 1297.

Robert de l'Ille-Adam/de lyle Adam/de lile Adam, *librere*. 1292–1300. Rue neuve Notre Dame. (1292 taille, p. 149; 1299 taille, fol. 214v; 1300 taille, fol. 288v).

Robertus Scoti, *librarius* or *stationarius*. 1342. (CUP 2.532, corporate oath). Possibly kinsman and successor of *Nicolaus de Scottia.

Robertus de Wigornia, *librarius* or *stationarius*. 1316 (CUP 2.180, blacklist).

Rogerinus Marcote, *librarius*. 1351. (CUP 2.658n, individual oath).

Stephanus Hibernicus, *librarius* or *stationarius*. 1316. (CUP 2.180, blacklist). He is perhaps to be identified with Estienne le roy (= l'Irois?), lieeur de livres, on the Rue Erembourc de Brie in 1297 (taille, p. 402). Stephanus may be a kinsman of the later *Nicolaus de Ybernia.

Stephanus Savage/dictus Sauvage, *librarius* or *stationarius*. 1316–1323. Rue Erembourc de Brie. (CUP 2.180, blacklist; CUP 2.192, CUP 2.273n, corporate oaths).

Symon dictus l'Escolier, *librarius*. 1342. (CUP 2.189n, individual oath; CUP 2.532, corporate oath).

Thomas Anglicus, *librarius* or *stationarius*. 1342. (CUP 2.532, corporate oath). Possibly to be identified with *Thomas de Wymondswold, Anglicus.

Thomas de Malbodio/Thomas de Maubeuge, *librarius*. 1316–1323. Rue neuve Notre Dame. (CUP 2.180, blacklist; CUP 2.189n, individual oath; CUP 2.191, CUP 2.273n, corporate oaths). Concerning his manuscripts, see pt. I-C above.

Thomas de Mante/de Maante, *librere*. 1292–1313. In the section of the parish of St-Sevrin near the Petit-Pont, street not specified. (1292 taille, p. 153; 1296 taille, p. 221; 1297 taille, p. 204; 1313 taille, p. 219). Thomas is one of only three *libreres* taxed in 1313 (along with *Nicolaus dictus Petit-clerc and *Thomas de Sens), in his case probably because his wife had an income as a "lingiere" (1296) or "ferpiere" (1313).

†Thomas le Normant/Thomas Normannus, *stationarius et librarius*. 1297–1323. Rue neuve Notre Dame. (1297 taille, p. 199; 1298 taille, fol. 214v; 1300 taille, fol. 288v; CUP 2.180, blacklist; CUP 2.189n, individual oath; CUP 2.191, CUP 2.273n, corporate oaths). Thomas takes his oath as a stationer only in 1316. He is perhaps kinsman and predecessor of the later *Gaufridus dictus le Normant and the still later *Johannes dictus le Normant.

Thomas de Saint-Pol, *librere*. 1296–1300. Rue neuve Notre Dame. (1296 taille,
    p. 214; 1297 taille, p. 198; 1300 taille, fol. 288v). Probably kinsman and
    predecessor of *Johannes Brito alias de Sancto Paulo.

†Thomas de Senonis/dictus de Zenonis/Thomas de Senz, *stationarius et
    librarius*. 1313–1342. Rue St-Jacques. (1313 taille, p. 234; CUP 2.171, indi-
    vidual oath; CUP 2.179, mention; CUP 2.180, blacklist; CUP 2.192, CUP
    2.273n, CUP 2.531, corporate oaths). Concerning Thomas and other mem-
    bers of his family *Andreas, *Guillelmus, and *Marguerite de Sens, see
    above, pt. I-D.

Thomas de Wymonduswold, Anglicus, *librarius* or *stationarius*. [1314–] 1323
    [–1342?]. (CUP 2.273n, corporate oath). Possibly to be identified with the
    *Thomas Anglicus who took oath in 1342. Concerning Wymonduswold's
    manuscripts, see pt. I-C above.

Yvo dictus Brito/Yvo dictus le Breton, *clericus, librarius*. 1342. (CUP 2.189n,
    individual oath; CUP 2.532, corporate oath).

Yvo Greal/Yvo dictus Greal, *librarius* or *stationarius*. 1342. (CUP 2.532). Yvo
    was one of the four *taxatores* for the year.

Medieval Libraries

9. The Early Library of the Sorbonne*

It is generally recognized that the Sorbonne library contained one of the largest collections of books brought together in a medieval institution, and that it was an influential collection as well.[1] The Sorbonne by the end of the thirteenth century was a major center of theological study at the University of Paris and its library was used not only by its own fellows, but also by the other masters of the Faculty of Theology. The influence of the collection extended beyond Paris to the Italian humanists; for it was at the Sorbonne that Petrarch and through him Salutati acquired their texts of Propertius, Plato's *Phaedo*, and perhaps Tibullus.[2] The catalogs compiled in the late thirteenth and early fourteenth centuries testify to the richness and variety of the Sorbonne's manuscripts. They testify also to the inventiveness of the individuals who compiled them, as regards both the detail of information supplied and the catalogers' ability to describe the contents of composite manuscripts.

---

*Originally published in *Scriptorium* 21 (1967) 42–71, 227–251 and plates.

I am grateful to Professor André Vernet of the Ecole Nationale des Chartes who read this article in typescript and made a number of valuable suggestions.

Addendum: For a shorter survey of the Sorbonne Library over a longer period of time, see R. H. Rouse and M. A. Rouse, "La bibliothèque du collège de Sorbonne," in *Histoire des bibliothèques françaises: Les bibliothèques médiévales du VIᵉ siècle à 1530*, ed. A. Vernet (Paris 1989) 112–123.

[1] For the sake of comparison in regard to the relative size of the collection: The Sorbonne had 1,017 and 1,722 codices in 1290 and 1338 respectively. The papal library had from 483 to 645 volumes at the time of Boniface VIII and would grow to 2,059 volumes by 1369. Christ Church, Canterbury, contained 1,850 volumes in 1331. The largest monastic collections of this period contained between four and five hundred volumes. See J. de Ghellinck, "Les Bibliothèques Médiévales," *Nouvelle Revue Théologique* 65 (1938) 45–46, 50, 52.

[2] Berthold Ullman, "The Library of the Sorbonne in the Fourteenth Century," *The Septicentennial Celebration of the Founding of the Sorbonne College in the University of Paris* (Chapel Hill 1953) 33–47; reprinted as "The Sorbonne Library and the Italian Renaissance," in his *Studies in the Italian Renaissance* (Rome 1955) 41–53.

Library catalogs such as these have long been used as sources for literary and intellectual history. In instances when their purpose and method of construction are understood and when they are as precisely dated as possible, the catalogs of an institution can render service in understanding the growth and development of that institution, and in dating the people whose names are associated with the institution's books. This is particularly true of the Sorbonne, because it produced such an array of complex catalogs during the first eighty years of its existence.

Four medieval catalogs of the Sorbonne library survive: a small fragment of a very early catalog of the collection; a shelf list and an analytical catalog of the chained codices in the *magna libraria*; and a catalog of the unchained codices in the *parva libraria*, completed in 1338. Mention is made of two other general catalogs, in 1290 and 1321.[3] These catalogs, along with over 1,500 surviving manuscripts and a number of college provisions relating to the library, are the sources from which the library has been studied.

The pioneer study of the Sorbonne and its library was written by Alfred Franklin in 1867.[4] Interesting for its time, his work is nevertheless a well-spring of misinformation. Franklin believed that the library, from its inception, consisted of two repositories of books, one containing chained codices, the other unchained codices. He attributed the 1338 catalog to 1289, and the fourteenth-century catalogs of the chained codices to 1290. Being unaware of the chronology of the Sorbonne statutes, he attributed the descriptions of the new library begun in 1481 to the library of 1290. Unfortunately, Franklin is still used as an authority on the

---

[3] Also to be noted is the list of forty-four manuscripts in the *magna libraria*, principally Aristoteliana and philosophy, made in the mid-fourteenth century by Master Adalbertus Ranconis de Ericinio, rector of the university, which survives in Prague, Metrop. Kap. MS. N. VIII (1532) f. 42ᵛ–43. The list begins, "Libri librarie de Sorbonna Parisius registrati per Albertum de Bohemia, magistrum in artibus, socium predicte domus de Sorbona," and is discussed and edited by Paul Lehmann, "Mitteilungen aus Handschriften VII," *Sitzungsberichte der Bayerischen Akademie der Wissenschaften, Phil.-Hist. Abteilung* 10 (Munich 1942) 3–28. Concerning Adalbert's library see Ivan Hlavácek, "Studie K. Dejinám Knihoven v Českém Státě v Době Predhusitshé" ("Studien zur Geschichte der Bibliotheken im Boemischen Staat in Vorhussitscherzeit"), *Acta Universitatis Carolinae. Historia Universitatis Carolinae Pragensis* 6 (1965) 47–87; summary in German. Hlavácek edits a list of books which Adalbert purchased in Avignon and sent to Prague. I am grateful to Professor Vernet for these references.

[4] Alfred Franklin, *Les Anciennes Bibliothèques de Paris* I (Paris 1867) 221–317; 2nd ed., *La Sorbonne, ses Origines, sa Bibliothèque* (Paris 1875). Mention should also be made of the materials collected by the seventeenth-century historian and librarian of the college (1638–46) Claude Héméré, and the chapter devoted to the library in his *Sorbonae origines, disciplina, viri illustres*, B.N. MS. lat. 5493 f. 96–107.

library,[5] in spite of the existence of the vastly superior study of the library published by Leopold Delisle in 1874.[6] Delisle asserts, "En 1289, la bibliothèque de la Sorbonne fût organisée sur des bases qu'on n'eût pas besoin de changer avant l'invention de l'imprimerie."[7] At the time of its organization, he adds, the library was divided into two collections, the *magna libraria* in which were chained the most frequently used books and the *parva libraria* which contained the duplicates, works seldom used and in general the books which circulated among the masters.[8] He discovered the fragment of the oldest catalog of the library, and indicated that the catalogs made in 1290 and 1321 do not survive. He attributed the shelf list and the analytical catalog of the chained library to the beginning of the fourteenth century, and the catalog of the *parva libraria* to 1338. As an appendix to the study, Delisle edited the catalogs of the *magna libraria* and the *parva libraria* from B.N. MS. Nouv. acq. lat. 99, p. 1–353.[9] Delisle's work provided the basis for a brief but critical description of the library and its catalogs by Alexander Birkenmajer published in 1922, in connection with his study on the manuscripts of Richard de Fournival at the Sorbonne.[10] Birkenmajer suggested that the fragment of

[5] To pick one example, Edgar Lehmann follows Franklin in applying Héméré's description of the 1481 library to the medieval library of 1289; *Die Bibliotheksräume der deutschen Klöster im Mittelalter* (Deutsche Akademie der Wissenschaften zu Berlin, Schriften zur Kunstgeschichte, 2) (Berlin 1957) 8, 41.

[6] Léopold Delisle, *Le Cabinet des Manuscrits de la Bibliothèque Nationale* II (Paris 1874), 142–208.

[7] Ibid., 181.

[8] H. J. de Vleeschauwer has emphasized that the chained collection was a reference library containing those books heavily used by masters and students for "course work" — that it was, namely, a teaching library — and that the unchained collection contained not only the duplicates but also the more specialized materials needed for research; *Libraria Magna et Libraria Parva dans la Bibliothèque Universitaire du XIIIe Siècle* (*Mousaion*, 7) (Pretoria 1956).

[9] Formerly Paris, Arsenal MS. 855; Delisle, III (1881) 9–114. Theodor Gottlieb used both Franklin and Delisle in compiling his notice on the catalogs of the Sorbonne: no. 347, undated fragment from B.N. MS. lat. 6412 (i.e., 16412); no. 348, catalog of 1290, for which he supplies the note from the end of the 1338 catalog and the first and last rubrics of the analytical catalog; no. 349, the catalog of 1338; no. 350, the shelf list of the *magna libraria*; no. 351, the analytical catalog. *Über Mittelalterliche Bibliotheken* (Leipzig 1890) 126–127.

[10] This article and an earlier treatment of this topic by Birkenmajer are difficult to obtain: A. Birkenmajer, "Studja nad Witelonem," part 1, *Archiwum Komisji do Badania Historji Filozofji w Polsce* 2 (1921) 5–9; idem, *Bibljoteka Ryszarda de Fournival* (Polska Akademja Umiejętności, Wydział Filologiczny, Rozprawy 60, 4) (Krakow 1922) especially pp. 16–18. I am grateful to Miss Sophie Kwiatkowski who translated the latter article for me. A brief French summary of the article appears in the *Bulletin International de l'Académie Polonaise des Sciences et des Lettres, Classe de Philologie* . . . (Krakow 1922) 4–8.

the earliest catalog dates from shortly after 1271; and he postulated that
between the date of this first catalog and the lost catalog of 1290 another
general catalog was made. At the time when this second and hypothetical catalog was written, the Sorbonne's books were numbered and were
classified by subject. Following Delisle, he dated the formation of the
magna libraria in 1289, and the two catalogs of it in the early fourteenth
century. However, Birkenmajer suggested that the analytical catalog was
made sometime after 1328. One of the most valuable parts of his study is
an extensive comparison of the contents of the shelf list of the *magna
libraria* with those of the analytical catalog. The most recent examination of the library and the most detailed since Delisle's is that published
in 1966 by Mgr. Glorieux as part of his study on the origins of the college.[11] Glorieux sees, with Delisle, the establishment of a fullgrown dual
collection in the years 1289–90. He identifies the fragment of the earliest
catalog with the catalog made in 1290, and he prints portions of thirteen
entries from it. The shelf list of the chained collection he dates ca. 1310.
He states that in 1321 a new catalog of the whole collection was made,
which no longer survives but which can still be discerned in the text of
the catalog made in 1338. Finally, Glorieux suggests that the analytical
catalog of the chained library is contemporary with the 1338 catalog of
the unchained collection. Glorieux uses his dating of the catalogs as an
aid in dating a large number of the early fourteenth-century donors to
the college.

These studies, taken as a whole, have provided a considerable fund
of knowledge concerning many aspects of the Sorbonne library. At the
same time, however, they have by no means told the whole story nor
answered all the questions. They present seriously conflicting opinions
on the dates of the Sorbonne's catalogs. To one degree or another, they
date the beginning of the library as a functioning entity with the creation
of the *magna libraria* in 1289, thirty-two years after the opening of the
college. For the most part they depict the library as a static institution,
born full grown, with little indication that the library might have been
reshaped by the masters to meet their needs as it grew. They have generally dealt with the library in isolation from other libraries of the same
period, without attempting to place it in a perspective. There is thus
room and need for further investigation of the subject.

A reexamination of the combined evidence of the Sorbonne's records
and of the extant catalogs themselves permits us, first of all, to fix more

---

[11] Palémon Glorieux, *Aux Origines de la Sorbonne, I. Robert de Sorbon* (Études de
Philosophie Médiévale, 53) (Paris 1966) cited hereafter as Glorieux I. See particularly 82–83,
239–289, 294.

precisely the date of the fragment of the earliest catalog; to identify the
text of the lost 1290 catalog in the text of the 1338 catalog; and to redate
the shelf list and the analytical catalog of the chained library. These precisions in turn will permit us to provide a terminal date of 1290 for some
thirty-five donors of books and to see the relative order of the some
forty-five bequests left to the college between 1290 and 1338; and to single out the periods 1289–92 and 1321–38 as the focal points of change in
the development of the library. The present article will not attempt to
write a new general history of the library, nor to describe in any detail
how it functioned; for Delisle's study, despite its age, remains more than
adequate in these areas. Instead this article will attempt to supplement
the picture Delisle presented by focusing principally on the development
of the library in its first eighty years, on the basis of the information
provided by its catalogs. It will serve in addition to introduce the fragment of the oldest known catalog of the Sorbonne manuscripts, which is
edited below.

*   *   *

When the Sorbonne was founded in 1257 its common store of
manuscripts, if it had any, could scarcely have merited being called a
book collection.[12] By 1290, when we have the first relatively complete
picture, the Sorbonne possessed one of the most significant libraries in
Europe and possibly the best in Paris. Such a rise in thirty-three years is
exceptional in any age, particularly in one usually noted for its conser-
vatism. This rapid growth is part and parcel of the growth of the college,
brought about largely by Robert of Sorbon's successful efforts during
thirteen years to enlist support for his new institution and to lay the
organizational basis for its administration. The early growth of the library
stemmed almost entirely from donations large and small. Some of these,
most notably that of Robert of Douai, physician to Queen Marguerite,
no doubt resulted from Robert's position at court among the wealthy
and influential. Other bequests, though doubtless few in the early years,
came from the fellows of the college itself. While these remained relatively small in number, they were consistent and significant, and reflect a
sense of responsibility for the college instilled by its founder. The majority of early bequests, however, came from the masters in the Faculty of

---

[12] Concerning the early history of the Sorbonne, see P. Glorieux, op. cit.; idem, in *Dictionnaire de Théologie Catholique* 14 (Paris 1941) cols. 2383–2394; A. L. Gabriel, "The
Spiritual Portrayal of Robert de Sorbonne," in *The Septicentennial Celebration . . .*, 13–32;
P. Glorieux, *Les Origines du Collège de Sorbonne* (Texts and Studies in the History of Mediaeval Education, VIII) (Notre Dame 1959); idem, *Aux Origines de la Sorbonne, II. Le Cartulaire* (Études de Philosophie Médiévale, 54) (Paris, 1965); cited hereafter as Glorieux, II.

Theology. For them the new college, which was the first collegiate institution formed for students of theology, filled a void and served as a catalyst if not a home. One need only remember that one of the most influential among them, Gerard of Abbeville, was from the beginning a close associate of Robert's, and he also left the most significant bequest of books to the college. The masters of theology left their worldly goods to the college for the benefit and use of the poor secular clerks such as they had once been. Often their wills contained books; and from these gifts the book collection of the Sorbonne became the equal of that of Notre Dame, St. Jacques, St. Germain-des-Prés, St. Victor or Ste. Geneviève, by the time of Robert's death.

It is not known whether the college was founded with any initial store of books, as a new monastery might have received from its mother institution. The slow but steady stream of bequests, however, started very soon after the college began to function.[13] In May of 1258 the physician Robert of Douai drew up his will which, in addition to the sizeable sum of 1500 pounds Parisian, bequeathed to the Sorbonne "omnes libros meos de theologia, tam biblias, tam originalia, quam alios libros glosatos," books which came to the Sorbonne some four years later; Robert of Sorbon was the first named among the executors of his will.[14] Already in 1260, Gerard of Abbeville, acting as executor for the estate of another Master Robert of Douai, clerk of the Prince of Achaea, gave to the Sorbonne some of his own books to the value of seventy pounds Parisian, which represented evidently a sum owed by him to the estate of Robert of Douai.[15] Master John of Gondricourt, canon of St. John's in Liège, left a Bible to the college in 1262, and in 1264 Master Nicholas of Vrigny, canon and penitentiary of Coutances, left thirteen books and 100 sous Tournois. Two years later four books and 500 pounds Parisian were given by Nicholas, archdeacon of Tournai, to provide for and be used by Flemish students at the college. In 1270, Lambert, dean of Soignies, left to the college a glossed copy of the Pauline epistles and the gospels of Luke and John, in addition to other goods; Robert of Sorbon again was the executor of the will. Robert was also one of the executors for the will of Miles of Corbeil, who left the college a missal and 100 pounds Parisian in 1271.[16]

---

[13] Delisle, II, 143–178, identified 168 early donors to the library through his examination of the surviving manuscripts and the 1338 catalog.

[14] *Chartularium Universitatis Parisiensis*, ed. H. Denifle and E. Chatelain 1 (Paris 1889) 372–375; Glorieux, II, 181–184.

[15] *Chartularium*, I, 411; Glorieux, II, 217.

[16] Delisle, loc cit.; Glorieux, II, 324–325.

With the probable exception of that of the physician Robert of Douai, these bequests—and doubtless dozens of other gifts and bequests of books which have left no record—were unexceptional in quantity and quality. Nevertheless, they form the beginning of what will later be called the *parva libraria*, and before the founder's death rudimentary rules existed regulating the use of these books. The first statutes of the house, which are dated ca. 1268–1270 and are probably the work of Robert himself, stipulate that "no one be accepted into the house unless he swears that, if he receives books from the community, he will treat them as carefully as if they were his own; that under no circumstances will he take them, or permit them to be taken, outside the house; and that he will return them whole, whensoever they are demanded of him, and when he must leave the city."[17] That we see no evidence of any more formal organization of the Sorbonne book collection at this date should not be surprising. Those books not in use were probably kept in *archae* or chests; the crux of the matter is that during these early years there can hardly have been many books which were not in use. The books were apportioned out among the masters of the Sorbonne for their own personal use, to be accounted for perhaps on an annual basis, and to be deposited in the common store or chests whenever the scholar left the city. The terms of the bequests occasionally reveal unmistakably that the donors intended the books to be kept for the most part in the hands of individual scholars—for example, the bequest of Archdeacon Nicholas mentioned above; or that of the physician Robert of Douai, who says that he leaves his books to the scholars "et assignabuntur eis coram magistris theologie. . . ." Indeed, in the middle of the thirteenth century it would be normal for the books of an institution, whether cloistered or secular, to be loaned out to the members of the institution rather than being kept together. This informal and very practical procedure was undoubtedly viable at the Sorbonne during the lean years when the number of books was small; the increasing number of books acquired by the Sorbonne during the 1260s made the arrangement more cumbersome, but the growth was so gradual as to allow the system to absorb the increase.

A transformation in the nature of the Sorbonne's collection—the point at which quantitative change became a qualitative one as well—

---

[17] "Item nullus recipiatur in domo, nisi fidem prestet, quod si contigerit ipsum libros de communi recipere, quod sicut suos ita illos fideliter observabit, et nullo modo distrahet nec accommodabit extra domum, et per integrum reddet eos quandocumque exigentur ab eo et quando contigerit eum villam exire." *Chartularium*, I, 507; Glorieux, I, 194.

came with the bequest of Gerard of Abbeville.[18] Approximately three hundred manuscripts passed to the Sorbonne when he died in 1272.[19]

Gerard of Abbeville was a master of theology at Paris, well endowed with ecclesiastical benefices and active in university politics. Probably a canon of Amiens by 1260, during this same decade he held the lucrative posts of archdeacon of Ponthieu in the diocese of Amiens and archdeacon of Cambrai. He was a regent master in theology at Paris from 1257 until his death, and in 1262 he was also protector of the privileges of the university. Gerard is best known for his polemical writings against the Mendicants during the struggle between secular masters and friars for control of the Theology Faculty.[20] Gerard was no doubt moved to make his magnificent bequest to the Sorbonne because of his friendship with its founder, Robert of Sorbon; but as a leader of the anti-Mendicant group in the university, Gerard was probably motivated as well by his desire to support the young college which was providing the secular challenge of the friar's preeminence in the teaching of theology.

The Abbeville bequest of some 300 books made a dramatic change in the Sorbonne library, just in terms of the sheer number of codices. We know that eighteen years later, in 1290, the collection contained 1,017 books.[21] It seems a reasonable conjecture that, at the time it was received, Gerard's bequest doubled the size of the library at one blow.

The gift was unique not only because of its size, but also because of the quality of the manuscripts it contained. In 1919 Birkenmajer discovered that a large portion of Abbeville's manuscripts came en bloc from the library of Richard de Fournival, poet, physician and chancellor of the cathedral at Amiens.[22] Fournival (1201–ca. 1260) had amassed in

---

[18] Concerning Gerard of Abbeville, see P. Glorieux, *Répertoire des Maîtres en Théologie de Paris au XIIIᵉ Siècle*, I (Études de Philosophie Médiévale 17) (Paris 1933) 356–360; and Ph. Grand, "Le Quodlibet XIV de Gérard d'Abbeville," *Archives d'histoire doctrinale et littéraire du moyen âge* 31 (1964) 207–269. It might be noted that when Grand refers to the "1290 catalog" on pp. 207, 212, he is in actuality citing the 1338 catalog.

[19] Gerard's obituary notes, "Obiit magister Geraudus de Abbatisvilla qui nobis legavit quasi iiiᵉ volumina librorum tam in theologia quam in philosophia, et omnia ornamenta que pertinent ad capellam;" Glorieux, I, 176.

[20] See L. Bongianino, "Le Questioni Quodlibetali di Gerardo di Abbeville contro i Mendicanti," *Collectanea Franciscana* 32 (1962) 5– 55. The best recent survey of the struggle in its broader aspects is Peter R. McKeon, "The Status of the University of Paris as *Parens Scientiarum* . . .," *Speculum* 39 (1964) 651–675.

[21] Delisle, III, 71.

[22] The life and varied works of Fournival have not as yet been dealt with as a whole, but see P. Paris, *Histoire Littéraire de la France* 23 (1856) 708–733; S. Vitte, "Richard de Fournival. Étude sur sa vie et ses œuvres, suivie de l'Édition du *Bestiaire d'Amour*, de la *Réponse de la Dame* et des *Chansons*," summarized in *École Nationale des Chartes, Positions des Thèses* (Paris 1929) 223–227; Cesare Segre, ed., *Li 'Bestiaires d'Amours' di Maistre*

his lifetime what must rank as one of the most elaborate private book collections of the Middle Ages.[23] It contained perhaps 300 volumes, whose contents ranged through the trivium and quadrivium, metaphysics, philosophy, poetry, medicine, civil and canon law, the scriptures and scriptural commentary and the writings of the fathers and doctors of the Church. Among these are a number of texts which range from rare to virtually unknown in the thirteenth century such as the *Elegiae* of Tibullus and Propertius, Plato's *Phaedo*, Cicero's philosophical works in the order of the Leiden corpus, his *Epistolae familiares*, a collection of gromatic materials known as the *Agrimensores*, and a collection of aphorisms by Publilius Syrus under the name of Censorinus. The late Berthold Ullman has suggested that Richard acquired at least some of his texts from the ancient abbey of Corbie which lay just fifteen kilometers from Amiens.[24]

Richart de Fournival e li 'Response du Bestiaire' (Milan 1957); idem, "Richard de Fournival," in *Dictionnaire des Lettres Françaises, Le Moyen Age* (Paris 1964) 635.

[23] Concerning the library and its passage through Abbeville to the Sorbonne, see Birkenmajer, op. cit. Delisle had noticed that item no. 66 in the *Biblionomia* corresponded to B.N. MS. lat. 16613 (Sorbonne, s. xiii), but he did not see the relationship between the two collections; Delisle, III, 387. The late Berthold Ullman had also noticed the similarity of Abbeville's and Fournival's books and had planned a formal analysis of the two collections; see his "The Library of the Sorbonne. . . ." The whole subject was recently reviewed by P. Glorieux, "Études sur la 'Biblionomia' de Richard de Fournival," *Recherches de théologie ancienne et médiévale* 30 (1963) 205–231; besides the comments of H. Sylvester in *Revue d'histoire ecclésiastique* 60 (1965) 231–232, the following corrections could be made: B.N. MSS. lat. 16142, 16249 and 16676 could not have belonged to Fournival, because the first was given to the Sorbonne by Henry Pistor, not Gerard of Abbeville, and the second dates from the fifteenth century and, along with the third, came to the Sorbonne with Cardinal Richelieu's bequest; B.N. MSS. lat. 16603, and 16581 are known to be part of the Abbeville bequest; for 11648, read 16648 part I; the identification of B.N. MS. lat. 15459 is doubtful since it bears no indication of having been given by Gerard, since it contains a not uncommon work, Avicenna's *Canones* III and IV, and since Gerard directed in his will that his medical books be sold. It is peculiar that the transmission of the Fournival books to the Sorbonne has been studied almost entirely on the basis of comparisons between the *Biblionomia* and the medieval catalogs of the Sorbonne. The actual Sorbonne manuscripts involved have seldom been touched in regard to this problem.

[24] On the origins of Fournival's library, see B. L. Ullman, "The Manuscripts of Propertius," *Classical Philology* 6 (1911) 282–310; idem, "The Library of the Sorbonne . . .;" idem, "A List of Classical Manuscripts . . . perhaps from Corbie," *Scriptorium* 8 (1954) 24–37; idem, "Petrarch's Acquaintance with Catullus, Tibullus, Propertius," in his *Studies . . .*"; idem, "Geometry in the Mediaeval Quadrivium," *Studi di Bibliografia e di Storia in Onore di Tammaro de Marinis* 4 (1964) 263–285. Ullman's attribution of the catalog in Berlin, Staatsbibliothek MS. Diez. B. Sant. 66 p. 218–219 to Corbie has been refuted by Bischoff in favor of the court library of Charlemagne; Bernhard Bischoff, "Hadoardus and the Manuscripts of Classical Authors from Corbie," in *Didascaliae. Studies in Honor of Anselm M. Albareda*, ed. Sesto Prete (New York 1961) 39–57; idem, "Die Hofbibliothek Karls des Grossen," in *Karl der Grosse: Lebenswerk und Nachleben, II. Das*

It is impossible to say just how or when Fournival's books passed into Abbeville's hands; however, it is interesting to note that Gerard was a significant figure and close associate of Robert of Sorbon in the years bordering on Fournival's death and that he had given books to the college in 1260. One might wonder if he did not acquire the Fournival books with the ultimate purpose in mind of giving them to the college. It is also unfortunately impossible to determine the extent to which Abbeville's bequest to the Sorbonne represents Fournival's library. For our knowledge of the latter comes only from the *Biblionomia*, Fournival's catalog of his collection; in it Fournival gives only cursory descriptions, or none at all, of the legal and theological books which constituted nearly half of his library.[25] It appears very probable, however, that with the exception of certain obvious items, the majority of Gerard's manuscripts came from Richard de Fournival's collection. The obvious exceptions are the manuscripts which date after 1260, and the specific university books such as those which Gerard mentions in his will as "all the summas of *questiones* and all the writings which I have compiled."[26]

Over 130 manuscripts survive from the Abbeville bequest.[27] While it is difficult to describe this collection as a whole, the manuscripts of the

---

Geistige Leben, ed. B. Bischoff (Dusseldorf 1965) 42–62. *Addendum:* See now R. H. Rouse, "Manuscripts belonging to Richard de Fournival," *Revue d'histoire des textes* 3 (1973) 256–269.

[25] The *Biblionomia* survives in a fifteenth-century manuscript, Paris, Bibliothèque de l'Université, MS. 636, which is printed by Delisle, II, 520–535. A few years ago A. Vernet discovered part of a single leaf containing the opening lines of the *Biblionomia* (now B.N. MSS. Don. no. 18845). The leaf was among Henri Omont's papers relating to his edition of the *Biblionomia*, but was evidently found by him after the edition appeared in 1884. The leaf is written in a northern French hand of the second half of the thirteenth century. It represents an unfinished, rather than a fragmentary, text. The brief portion of the text which it preserves is superior to its counterpart in Université MS. 636. The *Biblionomia* is generally thought to be a plan of, or guide to, Richard's library in Amiens. While it is a catalog of his books, I would doubt that his books were arranged in this fashion; more likely, they were kept in cupboards or chests, as was commonly done in libraries of this date.

[26] "Item omnes summas quaestionum et omnia scripta quae compilavi tam de quaestionibus quam de sermonibus. . . ." The will is printed by Grand 214–218; Glorieux, II, 354–358; *Chartularium,* I, 491–492. The main portion pertaining to his books is also printed by Delisle, II, 149.

[27] 119 of these were identified by Delisle among the Latin manuscripts in the Bibliothèque Nationale and are listed by him (miscounted as 118), II, 148. To these the following can be added with the help of the I.R.H.T.: Bern, Bürgerbibliothek MS. 332; Firenze, Biblioteca Medicea Laurenziana MS. Plut. 29. 19; Paris, Bibliothèque Nationale MSS. lat. 15289, 15662, 15983, 16362, 16371 ff. 288–434v, probably 16405, 16598; Città del Vaticano, MSS. Reg. lat. 72 I, 454 and 1572; the manuscripts now in Bern and in the Vatican are discussed in K. A. de Meyier, *Paul en Alexandre Petau en de Geschiedenis van hun Handschriften* (Dissertationes Inaugurales Batavae, V) (Leiden 1947) 117–120.

patristic, carolingian, school and early scholastic authors, the corpus with which I am most familiar, do reflect a certain uniformity. The majority of these date from the first half of the thirteenth century and are large volumes, with wide margins and with blank leaves between the texts. They are carefully rubricated, and bear contemporary tables of contents and running headlines in the hand of the scribe. They are uniformly and clearly written, with few corrections and little decoration. Their uniformity would suggest them to be the work of a limited number of scribes. The manuscripts of the authorities are good examples of the effort in the thirteenth century to compile collections of *originalia patrum* or whole works of the fathers, in contrast to the collections of sentences and extracts, or the codices containing only one or two works, which were more typical products of the twelfth century. All told, they suggest that considerable care was exercised in their collection and compilation. They must have constituted an impressive addition to the library.[28]

Gerard's will provided instructions for the use and care of his collection. The procurator of the Sorbonne was to be responsible for the books, and the masters were admonished to be diligent and cautious in caring for them. Each year the procurator was to take an inventory of the collection and give an account of it in the presence of the masters. Gerard directed that the books be made available even to scholars who were not members of the Sorbonne, namely to regent masters of arts, and to all secular scholars and secular masters of theology. True to his anti-Mendicant sentiments, Gerard, after emphasizing that he was leaving his books to secular theologians, went on to restrict the making of copies from his books to seculars only, "because the Religious have enough."[29] Possibly Gerard was aware that the care of his books in the prescribed manner would prove to be quite a task, for he bequeathed to the Sorbonne as a sort of recompense—"pro labore vero custodiae"— valuable fittings for a chapel. Also he gave the college his *armarium* and three of his better chests, in which to keep the books.[30]

---

[28] See Daniel A. Callus, "The Contribution to the Study of the Fathers made by the Thirteenth-Century Oxford Schools," *Journal of Ecclesiastical History* 5 (1954) 145–146.

[29] ". . . quia religiosi satis habent;" Grand, 215.

[30] Glorieux, following the standard reading, notes that Gerard requested the chaining of many books: ". . . quod omnes libri mei theologie et omnes libri iuris canonici quos habeo depositos in cistis apud dictos scolares et quos habeo penes me incatenati penes eos remaneant in perpetuum . . ."; Glorieux, II, 355; *Chartularium*, I, 492. Grand, 215, on the basis of the earlier text, Paris, Arsenal MS. 1228 f. 519ᵛ, emends the reading thus: ". . . et quos habeo penes me et Cameraci, penes eos remaneant. . . ." Since there is no evidence that any books were chained at the Sorbonne before 1289, and since the 1338 catalog shows

Upon the addition of the Abbeville bequest in 1272 to the Sorbonne's library, the problem of accounting for this increasingly significant and elusive part of the college's property must have become apparent. This would especially be the case, if the Sorbonne attempted to carry out Gerard's request for an annual inventory of the books. The necessity for creating an orderly record of the books was further increased, in 1274, when Robert of Sorbon bequeathed at least seventy more manuscripts to the college.[31] Robert's bequest, which ranks second in size only to Gerard's in the thirteenth century, added in particular to the Sorbonne's manuscripts of scriptural commentaries, contemporary theology and sermons. It was probably in response to this rapid growth of over 370 manuscripts in a two-year period that the masters drew up, early in the provisorate of William of Montmorency (1274–1286), the first inventory of the college books about which we have any knowledge.

Only a fragment of this catalog survives, but enough to present an interesting picture of the early library of the college. In his study of the medieval books of the Sorbonne, Delisle identified the two surviving leaves and published a small portion of one leaf, comprising the descriptions of four manuscripts, for the purpose of illustrating the method of the cataloger.[32] The two leaves have served as pastedowns and are now bound at the end of B.N. MS. lat. 16412, f. 323–324^v.[33] Sometime after the catalog was superseded in 1290, it was discarded and used as binder's scrap. The leaves have served as the pastedowns of MS. 16412 since at least the mid-fourteenth century when the manuscript was chained in the *magna libraria*, because the front leaf bears the same chain marks as the codex itself. They have suffered serious damage from the binder's knife

---

that a large proportion of Gerard's theological and legal texts were still unchained at that date, Grand's reading is the more probable.

[31] Delisle, II, 173.

[32] Delisle, II, 180–181. Portions of thirteen entries on f. 323^v–324^r are printed by Glorieux, I, 240–243; this text, however, should only be used with caution.

[33] The manuscript contains: f. 1^{rv}, binder's leaf; f. 2–3, table to the following text; f. 3–38^v, Simon of Hinton, Summa theologiae (Stegmüller, *Sent.*, no. 815), inc. *Ad instructionem minoribus (sic) quibus non . . .*, exp. *diligeretur tunc foret mortale*; f. 39–109^v, Ps.-Hugh of St. Cher, Filia magistri (Stegmüller, *Sent.*, no. 373), inc. *Scriptura sacra de duobus agit de creatore . . .*, exp. *per gratiam euaserunt*; f. 110^{rv}, blank; f. 111–118, table of the preceding work; f. 118^v, blank; f. 119–319, anonymous, Summa questionum sacre scripture (Stegmüller, *Sent.*, no. 1266), inc. *Quoniam modus in rebus forme retinet . . .*, exp. *honor et gloria per omnia in s. s. amen*; f. 319^v, blank; f. 320–322^v, Bonaventure, Breviloquium, prologus 1–5. 1 (Stegmüller, *Sent.*, no. 117), inc. *Flecto genua mea ad patrem . . .*, exp. *autentico reponuntur et hoc quidem satis recte . . .*; f. 323–324^v, two leaves from a catalog of Sorbonne manuscripts. Chain marks top and bottom center on f. 1 and 323 (formerly the front pastedown); f. 322^v, *Precii iiii^{or} librarum incathenetur in magna libraria*. Donor unknown. Modern binding, brown calf.

and the glue pot. Portions of the outer and lower edges of the text have been cropped, and the glue has rendered large portions of f. 323^r and 324^v almost illegible. However, enough of the text can be read that the manuscripts described therein can be identified among the some 1,500 surviving Sorbonne codices, or at least that a description of a given manuscript may be found in the Sorbonne catalog of 1338. With the aid of such a parallel description and/or the very codex being described, the effaced and missing portions of the text can be reconstructed with some degree of certainty. The two leaves are not conjunct, though they could have been part of the same gathering since they represent two separate but not distant portions of the catalog. The five descriptions on f. 323^r are lined through in red, and two of them are re-entered on the following page, f. 323^v (see Plate 8). All told, the two leaves contain twenty descriptions of eighteen codices, including the two which are rewritten. Of the eighteen codices, fifteen have been identified among the extant manuscripts of the college. Two of the three remaining codices are described in the catalog of 1338, leaving one for which there is no other source.[34]

There has been no agreement on the date of this catalog. Delisle cautiously calls it "l'un des premiers qui aient été rédigés," and makes no further attempt to date it. Birkenmajer, probably without having seen the manuscript itself, suggests the date 1271. Glorieux, in turn, identifies the fragment as part of the lost catalog of 1290.[35]

The fragment must, however, be earlier than the 1290 catalog, for the following reasons. We know that the descriptions in the 1290 catalog were numbered, the manuscripts having been described and numbered before certain of them were chained in the period 1289–92.[36] The descriptions in the fragment are not numbered, indicating that it must be something other than the 1290 catalog. Moreover, the order of the descriptions in the fragment is quite different from the order established by the numbering of 1290. Since the order of the descriptions once numbered remained constant through 1338, the catalog in the two leaves can only be earlier than the 1290 catalog. Further evidence that the fragment antedates 1290 is provided by the addition to the catalog of the descriptions of a mid-thirteenth century manuscript, B.N. MS. lat. 15654, which reappears in one of the 1290 portions of the 1338 catalog.[37]

---

[34] I wish to thank Mr. Leroy Dresbeck for arranging the analytical catalog by codex. This facilitated identifying descriptions of manuscripts located in the chained library.

[35] Delisle, II, 180; Birkenmajer, 16; Glorieux, I, 126, 240.

[36] For a discussion of the numbering, see below.

[37] 1275 catalog, no. 6; 1338 catalog, XXV. 8 (Delisle, III, 33).

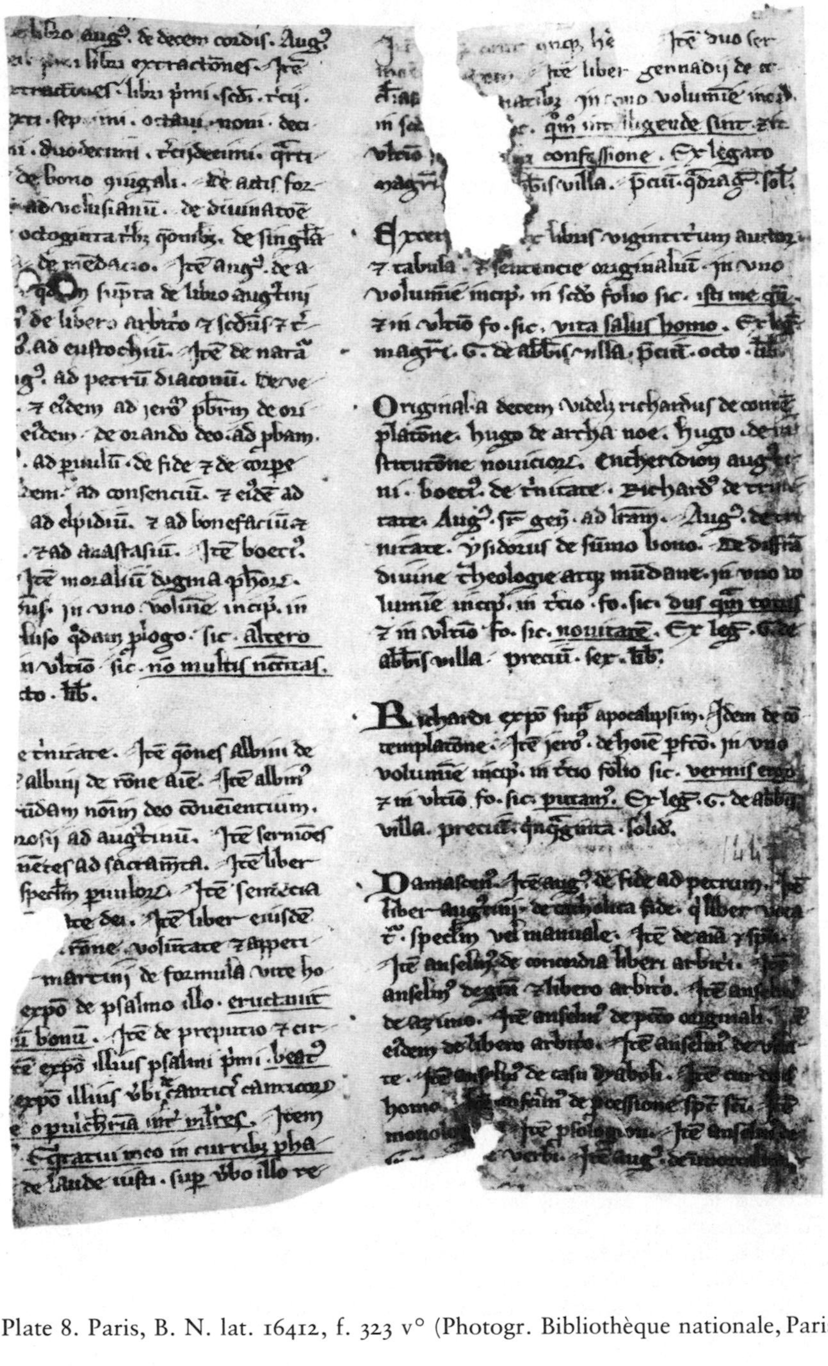

Plate 8. Paris, B. N. lat. 16412, f. 323 v° (Photogr. Bibliothèque nationale, Paris).

On the other hand, the catalog must have been compiled after 15 August 1274, since it contains a description of a manuscript bequeathed by Robert of Sorbon.[38] A date early in the last quarter of the thirteenth century is also suggested by the hand of the fragment itself. The catalog is written in a well-formed, somewhat cursive hand of the last third of the thirteenth century (see Plate 8), which exhibits the following distinguishing features: (1) the ascender of the minuscule *d* trails to the right; (2) the abbreviation for the genitive plural *-rum* is made in one stroke giving a strong S-curve to the vertical line; (3) the loop of the minuscule *g*, at times completed with a second stroke, is extended to the left and brought back to the letter with a descending loop, to form a horizontal figure eight. The same hand has added the *ex libris* notes to B.N. MSS. lat. 15315 f. 217^v, 16368 f. 1^v, 16413 f. 2^v and 16611 f. 1^v. These manuscripts were given by Gerard of Abbeville, which indicates that the writer of the catalog was associated with the college books at the time of the Abbeville bequest. While the absence of books from donors later in the 1270s and 1280s is not weighty evidence in itself, because of the limited size of the sample, when coupled with the hand of the writer it would strengthen the suggestion of a date soon after 1274 for the catalog.[39]

We can reconstruct the following picture of the early catalog on the basis of these two leaves. First of all, it was an inventory of college property. It reflects an effort to make an exact record of what belonged to the masters in common. For each codex in the library, the cataloger listed the author or title of every work it contained. He even went so far as to analyze codices of letters, as we can see from his treatment of two manuscripts of Augustine's letters included in the fragment. The cataloger apparently took his descriptions from the actual contents of the manuscript rather than relying merely on the contemporary tables of contents or the running headlines in the manuscripts which appear in so many of the Abbeville codices and which occasionally present discrepancies with the text itself. For the purpose of specific identification, he noted the opening words of the second or third, and the penultimate or ultimate, folios. These words would presumably be unique; and the codex could still be identified even if it lost its first or last folio, as was at

---

[38] 1275 catalog, no. 13.

[39] This is probably the catalog referred to in the note in B.N. MS. lat. 15629 f. 185, s. xiii, *Opera S. Dionysii* (Analytical cat., MS. Y. a.; 1338 cat., XXX, 1, *Cathenatus*): "Iste liber missus fuit ad domum de Serbonio per magistrum Danielem, socium domus predicte, a magistro Henrico de Gandauo [d. 1293], qui dicebat quod mutuatus sibi fuerat a quodam socio domus, qui sibi dixerat illum esse de libris domus, sed non inueniebatur in inuentorio uestro, sed antequam tradatur alicui, registretur." Delisle, II, 186, n. 2.

times the case. The catalog, to my knowledge, is the earliest example of this technique, which becomes common across Europe in the fourteenth century.[40] Finally, the cataloger added the name of the donor, if known, and the value of the codex or the sum for which it could be pledged. The descriptions, in sum, are exceptionally thorough.

The new catalog, however, was not a simple inventory alone, but it was also a classified catalog with a system of classification similar to that employed in the catalogs of 1290 and 1338. The two leaves preserve portions of two separate classes: f. 324 contains descriptions of nine manuscripts (nos. 1–9) from among the *originalia Augustini*; and f. 323 contains descriptions of nine manuscripts (nos. 10–20) from among the *originalia mixta sanctorum*.[41] They have been bound in reverse order in B.N. MS lat. 16412, but it is reasonable to assume that the *originalia Augustini* preceded the *originalia mixta sanctorum* in this catalog, as it did in those of 1290 and 1338. The cataloger apparently made some error in the section *originalia mixta sanctorum* which caused him to discard the page (f. 323^r) and begin the section, or at least part of it, afresh on the following page. The fourth description on the page is incomplete, the major part of the second column is left blank, and all five descriptions are lined through in red. Two of the entries (nos. 10 and 11) are rewritten on the following page (nos. 16 and 17) virtually without change, save that they are now in the midst of descriptions of different manuscripts. Presumably the other discarded descriptions were rewritten elsewhere in the catalog. Neither the fact that a description on the discarded page is incomplete, nor the suggestion that some manuscripts from this group may have been accidentally omitted, satisfactorily explains what happened here; and the answer remains a mystery.

---

[40] Karl Christ, *Handbuch der Bibliothekswissenschaft*, III, 1 *(Wiesbaden 1953) 269–270.*

[41] On f. 324, works numbered 1, 5–7 appear among the *originalia Augustini* in the 1338 catalog; nos. 2, 4 and 9 consist of Augustiniana and are cataloged with the *magna libraria*; no. 3 correctly appears among the *originalia mixta sanctorum* in the 1338 catalog, but is listed only by its first work, Augustine's *De academicis*, in the 1275 catalog; no. 8, *Cronica Augustini*, appears first among the *cronice* in the 1338 catalog.

On f. 323, works numbered 13, 15, 18–20 appear among the *originalia mixta sanctorum* in the 1338 catalog; nos. 10 and 11 appear in the catalog of the *magna libraria* only; no. 10 would appropriately be described as *originalia mixta sanctorum*, but no. 11 should be with the *flores originalium*, a classification which was apparently not used in 1275; no. 12 is among the *flores originalium* in the 1338 catalog; the description of no. 14 is for the most part illegible; and nos. 16–17 are recopied from nos. 10 and 11, respectively.

Concerning the changing meaning of "originalia" and its use in the thirteenth-century library catalogs, see J. de Ghellinck, " 'Originale' et 'Originalia' " *Archivum latinitatis medii aevi* (Bulletin Du Cange) 14 (1939) 95–105.

The catalog and related evidence afford a view of the organization and administration of the library in the 1270s and 1280s. It is quite possible that the division of the descriptions into categories reflects the actual physical grouping of the codices in the chests and *armaria* of the library. It would seem reasonable to suggest that the manuscripts were probably kept in upright chests or cupboards—*archae* or *armaria*—with shelves and dividers in them for the various classes of books, similar to the divisions described by Humbert of Romans writing around 1270: "Moreover, the cupboard in which the books are stored should be made of wood, so that they may be better preserved from decay or excessive dampness; and it should have many shelves and sections in which books and works are kept according to the branches of study; that is to say, different books and postils and treatises and the like which belong to the same subject should be kept separately and not intermingled, by means of signs made in writing which ought to be affixed to each section, so that one will know where to find what one seeks."[42] When the manuscripts were cataloged they were probably taken section by section and then described at random within each section. In order for these unnumbered descriptions in the catalog to serve readily as an inventory of property, one would think it must have been essential to have the books themselves grouped into corresponding categories. Some such topical grouping of the books would be desirable, as well, to enable the Sorbonne to store a large number of books in the *armaria* in a manner permitting a given book to be located when it was needed. One can well imagine that with Gerard of Abbeville's bequest in 1272, and that of Robert of Sorbon in 1274, the Sorbonne's bookchests in the library ceased to be mere entrepots and became instead repositories. By this date, a large number, possibly even a majority of the Sorbonne's books would be found, at a given time, in the college chests rather than in the hands of individual scholars. We can strongly suggest on the basis of the use made of the library by Thomas Hibernicus in the opening years of the fourteenth century that the books were then grouped according to a classification similar to that depicted in the catalogs of 1290 and 1338.[43] The evidence afforded by the early catalog permits one to extend this back to the library of the 1270s.

While we know nothing about its location in the college buildings, the library, or room which contained the book chests, was the store or repository for the college valuables. Besides housing the books when

---

[42] Humbert of Romans, *Instructiones de Officiis Ordinis*, in his *Opera . . .*, ed. J.J. Berthier, II (Turin 1956) 263.

[43] See below.

they were not in the possession of individual fellows, it contained the
chest with the college endowments. This latter, or perhaps a second
chest, at times also contained books which were deposited as security
for loans. The library was no doubt a small room, which was probably
kept locked. Access to it was gained through the officials responsible for
the books. While this repository for the books and other valuables of the
college must have existed from the earliest days of the college, there is no
known reference to it by name until 1319, when it is called the *libraria*;
the first known use of the term *parva libraria* was not until 1338.[44]

The library is a flourishing part of the college in the years following
the Abbeville bequest and the making of the first catalog. The books,
necessary to the life of the college, constituted one of its most significant
possessions, and efforts were made to guard and preserve this patri-
mony. The *ex libris* of the college was inscribed in each of the books.
This notice normally included the short title, the book's value, the name
of the donor, and at times an anathema against removal of the book.[45]
The donor's name was evidently not a regular feature of the *ex libris*
during the 1260s; this is most clearly exemplified by the fact that the
large bequest of Robert of Douai (1262) quickly lost its identity — there is
only one surviving manuscript which bears his name, and he is not mentioned as a donor in the surviving portions of the 1290 catalog. It is only
from the 1270s and 1280s, beginning with or shortly before the time of
Gerard of Abbeville's bequest, that one can begin to acquire a picture of
the flow of donations to the college on the basis of *ex legato* inscriptions.

The college put its mark of ownership on its books, in part for the
obvious reason that, probably more so than any other item of college
property, the books were susceptible to loss. To be sure, the strict admonition in Robert's statutes against the removal of books outside the college was incorporated in the oath taken by new members, promulgated
ca. 1280–1290, but not without an unconscious admission of changing
conditions; for the new members swore not to remove nor lend books
out of the college, without the permission of the provisor or his dep-
uty.[46] This concern with control of the circulation of books is reflected

---

[44] Ordinance of 1319: ". . . in archa que est in libraria in qua custodiri solet pecunia
legata pro redditibus emendis . . .;" ordinance of 1321: ". . . et hec vadia serventur in cista
ad hoc deputata;" Glorieux, I, 213, 215; see also II, 28, 30.

[45] "Iste liber est collegii pauperum magistrorum Parisius in theologica facultate studentium.
Ex legato magistri Geroudi de Abbatisuilla." (B.N. MS. lat. 16611 f. 1ᵛ). "Iste liber est
collegii pauperum magistrorum Parisius in theologica facultate studentium. Quicumque
delebit hunc titulum delebitur de libro uiuentium. Precium viii librarum" (B.N. MS. lat.
15829 f. 19ᵛ).

[46] Glorieux, I, 203.

in the earliest efforts to keep a record of the books which were in the possession of individual masters. A loan register of some sort was kept before 1321, but there is no indication of how early the practice began.[47] Instead, from the later decades of the thirteenth century we have two lists of quite different types. One of these, which survives on the back flyleaf of B.N. MS. lat. 15713, f. 148^v, is a very informal scratch sheet.[48] It contains brief entries in a variety of hands, jotted down helter-skelter in no apparent order, concerning the books in the possession of at least thirteen people. The name of the person and the short title of the book sufficed. There are also notices for books which Sorbonne masters borrowed from other institutions included in the list. The second record dating from this period is the list of twenty volumes in the possession of J. of Auxy, on the flyleaf of B.N. MS. lat. 15655, f. i.[49] Unlike the preceding example, which for all its informality was evidently a record of the college, the Auxy list is apparently intended to serve as a reminder to the possessor himself. Although Glorieux states, and Delisle implies,[50] that this list illustrates the ordinance of 1321 which stipulates that the loan register should be renewed, the list is certainly earlier, since it contains at least four manuscripts (Delisle ed. nos. 12, 13, 16 and 19) which by ca. 1321 were chained and, obviously, not in circulation. In addition, one text entered separately in Auxy's list, Bernardus super Cantica, had by ca. 1321 been bound at the end of a manuscript of Bernardiana, now B.N. MS. lat. 16371. This text is already associated with MS. 16371 by 1306, when Thomas Hibernicus lists it second among the works which comprise that manuscript, in the list of originalia appended to the Manipulus florum.[51]

J. of Auxy is otherwise unknown.[52] The list, however, is written in

---

[47] The 1321 statues state that the loan register should be renewed: ". . . renovent registrum . . .;" Glorieux, I, 215.

[48] This list is printed by Delisle, II, 195.

[49] Printed, Delisle, II, 187–188. The following can be added to Delisle's identifications: 1. 1338 cat. III. 7; 4. 1338 cat. X. 7; 8. 1338 cat. XIX. 3; 12. B.N. MS. lat. 16371 f. 288–434^v, Analytical cat. MS. Y. b., 1338 cat. probably XXIX. 2 Cathenatus; 13. B.N. MS. lat. 15585, Analytical cat. MS. T. i., 1338 cat. XVI. 1 Cathenatus; 15. B.N. MS. lat. 15328, not equivalent to 1338 cat. XXIV. 34 as stated in Delisle, III, 30; 16. B.N. MS. lat. 15295, Analytical cat. MS. T. g., 1338 cat. XXV. 10 Cathenatus; 17. 1338 cat. XXV. 11; 18. 1338 cat. XXXVII. 26; 19. 1275 cat. no. 9, Analytical cat. MS. Y. e.; 20. 1338 cat. XXXVI. 4.

[50] Delisle, loc. cit.; Glorieux, I, 244, and n. 4.

[51] Concerning Thomas Hibernicus, see below.

[52] The late John F. Benton suggested that "J. of Auxy" may be the Jean d'Auxois who became bishop of Troyes in 1314 (d. 1317); see P. B. Gams, Series episcoporum ecclesiae catholicae (Regensburg 1873–1886) 643.

a cursive hand which can date from the last decades of the thirteenth century, depending on the age and background of the writer. It contains six codices bequeathed by Gerard of Abbeville, one by Robert of Sorbon, one by Peter of Alberona who left his books to the college before 1290, and two bequeathed by Gerard of Rheims who is last heard of in 1282 and probably died soon thereafter.[53] In all, seventeen of the twenty manuscripts described can be shown to have been at the Sorbonne before 1290; and the date of the Sorbonne's acquisition of the other three is unknown. Five of the volumes were still unbound when the list was written, and ten of the twenty are of unknown origin, suggesting that they came to the college in the early years when donors' names were not regularly recorded. While, in sum, this is an argument *ex silencio*, it supports the evidence of the hand itself and is, I believe, strong enough to suggest a date soon after 1282.

The list appears to be rapidly though carefully written. It records, in the manner of the first catalog, the information necessary to identify precisely the manuscript involved, namely, brief contents, the name of the donor when known, value, opening words of the second and penultimate folios, and the number of quaternions when the manuscript was unbound. An effort was made to group the manuscripts by contents: [*glose*], *postille, originalia*. However, the list is the only one of this caliber known to survive. Even though lists such as the two described here were ephemeral and easily subject to destruction, the paucity of them suggests that no regularized or formal system of loan records was kept in the thirteenth century.

It is probably in the years surrounding the making of the first catalog that the Sorbonne began to assign to one or more of its members the responsibility of supervising the books. In the earlier years the books were probably treated as simply one category of the moveable property of the college, which the responsible officials, perhaps the lesser procurators, received, put into use, stored and accounted for, just as they would perform these same tasks for the fittings of the refectory or the chapel.[54] However, the execution of these tasks for the books must have demanded an ever-increasing percentage of their time. The fact that the first catalog was a sizeable undertaking, coupled with the fact that at least three *ex libris* notes survive in the hand of the cataloger, suggests that there was at least one official in the 1270s who inscribed *ex libris* notes, cataloged books, noted down (or required the borrower himself to

---

[53] See below note 69.

[54] The duties of these officials are described in the second part of Robert's statutes, Glorieux, I, 197–201.

note down) lists of books loaned, possessed the key to the door, and in general was responsible for this part of the college property. The office may have been one which rotated frequently, which was the custom at the Sorbonne for those tasks which were most onerous and time-consuming; certainly the thirteenth-century *ex libris* notes are written by a variety of individuals. One may suggest that the task of caring for the books fell under the authority of the two lesser procurators, and that they delegated the task to an individual or individuals who were responsible directly to them.

The number of the Sorbonne's books continued to grow steadily in the years following the completion of the first catalog, and with this growth came increased complications in controlling the use of the books. Among the major bequests were those of Gerard of Rheims, who gave some thirty manuscripts soon after 1282; John Claramboud of Gonesse, who left at least nine volumes in 1286; William of Montmorency (provisor 1274–1286) whose bequest of books valued at fifty pounds thirty-eight sous reached the Sorbonne in January of 1287; Stephen of Abbeville, a canon of Amiens, whose bequest of some forty codices came to the Sorbonne in November of 1288;[55] and Adenulph of Anagni, whose bequest in 1289 contained at least eighteen codices.[56] While these comprise the larger known gifts, perhaps as many as two or three hundred other books reached the Sorbonne from a constant stream of small bequests. A certain number of books also came to the college via other routes; some were left in payment of debts, others were purchased either with money left to the college or with revenue from the sale of other books.[57]

As the size and importance of the collection grew, there must have been a commensurate growth in the numbers of outsiders who made use of the Sorbonne's books. Gerard of Abbeville, in fact, had expressly stipulated in his will that his books be available to other secular masters and to the arts faculty. In so doing, he was merely putting into writing what was no doubt a common practice even by his day. The secular masters

---

[55] Ullman has identified the manuscript of Propertius left to the Sorbonne in 1288 by Stephen of Abbeville, and described in the 1338 catalog, with Leiden, Bibliotheek der Rijksuniversiteit MS. Voss. lat. 8° 38 f. 1–16ᵛ, on the basis of the opening words of the second folio. He goes on to assert that this was probably the manuscript described in the *Biblionomia* by Richard de Fournival, because of the similarity in titles; see his "The Manuscripts of Propertius," 284–285, and "The Library of the Sorbonne . . .", 40, 42–44. However, the hand of Voss. 8° 38, often dated ca. 1300, is too late to permit this. It would seem more likely that Voss. 8° 38 is a copy of Fournival's text made by Stephen of Abbeville, who was also a canon of Amiens.

[56] Delisle, II, 143, 147, 153, 157–58, 174.

[57] Delisle, II, 178–180.

evidently borrowed books from the Sorbonne, leaving pledges in their place. The number of such outside users is witnessed in part by the large percentage of bequests to the library from individuals who were never fellows of the college, and also, in part, by the very admonitions against permitting books to leave the college walls.

The general increase in the size and use of the collection may well have rendered it difficult for the fellows of the college to find the specific volumes which they desired at a given time, and it must also have made it more difficult to keep account of the books belonging to the college. This was a meaningful problem since the books formed an important portion of the Sorbonne's material wealth. Only a few years later, in 1292, they were valued at 3,812 pounds Parisian.[58] (For purposes of comparison, we might remember that Robert of Douai's bequest of 1,500 pounds caused him to be regarded as co-founder of the Sorbonne.) The problem was also significant because the college no doubt kept some form of annual account such as that specified in Gerard of Abbeville's will. The first catalog was a cumbersome tool for this purpose, since its descriptions and their corresponding manuscripts were not numbered. The college thus had the dual problem of assuring the availability of standard books for its fellows and of keeping account of what belonged to the fellows in common. Serious efforts to solve this problem can be seen in the making of a new catalog of the whole collection and in the establishment of a chained collection undertaken in the years 1289–1292, soon after the election of Peter of Villepreux (1286–1304) as provisor of the college.

The actions of 1289–92 have traditionally been used to mark the beginning of the Sorbonne library, since they were understood to have comprised the creation of the first library in the modern sense of the term and the compilation of the first catalog. Delisle saw the library established here in a form that would continue unchanged for almost two centuries. Glorieux saw the establishment in these years of rooms for both the chained and the unchained collections.[59] We have seen, however, that the Sorbonne in 1289 already had a flourishing library, i.e., a growing collection of approximately 1,000 manuscripts, possibly kept in a semi-organized fashion, with a detailed catalog and with certain regulations governing their use. Described in these terms, a library had existed since ca. 1275 if not, to one degree or another, from the earliest days of the college. The actions of 1289–92 should be seen as an

---

[58] Delisle, III, 71–72.
[59] Delisle, II, 181; Glorieux, I, 126.

effort on the part of the college to adapt the library to changing conditions, rather than as a beginning *ex nihilo*.

The point of departure for our knowledge of what happened in these years is a series of commemorative notes which were entered at the end of the 1290 catalog and which survive in the enlargement of that catalog made in 1338. The notice commemorating the establishment of a library for chained books reads, "Nota etiam quod anno Domini $M^0CC^0LXXX^0IX^0$ fuit primo institutum librarium in domo ista pro libris cathenatis ad communem sociorum utilitatem."[60] It indicates that a place was established where the availability of certain books would be assured to the fellows of the college—where they could at any time find, chained, manuscripts of certain standard texts such as the scriptures, the gloss, the sentences or the works of St. Thomas. In this way the fellows of the Sorbonne expanded their already extensive library provisions to include a room where certain of their books could be used. That this action did constitute the establishment of a second room for books is supported, in the absence of contemporary information, by evidence from the fourteenth century. The two libraries are designated by different names. By 1338 the unchained collection is referred to as the *parva libraria*. The chained library in the beginning is termed the *libraria communis*; by the second third of the fourteenth century it has acquired the name *magna libraria*, by which it is commonly known thereafter. They are obviously distinct rooms, because each library had its own keys. Keys to the *parva libraria* are mentioned in the statute of 1321; those to the *magna libraria* are mentioned in 1391, but in terms that indicate that they existed before this date.[61]

The books of the unchained collection, when they were not in use, continued to be kept in the *armaria* of the older library. We can say nothing more about the physical appearance of this room than has been suggested earlier. The library for chained books was probably a narrow room on the first floor near the rooms of the fellows, with one row of windows overlooking the street and the other the interior court.[62] Such a picture might be inferred, in the absence of contemporary evidence, from a notice of 1474, "Et erat in magna libraria, in bancca supra vicum, ante fenestras propinquiores camere magistri nostri Johannis Chien-

---

[60] Delisle, III, 71.

[61] Glorieux, I, 215, 233–234.

[62] Concerning French library architecture at the end of the Middle Ages, see the articles by André Masson in *Bulletin des Bibliothèques de France* 2 (1957) 95–110, 789–793; *Comptes rendus de l'Académie des Inscriptions et Belles-Lettres* (Paris 1959) 150–169; *Bulletin Monumental de la Société Française d'Archéologie* 117 (1959) 93–108.

nart."[63] While a picture of the deployment of the benches is afforded by the shelf list of the chained collection, it is dangerous to see the chained library of the 1290s in these terms.

The importance of the establishment of a chained library, in the broader picture, is that it established a place where books were not merely kept but where they were used, and used in common. This change at the Sorbonne in 1289–92 is part of a general trend to divide collections, which appears in Europe at the end of the thirteenth and continues through the fourteenth century.[64] Institutions began to divide their collections by causing certain commonly used works to be chained so that these would always be available to their members, while at the same time continuing to provide for the individual needs of their members and outsiders through a circulating collection. The Sorbonne probably provides the earliest clear example of this change taking place.

The notice commemorating the compilation of a new catalog of the college books reads, "Anno domini M^0CC^0 nonagesimo fuit istud registrum factum per socios de domo de libris in domo tunc inuentis quorum numerus mille et decem et septem. . . ."[65] No copy of this catalog has survived; however, one can reconstruct the majority of the 1290 catalog from the text of the catalog made in 1338.[66]

---

[63] Delisle, II, 198. John Chenart was librarian of the college 1467–1469.

[64] Concerning the division of libraries into two parts as a corollary to the appearance of the chained library, see K. W. Humphreys, *The Book Provisions of the Mediaeval Friars 1215–1400* (Studies in the History of Libraries and Librarianship, I) (Amsterdam 1964) 85–88. There are references to divided collections and chained books in Humbert of Romans ca. 1270, in records of Dominican chapters held in Sienna in 1306 and in Barcelona in 1323 (Humphreys, 85). This change may have been made at University College, Oxford, around 1292. The statutes of the college in that year stipulate, "Let there be put one book of every sort that the house has, in some common and secure place; that the fellows, and others with the consent of a fellow, may for the future have the benefit of it;" J. W. Clark, *The Care of Books* (Cambridge 1909) 127; see also R. W. Hunt, "The Manuscript Collection of University College, Oxford: Origins and Growth," *Bodleian Library Record* 3 (1950) 13–34. Other early lectern libraries are seen in the catalogs of St. Emmeram's and the Dominican and Augustinian houses at Regensburg compiled in 1347 and edited by M. Manitius, "Ungedruckte Bibliothekskataloge," *Centralblatt für Bibliothekswesen* 20 (1903) 3–16, 89–100. The way in which a divided library must have functioned at the Sorbonne and at Merton College is well described by F. M. Powicke, *The Medieval Books of Merton College* (Oxford 1931) 9–12. It might be noted that Powicke mistakenly thought that the ordinance of 1321 cited in n. 100 below dated from 1289. Also, there is no evidence that a formal system of distributing the books to the fellows, such as an annual *electio*, ever existed at the Sorbonne as it did at Merton College.

[65] Delisle, III, 71.

[66] Delisle seems to have suspected that was the case; he says, II, 182, that the 1290 catalog "ne nous est pas parvenu, mais la substance en est passée dans le catalogue de

At the beginning of a given classification or section of the 1338 catalog, one finds that the order in which the manuscripts are described bears no relationship to the donors of the manuscripts; neither the chronology nor the unity of bequests is preserved, but instead the descriptions of manuscripts from different donors are intermingled. A good example of this jumble, lengthy enough to be meaningful but not too long to summarize, is found at the beginning of classification XLII, *Summe morales*. There, in the first forty-four works, we find singly or in small groups manuscripts from the bequests of Robert of Sorbon, Gerard of Abbeville, Robert of Sorbon, Gerard of Rheims, Gerard of Abbeville, Stephen of Abbeville, John Persona, Gerard of Abbeville, John Persona, Robert of Sorbon.[67] Larger examples of this jumbled entry are the first fifty-six works in section XXIII, *Scripta et questiones supra sentencias*, and the first 134 in section XLIII, *Sermones*. Thereafter, in the sections of the 1338 catalog, we find that the descriptions of manuscripts are grouped by bequest, that the order in which the bequests are listed remains constant.[68] This division into two categories, the first disordered and the second in order, suggests strongly that the former category is composed of all the manuscripts received by the Sorbonne from whatever source, from the foundation of the college until the making of a catalog at some given time; and that the latter category consists of manuscripts received thereafter, added on to the end of each section of the original catalog at various times—perhaps at the very time each bequest was received, or perhaps at set intervals, such as once a year. That this primary catalog discernable in the 1338 catalog does indeed date from 1290 is a logical assumption, which is supported by the available evidence. There is, for example, the note copied onto the end of the 1338 catalog. "This register was made in 1290 . . .," a statement which obviously appeared in the document upon which the 1338 catalogers were basing their own register. Furthermore, there is the fact that there is no donor among those in the primary group who is known to have lived beyond 1290.[69] This is an argument *ex silencio* which proves little,

l'année 1338. . . ." Glorieux also sensed the presence of an earlier catalog within the catalog of 1338, but he concluded that his earlier catalog dated from the year 1321.

[67] To establish the order, in this case as well as in all others which will arise, it is necessary first to restore in their proper places the known donors of manuscripts for which there is a number but no description in the 1338 catalog. There will always remain, of course, many manuscripts and descriptions of manuscripts for which the donors are unknown.

[68] The order and names of these later donors are discussed below in detail.

[69] Gerard of Rheims is a possible exception; Glorieux says that Gerard was still alive in 1302, because a sermon of his appears in a sermon cycle, B.N. MS. lat. 3557, which he

in light of the number of unknown donors and unknown death-dates involved; it is, however, a necessary silence, without which the thesis would be untenable.[70] One can be certain, on the other hand, that the primary catalog does not date from before 1290, because the bequests of Stephen of Abbeville (1288) and Adenulph of Anagni (1289) form part of the original grouping.

It is evident, therefore, that when we distinguish this primary group in each of the sections of the 1338 catalog, we have a workable reproduction of the missing 1290 catalog. If we take the names of the donors supplied by the largest and most easily discernible examples of the original group, as a means by which to identify this group in the briefer sections of the catalog, we can with some certainty recover the 1290 portion from fifty-four of the fifty-nine categories listed in the 1338 catalog. Between the pre-1290 and post-1290 portions of a given classification there will normally remain a gray area, composed of descriptions of manuscripts for which the donor is unknown, or of manuscripts which come from bequests of only one or two books. Also the reconstruction of the 1290 catalog from the 1338 catalog must remain incomplete, for the latter does not reproduce the descriptions of those manuscripts which, in 1338, had been chained or lost. In spite of these qualifications, it is worth the effort to reconstruct what remains of the 1290 catalog, for the obvious reason that it will increase considerably the accuracy of our knowledge concerning the growth of the Sorbonne's library, and for the less obvious but perhaps equally important reason that it will serve as a useful aid in dating more precisely the donors whose names appear there.

The following is an indication, section by section, of those portions of the 1338 catalog which must have constituted the 1290 catalog.

---

dates from that year. Thomas Kaeppeli has questioned the chronological unity of this collection, since one of the sermons contained therein appears also in another collection of sermons which Glorieux has ascribed to the years 1273–74. If one discounts the dating of this sermon, the last known date in Gerard's life is 1282 (or 1281, according to Delisle) and he was presumed by Delisle to have died shortly thereafter. Glorieux, "Pour jalonner l'histoire littéraire du XIIIe siècle," in *Aus der Geisteswelt des Mittelalters,* I (Beiträge, Supp. III. 1) (Münster 1935) 497–499; idem, *Répertoire des Maîtres,* I, 372–273; Glorieux, I, 302; Th. Kaeppeli, "Praedicator Monoculus. Sermons parisiens de la fin du XIIIe siècle," *Archivum Fratrum Praedicatorum* 27 (1957) 151 n. 24; Delisle, II, 147.

[70] On the other hand, one does find occasionally a single manuscript from an early donor among the descriptions of manuscripts given by later donors. Presumably these manuscripts, only eight in all, were temporarily misplaced and thus escaped the catalogers in 1290. See the 1338 catalog, I. 49, Enguerrand of Cantiers; VIII. 31, Gerard of Abbeville; XXII. 31, Peter of Ausonne or Essonnes; XXII. 36, Enguerrand of Cantiers; XXIII. 112, G. Abbeville; XLIII. 206, Robert of Sorbon; XLV. 61, R. Sorbon; LIII. 42, G. Abbeville.

Any discrepancies or seeming discrepancies are discussed in notes as they arise. A number with a question mark, placed in parentheses at the end of the series, indicates that the 1290 catalog may have included these entries as well, but that there is no evidence one way or the other. For brevity's sake, each section is identified only by Roman numeral, corresponding to the section so numbered in Delisle's edition of the 1338 catalog:

I. 1–31(–39?);[71] II. 1–14(–17?); III. 1–2(–14?); IV. 1–11(–12?); V. 1–19(–22?); VI. 1–10(–13?); VII. 1–14; VIII. 1–12(–17?); IX. 1–9(–12?); X. 1–17(–18?); XI. 1–4(–5?); XII. 1–2(–5?); XIII. 1–5(–9?); XIIII. 1–7(–8?); XV. 1–10(–11?); XVI. 1–11(–17?); XVII. 1–8; XVIII. 1–7(–12?); XIX. 1–22(–24); XX. 1–2(–5?); XXI. 1–11(–14?); XXII. 1–25(–28?);[72] XXIII. 1–56(–69?);[73] XXIV. 1–43(–48?);[74] XXV. 1–22; XXVI. 1; XXVII. 1–2;

---

[71] Entry 34 describes B.N. MS. lat. 15470 which Delisle, II, 176, has mistakenly ascribed to the bequest of Thomas Hibernicus (d. post. 1316). The confusion doubtless arose from the fact that the flyleaf of B.N. MS. lat. 15797, recording Thomas's gift of that manuscript to the Sorbonne, is now bound in the front of MS. 15470, an error which Delisle himself has noted elsewhere (III, 29, n. 1). The donor of 15470 is unknown. The Bible ascribed in entry 38 to the gift of William Jafort (d. post 1307) was probably given before his death, to judge from its position relative to other bequests; this supposition is supported by the fact that no mention of this manuscript appears in Jafort's obituary (13th June; Glorieux, I, 167). However, one cannot say whether it was given before or after 1290.

[72] Entry 14 is a manuscript of the Sentences "ad usus Flamingorum, ex legato episcopi Tornacensis," now B.N. MS. lat. 15721. At the end of the manuscript, f. 240ᵛ, appears the note, "Hee sententie empte sunt per manus magistri Arnulphi de Hasnede, ad usus magistrorum Flamingorum, ex parte episcopatus Tornacensis, in domo de Sorbona." (An anonymous opponent of such particularism, by scraping off the passage "Flamingorum— domo," has adroitly changed this to read "ad usus magistrorum . . . de Sorbona.") Delisle suggests that the bishop of Tournai referred to is Michael Warenghien, who established an endowment at the Sorbonne to support two Flemish masters originating from Tournai. Warenghien died in 1291, slightly late for the inclusion of this manuscript in the 1290 catalog. The most likely explanation is that Arnold of Hasnede's purchase of this manuscript on behalf of the diocese of Tournai occurred, as the foundation for Flemish masters almost certainly did, during the lifetime of Bishop Warenghien rather than upon the occasion of his death; see Delisle, II, 163, and *Gallia christiana*, III, col. 222. A second possibility is that the manuscript did indeed come to the Sorbonne in 1291, and that the process of creating the catalog extended from 1290 through most of 1291; but I should hesitate to press this argument, on the basis of one instance. A third explanation is that it is not Warenghien but some previous bishop who is referred to here; since the manuscript itself refers not to the bishop, but the bishopric of Tournai, one might conjecture that this purchase may be related to the foundation endowed by Nicholas of Tournai (d. 1266) for Sorbonnists from that diocese; see above.

[73] Entry 16 describes the manuscript which is now B.N. MS. lat. 15822. Delisle, II, 158, identifies as its donor John of Essonnes, whose bequest dates from ca. 1306; but the flyleaf of the manuscript clearly says "P. de Essoniis," i.e., Peter of Ausonne or Essonnes, whose donation is consistently found in the 1290 portion of a given section. Entries 10–11 are

XXVIII. 1–6(–10?); XXIX. (–2?); XXX. 1–4; XXXI. (–2?); XXXII. 1–3(–4?); XXXIII. 1–3(–6?); XXXIV. 1(–3?); XXXV. 1–14; XXXVI. 1–4; XXXVII. 1–25(–26?); XXXVIII. 1–10(–17?); XXXIX. 1–13(–18?); XL. 1–8; XLI. 1–14(–17?); XLII. 1–44; XLIII. 1–134(–144?);[75] XLIIII. 1–16(–27?); XLV. 1–38(–41?); XLVI. 1–7; XLVII. 1–22; XLVIII. 1–3(–6?); XLIX. 1–9(–11?); L. 1(–6?); LI. 1–29(–30?); LII. 1–19(–20?); LIII. 1–17(–21?); LIIII. 1–10(–21?); LV. (–20?); LVI. 1–49(–54?); LVII. none;[76] LVIII. 1–28(–29?); LIX. (–7?).

The total of the minimum numbers from each section is 908 manuscript descriptions; the total of the maximum, 1, 111. The Sorbonne cat-

---

reported in the catalog "ex legato magistri G. de Fontibus" (and "ex legato eiusdem"); neither of these manuscripts is known to have survived. This early appearance of Godfrey's name (d. ca. 1306) may be explained by the fact that these two books (and a third, entry 36 in the following section) were given to the Sorbonne, perhaps while Godfrey was a student (before 1285), as replacement or exchange for books which he had lost. In the absence of the manuscripts themselves which might enlighten us on this point, such an explanation must remain a hypothesis, but I think a plausible one. Glorieux, I, 244–245, offers the alternative explanation that late acquisitions to the library were sometimes inserted in the 1290 catalog in place of books which had been lost; he adds, "Ainsi s'explique, par exemple, que de volumes légués par Godefroid des Fontaines (après 1306–09) se trouvent presque en tête de telle ou telle section." This suggestion contains some pitfalls: We should note, first, that Godfrey of Fontaines is not an example, but the only such case; and that only two sections of the catalog are involved. Secondly, inserting a new description into a catalog in place of the description of a book which is lost involves the physical problem of space: Does one squeeze the new descriptions into the margins, or does one scrape the parchment to efface the original descriptions and write the new in their place? It is difficult to believe that either of these unsatisfactory solutions would have been preferred over the simple and obvious solution of adding new descriptions to the end of the existing series. One might suggest that, instead, new descriptions were inserted in blank spaces which might have been left between the older descriptions. However, the descriptions in the Sorbonne catalog were numbered, with corresponding numbers being noted in the manuscripts, so that any insertion would render invalid all the numbers posterior to it.

[74] Entry 36 is recorded "ex legato magistri Godefredi de Fontibus." The manuscript described here is not known to have survived. I have suggested that this book (and two others, XXIII. 10–11) may have been given to the Sorbonne by Godfrey before 1290; see the preceding note.

[75] Entry 10, for which there is no description in the 1338 catalog (indicating that the book so numbered was unable to be located at the time that the catalog was made), is identified by Delisle in his edition as B.N. MS. lat. 16494, a manuscript given by John of Maroeuil (d. post 1311). This seems to be one of Delisle's rare mistakes—perhaps an error in transcription or typography, although I cannot suggest an emendation. This manuscript does not bear the notation "Inter sermones 10," the only means by which it could be identified with this spot in the catalog.

[76] It is not surprising to find that section LVII in the 1338 catalog, Libri Raymundi (Raymund Lull), did not exist in the 1290 catalog. This classification was probably created with the cataloging of the bequest of Peter of Limoges (d. 1306).

alog of 1290 contained 1,017 books. The similarity in numbers suggests that we have here a good approximation of the original document.

This reconstruction of the 1290 catalog, first of all, provides a *terminus ante quem* for the donors whose bequests it records. Although one cannot, on the basis of the catalog, range them in chronological order, one can at least say concerning the following people that their bequests were received by the Sorbonne before the year 1290: Adenulph of Anagni (d. 1289); the purchase of Arnold of Hasnede; Baudouin of Brinliva; Enguerrand of Cantiers; Gerard of Abbeville (d. 1272); Gerard of Rheims; Giles of Saumur; Godfrey of Limoges; Hugh of Pisa; John of Abbeville, archdeacon of Meaux; John the Chaplain; John Claramboud of Gonesse (d. 1286); John Persona; Joseph of Bruges; the archdeacon of Meuturepia (?); Michael Hellequin; Miles of Corbeil (d. 1271); Nicholas of Tournai (d. 1266); Odo of Châteauroux (d. 1273); Peter of Alberona; Peter of Ausonne or Essonnes; Peter of St. Martin (d. 1286); Philip, canon of Arras; Ponchard of Sorbon; Ralph of Châteauroux (d. ca. 1285); Reginald of Colant (? perhaps not a donor); Reginald of Grandchamp; Robert, brother of John the curate of St. Jacques of Rheims; Robert of Douai (d. 1262); Robert of Sorbon (d. 1274); Simon of Widelin (d. 1285); Stephen of Abbeville (bequest received in November, 1288); Walter of Douai; Warner of Moret (? perhaps not a donor); William of Montmorency (d. 1286); and William of Montreuil (de Mosterolio). Roger of Rheims may belong in this list; it is possible, however, that his only appearance among the 1290 donors (XLIII. 102) is an error, the copyist having written *R*. rather than *G*. (Gerard) *de Remis*. William of Moussy-le-Neuf (de Monchiaco; d. 1286) left his books to the Sorbonne with the condition that Master Adam of Villeron have use of them during his lifetime; most of them did not actually reach the Sorbonne until after 1290. Finally, there are six men, each of whose identifiable bequest consists of only one book which is described, in the 1338 catalog, in the gray area between the last of the known pre-1290 donors and the first of the known post-1290 donors: Bernard dean of St. Pierre, John of Boubier, John le Cercelier, Walter of Biencourt, William of Troyes and the gift (?) of William Jafort. In sum, the reconstructed catalog permits one to pose the date 1290 as a *terminus ante quem* for some twenty-two donors whose death-dates are unknown and who have, for the most part, hitherto been dated merely as "before 1338."

The reconstruction of the 1290 catalog, secondly, increases the accuracy of our knowledge about the library at the end of the thirteenth century, by providing information concerning the arrangement of the unchained books, about the manner in which the catalog was compiled, and about the establishment of the chained collection. It also serves to confirm a number of suggestions previously made about the condition of the library in the 1270s and 1280s.

We have seen that the first catalog of the college was classified; the text of the 1290 catalog provides a full view of this classification system. It was a system common to the intellectual world of the thirteenth century, namely, the Scriptures, glossed and postillated books; Peter Lombard's Sentences, and questions and summas on the Sentences; whole works of the saints and doctors of the Church; questions and distinctions of the masters; and whole works of the ancient philosophers, followed by works outside the realm of theology and philosophy—medicine, the quadrivium, jurisprudence and perhaps vernacular writings. In this schema, constructed for theologians, the works are arranged in descending order of their relative authority: Holy scripture, Doctors of the Church, modern masters, and ancient philosophers. This hierarchy of authority was detailed for example by St. Bonaventure: "Sunt ergo quatuor genera scripturarum, circa quae oportet ordinate exerceri. Primi libri sunt sacrae scripturae . . .; secundi libri sunt originalia sanctorum; tertii, sententiae magistrorum; quarti, doctrinarum mundialium sive philosophorum."[77] It was only natural that this hierarchy also appeared in the organization of medieval book collections such as that at the Sorbonne.

It has been suggested, furthermore, on the basis of the first catalog, that the books were grouped by subject and author in *armaria* similar to those described by Humbert of Romans ca. 1270,[78] and that the classification of the catalog is a reflection of this arrangement. It is impossible, however, to judge on the basis of the catalog alone whether or not it reflects the physical arrangement of the books themselves. We are fortunate in this instance to have collateral evidence which reveals the arrangement of certain books in the library just after the turn of the century.

In 1306, Thomas Hibernicus, a fellow of the Sorbonne, unintentionally but effectively preserved a picture of the arrangement of the manuscripts of the major authors in the *armaria*, in the process of completing his *Manipulus florum*.[79] This is a collection of extracts from the authorities grouped according to some 265 topics alphabetically arranged— *abstinencia, abusio, acceptio, accidia, adiutorium*, etc. Under each of the some 265 topics the extracts appear in a set order without significant

---

[77] *Hexameron*, collatio xix, 6; see also xix, 10–12; in *Opera Omnia*, Quaracchi 5 (1891) 421–422.

[78] See above.

[79] Concerning Thomas, see R.H. Rouse, "The List of Authorities Appended to the *Manipulus Florum*," *Archives d'histoire doctrinale et littéraire du moyen âge*, 32 (1965) 243–250.

variation: quotations from Augustine, Ambrose, Jerome, Gregory, Bernard, Hilary, Chrysostom, Isidore, and so on, concluding with the ancients. At the end of the *Manipulus florum* Thomas has appended a bibliography of 476 works, each with incipit and explicit, compiled from the Sorbonne's manuscripts. The authors in the bibliography are presented in virtually the same order as the extracts, works of Augustine, Ambrose, Jerome, etc.[80] The order preserved here, the order in which Thomas used the books, is apparently that of the grouping of the books in the *armaria* of the library. The order is virtually the same as the order of the authors in the catalogs of 1290 and 1338: *originalia Augustini, Ambrosii, Hieronimi, Gregorii, Bernardi,* etc.[81] The combined evidence of the 1290 catalog and the *Manipulus florum* certainly implies, if it does not prove, that the organization of the catalog reflects the physical arrangement of the manuscripts in *armaria*.

In 1290, the catalogers apparently cataloged the books section by section. They described the books within each section at random, the order of the descriptions reflecting merely the order in which the books were taken from the *armarium*. The descriptions were made according to the format which had been devised some fifteen years earlier for use in the first catalog: a relatively thorough list of the contents, the incipits of the second and penultimate folios, the name of the donor, and the monetary value of the codex. Variations in the descriptions of the same manuscripts in the 1275 and the 1290 catalogs suggest that the descriptions were to some degree made anew. The important change made at this juncture was that the descriptions in each class were numbered and the class and number were entered on the fly-leaves of the corresponding manuscripts, e.g., *Inter originalia Augustini 3*. With this number the description of any manuscript could be quickly located in the catalog. It had the long range effect of fixing the order of the descriptions and, therefore, the arrangement of the catalog, because once 1,000 codices

---

[80] The following authors appear in the list in this order: Beatus Dyonisius, B. Augustinus, B. Ambrosius, B. Ieronimus, B. Gregorius, B. Bernardus, B. Hylarius, Ysidorus, Iohannes Chrisostomus, Rabanus, Prosper, Damascenus, Anselmus, Ricardus de Sancto Victore, Hugo de Sancto Victore, Alquinus, Alanus, Plinius, Raby Moyses, Valerius Maximus, Macrobius, Tullius, Boetius, Seneca.

[81] XXV. Originalia Augustini, XXVI. O. Ambrosii, XXVII. O. Jeronimi, XXVIII. O. Gregorii, XXIX. O. Bernardi, XXX. O. Dyonisii, XXXI. O. Hilarii, XXXII. O. Crisostomi, XXXIII. O. Ysidori, XXXIV. O. Bede et Anselmi, XXXV. O. Hugonis, XXXVI. O. Richardi . . ., L. Libri Senece, LI. Lib. Tullii et Boecii, LII. Lib. Socratis, Platonis, Ciceronis, Valerii, Solini, Cassiodori, Plini et aliorum actorum; Delisle, III, 32–37, 60–62. Thomas varies from this order by placing Dionysius at the head of the list (perhaps since he was, we know, heavily influenced by Dionysian thought); by inverting Chrysostom and Isidore, and Hugh and Richard of St. Victor, and by reversing the order of the philosophers.

were numbered, no change could be made without a complete alteration. Thus new additions to the library were classified, and described at
the end of each classification in the catalog. In general, identification
marks such as these are rare in libraries before the later decades of the
fourteenth century, probably because most collections were not large
enough to require them.

It is interesting to see that no effort was made to preserve the order
of the entries established in the first catalog. The fact that these earlier
descriptions and their corresponding codices had not been numbered
would permit the order to be changed without undue difficulty; but
while the lack of numbers provides the opportunity, it does not explain
the motive for shuffling the order. A plausible, though purely conjectural, explanation is that the catalogers in 1290 created several additional or newly distinguished categories not found in the library or catalog before this time—that, for example, they substituted in some instances
a number of more narrowly defined classifications for one general classification. In so doing, they found that manuscripts previously cataloged
under a certain heading must now be placed in a different section, and
that in light of these necessary shifts it was simpler to ignore the order
found in the first catalog and to begin afresh. The surviving fragment of
the first catalog is too brief to provide much evidence on this point. It
does, however, permit the suggestion that one such change in the classification scheme in 1290 was the creation of a separate division for *flores
originalium*; for the collections of extracts, such as items 11 and 12,
which appear in the earlier catalog among the *originalia mixta
sanctorum*, have been culled out and grouped along with others in the
classification *flores originalium* in the 1290 catalog.

It is impossible to estimate how long it took to catalog in this thorough a fashion one thousand seventeen codices. One should, at least, be
aware that one cannot apply too literal an interpretation to the description of these events as recorded in the notes appended to the 1338 catalog, stating (A) that in 1290 the catalog was made; (B) that in 1289 a
chained library was first instituted; and (C) that in 1292 the value of the
books was 3,812 pounds Parisian. The last note, for example, implies
the possibility that the process of cataloging the whole collection may
not have been completed until 1292. And 1289 perhaps represents the
year when the decision was made, or even the year in which a room was
selected or built and furnished to serve as the chained library. But it
seems inevitable that the actual chaining of codices could not have begun
before the catalog was begun in 1290. One can see this from the fact
that, in each section of the catalog, the descriptions of codices subsequently chained are interspersed without pattern among the descriptions

of codices which remained unchained. It is difficult to give a meaningful example of this, because even though one restricts consideration to the 1,290 portions of the 1338 catalog, all the manuscripts marked *cathenatus* in 1338 were not necessarily chained in 1290. Nevertheless, if there had been manuscripts chained before the making of the catalog, one would expect the catalogers to have described them together in one place, perhaps at the beginning or end of each section, since one cannot envision them cataloging first one codex in the unchained library, then one in the chained library, and so on. For example, in section XXXVI, *Originalia Richardi*, works 1–4 were in the 1290 catalog; of these, no. 3 is marked (in 1338) *cathenatus*. This volume cannot practically have been chained when it was cataloged, since its position in the sequence of numbers shows that it was cataloged between two unchained manuscripts.

The choice of the first codices to be chained, in fact, was very likely made concomitantly with the cataloging of the whole collection. In all, the number so selected must have been relatively small. This is implied by the fact that the inventory of the *magna libraria*, ca. 1321, and the notation of chained volumes in the 1338 catalog, both show that the chained library contained approximately 312–340 codices, a total which included the major post-1290 additions to the *magna libraria*. The additions consisted, on the one hand, of all the chained codices derived from the early fourteenth century bequests, among which were the large gifts of Godfrey of Fontaines and Peter of Limoges; and, on the other hand, of all those manuscripts whether from early or late bequests which were chained in response to the college ordinances of 1321. Since the size of this latter addition is unknown, it is useless to suggest even an approximate number for the books chained in 1289–92. It is worth noting, however, that there is virtually no mention of books which are chained, before 1306.[82] The chaining of books was a considerable expense, and the concept of a chained collection was still new in Europe at the end of the thirteenth century.

The Sorbonne masters' interest in books, as displayed by the thoughtful organization of their own collection, extended beyond the college walls to the collections of other institutions in Paris. Just as outsiders used their books, they themselves no doubt used the book collections of Notre Dame, St. Victor, St. Jacques and other houses. The Sorbonne possessed in the latter decades of the century a collection of catalogs of the libraries of other Parisian houses, which the masters may have compiled in order to facilitate locating works which they needed. A fragment

---

[82] See below n. 94.

of this composite catalog survives in B.N. MS. lat. 16203, f. 71ᵛ–72;[83]
it has been printed by Delisle.[84] The fragment is a large leaf (12½″ ×
18½″) folded once, parallel to the lines of the text, by a later binder
who used it to form the back fly-leaf and pastedown in MS. 16203. The
leaf originally contained the whole catalog of the manuscripts of Ste.
Geneviève and the first portion of the catalog of St. Germain-des-Prés; it
was probably part of a larger work, since the completion of the catalog
of St. Germain at least would require another sheet. The hand of the
fragment, the only basis on which it can be dated, would suggest that it
was written in the last third of the thirteenth century. The text was written in three and four columns, but the left-hand column is almost entirely
lacking, having been trimmed off by the binder. The compiler evidently
copied the individual catalogs without any significant attempt to stan-
dardize them, and thus to a certain degree preserved the original form of
each catalog. The fragment is all the more interesting because the originals of these two catalogs are not known to have survived, and because
neither house is known to have produced any other medieval catalogs.

The copy of the catalog of Ste. Geneviève was written in three columns. Including the missing left-hand column, it must have contained
descriptions for approximately 226 volumes, of which forty-eight were
duplicates.[85] While the catalog is not classified, the descriptions were
with many exceptions roughly grouped according to broad categories —
scriptures and commentaries (missing), works of the fathers, works of
the twelfth-century authorities, law and philosophy. Entries consist simply of author and short title, followed by an indication of the number of
copies of the work belonging to the house. The majority of the codices
are listed as containing only one work, and none appears with more
than two. the late twelfth- and early thirteenth-century authors are relatively well represented, e.g., Alan of Lille, Stephen of Tournai, William
of Dacia, Prepositinus, Rigord, Peter of Chartres, Innocent III, Stephen
Langton and John of Abbeville. The latest identifiable work is Abbeville's
Summa or collection of *sermones de tempore*, which were probably

---

[83] The manuscript contains, f. 3–70ᵛ, Albumasar, Introductorium magnum in astrologiam,
tr. Johannes Hispalensis, inc. *In nomine domini pii . . ., Laus deo qui creauit . . .*, exp.
econuerso et proicitur ab ascendente; f. 71ʳ, blank; f. 71ᵛ– 72ʳ, fragment of a catalog of
books in Ste. Geneviève and St. Germain-des-Prés. s. xiii, ex leg. Gerard of Abbeville; 1338
catalog, LVI. 3, *Cathenatus* (Delisle, III, 67).

[84] Delisle, II, 513–515; noted in Gottlieb, 134–135, nos. 371– 372.

[85] A more accurate picture of this section of the catalog is presented in the edition by
Charles Kohler, *Catalogue des Manuscrits de la Bibliothèque Sainte-Geneviève* 1 (Paris
1893) lxxxviii-xci. To Kohler's identifications can be added, no. 150 (Delisle no. 49), probably B.N. MS. lat. 3247, s. xiii in.

given before 1216 and reworked in 1227. It would be hazardous to date the catalog much later than 1230–1240, because the absence of the authors who flourished in mid-thirteenth-century Paris, such as John of Rochelle, Alexander of Hales, William of Auvergne, Hugh of St. Cher and Averroes, speaks strongly in a catalog of as cosmopolitan an institution as Ste. Geneviève.

The catalog of St. Germain-des-Prés was written in four columns, the first of which again is lacking. The library is described codex by codex, e.g., "In uno uolumina: Ambrosius de officiis, Ambrosius de uita beata, Ambrosius de fide resurrectionis . . .," and so on.[86] Here the manuscripts may have been roughly grouped by author, since we have grouped five codices of Augustiniana, and two each of works of Ambrose and of Rabanus. Unfortunately, too little of the St. Germain catalog survives to permit any meaningful date to be determined for the original.

One cannot tell how many other catalogs, if any, the Sorbonne's collection included. However, if there were others, they may have been listed in alphabetical order, since Ste. Geneviève precedes St. Germain; but the evidence is obviously too slight to tell. The composite catalog was apparently in tabular rather than codex form, because it is quite large when unfolded, and is written on one side of the parchment only. Perhaps it was fastened to the wall or to one of the *armaria* in the library. This format, in turn, strengthens the belief that the collection of catalogs was not made by an individual for his own use, but rather that it was made at the direction of the college for the use of its members.

This collection of catalogs is interesting because the principal function of a medieval library catalog, even of a catalog which is a shelf list, is to serve as an inventory of property. This collection of catalogs had no inventorial purpose for the masters of the Sorbonne, but instead probably had the function of locating or finding books in other libraries.[87] It complements our picture of the bibliographic activity at the Sorbonne at the end of the thirteenth century.

The Sorbonne library as it was organized at the end of the thirteenth century served a whole generation of scholars, among them Godfrey of Fontaines, Raymond Lull, Peter Roger, and Sorbonnists Peter of

---

[86] The following identifications can be made: 2. B.N. MS. lat. 13366, s. ix; 7. B.N. MS. lat. 12138, s. xii; 9. probably B.N. MS. lat. 11683, s. ix; *11*. probably B.N. MS. lat. 13346 f. 1–112^v, s. ix; 12. probably B.N. MS. lat. 12322 f. 1–27, s. xi.

[87] Concerning other medieval location lists of books see Gottlieb, 328–329; Paul Lehmann, "Alte Vorläufer des Gesamtkatalogs," in *Festschrift Georg Leyh* (Leipzig 1937) 69–81, reprinted in his *Erforschung des Mittelalters* 4 (Stuttgart 1961) 172–183; and R. H. Rouse "Bostonus Buriensis and the Author of the *Catalogus Scriptorum Ecclesiae*," *Speculum* 41 (1966) 471–499.

Auvergne, Peter of Limoges, Thomas Hibernicus and John of Pouilly. The library remained basically unchanged until sufficient pressure built up from the difficulty of locating books, aggravated by increases in the size and use of the library, to cause the fellows to take the necessary steps to adapt it to the needs of the college. What must already have been a difficult situation for some years was the subject of detailed legislation in 1321.

The striking growth of the Sorbonne's book collection had continued in the early fourteenth century. We know the names of some twenty-five individuals who left books to the college between 1290 and 1321. The largest identifiable gifts were the bequest of Matthew Castelet, who left books to the value of sixty-two pounds Parisian in 1306;[88] that of Godfrey of Fontaines in 1306, of more than fifty codices;[89] that of Peter of Limoges, a fellow of the college, who in the same year left over 120 manuscripts, the second largest known gift to the medieval library;[90] that of Bernier of Nivella ca. 1307–1310, of twenty-five volumes;[91] that of William of Feuquières, of at least sixteen manuscripts;[92] and that of Stephen of Geneva, of some sixty manuscripts or more.[93] While there were no bequests in these years to equal that of Gerard of Abbeville, the steady flow of gifts of from one to twenty books compensated in total volume.

While the college library increased in size, there is no indication that the chained library grew apace with the collection as a whole. The chained library was evidently quite small in the opening years of the fourteenth century, when Thomas Hibernicus was compiling the *Manipulus florum*. The principal manuscripts which Thomas records, all of which were chained by the 1320s, are entered, in the list of *originalia* appended to the *Manipulus florum*, in the order in which the unchained books were shelved, implying that they were not chained when Thomas used them. The first evidence we have of an increase in the number of books chained occurs with the bequest of Godfrey of Fontaines in 1306. Perhaps some twenty of the thirty-eight manuscripts surviving from the bequest were evidently chained with their incorporation into the library, since the same hand which inscribed the *ex libris* of

[88] Delisle, II, 162.

[89] Ibid., 149–150. See also J. J. Duin, "La Bibliothèque Philosophique de Godefroid de Fontaines," *Estudios Lulianos* 3 (1959) 21–36, 137–160.

[90] Delisle, II, 167–169; Obituary, 3 November, Glorieux, I, 176. Concerning Peter, see A. Birkenmajer, "Pierre de Limoges, Commentateur de Richard de Fournival," *Isis* 40 (1949) 18–31.

[91] Delisle, II, 144–145.

[92] Ibid., 151.

[93] Ibid., 175–176.

the college wrote *cathenatus* on their flyleaves.[94] Only a few other sporadic references to the chained collection survive. Two volumes left by Nicaise of Plank are "in catenis" by 1307.[95] Raymond Lull gave the college a manuscript of his works in 1311, and requested that it be chained.[96] Sometime after 1306, and perhaps before 1321, Alan of Penrith gave the college a volume in replacement for a book given by Peter of Limoges which Penrith had lost, and he requested that the replacement be chained.[97] In all, thus, there is little indication that the chained library in its original form made a meaningful portion of the college books available to the community as a whole.

Instead of being ameliorated, the problems of making books available for the community of masters probably grew more serious in the opening decades of the fourteenth century. The Sorbonne's library, along with its hall, had been a strong factor in making the college the center of the Faculty of Theology in this period; and the use of its books by a growing number of outsiders, *hospites*, fellows and former fellows necessarily made it more difficult for the individual scholars to obtain the specific books they wanted. The natural desire among the fellows to have certain books in their possession prevailed, and books were granted to a fellow for the duration of his course or of his stay at the college, becoming *de facto* his personal property during that period. Other codices left the college, having been borrowed in return for a pledge by masters from the university at large. The loaning of books was not adequately supervised. At times pledges of insufficient value or even IOUs were left in the pledge chest in return for books borrowed. Whatever sort of loan register existed in the early fourteenth century, it was apparently too cursory and too informal to prevent the loss of books. Its weaknesses are implied in the 1321 statutes, in the detailed account of the pitfalls which are to be avoided in the new loan register. We know that there must have been one or more *librarii* who were charged with the care of the books; but it is apparent, from the precisions of the 1321 statutes, that their duties had not been suficiently well defined, and that their strict accountability to the community of fellows was not clearly established. In summary, the library had outgrown the customary procedures by which it had been governed hitherto.

---

[94] For example, B.N. MSS. lat. 15355, f. 251ᵛ, 15449, f. 1. This may also be the case with the bequest of Peter of Limoges, see B.N. MS. lat. 15554, f. 256ᵛ.

[95] Obituary, 13 June; Glorieux, I, 167.

[96] D. José Tarré, "Los Códices Lulianos de la Biblioteca Nacional de Paris," *Analecta Sacra Tarraconensia* 14 (1941) 6–10.

[97] B.N. MS. fr. 24780, f. 210ᵛ, Delisle, II, 143.

In order to remedy this situation, the masters promulgated a body of regulations in 1321 "for the benefit of the house and the better care of the books," which defined and rectified the book provisions of the college.[98] The election of Annibaldo Ceccano as provisor only a few months earlier may explain in part why significant legislation was undertaken at this particular date. In these provisions the masters are basically concerned with three matters of importance at the time and of significance to the subsequent development of the library: supervision of the loaning and of the general care of the circulating books; enlargement of the collection of chained books; and the making of a new catalog of the whole collection. These statutes, as is often the case, are a mixture of definition and codification of extant procedure with a considerable amount of direct innovation. In order that the provisions be successfully implemented, new librarians were elected and instructed to carry out these tasks.

At the head of the list was the stipulation that no book was to be loaned out of the house unless a pledge of greater value, whether book or precious metal, be left in its place in the pledge chest. The responsibility for the circulating books, the *libri vagantes* of the *parva libraria*, were placed in the hands of custodians of the books who were to be elected by the fellows. They were to account for books lost during their tenure, and to exercise strict control over the keys to the *parva libraria*. The loan register was to be renewed; in it, under the name of each individual borrower, the books which he had were to be precisely described, not only with author and short title but also with the value of the book and the incipit of its second folio.[99] The detail with which this procedure is described is indicative of the Sorbonne's concern in keeping as precise records of its books as possible, a concern similar to that exhibited in the detailed descriptions in the 1275 and 1290 catalogs of the library. Certain unbound manuscripts of little worth, such as collections of notes and sermons, were to be disposed of, and the proceeds used to buy books which the library lacked.

Having insured that adequate control would be maintained over the use and circulation of the unchained books, the statutes secondly insured that the major books would be available at all times. The legislation stipulated that henceforth the best manuscript of each work in the college was to be selected and chained in the *libraria communis*; all

---

[98] Glorieux, I, 214–215.

[99] Several leaves of this register survive from the mid-fourteenth century and are printed by Delisle, II, 188–191. The fifteenth-century loan list, utilized by Jacques Monfrin in "Les Lectures de Guillaume Fichet et de Jean Heynlin," *Bibliothèque d'Humanisme et Renaissance* 17 (1955) 7–32, is being edited from Mazarine MS. 3323 by †/Jeanne Vielliard and Jacques Monfrin.

books belonging to the college were subject to being impounded for
chaining, including those which might currently be on loan to individual
fellows, because the good of the community outweighs individual privilege.[100] This decision probably constituted a virtual refounding of the
magna libraria. The provision represents the first articulation, and probably the first formulation, of a rationale which was at the same time a
statement of the purpose of the chained collection and a basis for the
selection of books to be chained. While the college in 1289 had decided
that some books should be constantly available to all, it went on at this
juncture to insure that the right ones would be available. The years after
1321 in all probability saw a marked increase in the size of the chained
collection. For example, the great codices of *originalia* from the Abbeville
bequest, including those utilized by Thomas Hibernicus, were probably
chained at this time. It was, thus, in response to this legislation that the
magna libraria attained the state in which it is depicted in the inventory
and the analytical catalog.

The third matter of general significance in the statutes of 1321 was
the provision that a new catalog should be made of the whole collection,
because many of the books previously owned by the house could no
longer be found. No copy of this catalog survives, nor does any concrete
evidence exist indicating that a catalog was made at this date; Glorieux,
however, states that the 1321 catalog is discernible in the text of the 1338
catalog.[101] On the basis of his reconstruction of the 1321 catalog, he has
assigned the date 1321 as the *terminus ante quem* for a number of donors;
he has, in addition, drawn up a list of twenty-one donors whose bequests
can be dated 1321–1338 and whose names he has attempted to arrange in
the order of their appearance, an order which he treats as chronological.
However, Glorieux does not distinguish those portions of the 1338 catalog which represent his catalog of 1321; and his list of twenty-one donors
dated 1321–1338 is internally contradictory and inconsistent with the
facts. To cite a few examples: He has singled out Bernier of Nivella as
the latest donor to have his bequest recorded in the conjectural 1321 catalog; anyone whose bequest follows Nivella's in the 1338 catalog, therefore, Glorieux dates as post–1321. However, Nivella died 1307–1310, as
Glorieux observes elsewhere. This would indicate a period of from eleven
to fourteen years in which the Sorbonne received no gifts or bequests,

---

[100] Item quod de omni scientia et de libris omnibus in domo existentibus saltem unum
volumen, quod melius est, ponatur ad cathenas in libraria communi ut omnes possint
videre etiamsi unum tantum sit volumen, quia bonum commune divinius est quam bonum
unius; et ad hoc astringatur quilibet habens huiusmodi librum ponendum in libraria quod
sine contradictione eum tradat; Glorieux, I, 215.

[101] Glorieux, I, 244–246, 294 and n. 3.

followed by a period of seventeen years in which no fewer than twenty-one bequests were received. In Glorieux's list of twenty-one donors post–1321, Stephen of Geneva is third, William of Feuquières ninth in the order. However, in the eight sections of the 1338 catalog which record bequests of both men, Feuquières precedes Geneva seven times (sections I, VII, VIII, IX, XXV, XLVII, XLIX) and is listed immediately after him on the eighth occasion (section XXIV). First on Glorieux's list is William Patemoysi. However, only one manuscript of his, a Bible, can be located in the 1338 catalog; and in the record of the Sorbonne's Bibles (section I), Patemoysi's name follows those of four other donors from Glorieux's list (William of Feuquières, ninth; Stephen of Geneva, third; Ralph of Periers, eighteenth; and Peter Crespin, eleventh). Giles of Audenarde is only sixth, out of twenty-one, on the list; on this basis Glorieux suggests elsewhere (p. 303) that Audenarde died "peu après 1321." However, his only known gift to the Sorbonne is a manuscript for which the description has been added, at the end of section V, after the 1338 catalog was completed. These few examples are sufficient to indicate that the order of Glorieux's list of donors is unreliable.

In actuality, Glorieux's evidence for the existence of a 1321 catalog consists solely of indications in the 1338 catalog that the latter was copied from an earlier catalog.[102] Among these indications are the copying by mistake, on at least four occasions (XXIII. 101, LVIII. 62, LVI. 37, LVI. 43), of descriptions of manuscripts which in 1338 are not found in the *parva libraria*; the scribe has in each instance noticed his error and has added a note stating that the manuscript is chained, as in the first two cases, or is missing, as in the last two. Also, on very many occasions, after leaving the customary blank space beside the number of a manuscript which in 1338 is either chained or missing, the copyist describes the source of the succeeding manuscript as "ex legato eiusdem;" see, for example, XIII. 13, XIX. 28, XXIV. 73, 96–97. On the basis of this evidence one can be sure that the catalog of 1338 largely reproduces an earlier catalog, one which described indiscriminately the unchained codices and those which, by 1338, had been chained. But there is no justification on these grounds alone for asserting that the earlier catalog dates from 1321, rather than from 1290. As we have mentioned previously, all of the

---

[102] Glorieux's basic error was his assumption that the fragment found in B.N. MS. lat. 16412 formed part of the 1290 catalog. He correctly concluded that between the fragment and the 1338 catalog another catalog must have been made, one in which the order of the descriptions was changed and numbers were assigned to the descriptions; but as a result of his misdating of the fragment, he was forced to assume that these steps were not taken until 1321. See, for example, Glorieux, I, 137, where he suggests that it was 1321, at the earliest, when the books were classified.

post–1290 bequests are entered, in the 1338 catalog, in a constant order. Therefore, while we cannot rule out the possibility that a general catalog was made in 1321, we can see that if such a catalog was made it must have consisted simply of a fair copy of the 1290 catalog and its accumulated additions. As a result, any such 1321 general catalog would completely lose its identity in the 1338 catalog. It seems strange, though by no means impossible, that a second general catalog would be made in 1338 if one had been made just seventeen years earlier. It is also noteworthy that the 1338 catalog itself contains no reference to a 1321 catalog, while it does reproduce three notes describing the books and the catalog, 1289–92. In sum, we are left with the fact that the statutes of 1321 call for the making of a new catalog, but that there is no evidence confirming the execution of the decision at that date.

The 1321 statutes presented a basic program for the administration of the library in the 1320s and 1330s, if not for the balance of the century. To what extent and when the individual provisions were put into effect is, as indicated above, impossible to determine. Nevertheless, the provisions were apparently a successful *modus operandi* in the following years. Each of the items discussed in the statutes, a loan register, an enlarged chained collection, a general catalog of the library, are in existence by the middle of the century. In addition, two other significant catalogs were produced in the years immediately following the promulgation of the statutes.

These two catalogs, the inventory of the chained collection and the analytical catalog of the contents of these codices, may be regarded as indirect results of the 1321 legislation. The decision in that year regarding the chained books must have appreciably increased the size of the *magna libraria* and probably altered significantly the physical arrangement of the chained books. It was probably these changes in turn which, at least in part, motivated the making of the catalogs of the *magna libraria*.

The two comprise one manuscript, which is now bound with the 1338 catalog in B.N. MS. Nouv. acq. lat. 99, pp. 237–353. (See Plates 9–10). The analytical catalog is a *tabula* or subject guide to the contents of the major codices chained in the *libraria communis*.[103] Its compiler

---

[103] Glorieux (I, 248–289) has attempted to rearrange this catalog by codex, by grouping all those titles which bear the same pressmark. This task is hampered by the fact that many of the pressmarks in the analytical catalog are unreliable; see below. It is also necessary to use the manuscript of the catalog, since Delisle did not print all of it, omitting the majority of the sections containing Augustine's *originalia*, his letters, the letters of Bernard and Jerome, and the sermons of Augustine, Bernard, Leo and Maximus. While the list makes no pretense of being complete, the following corrections can be offered: A. g. is not

has arranged the works of each major codex according to fifty-two subjects. These subjects correspond to the divisions of the faculties: *arts*, containing grammar, logic, natural and moral philosophy, and the quadrivium; *medicine; theology,* containing the scriptures and commentaries, the *originalia* of the authorities, chronicles and miracles, the *originalia* of the modern doctors, sermons, commentaries on the sentences, and theological questions; and *law*.[104] In the larger sections the compiler has listed the works alphabetically by author. For each work he gives the pressmark, author, title and incipit; his pressmarks consist of a majuscule letter designating the bench, and a minuscule letter designating the place on the bench, where the codex containing the work is chained. As a necessary guide to the location of these codices, the compiler has provided a brief shelf list of the twenty-six benches of the library which is entered on pages 237–244, and which by its function completes the catalog.

The compiler explains his motives in a short prologue, taking as his base Ecclesiasticus xx, 32: "Hidden wisdom and unseen treasure — of what use is either?" He remarks that wisdom often lies hidden in libraries, because the people who own the books are unaware of precisely what they have — whether because of the multitude of their codices, or because of the large number of works contained within one codex, or because the titles of the works are defective. Such, in fact, is the case at the Sorbonne; what is even more intolerable, he says, is to see such a state of affairs in the chained library, in which a vast number of books on almost every subject are displayed for all to use, but where one can only with difficulty find what he seeks. This difficulty the compiler proposes to remedy; he will prepare an instrument which, if properly made, should enable anyone to locate in the chained library whatever he may wish. In taking this task upon himself, he does not hesitate to make the necessary sacrifice of his own interests for the common good, because

---

16193, since the donor Henry Pistor died toward the middle of the fourteenth century; *G. m.,* for XXXII. 13 read XXXVII. 13; for *H. c.* read *H. e.*; *H. f.*, final work is part of *H. e.*; for *N. c.* read *N; O* (Vincent of Beauvais), originally *L. h.* and *L. j.*; *T. r.* is not XXXVII. 23; *X. e.* is not 16142 (Henry Pistor); *X. f.* is not 16601 (Henry Pistor); *X. o.* is not 16249 (s. xv); *Y. c.* is not 15655, but rather 15294; AD. *m.* is not 16163 (Henry Pistor) — and the following additions can be made: *C. o.* = XXXVII. 28 = 15988; *I. g.* = LVIII. 52 = 15924; *L. o.* = 15377; *N. I.* = 15310; *O. k.* = VIII. 41; *Q. r.* = 15284; *S. e.* = 15983; *T. b.* = XXV. 20 = 15659; *T. c.* = 15288; *Y. e.* = 15655; *Y. g.* = XXV. *7 = 15662; Y. j.* (omitted) = 15653; *Y. k.* (omitted) = XXV. 19 = 15658; *Y. I.* = 15302; *Y. m.* = XXV. 1 = 15289; also, the descriptions of *D. o., F. e., T. s* and *Y. q.* should be added.

[104] The additional sections *Romancia uel libri in gallico* (p. 107), *Sermones usuales ad predicandum, Libri Raymundi philosophi barbati* (pp. 113–114), were probably added as afterthoughts — though not long after, since they are included in the table of contents.

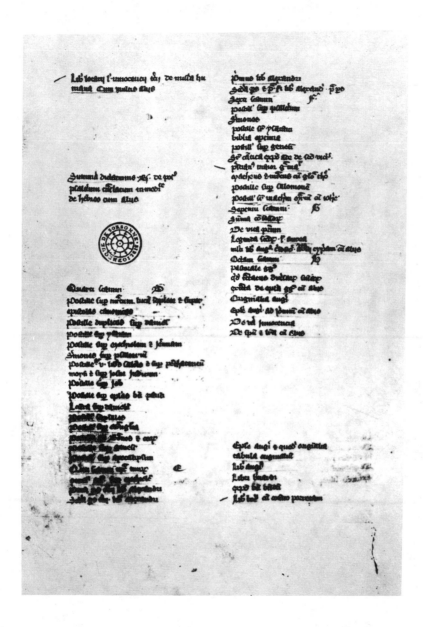

Plate 9. Paris, B. N., nouv. acq. lat. 99, p. 238, reduced.

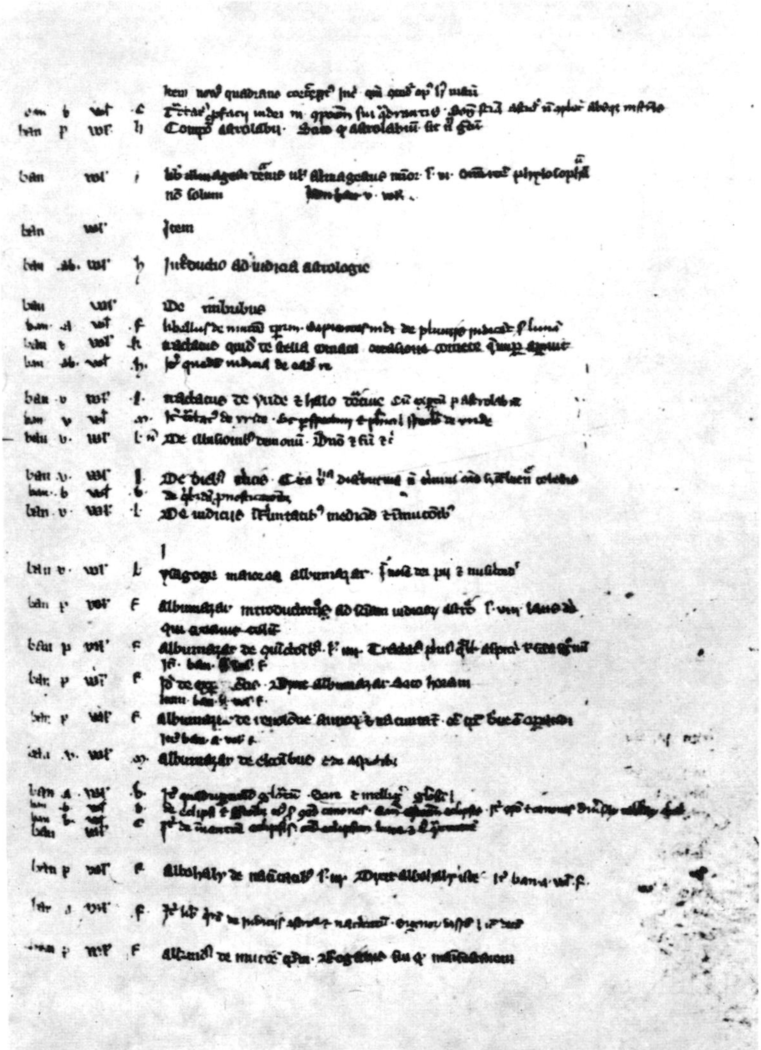

Plate 10. Paris, B. N., nouv. acq. lat. 99, p. 257, reduced.

"bonum quanto communius tanto diuinius." Thus, he says, he has undertaken alone by the best means he has been able to devise, the construction of a table to the contents of the numerous codices in the chained
library. Merely by looking at this table, anyone can quickly and easily
find what he wants, by means of either its title or its incipit, thus avoid-
ing a lengthy search. He hopes, therefore, that this work will benefit not
just himself but all who seek after learning. He concludes by commend-
ing his table to the college, asking that any errors be corrected, anything
missing be added, in the same charitable spirit with which the work has
been begun.

It is worth emphasizing that the basic purpose of this catalog, in
common with that of the composite catalog compiled at the Sorbonne in
the late thirteenth century, was not to serve as an inventory of property
but to enable the reader to locate materials. This catalog was, however, a
considerable advancement over the former, which was merely a collection of inventories; the present catalog, instead, involved an effort to
extract the individual texts contained in the manuscripts and rearrange
them in a meaningful order, while retaining their pressmarks. In other
words, it is an application of the subject index to the contents of the
library. The step is a natural one, since the principle of the index had
been successfully applied to gaining access to the *originalia* of the authorities in works such as the *tabulae* of Robert Kilwardby and the
Manipulus florum of Thomas Hibernicus. To my knowledge the catalog
represents the earliest effort to analyze the contents of manuscripts by
subject.[105] In doing so, it is a distant ancestor of the modern author and
subject catalog.

The analytical catalog was obviously the personal work of one
individual, in contrast to the general catalogs of the library which were,
instead, the impersonal inventions of the college. Its compiler describes
himself in the prologue as follows: ". . . Ego Iohannes, presentis collegii
de Sorbona quondam inter eius cetera membra unum de minimis ac
minus utile ad officia corporis exsequenda. . . ." Claude Hémeré and
Delisle after him tentatively identify this John with John of Pouilly, a
fellow of the Sorbonne and a regent master in the Faculty of Theology
whose writings were condemned by Pope John XXII on 24 July 1321.[106]

---

[105] The only other example I know of a medieval analytical catalog is pt. III of the
catalog of St. Martin's Priory, Dover, compiled in 1389 by the precentor of the priory, John
Whytefield, and partially edited by M. R. James, *The Ancient Libraries of Canterbury and
Dover* (Cambridge 1903) 407–496.

[106] Delisle, II, 160, 182. Concerning Pouilly see N. Valois, *Hist. Litt. de la France*,
XXXIV, 220–281; Glorieux, *Répertoire*, I, 450–452; J. Koch, "Der Prozess gegen den
Magister Johannes de Polliaco und seine Vorgeschichte (1312–21), *Recherches de théologie*

The basis of their identification was, apparently, the fact that Pouilly was the most important figure named John associated with the Sorbonne at the beginning of the fourteenth century. Pouilly, however, seems to be a doubtful choice. He was at the height of his career as a scholar and involved in the major disputes of his day by 1307, when he was a regent master. His condemnation and recantation in 1321, and a benefice accorded to him in the following year, are the last records we have of him; and the analytical catalog was produced ca. 1321. One would not expect one of the senior masters of the faculty to assume a task of this sort at the end of his career.

Previous studies have presented considerable disagreement, with one another as well as with the present account, concerning the dating of the inventory and the analytical catalog and concerning their relationship to each other. Delisle said merely that they can be dated "toward the beginning of the fourteenth century," and implied without comment that they were part of the same work. On the other hand, because they are now bound, and have been printed, with the 1338 catalog, later writers have occasionally assumed that the latter date applies to all three catalogs. Birkenmajer dated the analytical catalog after 1328, and the inventory several years before or after. Mgr. Glorieux separated the two by roughly twenty-eight years, dating the inventory ca. 1310 and the analytical catalog at around 1338.[107]

Any precise dating is obviously difficult. There are many manuscripts in these two catalogs whose donors are unknown; the catalogs do not provide this information, and we are thus forced to rely on information provided by those manuscripts which meet the dual requirements of survival and identifiability. There are as well many donors—in fact, thirty-nine out of the forty-six identifiable post–1290 donors—whose death dates are not known. Nevertheless, there is sufficient evidence, first, to show that the catalogs were written after 1321 and before the late 1320s; and, secondly, to suggest strongly that they were written by the same person and are part of one work.

Glorieux's date of 1310 for the inventory of the *magna libraria* is too early. His dating is based on the latest work which he has found in the inventory, the *Manipulus florum* of Thomas Hibernicus, completed

---

ancienne et médiévale 5 (1933) 391–422; and L. Hödl, "Die Aulien des Magisters Johannes von Polliaco und der scholastische Streit über die Begründung der menschlichen Willensfreiheit," *Scholastik* 35 (1960) 57–75.

[107]Delisle, II, 182; Birkenmajer, p. 17 n. 6, p. 23; Glorieux, I, 243–244, 246–247. See also, however, p. 83, where Glorieux says of the inventory, the analytical catalog and the 1338 catalog, "Ces trois documents sont à peu près de même époque. Ils permettent de se faire une idée exacte de la bibliothèque du Collège de Sorbonne vers 1338–1340."

in 1306. However, several manuscripts in the inventory came to the Sorbonne after that date. There is one from the bequest of Bernier of Nivella (d. 1307–1310); one from the bequest of James of Marli (living in 1307); at least one from the bequest of Nicholas of Bar-le-Duc (d. 1310); a manuscript from the donation of Raymond Lull, whose gift is dated 1311; and a *Summa confessorum*, donor unknown, which bears the date 1318.[108] The inventory also lists at least three manuscripts from the bequest of Stephen of Geneva,[109] whose death Glorieux himself dates at 1325; but this date is conjectural and cannot be used for precise dating. We are left, then, with a definite *terminus a quo* of 1318 for the inventory, and with a *terminus ad quem* of the date when the analytical catalog was drawn up.[110]

As for this latter, Glorieux for unstated reasons would date the analytical catalog in 1338 "ou peu s'en faut." However, the latest date-able work in this catalog is the *Summa confessorum*, 1318, mentioned above.[111] A further help in dating the catalog is the later addition of an entry for two manuscripts of "Questiones multe magistri Iohannis de Pouilli."[112] One of these, B.N. MS. lat. 15372, bears the date 1328, although the date of its coming to the Sorbonne is not known. It was on this evidence that Birkenmajer, not realizing that the entry was a later addition, based his dating of the analytical catalog. The other manuscript, B.N. MS. lat. 15371, completed shortly after 1321, was bequeathed to the Sorbonne by Pouilly himself; the date of his death is not known, but it presumably occurred in the 1320s, as both Glorieux and Valois have suggested.[113] We can see, then, that the analytical catalog was written after 1318 and before Pouilly's death in the (late?) 1320s.

---

[108] Nivella, Scamnum D, *Postille super Apocalipsim*, B.N. MS. lat. 15611; Marli, Scamnum O, *Quatuor ewangelia Thome*, 15270; Bar- le-Duc, Scamnum AB, *Questiones et exposicio fratris Egydii de generacione, Exposicio Petri de Alvernia . . .*, 16158; Lull, Scamnum Q, *De gentili et tribus sapientibus . . .*, 16111, from which also was copied the "Nota . . ." which follows, in Scamnum Q; *Summa confessorum,* Scamnum G, 15924.

[109] Scamni E, N and X, B.N. MSS. lat. 15676, 16293 and 15851.

[110] Birkenmajer, p. 23, noted that one cannot tell on the basis of their contents which of these catalogs precedes the other. However, the physical evidence afforded by the manuscript of the catalogs indicates that the inventory was completed first.

[111] Delisle, III, 113, with the pressmark *I. g.*, which is either a mistake for *G. i.* or the cataloger's misinterpretation of a notation that this volume was "1ªG."

[112] Delisle, III, 112, with pressmarks *H. I.* and AC.

[113] Valois, op. cit., 257–258; he lists 1322 as the last known date in Pouilly's life, but says that he must have lived a few years longer. Glorieux says (I, 316) that Pouilly was still alive in 1327, elsewhere (I, 331) that he died in 1327; he does not in either instance indicate the source of this information.

Glorieux and Birkenmajer have nevertheless pointed out that there are significant differences between the two catalogs which, to them, strongly suggest that the two were written at widely separated dates and that they represented the library at two different stages in its development. For example, the inventory lists some ninety-two codices which cannot be found in the analytical catalog. Conversely, the analytical catalog contains some seventy-five codices not found in the inventory,[114] as well as a number of codices whose bench marks are different from those given to the same codices in the inventory. These differences Glorieux and, to a lesser degree, Birkenmajer[115] believed to represent books lost,[116] books added, and books moved from one bench to another, during the time which passed between the making of the two catalogs. A fresh examination of the two catalogs indicates that the differences between them have been exaggerated and that there is good reason to suggest that they were written at the same time, probably shortly after the statutes of 1321.

The printed edition, excellent as it is, cannot be a substitute for the manuscript itself in regard to seeing how the catalogs were made, because it does not reflect the hand of the compiler at work. The most important fact in this regard is that the texts of the inventory and the analytical catalog are written in the same hand, and that this is probably the hand of the compiler of the latter.[117] This is strongly suggested by the fact that the text of the analytical catalog bears all indications of being the author's own working text which he drew up "alone, in the best way he could devise." Different portions of the text are in varying states of completeness, and there are numerous additions in the compiler's hand. He carefully wrote out the inventory and the basic structure of the analytical catalog in a text script, and then added numerous notes, a prologue and a table to the latter in a rapid cursive script. The result is a *tabula* in the process of construction and, quite clearly, not a scribe's fair copy. That the inventory is the compiler's own work, and not merely a copy of

---

[114] Both of these figures have been calculated primarily on the basis of Birkenmajer's tabular comparison between the contents of the two, pp. 19–23.

[115] Birkenmajer, 19–20, is aware that the analytical catalog contains a certain number of erroneous pressmarks.

[116] Some ninety volumes would represent a surprising loss from a chained collection; this thought is no doubt one of the factors which moved Glorieux to assign to the analytical catalog the latest date possible, 1338.

[117] Another text in his hand is the short metrical concordance to the gospels (Walther Nrs. 37, 15297) which is bound at the beginning of the Sorbonne's chained codex of Zacharias' *Super unum ex quattuor*, B.N. MS. lat. 15585, ff. 1–3^v, s. xiii, which had been bequeathed by Gerard of Abbeville. It was no doubt an aid to using Zacharias. The text bears the note "Ave Maria" at its head, as does the inventory.

someone else's catalog, is suggested by the fact that its date of composition is indistinguishable from that of the analytical catalog, and by the
fact that it is necessary to the use of that catalog since it is the means by
which the individual codices can be located, they themselves bearing no
pressmarks. The construction of the inventory was a simple task in comparison to the making of the *tabula*, and must have required not more
than a day or two to complete. The complier simply recorded the short
title of each major codex as he came to it, in the order in which they
were chained; in five instances he evidently began at the other end of the
bench and recorded the codices in reverse order.[118]

A second significant factor not reflected clearly in the printed edition is that the catalog was annotated by a number of later hands.[119]
Titles were added to the catalog by Master John and others for years
after it was made. In actuality, over one-third (twenty-eight) of the codices
contained in the analytical catalog but absent from the inventory consist
of additions to the former. Thus the physical evidence on the one hand
emphasizes their proximity in time and on the other diminishes their
differences in content. However, to understand the significance of the
differences which remain requires a more complex examination, including an attempt to understand the method and the mechanics of compiling the catalogs. Any attempt along these lines, short of a thorough re-
editing of them both, will never be wholly satisfactory. Nevertheless, it is
possible, within the limits of this study, to demonstrate that neither the
inventory nor the analytical catalog is complete; and that, in the latter,
there are multiple indications of error on the part of the compiler.

One can see from Delisle's edition of the inventory that this catalog
does not pretend to be complete, if only because of the summary nature
of its entries.[120] It is impossible to discern either the number, or the
specific contents, of codices described in an entry which says merely
"Multi libri Augustini, Crisostomi, Ambrosii, Cypriani, cum aliis." Given
the summary character of the inventory, it is possible that the compiler

---

[118] Scamni M, Q, V. AC, AD.

[119] For example, the entry which Glorieux, I, 244, uses as proof that books were lost
between the making of the two catalogs is *Romancium de rosa*, the last work in Scamnum
A (Delisle, III, 72), which appears in the analytical catalog (Delisle, III, 107) with the
pressmark *A. q.* and the notice "Perditus est." This note, however, is a later addition to the
analytical catalog.

[120] It was perhaps the summary nature of the entry in Scamnum X, *Multa quelibet et
questiones libri mag.* (Delisle, III, 77), which caused Glorieux, loc. cit., to state that the
quodlibets of Giles of Rome (*X. q.* in the analytical catalog, Delisle, III, 112) cannot be
found in the inventory. The manuscript represented by both of these entries is B.N. MS.
lat. 15851.

accidentally or deliberately omitted some volumes because of their insignificant size. Such might have been the case for the three small tracts
written by Thomas Hibernicus in 1316, which appear in the analytical
catalog with the pressmark S.c. but do not appear in the inventory.[121]
The manuscript of the inventory reveals an additional indication of incom-
pleteness. In each of some thirty instances in which the compiler has left
a blank space of from three to ten lines in the column, the entry preceding the blank concludes with the phrase "cum aliis" or "cum multis
aliis."[122] In only eleven instances is there no space left when an entry
concludes in this fashion. One wonders if the compiler expected that he
or someone else would eventually use these blanks to detail more clearly
what comprised the "many others." One may conjecture that some of
these blanks represent undescribed codices in the chained library. Taken
together, these factors go a long way toward explaining why one cannot
identify all the codices of the analytical catalog in the inventory.

The principal reason, however, for the differences between the two
catalogs can be found in the analytical catalog itself. It should first be
understood that the catalog is a selective list, not in any sense a complete
list, of the contents of the some 350 chained codices. We know this to be
true for a number of reasons. There are numerous occasions when the
compiler of the analytical catalog failed to note all the works contained
in a given codex; frequently, a later note inserted by himself or someone
else completed the description. Secondly, there are numerous occasions
of manuscripts, listed in the inventory but omitted from the analytical
catalog, which we know from other sources were still in the *magna
libraria* at a date posterior to the writing of the analytical catalog. For
example, most of the glossed books of the Bible listed in the inventory
on Scamnum O were not analyzed in the analytical catalog; yet all of
those for which a manuscript survives[123] are recorded as "cathenatus" in
the 1338 catalog—e.g., *Penthathecus glosatus* = B.N. MS. lat. 15186 =
1338 catalog, III. 14; *Libri hystoriales glosati* = B.N. MS. lat. 15190 =
1338 catalog, IV. 12; etc. In this instance, we have in addition to the
evidence of the 1338 catalog the testimony of a summary entry, added to
the analytical catalog: "Banco O, Item Biblia glosata in . . . uoluminibus

---

[121] B.N. MS. lat. 16397, ff. 1–18; the first tract is now missing form the manuscript.
Delisle, III, 108, incorrectly cites the pressmark of *De tribus hierarchiis* as *S. e.*

[122] There is one exception: the cataloger has left two lines blank between the last book
on Scamnum A and the heading for Scamnum B, indicating that he originally intended to
leave a bit of white space between the scamni.

[123] An entry in either the inventory or the analytical catalog cannot be identified with
an entry in the 1338 catalog except by means of the manuscript itself to which the entries refer.

supersignatis."[124] Lastly, the compiler neglects to list pressmarks which common sense insists must have existed. On bench E, for example, the analytical catalog lists only two codices, with the pressmarks E.a. and E.i.;[125] the seven intervening pressmarks are simply unaccounted for. On the basis of these indications of the compiler's selectivity, we can state that the fact that the analytical catalog omits works contained in the inventory is entirely without significance.

The seeming changes, between inventory and analytical catalog, in the pressmarks of certain chained volumes, are very likely all mistakes of some sort, most of them the compiler's. Since he was a pioneer in the field of analytical cataloging, the compiler no doubt created, and broke, his own rules of procedure as his work progressed; his procedures were frequently unsystematic, and are frequently, for us, unintelligible. The element which is most difficult to comprehend is the fact that, in almost half the entries in the analytical catalog, the compiler did not record the pressmark at the same time when the entry itself was written. In many of these cases the pressmarks are added, in a different ink; and many are, instead, left blank—at least seventy items in the printed version lack their pressmarks. The compiler apparently created the pressmarks specifically for the catalog, since none of the manuscripts of the *magna libraria* give any indication of having ever contained pressmarks similar to the ones he devised. It is this curious absence of pressmarks in the books corresponding to those in the catalog which necessitated the inclusion of a shelf list or synoptic picture of the collection as a whole, to enable one to find a given codex. As one might expect, the compiler made errors in his assigning of the pressmarks, rendering any comparison with the inventory difficult indeed. One sees, for example, P.f. for T.f.; I.g. for the first pressmark in Scamnum G, perhaps a mistranscription for "1ª G;" and H.f. probably for A.f.[126] A serious confusion of some sort has occurred with the compiler's cataloging of the books listed under Scamnum H in the inventory. On this bench, the inventory notes a dozen or more codices of patristic works. In the analytical catalog most of these can be identified with codices which are reported to be, instead, on bench Y (e.g., from Scamnum H, item 14 = Y.a.; 11–13 = Y.b.; 10 = Y.c.; 9 = Y.d.; etc.) It is hard to believe that all the patristic writings

---

[124] Delisle, III, 92.

[125] Delisle, III, 100, 113.

[126] Delisle, III, 93, *Item postille super Apocalipsim*; III, 113, *Summa confessorum*; III, 88, *Albumazar de coniunctibus . . . , Idem de experimentis.* Glorieux, I, 255, notes a third work with the pressmark *H. f., Morale sompnium Pharaonis . . .* ; this work actually bears the pressmark *H. e.* (Delisle, III, 108). Other mistaken pressmarks are noted by Birkenmajer; see note 115 above.

were moved en bloc from bench H to bench Y; it is especially hard, if one notes in consequence just what the compiler does record from Scamnum H. There is codex H.e., probably identifiable with the second item under H in the inventory;[127] H.f., probably an error for A.f.;[128] H.m. and H.n., which are later additions to the analytical catalog;[129] H.l., *Questiones multe magistri Iohannis de Poulli*,[130] which is also a later addition—but with the extra complication that this pressmark is given as well to *Quedam hystoria ecclesiastica dicta*, which not only is an unlikely companion for Pouilly's quodlibets but is not contained in the manuscript, which survives;[131] and lastly, H.g. and H.h., the *Summa* of Alexander of Hales, which according to the inventory should be found rather on bench E. In both of these latter entries, however, the H has been changed to a G by a later hand, and in addition a note inserted beside them says, "Item tres partes eius in quinque uoluminibus banco E";[132] one wonders whether this is really an additional set of the *Summa*, or whether the later writer is not making an unconscious correction to the original entry. When we make all these probable emendations, we are left with the fact that the analytical catalog reports one sole codex, H.e., on this bench, a result which makes the compiler's wholesale "transfer" of all the patristic works to bench Y seem highly suspect.

This analysis, itself far from complete, of the differences between the two catalogs concerning the codices on just one bench, can at least serve to indicate that the differences may not be taken at face value. In deliberately choosing the bench for which the two catalogs are at widest variance, I have hoped as well to indicate that a close examination suggests that the differences represent, not two different states or stages of the chained library, but human error on the part of the cataloger. To restore our sense of proportion, it might be well to take note of the similarities which exist between the two catalogs. For each of the benches E, L, N, O, AB and AD, the analytical catalog (unemended) notes only one additional codex. For bench M, all the codices noted in the analytical catalog can be found in the inventory. And for benches B, I and AC,

---

[127] Delisle, III, 108; erroneously listed as H. c. by Glorieux, loc. cit.

[128] Delisle, III, 88.

[129] Ibid., 112.

[130] Ibid., 106, 112.

[131] H. I. and AC, *Questiones multe* . . . (ibid., 112), correspond, not necessarily respectively, to B.N. MSS. lat. 15371–15372.

[132] Delisle, III, 111, omits the letter E, but prints instead a still later note, "2ª M," indicating no doubt that a copy of the *Secunda pars* was also on bench M, when the note was added.

the correspondence is exact between the codices listed in the inventory and those indexed in the analytical catalog.

In summary, then, I suggest that the seeming differences between the inventory and the analytical catalog are not of sufficient magnitude to justify the supposition that any significant period of time separates the two, and that their having both been written by the compiler of the analytical catalog indicates, to the contrary, that they were compiled at much the same time. Furthermore, the fact that they may be dated after 1318 but before the end of the 1320s permits the reasonable assumption that they were made pursuant to the major reorganization and enlargement of the *magna libraria* undertaken in 1321. The similarity between the number of codices listed in the inventory (approx. 312)[133] and the number which are called "cathenatus" in the 1338 catalog (approx. 340) confirms the belief that the former reflects the chained collection after, not before, its enlargement. Other, less tangible indications suggest that the catalogs were, in fact, made relatively soon after the library was expanded. The mistakes and confusions apparent in the analytical catalog, for example, may derive from the fact that the chained collection was still in the process of enlargement and had not as yet stabilized when the compiler was at work. The similarity of terminology used in the catalogs and the 1321 statutes is worth noting also. In the statute, in the inventory's title, and in the prologue to the analytical catalog, the chained library is designated by the term *libraria communis*. We cannot say precisely when, but soon after the changes wrought by the 1321 legislation, the chained collection became the *magna libraria* in both informal and formal usage. This was the case at least by 1338, when the store for unchained books was, in an obvious contrast, referred to as the *parva libraria*. Finally, we might note that the wording itself of several of the inventory's entries, "Decretum pulcrum . . ., Biblia optima . . ., Multi libri Anselmi et Augustini boni . . ., Liber sentenciarum optimus . . .," sound very much like conscious echoes of the statutes of 1321, ". . . quod de omni scientia et de libris omnibus . . . unum uolumen quod melius est ponatur ad cathenas. . . ."

It was probably very shortly after the election of Peter of Croso as provisor (1338?–1361)[134] that the college completed a new catalog of its circulating books in the *parva libraria*. Perhaps this catalog represents a

---

[133] This figure represents the number of codices indicated in the manuscript of the inventory. Delisle's edition frequently does not preserve the unity of the codices.

[134] Peter of Croso was perhaps elected provisor when the former provisor Peter Roger became a cardinal, 18 December 1338; however, Croso was acting provisor of the Sorbonne by October 1336, a position which he probably held without interruption until his election as provisor. See Glorieux, I, 139–141.

belated execution of the decision made in 1321 to catalog the general
collection, since there is no evidence that such a catalog was made at
that time. It is always possible, however, that a catalog was made in 1321
and that it was for some reason no longer satisfactory by 1338. The 1338
catalog was copied from its predecessor of 1290 (or 1321), including all
the later additions which had been entered in the earlier document.[135] It
retained the format of the description of manuscripts which dates back
to the earliest catalog, ca. 1275. However, the 1338 catalog was not simply a fair copy of its predecessor, because in 1338 the catalogers took
great care to describe only those manuscripts which were actually present
at that date in the *parva libraria*; books which were chained, and books
which, for the moment at least, could not be found, were not described,
although their numbers were recorded and sufficient space was left for
the description. This means that in 1338, possibly for the first time since
1290, the Sorbonne made an attempt to verify and to record the location
of every codex owned by the house. It is quite possible that this thorough
search uncovered a few volumes which had somehow managed to remain
at the Sorbonne for years without ever having been cataloged; this may
explain why, in some few instances, one finds a codex from the bequest
of Gerard of Abbeville (d. 1272), Robert of Sorbon (d. 1274), or Peter of
Limoges (d. 1306) noted at the end of a given classification. Although
they must have handled every codex described in the 1338 catalog, the
catalogers probably copied the descriptions themselves from the earlier
catalog.[136] At the end of the catalog the compilers copied several notes
from the 1290 catalog relating to the organization and cataloging of the
library at that date and the value of the codices which it contained. They
included as well a note of their onw, stating that all codices for which a
description is given were found in the *parva libraria* in 1338.[137] The cat-

---

[135] The manuscript of the 1338 catalog is written in two clear chancery hands. The
second, contemoprary with the first, begins on f. 199 and substitutes "defficit quia cathenatus"
for the "cathenatus" used by the first writer to designate books which have been moved to
the *magna libraria*. A few additions were made to the catalog in the fourteenth century,
but on the whole the manuscript is unusually clean and, compared with the analytical
catalog, gives relatively little sign of having been used.

[136] This practice is witnessed by the fact, mentioned above, that the copyist in two
instances reproduced the description of a codex which could not be found, and he had to
note at the end of his entry, "Vacat quia defficit."

[137] "Nota quod omnes libri in registro isto quotati secundo et penultimo foliis fuerunt
inventi in parva libraria anno Domini M⁰ CCC⁰ XXXVIII; illi vero ubi scribitur *defficit*
non fuerent inventi." This note is added in a different hand from the rest of the catalog, is
quite hastily written, and appears to have been erased. The other notes, which followed
this one, are carefully entered by the scribe who completed the manuscript; they have,
however, been crossed out.

alog indicates that the whole collection had grown to 1,722 volumes, an increase of 705 volumes in the forty-eight years which had elapsed since the account preserved from 1290.

The 1338 catalog has previously been used to provide a *terminus ante quem* for the donors whose names it contains. However, because it preserves the order of the additions to the preceding catalog, it also provides precise information about the relative dates of these bequests. As was stated earlier, most sections of the 1338 catalog begin with a portion which can be identified, with a high degree of certainty, as having composed the corresponding section in the 1290 catalog of the Sorbonne. The bequests in this portion are not listed in any order, nor are they preserved as units. Descriptions of post–1290 bequests, on the contrary, are largely grouped by donor, and the donations are largely entered in a perceivable order. As a result, one can establish a list, in order, of the bequests made between 1290 and 1338. Such a list as we have seen must be constructed with caution; and one must exercise caution in interpreting what the list means, once it is drawn up. There are forty-five or forty-six[138] donors whose bequests were recorded after 1290. Twenty-two of these can be ranged in a definite order, relative to one another. The constancy of this order suggests that it was customary at the Sorbonne to catalog each bequest as it was received. However, there are four instances in which the bequests of neighboring donors are sometimes intermingled, suggesting that the bequests were received, or at least were recorded, at the same time — or, perhaps, that the process of cataloging Master A's bequest was not completed before Master B's bequest was received. In these instances, the names are listed in the order which predominates, and the interconnection is noted in parentheses. In addition to these twenty-two, there are twenty-three or -four others whose place in the order can be merely approximated, since their names do not appear in conjunction with enough other names to establish their position precisely. Included in this latter group are all "one-book donors;" one must be extremely cautious in attaching any chronological significance to these single appearances, because we know, on the basis of the larger bequests, that isolated manuscripts remained uncataloged for years, or even decades.[139]

After the 1290 catalog was completed, bequests from the following donors were recorded, in this order: John of Mitry; Lawrence of Quesnes; the "payment" (*ex debito*) of William Breton; Gerard of Auvergne (? two

---

[138] If Stephen of Burgundy (XXIII. 101) is identifiable with Stephen of Geneva (Delisle, II, 176), then there are forty-five.

[139] See above, note 70.

manuscripts only); Reginald of Soissons; Peter of Farbu; Godfrey of
Fontaines (d. 1306–09); Peter of Limoges (d. 1306) and John of Essonnes
(these two bequests overlap slightly); Bernier of Nivella (d. 1307–10);
Nicholas of Bar-le-Duc (d. 1310); William of Feuquières; Stephen of
Besançon; Stephenof Geneva (in secton XXIV. 78–104, the bequests of
the five donors Nivella, Bar-le-Duc, Feuquières, Besançon, Geneva, are
intermingled); Ralph of Périers (his bequest overlaps, and is occasionally
confused with, S. Geneva's; see VII. 24, XXXVIII. 22); Peter Crespin;
Bernard of Pailly (de Parliaco; d. 1324);[140] Peter of Cuissy; John of Rua
(presumably not the John of Rua who died before 1271 but a fourteenth-
century namesake, whose existence was postulated by Delisle, II, 161);
Giles du Theil of Ghent and John of Maroeuil (it is impossible to say
which of these two precedes the other); and Robert Bernard of Normandy.

For the following bequests, only an approximate indication of their
place in the order is possible: *Walter of Aulnay*, before J. Mitry (if not
before 1290); *Evrard of Dijon, Stephen of Auvergne* (once), *Peter of
Auvergne* (d. 1304), not as a sequence, before G. Fontaines; *Giles of
Maintenay*, before P. Limoges; *Philip of Tours* (once) between L. Quesnes
and G. Fontaines; *Simon of Melta* (once), between P. Limoges and B.
Nivella; *Nicaise of Plank* (d. 1307?),[141] between P. Limoges and W.
Feuquières; *William* (?) *Graitepanthere* (once), between S. Geneva and
R. Périers; *Guy Breton* (once), between S. Geneva and P. Crespin;
Thomas Hibernicus (d. post 1316), between S. Geneva and J. Rua; in
sequence, *Simon of Velli* (once), *Simon of Furnes, Peter of St. Omer* and
Stephen of Burgundy (= Stephen of Geneva?) (once), between S. Geneva
and T. Hibernicus; in sequence, the master of *Orchaneteriis* (?), (once)
and *William Patemoysi* (once), between P. Crespin and J. Maroeuil;
William Epulcre of Normandy, between T. Hibernicus and J. Maroeuil;
Renier of Cologne (once), between G. du T. of Ghent and R. Bernard;
Raymond Lull (once, a gift ca. 1311), after P. Limoges; *Philip of Dunois*
(once), after P. Limoges; *James of Marli*, after S. Geneva; *Clarin of
Saulieu*, after T. Hibernicus; *William Amidouz* (d. post 1331) (once),
after G. du T. of Ghent. The two volumes (I. 55, between W. Patemoysi
and J. Maroeuil; XXII. 38, between B. Nivella and S. Geneva) given by
Firmin Deutart of Abbeville (d. post 1331), were evidently gifts made
during his lifetime. Lastly, if the "R. de Remis" recorded as the donor

---

[140]Glorieux, I, 297.

[141]Nicaise of Plank appears in the obituary for 13 June which, by a decision made in
1307, is the date for the commemoration in common of minor benefactors. It is probable
that the names enrolled in the initial entry represent bequests received only shortly before
the decision was taken; in addition to Plank, the date of ca. 1307 would thus apply to Giles
Dambries, Robert Lebort and Vincent of Molières. See Glorieux, I, 167.

for XLIII. 102 is a copyist's error for "G. de Remis," then one should add to the list of post–1290 bequests that of *Roger of Rheims*, between W. Feuquières and R. Périers. For some thirty-five of these post–1290 donors, in sum, the 1338 catalog provides more precise dates than we have from other sources. In addition to a *terminus ante quem* of 1338, it provides a *terminus a quo* of 1290; and because the names of the donors can be arranged in a presumably chronological order which contains occasional fixed dates, the catalog provides a relative indication of the dating of the individual bequests which fall within the boundaries 1290–1338.

The first century of the Sorbonne's existence witnessed a vital and recurrent effort on the part of the community of masters to care for the library and make it serve their specific and changing needs. The library created in these years was, thus, very much a product and a reflection of the unique intellectual environment it served. For this reason we could not, for example, expect to find such changes occurring in the library of the thirteenth-century monastery, where the purpose of study, determined by the purpose of monastic life itself, was ideally a continuous and unending search for God. Monastic study was to a much greater degree based on contemplation and meditation and focused upon the scriptures and the patristic commentators. A formal library and complex catalogs were not necessary to serve the needs of this community. These needs were essentially satisfied when the prior distributed the books of the house to the individual monks for the coming year, during the first week in Lent.[142]

Study in the thirteenth- and early fourteenth-century university placed an entirely different demand on the books of an institution.[143] It rested upon careful use of an extensive body of authority, for the purpose of arriving at answers to a large number of specific questions. This method of study demanded books not only of a variety of authors but also in multiple copies; and it required guides to these books and their contents. As the century progressed, the body of authority expanded considerably with the influx of translations from Greek and Arabic and with the flood of writings of the modern doctors produced by the new orders and by

---

[142] See Anscari Mundo, " 'Bibliotheca,' Bible et Lecture du Carême d'après Saint Benoît," *Revue bénédictine* 60 (1950) 65–92, and Karl Christ, "In Caput Quadragesimae," *Zentralblatt für Bibliothekswesen* 60 (1943) 33–59.

[143] On this point see also Joseph de Ghellinck, "En marge des Catalogues des Bibliothèques médiévales," in *Miscellanea Francesco Ehrle*, V (Studi e Testi, 41) (Rome 1924) 331–363; idem, "Les Bibliothèques . . .," 43–47; Christ, 267–269; and C. H. Talbot, "The Universities and the Mediaeval Library," in *The English Library before 1700*, eds. Francis Wormald and C. E. Wright (London 1958) 66–84.

the universities. The procedure of study also changed, evolving from the literal reading of the page, to the formulation of questions and the separation of these from the text, and finally to the public disputation. Under the stimulus of the new Aristotle and the Arabic commentators, the topics of controversy multiplied. Virtually every matter was subjected to scrutiny, "called into question," or disputed before the students and masters. This increasingly aggressive use of an expanding body of authority which characterizes the full bloom of scholasticism at the university basically altered the nature of book usage.

It was essential that this growing body of authority be accessible to the late thirteenth-century master. It was no longer feasible for a library to consist of a few hundred codices of the scriptures, the fathers and the liberal arts which, when not in the hands of individual users, were locked away in chests. Nor could the catalog remain merely an inventory of possessions. This system would have to be supplanted by a library in which books were kept in some order for the use of the community of fellows. This need for access to the whole works of the fathers, which on the one hand produced alphabetical concordances to their works such as those of Robert Kilwardby, on the other hand also required that inventories of possessions be supplanted by shelf lists which were guides to the collections, and analytical catalogs which helped the master to find the specific item he needed. In light of the demands placed upon book collections by the methods of late thirteenth- and early fourteenth-century scholarship, it is not surprising to see the university as the source of innovation in the development of new techniques and tools for the care of books, such as those created at the Sorbonne between ca. 1275 and 1338.

APPENDIX
Two Leaves from the Sorbonne Catalog of ca. 1275

[ORIGINALIA AUGUSTINI]

(f. 324ra) [Augustini liber locutionum de genesi. Item responsiones quinque contra Pelagianos. Item epistola Augustini ad Hylarium episcopum. Item de psalmo xxii. Item de sermone domini in monte. Liber contra Iulianum hereticum. Item Augustinus contra Maximinum hereticum. Item ad Cresconium gramaticum et Donatistam. Item contra Donatistam de baptismo libri vii. Item Augustinus contra perfidiam Arrianorum. Item de solutione sex questionum contra paganos. Item de questionibus ueteris et noui testamenti. Item liber] / Augustini super questionibus *(sic)* euangeliorum. Item liber / ad Ieronimum presbyterum de sentencia Iacobi a/postoli qua dicit: *si totam quis legem seruauerit*. Item / liber Arrianorum. Item liber beati Augustini episcopi contra / sermonem Arrianorum. In uno uolumine. Incipit / in secundo folio sic: *appellantur unius*, et ultimo / sic: *cepit ex tempore*. Ex legato G. de Abbatis/uilla. Precium sexdecim librarum.

(1. B.N. MS. lat. 15289, s. xiii; second folio: *appellentur*. Analytical Cat., M.S. Y. m.; 1338 Cat. XXV. 1, *Cathenatus*; Delisle, III, 32, 94. The first half of the description is reconstructed from MS. 15289.)

Duodecim libri Augustini super genesim ad litteram. / Item de consensu euangelistarum libri quatuor. Item / questiones euangeliorum libri tres. Item de utilita / te credendi. Item de gracia noui testamenti. Item / de natura boni. Item de opere monachorum. Item / soliloquiorum duo libri. Item de uera religione. / Item de agone christiano. Item contra epistolam / Manichei contra fundamentum. Item contra / Adimantum liber unus. Item epistole Augustini Vi/tali episcopo, item Desiderabili episcopo, item Consensio / episcopo, Marcellino, Maximino, item Marcel/lino, Espidio, Bonefacio, Nebridio, Seuero, / Felicitati et Rustico, Maxime, Anastasio, Se/bastiano, Victoriano, Marciano, Probe, / Bonefacio, Armentario et Pauline, clero / et senioribus et plebi Yponensis ecclesie, Man/datensibus (i.e., Maudarensibus). Ad Bonefacinos. Item sermones de / uerbis domini. In uno uolumine. Incipit in secundo / folio sic: *create primitus*, et in penultimo sic: / *enim tria habet*. Precium sexdecim librarum.

2. B.N. MS. lat. 15288, s. xiii. (Analytical Cat., MS. T. c.; Delisle, III, 103.)

Augustinus de achademicis. Incipit in tercio folio / exclusis capitulis sic: *memento*, et in ultimo sic: / *lenis constans*. Ex legato
magistri G. de Abbatisuilla. / Precium quadraginta solidorum.
(3. 1338 Cat., XXXVII. 15; Delisle, III, 38, where the incipits of the
second and penultimate folios are given instead.)

Augustinus contra epistolam fundamenti. Item contra / Ada-
mantium Manichei discipulum. Item liber / soliloquiorum. Item
de disciplina christiana. Item de / uita christiana. Item de natura
et origine anime ad / Vincentium. Item de baptismo paruulorum.
Item / questiones de ueteri et nouo testamento. Item de corre/
ctione et moribus Donatistarum ad Vincentium / partis Donati.
Item de correctione Donatistarum ad / Bonefacium. Item de
decem cordis. Item de uita / beata. Item acta contra Fortunatum
Manicheum. / Item de duabus animabus contra Manicheos.
Item / de achademicis. Item de ordine. Item de gene- /

(f. 324rb) (*outer margin cut off*)
si ad litteram contra Manicheos. [De moribus Ma]/nicheorum.
Item contra mendacium [Item de cura pro] / mortuis agenda.
Item regula [Augustini ad cleri]/cos. Item sermo Augustini ad
penit[entes. Item] / de penitencia. Item sermo eiusdem d[e
pastoribus o]/uibus. Item sermo eiusdem de [ouibus. Item de] /
mendacio. Item de duodecim grad[ibus abusionis.] / Item de
conflictu uiciorum et u[irtutum. Item de] / paciencia. Item de
utilitate cre[dendi. Item de gra]/cia noui testamenti. Item de
ca[thezizandis ru]/dibus. Item de quantitate anime. It[em de
adulterinis] / coniugiis. Item ad Renatum de [natura et origine]
/ anime. Item ad Petrum presbyterum d[e eadem re. Item] / de
orando deo. Item de uidend[o deo. Item de fi]/de et operibus.
Item sub qua cautel[a Manichei de]/bent recipi. Item de
perfectione [iusticie hominis. In uno] / uolumine. Incipit in tercio
folio sic: [*Nec illaque ad*]/*huc sequitur*, et in ultimo sic: [*dicis
misericordia gloriari*.] / Ex legato magistri G. de Abbatis[uilla.
Precium*] / triginta librarum.
(4. B.N. MS. lat. 15302, s. xiii; f. 324 rb, 1. 5, the rubric of this work in
MS. 15302 reads *Incipit sermo de pastoribus ouibus*. Analytical Cat.,
MS. Y. 1.; Delisle, III, 94.)

Augustinus de trinitate quindecim li[bri. Item super ge]/nesim
ad litteram duodecim libri. [Item de predestina] / tione diuina.
Item de natura boni. I[tem de libero ar]/bitrio libri tres. Item de
questionib[us Orosii ad Augus]/tinum. Item de mirabilibus sacre
[scripture libri tres.] / Item [epistola P]rosperi ad Aug[ustinum

de querela] / Ga[llo]rum. Item epistola sancti Hylar[ii ad Augustinum.] / Item de predestinatione et perseueran[cia sanctorum libri duo.] / Item de unico baptismo. In [uno uolumine.] / Incipit in secundo folio sic: *uel prof[ere sed qua*, et in ul]/timo sic: *nulla igitur ratio*. Ex l[egato magistri G. de Abbatis]/uilla. Precium duodecim li[brarum].

(5. B.N. MS. lat. 15659, s. xiii. Analytical Cat., MS. T. b.; 1338 Cat., XXV. 20, *Cathenatus*; Delisle, III, 33, 93–94.)

Item Augustinus super genesim ad litteram. Ench[eridion. Liber retracta]/tionum. Incipiens in secundo folio: *rata* [et in penultimo:] / *Iacob*. Precium centum solidorum.

(6. Inserted in an early 14th century hand. B.N. MS. lat. 15654, s. xiv. 1338 Cat., XXV. 8; Delisle, III, 33.)

Augustini in encheridio[n. Item Augustinus de] / inuisibilibus. Item Augustinus de ba[ptismo paruulorum.] / Item sermo Augustini de paciencia. [Item Augustinus de per]/fectione iusticie. Item Augustinus d[e natura et gracia fe]/liciter. Item Augustini epistola ad[Valentinum mona]/chum. Item Augustinus de g[racia et libero arbitrio. Item] / Augustinus de correctione et gracia. [Item epistola Prosperi] / ad Augustinum. Item de doc[trina christiana.] / Item Augustini epistola ad Volu[sianum.]

(f. 324va) (*outer margin cut off*)
[Item Volusianus ad Au]gustinum. . . . . (erased). . . . . /
[. . . . .] . . . . (erased) . . . . /
[. . . (erased?) . . . . It]em responsio Augustini ad Volu/[sianum. Item] de symbolo. Item Augustinus de quatuor / [uirtutibus caritatis.] Item Augustinum de cantico / [nouo. Item Augustinus de qua]rta feria. Item de cathaclismo. / [Item de mo]rte contempnenda. Item de tempore / [barbarico. It]em de trinitate dicta. Item de fide / [catholica. Item] Augustinus de prouerbiis super mulierem / [fortem. It]em Augustinus contra Iudeos, paganos / [et Arrianos. Item] sermo Augustini de oratione et ieiunio. / [Item sermo Augusti]ni de diuite. Item sermo Augustini / [de penitencia.] Item sermo Augustini de oratione do/[minica. Item A]ugustinus de fornicatione. Item Augustinus / [de spiritu et littera.] Item epistola Augustini ad plebiscitas. / [Item epistola Possi]dio episcopo. Item epistola Augustini Aure/[lio. Item episto]la Augustini Paulino et Therasie. / [Item epistola Augustini Bon]efacio. Item Donato. Item / [Olympio. Item] Selentiane. Item fratribus Atensibus (i.e., Cirtensibus) / [. . . . . I]tem Florentine. Item Ytalice. / [Item Pommach]io. Item Proculiano.

Item Vale/[rio. Item D]onato episcopo. Item Cornelio. Item /
[questiones Orosii ad] Augustinum. Item de cathezizan/[dis
rudibus. Item] de predestinatione. Item omelie / [de penitencia.
Item ser]mo Augustini quomodo factus est homo / [ad ymaginem
et similitud]inem dei. Item [admonitio / Augustini ut li]ngua et
moribus et operi[bus laudetur deus. / Item de dis]ciplina
christiana. Item Augustini / [liber diuersorum] questionum. Item
Augustini expositio / [quarundam propo]sitionum in epistola
ad Romanos. / [Item expositio] in epistola ad Galathas. Item /
[speculum Augustini.] Item Augustinus de bono coniugali. /
[Item Augustinus de uirginitate.] Hec omnia in uno uo / [lumine.
Incipit in secu]ndo folio sic: *cum ergo queritur*, et in ul/[timo
sic: *omnia peccata*.] Precium decem et septem librarum. / [In
hoc libr]o subtracta est unus quaternus de / [fine tercii et de
pri]ncipio quarti in libro de doctrina / [christiana.]

(7. B.N. MS. lat. 15657, s. xiii. Analytical Cat., MS. Y. g.; 1338 Cat.,
XXV. 7 [*Cathenatus*]; Delisle, III, 33, 95. The last note in the description, "In hoc libro . . . christiana," is completed from a similar note
which is added to the end of the table of contents in MS. 15657. The
text is actually complete; the confusion stems from an error in the
rubrication of the manuscript.)

[Cronica Augustini. I]ncipit in secundo folio exclusis / [. . . . . ?
capituli]s sic: *cis consultationibus*, et / [in penultimo sic: *pro*]
phanauit quod postea. / [Ex legato magistri] G. de Abbatisuilla.
Precium / [quinquaginta so]lidorum.

(8. B.N. MS. lat. 16551, s. xii. 1338 Cat., XL. 1; Delisle, III, 43. The
second folio reference is that of the second leaf of the text in this manuscript. It is preceded by a brief prologue, list of chapters and three
blank pages. The text lacks the opening lines of c. 1 and begins . . .
*tres apud iudeam extitisse reges quorum unus quisque uocatus est
Herodes*.)

(f. 324vb) [Epistola sancti] Augustini ad Eusebium. Ad Seue/rinum. Ad
Donatistas. Ad Ianuarium prime sedis / Donati. Ad Crispinum.
Ad Crispinianum scismaticum. / Ad Pascentium comitem Ar-
rianum. Item ad eun/dem Pascentium Arrianum. Item rescriptum
Pas/centii ad Augustinum. Item ad eundem Pascen/tium
comitem. Item ad Probam et Iulianam / de conuersione
Demetriadis. Item ad Honorat/um. Item ad Ytalicam. Ad
Bonefacium. Bo/nefacii ad Augustinum. Augustinus ad
Bonefacium. / Item Augustinus ad eundem. Item Bonefacii ad
Au/gustinum. Item Augustinus ad Bonefacium. Item Bo/nefacius

ad Augustinum. Item Augustinus ad eundem. / Item Bonifacius
ad Augustinum. Item Augustinus ad / Bonefacium. Item
Bonefacius ad Augustinum. Item Augustinus / ad Bonefacium.
Item Bonefacius ad Augustinum. / Item Augustinus ad
Bonefacium. Item Bonefacius ad Augustinum. / Item Augustinus
ad Fortunatianum Arrianum. Idem ad Edi/ciam. Ad Assellicum.
Ad Paulinum. Ad Bonefacium. / Item gesta Augustini quando
successorem sibi elegit. Item / Augustinus ad Paulinam. Ad
Optatum. Ad Ianuarium / due epistolas. Item Macedonii ad
Augustinum. Item / Augustini ad Macedonium. Item Macedonii
ad / Augustinum. Item Augustinus ad Bonefacium. Augustinus
ad Vin/centium. Augustinus ad Bonefacium. Item Discori ad
Augustinum. / Augustinus ad Discorum. Augustinus ad
Dardanum. Pau/lini ad Augustinum. Augustini ad Paulinum.
Necta/rii ad Augustinum. Augustinus ad Nectarium. Item ad
Ma/ximum Donatistam. Item ad Donatum. Ad Euo/dium. Ad
Probam. Ad Aulerium episcopum de uitan/dis conuiuis. Ad
Aulerium de monachis. Ad se/nem Alipium. Ad Eudoxium
abbatem. Ad Cele/stinum dyaconum. Ad Restitutum dyaconum.
Ad / Largum de ammonitione bonorum. Ad Bonefaci/um
comitem de exhortatione uite eterne. Ad / Crisinum. Item Alipii
et Augustini ad Peregrinum episcopum. / Augustinus ad Maxi-
mum episcopum medicum. Ad Esicium / de fine seculi. Esicii
ad Augustinum. Item Augustini ad / Esicium. Augustinus ad
Deutherium. Euodius ad / Augustinum. Item Euodii ad
Augustinum. Item Euodii ad Au/gustinum. Item Augustinus ad
Euodium. Item / eiusdem ad eundem. Item Consencii ad
Augustinum. / Item Augustinus ad Consencium. Ad Sixtum
Roma/ne urbis presbyterum. Item ad Sixtum presbyterum. Ad
/ Celestinum. Ad Gayum. Ad [Hermogenianum.]/
*(Bottom of the column; the remainder of the description is recon-
structed from B.N. MS. lat. 15655.)*
[Ad Romanianum. Ad Felicitatem et Rusticum de correptione.
Ad Tenobium. Item Nebridius ad Augustinum. Item ad eundem.
Item Augustinus ad Nebridium. Item Nebridius ad Augustinum.
Item Augustinus ad Nebridium. Item ad eundem. Item ad
eundem. Item ad eundem. Item Quoduultdeus dyaconus ad
Augustinum. Item Augustinus ad Quoduultdeum dyaconem. Item
Quoduultdeus ad Augustinum. Rescriptum Augustinus ad
eundem. Item Augustinus ad plebiscitas. Ad Possidium
episcopum. Ad Bonefacium episcopum. Ad Donatum. Ad
Olympium. Ad fratres Cirtentes. Ad Florentinam. Ad Ytalicam.

Ad Pommachium. Item ad Proculianum. Ad Valetium episcopum.
Ad Donatum episcopum. Ad Cornelium. Item Augustinus contra
Faustum Manicheum libri xxxiii. Item liber eiusdem de natura
et gracia. Item de gracia et libero arbitrio ad Valentinum. Item
Augustinus de correctione et gracia. Item de heresibus ad
Quoduultdeum. Item liber ypnosticon. Item sermo eiusdem de
oratione et ieiunio. Item contra Maximum hereticum libri duo.
Item sermo eiusdem quomodo factus est homo ad ymaginem et
similitudinem dei. Item liber eiusdem ad Ieronimum de origine
anime, et in fine ponitur rescriptio Ieronimi ad Augustinum.
Item de diuinatione demonum. Item de sancta uirginitate. Item
de perfectione sancte uiduitatis. Item de paciencia. Item de
elemosina. In uno uolumine. Incipit in secundo folio sic:
dominabitur gentium, et in penultimo folio sic: *post hec dicens*.
Ex legato magistri G. de Abbatisuilla. Precium uiginti librarum.]
(9. B.N. MS. lat. 15655, s. xiii. Analytical Cat., MS. Y. e.; Delisle, III,
94.)

[ORIGINALIA MIXTA SANCTORUM]

(f. 323ra) (*top of leaf missing*)
[Alcuinus de trinitate. Item questiones Albini de sancte / trinitate. Albini de ratione anime. Item Albinus de] / pro[prietate
quorundam nominum deo conuenientium.] / Questions Orosii
[ad Au]gustinum. Item sermones [Am]bro/sii pertinentes ad
[sac]ramenta. Item liber [qui dicitur] specu/lum paruulorum.
Item sentencia Iero[nimi de immensi]tate / dei. Item liber eiusdem
de tribus n[aturis anime, rati]one, / uoluntate, et appetitu. Item
[liber Marti]ni de for / mula uite honeste. Item exp[ositio de
psalmo il]lo: *Eru/ctauit cor meum uerbum bonum*. [Item de
prep]utio et / circumcisione. Item expositio ill[ius psalmi pri]mi:
Beatus uir / qui non abiit. Item expositio illius uerbi de canticis
/ canticorum: *Si ignoras te, o pulcherrima inter mu/lieres*. Item
expositio uerbi: *Equitatui meo in cur/ribus pharaonis*. Item de
laude iusti super uerbo illo / regum i.: *Fuit uir unus de*. Item de
uerbo illo can/ticorum: *Egredimi et uidete, etc.* item encheridi/on
Augustini. Item Augustinus de fide rerum inuisibilium. Item /
Augustinus contra quinque hereses. Item duo sermones / eiusdem.
Item liber Gennadii de ecclesiasticis dog/matibus. In uno
uolumine. Incipit in secundo folio / sic: *quomodo intelligenda
sint*, et in ultimo sic: *superius / placi confessione*. Ex legato
magistri G. de Ab/batisuilla. Precium quadraginta solidorum.

(10. This entry is lined through in red and rewritten on f. 323^{va-b}, no. 16 below. B.N. MS. lat. 16362, s. xiii. Analytical Cat., MS. T. r.; Delisle, III, 97. The final work, Gennadius' *De ecclesiasticis dogmatibus*, no longer appears in this codex, making it impossible to verify the beginning of the last folio.)

Excerptiones ex libris uiginti trium auctorum / et tabula et sentencie originalium. In uno uolumine. / Incipit in secundo folio sic: *isti me quando*, et in ultimo / folio sic: *uita salus homo*. Ex legato G. de Abbatis/uilla. Precium octo librarum.

(11. This entry is lined through in red and rewritten on f. 323vb, no. 17 below. B.N. MS. lat. 15983, s. xiii; last folio: *uita salus honor*. Analytical Cat., MS. S. e.; Delisle, III, 105.)

Excerpta de epistolis Ieronimi, Augustini et Gregorii. / In uno uolumine. Incipit in secundo folio sic: *que gloria / est*, et in ante penultimum sic: *studio quam infor*[. . .]. / Ex legato G. de Abbatisuilla. Precium sex solidorum.

(12. This entry is lined through in red. The manuscript described here has not been identified, but it is the codex described in 1338 Cat., XXXIX. 10; Delisle, III, 42. Since the beginning of the second folio references do not agree, one or the other must be taken from another folio, as is the case in no. 15 below.)

Anselmus de similitudinibus. Item cur deus homo est. / Item de ueritate. Item de casu diaboli. Item de azi/mo. Item de incarnatione uerbi. Item de concordia / predestinationis et presciencie. Item de gracia et libero / arbitrio. Item prosologion. Item de processione / spiritus sancti.

(13. This description is incomplete and lined through in red. B.N. MS. lat. 15686, s. xiii, Robert de Sorbon. 1338 Cat., XXXVII. 1, Delisle, III, 37, where the description continues as follows: Augustinus de predestinacione sanctorum, Damascenus de ineffabilitate Dei, Bernardus de concepcione Virginis, meditaciones Bernardi, Augustinus de spiritu et anima, idem encheridon, idem de ciuitate Dei libri xii extracti, idem de natura et origine anime libri duo, ex legato magistri Roberti de Sorbona. Incipit in 2° fol. *deliciosi*, in pen. *imperasti*. Precium VIII l.)

(f. 323rb) (*top of leaf and outer margin cut off*)

[. . . . . /

[. . . . . /

[. . . . . Hyldeberti Tu]/

ronensis archiepiscopi de . . . .

[. . . . .] / Hyldeberti episcopi de uita sancte Marie [Egyptiace]
/ et de passione sancti Laurentii martyris [et] / sancti Vincentii
martyris. Item liber [de la] / pidibus. Item de uestibus ecclesie.
I[tem e]/pistolarum sed(ecem?). In uno uolumin[e. Incipit in] /
secundo folio sic:. . . . . . et in [ultimo sic:] / *referet . . . .*
culcior (?). Precium sex [. . . . .]

(14. This entry is lined through in red. The manuscript described here
has not been identified. A similar collection of works is seen in
Montpellier, Fac. Méd., MS. 294, s. xii-xiii, Clairvaux. The remainder
of the column is blank.)

(f. 323va) (*top of leaf and outer margin cut off*)
[Iohannes Damascenus. Item Anselmus cur deus homo. Item /
moralitates breues super bibliam. Augustinus confessionum liber
/ abbreuiatus. Item Augustinus de operibus sex dierum extractas.
/ Excerpta] de libro Augustini de decem cordis. Augustinus /
[de ciuitate d]ei primi libri extractiones. Item / [de libro de
trinitate e]xtractiones libri primi, secundi, tercii, / [quarti, quinti,
s]exti, septimi, octaui, noni, deci/[mi, undecim]i, duodecimi,
terciidecimi, quarti / [decimi, quindecimi. Item] de bono
coniugali. De actis For/[tunati Manichei]. Ad Volusianum. De
diuinatione / [demonum. De] octoginta tribus questionibus. De
singula/[ritate clericorum]. De mendacio. Item Augustinus de
a/[nima et spiritu] et quedam sumpta de libro Augustini / [de
paciencia et prim]us de libero arbitrio et secundus et tercius. /
[Item Ieronimus] ad Eustochium. Item de natura / [boni. Item
Augustinus] ad Petrum diaconum de ue/[ra fide regula] et eiusdem
ad Ieronimum presbyterum de ori/[gine anime et rescriptum]
eiusdem. De orando deo ad Probam. / [Epistola Augustini] ad
Paruulum de fide et de corpore / [Christi. Item epistola eius]dem
ad Consencium, et eiusdem ad / [Publicolam et] ad Elpidium et
ad Bonefacium et / [ad Nebridium et ad Felicitatem] et ad
Anastasium. Item Boetius / [de trinitate]. Item moralium dogma
philosophorum. / [Item secundus philosoph]us. In uno uolumine.
Incipit in / [secundo folio exc]luso quodam prologo sic; *altero* /
[*in finite uero,* et i]n ultimo sic: *non multis necessitas.* / [Precium
o]cto librarum.

(15. B.N. MS. lat. 15829, s. xiii. 1338 Cat., XXXVII. 24, Delisle, III, 39,
where the description is abbreviated; the identification is positive since
the incipit "in secundo folio" is that of f. 23, and the incipit of the last
folio is that of f. 181. The works "De bono coniugali" through "De
mendacio" are missing from MS. 15829 and were perhaps lost before

1338, since they do not appear in the description of this manuscript in the 1338 catalog.)

[Alcuinus d]e trinitate. Item questiones Albini de / [sancte trinitate.] Albini de ratione anime. Item Albinus / [de proprietate quo]rundam nominum deo conuenientium. [Questiones] Orosii ad Augustinum. Item sermones / [Ambrosii perti]nentes ad sacramenta. Item liber / [qui dicitur] speculum paruulorum. Item sentencia / [Ieronimi de immensit]ate dei. Item liber eiusdem / [de tribus naturis anime,] ratione, uoluntate, et appeti/[tu. Item liber] Martini de formula uite ho/[neste. Item] expositio de psalmo illo: *Eructauit* / [*cor meum uerbu]m bonum*. Item de preputio et cir/[cumcisione. I]tem expositio illius psalmi primi: *Beatus* / [*uir qui non abiit.*] Expositio illius uerbi de canticis canticorum: / [*Si ignoras t]e, o pulcherrima inter mulieres*. Item / [expositio uerbi:] *Equitatui meo in curribus pha/[raonis*. Item] de laude iusti uerbo illo re- /

(f. 323vb) (*top of leaf cut off*)

[gum primo: *Fuit uir unus de*. Item de uerbo illo / canticorum: *Egredimini et uidete, etc.* Item encheridion / Augustini. Item Augustinus de fide rerum inuisibilium.] / Item [Augustinus] contra quinque he[reses]. Item duo ser/mones [eius]dem. Item liber Gennadii de ec / clesiast[icis dogm]atibus. In uno uolumine. Incipit / in se[cundo folio s]ic: *quomodo intelligenda sint*, et in / ultimo s[ic: *superius p]laci confessione*. Ex legato / magistri [G. de A]bbatisuilla. Precium quadraginta solidorum.

(16. This entry is rewritten from f. 323ra, no. 10 above.)

Excerp[tiones] ex libris uiginti trium auctorum / et tabula et sentencie originalium. In uno / uolumine. Incipit in secundo folio sic: *isti me quando*, / et in ultimo folio sic: *uita salus homo*. Ex legato / magistri G. de Abbatisuilla. Precium octo librarum.

(17. This entry is rewritten from f. 323ra, no. 11 above. Printed, Delisle, II, 180–181.)

Originalia decem, uidelicet Richardus de contem/platione, Hugo de archa Noe. Hugo de in/stitutione nouiciorum, encheridion Augusti/ni, Boetius de trinitate, Richardus de trini/tate, Augustinus super genesim ad litteram, Augustinus de tri/nitate, Ysidorus de summo bono, de differencia / diuine theologie atque mundane. In uno uo/lumine. Incipit in tercio folio sic: *dus quam totus*, / et in ultimo folio sic: *nouitatem*. Ex legato G. de / Abbatisuilla. Precium sex librarum.

(18. B.N. MS. lat. 15734, s. xiii. 1338 Cat., XXXVII. 6, Delisle, III, 37–38. Printed, Delisle, II, 181).

Richardi expositio supra (*sic*) apocalipsim. Idem de con/templatione. Item Ieronimus de homine perfecto. In uno / uolumine. Incipit in tercio folio sic: *uermis ergo*, / et in ultimo folio sic: *putamus*. Ex legato G. de Abbatis/uilla. Precium quinquaginta solidorum.

(19. B.N. MS. lat. 16380, s. xiii. Analytical Cat., MS. Q. t.; 1338 Cat. XXXVII. 2, *Cathenatus*; Delisle, III, 37, 103–104. Printed, Delisle, II, 181.)

Damascenus. Item Augustinus de fide ad Petrum. Item / liber Augustini de catholica fide, qui liber uoca/tur speculum uel manuale. Item de anima et spiritu. / Item Anselmus de concordia liberi arbitrii. Item / Anselmus de gracia et libero arbitrio. Item Anselmus / de azimo. Item Anselmus de peccato originali. Item / eiusdem de libero arbitrio. Item Anselmus de uerita/te. Item Anselmus de casu dyaboli. Item cur deus / homo. Item Anselmus de processione spiritus sancti. Item / monolog[ion]. Item prosologion. Item Anselmus de / [incarnatione] uerbi. Item Augustinus de immortalitate /
(*Bottom of the column; the remainder of the entry is recon-structed from B.N. MS. lat. 16359 and its description in the 1338 catalog.*)
[anime. Idem de diffinitionibus ecclesiasticorum dogmatum. Boetius de trinitate, epistola eiusdem utrum pater et filius et spiritus sanctus de deitate substancialiter predicentur, eiusdem breuis fidei christiane completio, eiusdem de persona et natura. Dissuasio Valerii ad Rufinum ne ducat uxorem. Incipit in secundo folio sic: *aliquo creatus*, et in penultimo sic: *cas aliam*. Precium decem librarum.]

(20. B.N. MS. lat. 16359, s. xiii. 1338 Cat., XXXVII. 11, Delisle, III, 38. Printed, Delisle, II, 181. The Boethian works listed between the *De trinitate* and the *Dissuasio Valerii* no longer appear in the manuscript.)

10. The Franciscans and Books: Lollard Accusations and the Franciscan Response[1]

The Middle Ages provide us with a number of theoretical statements about the value of books and libraries to learning and society. They range from brief proverbs — 'A monastery without books is like a castle without soldiers' — to full-length treatises such as Richard de Bury's *Philobiblon*. What we want to examine here is a series of statements regarding the practical value of access to books and libraries that form part of the litany of criticism aimed at the friars at the end of the fourteenth century, and the formal response of the Oxford Franciscans to these.

A number of Wycliffite texts contain a statement saying that the friars gather books and shut them up in their libraries, prohibiting others from having access to them and thus preventing secular clerks from preaching the word of God.[2] It should be understood at the outset that none of the tracts is focused on the matter of the availability of books. Instead, these remarks in each case are a minor part in an extended catalog of accusation against the mendicant orders.[3] Therefore, the ques-

Originally published in *From Ockham to Wyclif*, ed. A. Hudson and M. Wilks, Studies in Church History: Subsidia 5 (Oxford 1987) 369–384.

[1] We are grateful to Dr. Anne Hudson for suggesting this topic and for supplying us with references to many of the texts discussed, in addition to helpful suggestions at various stages.

[2] Curiously, no one, to our knowledge, has commented on these passages and the issue with which they deal.

[3] Regarding criticism of the friars, see H. Lippens, "Le droit nouveau des mendiants en conflit avec le droit coutumier du clergé seculier," *Archivum franciscanum historicum* 47 (1954) 241–292; L. Hammerich, *The Beginnings of the Strife Between Richard Fitzralph and the Mendicants* (Copenhagen 1938); C. Erikson, "The Fourteenth-Century Franciscans

tion immediately occurs, do the comments about books and libraries reflect a real grievance in a real place and time, or are they merely a *topos*, one more way to illustrate the basic duplicity of the friars, in being covetous and greedy instead of charitable with their books? So far, to the degree that these remarks have been considered at all, they have been taken as the latter. We should like to suggest instead that they describe an immediate situation in late fourteenth-century Oxford, and to consider why this complaint arose and to what extent it was justified.

The six treatises from which we quote are *Jack Upland, Fifty Heresies and Errors of the Friars, How Religious Men Should Keep Certain Articles* (i.e., rules), *Of Clerks Possessioners, Floretum,* and the *Opus Arduum*. As usual with Wycliffite texts they are anonymous, but they were probably all written between the condemnations of 1382 and the end of the century, the majority of them at Oxford. And again as usual, the number of surviving copies is not a reliable indication of their contemporary circulation. Three—*Fifty Heresies, Religious Men,* and *Clerks Possessioners*—survive in collections of Wycliffite materials: Cambridge Corpus Christi College 296 (X) and Dublin Trinity College 244 (C III 12) (AA), of the late fourteenth or early fifteenth century, while a third copy of *Fifty Heresies* (without the other two) appears in a third collection of a similar date, Oxford Bodleian Library Bodl. 647. *Jack Upland* survives in two late copies, London B. L. Harley 6641 (s. xv) and Cambridge University Library Ff. 6.2 (s. xvi in.), and the *Floretum* is known in five English manuscripts and several reduced or conflated versions. The *Opus Arduum* survives only in Central European manuscripts.

In the 1380s or 1390s a set of sixty-five Latin *quaestiones* severely critical of the friars circulated in England (again, probably originating in Oxford). It contained one *quaestio* devoted to books and libraries, and this work may account for the verbal similarities in our excerpts. Although it no longer survives, we come closest to it in the English enlargement called *Jack Upland*: 'Friar, what charity is it to gather up the books of God's word, many more than you need, and place them in your treasure room, and thus imprison them from secular clerks and curates, so that they are prevented from knowing God's word and from preaching the Gospel freely?'[4]

---

and Their Critics," *Franciscan Studies* 35 (1975) 107–135, 36 (1976) 108–147; and A. Gwynn, "Archbishop FitzRalph and the Friars," *Studies: An Irish Quarterly Review* 26 (1937) 50–67.

   [4]'Frere, what charite is it to gadere up þe bokis of Goddis lawe, many mo þanne nediþ ȝou, and putte hem in tresorie, and do prisone hem fro seculer preestis and curatis, wher bi þei ben lettid of kunnynge of Goddis lawe to preche þe gospel freli?' P. L. Heyworth,

In the Wycliffite *Fifty Heresies and Errors of the Friars*, which is early and may date from 1384, we find the following 'error' in chapter 42: 'Friars . . . rob curates of their offices . . . and prevent them from knowing God's word, by keeping books from them and by withholding from them the advantage of having books and learning.'[5]

The criticism appears again in the anonymous and undated *How Religious Men (i.e., regular clerics) Should Keep Certain Articles*. 'Article 17: That they should not withdraw noble books of Holy Writ and the holy doctors and other useful subjects from curates and clerks into their own cloisters, which are like the castles or palaces of kings and emperors, and permit them to be shut up there and rot, and neither give them nor lend them nor sell them to curates and clerks who might, could, and would learn Holy Writ and teach it freely for the love of men's souls.'[6]

The Franciscans and other friars were not the only villains, of course. The author of the anonymous *Of Clerks Possessioners*, as the title implies, is attacking the monks when he says, 'These possessioners are thieves, and destroyers of the clergy and of godly life in the people, because they have many books, especially of Holy Writ — some got by begging, and some by gifts and bequests, and some by other forms of cunning and deception — and hide them away from secular clerks, letting these noble books rot in their libraries. And they will neither sell them nor lend them to other clerks who would profit from studying them, and would teach Christian people the way to heaven.' But the author has saved his heaviest guns for the usual target; he goes on to say, 'In this fault, the mendicant orders are the principal thieves and heralds of Antichrist, so that seculars and curates can scarcely obtain any book of value. And in so doing — as Saint Richard primate of Ireland testifies — they seek to destroy the secular clergy and the true teaching of the people. Lord! Since these books are more necessary to man's godly life than gold or silver — and since a person is out of charity who can see his brother in need of worldly sustenance and fail to help when he easily could — how much more are these regular clerics out of charity, who do

---

ed., *Jack Upland, Friar Daw's Reply and Upland's Rejoinder* (London 1968) 70, lines 373–6. Heyworth (135–136) considered this comment to be in the nature of a general topos; he was unaware of its relation to Woodford's *Responsiones* described below.

   [5] 'Freris . . . robben curatis of hor offis and gostly worschip, and letten hom to knowe Gods lawe, by holdynge bokis fro hom, and wiþ drawinge of hor vauntages, by whoche þei schulden have bokes and lerne.' Edited by T. Arnold, *Select English Works of Wyclif* (Oxford 1869–71) 3.396–7; Arnold's suggested date (p. 338) should be regarded with caution.

   [6] F. D. Matthew, ed., *English Works of Wyclif Hitherto Unprinted*, Early English Text Society 74, rev. ed. (London 1902) p. 221/25–32.

not help secular clerks and curates to obtain these books, neither by gift nor by lending nor by selling for any amount of money.'[7]

The verbal parallels between this and the preceding excerpt (from *Religious Men*) are obviously close—the image of noble books shut up to rot, and the rhythmic 'neither give nor lend nor sell'—though we cannot say which came first, nor whether instead they derive separately from a common source.

The prologue to the *Floretum*, the great Wycliffite florilegium compiled between 1384 and 1396, rings the same chimes: 'Books filled with truth are manifold, but they have been imprisoned and chained up by the private religious in their communities . . . to such a point that poor clerks, . . . prevented from buying books by lack of money, . . . fear to take on the task of preaching.'[8]

The final excerpt, from the *Opus Arduum*, which was written between Christmas 1389 and Easter 1390, is especially interesting because it mentions specific books and places. The angle of attack is different from that of the previous excerpts: '[Friars think to defend themselves] by making off with the books of those who write against the friars' abuses, such as William of St. Amour, whose books are kept under lock and key at Oxford and at Salisbury, and also by making off with the books of William of Ockham against the Roman pope, and the books of brother John of Rupescissa, of brother Peter John Olivi on the Apocalypse, and other such.'[9] The alleged motive differs—censorship and coverup—but the accusation is the same: friars hide books.

The Wycliffites drew much of their material on various topics from Richard FitzRalph's anti-mendicant writings, as the reference to 'saint' Richard in the excerpt from *Clerks Possessioners* reminds us. The initial inspiration for attacking the book practices of the friars clearly comes

---

[7] Ibid., pp. 128/16–129/2.

[8] Regarding the *Floretum* and its Middle English translation see A. Hudson, "A Lollard Compilation and the Dissemination of Wycliffite Thought," *Journal of Theological Studies* ns. 23 (1972) 65–81; idem. "A Lollard Compilation in England and Bohemia," *Journal of Theological Studies* ns. 25 (1974) 129–140; and C. von Nolcken, *The Middle English Translation of the Rosarium Theologie* (Heidelberg 1979) 9–13. For the Latin text, see n. 30 below.

[9] '. . . per absconsionem librorum scriptorum contra abusiones suas et aliorum ecclesiasticorum, utpote Wilhelmi [Wiclef: MS] de Sancto Amore, cuius libri multis seris et vectibus clauduntur Oxonie et Sarum, necnon per absconsionem librorum Wilhelmi Occam contra papam Romanμm, fratris Johannis de Ripsissa, fratris Petri Johannis super Apokalipsim et talium'; unpublished. This transcription, from Brno U. L. MS Mk 28 fol. 174ᵛ, was provided by Dr. Anne Hudson. Regarding the *Opus arduum*, see A. Hudson, "A Neglected Wycliffite Text," *Journal of Ecclesiastical History* 29 (1978) 257–259.

from FitzRalph.[10] FitzRalph was already castigating the friars for their fine books in his London sermons early in 1357. In a sermon preached on 12 March at St. Paul's Cross, he said of the friars that 'they have more books, and finer books, than any prelate or doctor.'[11] This thought was embellished in his *Defensio Curatorum*, which was preached before pope and curia at Avignon the following November:

> There is another injury equally serious, which tends to destroy or take away the learning of the seculars of every faculty: namely, that these mendicant orders, because of the endless gains they have acquired by means of the aforementioned privileges of burial rights and of hearing confessions and other things, are so much increased in numbers of convents and of convent personnel that, in the common studies of the faculty of arts, of sacred theology, and of canon law—or even (as many report) of the faculty of medicine or of civil law—one can scarcely find any useful book for sale; for they have all been bought up by the friars, so that every convent has a large and noble library, and every friar with standing in the *studia* (and such people are countless nowadays) has a noble library. Thus, I sent three or four of my rectors to the schools, and I was told that they were unable to find there any usable Bible nor other books of theology suitable for them and so they returned home—or at least one of their number has already returned. Now: if this be not regarded as a great injury to the clergy, then nothing can be.[12]

---

[10] Regarding FitzRalph see K. Walsh, *A Fourteenth-Century Scholar and Primate: Richard FitzRalph in Oxford, Avignon and Armagh* (Oxford 1981) and the bibliography cited there, in particular (p. xv) those of Aubrey Gwynn, S.J., in *Proceedings of the Royal Irish Academy* 44C (1937) 1–57 and in *Studies . . .* in the 1930s.

[11] Cited from Gwynn, *Studies* 26 (1937) 59; noted by Erikson, 36 (1976) 114.

[12] 'Item aliud damnum tam graue, quod tendit ad consumptionem seu euacuationem doctrine in secularibus cuiuslibet facultatis est quod isti ordines mendicantium propter infinita lucra que mendiantibus predictis priuilegiis de sepulturis & confessionibus & aliis que acquirunt tantum multiplicati sunt in conuentibus & personis conuentuum quod non reperitur in studiis communibus de facultate artium, sacre theologie, & iuris canonici, aut etiam (ut fertur a pluribus) de facultate medicine aut de facultate iuris ciuilis (nisi raro) aliquis utilis multum liber uenalis: sed omnes emuntur a fratribus: ita ut in singulis conuentibus sit una grandis ac nobilis libraria, & singuli fratres habentes statum in studiis, quales sunt modo innumeri, nobilem habeant librariam. Vnde etiam de meis subiectis rectoribus tres aut quattuor misi ad studium: & dictum est michi quod nec bibliam eis utilem, nec libros alios theologie uenales eis congruos ibi poterant reperire, & ad suam patriam sunt reuersi, aut unus eorum saltem rediit iam. Si ista non sit in clero grandis iactura, nulla poterit in ipso esse.' Cited from Proctor 8811 (Rouen: Guillaume Talleur, n.d.) and Proctor 8611 (Lyon: Johann Trechsel, 1496). There is no earlier version of this passage in FitzRalph's *Propositio unusquisque* given on 5 July 1350 (edited by Hammerich, op. cit., p. 53ff.). One might wonder what FitzRalph's former patron Richard de Bury

FitzRalph's *Defensio* circulated widely; eighty-four manuscripts were known to his most recent biographer.[13] In addition, the work was translated into Middle English by John Trevisa. The influence of FitzRalph's argument is apparent in most of the Wycliffite excerpts, beginning of course with his choice of the topic itself, lack of books, as grounds for complaint against the friars. In particular, FitzRalph's phrase about loss of learning is echoed repeatedly in charges of 'prevention' or 'withholding' of learning.

More interesting than the similarities are the differences to be found in the Wycliffite framing of the problem. FitzRalph's statement that all useful books have been acquired by the friars was reshaped somewhat, to become the Wycliffite accusation that friars gathered up more books than they could possibly have a use for—*many mo þanne nediþ ȝou as Jack Upland* says, an idea implicit in the accusation that books in the friars' libraries simply sat there and rotted (*Religious Men, Clerks Possessioners*). Also, while FitzRalph speaks in general terms of injury or damage done to the secular clergy, several of the Wycliffite texts specify that the injury caused by a lack of books is its detrimental effect upon preaching, or teaching, which in context means the same thing.

The most significant Wycliffite addition to the argument, however, seems to have neither counterpart nor nucleus in FitzRalph's sermon. The *locus* of FitzRalph's complaint is the marketplace: secular clerks cannot buy books, there is no useful book for sale, the friars have bought up all the books, and so on. The Wycliffite excerpts quoted here, in contrast, complain specifically and unanimously about closed libraries—about the fact that, once having acquired books, the friars will not share the use of them. Any hint that friars could and should be expected to share their libraries is absent from FitzRalph's *Defensio*, while in all six of the Wycliffite texts that obligation is a common assumption. Even *Fifty Heresies*, the least specific on this point, accuses the friars of robbing seculars by 'withholding' books (*by holdynge bokis fro hom*), and the others are explicit in their language: friars gather up books and *putte hem in tresorie and do prisone him* (*Jack Upland*); they *suffre hem to be closed þere*, i.e., inside their communities (*Religious Men*); they *hyden hem from seculer clerkis* (*Clerks Possessioners*). The prison imagery, in *Jack Upland's* Middle English, occurs in the Latin texts as well: *libri multis seris et vectibus clauduntur* (*Opus Arduum*); *libri . . . incarcerati . . . conchatenati* (*Floretum*).

---

would have thought of these comments on the friars and their books; see A. Gwynn, "Richard FitzRalph at Avignon," *Studies* 22 (1933) 590–607.

[13] Walsh 469.

The Middle English translation of FitzRalph's *Defensio* by John Trevisa (d. 1402) is known in five manuscripts, and a sixth was seen as recently as 1845. They are all collections of Trevisa's translations, rather than collections of Lollard materials, and it is questionable whether Trevisa's version of the relevant passage actually influenced the Wycliffite texts quoted above.[14] The Wycliffite tracts lack specific verbal parallels with Trevisa's language. In particular, Trevisa's rendering 'damage þat vndoþ & distruyeþ þe seculers,' compared with the Latin 'damnum . . . quod tendit ad consumptionem seu euacuationem doctrine in secularibus,' is not a likely source for expressions like 'seculer preestis and curatis . . . ben lettid of kunnynge Goddis lawe' (*Jack Upland*). Nevertheless, FitzRalph's *Defensio* is rather different form the other works that Trevisa translated. We do not know when this translation was made, whether during Trevisa's years as a fellow at Queen's College (in the company of Wyclif and Nicholas Hereford, among others) in 1369–78, or at the end of his life as domestic chaplain of Berkeley Castle, or in the years between, most of which seem to have been spent in Oxford. Given that, his chaplaincy notwithstanding, Trevisa was still paying rent as a lodger at Queens' as late as 1396, one would suspect that his translating FitzRalph was a reflection of current Oxford interest in this text, and his Middle English version cannot but have helped to spread FitzRalph's word.

Read as a body, the Wycliffite excerpts may sound suspect, the repetition (with an added bit of embroidery) of a snatch of diatribe borrowed from FitzRalph—an accusation which, given the source, must have been hyperbole even in 1357 and which was merely a literary device by the 1390s. Even if this were the case, the excerpts would deserve our notice. The denial of access to books does not automatically spring to minds as one of the major sins, and so the fact that the Wycliffites repeat the accusation is a significant statement in itself.

In fact, however, the excerpts refer to a real and immediate situation, and particularly in the specifically Wycliffite complaint about closed libraries. Of this we have the most reliable evidence possible, the testimony of the friars themselves, in the person of the Franciscan William Woodford.[15] The Oxford Greyfriars took these and other charges seri-

---

[14] Edited by A. J. Perry, *Dialogus inter militem et clericum; Richard FitzRalph's Sermon . . . by John Trevisa*, Early English Text Society 167 (London 1925) p. 59/1–16. Regarding Tevisa see Emden (O) 1903–4; D. Fowler, "John Trevisa and the English Bible," *Modern Philology* 58 (1960) 81–98, and idem, "New LIght on Trevisa," *Traditio* 18 (1962) 289–317.

[15] Concerning Woodford, see Emden (O) 2081–2, and J. I. Catto, "William Woodford, O.F.M. (c. 1330–c. 1397)," D.Phil. diss., Oxford 1969.

ously, and responded to them categorically and in detail. Woodford was regent master of the Oxford Greyfriars ca. 1372–1373; he was in Oxford again in 1389 and 1390, serving in the latter year as vicar of the English provincial minister. It was obviously as the official voice of the order that, sometime between 1389 and 1396, he undertook an item-by-item reply to the sixty-five charges or *quaestiones* against the friars.[16] His response to the sixty-second of these—very close in its Latin wording to the Middle English version of *Jack Upland*—is a thorough-going defense of the library practices of the Oxford Greyfriars, worth quoting in full:

> *Question 62.* Friar, what charity is it to gather up books of sacred scripture and place them in your treasure room—and thus imprison them and exclude their use from priests and secular curates, and through locking them up prevent the seculars from preaching the word of God to the people. . . .?
>
> I reply and say, firstly, that . . . this question could be asked of the abbeys and priories of monks and canons, of the colleges all and singly, and of the cathedral churches, just as well as of the friars. For all such have libraries to keep their books in, whether works on Holy Scripture or on other subjects, which are closed up so that seculars are excluded, for the most part. The same question could as well be put to the masters of theology, who keep many books of sacred scripture shut up in their studies and their chambers, and also their books of sermons, which they do not share with other secular clerks in general, and scarcely even with their intimate friends.
>
> Also, I say that the friars gather up books of sacred scripture and keep them in their libraries in order to study them, and to use these books in preparing themselves to preach to the people—and that is an act of charity. But to say that friars lock up books in order to prevent secular clerks from preaching the word of God is plainly false. The friars do not do so for that reason, any more than do the cathedrals, or the people in the colleges.
>
> Rather, the friars do so for two reasons. One is, that their books are held in safekeeping so that they are not exposed to theft. For in some places where books have lain about in the open, and secular clerks had free access to them, the books frequently have been stealthily removed, in spite of their being sturdily chained; and some of the quires were cut out

---

[16] Woodford was a bibliographer at heart who revelled in documentation. In his *Defensio mendicitatis*, written in 1395–6, he frequently lists authors and documents every fact. The work concludes with a bibliography of forty-three learned doctors, to counter FitzRalph's contention that there had been more learned doctors before the friars came on the scene. See E. Doyle, "A Bibliographical List by William Woodford OFM," *Franciscan Studies* 35 (1975) 93–106.

of books, leaving only the binding and the chains. So it behoved the friars to hold onto their books and to keep them more securely locked up, or they would have done without the books which they ought to study. — I am not saying that secular clerks stole the books that disappeared, but that some persons or other disguised as clerks stole these books.

The second reason that the friars keep their books locked up is so that they can be immediately used by friars who need to study them. The same books cannot simultaneously serve the needs of both friars and seculars. — And there you have the response to the question.[17]

Woodford's response is exclusively concerned with that aspect of the argument which originates with the Wycliffites, not with FitzRalph —

---

[17] 'Sextagesima 2ᵃ questio. Frater, qualis est [caritas] congregare libros sacre scripture et reponere eos in thesauro et sic eos incarcerare et excludere a sacerdotibus eorum usum et a curatis secularibus et per cautelas impedire eos predicare populo verbum Dei? . . .

'Respondeo et dico, primo, quod pars prima huius questionis queri potest ab abathiis et prioratibus monachorum et canonicorum, a communitatibus collegiorum et unitatibus, et a cathedralibus ecclesiis equale sicud [secundum(?): MS] a fratribus. Nam quilibet predictorum habet librarias ad custodiendum libros in eisdem, tam de sacra scriptura quam de scientiis aliis, qui clauduntur, ita ut seculares ab eis excludantur pro maiori parte.

'Similiter, idem queri potest a magistris in theologia, qui in studiis et cameris suis multos libros sacre scripture clausos custodiunt, sermonum etiam libros consimiliter, quos non communicant aliis sacerdotibus secularibus communiter et vix aliquibus sibi bene notis.

'Item, dico quod congregant sibi libros sacre scripture et reponunt in suis librariis ad custodiendum ut in eis studeant et ad ordinandum et disponendum se ad predicandum populo, et illud est valde caritativum. Sed quod fratres claudent libros tales ad cautelam ut impediant sacerdotes seculares a predicatione verbi Dei est manifeste falsum. Nam illa de causa, sic non faciunt fratres plus quam ecclesie cathedrales vel alii in collegiis, sed propter duas causas faciunt, quarum una est ut libri habeantur in sacra custodia ne furto exponantur; nam in quibusdam locis ubi libri in loco aperto iacebant et sacerdotes seculares accessum liberum ad eos habuerunt, libri frequenter [ferquenter: MS] fuerunt furtive sublati, non obstante quod ipsi(?) fuerunt fortiter cathenati, et quaterni aliqui librorum fuerunt abscisi et cathene cum asseribus relicte remanserunt. Quapropter oportuit fratres tenere et servare libros suos melius clausos, vel defecissent eis libri in quibus studere oportebat. Non dico quod sacerdotes seculares furabantur libros sic sublatos, sed sub colore [colori: MS] tali illi vel alii tales libros furati sunt.

'Alia causa est quod fratres servant libros suos sub custodia clausos ut magis essent in promptu pro fratrum usibus ad custodiendum ut fratres ipsi studeant in eis et illi libri non possunt simul servire fratribus et secularibus. Unde patet responsio . . . questionis.' Unpublished; transcribed from the only surviving manuscript, Oxford Bodley 703 (SC 2766) fols. 41–57, questio 62 at 54ᵛ–55 (s. xiv/xv; Oxford Greyfriars). The edition of Woodford's Responsiones projected by Fr. E. Doyle did not appear. Portions of questio 62 are printed and translated by J. I. Catto, "New Light on Thomas Docking OFM," Medieval and Renaissance Studies 6 (1968) 147–148. Regarding the date of the Responsiones, see Catto, "William Woodford" 31–32. We thank Dr. Margaret Gibson for the suggested emendation of secundum.

Nowhere in his reply is there any suggestion that this is an inaccurate statement. Rather, Woodford's reply makes three points: (1) everybody else does it; (2) we must guard our books against theft and mutilation; and (3) our books must be kept available for our own study. Regarded objectively, the first is simply an excuse, while the other two comprise probably the earliest reasoned statement of the principles that justify a closed collection. Regarded historically, they reveal that the Wycliffite criticism struck a sensitive nerve at Oxford Greyfriars.

An envious awareness of Greyfriars' rich library must have been a constant irritant for scholars who did not have such wealth at their disposal. The library contained the books and notes of former great scholars of the house, from Adam Marsh and Robert Grosseteste down to 'the books of William of Ockham' mentioned by the *Opus Arduum*, as well as in-house instructional and pastoral tools compiled there for the use of the order, such as the biblical commentaries of Thomas Docking, the *Tabula septem custodiarum*, or the *Registrum Anglie de libris doctorum et auctorum veterum*. As Jeremy Catto has demonstrated, to the Franciscans their library and its books were an integral part of the house, which existed specifically for the use of its members in carrying out the Franciscan mission.[18] The Grosseteste archive was heavily used over the years. Thus, in a disputation in 1316 or 1317, Oxford's chancellor Henry of Harclay put forth as Grosseteste's an argument on Aristotle's *Physics*; and to this the Franciscan lector William of Alnwick retorted that the opinion in question occurred in the margins of Grosseteste's own copy of the *Physics*, not in a finished commentary, and that such marginalia could no more be regarded as Grosseteste's considered opinion than could his many jottings on slips of parchment 'which were all kept in the library of the Friars Minor at Oxford, as I have seen with my own eyes.'[19] Other Franciscan authors such as John Russell in the 1290s, John Ridevall (lector at Oxford in the 1330s), and John Lathbury (fl. 1329–1362) likewise quote from Grosseteste's marginalia in books at the Oxford convent. The authors cited by Lathbury, even though they need

---

[18] Regarding the library of Greyfriars the best survey is still Little, *Grey Friars*, 55–62. See also R. W. Hunt, "The Library of Robert Grosseteste," in *Robert Grosseteste Scholar and Bishop*, ed. D. A. Callus O.P. (Oxford 1955) 121–145; N. R. Ker, *Medieval Libraries of Great Britain*, ed. 2 rev. (London 1964) 141–142; K. W. Humphreys, *The Book Provisions of the Medieval Friars* (Amsterdam 1964) 46–66, 99–118; Catto, "Thomas Docking" 135–149; and M. Parkes's chapter on books and libraries in Oxford, in vol. 2 of *The History of the University of Oxford*, forthcoming. See also n. 32 below.

[19] Cited by Hunt, "Library of Grosseteste" 127.

not all have been at Greyfriars, imply a large and well-stocked library.[20] Lathbury refers to books as if they had fixed positions on shelves or reading desks, and as we have seen Woodford speaks of chains; doubtless, to judge from the practice of other contemporary libraries, another part of the collection was apportioned out among the friar-scholars. To this extent, at least, the Wycliffite criticisms describe an actual state of affairs at Oxford at the end of the fourteenth century.

Woodford's carefully phrased response, read in conjunction with the Wycliffite excerpts, suggests that there was a body of secular clerks at Oxford who did not, or at any rate felt that they did not, have sufficient access to books because the institutional libraries, whether of Merton, St. Frideswide, or Greyfriars, were for the use of members only.[21] These criticisms were written by a small minority among Oxford's 'secular clerks and curates,' but their complaints about books must have struck a responsive chord in a far larger audience. While the friars and colleges had their libraries, the majority of students were not members of colleges or orders but lived in the dozens of residence halls, without the advantage of an institutional library.[22] Bishop Thomas Cobham in ca. 1320 had ordered the building of a room on the north side of St. Mary's to house his books as a library 'for the use of poor scholars' ('libros nostros pauperum scolarium usui deputandos ibidem disposuimus collocari'). But the building work was not yet paid for at the time of his death in 1327, and his executors sold the books to the provost of Oriel, to cover the debt. Squabbles, sometimes unseemly, between Oriel and the university over the rights to these books continued through the century, indicating a continuing demand for a library not restricted to private groups. But the matter was only to be settled in the fifteenth century, and the

---

[20] B. Smalley, *English Friars and Antiquity in the Early Fourteenth Century* (Oxford 1960) 229, 365; idem, "John Russel O.F.M.," *Recherches de théologie ancienne et médiévale* 23 (1956) 309–310.

[21] The value of books to an Oxford scholar of this time is well illustrated by the fact that Trevisa carried off twenty-four books with him, when he was expelled from Queen's in 1378. The list of these is printed most recently by Fowler, *Modern Philology* 58 (1960) 94.

[22] The institutions in Oxford with libraries of their own would have included University, Balliol, Merton, Exeter, Oriel, Queen's and New Colleges, Canterbury, Durham, and Gloucester Colleges, the Augustinians of Osney and St. Frideswide, the Cistercians of Rewley and St. Bernard's, and the four friaries; regarding these libraries see N. R. Ker, "Oxford College Libraries before 1500," in *The Universities in the Late Middle Ages*, ed. J. Ijsewijn and J. Paquet (Louvain 1978) 298–311, reprinted in Ker's collected articles; and W. A. Pantin, "The Halls and Schools of Medieval Oxford . . ." in *Studies Presented to Daniel Callus*, OHS ns. 16 (Oxford 1964) 31–100. For a list of 123 academic halls in 1313, see *History of the University of Oxford* vol. 1, ed. J. I. Catto (Oxford 1984) xxxviii-xl.

university library did not open its doors until 1412. (Not surprisingly, perhaps, the statutes governing its use were worded in such a way as effectively to exclude the mendicants.[23]) In the 1390s, therefore, there was a large body of disgruntled 'outsiders' who would have said Amen! to the Wycliffite criticism of the closed libraries of the friars.

None of this explains why it should await the Wycliffites to criticize the friars' libraries. That the masses of students in residence halls lacked access to libraries is a condition that long antedated Wyclif. Also, just how difficult it actually was for secular clerks to obtain books in Oxford, and just how closed the libraries of institutions like Greyfriars actually were, are open questions. Yes, there clearly was an aggrieved audience, and Woodford was clearly on the defensive. But frequent institutional legislation fulminating against the lending of books without proper pledges suggests that one could always get into college libraries, if one knew the right people. It is apparent that some outsiders gained access to the Greyfriars library itself. As we have seen, Chancellor Harclay had used Grosseteste's books by 1317; Richard de Bury or his agents knew the library in the first half of the century;[24] Henry of Kirkestede, a Benedictine of Bury St. Edmunds, recorded titles from this library in his *Catalogus* in the 1370s;[25] and Wyclif himself appears to have had extended access to it.[26] And how did the seven-volume set of Gorham on the scriptures, which was copied for Greyfriars at the behest of William of Nottingham around 1312, leave the library to pass via Thomas Trillek and William Rede to the library of Merton?[27] Moreover, there is little indication in the contents of Wycliffite works to suggest that Lollards truly lacked libraries; to the contrary, one is struck by their access to written sources.[28]

What is new, we suggest, is an attitude. Quite clear between the lines of the Wycliffite texts quoted here is the unspoken assumption that books are the common possession of all, since they contain holy wisdom

---

[23] Regarding Cobham's foundation see E. H. Pearce, *Thomas de Cobham Bishop of Worcester 1317–1327* (London 1923) 244–248, and F. Madan, "Bishop Cobham's Library," *Bodleian Quarterly Record* 6 (1929) 50–51. The statutes are edited by H. Anstey, RS (London 1868) 1.264, and S. Gibson (Oxford 1931) p. 218.

[24] Ed. A. Altamura (Naples 1954) 102–103.

[25] Edition in progress by R.H. and M.A. Rouse, for the series Medieval Library Catalogues of Great Britain (British Academy); cited from Cambridge U.L. MS Add. 3470.

[26] See R. W. Southern, *Robert Grosseteste: The Growth of an English Mind in Medieval Europe* (Oxford 1986) 298–307.

[27] F. M. Powicke, *The Medieval Books of Merton College* (Oxford 1931) 171–176, nos. 551–3; it should be noted that, contrary to most references to these volumes, including Powicke's, they were not written by William but for him, in several different hands.

[28] See the comments of A. Hudson, *English Wycliffite Sermons* 1 (Oxford 1983) 189–202.

given to all and necessary for purveying to the faithful God's word. This tacit assumption is readily apparent, for example, in the *Fifty Heresies*, where the withholding of books is called robbery. The accusation occurs in a chapter that lists various sorts of robbery committed by the friars, a crime which they compound by hypocritically pretending to be poor. Thus, the indictment quoted above, 'Friars . . . rob curates . . . by keeping books from them and by withholding the advantage of books and learning,' continues on: 'They rob lords of their rents . . . and hypocritically take free annual rents from the lords' coffers, and they rob the common people of their livelihood . . . by hypocritical false begging, condemned by the word of God. And while at first they pretend to be the very poorest of clerks, in the end they surpass all others in great houses and costly libraries.'[29] This implication, that public access to books was a right, is in a sense an extension of Wyclif's rejection of 'private religion'. Wyclif meant by this term all those—monks, friars, canons regular—who lived apart in accordance with man-made rules instituted for peculiar (and self-centered) purposes, removing themselves from the community of the faithful who lived in accordance with the precepts instituted by Christ and, thereby, doing harm to the *res publica* of Christendom. In the Wycliffite excerpts, his followers rail against 'private religious' who have removed the written word of God from those who follow 'the common religion of Christ,' to the detriment of 'the public good'. All of this language, in the prologue to the *Floretum*, occurs with specific reference to the accessibility of the written word, as the compilers justify the making of their florilegium. Having characterized themselves as 'certain simple men' (*imbecilles quidam*) scurrying about to collect useful crumbs, just like Christ's disciples collected fragments after the Feeding of the Five Thousand, the compilers continue: 'Books filled with truth are manifold, but they have been imprisoned and chained up by private religious in their communities, while other books are too long drawn out with scholastic inquiry—to such a point that poor clerks, not seeking worldly goods but desiring the heavenly, prevented from buying books by lack of money and worn down by the obscure arguments of the doctors, are afraid to take on the task of preaching. Therefore these said simple men—not vowed to cells and cloisters nor adorned with masters' caps, but contented with the common religion of Christ—undertook . . . for the public good to put together for the household of faith this simple homely compilation. . . . They have decided, in a childlike way, to name their compilation *Floretum*, as

---

[29] Arnold, *English Works*, 3.97/4–9.

it were, little flowers growing in the meadow of Scripture.'[30] The authors assume the posture of simple men unfettered by theological complexities or mendicant cells, carrying out a God-given mandate because the religious, having locked away the books and distracted people from the truth by obfuscation, have prevented them from preaching the word of God. The situation at Oxford, then, was not new: some people (like Greyfriars) had books, and some did not; it had always been thus. The novel element was that the Wycliffites were not resigned to the situation. They did not see it as 'inevitable' or 'unfortunate' but as evil, and they said so bluntly.

Curiously enough, it seems that texts do emerge from Greyfriars, at the very end of the fourteenth century, for what reason we cannot say. This is based on the slender but suggestive evidence of the transmission of three Franciscan texts which adhere to a similar pattern: having been composed at the Oxford convent, they are known exclusively to Franciscans for many decades, only to emerge into the larger university world at the very end of the fourteenth century. Jeremy Catto has traced the fortunes of one of these, the biblical commentaries written by Thomas Docking, O.F.M., in the 1260s.[31] Thereafter Docking is mentioned or quoted by John Russell, O.F.M., about 1292, by William of Nottingham, O.F.M., about 1312, by John Lathbury, O.F.M., ca. 1350, and by William Woodford, O.F.M., around 1373; in addition there is a fragment of a student's *reportatio* of Docking on Luke in a late thirteenth-century Franciscan manuscript (London, B.L. Royal 4 A.xiii), and extracts from various Docking postills in another Franciscan manuscript (Paris B.N. lat. 3183). Then, a late fourteenth-century manuscript with extracts from Docking on Deuteronomy (Lincoln Dean and Chapter 229) appears in

---

[30] Et considerato . . . quod . . . veraces libri multiplicati sed religiosis priuatis incarcerati in collegiis conchatenati, aliqui curiositate scolastica nimis diffusi, ita quod pauperes sacerdotes terrena non ambientes, sed celestia desiderantes, tum propter penuriam pecunie libros emendi impediti, tum propter obscuras doctorum sententias fatigati, officium predicandi aggredi metuunt, dicti inbecilles antris & claustris non desponsati, cidaribus magistralibus non ornati, sed religione Christi communi contentati, istam facilem compilacionem domesticam pro fidei domesticis ex micis euangelicis doctorumque flosculis velut Ruth colligendo spicas propter bonum publicum Dei gracia conglutinari sunt connisi. Et . . . tanquam paruuli flores in prato scripture congerminantes suam conpilacionem . . . pueriliter *Floretum* decreuerunt nominari.' Unpublished; cited from the text in C. von Nolcken, "An Edition of Selected Parts of the Middle English Translation of the *Rosarium theologie*," D. Phil. diss. (Oxford 1976) ii 586–7. See now Christina von Nolcken, "Notes on Lollard Criticism of John Wyclif's Writings," *Journal of Theological Studies* n.s. 39 (1988) 411–437, edition on 432–433; we are grateful to Dr. von Nolcken for allowing us to compare our translation with her own.

[31] Catto, "Thomas Docking" 144–145.

the hands of Sir Thomas Carter, a secular clerk; and in the fifteenth century Docking is more widely known and appreciated (for example, Bishop Gray commissioned a set of his postills, Balliol MSS 28–30). A second text is the *Tabula septem custodiarum*, a guide to exegetical passages in the works of the Fathers, completed by the Oxford Franciscans probably in 1309. The only surviving manuscript from the first half of the century was written by a Franciscan, probably at Greyfriars, in 1339. But in the last decade of the century it suddenly came on the market and at least seven manuscripts survive that were written at Oxford before the middle of the fifteenth century: Harley 3858, written in the late 1390s by Robert Masham of Durham College Oxford; Merton 205, written at the end of the fourteenth century and bearing a note that it was corrected against the original at Greyfriars; Durham University Cosin V.ii.4, ca. 1400, copied from a draft version of the *Tabula* presumably at Greyfriars and owned by Thomas Clare, a Benedictine from Bury St. Edmunds studying at Oxford; Balliol 217, written at Oxford 1401–3 by Peter Wilhymleyd; Magdalen College MSS 78 and 150, written at Oxford in the first half of the fifteenth century; and Balliol 216, written at Oxford ca. 1451–65 for Bishop Gray by John Reynbold—not to mention two further copies at Cambridge, Peterhouse 169 (s. XIV ex./XV in.) and B.L. Royal 3 D.i (AD 1452). The third text, the *Registrum Anglie*, a location list of patristic works in libraries of the old orders, was compiled by the Oxford Greyfriars probably in the 1320s (before 1331); again, this tool appears not to have been known outside the house until near the end of the century. The only surviving copies are that made by William Dyngley between 1398 and 1444 at Peterhouse Cambridge (MS 169) and that made between 1428 and 1438 for Prior William Molash of Christ Church Canterbury (Bodleian Library Tanner 165).[32] Perhaps there are other texts whose transmissions follow this pattern, suggesting some slight relaxation of the practices at the library of the Oxford Greyfriars.

Our knowledge of these early tools casts an interesting light on the *Responsiones*. What was Woodford's purpose in writing this work? The apparent purpose was to give official and public rebuttal to external critics; yet the *Responsiones* survives in only one manuscript, which belonged to Oxford Greyfriars, and the work is not mentioned in the ongoing literary exchange. This permits the suggestion that the *Responsiones* may, instead, have been primarily intended as another of the sequence of in-house tools for the order—in this instance, a tool that prepared

---

[32] An edition of the *Registrum* is currently in progress by R.H. and M.A. Rouse for the series Medieval Library Catalogues of Great Britain (British Academy). The *Tabula Septem custodiarum* is discussed in the introduction to the edition.

Franciscans for the sorts of accusations they might face and provided a set of authoritative responses to them.[33]

We are aware, of course, that the accusations of denial of access to books, and Woodford's response to these, are part of a polemic, which means that considerable exaggeration was involved. Despite the polemical framework, however, the question of access to books was an intriguing choice, as grounds for claim and counter-claim. It was certainly true that the friars sequestered their books. It was clearly not true that the Wycliffites had been bereft of books as a consequence—although, by the 1390s, they could foresee lean years to come. Certainly the Wycliffites were interested in castigating the Franciscans for hypocritical behavior; but they were concerned as well with the real fate of real books, and their self-righteous outcry came close enough to the truth to provoke a Franciscan defense.

The loudness of the outcry and the response it produced are further indications, if any are needed, that Wyclif's effect in Oxford did not evaporate when he left for Lutterworth.[34] Though distance, and then death, cut off Wyclif's direct access to the university community, the influence of his ideas continued, engendering among other things a body of protest literature like that cited here. Whenever the protests of the Wycliffites coincided with the interests of a larger community who were not themselves Lollards—as the protest against book-hoarding surely did at Oxford—the impact was greatest. It produced, in this case, a defensive *apologia* by a spokesman for the Franciscans which forms the earliest detailed justification of the closed non-circulating library. Regardless of its ulterior motives, Woodford's thoughtful statement might well be heeded by modern librarians concerned for the preservation of their collections and for the needs of future readers to have access to the books of the past.

---

[33] We thank Sir Richard Southern for this suggestion.

[34] The disappearance of Wyclif as an issue at Oxford is implied, at least, by K. B. McFarlane, *John Wycliffe and the Beginnings of English Nonconformity* (London 1952).

Backgrounds to Print

11. Correction and Emendation of Texts in the Fifteenth Century and the Autograph of the *Opus Pacis* by "Oswaldus Anglicus"*

It is commonly held that medieval authors, scribes, and readers had no notion of emending a text, when they were confronted with an obvious error in their exemplars, other than by slavishly copying the readings of another text. This is the view set forth by the classicist E. J. Kenney in his studies of early textual criticism. "Copyists saw it as their task to reproduce the transmitted text, that of their exemplar; correction was limited to diorthosis and collation, criticism to choice between existing variants. Conjecture, so far as it played a part at all, was generated by the tradition itself, not by the mind of the corrector . . . Carolingian copyists did not innovate *ingenii ope*; on the contrary they seem to have been absurdly content to copy and to cross-copy gibberish with meticulous accuracy, but conjecture they would not . . . The manuscripts of Latin classical writers [were] copied with far less real care though with much more surface elegance as to text in the twelfth and thirteenth centuries." Most succinctly, he says, "Of conjectural criticism in anything like its modern sense the Middle Ages knew nothing," adding "Such an observation cries aloud for contradiction; it could be shaken

Originally published in *Scire litteras: Forschungen zum mittelalterlichen Geistesleben*, Festschrift Bernhard Bischoff, ed. S. Kramer and M. Bernhard, Abhandlungen der Bayerische Akad. d. Wissenschaften, Phil. = Hist. Kl.

*We thank Laura Light for her meticulous help with collating *Opus pacis* manuscripts. We are especially grateful to A. I. Doyle and Michael Sargent, who read an earlier draft of this piece and generously shared with us their knowledge of Carthusians and Carthusian writings.

by one positive example to the contrary."[1]

Well, yes, this opinion does indeed cry out for a contrary example; but no medievalist could provide one, if he consented to play by the restrictive ground rules laid down by classical philologists. For, of course, Kenney is referring exclusively to texts of the classics. In his supportive illustrations he names specifically the transmissions of Lucan, Livy, Tacitus, Apuleius, Caesar, Gellius, Cicero, Ovid, etc. Now, surely no one would maintain that these texts were central to the scholarly or literary interests of the Middle Ages.

Rather than split hairs on this point, however, we should like to consider the more general implication of Kenney's remarks—namely, that the Middle Ages was unable to cope with the problem of textual error, and of variant readings between manuscripts of the same text. Was this even recognized as a problem? Received opinion would answer no. If, in fact, the problem was recognized, what steps were taken to solve it? What were medieval attitudes toward textual accuracy, and how ingenious could medievals be, if pressed?

While these questions are important in the broader sense of probing the limitations of scribal culture in general, they have specific relevance to the interest in accuracy of text exhibited across Europe from the Brethren of the Common Life in Germany and the Netherlands to the Lollards in England. Anne Hudson, for example, in the first volume of her remarkable study of the Lollard sermon cycle ably demonstrated that while the manuscripts of the Lollard cycle display little or no surface uniformity in size, layout, script form, or decoration, and that literally dozens of different scribes produced them, nearly all of them share this in common: that they have been scrupulously and meticulously corrected, to a degree that one can explain only in terms of authoritative central direction. On this matter of correction, Hudson's research provides evidence of the most useful sort—numerous as to examples, yet neatly restricted in chronology and in the community concerned.[2] Until now, no one has thought that medievals had either the desire or the capacity to engage in such wholesale, disciplined pursuit of textual accuracy.

Where did this phenomenon come from, and when, and why? The correction of texts, of course, had a previous history in the Middle

---

[1] E. J. Kenney, "The Character of Humanist Philology," in *Classical Influences on European Culture, A.D. 500–1500*, ed. R. R. Bolgar (Cambridge 1971) 119–128 at 120.

[2] Anne Hudson, ed., *English Wycliffite Sermons* 1 (Oxford 1983) introd., esp. 149–151, 189–202. Among numerous examples demonstrating that, in Lollard works, "verbal accuracy was regarded as a matter of great importance," see especially Epistle-sermon 43, p. 656 lines 1–9 (" . . . trewe men shulden [note] eche uaryyng of Goddis word . . .").

Ages—ranging from the devoted attentions of atypical individuals, like
the learned (and always-cited) Lupus of Ferrières, to the universal (but
entirely pro-forma) corrections of the Paris stationers.[3] But the interest
in correcting blossomed in the fifteenth century as never before—and not
only in England, as witnessed by Hudson's Lollard scribes, but on the
Continent as well. It is in fact on the Continent where this activity is
most clearly and pervasively documented, among the groups that comprised the *Devotio moderna*—the Brethren of the Common Life and,
especially, the Windesheim Congregation.

In looking at attitudes toward the written page, in the Rhineland of
the fifteenth century, one cannot fail to be struck by the heavy emphasis
on the correction and emendation of texts. Whereas in an earlier century
it had been the careful and legible copying of texts that was held up as a
virtue to be admired and emulated, we find in the fifteenth century that
the correction and emendation of existing texts has been elevated to the
same high esteem, in the statutes, the histories, and the in-house biographies of these Rhineland groups. Johannes Busch, in his history of the
Windesheim congregation (1464), devotes two chapters to the correction
of books, in the section which describes the origins of the *Devotio
moderna*: All the service books of Windesheim ("Cuncta enim missali,
evangelaria, epistolaria, psalteria, lectionaria," etc.) were corrected, punctuated, ordered, and accented 'down to the last iota', so that, he boasts,
'no such correction of books has hitherto been found in any other order
in the world!' And, of course, he gives due notice of the Windesheimers'
stellar achievement, the establishment, through years of careful correction, of a new edition of the Bible.[4] In addition to the correcting activities of the Congregation in general, the Windesheim Chronicle often lists
the correction of books among the noteworthy accomplishments of individual luminaries of the order. Thus, a chapter on the life of subprior
Arnald Kalker is entitled, 'On His Authority and Diligence in the Correction of Books . . .',[5] and there are similar remarks concerning other
brothers. Most revealing perhaps, is a phrase that Busch applies to Johannes a Kempis, older brother of Thomas a Kempis and first prior of the

---

[3] The most recent discussion of the university stationers, with earlier bibliography,
occurs in the papers collected by L. J. Bataillon, B. Guyot, and R. H. Rouse, eds., *La
production du livre universitaire au Moyen Age* (Paris 1988).

[4] Johannes Busch, *Chronicon Windeshemense . . .*, ed. Karl Grube (Halle 1886). See
pt. B, *Liber de origine devotionis modernae* chap. 25, pp. 310–311 (service books), and
chap. 26, pp. 311–313 (Bible).

[5] Ibid. pt. A, *Liber de viris illustribus* chap. 5, p. 69, "De auctoritate et diligencia eius
in libris corrigendis et de interiori conversacione et morte prefati supprioris [scil. Kalker]."

daughter-house of Mount St. Agnes at the beginning of the fifteenth century. While Busch naturally recounts all the high-points of Prior John's eventful life, his first major achievement is introduced thus: 'He received from God a special grace, that of correcting books.'[6]

The emphasis upon scrupulously correct copying of books, which can be found in the surviving annals and statutes of virtually any house of the Brethren of the Common Life, is the expression in precept of that which Hudson has found in practice, on the English side of the Channel. It is very much a fifteenth-century, North-European phenomenon, pervading such diverse groups as the Lollards, the Brethren, and the Carthusians. For in spite of differences in rule and in doctrine, these groups clearly shared a dedication to textual accuracy. It was important to liturgical practice and to the very faith itself, that texts be uniform and free from error.

The passages we have mentioned from the Windesheim Chronicle, however, were chosen because they deal specifically with the correction of books already written: They do not describe measures taken to ensure that a newly composed work (like the English sermon cycle) preserves its accuracy in publication, but on the contrary they are concerned with the restoration of accuracy to texts that have deteriorated—with, in a word, emendation. We should not be surprised to find, then, that it is not in the classicists' realm of philology, but rather in the context of those groups who considered book-correction to be a God-given grace, that the principles of emendation are first codified. We refer to Brother Oswald's *Opus pacis*, the central topic of this paper.

The *Opus pacis* is the first medieval treatise—so far as we know, the first Latin treatise ever—to discuss the theoretical grounds for correcting and emending a text. It was written in 1417 at the Grande Chartreuse by the monk Oswald, vicar of the house. Well known throughout the fifteenth century, the work survives in at least thirteen copies, one of them in Oswald's hand.

In 1924, Paul Lehmann gave the *Opus pacis* its first serious attention in four hundred years. He listed the eight manuscripts known to him, described the work in some detail, and printed several sections, including the prologue, in his "Bücherliebe und Bücherpflege bei den Karthäusern".[7] While the article was reprinted in Lehmann's collected

---

[6] Ibid. chap. 35, p. 95, "Qui [scil. frater Iohannes de Kempis] graciam specialem suscepit a deo libros corrigendi et bene scribendi, diversa quoque exemplaria inter se repugnancia ad invicem concordandi et ea in formam propriam apte componendi."

[7] Paul Lehmann, "Bücherliebe und Bücherpflege bei den Karthäusern," in *Miscellanea F. Ehrle* 5 (Rome 1924) 364–389; we cite here the repr. in his *Erforschung des Mittelalters* 3 (Stuttgart 1960) 121–142.

studies, the *Opus pacis* was otherwise ignored; surprisingly, no one picked up on Lehmann's remarkable find. The author Oswald, on the contrary, fared better. Because of his correspondence with Jean Gerson, Oswald was highlighted by Palémon Glorieux, in three studies (1951–1961) leading to the edition of Gerson's works.

But here we come to a strange phenomenon: Lehmann, in 1924, of course, was unaware of the extensive correspondence between Oswald and Gerson. Glorieux, in 1951, published a previously unedited collection of Gerson's correspondence with the Chartreuse, probably compiled and circulated by Oswald himself — yet Glorieux was totally unaware of the *Opus pacis*' existence.[8] In 1955, Glorieux published the second of his three studies,[9] still ignorant of this other aspect of Oswald's life. In 1960, Georg Paul Köllner published an article examining the real identity of a work in a Wolfenbüttel manuscript mistakenly entitled "Ex opere pacis capitulo"; but while Köllner knew Lehmann's work well, he was oblivious of the French scholar's discoveries that had been published in the meanwhile.[10] Finally, in 1961, Glorieux published the last of his three articles,[11] still quite innocent of the work of his German colleagues.

The purpose of this digression is not to castigate past scholars but to point out that there is, in fact, a good deal to be known about Oswald, if the parts are put together. The information offered by various biographical dictionaries, from John Bale to the DNB, is so error-ridden that it is best ignored.

In addition, the earlier tradition confers a growing list of spurious works on Oswald. Bale attributes to Oswald the correspondence with Gerson, which survives, and two unknown works, *De remediis tentationum* and *Meditationes solitarias*; the fact that Bale does not record the opening words of these two means that he saw only the titles and not the works themselves. Possevinus, and the Carthusian bibliographer Petreius after him, treat these two (only) as the writings of an Oswaldus Anglicus, whom Petreius makes distinct from Oswald de Corda. John Pits, and Thomas Tanner after him, repeat Bale's list and add to it a *Portiforium* found in a Cambridge manuscript (Cambridge, Corpus

---

[8] Palémon Glorieux, "L'activité littéraire de Gerson à Lyon: Correspondance inédite avec la Grande-Chartreuse," *Recherches de théologie ancienne et médiévale* 18 (1951) 238–307.

[9] Palémon Glorieux, "Autour de la liste des oeuvres de Gerson," *Recherches de théologie ancienne et médiévale* 22 (1955) 95–109,

[10] Georg Paul Köllner, "Die Opus-pacis-Handschrift im Lectionarium des ehemaligen Benediktinerklosters St. Jakob vor den Mauern von Mainz," in *Universitas: Dienst an Wahrheit und Leben. Festschift für Bischof Dr. Albert Stohr . . . 2* (Mainz 1960) 258–273.

[11] Palémon Glorieux, "Gerson et les Chartreux," *Recherches de théologie ancienne et médiévale* 28 (1961) 115–153.

Christi College MS 391, an eleventh-century manuscript with an inscription that includes the name of Saint Oswald). None of them mentions the *Opus pacis*, though the Carthusian Petreius does note that Oswald "wrote a good deal for the benefit of correctors" (*complura scripsit in gratiam emendatoris*).[12] After putting the pieces of Oswald's life together, we found that James Hogg had done this in part in 1982;[13] but since he also missed some things, we will give our own version of Oswald's biography.

First, we have found no justification for the cognomen *Oswaldus Anglicus*. Whether our man has been conflated with a second Carthusian author named Oswald who came from England, we are not prepared to say; but we are rather skeptical of the latter's existence. In the records of the Grande Chartreuse, our Oswald is called *Oswaldus de Corda*; and he was Bavarian, perhaps from the region near the ethnic/linguistic border with Swabia.[14] Other evidence of his origin confirms the statement in the annals: In the *Opus pacis*, whenever he must cite a place-name as an example, it is invariably *Bavaria, Bavarus* (just as his example for a personal name is *Oswaldus*);[15] on a single occasion, where *Bavaria* will not illustrate his point, he gives another name, *Suevia*.[16] Moreover, the contemporary table of contents of a manuscript of the *Opus pacis* from Cologne (before 1439) observes (as shall we, in a moment) that Oswald was a prior in Scotland, and continues "licet Theutonicus fuerit et

---

[12] See the citation to Bale's 1559 *Scriptores* in n. 14 below (Oswald does not occur in Bale's *Index*); Antonio Possevino, *Apparatus sacri . . . tomus II* (Venice 1606) 544; Theodorus Petreius, *Bibliotheca Cartusiana . . .* (Cologne 1609) 250–251; John Pits, *Relationum historicarum de rebus anglicis tomus I* (Paris 1619) 644; Thomas Tanner, *Bibliotheca Britannico-Hibernica . . .* (London 1748).

[13] James Hogg, "Oswald de Corda: A Forgotten Carthusian of Nordlingen," in *Kartäusermystik und -mystiker* 3, Analecta Carthusiana 55 (Salzburg 1982) 181–185. See also R. B. Marks, *The Medieval Manuscript Library of the Charterhouse of St. Barbara in Cologne,* Analecta Carthusiana 21–22 (Salzburg 1974) 129–140, and M. G. Sargent, *James Grenehalgh as Textual Critic,* Analecta Carthusiana 85, 2 vols. (Salzburg 1984) vol. 1 chap. 1, "Textual Correction and Transmission among the Carthusians."

[14] See, for example, Charles Le Couteulx, *Annales Ordinis Cartusiensis . . .* 7 (Montreuilsur-Mer 1890) 582, "Oswaldus de Cordis, natione Bavarus." Although Lehmann, and other German scholars after him, state that Oswald was of "englischer Herkunft" (Lehmann 128, Köllner 258, Theele [cited n. 23 below] 257), Oswald's "Englishness" rests only upon the early bio-bibliographers. We have not traced it back any earlier than John Bale's *Scriptorum illustrium maioris Britanniae . . . Catalogus* (Basel 1559) 592.

[15] See, for example, *cautela* 12 of the *Opus pacis* (Huntington Library manuscript [hereafter "H"], fols. 10v–11v), in which "Oswaldus" and "Bavaria/Bavarus" are repeatedly used to illustrate points in the text.

[16] In *cautela* 17 (MS H, fols. 12v–14; Lehmann, Bücherliebe, 136–137), as an example of words in which the letter *u* is often replaced by a *w*.

Bavarus"—'though he was a German, from Bavaria'.[17] Finally, we know from his own words, in a letter to Gerson, that he took the habit at the Charterhouse of *Hortus Christi*[18] at Nördlingen near Augsburg—i.e., just at the Bavarian/Swabian border.

Oswald entered the order probably in 1405; for he tells Gerson that he remained at Hortus Christi 'about nine years' ("circa novem annos") before coming to the Grande Chartreuse 'a scant half-year before the opening of the Council of Constance' ("vix medium annum ante sacri Constanciensis consilii inchoatum")[19]—thus, late spring or early summer of 1414. At the Grande Chartreuse he was obviously deeply involved, perhaps in charge, of the correction and emendation of texts. Certainly his authority in such matters was quickly accepted at the Chartreuse, to judge from the *Opus pacis* itself—compiled, as the prologue says, in the year that the Schism ended (1417), under the priorship of *Johannes natione Theutonicus* (John of Greifenberg, d. 1420).[20] By the 1420s, Oswald had been named vicar of the mother house—perhaps before April 1424, date of the earliest known letter to him from Gerson, though he is not addressed as vicar in this letter itself. Glorieux has edited a sequence of Gerson's correspondence with the Grande Chartreuse, from 1424 to perhaps 1429, the year of Gerson's death; almost all are directed to Oswald as vicar, though occasionally they are replies to the questions of other Carthusians passed on to Gerson by means of Oswald. The only surviving manuscript of this correspondence comes from the Basel Charterhouse, and Glorieux plausibly argues thaat the collection must have been made and circulated by Oswald himself; unquestionably it would have required his permission, at least. Oswald was also responsible, it seems, for translating some of Gerson's Old French works into Latin.

John Bale says that Oswald met and became friends with Gerson at Paris, where Oswald studied before his monastic profession.[21] This is a plausible suggestion, but there seems to be no evidence to support it. It is obvious that Oswald's learning is great, of its kind; whether its kind is that of the University of Paris under Gerson, however, we are dubious. His 'questions of conscience' submitted to Gerson strike us as more earnest than profound; and the learning displayed in the *Opus pacis* is that

---

[17] Cologne, Hist. Arch. G. B. 4° 152, discussed below.

[18] Glorieux, *Recherches de théologie ancienne et médiévale* 18, no. XII, p. 291.

[19] Ibid.

[20] MS H, fol. 1v; Lehmann, *Bücherliebe*, 130.

[21] Bale, Scriptores, loc. cit. Michael Sargent suggests, more persuasively, that Oswald was "probably the monk of the Grande Chartreuse for whom Gerson's *De laude scriptorum* was written"; Sargent, *James Grenehalgh as Textual Critic* vol. 1, Analecta Cartusiana 85 (Salzburg 1984) 19–20 (following the hint dropped by Hogg, Oswald, 182).

of a very gifted—and compassionate—grammar-master. It is also strange, though perhaps just a trick of survival, that, if the two were friends from before 1405, their earliest dated exchange should take place twenty years later (and the undated letters are later still). In this first letter, of 1424, Gerson gracefully declines to meet Oswald face to face, on the grounds that the infirmities of his flesh might not measure up to Oswald's expectations from Gerson's 'spirit'.[22] This might imply that he fears Oswald will find him much changed since their former acquaintance; more likely, however, it implies that they have never met. Glorieux has documented Gerson's predilection, especially in later life, for the Celestines and Carthusians, so that an earlier friendship is not necessary to account for his correspondence with Oswald, vicar of the Grand Chartreuse.

Oswald was at Cologne, for an unknown length of time, in 1428. The evidence, though not the reason, for his presence there is provided by a lengthy note, added to an early manuscript of the *Opus pacis* at the Cologne house of the Crutched Friars, or Crosiers, now Cologne Hist. Arch. G.B. 4° 152. The text itself is not dated, but the note was written in 1439, when events of 1428 would still be a vivid memory. After sixteen lines' worth of discussion—identifying and praising Oswald and his work, while explaining that the work's Carthusian rules were not all applicable to the Croisiers—the note concludes, 'In the year 1428 this Oswald was at Cologne, and he must have lived a couple of years beyond that'. The contrast of the concrete information in the first half of this sentence, "Anno domini M° CCCC° XXVIII° isdem dominus Osualdus fuit Colonie," with the undisguised guesswork (wrong by a few years) of the second half, "et forte biennio supervixit" is convincing.[23] This is the same manuscript whose table of contents, contemporary with and perhaps in the hand of the text, identifies Oswald as Bavarian. We see no reason to doubt either of these statements.

We do not know why Oswald went to Cologne. Perhaps he was sent on visitation to the Cologne Charterhouse, although as vicar of his house it would seem more likely for him to have stayed in charge at the Chartreuse and for the prior to do the traveling. More likely, instead, Oswald's trip is connected with the last major event in his career.

In 1429, after some years of consideration, James I of Scotland founded the first (and only) Charterhouse in that realm, at Perth. Although the king's initial consultation with the order, and the direction of the

---

[22] Glorieux, *Recherches de théologie ancienne et médiévale* 18, no. 1, p. 244.

[23] The note at the end of the *Opus pacis* in Cologne G.B. 4° 152 was printed by Joseph Theele, "Aus der Bibliothek des Kölner Kreuzbrüderklosters," in: *Mittelalterliche Handschriften . . . Festgabe . . . Hermann Degering* (Leipzig 1926) 253–263, at 257.

construction, had been done through the agency of the English house at Mountgrace, the first monks (including at least one of the *conversi*) came from Continental houses, either because James wished, or because the Grande Chartreuse assumed he would wish, not to have Englishmen in his royal Scottish foundation. The general chapter in 1430 incorporated the house, and named Oswald as its first prior. He may, in fact, have been in Scotland from at least the preceding year, since, according to Margaret Thompson, general chapter 'rarely passed an act of incorporation of a house within the first twelve months of its existence'.[24] It may be that his presence at Cologne in 1428 (1429 N.S.?) occurred as he was journeying to Perth.

Perhaps Oswald was already a mature man, when he joined the order in 1405; or perhaps even the rigors of the Grande Chartreuse had not prepared him for the Scottish climate. In any event, he died in Perth, on 15 September 1434. The date (variously given in the secondary literature) is known from the observance of his death on the 17th Kalends of October, and from the fact that his death was recorded at the General chapter that met after Easter in 1435.[25]

Lehmann in 1924 knew eight surviving manuscripts of the *Opus pacis*, and knew of a ninth, from Buxheim, that he could not locate. His eight were these: Basel, Universitätsbibliothek F.IX.4 (s. xv; Basel Carthusians); Berlin, Staatsbibl. lat.qu. 630, ff. 182–219v, paper (s. xv; Erfurt Carthusians, O.94); Cues, Hospitalbibl. 12 ff. 53–69, paper (1449; Germany, Nicholas of Cues); Mainz, Stadtbibl. 151 (Mainz Carthusians); Trier, Stadtbibl. 1130 ff. 5–35 (s. xv; Trier Benedictines); Trier, Stadtbibl. 1924 ff. 161–193 (s. xv; Trier Carthusians); Utrecht, Universiteitsbibl. 824 ff. 102–163 (1470; Utrecht Carthusians); and Wolfenbüttel, Helm. 350 (= Lehmann's 316) ff. 7–8, extracts *De accentu* (s. xv; Mainz Benedictines). He discovered two more manuscripts: Berlin, Staatsbibl. lat. qu. 632 (s. xv; Erfurt Carthusians B.32) and Weimar, Thüringische Landesbibl. qu. 22 (s. xv; Erfurt Carthusians M.26), in the process of

---

[24] E. Margaret Thompson, *The Carthusian Order in England* (London 1930) 247. Glorieux interpreted a passage in one of Oswald's letters to mean that he had met, while at the Grande Chartreuse, a man who was on his way to the synod of the province of Sens, held at Paris in March-April 1429 (*Recherches de théologie ancienne et médiévale* 18, no. XII, p. 292 and n. 119); if Glorieux's interpretation is correct, that would of course eliminate the possibility that Oswald was already on his way to Perth in 1428 and his presence in Cologne in that year must have a different explanation. But the context suggests, instead, that the passage refers to an (undated) meeting of Franciscans that was held at Sens.

[25] We thank Ian Doyle for this information.

editing the early sixteenth-century catalog of Salvatorberg, the
Charterhouse of Erfurt.[26]

In 1960, G. P. Köllner brought Lehmann's list of ten up to date:
He reported that Mainz 151 had been lost (the library's only loss) in
World War II, and he demonstrated that the so-called "excerpt from the
Opus pacis" in the Wolfenbüttel manuscript is a different and anony-
mous work. On the plus side, Kollner added three manuscripts to
Lehmann's list: Mainz, Stadtbibl. II.276 ff. 28–71 belonged to the Mainz
Carthusians. Cologne, Historisches Archiv G.B. 4° 152 ff. 1–44v (before
1439; Cologne Crosiers), first reported by Joseph Theele in 1926, is the
manuscript that has provided such useful biographical information about
Oswald. The third, Basel Universitätsbibl. Inc. 5 ff. 2–56v, is the latest
known copy. Bound with an incunabulum, this *Opus pacis* was written
in 1514 by Johannes Lindower at the Basel Charterhouse.[27] Brief extracts
"ex opere pacis domni Oswaldi, quondam correctoris Cartusie," are
found on the final folio (fol. 146v) of Grenoble Bibliothèque municipale
46, a fifteenth-century manuscript from the Grande Chartreuse containing a glossary of words (probably the *Valde bonum*) from the martyrology
and the Bible according to the usage of the Carthusian Order. Finally,
James Hogg in 1982 indicated that the "missing" manuscript from Buxheim
is now at the Grande Chartreuse.[28] Including this one, that makes twelve
surviving manuscripts, and a thirteenth—Mainz 151—may reappear
someday.

A fourteenth manuscript, the most recent find and much the most
interesting, is the author's autograph.[29] This is a paper manuscript,
bound with a copy of Chrysostom's homilies printed at Brussels in 1479
for the Brethren of the Common Life; like the printed book, the manuscript belonged to Weidenbach, the house of the Brethren in Cologne,
and is now in the Huntington Library with the number 86299. On folio
1 of the manuscript, in a hand of the first half of the fifteenth century, is
an unfortunately garbled *ex libris*: "Liber domus presbyterorum zo
Wydenbach apud sanctum Pantheleonem in Colonia, et habent eum pro
alio libro ex isto scriptus fuerit." How should these last words be emended?
The simplest would be, ". . . libro *qui* ex isto scriptus fuerit"—they have

---

[26]Lehmann, Bücherliebe, 129.

[27]Köllner, Opus-pacis-Handschrift, 260–261 and passim.

[28]Hogg, Oswald, 182.

[29]The manuscript is briefly described in W. Bond and C. Faye, *Supplement to the
Census of Medieval and Renaissance Manuscripts in the United States and Canada* (New
York 1962) 23 and more fully in C. W. Dutschke, *Guide to Medieval and Renaissance
Manuscripts in the Huntington Library* 2 (San Marino 1987) 752–753. We thank Ms.
Dutschke for her help with this book.

it in exchange for another book which was copied from this one; but that seems odd, on the face of it—that someone would give them the original, in exchange for a copy. An alternative emendation, though more complicated, would be, "Habent eum . . . ex isto *a quo* scriptus fuerit"—they have it in exchange for another book, from the man by whom it was written. The other notes in this manuscript make the latter explanation the more likely.

The usual colophon, in the hand and script-form of the text, appears at the end of the work, "explicit opus pacis in Cartusia editum pro libris corrigendis, deserviens quibuslibet aliis domibus eiusdem Cartusiensis ordinis." The same hand, in an appreciably smaller script, inserts between the lines after "in Cartusia editum" the gloss "a fratre Osualdo ibidem monacho." And following the colophon, in this same small script, the same hand adds a seven-line paragraph: 'This book, upon the excessive persistence and importunity of Dom Johann Bernsau, I Brother Oswald relinquished to him, however much I needed it myself . . . (the next words, almost two full lines, have been thoroughly obliterated with red paint) . . . and let it be communicated to all those who piously desire to use it. This is written by my own hand, just as I wrote the book itself with my own hand.' Then there is a paragraph mark and the words, 'I have so ordered, on the Friday after *Reminiscere* in the year 1428' and another entire line painted out.[30]

We have not managed to identify Johannes Bernsau, and parts of the note are enigmatic, after the deliberate deletions. We are not even positive that the date means 5 March 1428, and not 25 February 1429 (New Style), though the former is more likely. Some things are clear, however: (1) This manuscript is an autograph of the author. Collation will eventually tell whether or not it is the archetype as well; preliminary comparisons have shown that it contains a very faithful text. (2) It is certainly one of the earliest manuscripts, given that the later note was itself written in 1428. (3) Surrendering this copy made Oswald unhappy, to put it mildly. "Ad nimiam instantiam et importunitatem domini Johannis" is not a very gracious phrasing of the usual formula for granting a book on request—especially when he adds, "quamvis mihi necessarius foret." The words after that, and further words at the end, have been

---

[30] MS H, fol. 42v: "Hunc librum ad nimiam instantiam et importunitatem d. Iohannis Bernsau ego Frater Osualdus dimisi ei quamuis mihi necessarius foret / [almost two lines obliterated] / communicetque omnibus pie desiderantibus. Scriptum manu propria sicut etiam ipsum librum manu propria scripsi. Feria sexta post Reminiscere anno 1428 ita ordinaui / [one line obliterated]."

covered with red, which makes one wonder if they were not even more ungracious.

Logically, one would assume that Oswald had written this manuscript at his home, the Grande Chartreuse; the watermarks of the paper—known at Colmar, Geneva, Basel, and possibly in the Vaucluse—tend likewise to suggest Grenoble rather than Cologne.[31] He must have written the added note at Cologne, however—since the manuscript belonged to the Cologne Brethren, and since we have other evidence that Oswald was there in 1428. The best sense we can make, from the garbled *ex libris* and the deliberately mutilated statement of the author, is that Oswald grudgingly surrendered his autograph to Dom Johann Bernsau, doubtless a member of the Weidenbach house, while he was at Cologne in 1428. We would further speculate that he was at that time carrying the autograph with him on his way to Perth; and that this incident explains why the *Opus pacis* did not accompany its author to the British Isles.

The *Opus pacis* fills about eighty-three pages in the Huntington autograph. The work is divided into two parts, of roughly equal length: part 1 deals with orthography, part 2 with accents. The whole is preceded by a prologue, and followed by a brief conclusion. We shall deal only briefly with part 2. Entitled 'Concerning Accents, as They Are Marked at the Chartreuse', part 2 sets forth systematically the Carthusian rules for accentuation, under such subheadings as 'On the Principal and Regular Accent', 'When One Vowed Follows Another', 'On Nouns in General', 'On Verbs in General', etc. The importance of consistency in accents for a community's liturgy requires no explanation; we will only add that, of course, the Grande Chartreuse bore the ultimate responsibillity of establishing the standard for the whole order. Our interest, however, is in the rest of the work.

Oswald explains his motive for compiling the *Opus pacis*—and reveals the compassion mentioned—in the opening words of his prologue: 'It is so very difficult to correct books in the way prescribed by our statutes—namely, that the Grande Chartreuse be able to provide the whole order with correct exemplars—that many of those who are among the most zealous of the order are filled with anxiety—not, I say, over a phrase, or a word, or a syllable, but over the changing or omission of a single letter—to the point that their peace of mind is often gravely upset, if not destroyed altogether'.[32] (This, Oswald says, is the devil's handi-

---

[31] Watermarks: circle surmounted by a cross, similar to Briquet 2952; hand, similar to Briquet 10635.

[32] MS H, fol. 1 (printed from Trier MS 1924 by Lehmann, *Bücherliebe*, 129; here, as elsewhere, we quote MS H): "Quoniam difficillimum est ad correctionem librorum iuxta

work: since he cannot defeat us on the grand scale, he tries to steal our tranquility in small matters.) Oswald's audience, then, is comprised of people like the English Lollard scribes, scrupulously meticulous to a fault—even, he implies, to the verge of neurosis.

The Carthusian statutes do indeed lay a heavy burden on correctors: on those at the Grande Chartreuse to establish correct texts, as well as on those of other Charterhouses to emend 'against the exemplars of our order'. To take an example from the *Statuta nova* of 1368 (the statutes Oswald would have had in mind), it is there prescribed that 'No one, without express permission of general chapter, shall presume to emend books of the Old and New Testament or the books with which divine offices are celebrated, save against the exemplars that have been emended by our Order . . . We say that same also for the books of the Doctors of the Church'. And in an earlier chapter on the divine office, there is a reminder that all houses of the order are to observe the saame rite, 'from exemplars corrected and emended against the books of the Grande Chartreuse', with the explicit provision that anyone who has the 'damnable presumption' to correct—'or rather, to corrupt'—the texts in any other manner shall publicly acknowledge his fault before the convent and shall be strictly disciplined for it by his prior.[33] One can well imagine how such a combination of injunctions and threats could thoroughly destroy a corrector's peace of mind.

It is, specifically, this peace of mind that Oswald intends to restore, with his *Work of Peace*, 'so that even in this part [i.e., correction of texts], we may lead a quiet and tranquil life, with the help of Him whose abode is peace', the proogue says. What he offers, first and foremost, is relief: 'that correctors of books shall not be eaten up by pointless labor, nor the books be debased by needless erasures and overcorrection'. And he concludes the prologue by explaining, 'This work is not to be taken as a command: "Do *this!*" but rather as an indulgence, a concession: "It suffices if *this* is done." For this reason, the willing whom it pleases may accept it, while the unwilling whom it displeases are free to reject it'.[34]

---

statutorum nostrorum tenorem per totum ordinem faciendam haberi posse exemplaria domus Cartusie originalia ac per hoc plurimorum zelum ordinis habencium sollicitetur animus, ita quod non numquam non dico propter orationis siue dictionis nec sillabe quidem sed et propter unius littere mutacionem uel diminucionem quies mentis etsi non subuertitur grauiter tamen plerumque perturbatur."

[33] Lehmann, Bücherliebe, 126, citing the edition of Basel 1510.

[34] MS H, fol. 1r-v (Lehmann 129–130): "Ut igitur eciam in hac parte quietam et tranquillam uitam agamus . . . ne librorum correctores frustrato labore ubi non oportet consumantur et libri sine causa radendo uel nimis emendando deturpentur . . . Non tamen est hoc opus secundum imperium ut ita fiat, sed secundum indulgenciam ut ita fieri uel factum esse

This is a promising beginning. We already suspect that this work is not going to consist merely of more and still more lists, regulations, and injunctions that the hapless corrector must add to his already cumbersome baggage—that there will be no encouragement of the careful reproduction of nonsense, nor of the flip-a-coin-and-pick-one school of correction, which supposedly are the only options available in medieval emendation.

The beginning of the work proper lives up to expectations. The very title is intriguing: 'General Cautions to Be Observed in the Correcting of Books'—the word is *Cautele*, 'Cautions', not *Regule*.[35] The first section provides two main 'general cautions', which serve as the sturdy philosophical foundation of the *Opus pacis*: (1) 'This is the first necessity for correctors: Whenever they find variant readings—for example, when they find, from one book to another, or within the same book, or even within a single chapter, that one and the same word, with the very same meaning, is written differently, now this way, now that way (for reasons explained below)—*that they not instantly set their hands to correcting*. Rather, like the wise man, let them deliberate carefully what is best to be done, especially on the basis of the information in this work. [2] Next, let them consider this fact: Just as there have been many different grammarians, so also these grammarians have had many different opinions, often on the very same questions, in orthography, in prosody, etc. As a result, correctors should not adhere exclusively to the rules and prescriptions of one set of grammarians, while believing that all other grammarians are in error or at least have not *quite* got it right'.[36] This is the quintessence of Oswald's philosophy: Use your judgment before (or instead of) your scraper and quill, in applying the rules; for rules are not absolute.

He complements his general principles with a few illustrative examples, all tending to demonstrate that, while practices may differ, the difference is not necessarily one of right *vs.* wrong. 'The prudent corrector

---

sufficiat. Ergo qua racione amplectitur a uolente cui placet, ea respui poterit a nolente cum illi displicet."

[35] MS H, fol. Iᵛ (Lehmann 130): "Cautele in correctione librorum obseruande generales."

[36] MS H, fols. Iᵛ-2 (Lehmann 130): "Primum quidem necessarium est correctoribus ut cum diuersa reppererint, sicut aliquando fit in diuersis libris aliquando in eodem libro immo eciam aliquando in eodem capitulo, ut una eademque dictio sub eodem significato aliter et aliter scripta habeatur, propter causas infra expressatas, non statim ad corrigendum mittant manum sed uelut sapientes quid agendum sit bene deliberent, presertim iuxta huius operis informacionem. Deinde considerent quod sicut diuersi fuerint gramatici (!) sic eciam diuerse nonnumquam de eadem materia eorum opiniones fuere (!) uarie, tam de ortographia quam prosodia etcetera. Propter quod non sic inhereant aliquorum regulis et dictis ut uel alios errasse aut minus bene dixisse putent."

should know that, because of diverse customs or languages of the different nations or because of the errors or habits of scribes, there are many words common in our Carthusian usage which the ancients either wrote differently or did not use at all, while many words commonly used by them are either rare or completely unknown to us'. For example, 'words which in ancient usages were indeclinable or partly defective may be the opposite with us—and vice versa. We may double a letter that was single with them, aspirate with an H where they did not, use Y where they used I—and vice versa.' (And note, he adds, that the ancients often differ among themselves on these matters.)' The corrector should not scurry around changing all modern spellings to conform to the ancients'. Conversely, correctors should know that the spelling in many Carthusian books—especially Bibles—is apt to be conservative, retaining forms that are no longer thought correct (e.g., *iuvavi, sonavi,* for the modern *iuvi, sonui*). The corrector should not automatically modernize archaic spellings such as these. Oswald then traces in exhaustive detail the variant spellings of a single biblical name (proper names, of course, are the bane of correctors, now as then)—*Euila, u* before *i,* vs. *Eiula, i* before *u.* He tracks its uses through five places in the Hebrew scriptures, through the *Interpretations of Hebrew Names,* and through three mentions in the dictionary of Papias (the authority Carthusians most relied on).[37]

He then concludes his general cautions and general examples with one general rule: 'Generally, therefore, correctors should know that, whenever they find the same Latin, vernacular, or Hebrew word written variously, in different books and chapters or even in the same book or chapter—whether because of possible scribal error, or through long usage, or due to the varieties of vernacular languages and the dissimilar ways of men's pronunciations—*provided* that in all this variation the sense and signification of the word is preserved, it is preferable in such cases to tolerate rather than to correct'.[38] This is Oswald's by-word, reappearing

---

[37] MS H, fols. 2–3v (Lehmann 130–132): "Sciat eciam prudens corrector multas dictiones in nostro usu consuetas, propter diuersarum nacionum uarias habitudines et linguas uel propter scriptorum uicia aut alias undecumque sic inolitas, que apud antiquos uel omnino non habebantur uel aliter scribebantur et proferebantur. Et econuerso illis consuete nobis penitus sint ignote siue minus usitate . . ."

[38] MS H, fol. 3v (Lehmann 132): "Generaliter igitur nouerint correctores quod ubicumque eadem dictio latina, barbara, siue hebraica in diuersis libris et capitulis seu eciam in eodem libro aut capitulo propter uicium scriptorum incertum aut propter usum inueteratum uel propter uarietates idiomatum et dissimiles habitudines hominum secundum suas linguas aliter et aliter pronunciancium siue alio quocumque modo uarie inuenitur scripta sensu tamen ac significacione propter huiusmodi uariacionem salua remanente ibi pocius est tolerandum quam aliquod corrigendum saltim ex necessitate."

in various terms throughout the work: *if* there is no possibility that a variant spelling will cause misunderstanding, "potius est tolerandum."

The preceding is sufficient to reveal the tenor of Oswald's discussion of orthography. But, of course, the correctors needed more concrete examples to help them apply the guiding principle. 'Now I shall descend from these general cautions on correction, to the more specific', Oswald says.[39] He treats the individual problems methodically, in twenty-four numbered chapters (*cautele*), each dealing with a separate matter (though they have no titles) and each designed to help the corrector distinguish those things that need correction from those which are insignificant. We shall spare you a step-by-step trudge through the whole, but we should at least like to summarize enough of the content to give the flavor of the work.

The first two chapters are representative: Thus, *Cautela* 1 says, if there is a difference of one letter — substitution (Jabes vs. Jabis), addition or subtraction (Johannes vs. Joannes), transposition (Ihesus I-H vs. Hiesus H-I), double letter vs. single letter — tolerance is better than correction *if the sense is not affected*. (And he gives a cautionary example: *annus* with double-N is different from the same with a single N.) *Cautela* 2 treats of aspirants — H or not (habundare vs. abundare), C before medial aspirant or not (mihi vs. michi): these are unimportant, *if* the word with or without is recognizably *the same*. And so on, all with numerous examples, and with sound common-sense observations. For example, in *Cautela* 6, he notes that the inversions of words is often without importance and may be left uncorrected; but one must take care that inversion does not alter the sense: "Omnia non sunt bona" (meaning *none* is good) is significantly different from "Non omnia sunt bona" (meaning that some *are* good).

He insists throughout, in other words, that the corrector must think, must use sound judgement, rather than slavish collation, to emend. Whenever there are cases, however, for which common sense alone would not suffice, he sets the rule. For instance, he states flatly, 'the diphthongs *oe* and *ae* are no longer in use';[40] and therefore, in correcting, one should not follow the ancient exemplars in this respect. Often, his pronouncements concern cases where specifically Carthusian practice varies from the norm — or some norms, at least. In these places, he will note,

---

[39] MS H, fol. 4 (Lehmann 132): "Nunc ab istis generalibus cautelis correcture descendam ad magis speciales."

[40] MS H, fol. 41ᵛ: "Est quoque sciendum quod diptongi oe et ae modo non sunt in usu, qua propter corrigendo et scribendo non oportet in his sequi antiqua exemplaria que sunt in Cartusia."

'The rules say, you should either do this, or that; now, in *our* order, we do it thus'. For example, in *Cautela* 10 (on rules for deleting and adding letters), he specifies that one should always write the plural *his, he*—not *hiis, hee*—'regardless of the usage of others';[41] for, while doubling the vowel does not change the sense, it does change the number of syllables, which causes difficulties in reading or singing aloud. (But, he adds, in texts which our order does *not* 'read', either spelling will do. This distinction between works 'read' and 'not read' is one that he makes repeatedly, the latter requiring only uniformity of sense, the former requiring in addition precise uniformity of working and pronunciation.)

One of the most interesting aspects of the *Opus pacis* is Oswald's recognition of national differences. This was surely not accidental. The Great Schism which had split the Western church had also profoundly divided the Carthusian Order. Carthusian allegiances to conflicting general priors had followed closely along national lines. The settlement in 1417 unavoidably left the houses of Germanophone regions under the tutelage of the French mother house and, understandably, resentful that they were required to 'correct' their texts according to exemplars from the Grande Chartreuse. This was doubly irksome because the Germans often felt that the Latin of the Grande Chartreuse was not necessarily better Latin, but merely 'French' Latin. Oswald—a native German, but a high official of the mother house in France—was ideally suited to offer balm to wounded national feelings within the order. Although he never mentions the fact, doubtless this sort of peace, as well as the 'peace of mind' that he explicitly considers, was one of Oswald's aims.[42]

His prologue specifically contrasts the *Opus pacis* with an earlier handbook immodestly called *Valde bonum*, compiled during the Schism under the priorship of Dom Guilhelmus. *Valde bonum*, a list of spellings for words in the Bible and the Carthusian martyrology, met with general resistance ("non sine causa a plerisque est refutatus") because 'it was not based on an established rule or rules' ("certo vel certis moderaminibus non est regulatus"), in Oswald's words—by which he means that it was arbitrary and capricious. Because of its unpopularity, no firmly identified copies of the *Valde bonum* are known to survive (though see Grenoble B. M. 46, mentioned above); simply from the description, however, it must have been the sort of document guaranteed to rouse national animosities. As a step toward peace in the order, Oswald advises that they

---

[41] MS H, fol. 10 (Lehmann 135): "Similiter, his et he in plurali debent scribi per simplicem uocalem sicut in libris correctis Cartusie diligenter cauetur, non obstante aliorum usu."

[42] We are grateful to Michael Sargent for this suggestion.

simply treat the *Valde bonum* as a dead issue.[43]

He alludes to national differences throughout the *Opus pacis*, but *Cautele* 17 and 18 are specifically devoted to the problem. To paraphrase this lengthy section: People *do* — whether they should or not — tend to spell as they pronounce, Carthusians as much as anybody else. And pronunciation differs from one nation to another, often strongly affected by the pronunciation of the local vernacular. After all, even the ancient Doctors of the Church *came* from somewhere, this nation or that, which explains why we find things in their books which vary from our usage. He cites some contemporary examples, including *lingua* (with U), *lingwa* (with W), and even *linga* — all stemming from national differences. Now, variants like this are significant, in works that are "read" in our order; and correctors should know that it is Carthusian practice to give full force to the U, for instance, in *suadeo* (four syllables: *su-a-de-o*) — it is not to be pronounced nor spelled *swadeo*. Otherwise, however (for books *not* read or sung aloud), at the Chartreuse such variation should be peacefully tolerated by men of divers nations, for our order is designed to *serve* all nations. In such (i.e., 'non-read') books, a corrector need not emend, to conform to the exemplar from the Grande Chartreuse, but rather should take the local or regional practice as his standard. (Even Oswald's tolerance has its limits, however; the double-N spelling of *donnus, colunnis,* etc. — for *domnus, columnis* — which comes from the vernacular, is "not Latin" and should always be emended.) In similar fashion, he acknowledges that centuries of use, and the transmission from nation to nation, have had their effect on the variant spellings of Hebrew names in the Bible, and he concludes that it is not to be wondered at, given that one can see from personal experience how, in the same language, the spelling and pronunciation of the same word can change, in the distance of a mile or so.

As the conclusion of part 1, after a restatement of his guiding principle, Oswald provides roughly eight pages of check-lists: The first is an alphabetical list of proper names, mostly biblical, with their preferred and accepted spellings; any spelling not offered is to be emended. The second, more complex, is an alphabetized list of words that have varying — or unusual, or defective — forms. Some of this is self-explanatory ('either this form or that is acceptable'), but some requires explanation:

---

[43] Since this article was written, two surviving manuscripts of the *Valde bonum* have been identified; see G. Ouy, "Le *Valdebonum* perdu et retrouvé,"*Scriptorium* 42 (1988) 198–205; in an earlier article, Ouy has printed extracts from the Huntington Library manuscript of the *Opus pacis*: "Orthographe et ponctuation dans yes manuscrits autographes des humanistes français des XIVe et XVe siècles," in *Interpunzione del latino nel medioevo*, ed. A. Maierù. (Rome 1984 [1987]) 167–206.

e.g., one may accept either *applicuit* or *applicavit*—but if the former, then the participle must be *applicitum*, and if the latter, *applicatum*. At the end of the lists, he returns yet again to his favorite theme: Consult the foregoing, in correcting books; but 'neither the writer nor the reader should surrender his own good judgment'.[44]

The text of the *Opus pacis* was disseminated through the houses of the Carthusian order, for which Oswald had intended it. Copies survive from the Charterhouses of Basel, Buxheim, Erfurt, Mainz, Trier, and Utrecht; there are in fact two copies each from Basel and Mainz, and three from Erfurt where they may once have been a fourth (the catalog description makes one suspect, rather, that this last was the anonymous piece described by Köllner).[45] The existence of two copies at Cologne, one at the house of the Crutched Friars and the other at Weidenbach, may be explained by Oswald's visit to the city, and by the close spiritual ties of the Crosiers and the Brethren of the Common Life with the Carthusians. The non-Carthusian Trier manuscript comes from the Trier Benedictines, who were part of the Bursfeld Congregation; they doubtless acquired their copy from the Trier Carthusians. That Nicholas of Cues owned a copy might be expected.

The surviving manuscripts reveal that the *Opus pacis* was not only copied but was put to practical use. The manuscripts that we have seen all contain frequent marginal annotations—*nota* marks, subject-headings, key words, cross-references—often in several different hands. Two separate, and thorough, indexes exist. A very early one, made by the Erfurt Carthusians in 1427, fills more than forty folios; it refers, by page- and line-number, to the *Opus pacis* which itself fills only thirty-seven folios in the same manuscript. A second index, with references to folios, was made some ninety years later at the Basel Charterhouse. At the Trier Charterhouse, a brief anonymous text on accents, beginning "Caveat corrector . . .," was appended to the *Opus pacis* as a supplement (it is related to the piece published by Köllner from the Wolfenbüttel manuscript). In manuscripts of whatever provenance, the *Opus pacis* is usually found in a codex with similar works, on orthography, punctuation,

---

[44] MS H, fol. 21ᵛ (Lehmann 139): "In omnibus supradictis correctioni librorum consulitur, non autem scribentis aut legentis arbitrium laxatur." Marks, loc. cit. (n. 13 above) notes that these principles influenced the St. Barbara's Carthusian Gobelinus Laridus in his 1530 Cologne edition of the scriptures.

[45] P. Lehmann, ed., *Mittelalterliche Bibliothekskataloge Deutschlands und der Schweiz* 2: *Bistum Mainz, Erfurt* (Munich 1928) 478 line 17, 503 line 29 (= 276 line 12), and (excerpts) 194 line 36. Probably not Oswald's is the work named on 373 line 5, "De accentibus aliquid cum quibus cautelis servandis, et videtur sumptum ex opere pacis"; cf. Köllner, Die Opus-pacis-Handschrift, passim.

emendation, etc. The manuscript of the Cologne Crosiers, written by their librarian Conrad Grunenberg, includes the prologue and bibliography from Thomas of Ireland's *Manipulus florum*, a text on orthography, and lengthy table to the *Catholicon*. Nicholas of Cues's mid-fifteenth-century manuscript opens with another treatise on correcting the scriptures, beginning "Assit deus et sanctus Panteleone . . ." The Trier Benedictines joined the *Opus pacis* with a Latin/German vocabulary, pts. 3–4 of the *Doctrinale*, and the *De nominibus* of Petrus Helias, while the Utrecht Carthusians in 1470 grouped it with rhetorical material, including a *De arte rhetorica,* Valla's *De ratione dicendi precepta,* and excerpts from Henry Kalkar's *Loquagium.*

The *Opus pacis* had a long life, for a practical manual; and its influence extended well beyond the Carthusian order. In the 1480s the records of the annual synods, or general chapters, of the Bursfeld Congregation of reformed Benedictines show that the *Opus pacis* had achieved the status of a standard—that it had become, so to speak, the generic name for works of its kind. The Bursfelders, meeting at Erfurt in 1480, decided to appoint a committee to draw up a *registrum*—a table or list—'like a little *Opus pacis*' ("tamquam pacis opusculum") dealing with doubtful passages, accents, ceremonies, notation of the chant, and similar things, tailored for the use of their houses.[46] Amusingly enough, they seem to have assumed that merely ordering this to be done was sufficient to ensure its immediate appearance; for they went on, in the same statute, to prescribe how this as yet nonexistent work should be circulated, and even to set penalties for ignoring it!—'Three copies shall be made, for the visitors of the three circuits to communicate to each of the monasteries that they visit; these monasteries in turn shall each make a copy, within a fortnight of receiving the opusculum, and shall at once begin to follow its precepts faithfully. Any abbot who fails to carry out this order of our annual chapter shall be condemned to drink the servants' drink, until such time as he obeys'.[47] It is either a tribute to Oswald's efficiency, or a sad commentary on authorship by committee, that this work, variously called 'the register named *Opusculum pacis*' or simply *Opus pacis*, dragged on for seven or eight years (Oswald cannot have spent more than three, at the most), with increasingly scathing com-

---

[46] P. Volk, ed., *Die Generalkapitels-Rezesse der Bursfelder Kongregation* 1: 1458–1530 (Siegburg 1955) 189 no. 13 (1480).

[47] Ibid.: "Hinc tripliciter excopiandum et per visitatores trium circariarum communicandum monasteriis per eosdem visitandis, in quibus idem opusculum, postquam receperint, infra quindenam excopiabunt et fideliter practicare incipiant. Prelatus vero quiscunque, qui hoc mandatum annalis capituli exegui neglexerit, potum servorum bibere sit astrictus, donec obediat."

ments by successive annual chapters, until a provisional text was submitted in 1486, to be confirmed as the observance in all houses of the Congregation by the chapter of 1487 (with revisions already being made in 1488).[48] One would expect, from all this legislation, to find manuscripts of a Bursfeld treatise called *Opus pacis* surviving from most houses of the congregation; but in practice, save for the excerpt printed by Köllner from the Wolfenbüttel manuscript (written at the Bursfeld house in Mainz), it seems to have left no trace at all.

The original *Opus pacis*, Oswald's work, continued meanwhile to be copied and used. A copy was made for the Utrecht Carthusians by Johannes Stertt in 1470; and it bears marginal annotations, in at least two different hands, on nearly every folio. The Rookloster union catalog (ca. 1470–1530) lists a copy of the work ("Oswaldus: Opus pacis etc., quoddam correctorium biblie"), although the work's location is not specified.[49]

The latest surviving manuscript of the *Opus pacis* was written at the Basel Charterhouse in 1514 by Johannes Lindower. He also created a sensible subject index to it, added from Bruno of Würzburg's commentary on the Psalms an extract that deals with emendation, and bound these with an incunable of similar nature, the *Vocabularius* of Johannes Altensteig—thus indicating that manuscript correction remained a living subject some sixty years into the printed era.

✻   ✻   ✻

We have set forth here the context, authorship, circulation, content, and afterlife of the *Opus pacis*, a medieval treatise on emendation. On the basis of these remarks, one can only conclude that Professor Kenney's observation, "Of conjectural criticism in anything like the modern sense the Middle Ages knew nothing"—an observation to be "shaken by one positive example to the contrary"—remains unshaken. For this is not conjectural criticism in the modern philologist's sense at all: But it is conjectural criticism nonetheless. Countless Carthusians and others read and attempted to apply the *Opus pacis*, with its repeated enjoinders to 'Wait', 'Reflect', 'Use your good judgment'. As for the further pronouncement, then, that 'Conjecture was not generated . . . by the mind of the corrector': Oswald's *Opus pacis*, in tenor, in toto, and in each least of its parts, comprises an 'example to the contrary'.

---

[48] Ibid., 221 no. 12 (1486), 227 no. 6 (1487), and 232 no. 17 (1488). See also 195 no. 6 (1481), 201 no. 8 (1482), 205 no. 6 (1483), 217 no. 9 (1485).

[49] Vienna, Nat. Bibl. MS 12,694, sub nom. Oswaldus. Concerning this and the related catalogs, see P. F. J. Obbema, "The Rookloster Register Reevaluated," *Quaerendo* 7 (1977) 326–353.

12. Backgrounds to Print: Aspects of the Manuscript Book in Northern Europe of the Fifteenth Century

The following observations will focus on the transition from manuscript to printed book, and have particular reference to the thesis of Elizabeth Eisenstein's book, *Print as an Agent of Change*, 2 vols. (Cambridge: University Press, 1979). Eisenstein attempts to demonstrate that the invention of printing was the single major factor which underlies the complex of social changes known as the Renaissance. In her view, the printing press enabled medieval people finally to carry out tasks at which they had been stymied for the previous five hundred years. The medieval world, shackled by the inaccurate single-copy handwritten book, was finally able to break loose and change. The body of Eisenstein's book is devoted to a definition and analysis of the types of change brought about by the press. While fascinating and provocative, the book suffers seriously from the fact that the author has not first come to grips with the nature of scribal culture, with the potentials and the limitations of the manuscript book as a vehicle of communication. If one has not defined scribal culture, how can one determine what changes printed culture brought about? It is not an impossible task, even though paleographers also have shied away from it. The written page, however, is an artifact from the past, a tangible piece of historical evidence, its changes in form reflecting social and intellectual change. This paper, therefore, will attempt to define (1) some aspects of the nature of the fifteenth-century handwritten book in Germany and the Low Countries,

Originally delivered as an address on 26 September 1981 to a plenary session of the Sixth Mid Atlantic States PMR Conference at Villanova University, and published in *Proceedings of the PMR Conference* 6 (1981) 37–49.

and (2) the relationship of the manuscript book to the invention of printing; and will conclude with (3) some comments on the change in the
book brought about by print.

I

The printing press was invented in Germany, Mainz to be precise,
and when it first appeared outside of Germany, it appeared in Italy,
where two German printers had migrated. Curious, then, that Eisenstein's
discussion of scribal culture should concentrate on England and France;
for by so doing, it eliminates from consideration the two communities of
the later Middle Ages that bring about dramatic changes in the nature of
the book, in adapting it to better serve their needs. These two are (1)
Italian humanists in Florence, and (2) the renewed religious orders of the
Modern Devotion in the Low Countries and Germany (in particular the
Windesheim Congregation, the Brethren of the Common Life, and the
reformed Benedictines and Austin Canons). The work of the humanists
has been well examined, and this paper therefore will focus on the
North, where print began.

The production of text manuscripts in Northern Europe in the fifteenth century—in Austria, Germany, and the Low Countries—is characterized by two contrasting qualities: (1) idiosyncrasy and individuality
to a degree never before seen, giving the period its bad name, and
reflecting the myriad of owner-produced books; (2) organization and
uniformity resulting from an urge for clarity, both bibliographic and
visual, the emanated from the rebirth of monastic scriptoria which had
lain dormant under the onslaught of university and mendicant book-
production for nearly a century and a half. These two characteristics
make the fifteenth century a distinguishable epoch in the history of the
manuscript book, and elevate it from its traditional and rather ignomin-
ious position as a chaotic period of scruffy paper books—poorly written
in ugly, crabbed, cursive hands of the decline of the Middle Ages—to
one on a par (as regards its distinctness) with the other great epochs of
the manuscript book: namely, the Carolingian, the twelfth-century Anglo-
Norman monastic, and the thirteenth-century university stationers' books.
The book usage of the reformed orders underlies not only the form of
the printed book but its acceptance in the fifteenth century, and for that
reason alone the book usage of these reformed orders merits closer examination.

This paper will deal with the more organized books, if only because
uniformity is more easily described than individuality. Such books are

the tangible signs of the renewal of northern European spirituality in the late fourteenth and fifteenth centuries. This renewal is first seen in the last quarter of the fourteenth century both in Carthusian and then Benedicting circles. The exemplary individuality of the Carthusians who move from their remote outposts to the city in the late fourteenth and fifteenth centuries is an important source for the new movements of lay piety, seen for example in the two elements of the Modern Devotion: the Windesheim Congregation and the Brethren of the Common Life. Traditional monastic orders, such as the Benedictines, undergo a series of internal reforms, among them (1) Abbot Nortweiner's renewal of Kastl in 1380, which spread through Bavaria; (2) the reforms initiated at the Council of Constance (1414–1418), from which the Austrian Danube houses, beginning with Melk, took on renewed vigor; and (3) efforts towards renewal emanating from the Council of Basel (1431–1449), which took form at Bursfeld and spread to the north and west of Germany, with the result that, before the end of the century, nearly two hundred Benedictine houses belonged to the Union of Bursfeld. Carthusians, Windesheimers, Brethren of the Common Life, Austin canons, Cistercians, or Benedictines—it is difficult and needless here to distinguish among their various interpretations of renewal—are closely linked and share in common the spirit of the Modern Devotion: a form of practical, individual search for a direct rapport with God through his written word and the interpretation of it. These orders shape the book to serve their needs. What emerges is a book distinctly different from anything the Middle Ages had hitherto seen—a book which in some ways has more in common with the printed book than with the products of the manuscript era that preceded it.

What, then, are the features of this new manuscript book, and how do we account for the abruptness of this change? The features can be grouped by function. *First*, the new book exhibits a vital concern for clarity of text, a concern seen in two aspects of the script: We see the formation of a new bookhand or text script termed *hybrida*, a combination of book and running scripts that would be written with the speed of *cursiva* but without the loss of legibility so often caused by the loopiness of cursive, with the *hybrida* substituting sharp angles for loops. The script takes shape in the Low Countries at the end of the fourteenth century, and blossoms in the first half of the fifteenth, becoming the common property of the various reformed scriptoria. Also, for the sake of visual clarity, we see reinstituted on occasion the practice of employing a hierarchy of scripts, to distinguish different sections of the text. Rubrics and colophons in particular are to be distinguished from the body of the text, because they contain the essential bibliographic information for identifying the work. The notion of a hierarchy of scripts, employed to such good effect in Carolingian books, had gradually passed out of use; so that by 1200, rubrics were written in letters of the same shape as the text script, only larger in size. A distinction in actual script-form for titles, rubrics, and colophons, is first reinstituted by early fifteenth-century Italian humanists, in imitation of the classicizing tendencies of the Carolingians. In the North, the earliest use of distinct scripts for title, rubrics and colophons is to be found in manuscripts of the Brethren in the Low Countries that date from the 1410s.

A *second* major feature which distinguished the books and book usage of the new orders was their concern for assuring the accuracy of the text. According to Eisenstein, the inability of the Middle Ages to produce an accurate copy was the most serious handicap of scribal culture and a major reason why scholarship never advanced. If, with each successive copying, one introduced new errors in transcription, how could one create an accurate text or accumulate corrections? In a world where the text partook both of an oral transmission and a single-copy scribal nature, how could one have the concept of an 'edition,' that is, a correct text? But in fact medievals could indeed have a sense of weeding out error and emending a text, when it was important to the community using the book.

The desire for textual accuracy among the Carthusians in the fifteenth century produced the first detailed codification of rules for textual emendation in Latin and vernacular texts, the *Opus pacis* written in 1428 by the German Carthusian Oswald de Corda, prior of the Grand Chartreuse. The *Opus pacis* pays careful attention to the punctuation of texts, for example, since for meaning to be clear a sentence must be divided into its proper grammatical parts. More important and interesting are the sections of the *Opus pacis* that deal with correct orthography. Oswald takes the sensible attitude that *no* corrections should be made when divergence in spelling merely reflects regional practice, without distorting the pronunciation or the meaning of the words. Thus, he says, while it is incorrect to insert *p* between *m* and *n*, in such words as *dampnum, columpna,* and so forth—"as the Bible in the choir at Chartreuse spells these"—nevertheless the intrusion does not affect pronunciation or meaning, and need not be corrected where it is already written. It is otherwise, however, with such matters as the spelling of the plural *hiis* and *hee* with a double vowel. While this misspelling does not change the meaning, it adds an extra syllable "which makes for diversity in chanting and in reading aloud." Therefore, such misspelling "is to be scrupulously corrected in Carthusian books—regardless of the practice of other people." The *Opus pacis* is particularly noteworthy for us, because an autograph manuscript of it is now in California, at the Huntington Library. This manuscript earlier belonged to the Brethren of the Common Life of Weidenbach in Cologne, having been given in response to their urgent request. The manuscript is bound with a printed book, Chrysostom's homilies on the Pauline epistles, which was printed for the Brethren of the Common Life in Brussels in 1479. Fittingly enough, the text of the printed book has been corrected throughout by hand.

The Windesheimers, also, attempted to emend the texts of their earlier Bibles and patristic authors. They wanted to correct them all uniformly (that is, the books of all the houses of the congregation) by comparing them with *exemplaria emendatiora*. By this they mean the combined readings of the oldest available manuscripts which they proposed to select on the basis of letter form: "tria aut quattuor . . . volumina vetutis litterarum figuris" (three or four volumes that contain early letterforms). Though they were very naive — for example, they thought they had someone's copy of Jerome's autograph of the Vulgate — still, as principles of emendation go, theirs and those posed in the *Opus pacis* are faultless, and might profitably have been adopted by early printers.

Another distinguishing feature of German fifteenth-century manuscripts is that they abound in aids to finding one's way about the text. None of these aids is invented or first reinstituted in the fifteenth century, as is the principle of a hierarchy of scripts; instead, the point is that these aids are used with increasing frequency and become increasingly complex. In specific, I am referring to the effective application of any or all of the following devices: (a) tables of contents for the codex, recorded by librarians on the pastedowns; (b) lists of chapters, either at the beginning of each book or gathered at the beginning of the whole work; (c) running headlines across the top of facing left- and right-hand pages, the 'opening,' giving the author and/or title and the number of book or chapter; and (d) foliation or pagination in arabic numerals, a practice which came into existence in the thirteenth century as a response to the need to order the leaves in a manuscript, and which became ubiquitous in the fifteenth century. (e) Perhaps the most striking change is the widespread appearance of subject indexes in fifteenth-century German manuscripts. New indexes are compiled to older texts, new texts appear with indexes, and older free-standing indexes acquire new life. Large freestanding alphabetically arranged reference compendia abound in the libraries of the reformed orders — for example, the *Lumen anime*, extracts from the authorities under about 100 alphabetically arranged topics on the subject of natural history, properly moralized, of which the Carthusians in Erfurt alone had nine copies representing three versions; Thomas of Ireland's *Manipulus florum* (6000 extracts under 265 alphabetized topics from *Abstinence* to *Christus*, spelled with an X); William of Montague's *Liber exceptionum ex libris viginti trium auctorum*; the anonymous *Liber pharetrae*, and the thirteenth-century table to the works of the authorities attributed to Walter of Bruges. These are all aids for using the works of the Church Fathers, whether in writing sermons or in the compilation of didactic and devotional treatises.

As there is a concern for clarity of text, there is a similar concern for bibliographic clarity exhibited in the expansion of the initial and final rubric or colophon. Rubrics have always existed to give the author and title of the text, and to signal the beginning and end of a text. It is, rather, the enlargement of the rubric, from one or two to eight or ten lines, and its distinction by means of separate letter-form, as well as the categories of information included, that are significant. Compare, for example, this early rubric:

> [Incipit]: *Here begins St. Augustine's* De patientia . . . [explicit]: *in the Lord's name, here ends St. Augustine's sermon* De patientia (Leiden Voss. Q.98, s. ixɪ).

—with a fifteenth-century rubric from a Cologne Charterhouse book now in Claremont:

> [Incipit]: *Here begins the prologue of the fourth book of sayings and stories of the holy Fathers, the start of which Pelagius, deacon of the Holy Roman Church, and the rest of which John the subdeacon translated from Greek into Latin. . . .* [explicit]: *Here ends the prologue.* [Incipit]: *Here begins the fourth book of the lives and sayings and stories of the holy Fathers divided into nineteen parts; the first part concerning monastic growth . . .* [explicit]: *Here ends the fourth book on the lives and sayings and stories of the saints.*

Or, consider the rubric in a manuscript of Bernard's sermons, written in the Netherlands in 1457:

> Hier begint dat derde stuck vanden sermoenen S. Bernaerts des abts van Clarendael, date eerste sermoen op S. Maria Magdalened dach. . . .
> (*Here begins the third part of the sermons of St. Bernard, abbot of Clairvaux; the first sermon is for the Feast os St. Mary Magdalene.*)

and the colophon:

> Dit boec is gescreven int jair ons Heren M CCCC ende LVII. Ende wert geeyndet op ten zesten dach in der maent van October. Een Ave Maria van mynnen om Gods will voer die onnutte scrijfster.

(This book was written in the year of Our Lord 1457. And it was finished on the sixth day of the month of October. For the love of God, say an Ave Maria for the worthless scribe.)

Desire for bibliographic detail extended even to the writer of the manuscript—I would rather use that expression that 'scribe,' because the latter implies an anonymity which is incongruous with the close association between writer and manuscript exuded by these books. Take, for example, the colophon of an English book written by a Netherlander far from home:

It ends, let it end; whoever wants to write more, let him write. Thanks to God, pray for the writer. Here ends the exposition of Bede the priest on the Tabernacle of God, begun and ended by me, Tielman, son of Cledwin and cleric of the diocese of Utrecht, Ad 1432, on the 21st day of the month of February, around 3 p.m. or thereabouts. (Cambridge, Gonville and Caius Coll. 114.)

These efforts directed toward bibliographic clarity and order are seen also in efforts to know about the texts available in the libraries, their own as well as those of others, through the making of bibliographies, subject catalogs, location lists and union catalogs. Bibliography is a wellknown medieval genre: in the form of the catalogs *De viris illustribus* and *De scriptoribus ecclesiasticis* of various orders, or the "lists of works quoted" that authors might include in their prologues. Such works circulated freely in fifteenth-century Germany, and they were often gathered together in something like a bibliographic corpus. One such is a manuscript of the Croziers in Cologne, which contained in a single volume the *Philobiblon*, Gerson's *De laude scriptorum*, the list of authors and works from the *Manipulus florum*, Bede's list of his own writings from the end of his *Historia ecclesiastica*, and the list of the books in the *Catholicon*. Besides gathering bibliographies, fifteenth-century librarians prepared massive catalogs, which in fact could be used as introductions to the numerous individual works available for use in the library. The catalog of the Erfurt Carthusians (fd. 1372) is the best example of this type of catalog. Completed at the end of the fifteenth century, it provides an introduction to the major works in the library, giving for each (along with its call number, author and title), the main intent of the work, what it is good for, and its main sections. The catalog is arranged by subject, and an ample supply of cross-references allows one to work back and forth with ease among the myriad texts described.

The following is the description of the above-mentioned *Opus pacis*, taken from the shelf-list of the Salvatorberg catalog for the MS

numbered M (vocabularies, grammar, properties of words) 26, now
Weimar Ms. qu 22.:

> M.26. Opus pacis ["Work of peace"]. It is called thus because it teaches
> one how to correct regularly and carefully (lest the spirit of some, who
> have a zeal for order and concord in correcting, be led astray into correct-
> ing incautiously), because often, by change, insertion or omission—I will
> not say of a phrase, word, or syllable, but even of single letter—one's
> peace of mind, if not entirely overset, may at least be gravely perturbed.
> This work is preceded in the codex by a certain little book called Valde
> bonum ["Very good"]. Whatever [text] is not regulated by certain rules is
> therefore, and not without cause, rejected by many; and unless the text be
> corrected according to the tenor of this work, it will be of little benefit, as
> experience has shown. This Valde bonum contains the vocabulary of
> martyrologies and the Bible; the former [Opus pacis] goes beyond that, to
> the correction of the works of the doctors of the Church. Valde bonum
> was collected by Dom Wilhelm during the time of the Schism; the former
> was compiled in the year the Schism ended by Dom Johann (i.e., Oswald),
> of German origin, prior of Chartreuse. (ed. P. Lehmann, Mittelalterliche
> Bibliotheks-Kataloge, II, 478.)

The description for H.36, a copy of the Manipulus florum, is even fuller
than the above:

> H.36. The Manipulus florum agrees with, and conforms very much to, the
> book called Pharetra ["Quiver"], both in its contents and in its manner of
> proceeding, though in the Pharetra the contents are much more extensive.
> This book contains diverse extracts, principally from the Holy Doctors
> but also from some other authors, who are listed on folio 5. The extracts
> are collected briefly from various books according to alphabetical order,
> in the fashion of a concordance, so that they may easily be found. For that
> reason this book is called Manipulus florum ["Sheaf of flowers" or
> "extracts"], since it has been gathered into one collection from the diverse
> "cornfields" of the authorities. Within its covers one finds promptly at
> hand the material that one could scarcely find in searching through many
> separate volumes. One finds listed here in alphabetical order, like a con-
> cordance, the more important and commonest topics that arise in both
> lectures and sermons, and, indeed, those topics which might be helpful to
> a man in all things. Thus, it should be apparent that the present book and
> the Pharetra complement one another very well, in both form and content.

Other contents of this codex are as follows:

> A table which lists all the topics treated herein; a list of the books of the
> Doctors, including their first and last words, so that whoever wishes to cite

them may do so with certainty and, if he chances upon them, can recognize them; a brief compendium on rhetorical colors; and a few quires of extracts from Seneca. (II, 390–91, Lehmann.)

Perhaps the most interesting experiment in cataloging, extending over a generation or more, is the effort to prepare a union catalog of books in the religious houses along the Rhine and in the Low Countries. The oldest extant version of this survives in a fragment of a few leaves now in Basel. From this, one can see that the Carthusians, probably in Cologne, began by compiling a basic list from a group of standard bibliographies—portions of the list of authors and works appended to the *Manipulus florum*, portions of a Dominican *De viris illustribus* list, and sections of other books. This composite bibliography was circulated among the various houses, and each added its siglum or symbol after the titles of those books found in its library. This list is related to the much larger catalogs compiled at Gaesdonck, St. Martin's of Louvain, and Rookloster between 1470 and 1530.

In all of the above—efforts toward clarity of text, toward access to texts through the application of both indexes and library catalogs, and toward textual accuracy, book production and library usage—the new movements of the fifteenth century distinguish themselves by their desire to formulate rules of procedure and to codify, a desire that reflects the sense of practicality that characterizes their work. This is seen in the rules for punctuation formulated by the Carthusians; in the *Opus pacis* or rules for textual emendation; in the extensive rules for writing and for the ordering of the library, seen in the statutes and customs of the Carthusians and the Brethren in the fifteenth century; and lastly, in treatises that incorporate the writing of text manuscripts into the framework of religious activity, such as Gerson's *De laude scriptorum* and Trithemius' work of the same title.

II

Having set out these features of the manuscript book and of book provisions which I feel make the fifteenth-century book a thing distinct from earlier forms of the manuscript book, I think one must ask why these changes occur, and what their significance is. These changes occur because the written page takes on a renewed, if not a new, meaning to religious communities in the fifteenth century. The scriptoria of Benedictine, Cistercian, and Augustinian houses, which had last produced books in quantity in the 1230s, before they were submerged by the flood of university and mendicant books, now resumed life. Libraries which had subsisted on the gifts of twelfth-, thirteenth- and fourteenth-century donors—libraries that had not actively acquired books since they were first established in the twelfth century—began once more to acquire texts. The renewal which took place was based squarely on the written word, and the believer's access to it.

The place of the written word, and of the physical process of writing, in the religious life of the Carthusians and, by extension, the Brethren and the Augustinian canons, can best be described in their own language and metaphors. "You shall eat the fruit of the labor of your hands, and you shall be blessed" (Psalm 128:2) is quoted by Jean Gerson (Chancellor of the University of Paris, 1395–1429) in his 1423 tract *De laude scriptorum*. The same phrase occurs as the scriptural "authority" for the chapter *De scripturario* in the statutes of the Munster house of the Brethren; the statute continues: "therefore, to avoid sloth (the root of all other vices) and to provide our necessities, we accept, as the principal and most fitting task laid upon us, the writing of sacred books."

One shall live by the fruit of one's labors—what does that mean? In one sense, this admonition is not particularly different from the traditional monastic principle that idleness is bad for the soul. But it means more than just that, as the wording of the Munster statute makes clear: not just *any* task, for the sake of occupation, but "writing sacred books" as the most fitting, suitable, and pious task. At the end of a collection of *sermones de tempore* printed for the Rostock Brethren in 1476, the latter are referred to as *Fratres non verbo sed scripto predicantes* ("Brethren who preach, not by speaking, but by writing"). Guigo of the Grande Chartreuse, who formed the oldest statutes of the Carthusian order (ca. 1112), said in them: "Since we are not able to speak, we preach with our hands." Beginning with the Carthusians, then—who were the principal spiritual 'source' for the reformed orders—writing was elevated to the level of preaching. We might profitably ask therefore what preaching meant to the ecclesiastics of the fifteenth century. To Guigo in the early twelfth century, the sermon may have been little more than a means by which the abbot spoke to the chapter. But by the 1400s—after the emphasis on preaching of the Fourth Lateran Council, and after the formation and expansion of preaching orders and the creation of a structure of pastoral theology in the schools—preaching and the sermon were not vague terms in the eyes of ecclesiastics. The sermon was *the* means by which the priest exhorted believers to confess, do penance, and take the sacraments. Preaching had become an indispensable part of the Church's ministry. The learned fifteenth-century doctor Geiler von Kayserberg is hired in Strasbourg not to give the sacraments, but to preach. And, in

Geiler's own words, "Mass without a sermon is much more injurious to a congregation's faith than a sermon without Mass." It is not surprising, hence, to see Thomas à Kempis (d. 1471) quote with approval the words of Gerhard Zerbolt: "These books preach and teach more than we are able to say. For sacred books are the lamps of our souls and our solace and the true healing balm of life, which we can no more do without, in our earthly pilgrimage, than we can the sacraments of the Church." If the form of spiritual writing has been elevated to the level of the sacraments of the Church, then the biblical text "You shall eat the fruit of the labor of your hands" takes on a new meaning.

The New Devotion (*Devotio moderna*) rested squarely on the reading of devotional texts—the works of Augustine, Bernard, and Bonaventure—for instruction. The written word, central to their faith, was raised to a level of importance seldom accorded it by earlier religious movements. And if the written word was important, then how equally important, how blessed, was the writing thereof. No wonder, then, that the statutes of the houses of the Brethren are often preceded not only by a brief history of the house but by biographies of their famous writers—*not*, in this case, their authors, but their praiseworthy scribes—listing the books they had copied, and the language and the script in which they were written. The following are two such biographies, the first of a writer and the second of an unlettered brother who found a useful niche in the production of books:

> Dom Jacob Enckhuysen (born of rather wealthy parents) was an agile and lively youth while he was attending the schools at Zwolle. Admitted to our house, he became the best of scribes, beloved of everyone because he was prompt and apt for all the exercises of our house. Finding strength in the flower of virginity, he remained robust and lively right up to the end of his life. Consequently, having become a good religious, and exceedingly faithful to the work of copying, he transcribed many books in cursive and fraktur script. In addition to missals, graduals, psalters, and canons, of which he copied many, he also wrote a Bible in fraktur, valued at fifty gold florins, which is at St. Mary's in Utrecht [now Utrecht University Library MS 31, written in six volumes during the years 1462–67], made at the expense of Master Hermann Droem from Paris, a dean of Utrecht and an able jurist. Dom Jacob was appointed for a short time as director of the Sisters at Ter Maet. But because that house, especially in those days, required a strict and rigorous regimen beyond his natural endowment, he was soon released from this task and assigned to the customary writing exercises of the cell. There in all his deeds and actions he was very diligent, so that he discharged those duties properly and in a quite perfect

manner. For whatever he wrote he did with due consideration, and he strove diligently to take into account and to provide for himself all the requisites for this. He was also for a long time, right up to his death, the custodian of books and the keeper of the clock. Such duties he performed most satisfactorily, because he always carried down, at the appropriate time, the book or books from which there was to be reading at table, preventing, when he could, the occurrence of anything out of the ordinary which might cause disturbance or discomfiture. Similarly, he tended the clock most competently, so that, while he was at hand, no untimely reveille occurred through his negligence. If the clock was ever out of order, he himself diligently saw to it that it was regulated before the time of our rising. He was always more than kind and considerate—and altogether affable. He had a good voice and was knowledgeable about chanting. But in speech he sometimes faltered by speaking too fast. Because of this he was embarrassed to make speeches in public. However, he made up for this defect through reading aloud, for very often he read for the laity and clergy in a clear and sonorous voice. At length, for four or five days before he died, he began to lose his appetite, and because of this he became so weak that he was hardly able to get about without a cane. Therefore we said to him, "Dom Jacob, perhaps you want to die." He responded, "Right, I have lived long enough. It is time for me to die." But he lived about three or four more days with his strength constantly failing, although none of us, nor he himself, knew the cause of his infirmity, except that the Lord was calling him. He was bedridden for less than two days; and the day before his death, when our brethren spoke to him about receiving the sacraments of the church, he replied, "When it pleases you." And then, late in the day, he received them devoutly and expired that same night, that he might rest from his labors. That was on [Saturday, September 20] the vigil of the blessed Apostle Matthew. He was buried at Windesheim alongside his brethren in the year of our Lord 1483.

*   *   *

In the same year, before Dom Jacob, there died our beloved brother Dom Hermann Corvodie, who was a relative of the father of our venerable father Dom Theoderic. As a favor to the latter, we received him [Dom Hermann] from the House of Paupers into our house, although he was somewhat deficient in letters (in spite of the fact that he [had] attended school long enough, he had not had much success). Wherefore, in our house he became a good binder of books, for he was very practical and thorough in such things as pertained to mechanical work, so much so that he was found to be suitable and showed himself to be amenable for carpentry both in the house and in the rooms of the brethren. Thereafter, because he sustained an injury, he became an illuminator of books, which he learned to do very well. Thus what he lacked in letters, he made up in practical and manual work. Because he was industrious and interested in all things, he knew how to respond to each person according to his condition and the things asked him. Because he formed his words aptly and sometimes even cleverly and jocularly, he was consequently pleasing to all who came there and spoke with him. Finally in Lent, specifically [March 13] *the day after* [the feast] *of Pope Gregory* [the Great], *he had a flux of the stomach* [and] *so he approached his end, daily failing in strength, but at all times bearing his infirmity patiently. At length, fortified by his sacraments, he expired on the second day of Easter, that is* [Monday, March 31, 1483] *the third day before the kalends of April, about the middle of the following night. He was buried at Windesheim alongside his brethren.* (Jacobus Traiecti alias de Voecht, *De inchoatione domus clericorum in Zwollis*, ed. M. Schoengen, Historisch Genootschap, 3rd ser., No. 13 [Amsterdam, 1908], pp. 190–94).

As they were not endowed with land but were opposed to begging for their livelihood, the Windesheimers and the Brethren made their living by commercial writing. They wrote anything from didactic and spiritual tracts to the expensive Bible produced for the dean of Utrecht by Jacob van Enkhuisen. The central importance of books and of writing to a Windesheim house is reflected in the workmanlike attention paid to all aspects of the process in their statutes—as in this example from the house at Zwolle, ca. 1427:

Concerning the Librarian

It is the custom to commit to one of the brothers (1) the care of our books, (2) the charge of writing and decorating, and (3) the custody of the parchment. (1) Concerning our books, let him take care that they are not maltreated nor improperly placed, and that whatever needs fixing, in the way of correction, binding, and the like, is fixed. He shall record each book distinctly in the register; let him consider carefully to whom he lends books, and diligently record their names and the length of the loan. If a book is missing, he should tell the rector; and if he himself is to blame, let him humbly beg forgiveness. So that scholars seeking books need not be dealt with every day, let him set them a fixed hour on feast days. Once in each year he shall collect all our books, and at the set hour all the brothers shall be called, with the rector present, to oversee, clean, and examine them. An associate shall be deputed to him for the books in the larger library, who shall keep the register for these and oversee the reading at the table; he shall not, however, lend any book outside the house without the knowledge of the librarian, and he shall not lend any of our deluxe books for longer than one day, without the permission of the rector. Also, one of those whom the rector will appoint shall sit beside the reader at the table as his corrector. Our own brothers within the house may remove one book from the library for study assigned to them by the rector, and shall sign their names on the tablet; but they may not take more with them to their chambers without the permission of the librarian or his associate. Also, once at the beginning of each month, the librarian's associate shall attend to the register and the tablet of books, and shall collect all the books from their various places, except the studies of the brothers, and replace them precisely in the library.

(2) Let the librarian take care, concerning the writing in our house, that all the brothers have enough to write; and all the same, let him not casually turn away someone who wishes to have a good book written, even though at that moment none of the brothers is free, but rather let him persuade the buyer to wait a little while. When someone asks to have a book written and we do have a writer available, let the librarian show him a sample of the writer's hand and come to an agreement with him for a certain price per quatern, unless he is content to rely on our own reckoning; but the librarian should not agree with anyone concerning the price of a deluxe book without taking advice of the rector, or of whomever the rector shall appoint for that purpose. The librarian should make a firm contract, especially with people unknown to us, so that we shall not get in to altercations after the fact; and according to his estimate he shall quote the man a price, and ask for a down payment in advance as the book is begun; and in cases where immediate payment in full cannot be relied on, he should not hand over the finished book before the balance is paid, or until someone we know goes surety. Let him forewarn the buyer, when occasion demands, if a given writer because of illness or other reasonable cause cannot finish a book, and ask that he agree to its being completed by another, similar hand. The librarian ought to take the greatest care to procure corrected exemplars for our writers, lest we burden our consciences by writing incorrect books. From time to time, he should admonish our brothers that they do their work faithfully and carefully oversee the writing of our brothers, especially of those who least know how to write formally, and of those who are beginning something new, providing them with a line or two of the better sort of script to keep before them as a model. Before the binding of books, inspect them to see that they are well corrected, and that the corrections have been entered without noticeably marring or disfiguring the books—which he should warn the brothers about beforehand. Let him provide our writers with the necessary tools, namely, penknives, pens, pumice, chalk, and the like. Also he must provide the illuminator and binder with the things that they need for their

work, and charge them that they inform him early enough of their needs so that he can buy these with the minimum of expense. He shall see to the mixing of the ink, along with his helper, and be sure that he makes only good ink, because good books may easily be brought to naught on account of bad ink.

(3) As for the care of the parchment: he must see to it that he procures parchment, vellum, and paper ahead of time and that he has a good supply on hand, so that he may dole them out according to the individual requirements of the books. Also, it seems more efficient that, with his helper, he prepare the greater part of the parchment all at once, so that he will not have to spend time preparing parchment every day; and in preparing it, he should beware of spots, missing corners, tears, and sewed places, as much as possible. For the purchase of parchment a sufficient sum will be given over to the librarian; what remains, after the settling of accounts each year, shall be given to the proctor. Let him not presume to give away to others the materials committed to his care — save scraps of parchment not useful for any bifolia *and other things like that, which he may dispose of as he likes. He should take care to record plainly and distinctly in his register all debts and receipts, and see to it that he claims in time the price of the books and what is owed to him, knowing himself deserving of correction should he be negligent in this, because we have often sustained loss from this sort of negligence. Once each year he shall make a reckoning, before the rector and the brothers, of his and his brothers' profit, and whatever gain of any sort he has in cash he shall promptly hand over to the proctor. The rest he shall pay little by little, as the cash comes to hand. Once the accounting has been done, he shall resign his register, purse, keys, and office and whatever pertains to it, humbly asking release from the rector and the brothers. Also every year, after the office has been committed to the same man again or newly committed to another, the rector, the librarian, and a third knowledgeable in these matters, shall take up the account book of the prices of our* bifolia, *both of the parchment itself and of the writing, and shall deliberate what is sufficient according to the changing value of money and the worth of our time, so that we do not take more nor less than what constitutes a just price.* (Jacobus Traiecti, op. cit., pp. 252–55)

The book provisions of the Carthusians and the *Devotio moderna* (Brethren of the Common Life, Windesheimers) were influential in the fifteenth century and became the models for reformed houses of Austin canons and Benedictines throughout Germany. It is due to the Windesheimers and the Brethren, most of all, that the "new book" achieved a dissemination far beyond the walls of ecclesiastical houses; for they were major participants in fifteenth-century commercial book production, having seized upon this as a sensible means both to earn their physical bread and to gain spiritual grace—to "eat the fruit of their labors" and "be blessed." Their enterprise has been called an "Apostolate of Writing." They were for good reason known as the *Broeder van den penne*.

What then is the relationship of this upsurge in the necessity of the word and the page to the invention of printing? The invention of printing and the acceptance of the printed book as the medium of communication are traditionally treated as a remarkable invention enthusiastically seized upon by a "technology-minded" Western society. That Gutenberg was a goldsmith rather than a scribe is stressed, as is the fact that he worked in a German city rather than at a university. All these assessments fail to recognize the relationship of the Modern Devotion to the invention of, and even more to the rapid acceptance of, printing. Between 1450 and 1500, it is estimated that some fifteen to twenty million copies were printed of some 40,000 editions, a very large number indeed—perhaps larger than the number of all the manuscripts produced in medieval Europe. The authors and titles published by incunable printers, to the puzzlement of modern scholars, were primarily copies of the Fathers, Bibles, liturgical books, medieval theologians and monastic writers—Augustine, Bernard, and Bonaventure. Only Caxton stands out as a publisher of romance. This fact has always puzzled historians, who wondered why the new invention published such "old stuff." Rudolf Hirsch, in *Printing, Selling and Reading, 1450–1550* (Wiesbaden: Harrassowitz, 1967), ventures the suggestion that it is because these texts were readily available in the old monasteries which dot the land.

No one invests in, and succeeds in selling, a produce simply because it is readily available; instead, the successful entrepreneur sells the commodity for which there is a demand. A look at virtually any monastic booklist of the second half of the fifteenth century reveals that the monasteries were lavish in purchasing printed books. The surviving incunabula indicate the same, over and over again; they bear the *ex-libris* marks of German religious houses: Melk, Bursfeld, Buxheim, Erfurt. The demand for books in the revived monastery was such that not only did it consume the output of commercial presses but that monasteries, houses of the Windesheim congregation and of the Brethren in particular, hired printers to publish for them. The printing press succeeded so quickly because the monastery was its market. The book provisions that we discussed earlier pertain to the whole of the fifteenth century; they treat printed and manuscript book alike, without distinction. Without the Modern Devotion and the reformed Benedictines, and their need for texts, printers would have gone broke. That goes far to explain why printing was so slow to establish in France and in England, and so rapid to expand in Germany and the Low Countries. At the end of the century, when Trithemius writes a treatise in praise of scribes, it is not to be taken (as it so often is) as a symbol of the persistence of scribal activity, but rather as an outcry against the invasion of monastic libraries by the printed book and the changes in the ways of doing things that comes with it.

III

Having attempted to define some features of the scribal culture that dominated that area of Europe which produced the printing press, I should like in conclusion to note three aspects of the book and its use that printing, for better or worse, drastically altered. That will return us to the starting point of these observations, *Print as an Agent of Change*; its author, curiously, does not treat these three aspects of change.

(1) With the growth of print as the normal medium of the page, the main medieval vehicle for relating new thought to inherited tradition disappears—namely, the gloss and the practice of glossing. To be sure, glossed books like the commentaries on the *Decretum*, the *Liber sextus*, or Nicholas de Lyra on the scriptures are often printed; but the printed book is not itself an object in which one writes long glosses. Perusal of Chatelain, *Paléographie des classiques latins* (Paris, 1884–92), will uncover pages of Virgils, Lucans, Juvenals and Horaces, the set texts of the *trivium*, covered with interlinear and marginal glosses of all dates. These manuscript books had in fact been laid out to be glossed, namely, with the text in large letters down the center of the page, surrounded by white space. In contrast, one can think of only a handful of printed books in which the page has been set up in type to be glossed by hand. What effect this had on processes of thought, methods of instruction, and the structured comparison of new ideas to old, would be interesting to work out.

(2) With the advent of print the book becomes a monolithic unit, compared to its handwritten predecessor. Medieval books, particularly those individualistic owner-produced volumes of the fifteenth century, are frequently made up of numerous pieces varying from one to several quires in length, which were initially kept in loose wrappers and were bound together by the institution which inherited the volume. A person interested in a given text could copy out what he wanted and no more: thus, of the two hundred manuscripts of the *Lumen anime*, only half can be classified according to one of three restructurings they represent,

while the other half are all hybrids, adaptations to the needs and desires of the individual owner-producer. In contrast, although printed books are on occasion copied by hand or sections of them are copied out, the average printed-book library is comprised of whole books. Not until the advent of the Xerox machine were individuals again easily able to make up books in sections or to produce tailor-made collections. It would be interesting to know what effect this had on patterns of reading.

(3) Up to about 1450, the main vehicle par excellence for painting was the manuscript book: the monuments of medieval painting are in Gospel books, Psalters, Pontificals, Breviaries and Books of Hours. The advent of printing forces painting out of the book. It is a desperate wrench. Owners of incunabula have them filled with beautiful minia-tures, printers hire illuminators to adorn books with initials and frontis-pieces, or to water-color woodcuts printed in Books of Hours, but it is a losing battle. By 1500–1520, the Book of Hours as the fifteenth century knew it is in the death throes of mannerism and sterility. With the excep-tion of the producers of woodcuts—Holbein, Duerer, Pieter Breughel, all of whom also painted—not a single major artist thereafter did his major work in the medium of the printed book. While panel painting as an art form clearly antedates the invention of printing, the transition to the printed page must have encouraged the growth of the new medium which was so important to Netherlandish art in the fifteenth and six-teenth centuries.

Epilogue

13. Bibliography before Print: The Medieval *De Viris Illustribus*

Bibliography is the study of who wrote what, and bibliographies are to lead their users to books. As *catalogues raisonnés* of given topics, they are finding devices or gates of access to literature. Defined thus, bibliography is normally considered to be a modern creation, necessitated by the great expansion in numbers of authors and titles brought about by the invention of printing. Some would hold, in fact, that the concepts of 'author' and 'title' could not exist without the printing press. To what extent, then, could bibliography as a literary genre exist in the Middle Ages? What forms did it take in the world of the manuscript book? And in what ways are these forms manifestations of changing intellectual and religious needs?

To provide some answers to the questions posed above, we wish in this article to follow the medieval fortunes of the major types of bibliography that were created in the patristic era, with special emphasis on the *De viris illustribus* but with consideration of other genres as well, noting the significant changes in form and function and examining some of the reasons for the changes.[1] To set the scene, let us consider a single example, one which spans the whole millenium that we regard as medieval:

Medieval bibliography has as its foundation the late fourth-century *De viris illustribus* of St. Jerome. Jerome's purpose, stated in his pro-

---

Originally published in *Bibliologia* 3: *The Role of the Book in Medieval Culture*, ed. P. Ganz (Turnhout, 1986) 133–154.

[1] P. Lehmann, *Literaturgeschichte im Mittelalter* (1912), reprinted in his *Erforschung des Mittelalters* I (Leipzig 1941) 82–113, is a dated but still indispensable survey, which provides a capsule description of a wide variety of medieval bibliographies, booklists, *accessus* literature, and so on. The present study is both narrower than Lehmann's, in restricting itself to patristic bibliographic forms, and broader, in examining the effects of changing context upon both the purposes and the functions of bibliography.

logue, is well known: Paganism glowed with brilliant literary luminaries, while apostates and anti-Christian 'mad dogs' (*rabidi canes*) mocked that the Church had 'no philosophical thinkers, no eloquent writers, no men of learning' (*nullos philosophos et eloquentes, nullos doctores*).[2] Jerome's *De viris illustribus* was meant to show such scoffers how ignorant they themselves were, to give Christians a sense of pride. But Jerome's purpose—to bolster the morale of the outnumbered learned Christians of the late fourth century—does not at all explain the subsequent history of his *De viris illustribus*. Some 250 manuscripts survive (not counting extracts).[3] Of these, 50 were written in the twelfth century, 30 each in the thirteenth and fourteenth centuries, and over 80 in the fifteenth century. In diminishing numbers, manuscripts survive as well from each of the preceding centuries save (not surprisingly) the fifth. Thus, in these later centuries, when the entire community, learned and otherwise, was Christian, this was the most well-known and widely circulated of Jerome's writings.[4] It is obvious from this tally that Christian bibliography had developed uses different from any foreseen by Jerome.

This very particular combination of continuity and change, the perpetuation of older models combined with innovation in function and techniques, we should like to consider in three of its aspects. (1) Patristic bibliographies maintained a constant popularity throughout the Middle Ages; but the functions that they served changed through the centuries. (2) In addition, new bibliographies were created on strict patristic models, but their authors' aims were quite different from those of the Fathers. (3) And perhaps most interesting of all, the needs of the later medieval centuries, which fostered many new and technically sophisticated forms of bibliography, likewise led to the transformation of patristic models into something quite different in both purpose and function. These three are not chronological stages, but rather they are cumulative. The new supplements, rather than supplants, the old. As a result, in the fifteenth century we will find that patristic *De viris illustribus* are being reproduced by the hundreds; that the largest new *De viris illustribus*, on the patristic model, is compiled; and that an innovative new bibliography, the regional union catalog, is cast in the form of the *De viris illustribus*.

---

[2] Ed. E. C. Richardson, *Hieronymus, Liber de viris illustribus; Gennadius, Liber de viris illustribus*, Texte und Untersuchungen zur Geschichte der altchristlichen Literatur 14 (Leipzig 1896) 1–56; prologue, pp. 1–2.

[3] This statement and the subsequent statistics concerning manuscripts of Jerome's *De viris illustribus* are based on the data provided by B. Lambert, O.S.B., *Bibliotheca Hieronymia manuscripta* 2, Instrumenta patristica 4 (Steenbrugge 1969) 429–457.

[4] With the exception, of course, of the biblical prologues.

I. PATRISTIC BIBLIOGRAPHIES

A. *De viris illustribus*

The tradition of the Christian *De viris illustribus* began with Jerome, in the closing years of the fourth century, writing from the motives we have seen. Jerome's work, a bio-bibliography of some 135 authors, was evidently quite popular straightaway, in the course of the fifth century. Although no manuscripts survive from that date, contemporaries mention it, and the oldest surviving manuscripts display the sorts of variant readings and cross-contamination of the text that reveal that a lively circulation lay behind them. Both the availability and the eminence of Jerome's work are verified by the fact that Gennadius of Marseilles wrote a continuation of it, at the end of the fifth century (ca. 490). Gennadius's *De viris illustribus* adds some 91 writers, virtually all dating from the fifth century, to Jerome's original 135. From this time on, the two *De viris illustribus* usually traveled together in manuscripts: Gennadius's work, in particular, seems to have no independent textual tradition.[5]

Gennadius's purpose in compiling his *De viris illustribus* must be inferred, for he himself does not tell us. Doubtless his motives were similar to Jerome's—to blow the trumpet for Christian learning and literature, in a world where pagan writers, Greek and Latin, still were preeminent. But if similar, his motives could never be quite the same as Jerome's. Times had changed somewhat, for one thing; but even more important, Jerome had gone before. The field was no longer virgin. For Gennadius, and for every subsequent writer of a *De viris illustribus*, tradition played at least some part in the purpose of compilation: that is, Gennadius (as well as his successors) considered this a worthy activity because Jerome, that worthy man, had compiled a *De viris illustribus*. Indeed, one early manuscript, of the early eighth century from Corbie (Paris, B.N. lat. 12161; CLA V:624), contains a lengthy notice in praise of Jerome's learning and writings as a prologue to Gennadius; this prologue does not go back to Gennadius himself, but it is older than the manuscript in which

---

[5] Edited by Richardson, op. cit., pp. 58–97. Of the 101 chapters in the text as it survives, chaps. 30, 87, 93, and 95–101 are later additions. Concerning the manuscript tradition, see ibid. pp. ix-xli.

Eight surviving manuscripts of Jerome-Gennadius were written before ca. 900: CLA I: 114 (s. VIII, Italy); CLA II: 183 (s. VIII², N.E. France; Jerome only); CLA III: 303b (s. VIII–IX, Lucca) and 391 (s. VIII, Bobbio); CLA IV:469 (s. VIII, N. Italy) and 490 (s. VI, Verona); CLA V:624 (s. VII–VIII, N.E. France); and CLA VIII: 1031 (s. VI, S. Italy). Concerning CLA VIII: 1031 see F. Mütherich, "The Library of Otto III," in *The Role of the Book in Medieval Culture*, ed. P. Ganz, 2 vols. (Turnhout 1986) 2.11–26 at 21.

it survives.[6] Thus it demonstrates that by the eighth century, at latest, it was an acceptable assumption that Gennadius had compiled his own *De viris illustribus* largely, if not solely, to emulate and honor St. Jerome.

We must be aware, then, that once the genre of *De viris illustribus* had been initiated, its perpetuation—in the copying of existing *De viris*, and in the compilation of new ones—owes much to inertia: later compilers did it, because earlier ones had done it. Knowing this fact will not necessarily make more difficult our task of detecting purposes and uses: for it serves to heighten the importance of discernible changes in the pattern.

The last in the patristic trilogy of *De viris illustribus* is Isidore's, which adds thirty-three more writers to the combined list of Jerome and Gennadius.[7] Like the latter, Isidore did not leave a statement of his purpose in compiling a *De viris illustribus*; but we may confidently assume that, writing in Spain in the first quarter of the seventh century, Isidore had motives quite different from Jerome's. It has been said that Isidore in all his works was consciously loading 'a literary Noah's ark';[8] while this is going a bit far, obviously Isidore was concerned to improve the woeful state of learning in his region, and it is reasonable to assume that, in the *De viris illustribus*, he desired to preserve and foster the knowledge of orthodox writers, especially in the face of Arian heresy in Spain. And Isidore, even more than Gennadius, must have been motivated by the sense of carrying on a great tradition, of picking up where Jerome and Gennadius had left off. Whether or not he specifically envisaged his work as a continuation of the Jerome-Gennadius unit, in fact the earliest manuscripts of Isidore's *De viris* present it in conjunction with its two predecessors. The oldest, Montpellier École de médecine 406, a southern manuscript of the late eighth or early ninth century, contains the three in order. And a slightly later ninth-century hand has noted on the flyleaf of this manuscript, 'This is Jerome's book *De viris illustribus*; next to it should be written (*debet scribi*) Gennadius's book, and in the third position Isidore's; and they ought all three to be (*debent esse*) in one volume.' This note is not a quasi-table of contents, as earlier scholars have implied[9]—the force of the verbs (*debet scribi . . ., debent esse*) precludes

---

[6] There is a later gemellus, Paris, B.N. lat. 8961; see Richardson's introduction, especially pp. x, xii.

[7] Of the 46 chapters in the printed edition. *PL* 83.1081–1106, 13 were not attributed to Isidore until the fifteenth century. See H. Koeppler, "De viris illustribus and Isidore of Seville," *Journal of Theological Studies* 37 (1936) 16–34.

[8] Ibid. p. 32.

[9] See for example ibid. p. 16, and *Catalogue général des manuscrits des bibliothèques publiques des departements*, 4° ser., 1 (Paris 1849) 447.

that—but rather a note of direction, either to a specific scribe or to-whom-it-may-concern, designed to ensure that future copies maintained this corpus, in order and intact. By the end of the eighth century, then, and probably much earlier, the three *De viris illustribus*—without losing their individual identities—were treated as a unit in the manuscripts.

Isidore's *De viris* differed from Jerome's and Gennadius's in its provincialism: some one-third of his 'illustrious men' were Spaniards. His intent was to present a universal list, and he included those non-Spaniards that he knew and judged worthy. But his vantage point, from his corner of a shattered empire and a fragmenting Church, led him for example to include the Spanish bishops Justinianus and Justus while omitting the likes of Boethius and Cassiodorus. This was a signpost for the future: The work which would appear next on any chronological listing of *De viris illustribus* is that of Ildefonsus of Toledo,[10] only a generation or so later than Isidore's; but Ildefonsus's illustrious men are virtually all Spaniards—and half of them are from Toledo! At this turning point, then, we shall leave the *De viris illustribus* tradition and consider the purposes and uses of other types of patristic and early medieval bibliographies.

B. Bibliographies Devoted to a Single Author

Almost as old as the Christian *De viris* is Augustine's *Retractationes*.[11] It is the earliest of its kind. It is also, alas, the only of its kind. However, although Augustine's feat was not repeated by later writers, there are aspects of the *Retractationes* clearly pertinent to subsequent bibliographic work. In his early seventies (Ad 427) Augustine wrote these two books of 'Reconsiderations' of his major works, defending controversial statements, clarifying obscurities, and in particular singling out and modifying—or rejecting—those of his earlier positions which he no longer thought correct. In the process, he created a masterpiece of bibliography: he discussed his works in the chronological order of their creation, giving for each the work's proper title, a précis of its contents, and its *incipit* or opening words. Augustine's purpose was strictly to survey and reconsider his writings, in the light of his mature opinions. But we can see at once another major function this document performs: that of authentication or verification—a point certainly not lost on subsequent readers and copyists of the *Retractationes*. Here was a list, from

---

[10]Ed. F. Arévalo, *S. Isidori Hispalensis Opera omnia* 7 (Rome 1803) 165–178. See A. Braegelmann, *The Life and Writings of St. Ildefonsus of Toledo*, Catholic University of America Studies in Mediaeval History n.s. 4 (Washington 1942) 32–59.

[11]Knöll, ed., *CSEL* 36 (Turnhout 1902).

the author himself, that permitted undisputable identification of a work as Augustine's. It is no doubt regrettable that the list was not—and was known not to be—all-inclusive, which gave scope for the scores of spurious attributions. Nevertheless, it had the great positive value of permitting the authorship of a large number of important works to be settled beyond question.

If no later writer matched Augustine's auto-bibliography in detail, still the *Retractationes* is the earliest representative of one type of bibliography—the bibliography devoted to the works of a single author. Possidius's near-contemporary *Elenchus* of Augustine's works typifies a variant, the bibliography of a single author compiled as a tribute by a friend or disciple. Possidius's list of works classified by type and subject matter, almost certainly based on a list drawn up by Augustine himself, was appended to his *Vita* of Augustine, evidence of his pious motives.[12]

A third type of single-author bibliography in the patristic era stems from the genre of narrative history. Gregory of Tours (d. 594) devotes the last chapter of the last book of his *History of the Franks* to the bishops of Tours, giving for each his dates and a summary of his life and significant deeds. The last on the chronological list is of course himself; and among his deeds he names the five works he has written, beseeching that his successors in the see of Tours take care of his literary legacy and not permit them to be either revised or discarded.[13]

For the purpose of this article, we have accepted that a work is defined as a bibliography not by purpose or form, but by function. The passage from Gregory of Tours does not meet this standard, since later centuries did not use it as a bibliography in significant measure. It is important here, however, as a forerunner of Bede's bibliography, included at the end of his *Ecclesiastical History of the English People*.[14] What prompted Bede's compilation is an interesting question. Certainly his bare list of titles is not modeled on Augustine's *Retractationes*, a work that he evidently did not know firsthand. He knew Possidius's list of Augustine's works, but his motive obviously differed from that of Possidius, who wrote in praise of another (it is difficult to imagine Bede writing in praise of himself). Unlike Gregory of Tours, whose work must initially have been his model, Bede did not list his works as part of the *gesta* of a prelate.[15] His motives, rather, are revealed by the context

---

[12] A. Wilmart, ed., *Miscellanea agostiniana* 2 (Rome 1931) 149–233.

[13] *MGH Scriptores rerum merovingicarum* 1.1 (Hanover 1951²) 535–537.

[14] C. Plummer, ed., *Venerabilis Bedae Opera historica* I (Oxford 1896).

[15] For the works known to Bede, see M. L. W. Laistner, "The Library of the Venerable Bede," *Bede, His Life, Times, and Writings*, ed. A. H. Thompson (Oxford 1935) 237–266.

of his bibliography: Having set forth in five books the history of Christianity in Britain, he then, in the final chapter of Book 5, gives a shortlist of significant dates by way of recapitulation, recording principally the comings and goings of missionaries and the deaths of kings and bishops, a list that ends with A.D. 731. He concludes by identifying himself, in a concise biographical statement, and by listing the works that he had 'written for my own needs and those of my fellows' up to that date. His language in describing his literary achievement is characteristically humble: These are merely things which he has 'culled in brief from the works of the venerable Fathers,' as well as a few things he has added 'in accord with the meaning and the interpretation' established by patristic writers. Yet he must have been clearly aware of the singularity of his literary output, as he sat on the northern edge of what passed, in A.D. 731, for the 'civilized world'. We think he wrote his bibliography, just as he wrote his history, quite literally 'for the record' — *ob memoriam conservandam*, as he says at the beginning of this chapter. His activities as a writer formed, in his view, part of the ecclesiastical history of his people. Bede could not have foreseen that this little appendix, severed from the *History*, would enjoy a long and independent life as a bibliographic tool.[16]

C. Bibliographies of Acceptable Reading

This matter of authenticity — 'the record' — had already by Bede's time come to play an increasingly important role in both the production and the reproduction of bibliographies. In the use made of bibliographies, an important aspect — or perhaps we mean 'type' — of authenticity was orthodoxy: Christian bibliography of this era was concerned not merely with who wrote a work, but with the question of whether or not the work itself was acceptable. Jerome and Gennadius included heretics among their 'illustrious men', but they carefully labeled them as such. Augustine took care to revise or renounce opinions of his younger days which he had come to feel were incorrect. For the anonymous compiler of the *Decretum Gelasianum*, the question of orthodoxy was the sole motive for making a bibliography.[17] This little work, probably compiled in southern Gaul in the early sixth century, is usually entitled in the

---

[16] M. L. W. Laistner, *A Hand-List of Bede Manuscripts* (Ithaca, N.Y. 1943), lists 18 surviving manuscripts of the bibliography independent of the *Historia*. For examples of its use, see below.

[17] *Decretum Gelasianum de libris recipiendis et non recipiendis*, ed. E. von Dobschütz, Texte und Untersuchungen zur Geschichte der altchristlichen Literatur 38.4 (Leipzig 1912).

manuscripts 'On Books That Are to be Accepted, and Those That Are Not' (*De libris recipiendis et non recipiendis*). It draws a sharp clear line: canonical books of the Bible and orthodox writings on one side, apocryphal scriptures and heretical works on the other. The *Decretum Gelasianum* can be as adamant in its recommendation of the orthodox as in its condemnation of the heretical, in one instance threatening with anathema 'anyone who disputes one iota of this text or fails to accept it reverently in its entirety'![18]

Cassiodorus's 'Introduction to Divine Letters' is Book I of his *Institutiones*, the two books of which (the second dealing with secular learning) circulated separately.[19] Written in the mid-sixth century, it is unlike any of the previously mentioned works, in that it is organized by subject matter; it is an annotated subject bibliography subdivided according to the parts of the Old and New Testaments, along with a few types of patristic literature. The 'Introduction to Divine Letters' was written to guide the studies of the monks at Cassiodorus's monastery of Vivarium. In writing on Christian literature Cassiodorus, like the compiler of the *Decretum Gelasianum*, was concerned with the question of which books were acceptable—but only with the positive side of the question. This same question, which led the compiler of the *Decretum Gelasianum* to separate emphatically the sheep from the goats, prompted Cassiodorus to write a critical reading list. Given its discursive format, and given the amount of non-bibliographic matter it contains (e.g., a chapter on the physical setting of Vivarium, a disquisition in praise of medical doctors), we may seem to be stretching the definition to label this work a bibliography at all. But we do so with justification: the Middle Ages regarded Cassiodorus's work as a bibliography, and used it as such.

II. PERPETUATION OF THE PATRISTIC TRADITION, CA. 800–1500

A. Carolingian Collections and Their Uses

These are the principal sorts of bibliographic composition that passed from the patristic period to the Middle Ages. It is useful to treat these as two separate eras in bibliography, because the disruptions in political,

---

[18] Sub nom. Leo papa, Epistola ad Flavianum: ". . . quispiam si usque ad unum iota disputaverit, et non eam in omnibus venerabiliter receperit, anathema sit.'

[19] *Cassiodori Senatoris Institutiones*, ed. R. A. B. Mynors (Oxford 1937). See Mynors's discussion of the manuscript tradition, pp. x-xxxix.

economic, and intellectual life of the late seventh and the eighth centuries likewise created a gulf in the bibliographic tradition that was tacitly recognized by the Carolingians. Carolingian scholars did not 'carry on' the patristic tradition: for example, they did not compile their own *De viris illustribus*, nor did Alcuin and his successors leave a bibliography of their own literary works. Instead, the Carolingians gathered, reproduced, and used the patristic book-lore that had come down to them.

The practice of collecting the three major *De viris illustribus* works in one codex goes back to the time of Isidore; still earlier, it had been customary to preserve the *De viris* of Jerome and Gennadius as a unit. Moreover, the oldest surviving text of Possidius's Augustine bibliography (s. VI, after A.D. 555) occurs as an interpolation in the Augustine chapter of Gennadius's *De viris*;[20] combining these works, in other words, was not new. It was the Carolingians, though, who carried this inherited practice to its logical conclusion, in creating a corpus—or corpuses, for the contents varied slightly—of patristic bibliography. The earliest surviving such collection belongs now to Hereford Cathedral (MS O.iii.2), but it was written at an Insular center on the Continent, in the second half of the ninth century. This particular collection includes, on fols. 2–163, Jerome *De viris illustribus*, the *Decretum Gelasianum,* Gennadius *De viris illustribus*, Isidore *De viris illustribus*, Augustine *Retractationes*, and Cassiodorus Book I (Divine Letters), followed by a further 40 folios of Isidorian works and extracts that discuss the books of the Bible. There were doubtless many other codices with the same or similar contents; although no other early manuscripts survive, the corpus was disseminated widely enough to engender literally dozens of later copies, and additional dozens of mentions in catalogs and inventories, which survive from the eleventh or twelfth century onwards, both on the Continent and in England. Some of the twelfth-century Continental copies also include the Bede bibliography from the *Historia ecclesiastica*, an inclusion that may likewise reflect earlier corpuses.[21]

What impelled the Carolingians to compile, and in later centuries to reproduce, this body of works? Of what use to them was a corpus comprised of patristic bibliographies that had originally been written at different times and places, for a variety of differing purposes? Such collections, for one thing, no doubt served as reference books, or encyclopedias, of Christian literary history. While there was no longer any sense that Christian letters were under siege from the proponents of pagan

---

[20] Verona MS XXII (20); *CLA* IV: 490. See Wilmart, *Miscellanea agostiniana* 2 pp. 153–155.

[21] Concerning this bibliographic corpus see Mynors, ed. cit., pp. xxxix-xlix.

literature, there was a real sense among Carolingian scholars that literacy itself was beleaguered; a bibliographic corpus like the Hereford manuscript served as a reassuring monument, to the literate world which Christendom had been in former times and would, *Deo volente*, become again. We do not doubt, in this context, that parts at least of the corpus were simply read, as history—though the Pseudo-Gelasian *Decretum* fits poorly into this picture.

A more important function of such a corpus was as a list of desiderata for the growing monastic libraries. Many monasteries, both Carolingian foundations and older houses, were actively building book collections in the Carolingian period, and a number of these have left us ninth-, tenth-, and eleventh-century catalogs of their books. Despite the large amount of 'dead wood' in the bibliographic corpus—the works of obscure second-century Greeks that even Jerome knew only by hearsay, or works in Augustine's *Retractationes* that had not survived the centuries of upheaval—nevertheless, one can easily see how this collection of patristic bibliographies could have served as a guide to the Christian literature that a monastic library should attempt to acquire. Documentation of this use of the collection is provided by the well-known catalog of Murbach (ca. 840), which not only records the books of the house but also goes on to list for an individual author those of his books that Murbach did not, as yet, possess: 'Sequentes libros adhuc non habemus:. . . .' these added titles, it has been established, were taken from various works that usually formed part of the bibliographic corpus, including Bede's list, the *Retractationes*, and especially Cassiodorus.[22]

Certainly, the bibliographies in this corpus were used for the purpose of authentication—especially, authentication in the sense of identification. For instance, the earliest surviving example of the Bede biobibliography as an independent item, divorced from the 'Ecclesiastical History', occurs in a ninth-century Reichenau compendium of Bede's works, where it serves to introduce the author and to vouch for his authority.[23] The practice of excerpting the relevant chapter from Jerome's *De viris*, to serve as introduction to an author's works, also goes back to the ninth century (indeed, one example survives from the eighth). Thus, e.g., a ninth-century manuscript from Corbie (now Leningrad Public Library Q.v.I.20) inserts, before Jerome's prologue to Eusebius, chapter 135 of the *De viris illustribus*: Jerome's chapter on himself. Sometimes, doubtless, these capsule biographies from Jerome served to introduce a

---

[22] See W. Milde, *Der Bibliothekskatalog des Klosters Murbach aus dem 9. Jahrhundert: Ausgabe und Untersuchung von Beziehungen zu Cassiodors* Institutiones (Heidelberg 1968).

[23] Karlsruhe, Landesbibliothek Aug. 167.

writer who was little known: this is the case, for example, of the ninth-
century manuscript (Paris, BN lat. 152) that includes Jerome's chapter
117 on Gregory of Nazianzus. But these excerpts served in addition as
'character references' for questionable authors and works. This is apparent from the fact that much the commonest excerpt is Jerome's chapter
12, on Seneca; and it is copied, almost invariably, to precede texts of the
very popular exchange of letters between 'Seneca' and 'St. Paul'—a venerable bit of spuria whose authenticity Jerome vouched for in all good
faith. There are 2 surviving ninth-century examples; and in all, from the
ninth century through the fifteenth, there are 96 surviving manuscript
copies of this one chapter. This use of Jerome's bibliography continued
unabated—indeed, it increased—throughout the Middle Ages (some 205
single-chapter excerpts survive); and when, in the fifteenth century, there
was a great revival of interest in Lactantius, whose work was rare in
previous centuries, scribes and scholars went yet again to Jerome for the
chapter that would identify, and vouch for, this little-known writer: 31
fifteenth-century manuscripts of Lactantius are introduced by chapter 80
of Jerome's *De viris illustribus*.[24]

The use of Augustine's *Retractationes* in similar fashion may not
have begun as early; at least, we know of no early examples. But it
became a common practice in the twelfth and later centuries, in copying
manuscripts of Augustine's works, to preface each work with the pertinent chapter from the *Retractationes*. In addition, beginning at latest in
the twelfth century, Augustine's bibliography was used as the organizing
principle for attempts to collect, in order, all of Augustine's surviving
works.[25] The works are arranged according to the sequence given in the
Retractationes, for example, in codices recorded in the catalog of Christ
Church, Canterbury.[26] Much the most impressive survivor of this sort is
from twelfth-century Clairvaux: six manuscript volumes survive, from a

---

[24] See n. 3 above.

[25] As early as the ninth century the *Retractationes*-sequence appears in library catalogs,
but it is unclear whether the codices themselves adhered to this order. See Milde, op. cit.;
and K. W. Humphreys, "The Early Medieval Library," *Paläographie* 1981, ed. G. Silagi,
Münchener Beiträge zur Mediävistik und Renaissance-Forschung 32 (Munich 1982) 59–70
at 66–67.

Addendum: For a more detailed treatment, see now Rosamund McKitterick, *The Carolingians and the Written Word* (Cambridge 1989), esp. "The Role of the 'De viris illustribus,'
the 'De libris recipiendis' and Other Early Mediaeval Bibliographical Guides" and "Carolingian Bibliographical Handbooks" on pp. 200–210.

[26] The catalog of Henry of Eastry, prior (1284–1331) of Christ Church, is edited by M.
R. James, *The Ancient Libraries of Canterbury and Dover* (Cambridge 1903) 13–142; see
especially no. 932, and see also nos. 22, 26, 933, 1654. A new edition of all the medieval
catalogs of Christ Church is being prepared by M. T. Gibson, University of Liverpool.

seven-volume edition of Augustine's works; arranged in the order of the
Retractationes (which itself heads the collection), the individual works
are frequently preceded by the relevant *Retractatio* as well.[27]

The availability and, especially, the authority of the *Retractationes*
is attested by its repeated use through the rest of the Middle Ages, in
organizing codices and booklists alike. As instances of the latter, let us
mention the fourteenth-century *Registrum* of the Oxford Franciscans
and the list of works appended to the *Manipulus florum* of the Sorbonnist Thomas of Ireland (1306). We need not describe these two works
here; it is sufficient to explain that each of these booklists, the *Registrum*
and the *Manipulus florum*'s, is a catalog of sorts, not based on hearsay
but representing actual manuscripts seen and recorded by the compilers—except for their respective lists of Augustine's works. For Augustine,
both Thomas of Ireland and the compilers of the *Registrum* dutifully
record the 94 titles, in the order and with the incipits, provided by the
Retractationes, thereby including in their catalogs of 'manuscripts' the
titles of works which had been irrevocably lost centuries before.[28] The
immense authority of Augustine's auto-bibliography was sufficient, in
both cases, to override their otherwise reliable methods of procedure.

B. *The revival of Patristic Forms, ca. 1100–1500*

In leapfrogging from the ninth century to the twelfth, we are consciously disregarding the growth of *accessus* or proto-*accessus* literature,
such as the often-cited example from the Ottonian bishop of Liège,
Notker. These works, though they clearly belong to *Literaturgeschichte*

---

[27] Troyes, Bibl. mun. 40.I–III, 40.VI, 40.IX–X. See J. de Ghellinch, "Une édition ou
une collection médiévale des opera omnia de saint Augustin," *Liber floridus: Mittellateinische
Studien Paul Lehmann gewidmet*, ed B. Bischoff and S. Brechter (St. Ottilien 1950) 63–82.
Concerning the manuscripts of Clairvuax see A. Vernet, ed., *La bibliothèque de l'abbaye
de Clairvaux du XIIe au XVIIIe siècle I (Paris 1979)*, especially pp. 349–350, 130–132.

[28] The most recent description of the *Registrum* in print is by R. H. and M. A. Rouse,
Preachers, Florilegia and Sermons: Studies on the Manipulus florum *of Thomas of Ireland*,
Pontifical Institute of Mediaeval Studies, Studies and Texts 47 (Toronto 1979) 24–25; the
Rouses are preparing an edition of the *Registrum*. The list of works appended to the
Manipulus florum is also discussed (pp. 156–160) and edited (251–301) there. In contrast to
the practice of the *Registrum*, which lists all of the *Retractationes* titles in sequence,
Thomas of Ireland uses the *Retractationes* only to supplement, without duplicating, his list
of the works that he had found in Sorbonne manuscripts; but he adheres to Augustine's
order as he records them. See nos. 89–100, 109–132, under the heading 'Libri beati Augustini'
(pp. 253–270). Thomas acknowledges his use of the *Retractationes* in the preface to his
bibliography (p. 251): 'Notandum quod libros originalium sanctorum ac doctorum quantum ad principia et fines . . ., hic signare curaui . . . Quorumdam autem librorum Augustini,
precipue quos ipse in suo libro retractationum enumerat, fines non uidi.'

as evidence of the 'book knowledge' of an era, are not bibliographies but schoolbooks, introductions to readings in the *artes*. We exclude them here on these grounds: (1) The authors considered in the *accessus* tradition date only from classical antiquity or the Early Christian period; (2) they are, especially in the early *accessus*, poets only; (3) they are treated from the standpoint of their helpfulness for students in the students' own Latin composition (especially metric, but later prose as well); and, most telling objection, (4) the *accessus* literature never adds new names to the canon of writers. In fact, since the *accessus* tradition is very selective, its effect is to diminish, rather than to increase, the number of authors and works that are considered worthy of notice. On the same grounds we shall not consider later practitioners of Notker's art, such as Conrad of Hirsau and Hugo of Trimberg.[29] It may seem arbitrary to exclude these while including Cassiodorus's work which, though it differs in most respects from *accessus* literature, is nevertheless a 'schoolbook' and not a proper bibliography. The deciding factor, as always, is use. Whether Cassiodorus intended it as such or not, his Book I was used as a bibliography, while the *accessus* literature was not.

The twelfth century saw a revival of bibliographic traditions that had lain dormant since the patristic age, though none of these rejuvenated types of bibliography approached their patristic forebears either in scope or in popularity. Bibliographies—usually just lists of titles, without incipits—of individual authors were compiled with frequency.[30] A few of these, like the *Indiculum* of the works of Hugh of St. Victor, were formal and extensive. The *Indiculum*, a list complete with incipits and explicits, was drawn up shortly after Hugh's death (1141) by Gilduin, abbot of St. Victor, to accompany the abbey's 'authorized edition' of the works of its most famous son. We doubt that this *Indiculum* circulated extensively; the one surviving manuscript was written in fifteenth-century England.[31] Other single-author bibliographies were quite informal, compiled perhaps on the flyleaf of a manuscript, recording for his own information or for future use elsewhere the manuscript-owner's knowledge of a given author's literary *oeuvre*. Such, for example, is the flyleaf list of the works of Boethius compiled from several sources by Henry of

---

[29] Concerning *accessus* literature see Lehmann, *Literaturgeschichte*; and R. B. C. Huygens, *Accessus ad auctores, Bernard d'Utrecht, Conrad d'Hirsau* . . . (Leiden 1970).

[30] Although it belongs to a quite different tradition from those considered here, we should give at least passing mention to the rhymed, vernacular bibliography of his own works included by Chrétien de Troyes in the first seven verses of *Cligés*.

[31] The *Indiculum* is edited by J. de Ghellinck, "La table des matières de la première édition des œuvres de Hugues de S.- Victor," *Recherches de science religieuse* 1 (1910) 270–289, 385–396.

Kirkestede (d. ca. 1380), to be incorporated later in his large *Catalogus* of writers.[32]

The patristic genre of *De viris illustribus* revived, beginning in the twelfth century, and reappeared in many different guises over the next 400 years. These works tended to be both parochial and derivative, and for the most part they survive in a half-dozen copies at most, of localized circulation. Some, indeed, of the twelfth-century *De viris illustribus* most widely known in our own century, such as those of Honorius Augustodunensis[33] and Wolfger of Prüfening ('Anonymous of Melk'),[34] were unknown outside their immediate neighborhoods during the Middle Ages. As typical of the traditional *De viris illustribus* of the twelfth through the fifteenth centuries, and as exemplifying particular aspects of the continuing tradition, we shall consider a localized collection that continued to grow over a period of two centuries; the foremost example of a specialized *De viris illustribus*; and the first *De viris* to owe its circulation to the printing press.

1. *A Belgian corpus of* De viris illustribus

The earliest of the twelfth-century *De viris*—the first such since Isidore's, if one discounts the parochial effort of Ildefonsus—was compiled in the first decade of the twelfth century by Sigebert, monk of Gembloux (d. 1112). Sigebert's work is an ambitious one; he lists 172 writers, from East and West, and from patristic times to his own day, with very little local bias evident in his selection. His *De viris* is a testimony to the contents of the library at Gembloux—but not, perhaps, in

---

[32] Lambeth Palace MS 67 fol. i^v; the list was put together from Vincent of Beauvais's *Speculum historiale*, the *Manipulus florum*, the *Registrum*, and the contents of MS 67 itself. Concerning the *Catalogus*, see below.

[33] Honorius Augustodunensis, *De luminaribus ecclesiae* (PL 172: 197–234), written probably in the 1130s, is almost entirely derived from Jerome, Gennadius, Isidore, and Bede. Surviving in only five Central European manuscripts, it is noteworthy for its chronological listing of Honorius's own works—and for what is surely the most paranoid prologue ever affixed to so innocuous a document. For a recent discussion and bibliography concerning Honorius, see V. I. J. Flint, "The Career of Honorius Augustodunensis: Some Fresh Evidence," *Revue bénédictine* 82 (1972) 63–86, and "The Chronology of the Works of Honorius Augustodunensis," ibid. 215–242.

[34] *Der sog. Anonymus Mellicensis De scriptoribus ecclesiasticis*, ed. E. Ettlinger (Karlsruhe 1896), composed perhaps in the 1160s. This work, which contains a greater portion of original material than Honorius's, survives in only six manuscripts, all written at various houses ranged along the Danube between Prüfening and Vienna. Wolfger did not know Honorius's compilation. For discussion, bibliography, and list of manuscripts, see B. Bischoff, in *Verfasserlexikon* 4 (1953) 1051–1058.

the way one would expect. For he took a great deal of information at second hand, scraping facts together from unlikely sources. Thus, for example, the rubric to Book 5 chap. 21 of Bede's *Historia ecclesiastica* reads 'How Abbot Ceolfrith sent to the king of the Picts architects for his church, along with a letter on the Catholic Easter and on tonsure.' From this snippet comes Sigebert's chapter 67: 'Ceolfrith, abbot of the Scots, wrote a useful letter on the correct observation of Easter, and on the tonsure of clerics, at the request of the king of the Picts.' There is much more of the same sort. (It is interesting to note, in passing, that five of the nine surviving manuscripts of Sigebert have, as an interpolation in the chapter on Bede, Bede's bibliography from the end of the *Historia*.[35])

What moved Sigebert to resurrect this tradition, to compile a bibliography of illustrious writers? He knew that no such thing had been compiled for a very long time; and, in fact, he was unaware of Isidore's *De viris illustribus*.[36] The Gembloux bibliographic codex must have contained only Jerome and Gennadius, whom Sigebert names as his models ('Imitatus etiam Hieronimum et Gennadium . . .'). But the specific motive must have been similar, instead, to Bede's, i.e., a sense of history, and of the historical importance of writers in the continuing development of Christendom. Sigebert wrote a Chronicle (it ended, like his *De viris*, in A.D. 1111, the year before his death), in imitation, he says, of Eusebius; and in it he names, with their works, some two-fifths of the authors that appear as well in his *De viris illustribus*.[37] As he imitated and continued Eusebius in the Chronicle, so he imitated and continued Jerome and Gennadius in the *De viris*. The names of these illustrious men and their works deserved to be remembered and, thus, to be recorded.

The *De viris illustribus* of Sigebert of Gembloux had a very local circulation. Anyone who took a map of Europe and put a thumb on Gembloux would cover the *Schriftheimat* of each of the nine surviving manuscripts, none of them—not even the fifteenth-century copies—having been written farther than seventy miles from Gembloux. Sigebert, in fact, was the progenitor of a small Belgian species of the *De viris* genus: Toward the end of the twelfth century, possibly as early as the 1160s, an anonymous monk compiled a list of thirteen twelfth-century writers,

---

[35] *Catalogus Sigeberti Gemblacensis monachi De viris illustribus*, ed. R. Witte, Lateinische Sprache und Literatur des Mittelalters 1 (Frankfurt a.M. 1974).

[36] Ibid. 19.

[37] Ibid. 14. The Chronicle was edited by L. C. Bethmann, *MGH Scriptores* 6 (1844) 300–374.

including Anselm of Laon, Abelard, Bernard, Hugh of St. Victor, and Peter Lombard.[38] Though there is no apparent Low-Countries bias in the choice of authors, and though the compiler is unidentified, it is clear that this so-called *Auctarium* was written in the neighborhood of Gembloux and that it was regarded from its inception as a continuation of Sigebert: The *Auctarium* begins chronologically where Sigebert had left off; and the *Auctarium* survives only as an accompaniment to Sigebert's *De viris*—it is found in eight of the manuscripts of Sigebert, and was almost certainly in the ninth as well (the last quire of that manuscript is lost). Some hundred years later, yet another and more extensive Belgian *De viris illustribus* was compiled (ca. 1270) by a monk at Affligem, probably Henry of Brussels.[39] The author of the Affligem bibliography seems to have been ignorant of the *Auctarium*; however, he not only knew of Sigebert's *De viris*, but considered his work as its continuation, as he states explicitly: 'The catalog of illustrious men begun by Saint Jerome, and later brought up to his own day by Sigebert, monk of Gembloux, I have undertaken to extend further, to our time'. The sixty authors in the Affligem *De viris* include most of the twelfth- and thirteenth-century notables one would expect to find; but it also includes, in an access of local pride, one abbot and three monks from Affligem itself.

These three works went into the making of a bibliographic corpus restricted solely to *De viris illustribus*—without the addition of other types of bibliography, such as the *Retractationes* or Cassiodorus—that circulated in what is now Belgium. The contents varied only slightly, and were arranged in this order: Jerome, Gennadius, Isidore, Sigebert, the *Auctarium*, the Affligem *De viris*. Each of the nine copies of Sigebert's *De viris* survives as part of such a corpus.[40]

2. Bibliographies of Dominican writers

A significant trend in the *De viris illustribus* bibliographies of the fourteenth and fifteenth centuries lay in specialization—no longer Illustrious Men, but Illustrious Benedictines (or Franciscans, or . . .).[41] While

---

[38] The *Auctarium* or 'Appendix' is discussed and edited by N. Häring, "Two Catalogues of Mediaeval Authors," *Franciscan Studies* 26 (1966) 195–211.

[39] See N. Häring, "Der Literaturkatalog von Affligem," *Revue bénédictine* 80 (1970) 64–96 (edition, 76–96).

[40] See Witte's study of the manuscripts of the corpus in *Catalogus Sigeberti* pp. 25–48. — E. Dekkers, "Sigebert van Gembloux en zijn 'De viris illustribus'," *Sacris Erudiri* 26 (1983) 57–102.

[41] The largest catalog of Benedictine writers was that of Trithemius, discussed below. The Franciscans likewise compiled lists of their writers in the fifteenth century; perhaps

many *De viris* compilations were limited, parochial, due to the unavoidable limits of their compilers' knowledge, these specialized bibliographies were intentionally and overtly restricted to writers that belonged in
one specific category.

The most thoroughly studied body of such works is the group of
catalogs of Dominican writers.[42] It seems that an original compendium
of Dominican writers, drafted probably ca. 1300, probably at Paris,
served as base for the tradition. Compilers of subsequent catalogs retained
most or all of this core bibliography, and added others, mostly consisting of authors from the compiler's own Dominican province. Thus, a
given list will show Norman additions, or Dacian, or Parisian, or the
like. It is apparent that the Dominican lists were not made as advertise-
ments for the Order; rather, their intended readership was internal, a
record *about* Dominicans compiled *for* Dominicans, 'in piam memoriam'
as it were. Most survive in manuscripts in company with other Dominican records, such as lists of Masters General, of Priors Provincial, or of
place and date of General Chapters. The fifteenth-century catalog written by Laurence Pignon, O.P., is prefaced with the quotation 'Let us
now praise famous men, our fathers . . . [Ecclus. 44.1],' and Pignon
states that the purpose of his bibliography is to let contemporary Dominicans know what sorts of sons the order of St. Dominic had engendered
in the past, that they might see what they have to live up to.[43]

Despite this internal target, however, these lists were too full of useful bibliographic information for outsiders to ignore. Thus, the sole text
of Pignon's list survives in a manuscript from the Augustinians of St.
Victor.[44] Thus, too, our only witness to the list made in the English
province is its use by a Benedictine, Henry of Kirkestede, to compile his
Catalogus in the 1370s. Although Kirkestede integrated his Dominican
source with his other materials, it is possible to discern the original
shape of this list: a central core of important Dominican writers, shared
in common with the other surviving Dominican lists, and an added

---

more important were the Franciscan chroniclers, such as Bartholomaeus of Pisa and Marianus
of Florence, who gave major attention to the authors of their order and their works. For a
brief summary of the bibliographies of individual orders and for bibliography, see K.
Arnold, *Johannes Trithemius (1462–1516)*, Quellen und Forschungen zur Geschichte des
Bistums und Hochstifs Würzburg 23 (*Würzburg 1971*) *116, and notes.

[42] See G. Meersseman, O.P., ed., *Laurentii Pignon Catalogi et chronica, Catalogi
Stamsensis et Upsalensis scriptorum O.P.*, Monumenta Ordinis Fratrum Praedicatorum
historica 18 (Rome 1936); H.-D. Simonin, O.P., "Notes de bibliographie dominicaine,"
Archivum Fratrum Praedicatorum 8 (1938) 193–214.

[43] Meersseman, ed. cit., p. 2.

[44] Paris, B.N. MS lat. 14582, s. XV.

selection of English Dominicans whose names are absent from the Continental catalogs.[45]

3. The patristic model at the end of the Middle Ages: Trithemius

The last great *De viris illustribus* of the Middle Ages are those of the prolific abbot of Sponheim, Johannes Trithemius, in the 1490s. His universal *De scriptoribus ecclesiasticis*, printed in 1494, includes the names of some 963 authors ranged chronologically from the patristic age to his own.[46] His sources included the earlier compendia of Jerome, Gennadius, and Isidore, as well as the Affligem list of Henry of Brussels and, his single most important source, Sigebert of Gembloux; obviously, at least one manuscript of the Belgian *De viris* corpus had escaped the 'Gembloux cordon', to travel the some 150 miles to Sponheim. Besides information taken at second hand, Trithemius relied on the library of his own and neighboring abbeys to draft the articles about more recent writers. As a result, this compendium is distinguished from its predecessors by the not infrequent inclusion of incipits, as well as titles, to identify works.

In addition to this universal catalog, harking back to patristic tradition, Trithemius continued the late-medieval trend toward the specialized *De viris illustribus*, compiling a *De viris* of Benedictine writers that circulated in manuscript, and another devoted strictly to German authors (printed 1495).[47] In his motives for compiling the latter, Trithemius is apt to remind us most of the Founding Father of the tradition, St. Jerome. Just as Jerome defended Christian literature against the arrogant scorn of the pagans, so Trithemius wrote to demonstrate to the contemptuous French and (especially) Italians that Germany, too, had produced worthy writers; he names some 300. We should note that, while Trithemius is considered here as the culmination of medieval *De viris* works, from another perspective he was a beginning, for his work inspired numerous emulators, on into the sixteenth century.[48]

---

[45] Kirkestede derived eighty-two of his authors from this list. Concerning the *Catalogus*, see below.

[46] *Liber de Scriptoribus Ecclesiasticis* (Basel: J. Amerbach, 1494). Hain no. 15613. Concerning Trithemius see now K. Arnold, op. cit., especially chap. 8, "Die literarhistorischen Schriften," 114–143.

[47] *Cathalogus illustrium virorum Germania . . . exornantium* (Mainz: Peter of Friedberg, 1495), Hain no. 15615.

[48] See Arnold, 137–143.

III. MEDIEVAL INNOVATIONS IN BIBLIOGRAPHY,
ca. 1100–1500

Bibliographies in the patristic mold, then, were at least as important in the fifteenth century as they had been in the fifth. New bibliographies were made along traditional lines, and the patristic ones continued to be reproduced in great numbers; for example, to extrapolate
from the number of surviving fourteenth- and fifteenth-century manuscripts of Jerome/Gennadius and of Augustine's *Retractationes*, the original figure must have been in the hundreds.

Beginning with the twelfth and thirteenth centuries, however, many
different types of bibliographies were produced that were distinct from
patristic forms. These bibliographies, often employing techniques of the
schoolroom, were tailored to the changing needs of schoolmen and preachers. The variety of bibliographies and book-related tools of the twelfth
through the fifteenth centuries is sufficient matter for a lengthy separate
study. We should like to focus our discussion here upon the works
whose contents and techniques were ultimately combined with the *De
viris illustribus* tradition, to serve a new purpose.

A. *Bibliographies of Works Cited*

One of the most significant bibliographic productions of the later
medieval centuries was an innovation with a modern ring to it: the 'bibliography of works cited'. Our remarks on this development must be
tentative, since much research remains to be done both to discover further examples and to make more precise the dating and localization of
known examples.

What we refer to is the list, either prefaced or appended to a given
text, that names the authors and works cited therein. This practice evidently begins in the twelfth century; but it origins very likely lie in the
practice of marginal citation of sources, the single word 'Augustinus' or
'Gregorius' recorded, as acknowledgment and *confirmatio*, alongside a
quotation from an author's works. We cannot say how old this practice
is; certainly Bede employed it in the early eighth century, in some of his
biblical commentaries, and Papias did so in his dictionary compiled in
the mid-eleventh century—but later copyists usually failed to preserve
these marginal references.[49] The practice does not come into frequent

---

[49] Concerning Bede, see M. L. W. Laistner, "Source-Marks in Bede Manuscripts,"
Journal of Theological Studies 34 (1933) 350–354; see also idem, *The Library of the Venerable Bede*, p. 240. Concerning the Papias references, see chap. 6, "*Statim invenire*: Schools,

use until the late twelfth or early thirteenth century, but the model did exist. The next step is that seen in the *Liber florum*, a largely patristic florilegium compiled at Bec or Canterbury in the first quarter of the twelfth century.[50] Here the florilegist was not content merely to note the names in the margins but, in addition, he listed at the end of his pro-logue the names of the authorities he has cited. The prologue explains his purpose: Although he himself is unimportant (he has not even left us his name), readers are not to assume from that fact that the *Liber florum* is unauthoritative, for it conveys the authority of all those whose words it quotes—hence, he lists their names.[51]

It is a short step—though one that was slow to be taken—for com-pilers to recognize that, if a bare list of names carries authority, then a list of authors and the titles of their works is still more impressive. We cannot give a date for the first true bibliography of works cited; but the wide diffusion of this practice in the thirteenth and fourteenth centuries suggests that some twelfth-century experimentation lay behind it. Such bibliographies are attached specifically to works of compilation, such as florilegia, world chronicles, topical indexes, and the like: for example, the *Abbreviationes chronicorum* of Radulfus de Diceto, dean of St. Paul's; the various recensions of the Cistercian *Flores paradysi*; the *Tractatus de diversis materiis predicabilibus* of Etienne de Bourbon; and the *Pharetra*, the *Mariale*, the *Manipulus florum*, the *Tabula septem custodiarum*, Higden's *Polychronicon*, and so on.[52]

The amount of detail in the bibliographic entries varies widely from one compendium to another. At one end of the scale is the *Mariale*, a florilegium of quotations lauding the Virgin Mary. Its compiler, an anon-ymous Englishman of the late thirteenth century, lists in his bibliogra-phy only the authors' names, for the most part (a half-dozen titles have

---

Preachers, and New Attitudes to the Page," and L. W. Daly, *Contributions to a History of Alphabetization in Antiquity and the Middle Ages*, Collection Latomus 90 (Brussels 1967) 71–72.

[50] See R. W. Hunt, "Liber florum: A Twelfth-Century Theological Florilegium," *'Sapientiae doctrina': Mélanges . . . Dom Hildebrand Bascour, O.S.B.* (Louvain 1980) 137–147.

[51] Quem si quis quia proprio carent auctoris nomine apocriphi nota presumpserit infamare, attendat quia tot eum auctores faciunt quot quibus componitur sententias ibi proponunt.' Hunt, p. 139.

[52] R. de Diceto, ed. W. Stubbs, Rolls Series 68.1 (London 1876); concerning E. de Bourbon see A. Lecoy de la Marche, *Anecdotes historiques, légendes et apologues tirés du recueil inédit d'Étienne de Bourbon* (Paris 1877), introduction, especially pp. xi–xiii; R. Higden, ed. C. Babington, Rolls Series 41.1 (London 1865); concerning the *Flores paradysi*, *Pharetra*, and *Manipulus florum*, see Rouse and Rouse, *Preachers*, 126–139, 204–205, and passim; for the *Mariale* and the *Tabula septem custodiarum*, see below.

crept in); but he apologizes for his laxness, due to the pressure of other business, and refers his readers to the citations of the titles of the works, to be found in the margins.[53] At the other extreme is the bibliography of the *Tabula septem custodiarum*, a vast collection of references to incidental passages of biblical exegesis from the works of the Fathers and Doctors of the Church. The *Tabula*, compiled by Franciscans at Oxford at the beginning of the fourteenth century, concludes with a bibliography that often goes beyond the norm; for example, instead of being content with listing 'Bernardus, *Sermones*' as a source, the bibliography of the *Tabula* specifies the individual sermons cited, and identifies each by both title and incipit.[54]

B. Bibliographies of Recommended Reading

There is a curious effect, or at least concomitant, of identifying both the authors and their works in a bibliography. Such lists are no longer intended merely to impress and to verify; they become as well, in some cases overtly, in some tacitly, 'references for further reading'. In one of the earliest of all, the list which accompanies de Diceto's *Abbreviationes chronicorum* (end of the twelfth century), the bibliography actually is presented in the form of a chronological *De viris illustribus*, although the list is in practice restricted to the historical works that he has used in compiling his *Chronicle*.[55] The bibliography accompanying the *Tabula septem custodiarum* must unquestionably be considered a reading list, because the *Tabula* compiles only references (author, title, book, chapter, lemma) to the works, and not excerpts from them.[56]

It is explicitly stated by the prologue to Thomas of Ireland's *Manipulus florum* (1306) that his bibliography is meant to direct the reader from the collection of excerpts to the full texts from which the excerpts came: 'Do not, for the sake of these modest gleanings, disdain the fertile field of the complete works, a man is a fool if he ignores the

---

[53] This work is found in Cambridge, Pembroke College MS 22 (s. XIV, Bury St. Edmunds); London, Lambeth Palace MS 52 (s. XIV); Salisbury Cathedral MS 62 (s. XIII ex.); and San Marino (Calif.), Huntington Library MS HM 26560 (s. XIV med.). The compiler's comments are paraphrased from Huntington 26560 fols. 311v–312.

[54] For a list of manuscripts see Rouse and Rouse, *Preachers*, p. 19 n. 36.

[55] See Stubbs's introduction to the second volume of de Diceto's historical works, Rolls Series 68.2 pp. xvii-xviii.

[56] The scribe of British Library MS Harley 3858 (s. xv; Durham) makes mention of the fact that the *Tabula* is useless without an accompanying library; fol. 62, 'Si hos . . . doctores aut aliquos ex hiis habueris, valde utilis ad predicandum presens liber [scil. the *Tabula*] tibi sit; sin autem, nescio quid tibi valebit.'

fire and tries to warm himself merely with sparks'. So that these complete works may be readily identified (*ut facilius possent cognosci et securius allegari*), he explains, 'At the end of this work I have listed the books of these authors, with their first and last words, their titles, and the number of parts in each'.[57] The result is a bibliography which describes the works so precisely that, in large part, one can identify the very manuscripts from which he took his information. Thomas's bibliography was so useful, not only to his contemporaries but to later generations, that it often circulated by itself, apart from the florilegium that prompted its creation.[58]

To consider medieval bibliographies from the standpoint of recommendations for reading leads us to the no-man's-land separating proper bibliographies from 'works which talk about books'. How shall one categorize, say, Vincent of Beauvais? His *Speculum historiale* certainly cannot be called a bibliography, yet it contains massive amounts of bibliographic information, which was quoted and used by others for essentially bibliographic purposes, the determination of who wrote what. To cite just two examples: Vincent's work was excerpted to create the anonymous bibliography of twenty-nine authors, the so-called *Brevis annotatio quorumdam sacrorum doctorum et de eorum libris*, which survives in two fourteenth-century French manuscripts;[59] and the English *Catalogus* of Henry of Kirkestede made exhaustive use of the *Speculum historiale*.[60] There are scientific works that surely fall near, if not across, the borderline. A prime example is the thirteenth-century *Speculum astronomiae* attributed (on uncertain grounds) to Albertus Magnus. In explaining and discussing the different sciences that comprise astronomy, the author introduces each topic with a description of the existing

---

[57]'Istorum autem auctorum libros quantum ad principia et fines et nomina et parcialium librorum numerum in fine huius operis signaui. . . . Propter has autem modicas spicas agrum fertilem originalium non despicias; improuidus enim est qui neglecto igne se per scintillas nititur calefacere'; Rouse and Rouse, *Preachers*, 238.

[58]There are at least fifteen surviving manuscripts of the list alone, and traces of others now lost. See ibid. pp. 216–224.

[59]Paris, B.N. MSS lat. 14578 fols. 368v–370v (St. Victor) and 15246 fols. 2–3v (Sorbonne); the title is that added, for convenience, to MS lat. 14578 by St. Victor's fifteenth-century librarian Claude de Grandrue; see A. Vernet, "Rapports sur les conférences: Philologie," in the *Annuaire* of the *École des chartes, année 1960–1961* (1961–1962) 81. We are grateful to Colette Jeudy for this reference.

[60]Kirkestede cites Vincent by book and chapter, and often lists an author's works in the sequence furnished by the *Speculum*; concerning his *Catalogus*, see below.

literature, giving author, title, incipit, and capsule characterization.[61] Again, as with Vincent, this sort of thing is not a bibliography, but certainly bibliographic. Countless other thirteenth- and fourteenth-century works attest a keen interest in precise knowledge about books, especially at the schools: the careful descriptions in the library catalogs of the Sorbonne;[62] the *Capitulationes* (lists of chapters, identified by their opening words) which Kilwardby compiled for the Fathers, and which anonymous Parisian scholars compiled for the translated Aristotle;[63] or the Oxford Franciscan *Registrum*. This last is an early fourteenth-century location list of books found in English ecclesiastical libraries, and thus from one point of view a union catalog; but it is selective in its list of authors, and thus from another point of view it is a bibliography.[64]

IV. NEW WINE IN OLD BOTTLES: THE *DE VIRIS ILLUSTRIBUS* AS UNION CATALOG, ca. 1375–1500

Rather than continue to belabor the obvious—that schoolmen made booklists—we should like to conclude with two late medieval bibliographies from outside the university milieu, works different from one another in many respects yet joined by a common denominator, their interest in locating books. The earlier of these we have previously mentioned in passing, the *Catalogus scriptorum ecclesiae* compiled ca. 1375 by Henry of Kirkestede, monk of Bury St. Edmunds (so-called Boston of Bury).[65] Kirkestede's universal bibliography contains an alphabetical list of 674 authors, who are described in the style of the *De viris illustribus*: 'X, bishop of Y, flourished in the year Z, and wrote the following:' The works are then listed, with their opening and closing words for identification. He combed every bibliographic source he could lay hands on— the patristic bibliographies in the Carolingian corpus (Bury's twelfth-century copy survives), Thomas of Ireland's bibliography and the lists of authorities (and even the marginal references) in other florilegia, Vincent of Beauvais, the Dominican *De viris illustribus* of the English province

---

[61] The *Speculum astronomiae* has most recently been edited by S. Caroti et al. (Pisa 1977), attributed to Albertus; but see the review of James Weisheipl in *Isis* 69 (1978) 616–618.

[62] See chap. 9, "The Early Library of the Sorbonne."

[63] See Rouse and Rouse, *Preachers*, 13–14, 19–20.

[64] See n. 28 above.

[65] R. H. Rouse, "Bostonus Buriensis and the Author of the Catalogus scriptorum ecclesiae," *Speculum* 41 (1966) 471–499. R. H. and M. A. Rouse are preparing an edition of the *Catalogus*.

(he cites his sources regularly)—and he ransacked the manuscripts of the Bury library. One of his primary sources of information, the Franciscan union catalog or *Registrum*, likewise provided the motive for his bibliography: He intended not merely to list every work by every author he knew of, but also to indicate where copies of these works could be found. He did this via a series of numbers after each work, referring to a key—a numbered list of monastic and cathedral libraries around England; this device also he borrowed from the *Registrum*. Kirkestede's ambitious scheme fell far short of accomplishment; he borrowed much of the *Registrum's* reference to the location of books, but he was able to add information concerning only a few libraries in East Anglia, including Bury itself. Nevertheless he hoped (vainly) that others would continue where he had left off, entering further 'location numbers' in the spaces left vacant for the purpose.

The second example is Continental, and a group effort. Houses of the Windesheim Congregation, from about 1470 to at least the 1530s, made a group of related bibliographies that contained information about the location of books.[66] Our knowledge about these is partly speculative, based upon the interpretation of the scanty remains: one complete manuscript (Vienna Nat. bib. 12694) from Rookloster, ca. 1530; the fragment of another, ca. 1470, from Cologne (Basel Univ. F.VI.53); the mention, in 1525, of a third at Groenendaal; early modern descriptions of a fourth made by Gerard Roelants (d. 1490) at St. Martin's, Louvain; and the traces (in the Rookloster catalog) of a fifth, from the Windesheimers at Gaesdonck in Guelders. Their history is something like this: A bibliography was compiled from the *De viris illustribus*, arranged roughly alphabetically by author, with a brief biographical notice for each, followed by the list of his works. This information was then fleshed out, from the manuscripts in the compiler's library, with incipits and sometimes explicits added to the titles. The distinctive element is the marginal annotation beside the titles of works of the different nearby houses—of various orders, not just Windesheim foundations—where the work was to be found. These were named in abbreviated form or 'syllables,' as the Vienna manuscript calls them, which are spelled out in the list of houses at the head of the catalog. Once this useful document had been made, it could be copied by the brothers at another Windesheim house—as, it seems, the Gaesdonck bibliography was copied at St. Martin's in Louvain, and the Louvain bibliography in turn copied at Rookloster. At each successive copying, however, the original bibliography was expanded. New

---

[66] See the discussion and bibliography of P.F.J. Obbema, "The Rookloster Register Reevaluated," *Quaerendo* 7 (1977) 326–353.

authors and titles were added, from the manuscripts in the house library and from other booklists; thus, for example, the Rookloster bibliography has added lists of works taken from Trithemius, and the Cologne bibliography has incorporated the bibliography from the *Manipulus florum*. And new location data were added, from the area surrounding the new home of the bibliography: locations in and around Louvain are added at St. Martin's, locations around Rookloster form a second layer of additions in the Rookloster version, and so on.

* * *

We end, in a sense, where we began, with the *De viris illustribus*, direct descendant of St. Jerome's: the author is named, with his station, locality, and date, and his works are listed. But the differences are more important than the similarities. In the intervening ten centuries much that is new has occurred in the field of bibliography, ranging from Augustine's *Retractationes* to Thomas of Ireland's precise 'recommendations for further reading'. The fact that Trithemius's *De viris* names more than seven times as many authors as Jerome's can perhaps be attributed to the mere passage of time. Yet Trithemius, superficially faithful to the patristic model, nevertheless takes it for granted that one must supply, not just a vaguely descriptive title, but also the opening words of the text, in order to identify a work properly. This difference we must attribute to the changing needs, expectations, and practices of medieval makers and users of bibliographies.

The early Fathers did not have to locate books. Their libraries, the product of the Roman book trade, were well stocked and relatively satisfactory to their needs. The canon of pagan literature, well defined and well known, was available in the great libraries of Milan, Rome, and Carthage. Jerome, progenitor of the Christian *De viris illustribus*, was not concerned with preserving written literature for the next generation, as was Cassiodorus; nor was he lending order to chaos, as were the Carolingians Alcuin and Theodulph, and their codifying successors, Gratian and Peter Lombard, in the twelfth century; nor was he faced with organizing the outpourings of a new spiritual movement, as were the monastic librarians of reformed houses in the fifteenth century. In the relative order of cosmopolitan Rome in the fourth century, bibliography in its modern form was basically unnecessary.

As for Kirkestede's *Catalogus* and the Windesheimer catalogs, it is apparent to the most casual glance that they represent a completely different outlook from Jerome's fourth-century defensiveness. They were utilitarian in purpose, 'utilitati studentium et predicatorum', as Kirkestede says. They are not meant to be read, but to be consulted; therefore, they are arranged alphabetically. Concern for precise identification of works is displayed by the use of incipits and explicits. And, most significant change of all, it was not intended that one should use these bibliographies as a polemic or apologetic, taking either pride or comfort in the fact that such fine books had been written. Rather, Kirkestede's *Catalogus* and the Windesheim bibliographies were goads: 'Go out and find these books, and keep worrying about the ones you have not found yet!'

St. Jerome would not have recognized this grandchild.

Subject Index

Abelard, Peter, 151, 484. *Sic et non*, 142, 192

Abu Ma'shar, 163

Adalbertus Ranconis de Ercino, rector of Prague, 172n. 76, 342n. 3

Adam of St. Victor, 151

Adam of Villeron, 369

Adelard of Bath, 48. *Natural Questions*, 53

Adenulph of Anagni, 361, 366, 369

Adrian IV, pope, 119

Ænigmata Aristotilis, 105, 134

Aesop, 186

Affligem, 484, 486

Agrimensores, 349

Agustin, Antonio, archbishop of Tarragona, 90

Aicher, Laurentius, librarian of St. Emmeram, 14

Ailly, Pierre d', 72–73

Aix-la-Chapelle, 182

Alan of Lille, 144, 202, 203, 205, 207, 223, 247, 374

Alan of Penrith, 377

Albero, bishop of Liège, 40

Albert of Cologne (*Albertus Magnus*), 202n. 28, 241, 285, 287, 490

Albert of Mantua, 246

Alcuin, 180, 477, 493

Aldgate, Austin Canons, 207

Aldhelm, St., 37

Alexander III, pope, 44, 119–122, 155, 158

Alexander Atheniensibus, 104, 106, 135

Alexander, bishop of Lincoln, 37, 52

Alexander of Aphrodisias, 90

Alexander of Hales, 217, 244, 375, 392

Alexander of Villedieu, 202n. 26. *Doctrinale*, 446

Alexander the Great, 186

Alphabetum narrationum, 241, 252

Altensteig, Johannes, 447

Alvear, D. L., 14n. 3

Alverny, Maria Thérèse d', 207, 249

Amadas et Ydoire, 26

Ambrose of Milan, 48, 143, 147, 234, 249, 371, 375

Ambrosiana Virgil, 88

Amiens, 78

Andrew of Sens, 282–310 *passim*, 324, 327

Andromeda, 254

Ansbold of Prum, 163

Anselm of Bec, 234, 304, 322

Anselm of Laon, 484

Anthony of Padua, 203

Antichrist, 411

Antiochus, 64

Aper, 169

Apuleius, 84, 109–110, 114, 155–156, 169, 171, 428. *Asclepius*, 108–110, 132. *De deo Socratis*, 76, 105, 108–110, 132. *De magia*, 95. *De mundo*, 108–110, 132. *De Platone et eius dogmate*, 76, 108, 132.

Aquinas, Thomas, 28, 232, 259, 286, 301–307 *passim*, 319, 363. *De perfectione spiritualis vitae*, 307. *De potentia Dei*, 294. *Expositio super Isaiam*, 304. *Expositio super Job*, 313. *Quaestiones disputatae de veritate*, 304. *Sententia libri Ethicorum*, 313. *Summa contra gentiles*, 294–295. *Summa theologiae*, 14. Commentary on

Book III of the *Sentences*, 285, 288, 306, 313–316.

Archives Nationales, 323

Arians, 472

Aristotle, 147, 192, 221, 222, 229, 231, 251, 317, 397, 491. *Analytics*, 230. *De animalibus*, 230. *Ethics*, 229–230, 252. *Libri naturales*, 230. *Physics*, 418.

Arnold of Hasnede, 369

Arnold of Liège, 186, 276

Arnulf, bishop of Orléans, 111, 157

Arnulf of Lisieux, bishop of Lisieux, 34, 36, 40, 42–45, 53, 55–59, 172n. 75

Arnulfus, *Speculum monachorum*, 141

Arras, 291

Ashridge, Bonshommes of BVM, 152, 187

Astronomy of Nimrod, 163

Atticus, 61, 163

Auctarium of Gembloux, 484

Augustine of Hippo, 48, 75, 143, 149, 215, 221, 230, 240, 254, 255, 304, 355, 371, 375, 459, 464. *Confessiones*, 43n. 37. *Contra academicos*, 62, 82. *De catechizandis rudibus*, 141. *De civitate Dei*, 43n. 37, 81. *Retractiones*, 473–474, 478, 479–480, 484, 487, 493

Augustinian canons, 247, 450 458, 463

Averroes, 375

Avian, 128

Avicenna, 277

Avignon, 5, 73, 74, 92–93, 98, 107n. 5, 182, 413

Avril, François, 278

Badia, 70

Bale, John, 431, 433

Bamberg, 65

Barbato, 88, 93, 98

Barcelona, 364n. 64

Bari atelier, 281

Barlow, Claude, 107, 111–112, 156, 158

Baron, F., 325

Bartholomaeus Anglicus, *De proprietatibus rerum*, 287, 300

Bartholomew of Pisa, 484n. 41

Basel, 438, 457. Council of, 451. Carthusians, 433, 436, 445, 447

Baudouin of Brinliva, 369

Bayeux Cathedral and diocese, 38–58 passim. *Livre noir*, 41–42. Bishops: *see*

Hugh II; Odo; Philip of Harcourt; Richard II; Richard III

Beaumont-le-Roger, dependency of Lincoln Cathedral, 37

Bec (O.S.B.), 34, 51–56 passim, 63, 76–79, 84, 114n. 30, 117, 119, 156n. 6, 165, 237, 488.

Bede, 180, 487. *De orthographia*, 168. *Historia ecclesiastica*, 455, 474–475, 477–478, 483

Beeson, C. H., 122

Bela III, king of Hungary, 67

Bellaise, J., 237

Benedict XII, antipope, 73

Benedict, bishop of Orléans, 40

Benedict of Nursia, 180

Benedictines, 485. *See also* Bursfeld Congregation.

Berger, Elie, 57

Berkeley Castle, 415

Bernard, Robert, 396

Bernard II, archbishop of Santiago de Compostela, 34n. 3

Bernard, bishop of Saragossa, 40

Bernard, dean of St. Pierre, 369

Bernard of Clairvaux, 43, 48, 53, 119, 216, 249, 304, 322, 371, 454, 459, 464, 484. *Sermones in Cantica Canticorum*, 197, 359

Bernard of Pailly, 396

Bernier of Nivella, 376, 379, 387, 396

Bernsau, Johannes, 437

Bersuire, *Ovide moralisée*, 253, 254

Bertram of Middleton, 265

Beutelbücher, 26

Biard, Nicholas, 224, 252, 286, 287

Bible, 3, 7, 198–205 passim, 214–215, 217, 231, 263, 265, 284, 363, 429. Gloss (*Glossa Ordinaria*), 191–201 passim, 216, 217, 221, 363. Verbal concordance, 191, 202–204, 209, 215, 218, 221–226, 230, 236, 244, 248, 251, 252, 286, 287, 306, 319

Bicchieri, Cardinal Guala, 34n. 3, 143n. 80

Billanovich, G., 88, 92, 107, 156

Birkenmajer, Alexander, 343–344, 348, 353, 387–388

Bischoff, Bernhard, 26, 65, 161

Black Death, 318

Bodel, Jean, 22

Boethius, 74, 128, 185, 235, 473, 481.
Comm. on Cicero, *Topica*, 91. *De
consolatione Philosophiae*, 147, 230.
De differentiis topicis, 229. *De
divisionibus*, 229.
Pseudo-Boethius, *De disciplina
scholarium*, 170
Bologna, 49, 87, 153, 236, 247, 265, 266n.
20, 270n. 26, 318, 319
Bonaventure, 370, 459, 464
Bongars, Jacques, 168, 170
Boniface VIII, pope, 341n. 1
Bonifacius, Johannes Bernardinus, marquis
of Oria, 95
Books of Hours, 466
Bourrienne, V, 41
Boyle, Leonard, O.P., 187
Branner, Robert, 260, 282
Brethren of the Common Life, 9, 428,
430, 436, 450–453, 458–464 *passim*
Breughel, Pieter, 466
Breviaries, 466
*Brevis annotatio quorumdam sacrorum
doctorum et de eorum libris*, 490
Brito, Warinus, 52
Brito, William, 202n. 26, 240, 253, 285
Brittany, 73
Bruges, Cistercians. *See* Ter Duinen
Bruno of Würzburg, 447
Brussels, Brethren of the Common Life,
453
Bullrich, Eduardo J., 14n. 3
Burchard of Worms, 49
Burleigh, Walter, *De vita et moribus
philosophorum*, 148, 186
Bursfeld Congregation, 445–447, 451, 464
Bury St. Edmunds, 420, 423, 491
Busch, Johannes, *Windesheim Chronicle*,
429–430
Buxheim, Carthusians, 181, 435, 445, 464

'Caecilius Balbus', 122, 131, 134
Caen, 56
Caesarian orations, 34
Calpurnius Siculus, 155, 169, 172–173.
Eclogues, 165
Cam, Helen, 27
Cambrai, 291
Canterbury, 50, 488. *See also* Christ
Church, Canterbury

Carit, Bernard, 94
*Carmen de Timone comite et de miraculo
fontis Sancti Corbiniani*, 25
Carolingians, 450, 452, 477, 491
Carter, Sir Thomas, 423
Carthage, 493
Carthusians, 9, 430–447 *passim*, 451, 452,
455, 457, 458, 463
Cassiodorus, 195, 473, 484. *Institutiones*,
476, 477, 481, 484, 493. *Historia
tripartita*, 50
Castelet, Matthew, 376
Cathars, 215, 247
Catholicon, 446, 455
Cato, 128
Catto, Jeremy, 418, 422
Catullus, 87
Caxton, William, 464
Ceccano, Annibaldo, 378
Celestine III, pope, 34n. 3
Celestines, 434
Censorinus, *De die natali*, 105, 106–108,
122–123, 134, 155–156, 169, 171, 349
Ceolfrith, 483
Champagne, 53
Charlemagne, 114, 176, 349n. 24
Charles the Fat, 29
Chartres, 36, 77, 84, 165
Chatelain, E., 321, 322, 465
Chaucer, Geoffrey, 263. *Canterbury Tales*,
4. *Tale of Melibee*, 254
Chenu, Marie-Dominique, 319, 124, 153
Chrétien de Troyes, 481n. 30
Chrysostom, John, 234, 371, 436, 453
Christ Church, Canterbury, 199n. 20,
341n. 1, 423, 479
Ciceri, Francesco, 90
Cicero, 34, 48, 61–98 *passim*, 101, 104,
108, 110, 112, 114–115, 120, 125, 138,
141, 155, 156, 159–160, 164, 166–169,
171, 173, 174, 175, 176, 185, 186, 349,
428. *Academics*, 34. 'Posterior
Academics', 61–98 *passim*, 167. 'Prior
Academics', 62, 88, 90, 91, 92, 94, 173.
Ad familiares, 71, 164, 167, 169.
Brutus, 95, 96, 159. *Cum senatui
gratias egit*, 132, 171. *De Amicitia*, 72,
90, 95, 96, 128, 138. *De divinatione*,
72, 78, 81, 90, 91, 95, 165–166, 173. *De
domo sua*, 108, 132, 160. *De fato*, 72,

90, 91, 95, 96, 166, 173. *De finibus bonorum et malorum*, 34, 64–98 *passim*, 167, 169, 174, 175. *De haruspicum responso*, 90, 108, 133, 160. *De inventione*, 115, 162n. 31. *De legibus*, 62, 72, 85, 90, 96, 164, 165–166, 169, 173. *De natura deorum*, 62, 72, 90, 95, 164, 173. *De officiis*, 72, 90, 128, 138, 166. *De oratore*, 71, 90, 95, 96, 159, 169, 174. *De paradoxa*, 72, 90, 95, 128, 173. *De provinciis consularibus*, 108, 133, 160. *De re militari*, 94, 96. *De senectute*, 72, 90, 95, 96, 128, 138, 141. *Hortensius*, 88. *In Catilinam*, 90, 94, 160. *In Q. Caecilium*, 94. *In Vatinium*, 108, 133, 160. *In Verrum*, 94, 101, 104, 110, 114–115, 134, 164, 169, 173. *Orator*, 95, 96, 159. *Partitiones oratoriae*, 96. *Philippics*, 76, 84, 90, 93, 160, 164–165, 169, 173, 174. *Post reditum ad Quirites*, 108, 133, 160. *Post reditum in senatu*, 77, 90, 108, 133, 160. *Pro Archia*, 77, 95. *Pro Balbo*, 108, 133, 160. *Pro Caelio*, 108, 133, 160. *Pro Cluentio*, 77. *Pro Ligario*, 90, 94, 160. *Pro Marcello*, 90, 94, 160. *Pro rege Deiotario*, 90, 94, 160. *Pro Sestio*, 108, 133, 160, 161. *Somnium Scipionis*, 95. *Timaeus*, 74, 78, 79, 90, 91, 94, 95, 96, 173. *Topica*, 95, 168. *Tusculan Disputations*, 72, 76, 90, 93, 95, 104, 171.

Pseudo-Cicero, *Ad Herennium*, 95. *De optimo genere oratorum*, 96. *Invectiva in Sallustrium*, 94, 160. *Pridie quam in exilium iret*, 108, 119, 132, 160

Cipriani, R., 90

Cistercians, 226–227, 236, 247, 451, 457–458

Cittadini, Celso, 114n. 31

Clairmarais (O.Cist.), 211n. 51

Clairvaux (O.Cist.), 154, 172, 184, 211n. 51, 226–227, 406, 479

Clare, Thomas, 423

Clarin of Saulieu, 396

Clark, A. C., 160, 165–166

Claudian, 128, 138, 180

Clemence of Hungary, 278

Clement IV, pope, 175

Clement VI, pope (Peter Roger), 375

Pseudo-Clement, 50

Cluny, 114–115, 102n. 2, 164, 176

Cobham, Thomas, 419

Codex of Roman Law, 49

Colete, Thomas, *Ars notaria*, 148

Collège de Montagu, 109n. 14

Collège de Saint-Bernard, 229, 246

Colmar, 438

Colocci, Angelo, 165

Cologne, 65, 115, 164, 176, 434, 436, 438, 492. Brethren of the Common Life (Weidenbach), 436, 445, 453. Carthusians (St. Barbara's), 435–436, 445n. 44, 454, 457. Crosiers, 434, 436, 446, 455

Columba, St., 85

Concordanciae anglicanae, 225

Concordantiae morales bibliorum, 203

Conrad of Halberstadt, 225

Conrad of Hirsau, 481

Conrad of Würzburg, 25

Constance, Council of, 72–73, 91n. 81, 433, 451

Corbie, 116, 159, 171, 349, 471, 478

Corbinelli, Antonio, 70

Corvey, 110, 118

Corvodie, Hermann, 460

Coutances. *See* Richard I de Bohun; William III de Tournebu

Crespin, Peter, 380, 396

Crosiers, 9

Cuissy Premonstratensians, 181

Curtius Rufus (Quintus), *History of Alexander the Great*, 106, 135, 186

Cyprian, 139

Daly, Lloyd, 240

Damascenus, 234

Daniel, Pierre, 111–113, 118, 156–158, 162, 167–168, 169n. 68, 170, 181

Dante Alighieri, 87

De arte rhetorica, 446

Decretum Gelasianum, 475–477

De ecclesiastica correctione, 146

Delalain, Paul, 261

Delisle, Léopold, 57, 111, 311, 343–344, 345, 352–353, 359, 362, 367, 373, 385, 386, 389

Denifle, H., 321, 323

De remediis tentationum, 431

Destrez, Jean, 228, 259–266, 303, 306, 308, 320, 322

Deusdedit, cardinal, 193, 194–195
Deutart, Firmin, of Abbeville, 396
De viris illustribus, 457, 469–494 passim
Dialogus creaturarum, 186
Dialogus inter philosophum ludaeum et
 Christianum, 142
Diomede, 169
Distinctiones monasticae, 118n. 50, 223
Dictionary of National Biography, 431
Docking, Thomas, O.F.M., 418, 422–423
Dominic, St., 192
Dominicans, 247–248, 485, 491. See also:
 St-Jacques in Paris; Mendicant orders
Donatus (Aelius), 170
Donatus (Ti. Claudius), 170
Dondaine, H.-F., 304
Douglas, A. E., 62
Doyle, A. I., 363
Droem, Hermann, dean of Utrecht, 459
Duin, J. J., 232
Dunsby, Lincolnshire, 187
Dupuy, Jacques, 66
Dupuy, Pierre, 66
Durand of Huesca, 211n. 51
Dürer, Albrecht, 466
Durham Cathedral, 116, 171, 233n. 29, 265
Durham College, Oxford, 423
Dux Moraud, 27
Dyngley, William, 423

Eberhard of Béthune, Graecismus, 153,
 202n. 26
Échard, J., 224
Egres, 67
Einhard, 159
Eisenstein, Elizabeth, 449, 452, 465
Ellesmere Chaucer, 4
Enguerrand of Cantiers, 369
Ennodius, bishop of Pavia, 6, 48, 55, 56,
 84, 101, 104–105, 114, 116–117, 119,
 128, 134, 138, 155, 169, 171, 172, 185
Epicurean school, 61, 64
Epitaphium Senecae, 69, 141
Erfurt, 445. Carthusians (Salvatorberg),
 435, 445, 452, 455, 464
Etienne de Bourbon, 244, 488
Eugenius III, pope, 40, 53, 56, 119
Eusebius, 45, 214, 478, 483
Eutropius, 76, 77
Euvrie, Guillaume d', 73n. 34, 166

Evangelists, 22, 23
Evesham, 234
Evrard of Dijon, 396
Évreux, 35, 37
Exultet Rolls, 27n. 37

Faubourg St. Germain-des-Prés, 71
Fécamp (O.S.B.), 39, 56
Festus (S. Pompeius), 169
Fifty Heresies and Errors of the Friars,
 411, 414, 421
Filastre, William, cardinal, 9n. 81
Firmicus Maternus Junior, 112
Fishacre, Richard, 231, 235, 251
FitzRalph, Richard, 412–415, 417
Fleury, 84, 85, 111, 112, 157–158, 164, 167,
 168, 170, 179–181
Florence, 70, 71, 450
Flores Bernardi. See William of Montague
Flores paradysi, 127, 184–185, 227, 254,
 488
Floretum, 410, 412, 421
Florilegium Angelicum, 6, 55, 101–152 pas-
 sim, 158–165, 170–177, 184–188 passim,
 248
Florilegium Gallicum, 84, 101, 107–108,
 117–118, 127, 153–162, 170–188 passim,
 248
Florilegium Saint-Gratien, 166
Florus, Epitome, 50, 76–77
Foliot, Gilbert, bishop of London, 34,
 206–208
Fortunatus, 75
Fountains Abbey (O. Cist.), 116, 171
Francis of Assisi, 192
Franciscans, 247, 411. See also: Oxford
 Franciscans (Greyfriars); Mendicant
 Orders
Franklin, Alfred, 242–243
Freculf of Lisieux, 50
Frederick II, 13
Freising, 118n. 51, 179–180
Frontinus, 76–77
Fugger Library, 74, 169
Fulda, 159
Fulgentius, 138. Mythologia, 112
Fumée, Lugas, 149

Gabriel, 21
Gaesdonck, 457, 492

Gagnér, A., 107, 158
Gallican Psalter, 199
Ganymede and Helena, 25
Gaufridus dictus le Normant, 276
Gaufridus Lotharingus, 273
Gauthier, R., 313, 317
Geiler of Keiserburg, 458
Gellius (Aulus), *Noctes Atticae*, 74,
    104–105, 113, 126, 134, 155, 158, 160,
    169, 171, 173, 174, 177, 178–179, 428
Gembloux, 110, 160n. 26, 483
Geneva, 438
Gennadius of Marseilles, *De viris
    illustribus*, 471–477 *passim*, 483, 487
Geoffrey de Lêves, bishop of Chartres,
    36n. 9
Geoffrey de St-Léger, 262, 269, 277–282
Geoffrey of Anjou, 38, 39–41
Geoffrey of Auxerre, 216, 249
Geoffrey of Monmouth, 48, 52. *Historia
    regum Britanniae*, 35
Geoffrey of Vinsauf, 111, 153
Gerald of Wales, bishop-elect of St.
    Davids, 6, 34, 124–127
Gerald of York, 48
Gerard of Abbeville, 78, 115, 162n. 31,
    163, 175–176, 230–231, 236, 288, 307,
    346, 348–352, 355, 357, 358, 360, 361,
    365, 369, 376, 394
Gerard of Auvergne, 395
Gerard of Rheims, 360, 361, 365, 369
Gerardus de Fracheto, 289n. 81
Géraud, H., 321
Gerson, Jean, 431, 433–434, 458. *De laude
    scriptorum*, 455, 457
Gesta Caesarum, 50
Ghellinck, J. de, 252
Giacomo, Niccolò di, 90
Gilbert Crispin, 48
Gilbert de la Porrée, chancellor of
    Chartres, 36n. 12, 48
Gilbert of Poitiers, 193, 216, 249; *Com-
    mentary on the Psalms*, 195–196, 199
Gilduin, abbot of St. Victor, 481
Giles du Theil of Ghent, 396
Giles of Audenarde, 380
Giles of Maintenay, 396
Giles of Rome, *De regimine principum*, 137
Giles of Saumur, 369
Gils, P. M., 288

Glanvill, 217n. 67, 246n. 55
Glauning, O., 16
Glorieux, Palémon, 343, 353, 362,
    379–380, 385–388, 431, 433
Gloss (*Glossa Ordinaria*). *See* Bible
Godfrey of Fontaines, 231, 232, 373, 375,
    396
Godfrey of Limoges, 369
Gorran, Nicholas, 224, 252
Gospel books, 466
Gower, John, 363
Grabmann, M., 230
Graevius, J. G., 164
Graitepanthere, William, 396
Grande Chartreuse, 430–439 *passim*, 444,
    452
Grandes chroniques de France, 279–280
Grandrue, Claude de, 71, 118n. 49, 143,
    146, 154n. 3, 162n. 30, 490n. 59
Gratian, *Decretum*, 48, 49–50, 191, 192,
    196, 200, 221, 276, 465, 493
Great Schism, 443
Gregorian reform, 3, 194
Gregory I, pope, 48, 131, 143, 155, 185,
    322, 371. *Epistolae*, 103, 104, 105–106,
    128, 131. *In Ezechielem*, 108. *Moralia
    in Job*, 217, 245
Gregory XI, pope, 94
Gregory of Nazianzus, 479
Gregory of Tours, *History of the Franks*,
    50, 474
Grenoble, 438
Grey, Bishop Richard, 423
Grey, William, 233n. 29
Grillius, 163
Groenendaal, 492
Groschedel, Bernhard, 65
Grosseteste, Robert, 196, 203, 232, 233,
    245, 251, 418, 420
'Grunelle', 73
Grunenberg, Conrad, 446
Gruter, Jan, 70
Guiart de Moulins, *Bible historiale*, 279
Gui de la Tour, bishop of Clermont, 282
Guido Aretinus, *Regulae rhythmicae*, 148
Guido I, prior of the Grande Chartreuse,
    458
Guilelmus de Militona, 285
Guilhelmus de Raynald, prior of the
    Grande Chartreuse, 443

Guillaume d'Auvergne, *librere*, 326
Guillaume de Machaut, 22
Guillaume *le librere, enlumineeur*, 326
Guillelmus de Boldensele, *Peregrinatio ad
    terram sanctam*, 141
Guillelmus de Curia, 273
Guillelmus le Grant, 273
Gutenberg, Johannes, 464
Guy Breton, 396

Hadoard of Corbie, 62, 122–123, 159
Hall, F. W. 154
Halm, C., 63
Hamacher, J., 181
Hamel, Christopher de, 198, 200, 282
Harcourt. *See* Philip of Harcourt; Robert I
    fitz Anschetil; Waleran, count of
    Meulan
Harley lyrics, 23
Haskins, C. H., 40
Haunolt, Conrad, 65
Heaver, John, 178
Hebrew Psalter, 199
Pseudo-Hegesippus, 137
Heidelberg, 65, 70, 148
Heiric of Auxerre, 106–107, 112, 156–157,
    161, 164, 188
Helinand of Froidmont, 111, 153
Hellequin, Michael, 369
Héméré, Claude, 342n. 4, 343n. 5, 385
Henri François of Orléans, 182
Henri, le petit, *librere*, 326
Henricus Anglicus, 295
Henricus Ariminensis, 14
Henricus Aristippus, 174
Henricus Guilloti, 323
Henry I, king of England, 39, 41–42
Henry II, duke of Normandy, king of
    England, 39, 40, 43–45, 52, 57, 84
Henry VI, emperor, 21
Henry, son of Frederick II, 13
Henry, cardinal priest of Sts. Nereus and
    Achilles, 172n. 75
Henry of Andely, 153. *Battle of the Seven
    Liberal Arts*, 111, 183
Henry of Brussels, *De viris illustribus*,
    484, 486
Henry of Ghent, 232
Henry of Harclay, 418, 420
Henry of Huntingdon, *Historia*, 50–53

Henry of Kirkestede, 420, 481, 485.
    Catalogus scriptorum ecclesiae,
    491–492, 493
Henry of Pisa, papal legate to France,
    55–56
Henry the Liberal, count of Champagne,
    50, 53
Herbert of Bosham, 199–200, 213
Hereford, Nicholas, 415
Herman von der Dhame, 19
Herneis *le romanceeur*, 281
Hesdin, 279
Higden, Ranulf, *Polychronicon*, 488
Hilary of Poitiers, 77n. 43, 117n. 49, 371
Hildebert of Le Mans, 48, 54, 126n. 62,
    166, 207n. 35
Hirsch, Rudolf, 464
Histoire de Troie, 280
Historia scholastica. See Peter Comestor.
Hogg, James, 432, 436
Holbein, Hans, 466
Holder, A., 167–168
Honoré, French miniaturist, 279
Honorius of Autun, 482
Horace, 128, 138, 147, 167, 185, 207,
    468
*How Religious Men Should Keep Certain
    Articles*, 410–414
Hudson, Anne, 428, 430
Hugh, archbishop of Sens, 40
Hugh II, bishop of Bayeaux, 42
Hugh, archdeacon of Leicester, 50
Hugh of Amiens, archbishop of Rouen,
    34, 37n. 18, 42, 48
Hugh of Mâcon, bishop of Auxerre, 53
Hugh of Pisa, 369
Hugh of St-Cher, 203, 224, 265, 290, 319,
    375
Hugh of St-Victor, 48, 322, 481, 484. *De
    institutione noviciorum*, 141. *De tribus
    maximis circumstantiis gestorum*, 193.
    Didascalicon, 193, 234
Hugh Primas of Orléans, 84
Hugo of Trimberg, 481
Huguccio, 85, 168, 202n. 26, 240
Humbert of Romans, 239, 357, 370
Hunt, Richard W., 1, 234
Hunt, T.J., 63–64, 67–73 *passim*, 86, 94,
    96, 97
Hyginus, 74

Ildefonsus of Toledo, 473, 482
Inforciatum, 49
Innocent III, pope, 119, 187, 210, 247, 374
Institutes of Roman law, 49
*Instructio pie vivendi et superna
    meditandi*, 141
Interludum de clerico et puella, 26
Isidore of Seville, 75, 234, 322, 371. *De
    viris illustribus*, 472–473, 477, 482, 486.
    Etymologiae, 43n. 37, 168, 170.
    Expositio in Genesim et Exodum, 142.
    Quaestiones in Vetus Testamentum,
    138
Pseudo-Isidore, *Decretals*, 117
Itier, Bernard, 114n. 30, 117n. 49
Ivo of Chartres, 49, 150

Jack Upland, 410, 414, 415, 416
Jacob van Enckhuysen, 459–460, 461
Jacobus de Cessolis, 186
Jacobus de Troanco, 273
Jafort, William, 367n. 71, 369
James I, king of Scotland, 434
James of Marli, 387, 396
James of Voragine, 288
Jean d'Auxois, 359n. 52
Jean de Chalons, 253
Jean of Gonesse, 312, 317, 361, 369
Jean de Montreuil, 164
Jean de Nemours, 181
Jean de Varzy, 285
Jean de Vignay, 280
Jeanne of Burgundy, queen of France, 278,
    280
Jeanne of Flanders and Hainaut, 290
Jehan *le librere*, 326
Jerome, 48, 125, 128, 137–150 *passim*, 155,
    170, 185, 217, 371, 453. *De viris
    illustribus*, 69, 141, 150, 469–479 *pas-
    sim*, 483, 486, 493. *Epistolae*, 43n. 37,
    102, 103, 104, 105, 131, 137, 139, 145.
    Interpretations of Hebrew Names, 144,
    215, 441
Jocelin, bishop of Salisbury, 37n. 18
Johannes à Kempis, 429
Johannes Belvantessis, *Summa
    grammaticalis*, 151
Johannes Brito alias de Sancto Paulo, 273
Johannes de Clyra, 235n. 34
Johannes de Deo, 187

Johannes de Garlandia, 273
Johannes de Pointona, 276
Johannes de Remis, 277
Johannes de St-Léger, 278
Johannes de Siccavilla, 286
Johannes dictus le Normant, 276
John XXII, pope, 385
John, bishop of Séez, 36n. 9
John the Good, king of France, 279, 280
John, duke of Berry, 166
John de Burgh, 187
John *le Cercelier*, 369
John the Chaplain, 369
John of Abbeville, archdeacon of Meaux,
    369, 374
John of Boubier, 369
John of Cornwall, 122n. 55
John of Essonnes, 396
John of Ferrara, 186
John of Freiburg, *Summa confessorum*,
    236
John of Garland, 111, 153. *Epithalamium
    B. Mariae Virginis*, 175
John of Gondricourt, 346
John of Greifenberg, prior of the Grande
    Chartreuse, 433
John of Guignecourt, 168
John of Hauteville, 287
John of London, 152
John of Maroeuil, 368n. 75, 396
John of Meilac, 298
John of Mitry, 395
John of Pouilly, 376, 385–386, 387, 392
John of Rochelle, 375
John of Rua, 396
John of Rupescissa, 412
John of Salisbury, bishop of Chartres, 34,
    36, 50; *Policraticus*, 82, 179n. 99;
    Metalogicon, 82
John of Schoonhoven, 253
John of Wales, 175
Joly, Claude, 75
Jordanus of Saxony, 218
Joseph of Bruges, 369
Josephus, 50
Julius Caesar, 177, 428
Julius Paris, *Epitome* of Valerius
    Maximus, 103, 105, 106–108, 135,
    156–157
Julius Valerius, 106

Jumièges (O.S.B.), 225, 237
Justinian, 112, 281
Justinianus, 473
Justinus, 70n. 25
Justus, 473
Juvenal, 128, 186, 465

Kalkar, Henry, *Loquagium*, 446
Kalker, Arnald, 429
Kastl (O.S.B.), 451
Kenney, E. J., 427, 447
Ker, Neil, 234, 245
Kilwardby, Robert, 203, 215, 230, 234,
    240, 244, 251, 255, 288, 385, 398, 491
Knust, H., 82n. 55
Köllner, Georg Paul, 431, 436, 445, 447

Lactantius, 62, 217n. 67, 246n. 55, 479
Ladislas of Hungary, king of Naples, 95
La Ferté-sur-Grosne (O. Cist.), 211n. 51
Lambert, dean of Soignies, 346
Lambin, Denys, 168
Lancelot, 280
Landriani, Gerardo, 159
Langton, Stephen, 214, 216–217, 244, 247,
    250, 374
Laon, 42, 48–49, 196
Laridus, Gobelinus, 445n. 44
Lateran IV (Fourth Lateran Council), 247,
    458
Lathbury, John, O.F.M., 418–419, 422
Laus Pisonis, 159
Lawrence of Amalfi, 179
Lawrence of Quesnes, 395
Légende dorée, 280
Lehmann, Paul, 168, 430–431, 435
Le Mans, 56
Leonine Commission, 259, 294, 301
Leopold VI, 13
Liber authenticorum, 49
Liber Catonis, 128, 188
Liber exceptionum. See William of Montague
Liber florum, 488
Liber pharetrae, 252, 454, 456, 488
Liber sextus, 465
Liederhandschriften, 21. See also Index of
    Manuscripts, Heidelberg,
    Universitätsbibliothek germ. 350
    (Liederhandschrift D) and germ. 848
    (Liederhandschrift C).

Lieftinck, G. I., 228
Liège, 291. Carthusians, 138. Jesuits, 138
Lincoln Cathedral and diocese, 37, 50, 52,
    53, 65, 195
Lindenbrog, Friedrich, 117n. 49
Lindower, Johannes, 436, 447
Lisieux, 35. *See also* Arnulf, bishop of
    Lisieux.
Liutward, bishop of Vercelli, abbot of
    Bobbio, 29
Livre noir. See Bayeux Cathedral and
    diocese
Livy, 428
Lodi, 159
Logica Algazelis, 90
Lollards, 10, 409–424 *passim*, 430, 439
London, 263
Loos (O.Cist.), 289, 290
Lorsch, 65, 116, 171
Louis X, king of France, 278
Louis I, duc de Bourbon, 279
Lucan, 428, 465
Lucius II, pope, 40
Lucius, Desiderius, 90
Lumen anime, 453, 465
Lupus of Ferrières, 62, 73n. 38, 84, 115,
    156, 159, 163, 167, 176, 188, 429
Lutterworth, 424
Lyre (O.S.B.), 114n. 30, 140, 156n. 6

Mabillon, Jean, 114n. 31
Macrobius (Ambrosius Theodosius), 126,
    155. Comm. on Cicero, *Somnium
    Scipionis*, 91. *Saturnalia*, 105, 131, 171
Maffei, Bernardino, 90
Mahaut, countess of Artois and Burgundy,
    278–279
Mahaut of Béthune, 290
Mainz, 13, 450. Benedictines, 435.
    Carthusains, 435, 445
Manesse Codex. *See* Index of
    Manuscripts, Heidelberg,
    Universitätsbibliothek germ. 848
Manichees, 215
Manitius, M., 122
Manuscripts. *See* Index of Manuscripts
Map, Walter, 125, 127
Marchanova, Ioannes, 91
Marchiennes (O.S.B.), 211n. 51
Mareste, M. de, 145

Margaret of Sens, 282–295, 302, 308, 327
Marguerite, queen of France, 395
Marguerite of Flanders and Hainaut, 290
Mariale, 488
Marianus of Florence, 484n. 41
Marsh, Adam, 233, 418
Martha, Jules, 80, 97
Martial, 173
Martim Codax, 25
Martin V, pope, 72
Martin of Braga, De formula honestae vitae, 105, 134, 141, 144, 151, 155, 185
Martinus Polonus, 195n. 10
Masham, Robert, 423
Matelica, Girolamo da, 171
Matheus Vavassor, 277
Mathurins, 264, 267, 283
Matthew of Vendôme, 111, 153
Maurice of Provins, 234, 252, 286
Maurists, 255
Maximianus, 128
Mazarin, cardinal, 168
Meditationes solitarias, 431
Meissen, 13
Mela (Pomponius), De chorographia, 34, 77n. 43, 84, 107, 117, 119, 156, 162, 172
Melk, 451, 464
Mendicant orders, 219, 222, 307, 348, 351
Menger, Dionysius, librarian of St. Emmeram, 14
Merton College, 364n. 64, 420
Merton Priory, Surry, 142
Methodius, 150
Michael of Neuvirelle, 290–291
Michaelsberg, 65
Michaëlsson, Karl, 321, 324
Michael Scott, 230
Micy St. Mesmin, 107n. 5
Migne, J.-P., 255
Milan, 493
Miles of Corbeil, 346, 369
Minnesänger, 10, 13. See also Reinmar von Zweter.
Modern Devotion, 429, 451, 459, 464
Moerbeke, 230
Molash, William, 423
Molinet, Claude du, 237
Monte Cassino, 118n. 51, 175, 179–180
Montpellier, 318

Mont-St-Michel, 45, 51, 54, 77n. 43, 114n. 30, 117n. 49, 159, 237
Moralium dogma philosophorum, 126n. 62, 140, 144, 158
Morel, Guillaume, 75–76, 98
Mortemer (O.S.B.), 145
Möser fragments. See Index of Manuscripts, Berlin, Staatsbibliothek Preussischer Kulturbesitz germ. qu. 795
Mountgrace (O.Cart.), 435
Mount St. Agnes, 430
Münster, Brethren of the Common Life, 458
Murbach, 478
Musée de Castre, 280

Naples, 88
Neckham, Alexander, 111, 153
Nemesianus, 153, 169, 172
Nennius, 50
New Academy, 61
New Digest, 49
Newton, F., 179
Nicaise of Plank, 377, 396
Niccoli, Niccolò, 70n. 25
Nicholas, archdeacon of Tournai, 346, 347, 367n. 72, 369
Nicholas of Amiens, 163
Nicholas of Bar-le-Duc, 387, 396
Nicholas of Clamanges, 73n. 34, 112, 115, 156, 164, 166, 188
Nicholas of Cues, 435, 446
Nicholas of Gorham, 287, 420
Nicholas of Lisieux, 307
Nicholas of Lyra, 465
Nicholas of Vrigny, 346
Nicholson, Sir Charles, 148
Nicolaus dictus Petit-clerc, 276
Nicolaus Lombardus, 282
Nonius Marcellus, 169
Nördlingen Carthusians (Hortus Christi), 433
Nortweiner, abbot of Kastl, 451
Notker, bishop of Liège, 480–481
Notker of St. Gall, Liber ymnorum, 28–29
Notre Dame de Paris, 75, 85, 102n. 2, 154, 266, 285, 301, 324, 346, 373
Novati, F., 182

Obiectiones contra iudeos, 148

Odo, bishop of Bayeux, 39–43 *passim*
Odo of Châteauroux, 369
Of Clerks Possessioners, 409–411, 412, 414
Ogden, G. K., 14n. 3
Old Academy, 61, 64
Old Digest, 49
Olivi, Peter John, 412
Omont, H., 165
Ong, Walter, 255
Opus Arduum, 410, 412, 414, 418
Orestes, 181
Oriel College, Oxford, 419
Orléans, 36, 84–86, 110–122 *passim*,
    153–188 *passim*
Orosius, 50
Osmund, St., 38
Oswald, St., 432
Oswald de Corda, *Opis Pacis*, 430–447
    passim, 452–453, 455–456, 457
Ouy, Gilbert, 72
Ovid, 159, 182, 428
Oxford, 10, 56, 226, 227, 229–239 *passim*,
    242, 409–424 *passim*. Franciscans
    (Greyfriars), 232–239, 409–424 *passim*,
    480, 489, 491

Padua, 265, 318
Paetow, L. J., 183
Pamphilianius, 128
Papias, *Elementarium doctrinae*
    erudimentum, 85, 167–168, 193–194,
    240, 441, 487
Paris, 73, 153, 225, 228–229, 230–231, 251,
    259–338 *passim*, 345, 373, 429. Univer-
    sity, 4, 196, 198, 226–236, 247, 259–338
    passim, 341, 433. *See also* Sorbonne.
    Celestines, 181. Carmelites, 211n. 51.
    Dominicans. *See* St-Jacques
Parkes, M. B., 263
Parma, 247
Parrhasius, Ianus, of Cosenza, 96
Parrott, M. M., 54
Passio sancti Albani, 66
Pease, A. S., 166
Pelster, F., 234, 235
Peniscola, 93–94, 152, 187
Périgueux, 44, 56
Perion, Joachim, 109n. 14
Perseus, 254
Persius, 128, 185, 186

Persona, John, 365, 369
Perth Carthusians, 434, 438
Petau, Alexander, 149, 150
Petau, Paul, 149
Peter Comestor, 48, 207. *Historia*
    scholastica, 234, 312
Peter Lombard, 206–207, 208, 210, 484,
    493. *Comm. on Psalms and the Pauline*
    Epistles, 199. *Magna glosatura*, 199,
    200. *See also* Henry of Bosham.
    Sentences, 191, 192, 196, 197, 198,
    204, 217, 221, 234, 244, 248, 252, 363,
    370
Peter of Alberona, 360, 369
Peter of Ausonne, 369
Peter of Auvergne, 375, 396
Peter of Blois, 127, 207, 249, 260
Peter of Capau, *Alphabetum*, 202,
    203–209, 211–214, 218, 223
Peter of Chartres, 374
Peter of Cornwall, 203, 205, 207
Peter of Croso, 393
Peter of Cuissy, 396
Peter of Farbu, 396
Peter of Limoges, 286, 288, 299, 373, 376,
    394, 396
Peter of Peronne, 298
Peter of Poitiers, 202, 203, 205, 206, 311
Peter of St. Martin, 369
Peter of St. Omer, 396
Peter of Villepreux, 362
Peter the Chanter, 202, 203, 247; *Summa*
    Abel, 205, 223; *Verbum abbreviatum*,
    126n. 62, 203, 206
Petersen, W., 156, 160
Petrarch (Francesco Petrarca), 89–98 *pas-*
    sim, 107n. 5, 160n. 26, 165, 179, 183,
    188, 341
Petreius, T., 431–432
Petronius, *Satyrica*, 159, 165–166, 169, 172,
    173
Petrus Alfonsus, 48, 76
Petrus dictus Bonenfant, 276
Petrus Helias, *De nominibus*, 446
Petzet, E., 16
Philip, canon of Arras, 369
Philip of Briouze, lord of Bramber, 35, 37
Philip of Dunois, 396
Philip of Harcourt, chancellor of England,
    bishop of Bayeux, 33–59 *passim*, 63,

76–86 passim, 96, 98, 117, 119n. 30, 156n. 6, 165, 171, 188
Philip of Tours, 396
Philip the Chancellor, 263
Philip IV (the Fair), 272, 324
Philip VI, king of France, 278, 280
Philippes de Barac'h, 73
Pierre de Joigny, 102n. 2
Pignon, Laurence, O.P., 485
Pisa, Council of, 73
Pisan, Christine de, 253–254
Pistor, Henry, 349n. 23, 381n. 103
Pithiviers, 111
Pithou, Pierre, 113
Pits, John, 431
Plasberg, Otto, 63, 67–68, 86
Plato, Meno, 174. Phaedo, 83, 91, 174, 341, 349. Timaeus, 230
Pseudo-Plautus. See Querolus
Pliny the Elder, Natural History, 43n. 37
Pliny the Younger, Epistolae, 34, 48, 76, 84, 87, 101–103, 105, 108–110, 114, 119, 124–125, 132, 155–156, 169, 171, 172
Poema ad coniugem, 180
Pollard, Graham, 234, 265
Ponchard of Sorbon, 369
Pontificals, 466
Pontigny (O. Cist.), 63, 66–67, 69–70, 137
Porte St-Jacques, 282–283, 285, 293
Possevinus, A., 431
Possidius, 474, 477
Praecepta Pithagorae, 105, 134
Prepositinus, 202, 203, 205, 206, 374
Prévostin of Cremona, 247
Proba, 54
Propertius, 84, 155, 169, 174, 182, 341, 349
Protestant reformation, 3
Proverbia philosophorum, 105, 131, 155. See also Caecilius Balbus
Prudentius, 147, 185. Psychomachia, 128
Psalters, 466
Publilius 'Syrus', 122, 140, 349
Pucelle, Jean, 279

Queen's College, Oxford, 415
Querolus (Pseudo-Plautus), 101, 105, 106–112 passim, 123, 134, 155–157, 160–162, 169, 170, 172, 180
Quétif, J., 224

Quintilian, Institutio oratoria, 84, 106, 123, 173, 178
Pseudo-Quintilian, Declamationes maiores, 106, 135

Rabanus Maurus, 143, 180, 375
Radbert of Corbie, 116
Radulphus de Diceto, 488
Ralph Niger, 216–217, 250
Ralph of Châteauroux, 369
Ralph of Périers, 380, 396
Ranstrand, G., 107–108
Raphanellis, Marcus de, 90
Ravenna, 107
Raymond Lull, 375, 387, 396
Raymond of Pennafort, 235, 236, 322
Reading, 42
Reginald of Colant, 369
Reginald of Grandchamp, 369
Reginald of Soissons, 396
Reginsburg, 364n. 64
Registrum Anglie de libris doctorum et auctorum veterum, 237–238, 418, 423, 480, 491, 492
Regula canonicorum, 149
Reichenau, 478
Reid, James, 63
Reid, L., 304
Reims, 117, 216, 249
Reinmar von Zweter, 13–29 passim
Remegius, 180
Renaissance, 98, 188, 449
Renaud de Louens, 254
Renier of Cologne, 396
Reynbold, John, 423
Reynolds, Leighton D., 69, 154
Rhineland, 74, 429
Richard, St., 411
Richard II, bishop of Bayeux, 39, 53
Richard III, bishop of Bayeux, 39
Richard I de Bohun, dean of Bayeux, bishop of Coutances, 42
Richard de Bury, 420. Philobiblon, 409, 455
Richard de Fournival, 78–81, 84–86, 94, 96, 98, 115, 162–167, 170–198 passim, 249, 343. Bestiaire d'amour, 22, 162. Bibliomania, 63, 78, 84, 102, 120–123, 153, 155, 163, 175, 350. Bibliomania no. 84 (Florilegium Angelicum), 101–102, 105–107, 151. De vetula, 162, 182

Richard de Montbaston, 262, 269, 280, 281, 323
Richard of Gerberoy, 163
Richard of Stavensby, 225
Richelieu, cardinal, 349n. 23
Ridevall, John, 418
Rigord, 374
Ringstead, Thomas, 187
Rivallon, archdeacon of Nantes, 165
Robert, earl of Leicester, 35
Robert, earl of Gloucester, illegitimate son of Henry I, 39, 41
Robert I fitz Anschetil, 35
Robert de Chesney, 195
Robert de Neubourg, seneschal of Normandy, 44
Robert de Sorbon, 79, 163, 266, 345, 346, 348, 350, 352, 355, 357, 360, 365, 369, 394, 405
Robert of Adington, 200n. 23
Robert of Douai, physician, 345–346, 347, 358, 362, 369
Robert of Douai, clerk of the Prince of Achaea, 346
Robert of Paris, 231
Robert of Rheims, 369
Robert of Torigny, *Chronicle*, 45–46, 50–52, 56
Robert of Worcester, 294
Robert Scoti, 294
De Rochefort, Parisian family, 91
Roelants, Gerard, 492
Roethe, Gustav, 17–20
Roger, Peter. *See* Clement VI, pope
Roger Bacon, 83, 175, 265
Roger, bishop of Salisbury, 37
Roger of Rheims, 369, 397
Rolduc (Liège), 164n. 44
Roman book trade and manuscripts, 4–5
Roman de Fauvel, 278
Roman de Godefroi de Bouillon et de Saladin, 280
Roman de Graal, 280
Roman de Poire, 281n. 56
Roman de Thèbes, 280
Roman law, 49–50
Rome, 50, 52, 493
Rookloster, 447, 455, 492–493
Rostock, Brethren of the Common Life, 458

Rotrou of Rouen, bishop of Evreux, archbishop of Rouen, 34, 36, 37n. 18, 42–44, 57–59
Rottendorf, Bernard, 74, 177
Rouen, 34, 42–44, 56. *See also:* Hugh of Amiens, archbishop; Rotrou of Rouen, archbishop
Royaumont (O. Cist.), 211n. 51
Rue aux Porees, 317
Rue Erembourc de Brie, 273
Rue neuve Notre-Dame, 281, 297, 308, 326
Rue St-Jacques, 282, 283, 289, 302
Russell, John, O.F.M., 418, 422
Rusticius Helpidius Domnulus, 197, 156
Ruysbroeck, John, 253

S. Andrea (Vercelli), 143n. 80
St-Aubin (Angers), 114n. 30
St. Augustine's, Canterbury, 152, 162n. 31
St-Colombe (Sens), 170
Ste-Croix (Orléans), 170
St. Davids. *See* Gerald of Wales
St. Emmeram, 14, 16, 364n. 64
St-Etienne (Caen, O.S.B.), 237
St. Frideswide, 419
Ste-Geneviève (Paris, O.S.A.), 154, 237, 346, 374
Ste-Geneviève-la-Grande, 283
St-Germain-des-Prés (Paris, O.S.B.), 211n. 51, 237, 346, 374–375
Saints-Gervais-et-Protais, 118n. 50
S. Giovanni a Carbonara (O.S.A.), 96
St-Jacques (Liège, O.S.B.), 141
St-Jacques (Lille, O.P.), 288, 290
St-Jacques (Paris, O.P.), 203, 211n. 51, 214, 224–226, 234, 238, 248, 251, 264, 284–285, 287–295 *passim*, 306, 318, 346, 373, 485
St. John (Viridario), 91
St-Julien-le-Pauvre, 264
St. Martial (Limoges) 42, 114n. 30, 117n. 49, 156n. 6
St. Martin (Louvain, O.S.A.), 457, 492
St. Martin (Marmoutiers, near Tours), 164
St. Martin's Priory, Dover, 385n. 105
St. Mary's (Oxford), 419
St-Maur-des-Fosses, 181
St-Pierre (Chartres), 165
Saint Pons, 183

St. Sulpice, 117
St. Victor (Marseilles), 164n. 44
St. Victor (Paris, O.S.A.), 45, 53, 56, 71,
    102, 113, 115, 117, 143, 144, 145, 154,
    162n. 30, 163, 166, 181, 182, 346, 373,
    485
Salerno, 153
Salimbene de Adam, 247
Salisbury Cathedral, 37, 412. See also:
    Jocelin, bishop; Roger, bishop
Sallust, 70n. 25, 94, 128, 173, 185, 186.
    Catilina, 141
Pseudo-Sallust, Invectiva in Ciceronem,
    94, 160
Salutati, Coluccio, 90, 91, 164, 341
Sarton, George, 242
Savigny, 237
Schiche, T., 80, 97
Schmidt, P. L., 92–93, 166
Kloster Schönrain, 17
Schriftbänder, 21
'Sellarii', 73
Seneca the Younger, 140–151 passim, 185,
    De beneficiis, 66, 69, 102, 105, 126, 131
    150, 151, 155, 171. De clementia, 66, 69,
    151. De remediis fortuitorum, 66, 69,
    141, 150, 151. Dialogues, 175. Epistolae
    Morales ad Lucilium, 69, 105, 123, 133,
    141, 151, 155, 171. Natural Questions,
    34, 53. Tragedies, 141, 169, 174
Pseudo-Seneca, 145. Epistolae ad Paulum,
    69, 141, 479. De moribus, 134, 151
Sententiae philosophorum, 105, 122, 134,
    155. See also Caecilius Balbus
Seripando, Antonio, 96
Sermo de beato Arsenio anachoreta, 141
Servius, 169
Sidonius Apollinaris, 104, 105, 122, 125,
    126, 133, 155, 171, 185
Sienna, 364n. 64
Sigebert of Gembloux, Chronicle, 483. De
    viris illustribus, 482–484, 486
Signy (O. Cist.), 211n. 51
Simon Chevre d'Or, 48, 53, 54
Simon de Plumetot, 115
Simon of Furnes, 396
Simon of Melta, 396
Simon of Velli, 396
Simon of Widelin, 369
Solinus, 138, 139

Sompting, rectory in Sussex, 37
Song of the Barons, 25
Sorbonne, college and library, 78–79, 83,
    94, 115, 128, 162n. 31, 163, 175, 178,
    185, 232, 237, 239, 287, 288, 341–408
    passim, 491.
Southern, Sir Richard, 33
Speculum astronomiae, 490
Speculum iaicorum, 186
Sponheim, 490
Spruchbänder, 21
Statius, 128
Stephanus dictus Sauvage, 276
Stephen, king of England, 37, 39, 45
Stephen of Abbeville, 361, 365, 366, 369
Stephen of Auvergne, 396
Stephen of Besançon, 396
Stephen of Burgundy, 396
Stephen of Geneva, 376, 380, 387, 396
Stephen of Rouen, 84
Stephen of Tournai, 122n. 55, 158n. 18,
    374
Stertt, Johannes, 447
Stoic school, 61, 64
Strasbourg, 14, 458
Strozzi, Carlo di Tommaso, 141
Suetonius, 63. Lives of the Caesars, 50,
    173
Suger of St-Denis, 53
Summa confessorum, 387
Symmachus, 126, 139, 149; Florilegium of,
    126

Tabula septem custodiarum super Bibliam,
    233, 237, 418, 423, 488
Tacitus, 428
Talmud, 287n. 75
Tanner, Thomas, 431
Tegernpeck, John II, abbot of St.
    Emmeram, 14
Ter Doest (Bruges, O. Cist.), 227–228
Ter Duinen (Bruges, O. Cist.), 211n. 51,
    227–228, 242, 244
Ter Maet, Sisters of the Common Life, 459
Terence, 128, 185
Theele, Joseph, 436
Theobald, archbishop of Canterbury, 37n.
    18, 52
Theobald, Pharetra fidei contra iudeos,
    148

Theodulph, 493
Theophilus, 128
Theoretica geometria, 74
Thibaut, count of Blois, 53
Thomas à Kempis, 429, 459
Thomas Becket, 53
Thomas de Maubeuge, 262, 269, 278–281
Thomas de St-Pol, 273
Thomas de Wymonduswold, 276
Thomas of Hales, 23
Thomas of Ireland, *Manipulus florum*, 79,
    128, 175, 178, 185, 241, 243, 251–254,
    301, 306–307, 317, 357, 359, 370–371,
    376, 379, 385, 386, 390, 396, 446, 453–
    454, 456–457, 480, 489–490, 491, 493
Thomas of Sens, 272, 276, 283–295, 298,
    302, 308, 323, 327
Thomas of Vercelli (Thomas Gallus),
    143n. 80
Thomas the Norman, 276, 298, 308
Thompson, Margaret, 435
Thomson, S. Harrison, 232–233
Tibullus, *Elegies*, 84, 112, 118, 155, 157,
    159, 169, 172–182 *passim*, 341, 349
Toledo, 153, 473
Toulouse, 318. Franciscans, 211n. 51
Tournai, 291
Tours, 102, 115, 164, 176, 177, 263, 474.
    Miniscule, 75
Transmundus of Clairvaux, 67n. 19
Tres partes, 49
Trevisa, John, 414, 415
Trier Benedictines, 435, 445. Carthusians,
    435, 445
Trillek, Thomas, bishop of Rochester,
    84n. 65, 166, 420
Trithemius, Johannes, abbot of Sponheim,
    225, 457, 465, 486, 493. *De laude
    scriptorium*, 457, 465. *De scriptoribus
    ecclesiasticis*, 486, 493
Troarn, 39
Trojan War, 53
Truchsess of St. Gall, 18
Twelfth-Century Renaissance, 34

Ugolinus, Thadeus, 173
Ullman, B. L., 120, 158, 179, 181, 186, 349
University College, Oxford, 364n. 64
Urban IV, pope, 290
Utrecht Carthusians, 435, 445, 447

Valde bonum, 436, 443, 456
Valerius Flaccus, 159
Valerius Maximus, 108, 140, 177
Valla, Lorenzo, *De ratione dicendi
    precepta*, 446
Valois, N., 387
Van den Bruwaene, M., 164, 166
Varro, 70n. 25, 81, 88, 186
Vauluisant (O.Cist.), 306
Vegetius, 63, 90, 145
Versus Ciceronis, 131
Vespasiano da Bisticci, 71
Vibius Sequester, *De fluminibus*, 107, 111,
    156
Vie des sains, 279
Villers-en-Brabant (O. Cist.), 127, 184,
    226, 227
Vincent of Beauvais, *Speculum historiale*,
    83, 98, 185–186, 200, 490–491
Virgil, 128, 185, 465
Virgil the Grammarian, 169
Visconti-Sforza library, 89, 90
Vitalis, abbot of Savigny, 27n. 35
Vitruvius, 43n. 37
Vivarium, 476
Voeux de Paon, 278
Vogel, F., 116–117
Von den Steinen, W., 29

Waleran, count of Meulan, 35–38
Walter of Aulnay, 396
Walter of Bibbesworth, 26
Walter of Biencourt, 369
Walter of Bruges, 454
Walter of Chatillon, 187n. 126
Walter of Douai, 369
Walther von der Vogelweide, 13
Warenghien, Michael, 367n. 72
Warner of Langres, 233, 247
Warner of Moret, 369
Wartburg-Krieg, 25
Webb, C. C. J., 82
Weihenstephen, 25
Weingarten manuscript, 21
Wenzel I, 13
Westminster, 56
Whytefield, John, 385n. 105
Wibald of Corvey, 65, 110, 115, 160n. 26,
    176
Wilhymleyd, Peter, 423

Wilkins, A. S., 168
William Amidouz, 396
William Breton, 395
William de Malliaco, 288
William de Montibus, 247
William III de Tournebu, dean of Bayeux,
     bishop of Coutances, 42
William Epulcre, 396
William of Alnwick, 418
William of Auvergne, 375
William of Conches, 77n. 43
William of Dacia, 374
William of Feuquières, 376, 380, 396
William of Jumièges, 50
William of Malmesbury, 38n. 19, 81, 187
William of Montague, abbot of
     Clairvaux, 185, 226, 453. *Liber
     exceptionum ex libris viginti trium
     auctorum*, 185, 226, 231, 453. *Flores
     Bernardi*, 226
William of Montmorency, 352, 361, 369
William of Montreuil, 369
William of Moussy-le-Neuf, 369
William of Nottingham, O.F.M., 420, 422
William of Ockham, 412, 418
William of Pagula, 187
William of Rennes, 236

William of St. Amour, 412
William of Sens, 285–294, 300–308 *pas-
     sim*, 313–316, 318–319, 324, 327
William of Troyes, 369
William Patemoysi, 380, 396
William Rede, 84n. 65, 420
Wilmart, A., 166, 222, 321
Wilson, Nigel G., 154
Wilson, R. M., 27
Windesheim, 460, 461. Congregation, 9,
     428–430, 450–451, 452, 453, 461–464,
     492, 494
Winter, P. M. de, 163, 325
Wittenberg, 19
Wolfger of Prüfening, 482
Woodford, William, O.F.M., 415–420,
     422, 423, 424
Worcester, 234
Wright, Thomas, 26
Wyclif, John, 409–424 *passim*
Wycliffites. *See* Lollards

York, 44, 56. Austin Friars, 233n. 29

Zacharias Chrysopolitanus, 48–49
Zerbolt, Gerhard, 459
Zwolle, 459, 461

Manuscript Index

Amsterdam, Universiteitsbibliothek
77: 66–74, 81, 98
80: 68
Arras, Bibliothèque Municipale
64: 159n. 20
305: 159n. 20
Auxerre, Bibliothèque Municipale
234: 102–108 *passim*, 137
Avranches, Bibliothèque Municipale
93: 54
159: 45–46, 52
162: 159n. 24
238: 159

Basel, öffentliche Bibliothek der
Universität
D IV 4: 181
N I 3, n. 145: 18
F IV 12: 25
F IV 26: 168
F VI 53: 492
F IX 4: 435
Inc. 5: 436
Berlin (East), Deutsche Staatbibliothek
Diez B Sant. 60: 159n. 20, 181
66: 114, 180, 349n. 24
germ. 923: 18
lat. 201 (Phill.): 73n. 34, 84
qu. 630: 435
632: 435
Phillipps 1715: 116, 171 (Rose 172)
1794: 165, 173 (Rose 201)
1813: 181
Berlin (West), Staatsbibliothek der Stiftung
Preussischer Kulturbesitz
xx. HA St. A. Königsberg 33.11: 25

germ. qu. 795 (Möser fragments):
19–20
lat. fol. 47: 175n. 84
252: 65, 110, 115, 159–160,
160n. 26, 176
Bern, Burgerbibliothek
45: 181
123: 169n. 68
136: 108–110, 112, 113, 119, 132,
155–156, 160–161
161: 83, 186
C 219 pt. 1: 168, 170
276: 85, 86, 98, 155, 168–173 *passim*,
178, 180, 182
291: 168, 170
327: 181n. 114
332: 350n. 27
351: 84
395: 110n. 16
433: 167n. 60
633: 113, 158
Bologna, Biblioteca Universitaria
1546: 235n. 33
Bourges, Bibliothèque Municipale
400: 117
Brno, Universitni Knihovna
Mk 28: 412n. 9
Brugge (Bruges), Bibliothèque de la Ville
253: 211n. 51
Bruxelles (Brussels), Bibliothèque Royale
Albert Ier
4785–4793: 184, 227
5345: 110, 160n. 26
9845–8: 116, 171
10007–10011: 90n. 81
10030–10032: 127

10098–10105: 102, 116n. 40, 138
20030–32: 184, 227n. 8, 248n. 61
II 1635: 119
Schloss Büdingen, Ysenburgisches Archiv
  Fürstlich Ysenburg-Büdingensches
    Archiv 54: 17–18

Cambrai, Bibliothèque Municipale
  954: 72
Cambridge, University Library
  Dd. 13. 2: 82n. 53
  Ff. 6. 2: 410
  Gg. 2. 21: 51, 47n. 55
  Add. 3470: 420n. 25
Cambridge, Clare College
  26: 178
Cambridge, Corpus Christi College
  296: 410
  391: 431–432
Cambridge, Gonville and Caius College
  114: 455
  329: 235n. 33
Cambridge, Peterhouse
  169: 233n. 29, 238n. 42, 423
Cambridge, Pembroke College
  22: 489n. 53
Cambridge, St. John's College
  97: 152, 187
Cambridge, Trinity College
  150: 199n. 20
  152: 199n. 20
  153: 199n. 20
Cambridge, Mass., Harvard University,
  Houghton Library
  198: 25
Cesena, Biblioteca Malatestiana
  S. XXIV.4: 317
Chalon-sur-Saône, Bibliothèque
  Municipale
  15: 211n. 51
Charleville, Bibliothèque Municipale
  230: 211n. 51
Clairvaux
  E. 45, I. 22, I. 23, L. 50: see Troyes
    658, 461, 469, 186
Copenhagen: see København

Dijon, Bibliothèque Municipale
  646 (386): 75n. 19
Douai, Bibliothèque Municipale

433: 211n. 51
Dublin, Trinity College
  244 (C III 12): 410
Durham, Cathedral Library
  A.III.4: 199n. 19
  A.III.17: 200n. 23
Durham, University Library
  Cosin V.ii.4: 423
Durham, N. C., Duke University Library
  104: 211n. 51

Erlangen, Universitätsbibliothek
  847: 65
  848: 159
Escorial, El, Real Biblioteca
  O.III.2: 54
  Q.I.14: 159n. 20
  R.I.2: 93, 94n. 90
  T.III.18: 95
  V.III.6: 90, 92
Eton, College Library
  13: 245
Èvreux, Bibliothèque Municipale
  1: 102–111 passim, 139–140
  92: 43n. 37

Firenze (Florence), Archivio di Stato
  Carte Strozziane, ser. 3 no. 46: 90
Firenze, Biblioteca Medicea Laurenziana
  plut. 29.19: 350n. 27
    48.29: 114n. 31
    51.4: 70n. 25
    90.12 infra: 173
  Conv. Soppr. 111: 70n. 25
    131: 66–74
    224: 96
    399: 71n. 30
  S. Marco 284: 84, 109, 113, 156, 182
  Strozzi 37: 95
    75: 101–111 passim, 140–141
Firenze, Biblioteca Nazionale Centrale
  Magl. XXI.30: 95
    XXXIX.199: 90
Frankfurt, Stadt- und Universitätsbibli-
  othek
  Barth. 110: 182

Gdansk (Danzig), Biblioteka Gdanska
  Polskiej Akademii Nauk
  2388 (IXq.B.11): 95

Genève, Bibliothèque Publique et
Universitaire
lat. 41: 43 n. 37
169: 115
Giessen, Universitätsbibliothek
945: 281
Glasgow, University Library
Hunter T.2.14 (56): 90
V.2.17 (397): 90
Grenoble, Bibliothèque Municipale
46: 443

Halle, Leopoldinisch-Carolinische
Akademie der Naturforscher bifolium
containing Sprüche of Reinmar von
Zweter: 18–20
Hamburg, Staats- und Universitäts-
Bibliothek
53c in scrinio: 117 n. 49, 162 n.
30
Heidelberg, Universitätsbibliothek
Germ. 350 (Liederhandschrift D):
13–29 passim
357: 18–20
848 (Liederhandschrift C)
(Manesse codex): 13–29
passim
Sal. 9.62: 159 n. 20, 181
Hereford, Cathedral Library
P.VI.6: 211 n. 51
O.III.2: 478

København (Copenhagen), Kongelige
Bibliotek
Gl. Kgl. 546 fol: 54
Köln (Cologne), Historisches Archiv
G.B. qu. 152: 433–434, 436
Kues, Hospitalbibliothek
12: 435

Lambeth Palace: see London.
Laon, Bibliothèque Municipale
193: 181
461: 181
Leiden, Bibliotheek der Rijksuniversiteit
B.P.L. 20: 47 n. 54, 50 n. 66
191B: 102, 104, 141–142
199: 114 n. 30, 156 n. 6
Gronovius 21: 66–74, 96–97, 177–179
Periz. F.25: 67, 72, 74

Voss. Lat. F.67: 110 n. 16, 161
Q.2: 118 n. 50, 162 n. 29
Q.83: 111, 157
Q.98 454
Q.103: 162 n. 31
O.26: 159
O.38: 174, 182, 361 n. 55
Vulc. 48: 181
Leipzig, Ratsbibliothek
421: 19
Leningrad, Publichnaja Biblioteka im.
M.E. Saltykova-Shchedrina Lat.
Q.v.I.20: 478
Léon, Biblioteca de la Catedral
33: 171 n. 71
Lille, Bibliothèque Municipale
835–838: 289–291
Lincoln, Cathedral Chapter Library
229: 422
London, British Library
Add. 17304: 321
23986: 26
25104: 102–108 passim, 142–143
47678 (formerly Holkham Hall
387): 114, 115 n. 34, 176
Harley 2682: 65, 115, 176
2687: 114 n. 31
2736: 159–160
2745: 181
2773: 164
3858: 233 n. 29, 238 n. 43, 423,
489 n. 56
4927: 92, 110, 160 n. 26, 161
6641: 410
Royal 4.A.xiii: 422
10.B.viii: 235 n. 33
6.C.ix: 235n.35
3.D.i: 233 n. 29, 238 n. 42, 423
8.E.iv: 117
11.A.v: 102, 142
Sloane 809: 26
London, Lambeth Palace
52: 489 n. 53
67: 482 n. 32
325: 116, 171
347: 235 n. 35
Los Angeles, University of California
Research Library
AiT 36s: 14
Strip I: 14–29 passim

Strip II: 14–29 *passim*
170/348: 215 n. 60
Lyon, Bibliothèque Municipale
414: 196 n. 13, 232

Madrid, Biblioteca Nacional
9116: 95
Mainz, Stadtbibliothek
151: 435
II.276: 436
Manesse codex: *see* Heidelberg,
Universitätsbibliothek, Germ. 848.
Marburg, Hessisches Staatsarchiv
2 leaves containing *Sprüche* of
Reinmar von Zweter: 18
Milano, Biblioteca Ambrosiana
E.15 inf.: 90, 92
H 14 inf.: 107 n. 5
S.64 sup.: 90, 92
Modena, Biblioteca Estense ed
Universitaria
Lat. 213: 95
Monte Cassino, Biblioteca dell'Abbazia
355: 211 n. 51
361: 144 n. 31
Montpellier, Bibliothèque de la Faculté de
Médicine
12: 67 n. 17
132: 69
294: 405–406
359: 71 n. 28
406: 472
Möser fragments: *see* Berlin (West),
Staatsbibliothek der Stiftung
Preussischer Kulturbesitz germ. qu.
795.
München, Bayerische Staatsbibliothek
Clm 3743: 277
6292: 180
6929: 118 n. 51
13582: 19
15958: 96
21571: 25
29110a: 181
Cgm 189: 25

Napoli, Biblioteca Nazionale
IV.G.43: 95, 97
IV.G.46: 96
V.A.8: 173

New Haven, Conn., Yale University,
Beinecke Library
207: 313–317
Marston: 211 n. 51
New York, Pierpont Morgan Library
Morgan 819: 22
New York, New York Academy of Medi-
cine
Safe: 162 n. 31

Oxford, Bodleian Library
Add. 208: 181
Auct. E infra 6: 199 n. 20
Bodl. 647: 410
685: 233 n. 29
703: 417 n. 17
Canon. Pat. Lat. 131: 217 n. 67
176: 71 n. 30
Douce 308: 22
Eng. Poet: 28
Hatton 11: 235 n. 34
Selden supra 48: 235 n. 36
Tanner 165: 238 n. 42, 423
Oxford, Balliol College
28–30: 423
36: 195
216: 233 n. 29, 423
217: 233 n. 29, 423
Oxford, Keble College
Roll I: 27
Oxford, Lincoln College
lat. 83: 208 n. 40
Oxford, Magdalen College
78: 233 n. 29, 423
150: 233 n. 29, 423
Oxford, Merton College
205: 233 n. 29, 423
311: 84 n. 65, 166
Oxford, New College
31: 235 n. 33
112: 235 nn. 33, 37
315: 233 n. 29
Oxford, Oriel College
43: 235 n. 33
77: 196
Oxford, St. John's College
31: 208 n. 42
Oxford, Trinity College
18: 152, 187
Oxford, University College

21: 235n. 36

Pamplona, Biblioteca de la Catedral
  51: 285, 288–289, 313
Paris, Archives Nationales
  KK.283: 324, 327
Paris, Bibliothèque de l'Arsenal
  711: 117, 162, 159n. 20
  855: 343n. 9
  1116E: 102–111 passim, 143
  3142: 22
  3481: 280
Paris, Bibliothèque Mazarine
  37: 284–285
  281: 285–286
  333: 285
  1007: 211n. 51
  1008: 211n. 51
  3323: 378n. 99
Paris, Bibliothèque Nationale
  Don. no. 18845: 350n. 25
  fr. 60: 280
    146: 278
    241: 280
    899: 281n. 56
    1586: 23
    2186: 281n. 56
    9123: 280
    10132: 279
    22495: 280
    24780: 377n. 97
  lat. 152: 47n. 55, 479
    174: 215n. 60
    1685: 47n. 54
    1860: 102, 106, 128, 144–145, 185,
      186, 248n. 61
    2201: 88
  lat. 3107: 294
    3183: 422
    3247: 374n. 85
    3557: 365n. 69
    3893: 276
    5493: 342n. 4
    5765: 177, 179
    5802: 36n. 13, 47n. 55, 77, 84, 92,
      165
    6042: 51
    6331: 66–74, 81, 87
    6375: 90
    6379: 175n. 84

6412: 343n. 9
6602: 165
6621: 84
7647: 118, 162, 159n. 20
7774A: 176
7775: 94, 115–116, 177
7776: 114n. 31
7783: 71n. 28
7794: 91n. 81, 109, 114, 156,
  160–161, 182
7823: 94, 115
7973: 167, 182
8049: 166, 173
8089: 159n. 20
8213: 167, 170
8260: 174
8961: 472n. 6
9085: 282
11648: 349n. 23
11683: 375n. 86
12138: 375n. 86
12161: 471
12211: 47nn. 54, 55
12322: 375n. 86
13346: 375n. 86
13366: 375n. 86
13582: 181
14318: 276
14578: 490n. 59
14580: 253n. 72
14582: 485n. 44
14749: 112, 156n. 8
14761: 67–72
14909: 253n. 72
15084: 73n. 34, 166
15086: 175n. 84
15155: 174, 181, 182
15172: 102, 106, 145–146, 159n. 20
15173: 253n. 72
15186: 390
15190: 390
15246: 490n. 59
15270: 387n. 108
15284: 381n. 103
15288: 381n. 103, 399
15289: 350n. 27, 381n. 103, 399
15294: 381n. 103
15295: 359n. 49
15302: 381n. 103, 400
15310: 381n. 103

15315: 355
15328: 359 n. 49
15350: 232
15355: 377 n. 94
15371: 387
15372: 387
15377: 381 n. 103
15449: 377 n. 94
15459: 349 n. 23
15470: 367 n. 71
15554: 377 n. 94
15569: 230 n. 18
15585: 359 n. 49, 388 n. 117
15611: 387 n. 108
15629: 355 n. 39
15641: 249
15653: 381 n. 103
15654: 353, 401
15655: 359, 381 n. 103, 402–404
15657: 401–402
15658: 381 n. 103
15659: 381 n. 103, 400–401
15662: 350 n. 27, 381 n. 103
15676: 387 n. 109
15686: 406
15713: 359
15721: 367 n. 71
15734: 408
15754: 213 n. 24, 235 n. 33
15773: 288
15797: 367 n. 71
15811: 232
15819: 232
15822: 367 n. 73
15829: 358 n. 45, 406–407
15848: 232
15851: 387 n. 109, 389 n. 120
15924: 381 n. 103, 387 n. 108
15982: 184
15983: 230 nn. 16, 20, 231 n. 22,
     350 n. 27, 381 n.103, 405
15984: 230 n. 19
15988: 381 n. 103
16099: 287
16111: 387 n. 108
16142: 439 n. 23, 381 n. 103
16147: 231 n. 23
16158: 387 n. 108
16163: 381 n. 103
16193: 381 n. 103

16203: 374–375
16208: 84 n. 66
16249: 349 n. 23, 381 n. 103
16293: 387 n. 109
16334: 231 n. 21
16359: 407
16362: 350 n. 27, 404–405
16368: 355
16371: 350 n. 27, 359
16380: 408
16387: 263, 265
16397: 390 n. 121
16399: 296 n. 99
16405: 350 n. 27
16412: 352–356, 380 n. 102
16413: 355
16492: 232
16493: 232
16494: 368 n. 75
16551: 402
16558: 287 n. 75
16581: 175, 349 n. 23
16598: 350 n. 27
16601: 381 n. 103
16603: 349 n. 23
16611: 355, 358 n. 45
16613: 349 n. 23
16648: 349 n. 23
16676: 349 n. 23
16719–22: 291
16894: 211 n. 51
16896: 211 n. 51
16906: 232
17162: 194
17812: 164
17903: 126 n. 62, 159 n. 20, 186
18104: 75–78, 81, 97–98, 114 n.
     30, 156 n. 6
nouv. acq. lat. 99: 343, 381
              340: 110 n. 16
              514: 235
              540: 196 n. 13
Paris, Bibliothèque Sainte Geneviève
     22: 278
Paris, Bibliothèque de l'Université
     9: 276
     130: 277
     636: 350 n. 25
Pisa, Seminario Arcivescovile, Biblioteca
     Cateriniana

124: 229–230
Praha (Prague), Knihovna Metropolitni
　　Kapituli
　　N. VIII: 342n. 3

Reims, Bibliothèque Municipale
　　862: 91n. 81
　　1110: 91n. 81
　　1400: 67n. 19
Roma, Biblioteca Angelica
　　505: 175n. 84
　　720: 102, 109, 127, 146, 185, 248n. 61
　　1895: 101–108 passim, 129–130, 131,
　　　　146–147, 155
Rouen, Bibliothèque Municipale
　　1040: 110n. 16
　　1041: 166
　　1111: 114n. 30, 156n. 6

St-Omer, Bibliothèque Municipale
　　217: 211n. 51
Salamanca, Biblioteca Universitaria
　　2306: 159n. 20
Salisbury, Cathedral Library
　　62: 489n. 53
San Marino, California, Henry E.
　　Huntington Library
　　Huntington Bible: 233, 245
　　HM 26061: 196n. 13
　　　　26560: 489n. 53
　　RB 86299: 436–438, 453
Sydney, University Library
　　Nicholson 2: 102–108 passim, 147–148

Tortosa, Biblioteca de la Catedral
　　80: 159n. 20
Toulouse, Bibliothèque Municipale
　　211: 211n. 51
Tours, Bibliothèque Municipale
　　688: 166
Trier, Stadtbibliothek
　　721: 211n. 51
　　1130: 435
　　1924: 435
Troyes, Bibliothèque Municipale
　　40: 480n. 27
　　114: 211n. 51
　　186: 184, 226n. 7
　　461: 116, 172
　　469: 116, 172

497: 226n. 7
546: 285, 312n. 139
658: 116, 172
667: 285
1037: 227

Utrecht, Bibliotheek der Universiteit
　　31: 459
　　824: 435

Vaticano, Città del, Biblioteca Apostolica
　　Vaticana
　　Arch. S. Pietro H.23: 90–91
　　Borgh. lat. 134: 285
　　Chigi H.V.153: 175n. 84
　　Ottob. lat. 294: 235n. 33
　　Pal. lat. 957: 101–111 passim, 119, 148,
　　　　157
　　　　1511: 60, 67, 72–74
　　　　1513: 65
　　　　1514: 168, 171
　　　　1525: 65
　　Reg. lat. 72: 350n. 27
　　　　129: 172
　　　　314 pt. VI: 107n. 5
　　　　358: 102, 149
　　　　406: 267n. 22, 321
　　　　454: 350n. 27
　　　　585: 54
　　　　1554: 287
　　　　1561: 111, 157
　　　　1572: 350n. 27
　　　　1575: 101–111 passim, 126,
　　　　　　149–150
　　　　1625: 181
　　　　1762: 159
　　　　2120: 174, 181n. 114
　　Rossi 559: 70n. 24
　　Vat. lat. 1720: 95, 96
　　　　3087: 102–111 passim, 150–151
　　　　3452: 177, 179
　　　　3803: 116, 171
　　　　4304: 211n. 51
　　　　4929: 84, 106–109, 111, 112,
　　　　　　117, 118, 119, 135, 157, 158,
　　　　　　160, 171, 180, 182
　　　　5994: 152
Vendôme, Bibliothèque Municipale
　　181: 276
　　189: 76n. 43, 117n. 49

Venezia (Venice), Biblioteca Nazionale
   Marciana
     Lat. cl.II.40 (2195): 152
     Lat. VI.81 (3036): 91
Vienna: *see* Wien

Weimar, Thüringische Landesbibliothek
   qu. 22: 435, 456
Wien (Vienna), österreichische
   Nationalbibliothek

   12: 447 n. 49
   189: 73 n. 34, 85, 166–167
   745: 172
   1380: 211 n. 51
   1536: 294
   12694: 492
Wolfenbüttel, Herzog-August-Bibliothek
   Gud. lat. 2: 91–92
       224: 174, 182
   Helmst. 350: 435, 444